How to Get Rich in
MAIL ORDER

Melvin Powers, Mail Order Consultant

Melvin Powers
Wilshire Book Company

12015 Sherman Road, No. Hollywood, CA 91605

Printed in the United States of America
Library of Congress Catalog Card Number: 79-67122
ISBN 0-87980-373-8

Contents

PROFILE

'Get-rich-quick' book helps D.M. men sell mail-order pipe tobacco

By STEVE BALLARD
Register Business Writer

In just one year, two Des Moines men have parlayed $1,200 in cash and advice from a book called "How to Get Rich in Mail Order" into a business that sells pipe tobacco to thousands of smokers across the nation and to 80 retail outlets in central Iowa.

"I've done everything it says in that book except advertising," said co-owner Chuck Foote. "But I don't want to get rich, I just want to be happy."

The business, Tobacco Outlet, 3814 Douglas Ave., is owned by Foote and Dallas Fisher, who decided Foote's unique skill at blending tobacco was too good to keep quiet. Foote, who placed sixth in a world pipe-smoking contest eight years ago, ran smoke shops for Younkers department stores here and in Omaha for 12 years before retiring last year.

"I thought I'd retire and take it easy," said Foote, 61.

But taking it easy isn't what sold 6,000 pounds of tobacco in the last year or what will thrust his business into the range of $50,000 in gross receipts this year.

Drawing upon loyal customers from his days at Younkers, Foote compiled a list last June of 4,000 smokers in 47 states who savored the taste and aroma of his most popular brand, "Chuck Foote's Favorite Blend," which he sold at Younkers under a different name.

Taking instructions from "How to Get Rich in Mail Order," by Melvin Powers, Foote tapped into loyal customers from his days at Younkers. He mailed a letter saying he had left the department store, and included a pamphlet and order form to begin the venture.

The letter and pamphlet effort are the only advertising Tobacco Outlet has done, a violation of the how-to book, which implores its disciples to take out ad space in local newspapers and magazines, Foote said.

Foote gets his tobacco from North Carolina, Virginia and Georgia, mixes it, and places it in plastic pouches. A custom-printed label is attached to the bags and the product is ready for sale.

The blend and Tobacco Outlet's 29 other offerings are sold in 1-ounce, 2-ounce, 8-ounce and 16-ounce packages, for 80 cents, $1.54, $5.15 and $9.60 respectively. Walk-in customers pay the same as those who order through the mail, Foote said, eyeing a desk-top sized cardboard box lid brimming with orders.

A marketplace fence-sitter, Foote sells "Hawkeye" and "Cyclone" blends, with packages carrying sketches of Herky and Cy puffing on pipes.

As rock stars have groupies, Chuck Foote has dozens of letters from customers lauding his blends, and he supplied a member of the U.S. Embassy in Athens, Greece, with smoke before the man ended his tour. Each month, Footes ships 25 customers a 30-day allotment of tobacco.

Foote won't disclose the contents and proportions of his blends, but he does humbly admit their popularity.

"It's just like cooking I guess — not too many people can do it well," he said. "I've been in it so many years, I just know how to blend it."

When Foote and Fisher opened their mail-order business, still Tobacco Outlet's staple, they didn't imagine that a year later they would be displaying their wares on the counters of Hy-Vee and Super Valu food stores, Drug Towns, and Sun Drugs in Des Moines, Perry, Chariton, Newton, Ames and Johnston.

But, following a section of the mail-order primer, the entrepreneurs tackled the wholesale tobacco market.

"I didn't plan a market like that, I just planned on selling a few by mail and it just mushroomed," Foote said.

He attributed Tobacco Outlet's growth to the "romanticism" associated with pipe smoking, and the nationwide decline in cigarette smoking among males in the United States. The store also sells, "Down Home Iowa Chew," a chewing tobacco.

The only other employee at Tobacco Outlet, Dennis Stecker, is the company's sales representative. Last month, he trekked to Waterloo and Cedar Falls to peddle tobacco, and he makes weekly visits to stores that carry Foote's blends. His plans are to have Foote's blends on store shelves in every Iowa county.

"We just saw wholesaling as an ideal source of income in these small towns where you can't find good, fresh tobacco," Stecker said. "Other store tobacco is dry."

"We're going to cover the state with retail outlets," Foote said.

Pipe tobacco, while not an item of great excitement to most store managers, can be found in most supermarkets and drug stores, so why not give a local product a shot, several managers wondered?

"It's not a big product any way you look at it," said Mike McKinley, assistant manager at Hy-Vee Harding Hills, 3330 Harding Road. "But if you can put a local product in, that's always a good deal for everybody concerned."

Foote entered the wholesale business last August through his partner, Fisher, who is a shift manager at the Hy-Vee at 2559 E. Euclid Ave., and has since distributed 7,000 2-ounce pouches of tobacco through 25 of the chain's stores. Tobacco Outlet is currently talking with a 524-unit convenience store chain in Iowa about stocking its stores with Foote's tobacco.

In addition to blending tobaccos, Tobacco Outlet sells pipes, lighters and pouches from a New York wholesaler to its mail-order customers, and the company is working on a blender Foote invented to market to other smoke shops.

"It's a simple idea, but nobody ever thought of it," Stecker said.

Foote has applied for a patent for his machines, which are made of Lucite by Central Iowa Plastics, and said he thinks he can sell 1,500 of them for $300 each.

Chapter One

How to Develop Your Mail Order Expertise

Welcome to the wonderful world of mail order!

You are about to embark on what could prove to be one of the most fascinating and challenging enterprises you have ever undertaken. But this is just part of the story—the rest deals with the prospect of financial gain exceeding anything you might have imagined. It is the drama inherent in the mail order business, a world of activity whose branches reach out into the commerce of virtually every nation on the face of the earth.

Like most businesses, the world of mail order is one in which there is a direct correlation between what you are prepared to put into it and what you will eventually take away from it. But unlike many, it is a game unfettered with restrictions and qualifications—and for that reason it could be the best game in town. The opportunity for success is available to all. There is no distinction in terms of social background, job, or affluence. No particular skills are necessary nor is education required beyond that which is provided in this book and the supplemental reading program suggested. Play by the rules, follow the guidelines, meet the challenges squarely, and the only limit on how much you can earn is that which you set.

As with anything else, the prime catalyst for accomplishment in the mail order field is *motivation*. Given this incentive and determination to succeed and the guiding hand of one who has already successfully established a business, you are well on your way.

It is this book which will provide the guiding hand, the link between motivation and achievement. It is unique in the sense that I candidly share all I have learned about the intricacies and ramifications of the mail order business so you might achieve the goals of wealth and success set for yourself. Through its pages, my know-how will become yours. You will learn much about my philosophy, my avocations, hobbies, interests, and business thinking. I have tried to invest the book with my own personality, to establish between us—author and reader—a sense of rapport. By creating this relationship at the outset, I will assume we are conferring on a personal level. Feel free to communicate with me whenever you wish, with the positive assurance that you will be heard. If you feel so inclined, don't hesitate to write, phone, or visit me at my office. Mail order is a hobby with me as well as a business, and I find talking about it is pleasurable and stimulating.

In effect, we will be working together, and since I have made various claims about my ability to enhance your chances for wealth and success in the mail order business, you should know my credentials. Briefly, I am Melvin Powers—writer, editor, publisher, lecturer, and executive head of the Wilshire Book Company, specializing in self-improvement books. I have been a book publisher and mail order entrepreneur for more than 25 years, selling millions of dollars worth of books and products, utilizing mail order techniques almost exclusively.

During those years I have learned that the mail order business, despite its mundane image, is a highly creative endeavor. You will better understand this once you start to open the envelopes and watch the money pour out.

Now that we have established the nature of our relationship and have determined that our mutual objective is your success, let's get down to business.

This book is a practical, realistic, no-frills approach to the mail order business. In it, we will explore in detail the methods and devices I have employed as mail order techniques to exact from the business the maximum financial return that is commensurate with the time and effort expended. We will examine the potential peaks and valleys and I'll post storm warnings about the pitfalls, call the shots as I see them, and stick to fundamentals.

Imagine you are seated with me in my office, and I am explaining what I am doing and why. With patience and concentration, you will gradually begin to absorb the essentials and develop an understanding of the mail order business. Your efforts to conscientiously follow my instructions will eventually bear fruit until, almost without realizing it, you will have transferred them from theory to an operational understanding of the business, enabling you to undertake your own mail order project. I can assure you that you will become successful.

To implement the practical aspects of the book, I have included a wide variety of mail order ads, direct mail literature, and magazine and newspaper articles, all designed to better enable you to comprehend the mail order business. Once you see the overall picture and become attuned to the multiplicity of operational techniques involved, it will be easier for me to demonstrate success patterns to you and explain how you can emulate your predecessors who have already reached the pinnacle of success.

Having initially launched your career with the prime propellant—motivation, the next important step to be considered in your drive to success is an element called *creativity.* In the context of the subject with which we are dealing, creativity refers to the ingenuity exercised in promoting a service or a product—the inventive or innovative design one employs to spark the interest of a potential customer. The degree to which one exerts his powers of creativity is, more than likely, the difference between success and failure.

To help nurture your powers of creativity, I'll explain the rationale of specific successful mail order operations, the success of specific mail order ads, and recommend a series of books for supplemental reading that can be obtained at your local library. It may prove helpful to read others of the same genre. The purpose is to start your creative processes churning, and this requires that you become involved in a continuous reading program. To this day, I pursue a program of this nature, reading books on mail order, advertising, business creativity, psychology, and motivation incessantly. It's a preoccupation that keeps me perpetually stimulated. I welcome reading recommendations from any legitimate source, so if you should happen to read an exceptionally interesting book, I'd appreciate hearing from you.

Above all, you must learn to believe in yourself and in your ability to succeed. A success formula in any field of endeavor starts with the individual and an unyielding conviction that he will make the grade, no matter how small or unimpressive his beginning. Books are filled with stories of men and women who have pyramided a kitchen table operation into a corporate giant. A case in point is the story of Leonard Carlson, who sold a $1 personalized rubber stamp, and parlayed it into Sunset House, the multi-million dollar, gadget mail order house. It could happen to you, but not without drive, perseverance, ingenuity, and an excellent self-image.

Patience is another virtue which plays a dynamic role in your success drama. Bear in mind that careers are not built overnight. They are laid on a solid foundation comprised of many qualifying layers of hard work, tenacity, ingenuity, and motivation. There are bound to be failings along the way, but failings do not add up to failure unless you succumb to them, allowing them to destroy your determination to reach the goal set for yourself.

A villain in the picture is an inclination to dwell on past mistakes. This can be a fiendish antidote to success. Don't allow it to happen. It will destroy your self-image, and that can be fatal. Mistakes are just as much a part of the growth process as anything else, and they must not be given disproportionate importance by allowing them to assume a bigger-than-life role in your scheme of things. Remember, you're in charge. Only you can get rid of the dead wood. To quote Hal Leighton, prominent Los Angeles printing executive, "The success of the business is usually determined by one guiding individual. He's like the captain of a ship, pulling all the elements together for a smooth trip. In a storm, he can't falter. He needs to be resolute in what he's doing."

To make you the captain of your ship is what we have set out to accomplish in your sail to success as a mail order entrepreneur. An inquisitive person with a willingness to learn can be guided to success. If properly applied, the knowledge you'll gain from this book and those I recommend to you will inevitably underwrite that success. I want you to adopt the attitude that if others have been successful, so can you. Emulate their success patterns. Start thinking of yourself as a professional. If you have doubts about yourself, dispel them by thinking about the vast number of men and women who have made it to the top in myriad fields of endeavor. If they share a common virtue, it is determination, the single most indestructible weapon in man's drive for conquest and recognition. Without it, the road may never lead to success.

We have touched on the importance of building a good self-image. This self-image is not difficult to maintain when one is successful, but what becomes of the self-image in the face of adversity? Hold on to it! It's just as important to maintain that good, confident, self-assured image of yourself when you're waiting for success as when you have achieved it. Once you have experienced the satisfaction of knowing you've given your best effort to the project at hand, your self-image will feed on the anticipation of good things to come.

Don't be afraid to dream. You'd be amazed to know how much of tomorrow's success is made of today's dreams. They give spark and meaning to our daily existence. I, too, have my dreams. One of them is to help you achieve personal and monetary satisfaction from the unlimited scope and stimulating challenge of the mail order business. It is a dream that, when it turns to reality, will make you independent and beholden only to yourself.

Achieving success is never easy, but it will be a great deal easier if you equip yourself with the proper tools. If you conscientiously follow the instructions in this book and pursue the leads I give you, your chances for success will be greatly enhanced. You'll discover a unique way of merchandising a product or a service. You'll write an advertisement that will pull in orders exceeding amounts you might have imagined not possible. You'll produce a catalog that will prove remunerative. You'll make money just renting your list of customers to others. And then comes that great feeling ... the glorious, daily ritual of shaking checks, cash, and money orders out of the envelopes!

Each of us is unique. Each of us has a personality and temperament distinct from others. We each have individual hopes, desires, and ambitions. It is by virtue of these individualities that each of us brings to a business venture a different approach from that used by someone else. It is this uniqueness I want to encourage and develop, for it is the element which will eventually spell success. If you have not yet been as successful as you would like to be, don't be discouraged. In reading this book, at least you are doing something about it—taking constructive steps to bring it about. A failure in the past does not preclude a future that can be extremely successful. Monetary and personal success begin with a correct mental attitude. Knowing someone is successfully mail ordering lobsters from Maine and oranges from Florida, or selling apples from the state of Washington, should be good news for you. If they can do it, so can you.

In my earlier remarks, I stated that success in mail order is not determined by how much money you have to invest in your venture. It is advisable for the uninitiated to start in a small way with a few products, constantly testing results against various factors, such as layout of advertisements, headlines, prices, media where ads are placed, classified and display ads, direct mail, mailing lists, and so on.

Bear in mind that one of your prime goals is to develop your powers of creativity and innovation. The creative process is developing an idea to its maximum potential. Can you look at a product and envision a new use for it? Can you foresee a way to increase its functional use by making it smaller or larger? Is there some way you can improve on it? Can you romanticize or dramatize it in

advertising copy? Can you evaluate the sales potential of a product or service?

If you could answer all these questions affirmatively, there would be no need for you to read this book. Even I cannot always supply the answer to every question. So, obviously, we can both continue to educate ourselves and be prepared when an opportunity to employ our creative talents presents itself. Become an innovator in dealing with products and services, not just a follower. Be original. The inventive thinker and doer makes the money. We are endowed with resources enabling us to be creative, productive, and analytical, and to develop the capacity for making a success of our lives. I want you to experience the pleasure inherent in the challenge of making money in the mail order field.

I am constantly stimulated by the unlimited opportunities that exist for making money in the mail order field. I want you to savor the same stimulation, be caught up in the excitement of making more money than you ever thought possible. And I want you to have a good time doing it. Once you experience the challenge, a stream of conscious and subconscious influences will appreciably enhance your creative thinking.

As in any other progressive move, there are some calculated risks in being an innovator and a non-conformist. Not all our ideas can be money makers. Our goal is to come up with a winner. My goal with this book, and those I recommend to you, is to bolster your self-confidence in a valid way and suggest ideas which will enable you to find and create products. I will give you the basic guidelines to outline, organize, and develop a mail order plan which will stir your creativity and give you a sense of personal pride and fulfillment money can't buy. When you achieve this, please let me hear from you so that I may share with you the incomparable gratification attending your well-earned success.

In the beginning, do not place your goalposts too far back. Set realistic aims for yourself and try to meet them. Even the smallest degree of success as a mail order entrepreneur will bolster your self-confidence. Having reached your initial goal, you can now train your sights on a more challenging accomplishment. Reach one plateau—the next will be a great deal easier. Should your second attempt falter, keep your confidence unshaken. Remember, you have a self-image that has known success.

Don't expect success with every mail order campaign. It just doesn't happen, not even to the experts. If you have given your best effort to a mail order idea and it doesn't work, put your energy into the next project. Don't be too tough on yourself. An error predicated on honest judgment is no reason for self-chastisement. Celebrate every success, no matter how small, which, appropriately, brings to mind the remark of Dr. Erich Fromm, author of *Man for Himself.* In commenting on the phenomenon of finding happiness, he said, "Man's main task in life is to give birth to himself, to become what he potentially is."

The following comprises my initial list of books for recommended reading. These books and many others on the same subject are available at your local library. If you have especially enjoyed one of the books that I have recommended, I would appreciate your comments.

How I Made a Million Dollars with Ideas by George J. Abrams
A self-made marketing genius tells all about ideas—how to get them, how to use them, how to make money from them.

How To Turn Your Idea into a Million Dollars by Don Kracke
Fads and fancies, amusing gadgets, clever devices. What do you do when you have an idea for a new product or invention—maybe even a million-dollar idea? Hardly anyone has a clue about what to do next. It tells you everything you need to know in complete detail to turn your bright idea into a big success.

The Techniques of Creative Thinking by Robert P. Crawford
How to use your ideas to achieve success. Uncovers the hidden power of the mind, shows how it works, demonstrates how to take random thoughts and turn them into practical ideas that produce positive results.

Brainstorming by Charles Clark
A dynamic way to create successful ideas. Brainstorming is a method of tapping the hidden brain power and drawing creative ideas from the subconscious mind.

The following are my favorite inspirational books. I recommend them to you.

Exuberance—Your Guide to Happiness and Fulfillment by Paul Kurtz, Ph.D.

How To Attract Good Luck by A.H.Z. Carr

How You Can Have Confidence & Power In Dealing with People by Les Giblin

Magic of Thinking Big by David J. Schwartz, Ph.D.

New Guide To Rational Living by Albert Ellis, Ph.D. and Robert Harper, Ph.D.

Psycho-Cybernetics by Maxwell Maltz, M.D.

Your Subconscious Power by Charles M. Simmons

10 Days To a Great New Life by William E. Edwards

I Am a Compleat Woman—An Adventure in Self-Discovery by Doris Hagopian and Karen O'Connor Sweeney

Chapter Two

How to Find a Unique Product or Service to Sell

Visit your library, bookstore, or newsstand. Examine the classified section of numerous magazines and tabloids. Your job is to search for something you would like to sell. Answer the classified ads that are of interest to you.

One of the easiest ways to find out about trade shows is to look on the Internet. If you don't have a computer, you can use one at your local public library or at a college or university library, if there is one near you. Librarians are familiar with the computer and will be glad to help you if you ask.

Practically every major city has a convention center. You can easily find the one nearest you and get a schedule of forthcoming shows and lots of other valuable information by entering on the computer the name of the city you live in, followed by the words *Convention Center;* for example, San Francisco Convention Center, Los Angeles Convention Center, Anaheim Convention Center, Chicago Convention Center, Dallas Convention Center, Boston Convention Center. You can also enter the names of nearby cities or cities you may be visiting to get lists of their shows.

If you are interested in a particular product category and want to find out about scheduled shows at various convention centers, you can do that, too. For instance, say

you want to learn of jewelry trade shows, sporting goods trade shows, or gift trade shows, you would enter *jewelry trade shows*, for example, on your favorite search engine. I have found Alta Vista to be the best for my purposes.

Whether or not you can get to a trade show, I urge you to go to the library and ask for the reference publication, *Business Publications Rates and Data.* It profiles more than 3,000 business, trade, and technical publications in the United States. They are arranged in 175 categories. Under the heading, *Giftware, section 57,* for example, you'll find a list of publications. You would then write to every magazine for a free sample copy, telling them you are in the mail order business.

Attend every kind of trade show where products are being exhibited. Many shows are held on Saturday and Sunday, making it convenient for people to attend. You never know when you are going to find a product that will capture your imagination. I liken the trade show to a treasure hunt. Sometimes a prize is found, sometimes not. In any event, it will stimulate your creative thinking and eventually you will find a great product to sell.

The Internet is also a great place to find products. See what other people are advertising. It's the greatest source of products that you can possibly imagine. This is where the action is in mail order. It's important for you to become familiar with the Internet and use it to look for products that you would enjoy selling.

You can surf the Internet and find thousands of products from all over the world. Three of the most comprehensive sources of supplies for your mail order business can be found at the following URL (Universal Resource Locator) addresses: http://www.miesys.com, http://www.tdc.org.hk, and http://www.wholesalecentral.com. The first is for products from Europe; the second, from Asia; and the third from the USA. They contain a gold mine of information.

You can immediately retrieve valuable information from the Internet. You will be able to search for a particular product or companies that offer products in a specific category. They will be pleased to cooperate with you, and you will enjoy dealing with companies all over the world.

Do the same with other categories that interest you. The possibilities are unlimited. This is the homework that will pay you big dividends. Think of yourself as a mail order detective in search of an item or line of items that will spell success for you.

Most people love to receive packages through the mail, especially from overseas. I was in Paris some years ago and found a company that sold perfume over-the-counter, as well as by mail order. Instead of carrying home the perfume, I had it sent to various women in my life. Ever since, I have been receiving the company's yearly catalog, and I still send perfume. The recipients are always telling me how they love getting these annual packages of perfume. It's the excitement of receiving the package, especially from the city of romance—Paris. You could make similar arrangements for drop-shipments from companies around the world. What about selling cheese, nuts, tea, coffee or a variety of food products and gifts from all over the world?

Another source of products is the business section of your local newspaper. Reading it diligently can be an extremely resourceful way of finding products that interest you. I'm reproducing an article that appeared in the *Los Angeles Times*. See page 21. As I read the article I said to myself, "That's the hottest mail order item I've seen in years." Sure enough, in the same section there was an advertisement for the translating calculator.

Obviously, the company selling this item knew about it before the article appeared in the paper. I think it's safe to assume they were instrumental in getting this publicity release. Running their ad in the same section at the same time is perfect mail order and retail merchandising strategy. It's a classic example of excellence.

Anastasios Kyriakides, the inventor, was on the Merv Griffin TV program talking about his fabulous success in selling the *Lexicon*. He's become a multi-millionaire in a very short period of time. It's a beautiful success story, based on the ingenuity and tenacity of one man.

Become intellectually curious about all types of business opportunities and products to sell. Keep an open mind in this pursuit. It will prove stimulating and will stimulate your creative thinking.

Should you want to find out more about the food industry, go to *Business Publications Rates* and *Data*. Under section 127, you'll find plenty of magazines to whet your appetite.

Here's my message to you: If others are doing it successfully, so can you. There are no secrets. You can send for their catalogs, you can purchase their products, and you can get on their mailing lists. If you are interested, you can duplicate what they are doing and, perhaps, even improve on it.

There are trade shows, seminars, trade publications, books, and retail publications in almost all areas of specialized mail order products. Your job is to learn from them and capitalize on all this information, transforming it into dollars for your business. It's all there waiting for you. Bring the elements together in an attractive mail order package and the world will beat a path to your door. Always keep in mind that if others are doing it successfully, so can you.

Regardless of what you are selling, the pattern is the same. I recommend you specialize in one particular area and become well-known for your expertise in that field. If that field is one that really interests you, or in which you would like to develop an interest, your business becomes your hobby. My business is my hobby and I take pleasure in each day's work schedule. That's the way I would like it to be with you.

Your library may have various directories of mail order companies. In it you'll find companies selling food products. Request their catalogs to aid in your research. Digest the offers, layouts, ad copy, and headlines. This is the work of successful merchandisers. With all this information, wouldn't it be easy to copy their success pattern? Better yet, can you come up with recipes for your own grandmother's fruit cake, jellies, candies, pickles, or homemade cheese? What about special tea or coffee blends, clam chowder, special Italian meat sauce (spicy and non-spicy), or what have you? If you like chocolates, send away to Charbonnel et Walker, 31 Old Bond Street, London W1, England, for their catalog. You'll gain five pounds just reading and looking at the pictures.

Go through the classified and display ads of the wide assortment of magazines at your library. You might stumble across something that will interest you. This takes time and energy, and should not be done in a cursory manner but with diligence.

Next, go to some out-of-print bookstores and look through the old magazines. Perhaps you'll find something there that will be of interest to you. You can always revitalize a winning idea. Look through the off-beat magazines as well.

Spend some time reading the Sunday classified business section. There may be a business for sale that has a perfect mail order product.

You might consider running the following one-inch ad in your local newspaper:

WANTED
Mail order products.
(Your name and address)
(Your phone number)

It might be a good idea to run the same ad in the *Wall Street Journal*, the *New York Times*, the *Los Angeles Times*, or any other major newspaper. If you prefer a variation on the above copy, the following could serve the purpose:

Mail order entrepreneur
looking for new products. Send details to:
(Your name and address)
(Your phone number)

Be sure to include your telephone area code and zip code.

Government-owned Patents

As a general rule, any U.S. government-owned patent is available on a non-exclusive, royalty-free basis. Some government agencies will issue a license with limited exclusivity if there has been no request for a license within two years of the date of publication of the patent. You can obtain information on government-owned patents from your local Small Business Administration office (check your local phone book), the closest field office of the U.S. Department of Commerce, or by writing to the U.S. Patent Office, Department of Commerce, Washington, D.C. 20231.

Patent Abstracts Bibliography (PAB)

Patent Abstracts Bibliography is a semi-annual periodical which lists NASA-owned patents and applications for patents. It is published as a service to those seeking new licensable products for the commercial market. Two issues of the PAB are available: the cumulative issue of abstracts (N74-20609) for $18.75 and the cumulative issue of indexes (N74-20610) for $4.50. They may be ordered from the National Technical Information Service (NTIS), U.S. Department of Commerce, Springfield, Virginia 22151.

Made in Europe

The very best source in the world for finding hundreds of new products is the magazine, *Made in Europe*. All successful mail order companies use this publication. As a bonus, the readers' service department of the magazine offers free personalized information in finding all types of specific mail order products.

I'm offering subscriptions on a one-year, money-back guarantee basis. A subscription for 12 issues costs $120. Sample copies cost $14 postpaid. Send your order to: Melvin Powers, 12015 Sherman Road, North Hollywood, California 91605.

Private Patents

The Official Gazette of the U.S. Patent Office is published weekly and lists all the patents granted by the U.S. Patent Office. Annual subscriptions are available from the Superintendent of Documents, Government Printing Office, Washington, D.C. 20402. The *Gazette* contains a one-time-only section that lists patents that are available for sale or licensing.

There are a number of private publications listing patents available for licensing or sale. Your local librarian can give you a complete listing of all such private publications.

Inventor's Shows

The Chamber of Commerce in large metropolitan areas generally sponsors an annual "Inventor's Show" to encourage manufacturers and inventors to meet and put new products on the market. Check with your local Chamber of Commerce for the date of its next show. One of these shows might have the ideal new product for your mail order business.

Foreign Licenses

The U.S. Department of Commerce publishes biweekly *Business America—The Magazine of International Trade.* This magazine contains a "Licensing Opportunities Section" listing foreign-made products for which the manufacturers seek U.S. firms to manufacture and sell the products in this country. The yearly subscription fee is $41. The publication may be ordered through the Department of Commerce local field office. Before you order, go to your local field office and examine previous issues that are available for public inspection. Your library may have copies as well.

American Export Register of Exporters & Importers, published by Thomas Publishing Company, 1 Pennsylvania Plaza, New York, New York 10001. The book contains a product index in English, Spanish, French, and German. Go through every page of the book. Write to companies telling them of your interest. It also contains the addresses of American Chambers of Commerce in foreign countries and foreign Chambers of Commerce and foreign embassies in the United States. You can write to them explaining you are in the mail order business and are looking for products. You may be sure you will receive an answer. An important part of their job is to promote trade.

Examine the *Thomas' Register of American Manufacturers,* published by the Thomas Publishing Company, 1 Pennsylvania Plaza, New York, New York 10001. This book is a great source of information. It has an extensive list of products, with the name of the manufacturer. Go through all the categories. Again, write to companies telling them you are in the mail order business and you are looking for unique products to sell.

The *Directory of New York Importers,* published by the Commerce & Industry Association Institute, Inc., 65 Liberty Street, New York 10005, is excellent, containing a list of products with names and addresses of importers.

It probably never occurred to you that the Yellow Pages of your local phone book is a source for products. Most libraries carry phone books of many of the major cities in the United States. Go through every page. You never know when a heading or an advertisement will appeal to you. When you find something, phone the listed party and say you are in the mail order business and, if the conversation generates further interest, set up an appointment.

I also recommend the magazine *Gifts & Decorative Accessories,* 51 Madison Avenue, New York, New York 10036.

When you write to the various consulates and embassies, tell them you are interested in new products from their country and that you'd like to receive trade publications. You'll receive literature from all over the world.

An excellent way of finding out what's going on in the field of mail order is to read trade publications. They contain articles about companies that are successfully selling various products. These articles contain a wealth of information for the astute mail order entrepreneur. If you are interested in a particular category of product, you can copycat marketing techniques used by the companies you read about, adding your creative touch.

Send away for complimentary copies of the following publications. Subscribe to those you find most helpful. I personally read them all every month.

Catalog Age
911 Hope Street
Six River Bend Center, PO Box 4949,
Stamford, Connecticut 06907-0949

Direct: The Magazine of Direct Marketing Management
911 Hope Street
Six River Bend Center, PO Box 4949,
Stamford, Connecticut 06907-4949

DM News: The Weekly Newspaper for Direct Marketers
19 W. 21st Street
New York, New York 10010

Target Marketing
401 N. Broad Street
Philadelphia, Pennsylvania 19108

Direct Marketing
224 17th Street
Garden City, New York 11530

With all the sources of reference I've given you, you should have little trouble coming up with some products you would like to sell. Let's look at some of the other leads I have for you.

On page 30 you'll find some ads for miniature horses. That sounds like an unusual business, and I assume the miniature horses make nice pets. If you are interested in mail ordering these horses, you could make arrangements for them to be sent by trailer to their destination. I'm in the Arabian horse business, and just today, in fact, as I'm writing this chapter, I received a sizable check from my partner for one of the horses we sold. You could easily publicize your business and that would result in your selling more and more miniature horses. Why couldn't you make arrangements with various pet shops to drop-ship them? It's worth a try. I'd be interested to learn the results of your effort.

See page 31. Bathing suits and bikinis sell very successfully if promoted properly via mail order. Many small town inhabitants are sensitive about advertising their personal needs to the local merchants and would welcome the opportunity to have these requirements supplied by mail.

The best products to sell are those that are consumable and need to be replaced with regularity. These include coffee supplies, personalized stationery, name-and-address labels, food, beverages, perfumes, make-up, personal products, and clothing.

The clothing field lends itself especially well to mail order. You could specialize in all shapes and sizes, a particular look, clothing for every kind of indoor-outdoor activity, sports apparel, and something to project that sexy look.

See page 32. Frederick's of Hollywood specializes in sexy underwear and clothing for women. They have been successful in this operation for many years. They also have retail outlets that have prospered. The women depicted in Frederick's catalog are always alluring. The catalog caters to the romantic fantasies of women and men. Every illustration is saying, in effect, "How can he possibly resist you in a revealing, exciting, enticing creation from Frederick's of Hollywood, couturier to the stars?" See page 33.

Frederick's publicity program is great. I've seen him many times on TV, talking about his sexy clothing while beautiful models show off their wares and his. The host is always in a jovial mood. Everyone has a good time looking at the models and talking about Frederick's sensuous clothing. Frederick receives thousands of dollars worth of free publicity. Here is a man who, with design and imagination, has turned the power of suggestion into a multi-million dollar business.

Note that Frederick charges for his catalog. This is an economically feasible way of qualifying his customers. Obviously, through trial and error, he had discovered that he was spending too much money sending free catalogs to mere curiosity seekers. When you add up the cost of the catalog, postage, and clerical time, the expense can become prohibitive, particularly if you are not pulling in sufficient orders.

You might want to consider selling some type of wearing apparel. I buy my shoes by mail. I've found a particular design of shoe that's good for me. It's called *Foot-so-Port* and has a built-in arch support. Wearing this shoe, I can walk around all day and not become tired. I know this sounds like a commercial, but it's true. I've tried all makes of shoes, but this shoe does wonders for me. I recently ordered three pairs. I simply write a letter and pay for the shoes after they arrive. The company maintains retail outlets. If you are ever in Colorado Springs, Colorado, and looking for a comfortable pair of shoes, see Fred Kaufman at Foot-so-Port, 323½ N. Tejon Street. Put out a good product and personal endorsements will keep it growing. It means more than the best advertising copy.

Do you have specialized knowledge or skill in any field? If so, the chances are you can run a successful mail order course teaching that subject. It could involve some phase of business or a profession.

Perhaps you have a hobby or avocation you could develop into a course of instruction. Here are some examples: playing guitar, playing piano, interior decorating, how to become an accountant, stamp and coin collecting, upholstering, watch repairing, invisible mending, locksmithing, television and radio repair, hotel management, meat cutting, taxidermy, gardening, growing orchids, commercial art, horticulture, baking, cooking, woodworking, piano tuning, candy making, writing, photography, baby-shoe metallizing, repairing electrical appliances, calligraphy, how to improve your English, voice-and-speech training, songwriting, teaching a sport, and dancing.

Magazines are filled with offers for these kinds of courses. Send for the literature, and if you are interested in publishing a course of instruction, send for those being sold, then improve upon it. Cassette tapes can be extremely useful when it comes to teaching and instruction. Take advantage of them. Use the telephone for a personal follow-up during the hours that the rates are low.

If you are selling a course of instruction in learning how to play the guitar, you might consider selling guitars as a follow-up. If it's a course in cooking, you might want to sell cooking utensils that you found especially useful. You would also want to carry a line of cookbooks in your particular specialty. You can buy books from all publishers at discounts from 40% to 50%.

I enjoy selling books by mail, and I'll talk extensively about it later in this book. I have been in the gift-and-gadget mail order business but had to give it up because I didn't have the time to devote to it. My advice is to specialize in whatever you decide to mail order.

Besides thinking of a saleable product, you should also give some thought to what would be the natural follow-up. Some time ago, I ran a series of advertisements selling golf books. One was titled, *The Secret of Perfect Putting,* and the other, *How to Play Better Golf Using Self-Hypnosis.* What would be the logical items to sell these buyers? Golf equipment. For the buyers of the second book, you would add books dealing with hypnosis. Although I didn't sell it, the perfect follow-up for the book, *The Secret of Perfect Putting,* might have been a specially designed putter, called "The Perfect Putter."

As it was, I sold thousands of sets of personalized golf balls. In my follow-up mail, I suggested it as a perfect gift for the golfer on any number of occasions, such as for a birthday, Valentine's Day, Father's Day, Mother's Day, anniversary, Christmas, Chanukah, and just to say, "I love you." The gift package was made up of a dozen good golf balls that were personalized with the individual's name and gift wrapped in a beautiful wooden box that could be saved and used. An attractive gift card was enclosed with every order that was drop-shipped by the manufacturer. It was a great re-order item, and I received many multiple orders, virtually all to be sent as gifts.

The ideal product is one that is reasonably priced, light weight (to keep the postage at a minimum), and unbreakable in transit. It follows that it should please the customer and lead to re-orders.

While we generally associate mail order with low-ticket items, we know that jewelers, furriers, exclusive department stores, such as Neiman-Marcus, and specialty mail order houses put out catalogs with items selling for thousands of dollars.

My philosophy has always been to sell at the lowest possible price and do a volume business. That's why most of the books I publish sell for two and three dollars. I've sold well over two million copies of the book *Psycho-Cybernetics* by Maxwell Maltz, M.D., at a price of $2. Let's assume I priced the book at $5. Do you suppose I would have sold just as many?

We know some perfume is purposely priced high for status, or snob appeal. For the same reason, certain restaurants, vacation spots, clothes, jewelry, cameras, and automobiles are similarly priced high. There are numerous people who equate high prices with excellence and are willing to pay for it.

See page 15. You've probably seen this ad and variations of it in many magazines and tabloids. I have investigated numerous sources for gifts and highly recommend Mail Order Associates, Inc. This company was founded in 1956 to supply mail order dealers with a reliable source of products from all over the world.

Mail Order Associates offers you the opportunity to get started in the fabulous mail order gift and gadget business without investing five cents in inventory. MOA has an effi-ciently trained staff of over 50 to help you make money. I am very impressed with the company's service and operation, and helpful attitude of the president, key personnel, and office and warehouse employees.

Does it sound like I am enthusiastic about MOA? I am. I would highly recommend that you write to: Mail Order Gift Catalog Division—Dept. 12, Mail Order Associates, Inc., 120 Chestnut Ridge Road, Montvale, New Jersey 07645. Their beautiful gift catalog is available with your imprint. Write for details. They'll send you information about 500 mail order products that they will drop-ship for you.

At the end of this chapter I'm including a list of associations, direct mail clubs, and contacts for you. Search out one of the organizations near you, introduce yourself, and start attending the meetings. You'll be in a climate of professionalism, and that's the best possible learning experience for you. As a result, you'll be able to progress that much quicker in your own business. Don't be reticent to tell them you are a beginner in mail order and want to learn as much as possible about the intricacies of the business. You'll establish important contacts, and you'll be able to get all kinds of professional assistance from people eager to help you. Let them know you are looking for products. You never know when someone will put you on the track of a mail order item that's just right for you.

Are you beginning to think, "This fellow, Melvin Powers, has me doing too much work. I just want to find an item, run an ad, and make a lot of money."? Let me remind you again, there's no easy road to success. There is plenty of creative energy behind every successful venture. If it's a product you want to mail order, your success will be directly correlated to the effort you put into following the sources of products I have enumerated in this chapter. Think of it as an exciting treasure hunt with a pot of gold at the end. For that's exactly what it is.

The rest of the book will give you further insight into how to merchandise products, books, services, or courses of instruction. Although I'll be mainly talking about books, the basic information is the same for whatever you are mail ordering.

I've given you enough leads to keep you busy for quite some time. Do not neglect your homework. Everything begins with the product. It's a continuous, unending search for winners, and to be successful you must, through diligent homework, be ready when that winner appears.

As for your reading program, I can recommend nothing better than *Direct Marketing News.* I have previously mentioned how rewarding its information can be to you.

How to get rich

TRADE CENTERS IN THE UNITED STATES

Atlanta Merchandise Mart
Peachtree Center
Atlanta GA 30303

Charlotte Merchandise Mart
2500 Independence Blvd
Charlotte NC 28205

Chicago Merchandise Mart
Merchandise Mart Plaza
Chicago IL 60654

Cleveland World Trade Assn
Burke Lakefront Airport
Cleveland OH 44181

Dallas Market Center
2100 Stemmons Freeway
Dallas TX 75207

Denver Merchandise Mart
451 East 58th Avenue
Denver CO 80216

Houston World Trade Association
328 World Trade Center
1520 Texas Avenue
Houston TX 77002

International Business Center of New England Inc
470 Atlantic Avenue
Boston MA 02210

International Trade Club of Chicago
Chicago IL

Los Angeles World Trade Center
333 South Flower Street
Los Angeles CA 90017

Maryland Port Administration
World Trade Center
Baltimore MD 21202

Philadelphia Civic Center
Boulevard at 34th Street
Philadelphia PA 19104

Port of New Orleans
P.O. Box 60046
New Orleans LA 70160

Seattle World Trade Center
Sea Tac International Airport
Seattle WA 98100

San Antonio International Trade Center Inc
PO Box 9264
San Antonio TX 78204

World Trade Centers Association Inc
One World Trade Center
63 West
New York NY 10048

International Trade Administration District Offices

Albuquerque, 87102, 505 Marquette Ave. N.W., Suite 1015 (505) 766-2386.

Anchorage, 99513, P.O. Box 32, 701 C St. (907) 271-5041.

Atlanta, 30309, Suite 600, 1365 Peachtree St., N.E. (404) 881-7000.

Baltimore, 21202, 415 U.S. Customhouse, Gay and Lombard Sts. (301) 962-3560.

Birmingham, 35205, Suite 200-201, 908 S. 20th St. (205) 254-1331.

Boston, 02116, 10th Floor, 441 Stuart St. (617) 223-2312.

Buffalo, 14202, 1312 Federal Bldg., 111 W. Huron St. (716) 846-4191.

Charleston, W.Va., 25301, 3000 New Federal Bldg., 500 Quarrier St. (304) 343-6181, Ext. 375.

Cheyenne, 82001, 6022 O'Mahoney Federal Center, 2120 Capitol Ave. (307) 778-2220, Ext. 2151.

Chicago, 60603, Room 1406, Mid-Continental Plaza Bldg., 55 E. Monroe St. (312) 353-4450.

Cincinnati, 45202, 10504 Federal Office Bldg., 550 Main St. (513) 684-2944.

Cleveland, 44114, Room 600, 666 Euclid Ave. (216) 522-4750.

Columbia, S.C., 29201, Strom Thurmond Federal Bldg., Suite 172, 1835 Assembly St. (803) 765-5345.

Dallas, 75242, Room 7A5, 1100 Commerce St. (214) 767-0542.

Denver, 80202, Room 177, U.S. Custom House, 721-19th St. (303) 837-3246.

Des Moines, 50309, 817 Federal Bldg., 210 Walnut St. (515) 284-4222.

Detroit, 48226, 445 Federal Bldg., 231 W. Lafayette (313) 226-3650.

Greensboro, N.C., 27402, 203 Federal Bldg., W. Market St., P.O. Box 1950 (919) 378-5345.

Hartford, 06103, Room 610-B, Federal Office Bldg., 450 Main St. (203) 244-3530.

Honolulu, 96850, 4106 Federal Bldg., P.O. Box 50026, 300 Ala Moana Blvd., (808) 546-8694.

Houston, 77002, 2625 Federal Bldg., Courthouse, 515 Rusk Ave. (713) 226-4231.

Indianapolis, 46204, 357 U.S. Courthouse & Federal Office Bldg., 46 E. Ohio St. (317) 269-6214.

Jackson, Miss., 39201, City Center Plaza, Suite 550, 200 E. Pascagoula (601) 960-4388.

Kansas City, Mo. 64106, Room 1840, 601 E. 12th St. (816) 374-3142.

Little Rock, 72201, Suite 635, Savers Federal Bldg., 320 W. Capitol Ave. (501) 378-5794.

Los Angeles, 90049, Room 800, 11777 San Vicente Blvd. (213) 824-7591.

Louisville, 40202, Room 636B, U.S. Post Office and Court House Bldg. (502) 582-5066.

Memphis, 38103, Room 710, 147 Jefferson Ave. (901) 521-3213.

Miami, 33130, Room 821, City National Bank Bldg., 25 W. Flagler St. (305) 350-5267.

Milwaukee, 53202, Federal Bldg./U.S. Courthouse, 517 E. Wisconsin Ave. (414) 291-3473.

Minneapolis, 55401, 218 Federal Bldg., 110 S. Fourth St. (612) 725-2133.

New Orleans, 70130, Room 432, International Trade Mart, No. 2 Canal St. (504) 589-6546.

New York, 10278, Room 3718, Federal Office Bldg., 26 Federal Plaza, Foley Sq. (212) 264-0634.

Newark, 07102, 4th Floor, Gateway Bldg., Market St. & Penn Plaza (201) 645-6214.

Omaha, 68102, Empire State Bldg., 1st Floor, 300 S. 19th St. (402) 221-3664.

Philadelphia, 19106, 9448 Federal Bldg., 600 Arch St. (215) 597-2866.

Phoenix, 85073, 2950 Valley Bank Center, 201 N. Central Ave. (602) 261-3285.

Pittsburgh, 15222, 2002 Federal Bldg., 1000 Liberty Ave. (412) 644-2850.

Portland, Ore., 97204, Room 618, 1220 S.W. 3rd Ave. (503) 221-3001.

Reno, Nev., 89503, 777 W. 2nd St., Room 120 (702) 784-5203.

Richmond, 23240, 8010 Federal Bldg., 400 N. 8th St. (804) 771-2246.

St. Louis, 63105, 120 S. Central Ave. (314) 425-3302.

Salt Lake City, 84101, U.S. Courthouse, 350 S. Main St. (801) 524-5116.

San Francisco, 94102, Federal Bldg., Box 36013, 450 Golden Gate Ave. (415) 556-5860.

San Juan, P.R., 00918, Room 659, Federal Bldg., Hato Rey (809) 753-4555, Ext. 555.

Savannah, 31412, 222 U.S. Courthouse & P.O. Box 9746, 125-29 Bull St. (912) 944-4204.

Seattle, 98109, Room 706, Lake Union Bldg., 1700 Westlake Ave. North (206) 442-5616.

GOLF ITEMS
NAUTICAL GIFTS
RADIOS
SPECIALTY PRODUCTS
WIND CHIMES
SMOKERS ITEMS
RAINGAUGES
MEXICAN ITEMS
KNIVES
GIFTWARE
GERMAN NOVELTIES
FISHING ITEMS
ELECTRONICS
BURGLAR ALARMS
ADULT GAMES
BINOCULARS
BOOKS
GREENHOUSE KITS
LAMPS
ORIENTAL GIFTS
NOVELTIES
MATH KITS
RECORDS & STEREO
SAUNA ITEMS
TOOLS
WIGS
SPORTING GOODS
SELF-IMPROVEMENT
RUBBER STAMPS
PREMIUMS
MINERALS & GEMS
PERFUME
GEN MERCH
PET PRODUCTS
KITES
HANDICRAFTS
HEALTH ITEMS
GLASSWARE
FOOT MASSAGE
RAZORS & SHAVERS
COAT-OF-ARMS
CANDLE MAKING
CASSETTES
YOGURT-MAKER
WATCHES, CLOCKS
JEWELRY
SHIRTS
TOYS
UNIQUE PRODUCTS
IMPORTS
TROPICAL KITS
SAFARI GRILLS
PRO SPORTS ITEMS
MEDICAL AIDS
LAWN & GARDEN
INCENSE, LOVE OIL
JIGSAW PUZZLES
GOURMET FOODS
HOME STUDY ITEMS
HYPNOTISM
FLAGS
ENCYCLOPEDIA
CANDLES
COIN JEWELRY
JAPANESE ITEMS
BABY CATALOGS
AUTO ACCESSORIES
COSMETICS
EDUCATIONAL
FLASHLIGHTS
HOBBY KITS
LUGGAGE
MUSICAL ITEMS
MIMEOGRAPHS
MOVIES
LEATHER ITEMS
HAND-PAINTEDS
JEWISH PRODUCTS
MAGIC TRICKS
OUTDOOR ITEMS
HISTORICAL ITEMS
LANTERNS

HEIRLOOMS
FAMILY HISTORY
FIGURINES
ELEC APPLIANCES
CAR CADDY
PLAQUES
DOCUMENTS
BIRD MOTEL
BIRDS, LIVE
GUN RACKS
LEISURE TIME
MEN'S PERSONAL
PHONE ACCESSORIES
YOGURT KITS
BLACKLITE
HERBS, TEAS
RACK GOODS
BOATERS ITEMS
BIBLES
DOLLS, BISQUE
ETHNIC ITEMS
GOLD PAN KIT
HAND-CARVEDS
HOME SECURITY
HOME GADGETS
PERSONALIZED'S
DESK SETS
NAME PLATES
CURIOS
SKI ITEMS
SLEEP PRODUCTS
SPACE TOOLS
STAMP KITS
WOOD SHIP MODELS
MOBILE HOME ITEMS
LIQUOR ITEMS
FAR EAST PRODUCTS
CAR CADDY'S
ALPHA-BLOCKS
BATHROOM ITEMS
CAR STEREO
SMALL TV'S
HONG KONG ITEMS
COLOGNES
DATE BOOKS
DRUG, HEALTH AID
FIRST AID KITS
OLD RADIO TAPES
MAGNETIC NOVELTIES
NOSTALGIA
MAIL BOX, UNIQUE
PHOTO ALBUMS
SAUSAGE KITS
PHOTO LABELS
SUNDRIES
WOODENWARE
MAIL ORDER BOOKS
FOREIGN PRODUCTS
VITAMINS

PLUS 100'S MORE!
AVAILABILITY
OF ITEMS LISTED
SUBJECT TO CHANGE
IN EACH EDITION.

Hot Off The Press!   All Fresh Listings!

AMERICAN DROP-SHIPPERS DIRECTORY

LARGEST WHOLESALE DROP-SHIPMENT GUIDE PUBLISHED IN U.S. TODAY!

NOW - SELL BY MAIL!

NOW AVAILABLE - A complete guide to show how to sell *without* any cash outlay; *without* any merchandise investment; *without* any inventory expense! The new "American Drop-Shippers Directory" is the most complete wholesale buying guide to U.S. drop-shipment sources published today. You'll find thousands of unique, profitable items at terrific drop-ship wholesale prices in this giant directory of little-known sources. A tremendous guide to PROFITS for you!

SAVE TIME AND MONEY!

The "American Drop-Shippers Directory" is the quickest guide to valuable contacts in the field of wholesale buying available now. Save yourself both time and money: No costly franchises; no expensive courses; no time-consuming searches through dozens of catalogs - just the straightforward, practical information you need about the HOW and WHERE of wholesale buying by the no-investment, drop-ship method in one complete directory!

NEW LINES - BUYING CONNECTIONS!

New products... New ideas... New inventions... New premiums... New imports - The "American Drop-Shippers Directory" is a MUST for the latest information on exciting new products and services. It puts you in direct contact with top U.S. Manufacturers and Distributors of new, fast-selling items at unbelievably low prices. Complete information to have single-item orders shipped direct to you or your best customers!

Start TODAY to earn profits by the no-investment, drop-ship method! An order will bring your personal directory of new products to sell, new buying connections, low wholesale prices, proven knowledge and little-known sources of supply to save you time and money. The "American Drop-Shippers Directory" - you owe it to yourself to buy one! Order your copy today while this wholesale drop-shipment directory is still available for this low price.

BONUS FEATURE!

You'll get a special bonus for ordering NOW - your own free copy of "Wholesale Sources" - and exclusive, confidential list of the leading sources-of-supply for hundreds of items at low wholesale prices. You will receive the complete names and addresses of suppliers who will fill your quantity orders at low, low wholesale prices! Don't hesitate... order your copy of "American Drop-Shippers Directory" TODAY and receive this valuable "Wholesale Sources" information list free. Watch for it! It's bound right into the back pages of your personal copy of "American Drop-Shippers Directory!"

Only $10.00 ppd.

New Edition - Revised, Expanded!

YOUR KEY TO FABULOUS DROP-SHIP BARGAINS FABULOUS DROP-SHIP PROFITS!

ORDER FORM

Send orders to:
**Melvin Powers
12015 Sherman Road
No. Hollywood, CA 91605**

BUY DIRECT

RUSH my copy of "American Drop-Shippers" Directory for $10 prepaid which is enclosed.

Name _____

Address _____

City _____ State _____ Zip _____

18

INTERNATIONAL DATA & MAIL MANAGEMENT

NuPost International, 10526 W. Cermack, Westchester, IL 60154 800-449-2710

INTERNATIONAL DISTRIBUTION SERVICES

DISTRIMAIL DIV. OF INT'L DISTRIBUTION & MAILING SERVICE, INC.
P.O. Box 7195, Garden City, NY 11530 ....FAX 516-747-0854, 516-747-0333
Serving the publications community since 1974. Our overseas mailing and lettershop facilities process all types of publications and printed matter efficiently and expeditiously. Cost studies prepared upon request.
Global Mail Ltd., 22455 Davis Dr., Sterling, VA 20164 800-545-8794
Milne & Craighead Customs Brokers, 19th Floor,112-4th Avenue S.W.,Calgary,AB T2P 0H3 ..403-263-7856

INTERNATIONAL MAILINGS

Curtis Industrial, Central America ....FAX: 011-(503)-98-2814
GENESIS CORPORATION, 225 Moonstone St., Manhattan Beach, CA 90266 ....FAX (310)-796-0621
HOT Japanese Consumer Response and B to B List, Database Management.
K&D BOND INTERNATIONAL PTY. LTD.
Level 3 8-24 Kippax Street, Surry Hills, NSW 2010 AUSTRALIA ..(02) 288-9000, (F)(02) 281-6121
PERMAIL PTY LIMITED , 11-13 Campbell St., Artarmon, NSW 2064 Australia
Letter Shop, Medical List Rental, Consultancy Tel AA126736 ..Phone 61-2-437 6251 Fax: 61-2-436 3163
RESPONSE MARKETING INTERNATIONAL, LTD. ....FAX (0784)240241
2 Station Parade, ASHFORD, Middlesex TW1 5 2RX England 0784-240400
SPAIN DIRECT MARKETING SERVICES— PUBLIPOST, S.L.
Antonio Lopez, 233.28041 Madrid, Spain.P 34 1 4766363 F-34 1 4758402
Full DM Services in Europe: Database Services, List Rental, Letter Shop, Telemarketing, Fulfillment, Printing, Media Research.
WORLD WIDE MARKETING,
1216 Eleventh Avenue, Altoona, PA 11601-3416 800-445-2522
US/European List Brokers; Printing, Laser, A-Z, Factory Direct Savings .... FAX: 800-621-2011

INTERNATIONAL MAILING LISTS

MEXICO — 65,000 personal names "MEXTOPEXEC" : Direcciones S.A. 011-525-527-0398
PO Box 17-591, Mexico 17 D.F. Mexico 11411 ....FAX: 011-525-399-0558
GREAT AUSTRALIAN LIST CO., P.O. Box 313 Darlinghurst NSW 2010 Australia PH:61-2-5198250; FAX; 61-2-5195147
Mailing List of Venezuela, Box 69527 Caracas 1063A, Vzla ....(F)58-2-7932324; (PH)58-14-223880
Moore Information Management Services ....FAX: 64-9-5735065
6 Donnor Place, Mt. Wellington, Auckland, New Zealand 64-9-5735110
Namebank International, 824 E. Baltimore St., Baltimore, MD 21202 410-234-0999
Worldwide consumer names of subscribers to financial & travel newsletters, reports, & books.

EUROPEAN PRINT PROJECT MANAGEMENT

PMG INTERNATIONAL (USA), 1360 Melanie Dr., Ste. 8, Uniontown, OH 44685 216-896-2070
Multi-Lingual Print Management: Translation, Print-Buying, Warehousing, Distribution and Mailing.

ASSOCIATIONS & CLUBS

ARIZONA
Phoenix Direct Marketing Club-Pres. Murray Hill 602-990-8868
c/o The Listworks Corporation, 4430 Civic Ctr Plz, Ste 103, Scottsdale, AZ 85251
CALIFORNIA
American Telemarketing Assoc..-Pres. Joan Mullen 818-995-7338
5000 Van Nuys Blvd, Suite 400, Van Nuys, CA 91403
DM Assoc. of Orange County-Pres. Al Ingallinera 714-939-1785
5942 Edinger Avenue, Ste 113, Huntington Beach, CA 92649
DM Club of Southern California-Pres. Jan Edwards-Pullin ....310-374-7499: FAX: 310-374-3342
2401 Pacific Coast Hwy, Ste. 102, Hermosa Beach, CA 90254
North California Direct Marketing Club-Pres. Walt D. Abraham 415-434-1696
c/o Communicolor, 500 Sutter Street, Suite 906, San Francisco, CA 94102
San Diego Direct Marketing Club-Pres. Gil Mombach 619-270-6230
c/o The Adcentive Group, 2252 Caminito Preciosa Sur, La Jolla, CA 92037
Western Fulfilment Mgmt. Assoc. -Pres. Glen Giles 818-567-2885
PO Box 4102, Los Angeles, CA 90028
COLORADO
Rocky Mountain DM Assoc.-Pres. Sabrina Luce 303-534-2508
c/o Bioenergy Nutrients, 6395 Gunpark Drive, Ste A, Boulder, CO 80301
CONNECTICUT
New England Mail Order Assoc.-Pres. Ned Haley 203-691-1260
c/o Joan McLaughlin, 14 Faulkner Dr.,Niantic, CT 06357
DISTRICT OF COLUMBIA
Direct Mktg. Assoc. of Washington, DC-Exec. Dir..Sherryl Marshall 703-821-3629
8229 Boone Blvd, Ste 740, Vienna, VA 22182-2623
Advertising Mail Marketing Association-Gene A. Del Polito 202-347-0055
1333 F St. NW 710, Washington, DC 20004-1108
National Infomercial Marketing Assoc., ...202-962-8342
NIMA, 1201 New York Ave., N.W., #1000, Washington, DC 20005
Woman's Direct Response Group- Washington-Pres. Eva Watson 301-249-7800
c/o The Mail Bag, 201 Commerce Drive, Upper Marlboro, MD
FLORIDA
Florida Direct Marketing Assoc. ,-Pres. Robert Dunhill 407-347-0200
1951 NW 19th St.,Boca Raton, FL 33431
Florida Direct Marketing Assoc., Gold Coast Chapter.-Pres. Betty Kaufman 305-472-6374
8851 NW 10th Place, Plantation, FL 33322
Florida Direct Marketing Assoc.,Central Florida Chapter -Pres. Debi Bushnell 407-352-3207
P O Box 10000, Lake Buena, FL 32830
Florida Direct Marketing Assoc., Southwest Chapter- Pres. Anthony Correnti 813-278-5778
6240 Arc Way, Fort Myers, FL 33912
Florida Direct Marketing Assoc., Sun Coast Chapter -Pres. Danene Martinez 813-447-8406
c/o Direct Approach, Inc., 1962 Ripon, Clearwater, FL 34624
ILLINOIS
Chicago Assoc. of Direct Marketing-Pres Rob Jackson 312-761-1232
c/o Westvaco Envelope Division, Sheridan Rd. & 10th St. P O Box 363, N. Chicago, IL 60064
Women s Direct Response Group-Pres Pat Wheelless 312-642-1377
c/o The Wheelless Group, 49 East Elm St.., Chicago, IL 60611
INDIANA
Indianapolis Direct Marketing Assoc.-Pres. Scott Macy ....(F)317-471-8246
c/o Service Graphics,8350 Allison Ave, Indianapolis, IN 46241
KENTUCKY
Louisville Direct Marketing Assoc.- Pres. Larry Kass 502-585-3403
c/o Halbleib/Beggs, Inc., 635 W. Main St., Louisville, KY 40202-2987
MARYLAND
Fulfillment Mgmt. Assoc./Wash.-Pres.Terri LaGoe 301-559-5715
PO Box 67, Hyattsville, MD 20781
Mail Order Assoc. Of Nurseries 301-490-9143
Ms. Camille Chioini, 8683 Doves Flyaway, Laurel, MD 20707
Maryland Direct Marketing Association 800-441-1850
P.O. Box 314 ,Riderwood, MD 21139-9982
MASSACHUSETTS
New England Direct Marketing Assoc.-Pres. Gregory Sullivan 508-473-8643
c/o Mc Carthy & King Direct, 8 Esther Dr., Milford, MA 01757
MICHIGAN
Direct Marketing Assoc. of Detroit-Pres. Duane E. Dub 313-292-3200
c/o Polk Direct, 6400 Monroe Blvd., Taylor, MI 48180-1884
MINNESOTA
Midwest Direct Marketing Assoc,-Pres. Mark Lamberty 612-339-8141
800 Hennepin Ave., Minneapolis, MN 55403
MISSOURI
Direct Marketing Association of St. Louis-Pres. Margaret Forster 314-291-3144
12686 Lonsdale Drive, Bridgeton, MO 63044-1507
Kansas City Direct Marketing Assoc.- Pres John Goodman 913-236-6699
3101 Broadsway, Suite 585, Kansas City, MO 64111
NEBRASKA
Mid America Direct Marketing Association-Pres. Tom Dudycha 402-333-4777
c/o Dudycha, Inc., 3606 D Street, Omaha, NE 68107-1342
NEW YORK
ASSN. OF AMERICAN PUBLISHERS-Pres.Nicholas Veliotes 212-689-8920
220 East 23rd Street, New York, NY 10010
Direct Marketing Association-Pres. Jonah Gitlitz 212-768-7277
11 West 42nd Street, New York, NY 10036
Direct Marketing Club of NY 516-746-6700
224 Seventh Street, Garden City, NY 11530
Direct Marketing Creative Guild-Pres. Stan Winston 212-645-0344
516 Fifth Avenue, New York ,NY 10036
Fulfillment Management Assn.-Pres. Ken Ketzler 212-661-1410
60 East 42nd Street, Suite 1146, New York, NY 10165
Hudson Valley DM Assoc.-Pres. Hunter M. Marvel 203-637-4777
c/o Marvel Assoc., 199 Sound Beach Ave., Old Greenwich, CT 06870
Long Island Direct Mktg. Assoc.-Pres. Susan Johnson-Soules 516-868-1732
c/o 49th Parallel Direct Marketing, 2572 Central Ave.,Baldwin, NY 11510
Nat'l Business Circulation Assoc.- Pres. Ms. Susan Sherwood 212-536-5185
c/o BPI Communications, 1515 Broadway ,New York, NY 10036
Women's Direct Response Group- Pres. Phyllis Kusel 212-675-4250
c/o Johnson & Hayward, Inc., 516 W. 19th St., New York, NY 10011-2876
OHIO
Cincinnati Direct Marketing Assoc.-Pres. David Rose 513-397-7227
c/o Cincinnati Bell, 201 East 4th Street, Cincinnati OH 45202
Direct Marketing Assoc of Dayton-Pres. Marilyn Smith 513-294-4000
c/o Yeck Bros., 2222 Arbor Blvd., Dayton, OH 45439
Mid-Ohio Direct Marketing Association- Pres. Don Nichols 614-846-1800
P.O. Box 2543, Columbus, OH 43216
OREGON
Oregon Direct Marketing Day-Pres. Richard Rosen 503-228-4000
319 SW Washington Ave, Suite 1100, Portland,OR
PENNSYLVANIA
Philadelphia Direct Marketing Assoc.-Exec. Admin., Arlene Claffee 215-540-2257
1787 Sentry Pkwy. W., Suite 1, Blue Bell, PA 19422
TEXAS
Direct Marketing Assoc. of North TX-Pres. Blair Y. Stephenson 817-640-7018
4020 Mc Ewen, Suite 105, Dallas, TX 75244-5019
Houston Direct Marketing Assoc.- Pres. David E. Mackey 713-869-8551
2299 White Street, Houston, TX 77007
VERMONT
Vermont/New Hampshire Direct Marketing Group-Pres. Sam Cutting IV 802-655-4442
c/o Dakin Farm, Rt. #7, Ferrisburg, VT 05456
VIRGINIA
Graphics Communications Assn.-Pres. Norman Scharpl 703-519-8160
100 Dangerfield Rd. ,Alexandria, VA 22314-2804
MASA International-Pres. David Weaver 703-836-9200
1421 Prince Street, Suite 200, Alexandria, VA 22314-2806
WASHINGTON
Seattle Direct Marketing Assn.-Pres Jeanne Davis 703-821-DMAW
c/o The Mailhandlers, Inc., 520 S. Front St., Seattle, WA 98108
WISCONSIN
Wisconsin Direct Marketing Assoc.-Pres. Grant A. Johnson 414-873-9362
2830 N. 48th St., Milwaukee, WI 53210
CANADA
Canadian Direct Marketing Assn./QU- Montreal Chapter,Pres Paul Poulin 514-281-5725
c/ o Cicoma Inc., 666 Sherbrooke St. West, Bureau 2100,Quebec H3A 1E7 CANADA
Canadian Direct Mktg. Assn./VAN- B.C. Chapter,Pres Cathi Flanigan 604-736-3024
c/ o Taylor-Tarpay West, 101-1965 West 4th Ave., Vancouver, BC V6J 1M8 Canada
Canadian Direct Marketing- National Headquarters, Pres. J. Gustavson. 416-391-2362
#1 Concorde Gate, Suite 607, Don Mills, ON M3C 3N6 Canada
Direct Mktg. Assoc. of Toronto-Pres. Luci Furtado 416-502-0433
c/o DMAT, 200 Consumers Rd., Suite 200, North York,ON M2J 4R4, Canada
AUSTRALIA
Australian Direct Marketing Association, Level 7, 22-30 Bridge St., Sydney NSW 2000 Australia FAX: 02-247-4919
BELGIUM
Belgian Association du Marketing Direct, rue de Stalle 65, 1180 Brussels, Belgium ....FAX: 02-332-10-70
European Direct Marketing Assn.-Pres. Michael J. O. Sutherland 322 21 76309
36 Rue du Gouvernement Prov., Brussels B1000 Belgium
ENGLAND
British Direct Marketing Assn., Dir. General, Richard Genochio ....FAX 71-321 0191,71-321 2525

TRANSLATING CALCULATOR

Lost for Words? Push the Buttons and Voila!

BY PATT MORRISON
Times Staff Writer

A stranger in a strange land?

No more. You want your pants pressed at your hotel in Venice and don't speak the language? Just push the right buttons and, ecco! Creases, too.

You've sliced your foot on a fish-hook in Marseille and you'd like the cabbie to take you to to a hospital? Hit the proper keys, and voila! The emergency ward.

For Americans who have struggled with phrasebooks in incomprehensible foreign tongues for years, there is now help: a pocket-sized, solid-state dragoman, a computer translator, the 17-year dream of a Greek immigrant who says modestly that his device is popular: it is back-ordered by a million.

It is called Lexicon LK-3000, it costs $225, and on its keyboard are the letters of the alphabet. Slip in a small cartridge for Italian, or French, or Greek, Spanish, Portuguese or German, and you have access to 1,500 words in that language, and the equivalent 1,500 in English. Learn the rules, type in the sentence or phrase in English, and see its other-language translation across the keyboard in red letters, or vice versa.

There is competition for Lexicon—The Translator, from Craig Corp. of Compton, with "capsules" for five languages and plans for others—including advanced vocabulary, phonetic pronunciation and a calorie counter.

Like the Lexicon system, the Craig device, called an M-100, has a vocabulary of about 1,500 words for each language, and 50 common phrases in Spanish, French, Italian, German and Japanese.

It isn't as romantic as Musset, or as compelling as Dante. Its sometimes-clumsy, strictly-pidgin translations won't go far if you're trying to romance an Italian or argue existentialism with a Frenchman.

On the other hand, it will keep you from ordering baked fenceposts on toast or from saying you're pregnant (embarazada) when you mean embarrassed (avergonzada).

That is exactly what Lexicon's "father" wanted it to do.

Now 31 and very rich ("Each time the stock market goes up, I get more girlfriends"), Anastasios Kyriakides, of Miami, Fla., followed the Hollywood formula for success, coming here from Athens at the age of 15 with $72 in his pocket.

"When I came here, I didn't speak any English at all—I was constantly searching for something useful," he said, finding guidebooks unwieldy, stilted or just wrong.

Still struggling with the language, he began working in a bank, and in his scientific naivete, he associated existing calculator possibilities with an electronic dictionary.

"Thank God I have no knowledge of electronics," he recalled. "If I had, I'd have given it up as impossible."

His ignorance, though, left him blissfully creative, and the first Lexicon ancestor, as big as a typewriter, translated a few words into Greek and back again.

By 1977, with Kyriakides financing the effort, a research team developed a rather larger working prototype. Further work required more money, and a public offering of Lexicon units early in 1978 raised $500,000 for legal, administrative and research costs. As designs were completed, patents were applied for.

Now, 16 years after his arrival, the state of the electronic art and Kyriakides have both progressed. The Lexicon, with a memory chip measuring not quite four-hundreths of an inch square, "can do about everything but drive a car," he says proudly.

He believes it is limitless in its possibilities. Cartridges, at about $60 each, now exist for six languages. Upcoming are cartridges for currency exchange rates, the metric system, Russian —for the Olympics—Polish, Chinese, Swedish, Japanese, and a special one for Olympic records.

"It's one of our best-selling items," said salesman Mike Barnhart. "It's neat for people who want to travel—they can go and not get stuck. A couple of people got one just because they had a Spanish-speaking servant or something."

Because of its vocabulary and idiomatic limitations, Lexicon has to be addressed as one would talk to a child —simple words, present tense. "The main thing to remember is not to be discouraged . . . try simplifying your thoughts, rephrasing them and entering them again," advises the owner's manual.

AVAILABLE·NOW

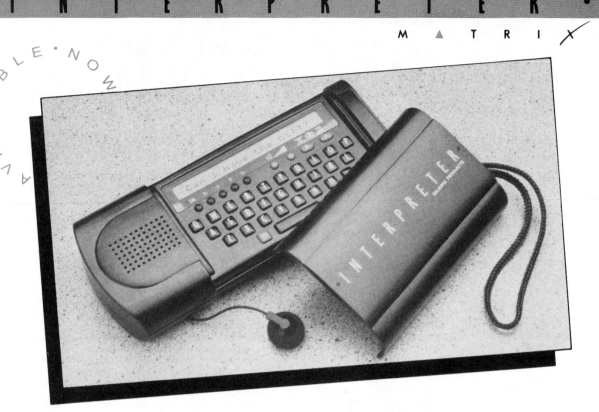

The world's first multi-lingual *TALKING* translator

WORLDS FIRST

On the 16th of October 1989, at the International Electronics Show in Hong Kong, a new product was unveiled that overnight took the world's major electronics manufacturers by storm.

The reason for the unprecedented excitement was the new **TALKING INTERPRETER** — the **first multi-lingual talking translation machine in the world.**

REMARKABLE

This remarkable product, probably the most exciting to be launched in years, heralds a new era in language learning and international communication and a major breakthrough in microchip technology. Not only does it store over 13,000 phrases in each of 5 languages — English, French, Spanish, German and Italian — an incredible 65,000 in all, and show you each one on the display, but it also speaks each phrase out loud with an electronic voice that's amazingly clear and distinct, even the accents sound authentic.

SPEAKS FIVE LANGUAGES

Because you see **and** hear a foreign language being spoken at the same time, its makes learning it so much easier, vital with 1992 looming.

65,000 PHRASES

And it's so easy to operate. Simply type in the required word in any one of the five languages on the 'QWERTY' keyboard, and push your chosen language button. **INTERPRETER** will immediately display your word and translate it through its built-in speaker, you can then create phrases around the word that you have chosen. You can use an earpiece too — ideal for learning a language while travelling.

BUSINESS, TRAVEL, EDUCATION

Other features include: a "look listen and speak" mode for easy learning alternative word meanings; a wordfinder feature; male and female voice option; 22 character dot matrix display with scroll. It measures a remarkably compact 18cm × 7.5cm × 2.5cm, comes complete with protective carry case and takes 4 AAA batteries.

With increased international communication, the revolutionary **INTERPRETER** will fast become the essential personal language assistant of the 90's for business and travel. The combined project development team of Pan Star and Innovations International do it again.

FEATURES

- World first
- Interpreter actually speaks your required phrase
- Translates across 5 languages: English, French, Spanish, German and Italian
- Versatile language database developed by expert linguists
- Natural voice reproduction in each language
- 65,000 phrases + 10,500 individual words
- 50 commonly-used phrases on instant access
- Teach mode: speak and learn random words
- Alternative meanings displayed automatically
- Male and female voice option
- Speech by built-in speaker or earphone
- Automatically displays correct accents such as é, ü etc
- Ideal for business, leisure and education
- 22 character dot matrix display with scroll facility
- Comes complete with protective carrying case, carry strap, earphone and multi-lingual instruction manual
- Powered by 4 × AAA batteries (not supplied) or optional AC mains adaptor.

For further information please contact:

Hong Kong Office

Pan Star Ltd,
5/F Aubin House,
171-172 Gloucester Road,
Wan Chai, H.K.
Tel: 852 8911923
Fax: 852 8384825

European Office
INNOVATIONS
INTERNATIONAL

Innovations International Ltd,
NSP House, 211,
Lower Richmond Road,
Richmond,
Surrey, UK. TW9 4LN.
Tel: 44 81 878 9111
Fax: 44 81 878 9582
Contact: Peter Channell

INTERPRETER has been exclusively designed, provided for and distributed by Innovations International - a member of the NSP Group of companies.

MARKET SHARE

3455 Commercial Avenue, Northbrook, Illinois 60062
Phone: **(708) 559-0800** Fax: **(708) 559-0901**

| Mail Order Communications | College Financial Planning Service | Educational Services of America |

February 25, 1992

Larry Organ
President

Mr. Melvin Powers
Mail Order Consultant
WILSHIRE BOOK COMPANY
12015 Sherman Road
North Hollywood, CA 91605

Dear Mr. Powers:

In early 1987, I purchased your book entitled, "How to Get Rich in Mail Order".

Armed with a yellow highlighter, I went through it meticulously and enthusiastically to learn about a topic which had always fascinated me.

Using many of the techniques and inspiration provided by your book, I started my own mail order firm.

In my first year, I employed only myself and had sales revenues totaling approximately $5,000.00. At present, we have a staff of 65 full-time employees and will have revenues in excess of $20,000,000.00 in 1992.

Mr. Powers, please add me to the list of people whose lives have been changed through your writing.

Sincerely,
MARKET SHARE

Larry Organ

LO/erl

JOIN ME IN MAKING MONEY
WITH THE EASIEST PRODUCT I'VE EVER SOLD

One of my associates, Shel Swartz, who has his own weekly, syndicated radio-opportunity show, called me from Florida raving about some new, wonder herbal-vitamin-mineral tablets called One Life. He wanted me to get involved in marketing them. My initial reaction was "Oh no, not another vitamin product! There are so many out there already." Shel replied that everyone who tries this unique formulation, loves it. People reorder again and again.

"What makes these particular herbal-vitamin-minerals so special?" I asked. He told me that he had been as skeptical as I was until he and his wife tried them. Within a few weeks his recurring headaches miraculously disappeared and her aches and pains were subsiding. They both felt better than they had in years. I said I was happy they were feeling so well, but that I wasn't interested in selling any kind of health products.

Undaunted, he continued. "This product is one of a kind. It contains an herb called echinacea that's said to have special healing properties, and there are vitamins and minerals, including antioxidants and other ingredients that somehow produce an incredible effect. It works! People feel a difference when they take it. Many are convinced that it rid them of nagging physical conditions that were unaffected by any of the other treatments they tried. I don't know exactly *how* it works—I just know that it *does!"* I still wasn't interested.

Shel persisted. He enthusiastically told me that he was receiving unbelievable testimonials from people all over the country. To end the conversation, I finally asked him to send me some literature. "I'd rather send you a month's supply of the product," he responded. "It's the only way you'll be able to feel the difference yourself. Then, if you want literature, I'll send you tons of it, OK?"

I relented. "All right, send me three bottles and I'll have my friend and her son try it, too. They're both into health and nutrition, and they'll know if there's anything special about this product. I don't take vitamins or any other supplements. I don't think I need them. I'll try the ones you're sending me, but don't expect too much."

Soon after starting One Life, to my amazement, I felt more energetic, my stamina was noticeably improved, and my usual sense of well-being was heightened. My friend was convinced that it boosted her immune system, as her resistance to colds and flus improved dramatically and some longstanding allergies cleared up. Her son, the lead singer in the rock band Superfine, had a persistent sore throat that was hampering his ability to perform. After three days of taking One Life, the sore throat vanished and didn't come back.

My cousin, who is in her eighties, had been suffering with arthritis every day for many years. Various prescriptions prescribed by her physician had not helped. I gave her a bottle of One Life, and believe it or not her pain completely disappeared. She's now feeling great, has been given a new lease on life, and is shouting the praises of One Life to family and friends.

My masseur had been complaining about an intermittent sinus condition and a lethargic feeling that he couldn't shake for months. None of the medicine his doctors prescribed had worked. He was very discouraged and reluctantly agreed to try One Life. I ordered a bottle and gave it to him. In one week he was feeling great. The sinus condition was gone, and he had more energy than ever before. He now takes One Life regularly and is enthusiastically recommending it to others.

I called Shel and told him of the fabulous results. We had a good laugh about my change in attitude. I had become a believer and so had my friend, her son, my cousin, and my masseur. We were all so thrilled that we began ordering One Life for our friends and family members. They began ordering for their spouses, friends, and family members. Although no one is trying to sell anything, a lot of One Life is being sold. The product sells itself based on results.

DO YOUR BODY AND YOUR WALLET A BIG FAVOR

Millions of dollars worth of vitamin-mineral products are sold every week in the United States, and millions more are sold around the world. Wouldn't it be nice to get your slice of the pie? All you have to do is try one bottle of One Life, feel the difference, and tell people about the results you're getting. There is no canned sales pitch. Simply share your enthusiasm with others. It's that easy.

There is a lot of money to be made with One Life. Because the product is so outstanding, people are selling it who previously never considered offering anything for sale. They say that the extra money is great and so is the satisfaction they feel from helping people to feel better.

Join my family of wealth builders, and you'll get guidance that will help you make money fast. Get started now. Send for your first bottle of One Life. Its ingredients are derived from natural sources. It is 100% safe and 100% guaranteed. Use the product and you'll see for yourself that everything I've been saying is absolutely true. Then call me, and I'll get you started on the road to riches and teach you how to acquire the Midas touch!

ORDER FORM

Date_____

YES, I want to join the Melvin Powers family of wealth builders.

( ) Please send me a bottle of One Life (90 tablets—30-day supply) for $18.00 postpaid.

Enclosed is my ( ) cashier's check ( ) money order ( ) personal check payable to Melvin Powers.

Charge to my ( ) Visa ( ) MasterCard. To charge by phone, call (818) 765-8529.

Number_____ Expiration date_____

Name_____
(PLEASE PRINT)

Address_____
(STREET ADDRESS FOR UPS DELIVERY)

City_____State_____Zip_____

Mail to:

Melvin Powers
12015 Sherman Road
No. Hollywood, CA 91605

FREE SOURCING SERVICE

Hong Kong Enterprise, a Hong Kong Trade Development Council monthly publication, provides free trade publicity or enquiry services to overseas business concerns interested in trading with Hong Kong. Your request will be published in a special Hong Kong Enterprise local supplement reaching thousands of manufacturers and traders; and firms interested in your enquiry will contact you direct.

Please fill in the reply form below and return to us for publication.

Company: _____

Address: _____

_____

Postal Code: _____ Country: _____

Tel: _____ Telex: _____ Fax: _____

Person to contact: _____

Banker: _____

Interested in:

☐ exporting to Hong Kong

☐ importing from Hong Kong

Product(s): _____

_____

HONG KONG TRADE DEVELOPMENT COUNCIL
Field Manager/Publications Advertising Section

Convention Plaza, 36/F., Office Tower
1 Harbour Road
Hong Kong

Melvin Powers
Wilshire Book Company

12015 Sherman Road
No. Hollywood, CA 91605

(818) 765-8579
FAX (818) 765-2922

MARKETERS FORUM
A Wholesale Buyers' Guide

Every successful mail order entrepreneur invests time in finding products to sell. We think of that search as an exciting treasure hunt with a pot of gold at the end—because that's exactly what it is. Be diligent in looking for your first product. It is the one that will launch your new business and finding it can be a most exhilarating experience.

One of the best monthly magazines in which to find descriptions of products from Taiwan, Hong Kong, Singapore, Korea, and China is the United States published *Marketers Forum.* It's an encyclopedic source that will stimulate you to find a money-making product with which to begin your mail order business.

The pages are filled with illustrations of excellent mail order products and with names and addresses of hundreds of sources in the United States where you can buy merchandise at the lowest prices possible. Send for a copy or subscribe today.

When you receive your copy of *Marketers Forum*, mark each of the merchandising companies located near you. Visit them, introducing yourself (you'll be establishing valuable contacts) and exploring their products. In addition, write to the non-local companies that carry items in your field of interest or call their toll free 800 numbers. Ask every company to place your name on its mailing list so you will receive announcements of new products. It's a good way to find out about unique items before they are advertised to the general public.

Print business cards with your name, address, and telephone number to leave with your contacts and to hand out at trade shows. If you do not have a company name, print Mail Order Entrepreneur under your own name. Not only will you present a good business image to others, but every time you look at your card, you'll be programming yourself for success.

Follow these suggestions and you'll be proceeding in a logical, business-like manner that will eventually spell success for you.

To start your mail order career, invest $5.00 for a sample copy of *Marketers Forum* or send $30.00 for a full year's subscription (Canada—$60.00 in United States funds). Make your check payable to Melvin Powers and send to:

Melvin Powers, 12015 Sherman Road, No. Hollywood, California 91605

HONG KONG

enterprise

HONG KONG TRADE DEVELOPMENT COUNCIL

THE ONE STOP
SHOP

HK DIC The Hong Kong Trade Development Council has everything the trader needs — and all under one roof.

From trade enquiries and economic advice to trade promotions and product magazines, every HKTDC office has it all.

With a chain of international offices spanning the globe, the HKTDC provides a vital reference point for dedicated Hong Kong traders.

They know that the experienced staff can answer all their queries and keep them informed of possible business opportunities, upcoming events and business group visits.

The entire service is free, but the opportunities are unlimited, so don't delay — call the Hong Kong Trade Development Council today!

HONG KONG

Great Eagle Centre, 31st Fl.
23 Harbour Road, Hong Kong
Telephone: (5) 833-4333
Cable: CONOTRAD HONG KONG
Telex: 73595 CONHK HX
Facsimile: 852-5-730249

Sub-Offices:
Fou Wah Centre, 1st Floor
210 Castle Peak Road, Tsuen Wan
New Territories, Hong Kong
Telephone: (0) 498-1602

Chung Nam Centre, Ground Floor
414 Kwun Tong Road, Kwun Tong
Kowloon, Hong Kong
Telephone: (3) 412314/7

EUROPE

Amsterdam
Prinsengracht 771-773 g/f
1017 JZ Amsterdam
The Netherlands
Telephone: (020) 277101
Cable: CONOTRAD AMSTERDAM
Telex: 15081 HKTDC NL
Facsimile: 31-20-228529

Athens
2, Vassileos Alexandrou Str.
Athens 11634, Greece
Telephone: (301) 7246723/4/5
Telex: 219591 GRAD GR.
Facsimile: (301) 724-8922

Barcelona
Balmes 184
Barcelona 08006, Spain
Telephone: (3) 217-6250
Answerphone night service:
(3) 217-6654
Cable: PUBLICRELATIONS
        BARCELONA 6 (Spain)
Telex: 97862 SARP E
Facsimile: (3) 237-92-26

Frankfurt
Bockenheimer Landstrasse 93
D-6000 Frankfurt/Main
Federal Republic of Germany
Telephone: (069) 740161
Cable: CONOTRAD FRANKFURT
Telex: 414705 COFRA D
Facsimile: 069-745124
Postal Address: P.O. Box 17 03 52
6000 Frankfurt 1
Federal Republic of Germany

Hamburg
Brodschrangen 9
D-2000 Hamburg 11
Federal Republic of Germany
Telephone: (49)-040-321838
Facsimile: (49)-040-321867
Telex: 214352 CONHA D
Cable: CONOTRAD HAMBURG

Istanbul
Ankara Cad. No. 74
Ankara Han Kat
1 Istanbul, Turkey
Telephone: (901) 5114624, 5208050
Facsimile: 901-527-48-65

London
8 St. James's Square
London SW1Y 4JZ, England
Telephone: (01) 930-7955
Cable: CONOTRAD LONDON SW1
Telex: 916923 CONLON G
Facsimile: 44-1-930-4742

Milan
2 Piazzetta Pattari
20122 Milan, Italy
Telephone: (02) 865405, 865715
Cable: CONOTRAD MILAN
Telex: 333508 HKTDC I
Facsimile: 39-2-860304

Paris
18 rue D'Aguesseau
75008 Paris, France
Telephone: (01) 47 42 41 50
Telex: 283098 HKTDC F
Facsimile: 33-1-47427744

Stockholm
Kungsgatan 6
S-111 43 Stockholm, Sweden
Telephone: (08) 100677, 115690
Cable: CONOTRAD STOCKHOLM
Telex: 11993 TDC S
Facsimile: 46-8-7231630

Vienna
Rotenturmstrasse 1-3/8/24
A-1010 Vienna, Austria
Telephone: (0222) 5339818
Cable: CONOTRADREP WIEN
Telex: 115079 HKTDC A
Facsimile: 43-222-5353156

Zurich
Bellerivestrasse 3
8008 Zurich, Switzerland
Telephone: (01) 251 01 85
Cable: CONOTRAD ZURICH
Telex: 817850 CONZ CH
Facsimile: 41-1-251-08-14

NORTH AMERICA

Chicago
333 N. Michigan Ave. Suite 2028
Chicago, IL 60601, U.S.A.
Telephone: (312) 726-4515
Cable: CONOTRAD CHICAGO
Telex: 728335 HONG KONG CGO
Facsimile: 1-312-7262441

Dallas
166 World Trade Center
2050 Stemmons Freeway
Dallas, TX 75207, U.S.A.
Telephone: (214) 748-8162
Cable: HONGTRADS DALLAS
Telex: 791719 HKTDC DAL
Facsimile: 1-214-7426701
Postal Address: P.O. Box 58329
Dallas, TX 75258, U.S.A.

Los Angeles
350 S. Figueroa St., Suite #282
Los Angeles, CA 90071, U.S.A.
Telephone: (213) 622-3194/5
            622-0082
Cable: CONOTRAD LOS ANGELES
Telex: 194288 HKTDC LA LSA
Facsimile: (213) 613-1490

New York
673 Fifth Avenue, 4th Floor
New York, NY 10022 U.S.A.
Telephone: (212) 838-8688 ,8801
Telex: 710 838-8959 HKTDC NYK
Facsimile: 1-212-838-8941

Toronto
Suite 1100, National Building
347 Bay Street, Toronto
Ont. M5H 2R7, Canada
Telephone: (416) 366-3594
Cable: CONOTRAD TORONTO
Telex: 06218056 HKTDC TOR
Facsimile: 1-416-366-1569

CENTRAL AMERICA

Panama City
Condominio Plaza Internacional
Primer Alto, Oficina No. 27
Edificio del Banco Nacional de
Panama, Via Espana y Calle 55
Panama City, Republica de Panama
Telephone: (507) 695894, 695611,
            695109
Telex: 2989 HKTDCP PG
        (From USA 3682989
         From other countries
         3792989)
Facsimile: (507) 69-6183
Postal Address:
Apartado Postal 6-4510
El Dorado
Panama City, Republica de Panama

ASIA

Beijing
Room 28-A, 28th Floor
CITIC Building
19 Jianguomenwai Dajie
Beijing China
Telephone: (86)-1-500-3285
Telex: 22927 HKTDC CN
Facsimile: (86)-1-5003285

Osaka
Osaka Ekimae Dai-San Bldg.
6th Floor, 1-1-3 Umeda, Kita-ku
Osaka 530, Japan
Telephone: (06) 344-5211/4
Cable: CONNOTRADD OSAKA
Telex: J26917 HKTDCT
Facsimile: (06) 347-0791

Shanghai
Room 104, 1/F.
Shanghai Union Building
100 Yanan Dong Lu
Shanghai, China
Telephone: (21) 264196, 265935
Telex: 30175 TDCSH CN
Facsimile: (86)-21-264200

Taipei
12/F., Quanta Place
678 Tun Hwa South Road
Taipei, Taiwan
Telephone: (886) 02-705-9333
Telex: 23288 QUANTA
Facsimile: 886-02-705-9222

Tokyo
Toho Twin Tower Building
4th Fl., 1-5-2 Yurakucho
Chiyoda-ku, Tokyo 100, Japan
Telephone: (03) 502-3251/5
Cable: CONNOTRADD TOKYO
Telex: J26917 HKTDCT
Facsimile: (03) 591-6484

AUSTRALIA

Sydney
71 York Street
Sydney, NSW 2000, Australia
Telephone: (02) 298343/6
Cable: HONGKONREP SYDNEY
Telex: AA121313 CONSYD
Facsimile: 61-2-290 1889
Postal Address: G.P.O. Box 3877
Sydney, NSW 2001, Australia

MIDDLE EAST

Dubai
Dubai Pearl Building, 14th Fl.
Dubai, U.A.E.
Telephone: 284236
Telex: 47200 MACOM EM
Facsimile: (9714) 285217
Postal Address: P.O. Box 3347
Dubai, U.A.E.

Hong Kong Convention &
Exhibition Centre

LOOKING FOR SOMETHING?

Find it here, on the Internet's Ultimate Searchable Directory of Wholesale Products & Suppliers!

Enter to WIN $100 worth of merchandise!

Find current suppliers of wholesale general merchandise...

Sunglasses

(Type a product, type of product, or company name.)

Or click a category to find wholesalers in that major category...

Apparel
As Seen On TV
Closeouts
Collectables
Dealer Supplies/Services
Electronics
Flowers
Footwear
General Merchandise
Gifts

Hair Accessories
Handbags / Luggage
HBA
Herbs / Vitamins
Housewares
Incense / Potpourri
Jewelry
Knives
Leather
Music

Novelties
Perfume
Self-Defense Products
Software
Sporting Goods
Sunglasses
Toys
Trade Publications
Watches

Now you can find wholesale and closeout sources for the products you sell easily and quickly --
on the internet! At **WHOLESALE CENTRAL** you can search our huge database for just the products
you want. Or search for your favorite wholesalers to find their current specials and offerings.
WHOLESALE CENTRAL is the easiest to use, most information-packed web site in the industry.
Thousands of products, industry news, hot links, and much more!
Visit the superhighway to profits today!

"WHOLESALE CENTRAL"
http://wholesalecentral.com

Sumner Communications, Inc.
24 Grassy Plain Street, Bethel, CT 06801-1725
For advertising information, call **1-800-999-8281**

World's Smallest

We are the oldest breeder of small horses in the United States, having spent 40 years in breeding and development of a herd of the smallest horses in the world.

BOND MINIATURE HORSE FARM
Lavonia, Georgia 30553
Ph. 404-356-1143 or 356-4449

**Komoko's Little Hussler
5-year-old stallion, 26½" tall.**

Choose a pet or breeding stock from the largest herd of the smallest horses in the U.S.A. 300 head of perfect little horses, all colors and ages. We ship anywhere in U.S.A. or abroad. From 1 to 100.

Komoko Miniature Horse Ranch
Newberry, Florida 32669
Phone 904-472-2828
All sales by appointment.

* * *

MINUSCULE MARKET: How about a mini-horse for a pet?

Breeding of miniature horses in the U.S. is just about a one-man effort by C. Moody Bond, a Lavonia, Ga., rancher involved in "going back full circle" in horse size to Eohippus, a 12-inch high animal that roamed the earth some 50 million years ago. Mr. Bond currently has a herd of some 100 miniatures. One named Tiny Tim is fully grown but stands only 19 inches high at the withers and weighs 80 pounds. And beyond the Bond herd, there isn't much of a supply. The recently formed American Miniature Horse Registry counts "about 180" registered horses which are 34 inches or less in height.

Demand for the animals is heavy. One Japanese businessman seeks 40 of the small horses. From time to time, Mr. Bond has sold some of his larger miniatures at prices ranging from $1,000 for a mare to $10,000 for a stallion. But the rancher claims he has turned down an offer of $50,000 for his knee-high Tiny Tim. He is being put to stud this spring in hopes of producing even smaller sizes.

Who are buyers of miniature horses? So far, says Mr. Bond, "90% of them are doctors."

* * *

Bikini Mail Order Budget Is Upped To $500,000

BALBOA ISLAND, CA—Just Bikinis, Inc., the firm which sells mix-and-match bikini bathing suits by mail order, has allocated $500,000 for its 1984 advertising budget. The firm entered mail order three years ago with an ad budget of $25,000.

The company's unique selling proposition is the offer of different size tops and bottoms, based on the fact that women's bodies are not all standard size. A woman with an opulently endowed bosom may find it paired with narrow hips. And, vice-versa.

Ben Osher, chairman of the board of Just Bikinis, said that test-marketing has indicated the company can sell bikinis "off the page."

First attempts at national advertising involved four consumer magazines. Two of them, *Seventeen* and *Mademoiselle,* were aimed at the teenage audience.

"They bombed," Osher said. The firm learned that the bikini market involves women in more advanced age groups, the median age being 29. Consequently, the Just Bikinis campaign will appear in such magazines as *Vogue, Glamour, Cosmopolitan* and *Self.*

Television also will figure into the media mix. Two-minute commercials will be scheduled for cable exposure.

Advertising copy will promote the bikinis and the Just Bikini catalog which will have a cover price of $2. The $2 will be rebated on any first order.

Magazine ads will be four-color. They will feature coupons and telephone response will be available through a toll-free number, 1-800-BIKINIS.

Just Bikinis has developed a list of 15,000 repeat buyers who make purchases averaging $45 to $50. Its mail order business doubled after the first year, then expanded two-and-a-half times the following year.

The print and TV campaign will be preceded by a direct mail effort with the 1984 catalog going to 50,000 names.

Osher said the heaviest marketing period is the first six months of the year but the firm will advertise on a year-round basis. This is because women who buy bikinis often purchase them for wearing around the house, a comfort factor.

The Just Bikinis catalog includes a Bikini Style Guide which enables women to pick the correct top and bottom for their figures. It involves eight cardboard strips, four displaying different size bodies from the waist up and four showing bodies from the waist down. All are clad in different styles of tops and bottoms. A shopper can slip the strips through slots cut in a photo of a model to determine the sizes and styles for her particular figure.

Osher said the company does receive some requests for credit or refunds but most of them seem to stem from incorrect information being given about the customer's figure.

The Just Bikini bathing suits are designed by Joyce Holder, president of the firm, and are manufactured by the company.

Mail-Order Division Booming For Frederick's of Hollywood

By Larry Jaffee

Overcoming a 52 percent increase in paper costs, the Frederick's of Hollywood mail-order subsidiary reported pretax operating profits increased 53.1 percent to $3.7 million for the Sept. 2, 1995 fiscal year from $2.4 million last year.

According to Frederick's just-released annual report, net sales for the mail-order subsidiary, which contributes 47 percent of the company's total sales, rose 11.8 percent to $66.8 million from $59.8 million the previous fiscal year.

George Townson, Frederick's chairman/president/CEO, attributed the company's positive performance to expansion of successful marketing and merchandising concepts, as well as the installation of an efficiency-enhancing mainframe computer system.

Frederick's catalog operation was more profitable than the company's larger retail operation, for which the company's 204 stores in 39 states registered a pretax operating profit of $866,000 on net sales of $76.1 million. In fiscal 1994, the retail division experienced an operating loss of $3.6 million on net sales of $72.4 million.

The company as a whole registered a profit of $2.7 million, compared with the previous year's net loss of $903,000, principally related to certain store closings.

Frederick's distributed 48.6 million catalogs to households throughout the United States during the year, a 6 percent increase over fiscal 1994. The company plans to distribute about 49.5 million catalogs in fiscal 1996.

Townson estimated that the company is facing a 66 percent increase in the cost of producing its catalog during the current fiscal year, which will "test both our business acumen and creative skills."

Townson said that to help offset continuing increased postage and paper costs, estimated to exceed $2 million for the full fiscal year, some catalogs will have fewer pages and lighter paper.

The intimate apparel and sportswear cataloger/retailer also will evaluate customer order patterns carefully to either reduce the frequency of, or eliminate, certain mailings.

Townson noted that last month Frederick's brought out its first swimwear-collection catalog, which it hopes will attract new customers and provide added sales from existing ones.

In October, the company mailed an undis-

The 1995 annual report cover

closed number of its holiday catalogs to Canada, marking Frederick's first international foray. Townson said it was too early to determine the results.

Catalog sales from the company's Plus Size Collection rose 78 percent for the year with plus-size merchandise accounting for approximately 8 percent of mail-order sales.

Earlier this year, it became apparent that Frederick's was not experiencing the same profitability struggles plaguing other apparel catalogs ("Lingerie Untouched by Paper/Postage Hikes," *DM News* — Aug. 7). The company's positive performance was attributed to a product category that's

> Catalog sales from the company's Plus Size Collection rose 78 percent for the year, accounting for about 8 percent of MO sales.

always in demand.

The strength of lingerie as a category unsusceptible to catalog market pressures was also underscored by the revelation this fall that Victoria's Secret, a Frederick's of Hollywood competitor, had a last-12-month catalog-buyer file of 4.3 million customers.

Intimate Brands Inc., Victoria's Secret's parent company, was spun off by The Limited Inc. in October. ∎

Queen of mail-order catalogs started in the kitchen, ended up in the millions

By MARY DANIELS
Special to the Daily News

Catalogs have become favored forums for late 20th-century shopping sprees, and while some catalogs specialize in luxury items — furs, glitzy clothes, shoes, even custom cars and exotic pets — the Lillian Vernon catalog offers about 150 pages of answers to that seemingly impossible quest — finding clever, memorable but inexpensive gift items rarely seen in shopping malls anymore.

There is an actual Lillian Vernon, though the queen of mail order kitsch's real name is Katz. Lillian Katz' professional name derives from the city in which her business is based: Mount Vernon, N.Y. Next to her photograph on the inside front page of her new 1983 Christmas catalog, she boasts, "The fact is, you'll find more gifts here under $10 than most catalogs have gifts."

No exaggeration. Letting your fingers doing the walking through her pages is like a stroll through a narrow-aisled boutique piled high from floor to ceiling, where one has to peer carefully at everything in order not to miss that certain special something.

The gift items in the Lillian Vernon catalog have become a reflection of changing social trends. This is evident in the one area that has recently expanded greatly.

"Baby items in our catalog have become fantastic in the last two years," says this paradoxical woman, who is self-assured, sometimes even self-critical, sophisticated and intense but also cozy and homespun. She is an avowed traditionalist when it comes to husband, three children and home. But she is also a shrewd and consummate businesswoman.

The new catalog "has a 16- or 18-page spread of baby things," she adds. "Last year it was 12. There's a baby boom on right now."

The mothers-to-be, she says, "are women in their mid-30s who are working and making money, or feeling guilty for going back to their jobs and spending a lot of money on these things. It is really becoming an incredible category for us."

Formerly discontinued items have made "a comeback," such as a child's set of animal-faced dominoes.

"All these things you can't find anywhere else," says Vernon, pointing to a personalized, bus-shaped wooden clothes rack.

One new handcrafted item she is especially proud of this year is a growth chart to measure children's heights. The balloon height chart, which measures up to 5 feet and sells for $10.98, also can serve as kind of colorful soft-sculpture wall hanging. It is bright blue, yellow and red, in foam-plumped poly-cotton with matching wide grosgrain ribbons.

"It is made for us alone" (a phrase she often says with pride) by Third Age Folks from Chicago. This is a cottage industry sponsored by the local YMCA, she explains from notes she has taken in an earlier morning meeting with the company managers. The program is unique to the Chicago area "and designed to serve older and handicapped persons who cannot enter or re-enter the job market through ordinary avenues of employment." Started with a $100,000 grant by the Retirement Research Foundation, this group utilizes the sewing and handwork skills of a traditionally untapped work force.

Katz had come upon the growth chart at the Housewares Show in Chicago last January. "The Third Age Folks had a booth there," she says. "I met the lady and said: 'I'll buy it, but I want an exclusive. I need 5,000.' " She got it.

The Third Age Folks program has a work force of "200 people of all ethnic groups. They all have to know how to sew. But they teach them how to make each product. It's very professional. They give them a class first, then give them a sample. They cut it and bundle it at the Y, then take it home and sew it and bring it back. It is a real cottage industry.

"They have no quality-control problem. The production is perfect.

"These people didn't have enough money for food when government money dried up," she explains. "All of these grants dried up under the Reagan administration. Many of

> She has a staff of 300, which sometimes swells up to 1,000. 'Our company is devoted to women. If I'm not gonna give them a chance, who is?'

these women went to work after their husbands became unemployed when the steel mills closed. Their husbands are very supportive because the wives work at home.

"There is one woman worker who has multiple sclerosis, and another woman is 84. They look fabulous. My mother is 81, and she's so lonely and bored.

"When I do business in China and Europe, I see the wonderful respect they give to older people.

"First of all, when you go into the Canton Fair (where everything from garments to farm machinery is sold), there are many women who are the salespeople. It is the women who represent the sales combines. They wear no makeup; age seems to be no factor. I don't think we do that in America, and I'm guilty of that with my own mother. I don't think we take advantage of the skills of our older citizens."

Referring to herself, she says, "by being in your own business, you can keep going as long as you want." Perhaps because of what it means to older people who feel they no longer matter in our culture, Katz says, "I got really turned on to these people. I may put them on one page and do a whole story about them," she says, speaking of the first 1984 catalog. "I would love to start one (such program) in the community I do business in," she says, adding that she has already ordered more exclusive handcrafted items from Third Age Folks.

"We just really try hard to find things that would not find elsewhere," she continues. "I really am a snob about it. I travel 16 weeks all over the world, all the way into China," where she looks for what she calls "21st-century antiques" to sell in the catalog. (Approximately two-thirds of the approximately 3,000 products offered each year in her catalog are imported, and are found by scouring international trade shows and foreign design markets.)

Katz' exceptional talent lies in merchandis-

ing, selecting, pricing and photographing the more than 3,000 items offered each year. She oversees each aspect of this activity for the seven editions of the 50 million catalogs the company produces each year.

One of her most popular lines are brass Christmas tree ornaments designed by her, which can be dated and personalized with engraved names. Selling for less than $3 each, more than 55 million have been sold to date.

Banking, literally, on the birth of a panda at the Washington, D.C., zoo, Katz placed a picture of a panda from China on the cover of the Christmas catalog. Despite the subsequent death of the newborn panda, Katz says: "We'll make a donation to the World Wildlife Fund for every one of our panda items sold.

"I really have a wonderful world. I don't think we're only here to make money. I think we've got to give back some of what we get."

When one learns how she started her business, it is not difficult to understand why she is so supportive and exuberant about getting a simple item like the children's growth chart into her catalog.

Called "The No. 1 Woman in Mail Order," Vernon is not modest about her title. "I am the most prominent woman in mail order, no question about it. I'm probably the leading person in mail order."

Vernon founded her company in 1951 with the single offer of a monogrammed purse and belt.

The corporation's 1983 sales are expected to reach $100 million. She says things really took off in 1970 with the lessening of her family responsibilities. When the gasoline shortage came along in the mid-'70s and people began to do more of their shopping by mail, "I made my first million in sales," she says.

She says she has a staff of 300, which swells to 1,000 employees at peak season, and adds: "Our company is devoted totally to women. If I'm not gonna give them a chance, who is?

"We even have people who can't read," she says proudly. "We produce monogrammed pencils, and I have a typesetter for those who don't even read. He has worked for us 14 years. Imagine, what an indignity it is for a human being, not to be able to read!

"One of my children said to me that I have people in my company who didn't fit in anywhere else. They have ability, but they don't look corporate."

For instance, she has one woman employee who has been with her for 10 years, and who, she says, may not look corporate, but drives a red Porsche.

"Our garage guy asked her one day, 'What's a secretary like you doing driving a Porsche?' 'I happen to be the vice president of this $100 million dollar company!' she told him. 'Well, you could have fooled me,' he said," Katz says, chuckling.

Now for the most important question. Does she ever order items from her own catalog?

"Oh, God, yes, absolutely," she replies vehemently. "I use all the towels, I use the potholders, I use the phone. I found 24 things out of my catalog to send to my grandchildren," she says, flipping through the pages as if she were seeing the items for the first time, as an avid mail-order shopper.

— Chicago Tribune

Chapter Three

How to Make Money with Classified Ads

One of the easiest and least expensive ways of starting your mail order business is to place classified ads for your product or service. Go to the library and study the ads in a large variety of magazines. Study the classified ads in weekly newspapers such as *The National Enquirer, The Star,* and *Midnight Globe.* You'll find these at the checkout counter of your grocery store. Notice whether the ads ask you for money or ask you to send for further information.

As a rule, you'll be asked to send for further information. The ad is designed to arouse your interest. The principal function of a classified ad is to solicit inquiries, and then convert these inquiries into sales by the use of direct mail. The direct mail will usually take the form of literature about the product or service, personal letters, testimonials, photographs or illustrations, an order form, a return envelope, and guarantees.

Classified ads for products in newspapers generally do not pay off. The reason for this is two-fold. The life expectancy of a newspaper is, at the most, one day. And, as a rule, the general public is not in the habit of looking for mail order merchandise in the newspaper's classified section.

The first few words of the classified ad are usually set in capital letters, and you should try to make these words count by giving them impact. Make them attention-grabbers. The advantage of classified ads is you have reader curiosity working in your favor. You might want to change the classification under which your ad appears. Personal and Miscellaneous are two good classifications to consider if you are not getting anticipated results from the section where you would normally expect to find your ad.

When you get excellent results from your advertisements, run them on a "T.F." basis. T.F. means "til forbid." The publication will continue to run your ad until you cancel. It saves you time and paperwork. They'll also change the key every month if you wish.

Learn to write tight copy, succinct—to the point. Make every word count. A good practice is to pretend you're writing a telegram where every word is expensive. Eliminate the extraneous. By the end of the year, this can add up to a saving of hundreds, maybe thousands, of dollars.

You can sell your product on either a one-step plan or a two-step plan. One step means you want to sell the product right from the ad. The problem here is you are paying for each word of the ad and that can become prohibitive in terms of anticipated orders.

I use the two-step approach in selling the books in my catalog. Many mail order companies prefer to sell a single item and then include a catalog for further orders. Experiment with both techniques. My classified ad for books reads: "Free, interesting, illustrated, self-improvement book catalog. Write: Melvin Powers, Suite 711, 12015 Sherman Road, North Hollywood, California 91605." I've kept my ad to a minimum number of words and my message clearly states what I'm selling.

Suite 711 is the key for the particular magazine. It's important for me to know how many inquiries I received from the ad, how many were converted into sales, the amount of the sales, and the amount of the average order. I also want to know what percentage of inquiries turned into orders.

There are many ways to key an ad. The point is you want to know if your advertising dollars are paying off for you. If you send a return envelope with your return literature, you can unobtrusively mark the envelope Suite 711. You can also keep the original letters and cards, file them by state and in alphabetical order. You'll be able to check the original source of the inquiry immediately. These are just two suggestions. Use whatever system is convenient for you.

Over a period of time, you'll learn to recognize certain repeat classified advertisements, indicating these ads are paying their way and making money. Mail order advertising must pay off or the ads will stop. A non-paying ad doesn't pull any better because of repetition.

Perhaps you have on occasion made the statement, "How could anyone make money selling that?" Be assured they are, and to satisfy your mind on that score, send away for the offer. When you do, key your address, note the date you send away for the product, and the date you receive it. See if you get follow-ups and note whether you start getting mail from other companies with the key number. Keep a record of it. It's all valuable information, and you'll begin to appreciate it as you progress in your own mail order business.

You can sell your inquiry names as well as names of customers. The inquiry names sell for less, but there can be a good market for the rental of the names. That's the reason I want you to key your letters to other companies. You want to find out how many times your name has been rented and to whom.

Let's assume you paid $100 for a classified ad and received 100 inquiries. That means every lead costs you $1. Suppose you received 200 inquiries. Every name costs you 50¢. You might want to consider mailing your literature to someone else's inquiries or buyers, 1,000 inquiry or buyer names will run between $75 to $100 as an average. In each case, you must keep very careful records of the expenses and income from each source. Suppose the rental of outside names proves satisfactory. That might be the way to go with your proposal, as well as with classified ads. Those names would average about seven cents per name.

Let's say you are making money with your classified ad. Run the ad again, and gradually expand your coverage until your ad is running in as many magazines as you can manage and still have them pay off. To get a fast, overall view of the classified rates of magazines, write to: National Mail Order Classified, Dept. A-1, 2628 17th St., Sarasota, FL 34230. Telephone (813) 366-3003.

You might consider running a test classified ad in *The Star* or *The National Enquirer*. See pages 42 and 43 for rates and other information. I like these two publications because there's a six-week closing date and you'll be able to test your offer in a short time. It is not necessary to run in both publications. Pick one for your test. Run the advertisement one time and one time only. Sit back and watch the results.

You could run two different ads, one in each publication, if you wished. The point is to spend as little money as possible on your test. As a general rule, I would advise placing your ads in publications with long classified sections. They have a proven track record. However, this is not an inviolate rule. I've been running ads for years in magazines with very small classified sections, and they've paid off for me.

Assume you are making money with your classified ads. Try to get an even better response by adding a few descriptive words. Study other classified ads and see what key words they are using. Your initial words are important. Are you using such words as: free, new, exciting, extra income, make money, how to, save money, save, amazing, wanted, at last, introductory offer, sold only by mail, buy direct—save, study at home, free gift, free trial offer, secret, learn, better health, do-it-yourself, freedom from worry, happiness, prevent, protect, relief, romance, self-improvement, sex, power, success, and wealth?

Assume you are not making money on your ad, now what do you do? Try to improve the ad just as you would if the ad were making money. These are the variables to consider: you may be advertising in the wrong publication for your kind of offer, you have too much competition for the same product and sales are watered down, your price is either too high or too low, your follow-up literature doesn't tell the story effectively or succinctly, the offer isn't believable, your advertising copy doesn't generate excitement, you didn't answer the inquiry immediately, or your offer just doesn't initially make it. You've picked a loser.

Let me assure you, even though I'm credited with being a mail order expert, I still have my share of losers. I've put together a perfect package at times, but the only problem was the general public didn't realize it! Accept the loss as part of the expense of doing business, and go on to the next project. You never know when you can salvage part of a losing campaign and put some elements of it into a winning one.

Here's a mail order tip for you. Answer your inquiries the same day you receive them. As a beginner, you might be tempted to wait for the week-end to answer. You are busy and might be tired after a full day's work, but you can miss the boat by waiting. Your competition might be getting his literature to the same potential customer before you. By the time he receives your literature, he's already made his purchase. The rule is to catch the prospect when he's interested and hot. Don't let him cool off.

In my office, literature to inquiries stemming from my classified or display ads is the first mail to go out every day. The orders and correspondence can wait a day or two, but new business is what keeps things rolling. I've checked my competitors and some don't answer for several weeks. I'm sure you've had similar experiences with information you've sent for.

Let me illustrate this point, which is applicable to every business. I recently needed some steel shelving for my warehouse. The order came to over $6,000. I had my secretary call a dozen companies listed in the Yellow Pages of the phone book. Three representatives came the first week, six came the second week, and three came the third week. By the time the last representatives called on me, I had already purchased the shelving. It so happens the prices were virtually the same. I purchased the shelves from one of the first three salesmen who called on me, because his prompt response gave me the assurance that if I needed servicing, he would respond. The salesman, seeing a piano and guitar in my office, struck up a lively conversation with me, telling me he was a musician, and in his younger days traveled with some of the big bands. In retrospect, we spent more time talking about music than we did about the shelving. He truly struck a responsive chord with me. When he saw some of my songwriting awards in my office, he asked me to play a few of the songs. How could I resist buying from him!

Interestingly, only three of the salesmen followed up with phone calls or paid me a visit after I had received a written quotation. They all could have called back in person to meet or better the price and extoll the benefits and superiority of their shelving. Who knows, I might have changed my mind. In the meantime, I've recommended the shelving to a friend of mine, with the result the salesman got an additional sale. If your initial mailing doesn't produce a sale, you might want to consider follow-up letters and literature. This would largely depend on the dollar potential of your mail order program. Naturally, once you have a customer, you'll want to follow up with more products.

The following are questions and answers that most often come up in regard to running classified ads. The answers would also apply if you were running small display ads.

Question: In what magazines do I advertise?
Answer: In those patronized by other mail order companies. The magazines which consistently run their ads are the survivors of trial and error. The advertisers have tested the various magazines, and you can learn from their experience which are the best. That doesn't mean that you can't experiment. Hunch bets have been known

to pay off. But customers, by habit, have become programmed to look in certain publications for various classified offers, and you would be well advised to use them if you want the largest audience. Your challenge is to attract the attention of your competitors' customers, selling your product or service from the ad or by motivating them to send for further information.

Question: I think I have a great mail order idea. How many ads do I run?
Answer: Run one advertisement in the very best publication that would logically produce orders for you. Some publications will offer you the third or fourth advertisement free if you run the ad several times in succession. Forget it. Accept such an offer only after you have a winner. If you have an ad that isn't going to pay off, why waste the money? Generally speaking, the ad will not initially pull better with repetition. Running one time gives you the opportunity to revise and strengthen your ad as soon as you have determined it needs improvement. The rule in mail order is to keep testing to minimize your losses and maximize your earnings.

Question: What are the best months in which to advertise?
Answer: Many products have a well-established seasonal period. Don't try to buck it. Accept it as a general rule. The best mail order months are, in order of importance: October, November, September, January, February, and March. The first three months of the year are great because people are home much more during the winter than other times of the year. That means more time for reading, and especially to activate New Year's resolutions for self-improvement. Many mail order companies do the greatest percentage of their business during the months of September, October, and November. These months lead to a great volume of orders for the holiday season. It's the time of year that people are in the mood for buying gifts. If you are in a seasonal business, do some brainstorming to stimulate sales during the slow periods. I. J. Fox, a Boston furrier, turned the months of July and August into the biggest sales months for fur coats. How? By offering all kinds of sales incentives; mainly, saving money during the slow season. This idea was hammered home by radio and newspaper ads.

Question: How do you find out about advertising rates?
Answer: Many times the publication will carry that information at the beginning of the classified section. It will read something like this: *$2 per word. Minimum words— 15. Closing date, the 10th of the second month preceding publication.* That means you need to get the ad into the publication office by January 10th for the March issue, February 10th for the April issue, etc. There are also companies that specialize in selling classified ads. They'll send you all the rates and even place the ads for you. I recommend these agencies because they are reliable and can give valuable tips on where to advertise. Make it your business to get to know someone at the agency so you

always have an open line of communication with him. He'll help you make money with your ads because your success is his success. There is no charge for his service. He makes a 15% commission for placing the ad.

Question: Should I charge for the catalog or literature that I send?

Answer: For your initial ads, and until such time as you are really making money in your mail order business, I'd strongly recommend you send a free catalog. The self-addressed envelope, stamp, 25¢ or $1 you receive isn't going to spell the difference between failure and success. You want to receive as many requests as possible, and your job is to find out if you have a viable product or service to sell. Put your energy into the important part of your program. Asking for money for your literature will definitely cut down on your responses. Good advertising literature can turn curiosity seekers into buyers. The very fact they send for your literature indicates some interest. Take that interest seriously and do whatever you can to capitalize on it.

There are, of course, some firms that charge for their catalogs, but these are usually well-known established companies. Frederick's of Hollywood charges $2 for its catalog. See page 32. Neiman-Marcus, one of the most successful and prestigious department stores in the world, charges $5 for its catalog. You can be sure their reasons are valid. There are a number of companies that charge. But for the beginner, my advice is still to put your priorities in order by testing your offer and not worrying about a minor detail at this point.

Question: How do you charge the customer for postage? What's the best way?

Answer: Simply experiment. Run two ads. In one, charge $5.00 for your product; in the other charge $4.25, plus 75¢ postage. See if there's an appreciable difference in the response. I've done it both ways, and it doesn't seem to matter. I generally prefer $5.00, postpaid. There's less clutter. Every mail order buyer in the world knows he's paying for postage, regardless of how the price is stated. Most mail order companies list the price of the item and the postage separately. In running classified ads where you are selling a product directly from the advertisement, I suggest you use the $5 postpaid method. For one thing, it cuts down on the use of words. Actually, you could eliminate the "postpaid." It's self-evident, and you save a word. Use what you need to tell your story, but don't waste a single word. Words saved put dollars in your pocket.

Question: I'm using the two-step approach to selling my product. What is the optimum sales literature package?

Answer: Your objective is to develop a mailing package that will generate maximum response at the lowest cost. It may not be necessary to mail the optimum literature in response to an inquiry because of the expense in printing, envelopes, and postage. Keep testing to satisfy yourself

you are getting the best return at minimum cost. As an example, you might not need four-color circulars to sell your product. Black and white might suffice. You might not need coated stock for your mailing pieces.

Here's the literature that should comprise the classic response to an inquiry: a sales letter, advertising literature including photographs or art work of the product, testimonials, guarantee, credit card option, postage reply envelope, and incentive for prompt response.

Question: What do you include in the sales letter?

Answer: Thank the reader for making the inquiry, and briefly assure him he's going to enjoy, or benefit from, the product or service. Write your letter on a one-to-one basis, making it as personal as you can. If such is the case, you might want to tell him how the product helped you. If it's appropriate to do so, use a photograph of yourself or your family. I endorse this idea because it immediately creates a personal relationship between buyer and seller. Many of my customers have sent their pictures after doing business with me for a period of time. Why not? It's pleasant and sharing. I have pictures of my wife and myself on some literature and book covers, and our customers seem to enjoy it. I've shown a picture of my Arabian stallion. See page 264. In return, I've enjoyed receiving photographs from proud horse owners. All of this contributes to a sense of personal involvement, and there is no greater way to cement a relationship, be it personal or business. If at all possible, use a P.S. to your letter. This gives you another opportunity to accent your message or stress an important point.

Question: What do you include in the advertising literature?

Answer: You give as much information as you can about your product or service, making it as concise and understandable as possible. Talk about the benefits to be derived, supporting your representations with testimonials from authorities in the field or from satisfied customers. Include an illustration and specifications if it calls for it. State the price, postage, and guarantee. Ask for the order. If it ties in with the product, tell something about yourself or your company. If you are selling to teenagers, you might want to design a special sales message written with invisible ink which becomes legible only when the paper is wet. Talk about it in your sales letter, and tell them there's a very special offer or a message of importance they'll want to know about, or that there's a bonus gift earmarked for them.

Question: What about guarantees?

Answer: An important point to consider is the guarantee you offer for your product or service. Is it for 10 days, 30 days, 60 days, or more? Some mail order entrepreneurs guarantee satisfaction by allowing the purchaser to post-date his check for 30 days. If the product is not to his liking, he can then ask for the return of his check or cancel it. I've been selling some of my books on a 365-day, money-back guarantee. I do it to lend credibility to my offer, and I have yet to receive one request for a refund for any of my 365-day offers. Furthermore, I cannot recall a single instance when someone requested a refund on our 30-day, money-back guarantee offers. I know this may sound incredible, but it's a fact. Perhaps it's because I'm dealing with inexpensive books. If your product or service is worthwhile, the chances of a request for a refund are negligible. Be sure to always include the guarantee in your literature. If you do get a request for a refund, send back the money immediately. Include a self-addressed, stamped envelope, and politely ask the customer why, explaining that if there is a way to improve the product you would appreciate his cooperation in helping you to make the improvement. Too many requests for refunds are an indication that something is wrong with your product. It is then up to you to do something about making corrections.

Question: What should the order form include?
Answer: The order form can consist of a detachable part of your sales letter or advertising literature. It can also be a separate form. If it's a separate form, make sure your name and address are on it. Repeat the offer, the price, and guarantee. Leave sufficient space for the sender to print his name and address. Request it. This will save you the time and aggravation that comes from not being able to read the sender's handwriting. Use a key in the order form, such as a number, price, or color. You might want to offer a free gift for replying within a certain period of time. You might offer your special, money-saving price inducement good only until a certain date, when the price goes up or reverts to its originally higher level. If it's a new book, for example, the pre-publication price could be $10 as opposed to $15 once the book is published. You might call it a one-time offer at a special reduced price. You could have an inventory clearance sale, or offer a special price due to an anniversary or special event. Take your lead from the department stores. They have a valid reason for a sale every month. Have you ever been to Sears when they are not having a sale? Of course not. They are smart merchandisers, stressing the fact year after year that you save money by shopping at Sears. Think about it. Don't you really believe it?

Question: Should you furnish reply envelopes with your advertising literature?
Answer: In theory, reply envelopes should increase your sales by making it easy for the recipient to order. If you are selling an item priced at over $10, I'd say yes, generally include the envelopes. I'm not sold on it in my particular business research program, because I sell low-priced books. My average order amounts to $30.00. I no longer supply envelopes. They are expensive and add to the cost of mailings. Here, again, you have to determine through experimentation whether supplying envelopes is a worthwhile practice.

Question: What about paying postage on the return envelopes?
Answer: Most mail order companies do not pay for the postage because the postage rates have become so high. If I were selling expensive merchandise, I would take a different view. I'd suggest that you experiment with it. I would like to know the results of an offer to a mailing list with only the following variables: 5,000 with no return envelope, 5,000 with a prepaid envelope enclosed, and 5,000 where the customer pays for the postage. Only you can determine what is best in terms of sales and profit.

When you get into large mailings, the saving of pennies adds up to dollars, and the dollars can run into the hundreds and thousands. Be prudent about how you spend your hard-earned money. You might be able to get the same return with less of an expenditure. Those thousands of dollars that you will have saved by the end of the year will feel good in your pocket.

There are plenty of businesses running mainly from classified ads. You'll see their ads in virtually all magazines. Behind those few classified lines inviting you to send for a catalog or further information, there could easily stand a business doing millions of dollars a year in sales. Study those ads, send away for their literature and products, and become knowledgeable about their operations. Next, pick your own product or service and run classified ads.

There is a certain fascination attached to classified ads. You never know what your return will be. Remember, the classified reader is curious, and therefore open to suggestion. Can you spark enough interest in the ad to induce him to send you his order, or at least send for further information? I hope so. In any event, I wish you good luck as you begin your career in the fascinating world of mail order.

As you read the next chapter on display advertising, bear in mind much of the material dealing with classified advertising also applies to display advertising, and vice versa.

P.O. Box M
Swainsboro, GA 30401

Telephone (912) 237-2422
Fax (912) 237-3433

Prime Publishers, Inc.

NOW YOU CAN ALSO EARN A COMMISSION
ON NAMES YOU OBTAIN FOR YOUR OWN USE

Dear Sir or Madam:

You must have fresh responsive names to succeed in the Mailorder/MLM business. Have you found a reliable source? If you are experienced, you know it is almost impossible to find a dependable source for quality names.

If you are offering a worthwhile money-making opportunity, a publication directed to the work-at-home entrepreneur, or you are a name dealer, you really should take a few minutes to read this letter. If you have had bad experiences in the past with rented names, take a moment to learn why the names you received did not respond to your offer and why you had so many returned as undeliverable. Did any of the undeliverables say "Forwarding Order Expired"? If you have a continuing need for absolutely fresh responsive names, please read on.

As a client of Prime Publishers, Inc., you can earn a commission on all name orders you place for your own use as well as earn a commission on all orders placed by folks to whom you have recommended us.

EARN A FULL-TIME INCOME

Many of our regular customers are receiving a very healthy FULL-TIME INCOME by obtaining our names for their own use and by recommending our names to others. Each month they receive a very sizeable commission check. YOU CAN TOO! I know exactly how big these checks are because I have to sign all of them at the end of each month. Now you can receive the freshest, most responsive names available anywhere and at the same time earn large monthly commission checks just like our regular customers receive.

Prime Publishers, Inc. has become the leader in the name business by following one simple philosophy. We will offer only the freshest, most responsive names available anywhere. It's that simple - we have the best names. That is why most of our clients are repeat customers and include the biggest names in Mailorder/MLM. Many of our customers have been receiving names from us on a regular schedule for years.

Our names are reasonably priced. We want you to become a regular customer; we are not interested in overpriced "one-shot" sales like so many dealers are. We want you to succeed and become one of our regular customers for years to come. I feel this is the only way we can succeed in our business.

WHY ARE THERE SO MANY BAD NAMES BEING SOLD

Very few mail list dealers compile their own lists directly from the responses they receive from their own advertising efforts. Most dealers buy or swap lists to obtain the names they offer. The names they advertise as being fresh have often been traded back and forth between dealers for a very long time. When dealers say their names are less than thirty days old, more times than not what they are really saying is that they have received the names from some other dealer within the last thirty days. And you can be sure no dealer is going to trade his names until he has worked them to death to receive the last dollar they are capable of producing. This explains the poor response rate and high number of undeliverables.

HOW TO AVOID THE BAD GUYS

Every week we hear horror stories from our clients about experiences they have had in the past obtaining names. We hear about names that resulted in 30% to 40% undeliverables. Names that produced a very poor response. These stories do not seem to be the exception; they seem to be the rule. And these are names obained from some of the biggest and best know dealers in the country.

I am frequently asked how to avoid these name dealers who are selling all these old worn-out names. If you will follow a few simple rules you will eliminate most of the crooks.

1. Never do business with any individual or company that does not list their phone number in their advertising. How many reputable businesses are there in your home town that do not have a phone? If they have a phone number but all you get is a recording, don't do business with them.

2. Never obtain names from a source that does not compile their lists from their own inquiries or orders. Call and ask direct pointed questions. And be prepared for some pretty evasive answers.

3. Never obtain names from a dealer that only offers more names to replace undeliverables. A reputable dealer will offer a cash refund for nixies.

4. Never obtain names from a source that offers a refund (even if it is cash) only if undeliverables are returned within thirty days. This is the meanest trick of all. It is not possible to return nixies within thirty days. Figure it out yourself.

5. Stay away from dealers offering very low prices or fancy gimmicks such as two or three for the price of one.

6. Always deal with companies that accept credit cards. To obtain a merchant account, companies are thoroughly investigated by the banking industry. If a company does not accept credit cards, there must be a reason they were unable to get a merchant account.

WHY PROFESSIONALS OBTAIN THEIR NAMES FROM US

Because they are fresh, responsive, and accurate. As a result of national advertising in small town weekly newspapers, shoppers guides, penny savers, etc. we receive a steady stream of letters from "out of circle" newcomers every day. We have four girls sitting at four computer stations who do nothing else but enter these names into our computer system. These letters come from brand new folks who are trying to figure out how to make some extra money working at home. These new people are very eager to get started. They will immediately respond to worthwhile offers.

New names are entered each day as these responses to the advertising are received. We have a constant supply of new names. This assures that our names are never overworked and you will be receiving only fresh names. Our computer system makes it impossible for anyone to receive the same names on future reorders. Also, our computer system will prevent you from receiving the same names as another person working the same program.

We have in our computer system every single USPS approved mailing address in the United States. Every new address we enter is compared against the Post Office data base. Those which do not match perfectly are automatically deleted. Is it any wonder that undeliverables are not a problem when you order names from Prime Publishers, Inc.? Shouldn't you be receiving your names from the same source used by the professionals?

Stay away from old worn-out opportunity seeker, buyer, and MLM lists. These folks have already made a start in mailorder/MLM and their names have been circulated far and wide. They have already seen every offer out there many times. To get the response you want, you have to mail your offer to brand new people who have not already been drowned in a flood of circulars and offers.

FREE DEALERSHIP OPPORTUNITY

Not only will you be receiving the most responsive names yourself, you can earn a very worthwhile FULL-TIME INCOME by recommending our names to others.

When you send us the information we need to open your commission account, we will prepare a supply of our name circulars for you with your exclusive code number on each one of them. Just send these circulars out with each piece of outgoing mail. Suggest in your cover letter and sales literature that the reader obtain their names from us. Tell them about the good experiences you have had with our names. When the person sends in the name order form with your exclusive code number on it, you will receive a generous commission on each sale.

We do not offer this dealership to just anyone who happens along. While many dealerships cost $25, $50 or more, a Prime Names Dealership is ABSOLUTELY FREE.

In order to eliminate those who are not serious, we do set a minimum. It costs quite a lot in money and time for us to set up your dealership account and special handle your orders and your customer's orders.

Once you are signed up as a dealer, you will be eligible to receive a commission on all of your own retail purchases and also a commission on all our retail sales to those who order using the circular with your code number on it when the total number of all names ordered in any month reaches 2,000 names or more.

For example, if you place two retail orders for 500 names each and two other people each order 500 names using the circulars with your code number, your account will have reached the 2,000 minimum and you will receive commissions on all the orders. Or, we could receive four orders of 500 each from folks using your circular and the minimum would have been reached even if you did not order any names yourself. As soon as this minimum is reached, you will receive commissions on all of the orders received in your account for the entire month.

If you are a serious mailer, the 2,000 minimum will easily be exceeded in the first few days of each month.

We do all of the work for you. We handle all telephone inquiries, fill all orders, offer a guarantee, accept credit card orders, etc. We do all the work and you earn a very worthwhile commission check each month. All you have to do is mention Prime Publishers, Inc. in your cover letter or report and include your circular in every piece of mail you send out.

HOW MUCH CAN I EARN

At the end of each month in which you earn a commission, we will send you a statement showing all of the purchases during the month in your account including your own. The statement will show who ordered, how many names they ordered, and your commission on each sale. Enclosed with your statement will be your commission check for each and every order received during the month.

The following is a table showing the generous commissions you will earn:

Quantity	Retail	Commissions
250	$ 30.00	$ 10.00
500	40.00	20.00
1,000	70.00	30.00
2,000	125.00	50.00
5,000	275.00	75.00
10,000	400.00	100.00

As you can see from the commissions table above, it does not take very many orders each month for you to earn a very worthwhile income each month.

EVERYONE NEEDS FRESH RESPONSIVE NAMES

I'm sure by now you can see that you are holding in your hands a wonderful money-making opportunity. You can earn those big commission checks as our dealer while still working your present program. Just mention us in your cover letter, report, or other sales literature and include one of your circulars with your code number on it in every piece of mail you send out. You are, of course, still in complete control of your own business. All of your mailings will still go out with your return address on the mailing piece.

HOW DO I GET STARTED

To open your commission account, just place your initial order for circulars with your code number printed on each one and send us your personal name, your home address, your home phone number and your Social Security number. Send in the above information right now and get started receiving those big commission checks every month. This dealership opportunity is only open to U.S. citizens living in the continental 48 States.

Just tell us how many circulars you would like to start with and be sure to tell us the color of paper on which you would like to have your circulars printed. Colors available are: Canary, light green, light blue, goldenrod, ivory, grey, or salmon. Each of your circulars will have your exclusive code number already printed on it. If you include a money order, we can process your order immediately. Please allow time for your circulars to arrive. By phoning in your order, several days can be saved. The prices below are for colored paper and include all shipping charges direct to your home address. We can not ship circulars to a P.O. Box. Circulars are shipped by UPS truck to the 48 States only. As with any printing, the more you order, the lower is the unit cost. We suggest you order enough circulars to last several months.

Quantity	Price	Co-Op
500	$20.00	$16.00
1,000	26.00	21.00
2,000	44.00	35.00
3,000	63.00	50.00
4,000	80.00	64.00
5,000	96.00	77.00

Co-Op means we print your circular with your exclusive code number on the front and our non-conflicting printing advertisement on the back.

SAME DAY SERVICE

By using your credit card, we can take your order for names and/or circulars over the phone. This will save several days. Just call (912) 237-2422 for immediate service. Your order will be processed the same day you call.

YOUR SUCCESS IS ASSURED

The demand for good quality responsive names is growing each year. As an active name dealer for Prime Publishers, Inc., your success is assured. Absolutely fresh responsive names are very hard to find and you and your customers will be receiving the very best. Get started now! I would love to send you one of those big commission checks every month.

Send us the information we need to open your commission account right now. Or, if you have any questions, call me right now at (912) 237-2422.

JBD:dw

Respectfully,

James B. Dunn

James B. Dunn
List Manager

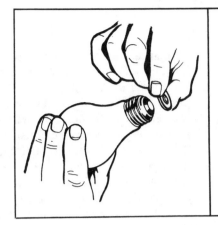

Chapter Four

How to Make Money with Display Ads

As with classified advertising, display advertising is a useful device for generating interest and promoting inquiries. Also, it is used effectively for selling the product or service directly from space advertising. In this and subsequent chapters, we'll deal solely with selling from display ads, and we'll explore those elements that, if properly applied, will help you to become successful in creating productive ads.

Ads will range from one inch, one column in size to a full page. As you begin to analyze display ads that are obvious winners because of their continuous appearance in print, try to determine what sets them apart. Why are they successful? Since these are the money-making ads, they can be extremely useful to you in designing a winning combination. Make a file of these winners for reference purposes so you can incorporate some of their captivating features into your own ads. Carefully note what they are selling, the illustration, if any, the heading, the body copy, the guarantee, testimonial or proof, and price.

If you want to get quick results from an ad, try running it in the shopping section of your local newspaper. That will give you some indication as to whether it will pay off in magazines. You might try running your ad on the television page, which has a large readership.

The following are the most frequently asked questions about display advertising:

Question: What is a display ad?
Answer: A display ad is a certain amount of space purchased in a publication for advertising purposes. This space can range from one inch in height by one column in width to a full page. You will encounter the term *junior page*. *Junior page* refers to two thirds of a page. Your daily newspaper and all magazines are filled with ads of many shapes and sizes. Your job is to analyze and experiment so you will eventually sell your product with the minimum amount of space—the more space you buy, the greater the cost. Running full-page ads does not insure success.

Question: Should I use an advertising agency?
Answer: Absolutely, when you can get one to work with you. You should make every effort to enlist the help of a local advertising agency. Tell them of your overall plans and try to generate in them some of the excitement that you feel about your projected operation. Advertising agencies make a commission of 15% on the cost of the ad, plus another 2% if they pay within 10 days from receipt of the bill. If the cost of the advertisement is $1,000, their commission is $150 plus another 2% of $850, which is $17 for prompt payment.

Question: What if I don't use an advertising agency?
Answer: You are in for some schooling that will be very good for you. I suggest you study the ads of mail order companies selling the type of product or service you have in mind. Take what you consider to be the strong elements and improve upon the ad.

Question: Should I use freelance copywriters?
Answer: Absolutely. No matter how small the size of your ads, take advantage of their expertise. They are specialists in the use of words that convey your message

with impact. Freelance copywriters write advertising copy for a flat fee. Advertising agencies employ staff as well as freelance copywriters. Many who work for the major advertising agencies do freelance work at a fraction of what they would have to charge as a firm employee. Should you be turned down by an agency, tell them you would appreciate their assistance in referring you to one in this field, as well as an artist. For the beginner especially, as well as for the advanced mail order entrepreneur, I highly recommend using their services. A change in a headline can make the difference between failure and success. I suggest you show your ad to as many people as you can to get the following feedback: On the basis of the advertising, would they send for the product or service you are trying to sell? Did the headline arouse their interest? Did the body copy hold their interest? Were the benefits clearly delineated? Did the price seem reasonable? In their opinion, what was the ad's chance of success? What comments would they care to volunteer?

Question: How long do you stay with an unproductive ad?

Answer: Drop it as quickly as you can. Just because you were once enthusiastic about it, don't let your ego induce you to put money into what is obviously a losing proposition. Once I've given an ad my best shot, I back off if it turns out to be a loser. I'll stay with an ad if the results are even marginal. I'll look for the critical element that will turn it into a winner. Or I'll assign the job to one of my copywriters. If, between us, we can't come up with a logical improvement, I'll drop the ad. You can spend only so much time, money, and energy on an ad, and then it's time to move. Like a jockey, you can't always bring home a winner. It's the percentages that count.

Question: How long do you stay with a winner?

Answer: Just as long as it continues to make money for you. Be careful not to schedule too heavily after the ad has been out for some time. The rule of thumb is the pulling power of an ad diminishes after a period of time. On the other hand, ads such as those on pages 93 and 97 seem to sustain their impact, increasing readership and orders by the sheer force of repetition. It seems repetition finally arouses enough curiosity in those who are marginal to get them to order.

When you have a winner, don't become overly complacent. See if you can't improve on your success with a new headline, perhaps a change of subtitle, use of an illustration, providing a toll-free number, and maybe by deleting the order blank. I, personally, like the order form if you have the space for it.

Give your ad to a freelance writer and challenge him to write a better ad. Suppose the new copy pulls better than the original. Go to still another freelance writer with the same assignment. The money you spend on rewriting is worthwhile, even though some writers will not improve the copy. When you use this technique, you'll finally hit

a bonanza. You or one of the copywriters will eventually come up with that critical element that will turn a winner into a gold mine.

Question: Where do you test an ad?

Answer: Since it's important to find out results as quickly as possible, I'd recommend using the daily newspaper. Remember, this is a test to determine whether or not there is a chance for success. The disadvantage of the newspaper is it has a life of only one day. If appropriate for your particular kind of product, *The Wall Street Journal* could be ideal. It's a great mail order paper, and you can test the ad regionally. It isn't necessary to buy the entire run. I like to test in *The National Enquirer* and *The Star*. There's a six-week closing date, and if you have a hit, you can go from there with your schedule.

Question: Where is the best place in the magazine or newspaper to advertise?

Answer: If you are prepared to spend big money, the back outside cover of a magazine is the choice location. Second to that are the front right-hand pages. Those are the odd numbers. Extensive tests tend to show that people respond better to the right-hand pages. If you are running a full-page ad, your coupon is usually going to be at the bottom of the third column and it's easier to cut it out on a right-hand page. You have the problem of the binding on the left-hand page. Make it easy for the customer to order. In some magazines, there is a premium for the up-front positions. You can request this position at no additional charge, but there's no guarantee you're going to get it.

If you plan to run in tabloids or newspapers, ask for the right-hand side of an up-front position, and be sure to specify you want your ad above the fold. Ads on the bottom, and especially running along the gutter, can be easily overlooked.

Question: How can I get good buys on space?

Answer: With publications other than those which obviously are very successful, you can ask for the special mail order rate. Publishers are aware that mail order businesses cannot pay the same rate as institutional ads from major companies. Many magazines, and most newspapers, have different rates according to the type of advertising. As you progress with your advertising experimentation, you'll learn about space brokers. Space brokers buy up large quantities of space, and they can give you a better deal than you could get buying directly from the publication. Magazines also have a quantity discount for the advertiser who runs three, six, and twelve times. Newspapers will give you a line rate for contracting for a given number of lines of advertising during a one-year period.

Question: What about P.I. (per inquiry) deals and help-if-needed deals?

Answer: A help-if-needed deal means the publication will rerun your ad free of charge if you don't meet expenses on the first ad. These arrangements are generally made with the salesmen representing the magazines. The major magazines won't budge on this score, but it is often possible to get this kind of deal with other publications. Don't expect to get it every time you run an ad, but it might be available when you ask for it.

P.I. deals are available with many magazines. They are usually made through the sales representative, although this isn't a hard-and-fast rule. In a P.I. deal, you agree to pay the publication what usually amounts to 50% of the price of the product you are selling, or perhaps even more. In turn, your advertisement is run free of charge. The mail is either sent directly to the publication or directly to you. The ad is keyed, and if the mail is sent to you, you remit to the publication once a week, once every month, or however you arrange. If the mail comes to the magazine, they pay you according to your arrangement.

Right now, as I write this chapter, I have several P.I. deals that are resulting in thousands of orders every week for my books. It's a nice feeling to see those orders coming in every day; it's like someone handing you dollar bills all day long. One of my magazine publishers is so delighted with the results that he's flying out to Los Angeles from the East to talk about an expansion of his advertising schedule.

When publications make up their pages, they are often left with an extra page or two that hasn't been sold for advertising. These are called *distressed, remnant,* or *standby pages* and are sold at greatly reduced prices. After you become known to the publications, you can make arrangements for these pages. Send them a full-page, glossy print of your ad with standby instructions to run it when they have a distressed page. From the publication point of view, it's better than running blank pages or public service announcements.

Keep in mind publications of all kinds want you to make money with your advertising program so you'll repeat the ads with them. Their existence is predicated on advertising revenue. They need to be competitive in the marketplace, and it's my experience they are willing to bend, give you a good deal, work with you equitably, and do whatever they can to be of service. They especially work this way with you when your advertising takes on a good schedule.

Question: How do I get free editorials on my products?
Answer: In Chapter 13 I'll talk more extensively about the art of acquiring free editorials when you are not paying for the ad. For now, let's assume you are paying for the ad. If the publication has an editorial section, do not hesitate to ask for a free editorial. Do more than ask for it; insist on it. You'll usually get it. When you do, I would advise you not to run the editorial for the product in the same month as your ad is being run. Run it next month. You might also want editorial mention for a new product. It is not imperative that you run the same item. I would test the saleability of a new product. If you happen to be living in a city covered by the advertising representative, ask him to arrange the editorial the next time he calls. It's to his advantage to help you in this regard. Since his commissions are based on the amount of money you spend for advertising, he'll be glad to work with you. Get to know him. He has a wealth of knowledge and information about the successes and failures of mail order ventures. His experience can help you.

Question: What about the use of credit cards and toll-free numbers?
Answer: There is no doubt credit cards will increase your business, but you have to decide if it's worth the paperwork involved, and if you are willing to lessen your profits to extend this privilege to your customers. Toll-free numbers will also produce results, but is it worth it? Until you have had more experience in the mail order business, I would suggest you forget both. After a while, let some tests help you make a valid judgment on the subject, and then act accordingly.

Question: What about C.O.D.'s?
Answer: I have discontinued the use of C.O.D. sales because it consumes too much clerical time. Very often, the order will be returned because the purchaser was not at home when the postman delivered the merchandise. When that happens, you've lost out on postage, paper work, and expense of the transaction. Stay away from C.O.D. shipments.

Question: How can I do something out of the ordinary in my mail order operation?
Answer: If it's in keeping with the character of your product, give your customers the option of having their purchases personalized. Depending on which process is most suitable, the individual's name can be printed, monogrammed, embroidered, or engraved on the product. Everyone likes to see his or her name in print, especially if it's on a gift. Wouldn't you like to receive a crate of oranges or apples marked, "Picked especially for (your name)?" A friend of mine is selling thousands of sunglasses that are personalized with the wearers' name. I've sold thousands of dozens of golf balls only because they were personalized. Think of all the personalized key chains and mugs that have been sold. My wife and I recently moved into a new home and last week we received a pair of monogrammed towels as a gift. My wife immediately put them into the guest bathroom to accent the room. The monogramming turned ordinary towels into special towels.

There's a local book company that sells children's books personalized with the child's name, address, name of pet, birthday, name of brother, sister, friend, or other members of the family. See page 54. The books are beautiful, and the product is an excellent way to stimulate a child's interest in reading. It works most effectively.

Imagine you have been called in as a mail order consultant to improve the response of this advertisement. Read it, study it, analyze it, and come up with some suggestions to improve it before you read my following critique.

This ad ran in *The National Enquirer*. The cost was $12,000. In my opinion, the ad lacks a strong headline. The prominent headline is *Take a minute to fill out this coupon.* This is putting the cart before the horse. Those instructions should be in small type at the bottom of the ad. The second headline, *Give your child hours of fun!*, doesn't pique my interest. The subheading, YOUR CHILD IS THE STAR OF THIS NEW 16-PAGE ME-BOOK, should really be the main heading, and the entire bottom part of the ad, which does the selling, should be on top. Using a split run, I'd like to see proof that the order form on top pulled better.

Let's go back to the copy. Does the ad have a strong enough hook to grab the reader? I know it doesn't. In the subheading, leave out 16-PAGE ME-BOOK. Put that copy elsewhere. The name of the company is not important to the reader and it gives no impact to the copy. Have that line read, *YOUR CHILD IS THE STAR OF THIS NEW PERSONALIZED BOOK THAT WILL EXCITE AND DELIGHT HIM.*

This line is an improvement, but we still haven't hit the heart of the ad. The hook is in the very last line of the ad: "A recent report gave startling evidence that personalized books improve reading retention and comprehension by 35%." This is the key to the whole ad—almost lost on the last line. Every parent wants his child to improve in reading, retention, and comprehension. Use it in the headline, shout it out loud and clear. WE GUARANTEE TO IMPROVE YOUR CHILD'S READING! Follow this with proof that personalized books stimulate a child's interest in reading and re-reading *his story* to others.

Next point. They have missed a basic precept in writing good advertising copy. Who is the authority stating personalized books improve reading retention and comprehension by 35%? The ad says "A recent report." Does this statement convince you? Not me! I want hard evidence this is true, preferably by facts from universities and people who have researched the matter. Let's assume there hasn't been any extensive research done along these lines. If I were running the Me-Books Publishing Company, I would fund some studies at Harvard or local universities. I would become involved with the inner-school reading program and give free personalized books to students. I'd involve principals, teachers, and other educators in the project. In doing so, I'd get tens of thousands of dollars worth of publicity that money can't buy, and I'd also wind up with plenty of concrete evidence to back up my claim.

I've gone into detail concerning this advertisement just to show you how my mind works when it comes to analyzing display ads. I want you to develop the ability to apply your own analyses in the same way. I have no idea how this ad pulled, but, regardless of how well it did, I certainly know that my suggestions for improving the ad are valid. I'm going to be showing you some of my advertisements, and I'd appreciate your judging them in the same manner I have this one. If you do a good job, I'll put you on the payroll for assignments. Let me know if you are interested. The point to remember is: have your ads criticized before you run them. This insures you the best possible chance for success. Before running my ads, I solicit feedback from a dozen or more competent people. I note each one's comments and constantly look to improve a line, a phrase, or word. Why not? I'm more interested in the end result than in the confirmation that I or my copywriters have written a great piece of copy.

You could run a well-paying mail order business that offers the service of evaluating advertisements for a fee. Assuming my comments on the personalized books were valid, wouldn't you, as the president of the company, be willing to pay my consultation fee of $100 for a full-page ad—the results of which could bring a return of thousands of dollars and save you thousands of dollars more in non-effective ads? You can do the same thing. Start writing letters offering your services to companies running ads. If you are good, you'll get as much business as you can possibly handle.

Question: What suggestions do you have for the mail order neophyte?

Answer: I realize you are not going to follow all my suggestions in operating a successful mail order operation, but there are some that are basic and will give you valuable information. Here's a Melvin Powers mail order technique:

Once I see an advertisement repeated over a period of time in the same or different publications, I assume it's a winner and send for the product. I always use a key in my name or address to find out what the company will try to sell as a follow-up, and how many times during the year, or for a period of years, my name will be rented.

Keep in mind it is in the back end of the mail order business where the big money is generally made. When you send for a product, tape the advertisement to the front of an 8½" x 11½" or larger envelope. On the back of the envelope, mark the date you sent away for the product and the date you received it. Put in all the follow-up mail, indicating dates. When you receive mail from some other source with your key, mark down the date, a brief description of it, and from whom it came. Save the literature.

Some time ago, I ordered a book on how to make a living playing poker. I used the name of Ace Powers. In one year, I received 35 outside offers, not only for other gambling systems, but for many types of merchandise, including a high percentage of pornographic literature.

Let's go a step further with our detective work. Since

I'm now getting mail from various companies, it's obvious the names are being rented. I can do one of two things to gauge the results of the original ad. I can write directly to the company using my company stationery, or I can write to my list broker, inquiring how many names are available for rent and what the cost is.

Let's assume I get an answer stating they have 25,000 customers, and the rental is $40 per thousand. To find out how much money they took in on the book, simply multiply 25,000 by the cost of the book. The book sells for $10. Therefore we know they took in $250,000. We can fairly well judge the cost of the book, but we don't know how much money was spent on advertising. Let's assume the book costs them $2 to mail and they spent $100,000 on ads. That leaves them with a profit of $100,000 for the year, and that's just on one book without the follow-ups and rental of names. Suppose I'm way off on the amount of money spent for advertising. Let's say they really spent $150,000 on advertising. That leaves them with a $50,000 profit. I gave you a figure of $2 in the mail for the book, but in truth the maximum the book would cost is $1.50 in the mail. Add another $12,500 to the $50,000.

Joe Karbo, in the eighth line of his prize-winning ad, *How to Get Rich the Lazy Man's Way* (see page 93), says, "What's more, I'm going to ask you to send me 10 dollars for something that'll cost me no more than 50 cents." If I had his book printing business, I'd be making money on that price.

Let's find out the approximate amount of money the company made on the rental of names. The list broker gets a commission of 15% of the $40-per-thousand rental. If it's a new ad, we know they built up the list to 25,000 names. For our example, we'll say they have 25,000 names and the ad is still running, adding even more names. The company is getting $34 per thousand each time the names are rented; 25 times $34 is $850. According to the literature I received, they rented the names 34 times. Multiply 34 times $850 and you get $28,900. Now estimate the income from the one book for the year at $91,400 as follows: $62,500 on the sale of the book and $28,900 from rental of names. If my calculations are off about one third the amount, I'll deduct $26,400, leaving at least $75,000 profit.

The importance of these calculations is to show you the viability of copycatting a program. It indicates success if you improve upon the advertisement, or, better still, stimulates you to create a program of your own. That's the real challenge, and meeting it will make you proud of yourself. That's your goal, that's your dream, and don't

think you can't realize it. You never know what will happen when you use your energies and talent creatively.

Look at the results of two successful campaigns. Read the write-ups on pages 92 and 99. Joe Karbo tells you in the interview he sold 173,000 copies of his book, *The Lazy Man's Way to Riches,* at $10 in one year. Mark Haroldsen tells you he has sold 350,000 copies of his book, *Financial Success.* See page 99. In his advertisement for the book he says 250,000 copies of the book were sold at $10 each in 1977. To paraphrase Mark Haroldsen's prize-winning headline, I'm saying, "Wake up the creative genius that sleeps within you."

Since I've been writing this book, my creative juices have really been flowing. My sixth sense tells me I've come up with some winning products and new book concepts for mail order. See pages 119 through 140. This is stemming from my subconscious mind without conscious effort. I can feel the creative forces at work within me. It will happen to you, too, as you consciously begin to put your energies to work. Read books on creativity. It's an exhilarating feeling to know that you've come up with a winner, and then prove it to yourself.

Regard your first attempts at mail order as a learning experiment. Spending your first dollars running your ads will put you in the mail order business. Once you get results, you'll have plenty of questions. If the ad didn't make money for you, why not? If it did, how can you improve your results? Once you develop a successful mail order formula, opportunities are limitless. How much money you make and how successful you become are determined only by the extent of your creative and business ambitions.

I'll talk more extensively about display advertisements and the factors that go toward making them winners. This chapter was intended merely to give you some of the basic elements.

Here is your second mail order quiz. Look at the two ads on page 55. Before you read the answer, see if you can reach a decision as to which one pulled more orders. What elements entered into your decision?

Throughout the book, I'll be challenging you. When I ask you to stop reading and look at the ads in question, why not do so? Have the fun of trying to assess the ads before you read the answer. It will be a good learning experience for you.

In the next chapter, I'll be discussing the use of direct mail to sell products and services. The potential is unlimited in its scope. Once you work out the right direct mail package, success is assured.

MORE BIDDERS THAN TAKERS FOR ACQUISITIONS

Everybody Wants to Sell by Mail

BY NANCY YOSHIHARA
Times Staff Writer

What do Parker Pen Co., Greyhound Corp., Quaker Oats Co., International Telephone & Telegraph Corp. and General Mills Inc. have in common?

Each is in the mail order business.

Parker Pen sells clothing by mail; Greyhound, gifts; Quaker Oats, yarn; IT&T, seeds and General Mills, stamps, coins and dresses.

Those are some of the surprising competitors in the mail order industry, according to a recent report by Maxwell Sroge Company Inc.

"Probably one of the most significant happenings in recent years in the mail order business, says Maxwell Sroge, president of the Chicago-based direct marketing, advertising and consulting firm, "is the entrance of large, publicly held corporations into the field.

"The consulting group of our company has received more inquiries about acquisitions within the past several months than at any time in our history."

Acquisition figures, however, are hard to come by because of the fragmented nature of the direct mail market-

---

A Word From The Sponsor	How and why of advertising and marketing.

---

ing industry. But direct mail sales are booming, thanks to the energy crunch and the increasing number of working women who are looking for short cuts in shopping.

The Sroge firm predicts that direct mail sales of consumer goods and services will total $26.3 billion this year compared with $21.5 billion last year.

"More and more companies are diversifying into directing marketing or direct mail," says Edward J. Pfeiffer, director of communications at the Direct Mail/Marketing Assn. in New York. "Marlboro, for example, is selling western clothing now, but you also have to include tops from cigarette packages."

The catalogue method of selling is attractive in uncertain economic times, according to Sroge, because the business requires little cash, profits are higher than in conventional retailing and selling can be tailored to special interest markets.

Pfeiffer says research shows that direct mail is third behind television and newspapers, and ranks ahead of radio and magazines.

"Its advantages are selectivity—you can really pick who you want to sell to and see results," he says.

Indeed, almost anything can be purchased by mail these days. The rapid development of special interest markets has spawned companies, which for example, may sell only large size men's clothing, left-handed products and sexy underwear.

Pfaelzer Bros., a unit of Greyhound, even offers complete dinners—from shrimp cocktail to dessert—which are delivered frozen through the mail.

All this has triggered growing interest from big companies.

Charles Hersheway, account supervisor in charge of acquisitions and limited partnerships at Maxwell Sroge, reports an increase in acquisition inquires from large firms listed on Fortune's list of the top 500 U.S. companies.

"Not only are we getting requests from U.S. firms, but also from foreign," including one of Japan's largest retailers, he says.

"In our file we also have requests from West German companies. Our problem is not finding prospective buyers, but finding prospective sellers."

Currently, about 30 of the Fortune 500 companies are involved in mail order selling or other forms of non-store marketing, according to Hersheway.

A newcomer to the field is Zenith Radio Corp., which recently purchased Heath Co., a mail order seller of electronics kits and how-to-do-it materials.

A major buyer of mail order businesses has been the privately owned S.C. Johnson & Co. Inc., the wax maker, and its affiliate, S.C.J. Investment Co., which own mail order operations selling everything from cheese (Wisconsin Cheesemakers Guild Ltd.), to fishing rods (Leonard Rod Inc.).

Neiman-Marcus Gift Out of This World

The featured gift in Neiman-Marcus' 1979 Christmas catalog is Homesat, a $35,000 antenna designed to pick up television signals from satellites. Sidney Topol, chairman of the Dallas-based chain, described Homesat as the first remote control, multi-satellite antenna available to individual consumers.

For those on a tighter budget, Neiman-Marcus has a ceramic cowboy boot filled with 20 pencils for $12 or four tubes of liquor flavored, nonintoxicating toothpaste for $10.

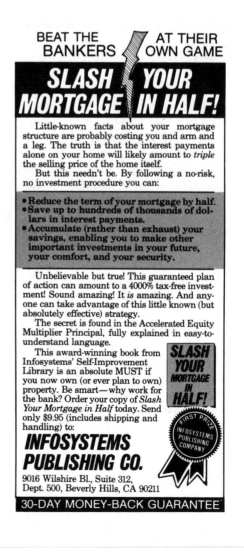

Have You Ever Taken A Practice Golf Swing At A Dandelion?

Have You Ever Taken A Practice Golf Swing At A Dandelion?

How You Can Play GOLF using SELF-HYPNOSIS

...How You Can Play Better Golf Using Self Hypnosis

(A) All-copy . . . or

These ads for the book "How You Can Play Better Golf Using Self-Hypnosis" appeared in the Wall Street Journal. Which ad pulled the largest number of coupon inquiries?

Ad A uses an all-copy approach. The headline is provocative; it asks: "Have You Ever Taken A Practice Golf Swing At A Dandelion?"

The copy explains: "What would your golf score be if you could hit golf balls like you hit dandelions? Pretty good? What would you say if we promised you that score? Unbelievable? If you are willing to keep an open mind for a new concept while you read this advertisement, we can point a way to help you improve your golf score immeasurably, as well as your enjoyment of the game.

"How many times have you heard the remark or, possibly, made it, 'I can take a practice swing I know is just right, but put a golf ball down and I freeze.'

"The pages of a new golf book are dedicated to the mental side of golf or, more specifically, to the use of self-hypnosis for control of the mechanical action of the golf swing. The use of self-hypnosis for golf is a new concept

(B) with picture?

and one that will help the golfer with all phases of his game. The reader will learn about the simplest, most effective technique ever devised to help him reduce his score.

"The average player knows the fundamental movements of the golf stroke, yet fails to play well. It must follow that his failure is in his mental play. Through hypnosis, the way to obtain a mental effect may be explained, understood and put to use. Self-hypnosis helps the golfer to attain 'the subconscious feel' which is imperative to good golf . . ."

Ad B uses the same headline and the same copy. The layout is a little different—and a picture of the book in its dust jacket is shown.

Basis of comparison: Both ads appeared in the Wall Street Journal. Ad A ran 405 lines in the edition of May 12, 1961. Ad B ran 280 lines in the edition of April 18, 1961. Which ad pulled the most coupon inquiries?

Answer appears upside down below

Examples such as this benefit all advertisers and agencies. Please send your case histories to Larrie O'Farrell, senior editor, PRINTERS' INK, 635 Madison Avenue, New York 22.

According to Melvin Powers of the Wilshire Book Co. in Hollywood, Calif., Ad A pulled three-to-one over Ad B. Readers of the Wall Street Journal read ad A because of the provocative headline and the newspaper format of the ad. Ad B, using the book as an illustration, told readers at a glance what the ad story was, and it is felt that the word "hypnosis" on the cover of the book deterred many readers from exploring further.

L.L. Bean, Freeport, Maine... Retail sales are 20% of its volume, mail order 80%... Last year's volume: more than $40 million... Store opened 24 hours a day, 365 days a year... Has 10,000 square feet for retail selling and 176,000 square feet for an on-hand inventory of $7 million... United Parcel's largest customer... Average daily order: 5,000. Peak daily order: 25,000... Packages mailed last year: more than one million... Still a best seller: the Maine Hunting Shoe. Store sells 165,000 pairs of footwear each year... Rushed boots and clothing to Israeli army during Yom Kippur War (only place in the world with enough on-hand inventory).

Caroll Reed, New Hampshire... Now has ten divisions and mails seven million catalogs a year... Its motto: "First Quality—Then Fashion, Last Price"... Direct mail is 70% of its sales which total more than $60 million... More than 800,000 names in-house... Has increased number of retail shops but limits growth to New England because "spreading too thin would be disastrous," says company president Fred Leighton.

Doll House Corner, Manchester, Vermont: Its first year's gross in 1966 was $21,500... Last year's volume: $1 million. The big difference: mail order... Started mailing in 1968 with 5,000 names from its guest book... Today mails 160,000 catalogs and charges $1 for each one... When asked, "Have you been hurt by the depressed economy?"; spokesman answered: "What depressed economy?"

MONTHLY RECORD OF AD RECEIPTS

Product	Selling Price	Key	
Publication	Circulation	Issue	On Sale
Cost	Size of Ad	Monthly Profit	Monthly Loss

Projection: Total Number of Orders   Total Cash

Month_____ Day of Month	Daily Number of Orders	Total Number of Orders	Daily Receipts	Total Receipts	
1					
2					
3					
4					
5					
6					
7					
8					
9					
10					
11					
12					
13					
14					
15					
16					
17					
18					
19					
20					
21					
22					
23					
24					
25					
26					
27					
28					
29					
30					
31					
Total					

Comments _____

French Leather Designer Builds A $2-Million Business In The U.S. Using Catalog Request Ads

SPACE AD for Jacques Vincent in the *New York Times Sunday Magazine*.

By Marlene Nadle

LITTLE NECK, NY—Jacques Vincent, a French leather clothing designer, has built a $2-million mail order business in the United States in only 10 months, using catalog request ads in a variety of publications. This year, the firm will raise its direct response space budget by 60 per cent, to $500,000.

"You can grow very quickly in this business," said Claude Socroun, president of the firm's U.S. division. "We have already had over 100,000 responses requesting catalogs from our ads. An average of eight-and-a-half to nine per cent of those are converted into sales. Our average sale is $225. The order is just as important as the re-order," he said, "because it means people are happy with your product. In this short time, our re-order rate has been three per cent."

New sales are averaging $350,000 a month, he continued.

The ad budget for 1985 was $250,000, and the publications used were: *The Village Voice, Esquire, Ebony*, the *Roth Report, Working Women, Success*, and *The New York Times*. The color ads emphasized the "factory direct" and "below wholesale" prices. Socroun said he got his best results from *New York Times* ads which produced 50,000 requests for catalogs and a 12 per cent order rate. *Ebony* produced 12,000 requests, but an order rate of under seven per cent.

In France, the order rate is 27 per cent because the firm is so well established there, Socroun said.

The 1986 space campaign will be changed in a number of ways, starting with a new ad agency, Tom Lennon Associates of New York.

"The old ads made us look too punk and too young," said Socroun. "They used backgrounds of subway trains. We are really selling a product for all ages. Our average customer is 34, makes over $25,000 and is often college educated. In the new campaign, we will not even be using professional models. Instead, they will be just average people. One of them, a friend of mine, is a CPA, 42 years old, and looks terrific in our clothes. So does my son, who is 20."

Another way the new campaign will be different is that it will be more directed at women by using such women's magazines as *Cosmopolitan* and by expanding the line of women's items available.

The old catalog showed 50 items for men and five for women. The new catalog will still have 50 items for men and 20 for women.

The catalog will also be expanded from 48 full-color pages to 62 full-color pages. Socroun still sees no need to purchase any mailing lists. He is, instead, planning to market his own 75,000-name list.

One of the techniques successfully used in France will also be used here. Vincent has 25 catalog stores in France, which have increased sales by 30 per cent.

"Customers come in carrying the catalog, try on or inspect the merchandise, and take it with them," said Socroun.

He opened one catalog showroom in the Little Neck office in September and, after a slow start, is now getting 20 to 30 people a day in the shop. He plans to open another showroom in Manhattan by March and build from there.

"We are dealing with a very hot item when we are dealing with leather jackets. I know that because when we put some on display in a window in Rockefeller Center, they were stolen and we already had a robbery at our office. That is either a very great compliment to our product or a very significant comment on American society," he concluded.

57

Sex, Fear and Big Ads Are a Winning Trio For New Publisher

* * *

Advertising Gets Much Credit For 2 Straight Best Sellers; Are All Generations 'Me'?

By Laurel Leff
Staff Reporter of The Wall Street Journal

"A mundane sex life can be compared to a frozen TV dinner: It will keep you alive but it's not a gourmet banquet served in a posh restaurant."

So teases a newspaper advertisement for "Nice Girls Do—and Now You Can Too!" a frothy sex guide by a Hollywood psychologist, Irene Kassorla. The ad is also chockfull of specific advice on how to share in the feast. So specific that several newspapers refused to run it. "We didn't think it was the right kind of copy for a family newspaper," says the general advertising manager for the Pittsburgh Press.

But newspapers' skittishness doesn't seem to have slowed sales of the book, which is near the top of the New York Times best-seller list. Nor has it intimidated the book's publisher, Robert J. Ringer, the controversial author of the 1970s book "Winning Through Intimidation." Mr. Ringer dismisses the newspapers' action as "relatively insignificant."

A few ads in a few markets may not be crucial to the success of "Nice Girls Do," but Mr. Ringer's overall advertising strategy certainly is. Largely as a result of flamboyant marketing maneuvers, Mr. Ringer's publishing house, Stratford Press of Beverly Hills, Calif., now is two for two—two books and two best sellers in just one year. The company was founded in January 1980.

Manhattan Amazed

Using a hard-sell approach, unabashed appeals to Americans' self-interest and an unusual form of advertising, Mr. Ringer pushed both Stratford books to the top of the best-seller lists in a matter of months. Stratford's first book, "Crisis Investing," a dour chronicle of "opportunities and profits in the coming great depression," was the best-selling nonfiction hard-cover book of 1980, selling over 400,000 copies. Priced at $12.50 for "Crisis Investing" and $9.95 for "Nice Girls Do," the two books have reaped about $5.4 million in revenues for Stratford.

The Manhattan publishing establishment is amazed. "Two books from a small West Coast publisher on the New York Times best-seller list at the same time, it's just remarkable," says Susan Ginsberg, executive editor of Gulf & Western Industries Inc.'s Pocket Books unit. "People were very surprised."

Mr. Ringer, however, wasn't. Ever since 1973, when he published "Winning Through Intimidation" himself, after all the major publishing houses had turned it down, Mr. Ringer has been beating his own path to the best-seller list. After "Winning Through Intimidation," he wrote "Looking Out for No. 1" and "Restoring the American Dream." They were all best sellers and were published by Mr. Ringer's Los Angeles Book Publishers Co., a forerunner of Stratford.

Sitting in Stratford's makeshift Beverly Hills office, the 43-year-old Mr. Ringer doesn't look or sound intimidating. (He does, however inform this reporter at the outset of an interview that he intends to tape it.) The former real-estate broker and all-around promoter doesn't even sport the "dress for success" look one would expect from the man who wrote that "posture is everything." Instead, he looks like an accountant on his day off, wearing a velour pullover, corduroy pants and gray suede shoes.

Reams of Words

If his manner is nonchalant, his marketing approach isn't. Mr. Ringer uses basically the same carefully executed strategy to promote all his books. First, he introduces the book with expensive full-page newspaper ads, each cooperatively financed by Stratford and a bookstore chain, usually B. Dalton Booksellers or Waldenbooks. Unlike most ads, which emphasize pretty pictures and splashy slogans, Mr. Ringer's ads feature reams of words and one small photo of the author. It's what the ads say—Mr. Ringer writes them himself—that counts.

"The ads are a remarkable piece of persuasion," says Oscar Dystel, formerly Bantam Books Inc.'s chairman and currently a consultant. "Once you're hooked into reading the ad, you figure you might as well try the book."

Mr. Ringer also makes it as easy as possible to get the book. While many publishers run cooperative ads with the chain stores, and others sell books through mail orders, Mr. Ringer is one of the few to combine the two methods: Each of his ads contains a mail-order coupon that the reader can clip and send to the store. "To be a legitimate publisher you have to sell through bookstores," Mr. Ringer says. "You can sell thousands of books through mail order, and the general public will never hear about it."

This merchandising method permits Stratford to concentrate sales in two major chains with best-seller lists of their own that are highly visible in the publishing trade. The method also provides, through the chains' computerized weekly sales lists, a quick measure of consumers' response to the ads.

The theory is that once the books appear on the chains' best-seller lists, other retailers will be encouraged to stock them and the authors will be invited to local talk shows and other promotional forums. Then it's only a matter of time before the books appear on more-widely-circulated best-seller lists.

J. Kendrick Noble, a publishing analyst for Paine Webber Mitchell Hutchins Inc., sees an additional reason for Mr. Ringer's success. "He has a gift for identifying books that buyers have a need for," Mr. Noble says. Mr. Ringer agrees and asserts that the public's appetite for self-interest books won't slacken.

"People in the media keep insisting that we're going through a period, that the 1970s were the 'me generation,'" Mr. Ringer says. "Every generation since neolithic times has been the 'me generation.'"

Mr. Ringer is particularly adept at identifying and playing on people's fears. Ads for "Crisis Investing," which he picked up from a small publisher who had sold it through mail orders, warn that you will probably "lose everything in the coming depression." But they assure you that if you read the book, you might be one of the "canny few that will not only survive, but prosper."

"Nice Girls Do" isn't exactly "my cup of tea," Mr. Ringer says, but he contends "there's a need for this kind of book." The book was in its fourth rewrite, and had been rejected by several publishers, when Mr. Ringer met Irene Kassorla at a party. He suggested that she borrow his editor, Ellen Shahan, to help with the book. The psychologist-author describes the resulting collaboration as "a miracle."

She is less pleased with the book's advertisements. "They're too, well, sexy," she says. "The book isn't sexy. I wanted to be represented as a research scholar with a revolutionary approach to female sexuality. I'm making one of the most important statements about sex in this century." She apparently hasn't been upset enough, though, to demand that Mr. Ringer alter the ads.

Based on the success of his first two books, Mr. Ringer plans to double his staff to 20 and move from his cramped quarters. He also plans to publish about a book a month beginning with an economics book, "The Alpha Strategy," in May. Mr. Ringer, who tends to talk in advertising slogans, describes "The Alpha Strategy" as "the greatest book ever written on the free-market philosophy."

Next summer he plans to publish a book for divorced fathers and another entitled "Living Alone and Liking It." He says he is "seriously negotiating" for six other books.

Chapter Five

The Unlimited Potential for Making Money with Direct Mail

When you find an American product, try to get an exclusive on it for mail order sales. If you are importing the product, try to get exclusive rights for the sale of it in the United States. When you do, exploit it to the fullest through mail order, wholesale, and trade sales. Read Chapter 12 for information on selling retail outlets and jobbers. If you still need some help, write or call me.

Direct mail and package insert programs are fascinating ways to sell products of all kinds. The first thing to do is to study and analyze the direct mail that comes to your home and office. Does the literature entice you to buy the product? If not, why not? How can the literature be improved? You can begin your own direct mail campaign with a modest mailing of one thousand names.

Try to find a product that credit card and oil companies would welcome when they bill their customers every month. The colorful printed inserts used by numerous other types of companies to sell merchandise to recipients of their bills runs into billions of dollars. There are hundreds of companies that will work with you in a statement stuffer or package insert program.

I've had great success with direct mail circulars selling various business opportunities. See pages 63 through 76. These mailing pieces are winners. Can you tell me why? Copy the style and formats when you find an appropriate product or service to sell.

Here's a thought to remember. Good advertising copy can make a winner of an ordinary product. Poor advertising copy can make a loser of an excellent product.

The enormous advantage of using inserts and statement stuffers is you can get a fast read-out about the possibility of success for your offer. When you have a winner, the money-making possibilities are staggering.

Start saving and studying every piece of literature that you receive with statements from gas companies, credit card companies, department stores, specialty shops, and mail order companies.

When you find your product and are ready to roll with it, you can copy a layout and design you feel would be appropriate. You'll also get an idea as to what is being sold, the price range of various products, payment plans, and other pertinent information.

You don't have to go to the giant companies to begin your operation. You can contact merchandisers in your community and try to make an equitable financial arrangement with them to include your inserts in their outgoing mail. This way, you can test the pulling power of your offer with small mailings. You might be able to interest some merchandisers in passing out one of your circulars with each purchase. You could also make arrangements for a small counter display containing your circular and sign reading "TAKE ONE." Go to the people with whom you are doing business. It does not matter whether or not the product ties in with what they are selling or the service they offer. Be sure to key each business establishment. Your purpose in doing this is to test the response of your offer at a minimal cost. Once you get good results, go to the major companies, and you'll be able to deal with them in an authoritative way.

Spencer Gifts, one of the country's leading gift-and-gadget mail order houses, welcomes your package inserts. They have 4,000,000 packages a year available for inserts. You have your challenge clearly spelled out. Find a product to pay off with those 4,000,000 packages. Once you do, there are dozens of other similar mail order houses with millions of more packages. You could become wealthy in a short period of time with the right product.

Once successful, look what happens: you develop your own mailing list, you produce a catalog for your mailings, and you start renting your names—which means more money in the bank. It's an exhilarating, never-ending cycle.

When you have produced a winning, package-insert mailing-piece, make the necessary changes to run display advertisements on it. It should pay off. The converse is also true. Be alert to the interchangeable relationship.

Did you know you can make arrangements to have your circulars inserted in egg cartons? Here again, the potential for making money never ends, and once you come up with a winner, the monetary figures are staggering. You need a product that will appeal to women as an impulse purchase. Your insert should consist of a four-color circular containing an illustration of the product, a brief description, and an order form. Just think of the possibilities once you hit. You can make arrangements to send out millions of circulars in egg cartons throughout the country. I've been privy to a wide variety of winners and to the amount of orders these inserts generate. The figures are mind boggling, and so beautiful for those who are raking in the dollars.

Once the package inserts work for you, you can go to the Sunday supplements that sell products and give coupon discounts for food and market items. Again, the figures run into the millions and it's an unending process. The companies producing such supplements have to fill out their catalog each week, and, as with the magazine distress-page opportunities, you can work out a good deal on a standby situation. They are open to joint ventures, and you might want to follow through on some equitable arrangement. Needless to say, you can buy space, but during the initial testing stages of your venture, the price could be prohibitive.

The opportunity for making money with package inserts and with Sunday supplements is truly exciting. You can start in a small way and gradually build up circulation numbers. As with any other phase of mail order, it is important that you keep informed as to what is happening and know this aspect of the business. Investigate it as you would any other phase of mail order. The fact that others make money at it is a promising sign you, too, could reap a financial harvest. Your initial and all-important task is to find the product ideally suited for this type of merchandising. Equipped with that, you might well have a winner.

To stimulate your creativity, study the mailing list categories available from Quality Lists on page 198. The possibilities for successful direct mail are limitless. Here is an exercise in brainstorming I use in my mail order classes. I suggest you try it. As you read each list, write down the name of mail order products or services that might do well in each category. Don't worry about the correctness of what you come up with. This is a free-wheeling, brainstorming

exercise. When you finish, go back and study your list of suggestions. Are you sufficiently confident to activate any of your ideas? If so, do it.

When you are at your main library, ask for and study the reference publication, *Direct Mail List Rates and Data*. It profiles over 30,000 mailing lists, including business lists, consumer lists, and farm lists. Also included is a complete list of co-op mailers and package inserters. My advice is to work with a mailing list broker. You want to be able to discuss the results of your mailings with someone who is knowledgeable. He can give you excellent feedback and suggestions for further mailing lists. He could be an invaluable aid to your complete operation.

Early in my book publishing career, I became a believer in the power of direct mail. I published a medical book entitled *Psychosomatic Gynecology* by William S. Kroger, M.D. I priced it at $10. I rented the names of gynecologists, obstetricians, general practitioners, osteopaths, chiropractors, nurses, psychiatrists, and psychologists. I produced an elaborate direct mailing piece and did extensive mailings. I easily sold out the first printing of 5,000 copies of the book in a relatively short period of time. In Chapter 10, you'll see how I used the same technique years later to sell several hundred thousand copies of the book, *Cybernetics Within Us*.

More technical and specialized books are sold by direct mail than in bookstores. Direct mail is very effective, as it pinpoints the target perfectly. Publishers in technical fields count very little on bookstore sales because of the highly specialized nature of their books. Mailing lists of all kinds are available, and the publishers are able to concentrate their marketing efforts.

Magazines derive most of their subscriptions from the use of direct mail techniques. Let one of your subscriptions run out and just watch how many letters you'll receive urging you to renew at special savings. Advertising revenues are based on their number of subscribers and newsstand sales. It's important they not lose a single subscriber.

Good direct mail literature contains the same elements as good display advertisements. With direct mail you have the advantage of not being confined to a limited amount of space. You can use as long a sales letter as you want to convince your customer that he will immeasurably improve his life once he orders your product. You have the option of a one-, two-, three-, or four-color brochure and choices of paper to run it on. The same applies to your outgoing and return envelopes. You can use special guarantee literature and a separate sheet containing the names and photographs of satisfied customers. You have your choice of sending your literature first class or third class. You might even want to use hand-written envelopes for special mailings, and, perhaps, even calligraphy. There is no end to the variety you can use.

My premise is you don't have to be pretentious in your solicitations. Tailor your mailing piece to your product, its price, and your audience. Keep your options open.

We know the average direct mailing piece contains an outside envelope, a return envelope, a personal letter, a brochure, and an order form. Ask yourself which of these elements you need to motivate your readers to respond. Be certain your name and address is on every piece of literature. You might elect to send out a self-mailer, in which case you can eliminate the outside envelope and the return envelope. You can then combine your sales letter, brochure, guarantee, and order form all on one sheet of paper. You'll see how I did this very effectively in Chapter 10.

In the final analysis, I personally believe it's the offer that's all-important, not the gingerbread that surrounds it. This should not prevent you from experimenting with different ways to improve your results—that's always a challenge.

If you have an exclusive product, your direct mail piece can serve a two-fold purpose. One, it can be used to sell your product to your prospective customer, and, second, it can be used to stimulate sales in appropriate retail outlets. That's exactly the procedure I followed in selling a book entitled *Psycho-Cybernetics*. The two-page circular, as shown on pages 81 and 82, including variations, was responsible for helping me sell over two million copies of the book.

I sent this circular, with a catalog of all my books and a postpaid business reply envelope, to a large number of business organizations. I got my initial mailing list from such magazines as *Specialty Salesmen* and *Opportunity Magazine*. I also used *The Thomas' Register of American Manufacturers* and the classified section of the phone book.

Let's examine the circular. It contains only a brief page of advertising copy. The backside contains further information, plus a photograph of the author and an illustration of the book. The headline on side one, plus the first sentence, contain the key elements of the sales letter. The two endorsements that immediately follow lend credibility to the statements. For emphasis, I reiterate my theme that the book will help make better salesmen of everyone on the company's sales force. Announcing that the book is available at all bookstores makes it easy for the purchaser to buy the book immediately. If the bookstore doesn't carry the book, you can be sure that after receiving a few requests they'll order some copies from me. For my part, not only will I sell them *Psycho-Cybernetics* but my entire line of books as well. It works beautifully in theory and in practice.

I was very successful sending this letter to real estate companies. The multiple sales were great. As a direct re-sult, it led to my teaching classes in *Psycho-Cybernetics* for many real estate organizations. Dr. Maxwell Maltz, the author, was in great demand as a speaker and taught many seminars.

I haven't spoken much about the use of mail order techniques to sell a service, but here is a perfect example of how productive it can be. I've had the same printer for 25 years. I've turned over all of my production to him, and I'm free to concentrate on the creative end of the business. During this period of time, I've personally given him many millions of dollars worth of printing, and, through recommendation to other publishers, millions more. It's become axiomatic among book publishers in California that if you want to print a book or catalog, "Call Hal Leighton."

The interesting part of all this, for purposes of our discussion, is that this tremendous volume of business was initiated with a simple, yet masterful, piece of direct mail. The pulling power of the mailing piece he has successfully used over a 25-year period, with slight variations, confirms my theory that direct mail literature doesn't have to be elaborate to be very effective.

I'm reproducing the mailing piece on page 83. It consists of a 5½" x 8½", coated, book stock card, exactly like the cover of this book. On one side he uses a picture of one of his clients and himself and on the other, a brief description of the person shown with him in the picture and his sales message. Let's analyze his mailing piece. We can learn a lot from it.

Primarily, Hal Leighton is looking for leads from his mailing piece. He's told me that over the years he has rarely lost a sale. Let's look at his sales message. His headline—the hook—is SAVE MONEY ON PRINTING. You can't argue with that. Who in the world doesn't want to save money? He immediately gives you a testimonial from one of his clients by showing his customer posing with him for a picture. Furthermore, he identifies him. That's proof! He isn't even concerned that another printer will go after his account. That's confidence!

Look how many times in this brief copy he makes the point you can save money by printing with him. That's his theme. Notice how effectively he uses a P.S. to hammer home his message again. Cleverly, he suggests in bold type—SAVE FOR FUTURE REFERENCE. Parenthetically, that's exactly what I did when I received this card in the mail. I called him for a price when I was ready to run my next book, and I remember parroting his theme when I spoke to him. Without identifying myself, my first words to Hal Leighton were, "I received your mailing piece and want to save money on printing." He caught the mood of my friendly referral to his pet theme and told me I had come to the right person. That was the beginning of a beautiful relationship and millions of dollars worth of business.

April 22, 1991

Mr. Melvin Powers
Wilshire Book Company
12015 Sherman Road
North Hollywood, CA 91605

Dear Mr. Powers:

Mail Order Millionaire has changed my life! It is without doubt one of the most helpful mail order programs I have ever purchased--and I've purchased most of those available.

Several years ago, I answered an advertisement for your course. Using your innovative, proven techniques and formulas, I sold over 1,000,000 Hotel Express discount travel club memberships through the mail in only two years. My sales last month alone were $200,000.

Your mail order instruction has helped me to succeed beyond my wildest dreams. I am now CEO of my own multi-million dollar a year mail order company. I have earned enough money to purchase a 5,000 square foot, ocean view home with an indoor swimming pool and five automobiles--and I've taken some fabulous vacations around the world.

I am living proof that the "good life" you suggest as a possibility for mail order entrepreneurs is more than just advertising hype--it's an attainable goal. Thank you for sharing the knowledge that made it all possible for me.

Sincerely,

Keith C. Monen
CEO Hotel Express

P.S. Mr. Powers, you have done for the mail order industry what John Wayne did for westerns. You are truly my star in Hollywood!

. . . This letter can change your life. It's from Melvin Powers—a multi-millionaire international marketing expert, mail order consultant, and publisher of such bestsellers as Think & Grow Rich *by Napoleon Hill and* Psycho-Cybernetics *by Maxwell Maltz, M.D.*

You Can Start with Less than $100 And Make Lots of Money With Classified Ads! I Did, and I'll Teach You How

Sound incredible? Maybe, but over 40 years ago, I started my mail order career with one small classified ad. Since then, I've run thousands upon thousands of ads, month after month, year after year and have made millions doing it. I've learned a lot about what works and what doesn't. I found that, as with most things, making money with classified ads is easy when you know how.

There are many "get rich quick" plans. Some are based on esoteric theories that simply don't work. Others are winners that have proven themselves over the years. These opportunities have stood the test of time. My techniques for making money with classified ads is one of them.

I can't promise that you will get rich overnight (although some people do) and I can't promise you the moon (although I have helped many people to reach it). What I can promise is that if you are willing to put some time and effort into doing as I suggest, you positively will become successful. How do I know for sure? Because my approach to success works. I've proven it again and again in the real world, first with myself and then with other people, just like you!

It's Your Turn for Success

Now you can assure your success by learning the winning mind-set and techniques I developed by trial-and-error during my four decades of experience as a successful mail order entrepreneur, consultant, book publisher, author, and instructor. Not only have I made me a fortune, but my proven techniques have made big money for many of the thousands of students who have taken the mail order courses I taught at colleges and universities in the Los Angeles area for over ten years. I have helped students to become successful entrepreneurs—in fact, to literally change their lives dramatically—so many times that I am absolutely positive it can be repeated by anyone who is willing to listen and follow through.

Make a Beautiful, New Life for Yourself

If you take my solid, proven techniques that have performed reliably day after day, year after year and put them to use, you will succeed in making a life in which you will no longer be dependent on a boss or a job or a salary that someone else dictates. You won't be at the mercy of inflation, recession, or other monetary fluctuations. When, where, and how you work will be entirely up to you. And so will how much money you make. You'll have control of your life and feel good every day about who you are and what you are doing. It's a gift like no other.

Can You Really Make Money Running Classified Ads?

You certainly can! Did you ever stop to wonder who's running the hundreds of classified ads you see in magazines and tabloids? It's people like you and me. Some are just starting out, others have been advertising for years. What does it mean when the same ads run again and again? It means they are making money. Behind those few classified lines inviting you to send for a catalog or further information could easily stand a business doing millions of dollars a year in sales. I ought to know. Some of my ads have been running every month for 25 years! If you are willing to learn what I have to teach, you can be saying the same thing 25 years from now.

The Melvin Powers Formula for Success

My new book, *Making Money with Classified Ads,* is a 240-page, 8½"x11½", fully illustrated guide to entrepreneurial success, jam-packed with details that systematically walk you through the steps necessary to make money—the same steps that are still making money for me.

It takes a practical, nuts-and-bolts approach to starting and running a mail order business based on classified ads. The book is easy to follow and fun to read. Yes, I said fun. (You'll see what I mean soon after you sit down in your easy chair, open the cover, and begin to read.) All you have to do is follow the step-by-step instructions and you may very well take what turns out to be the adventure of a lifetime.

Get Years' Worth of On-the-Job Experience
In Only a Few Weeks

Making Money with Classified Ads includes something you probably have never seen before. Copies of ads, circulars, sales letters, and other literature from dozens of actual advertising campaigns—some that proved their pulling power by bringing in thousands of dollars—and analyses of how and why they pulled and how you can make similar pieces work for you. I literally lay open the internal workings of my business and my mind, sharing my own mental processes as I choose a new product, plan the advertising campaign, prepare the literature, execute the plan, evaluate it, keep track of it, expand it, pull back when appropriate—and love every minute of it all.

You'll see the mechanics of how everything comes together from inception to the natural wind-down of successful and not-so-successful campaigns. I share some of my biggest winners and some losers. As a result of experiencing numerous mail order campaigns almost as if you had conducted them yourself, you'll gradually develop a sixth sense—an intuitive feeling about what works and what doesn't that usually takes years of trial-and-error to develop.

You'll learn how to find and use the same resources that I and other professionals use. You'll be reading the same magazines I read. Evaluating the same products I evaluate. Analyzing the competitions' ads as I analyze them. And finding great new ideas where I find them. You'll develop a business logic that will help you make the right decisions, and instincts that will make you, and save you, a lot of money.

Here's what else you'll get when you send for *Making Money with Classified Ads*:

▸ Names, addresses, and telephone numbers of dozens of my own business contacts and resources—my printer, graphic artist, copywriters, mailing list broker, individuals at various publications who place my ads, and more.

▸ Names and addresses of resource directories and trade publications that pros rely upon. Information on how to get free copies, and how to use them to find the source of proven products.

▸ Actual classified ads that are being used successfully to build a large multi-level business and instructions on how to use them to build an organization of your own.

And that's not all. You'll learn

▸ Where professionals find products and how they choose winners. How they know what's hot and what's not.

▸ Where to find invaluable free resources that contain thousands of products and how to choose those that are most likely to work.

▸ How to prepare advertising materials that pull orders and how to stay on top of the competitions' winners and losers.

▸ How to get started with a minimum expenditure of money.

▸ How, when, and where to advertise to have the best chance of success—and where and when not to advertise.

▸ How to get people to answer your ads. And how to get them to buy and continue to buy your products.

▸ How to ensure your success with full-page ads before you run them.

▸ How to pyramid your profits into an income that will mean financial security.

▸ How to think like an entrepreneur.

My Personal Guarantee to You

I guarantee that if you read *Making Money with Classified Ads* and you actively participate in the process it guides you through, your creativity will be sparked, your intuition developed, your business sense sharpened, and your feelings about yourself and your life transformed. You will establish yourself as a mail order entrepreneur with unlimited potential. If you listen and act upon what you learn, you can become rich both financially and personally. I know this for a fact.

There aren't any secrets. There are simply logical steps to take. But you must take them. My formula for success will only work for you if you work at it. The question is, are you sufficiently motivated to do what it takes? Is your determination to succeed strong enough to see you through the process that will ultimately get you what you want? If so, it's only a matter of time until you experience the joy of shaking out checks, cash, and money orders from stacks of mail sent to you every day.

Judge My Book at Absolutely No Risk

Does it sound too good to be true? You can be the sole judge of that on a 30-day, money-back guarantee basis. See for yourself that *Making Money with Classified Ads* is all I say it is. You have nothing to lose.

And in case you would like to "attend one of my seminars" in the privacy and comfort of your own home or automobile, I'll extend the same guarantee to my audio tape course, *Mail Order Millionaire,* which includes 11 cassettes, the bonus tape *50 Proven Mail Order Products*, plus the 352-page book *How to Get Rich in Mail Order.*

It will seem as if you are sitting in my classroom and I'm talking directly to you. You'll hear loads of invaluable, in-depth nitty-gritty information about how to make it in mail order. And you'll hear for yourself the upbeat, encouraging messages that have helped many students to overcome the inertia that often keeps capable people from realizing their potential.

Information-Packed Chapter Titles

l. Getting Started with Classified Ads 2. Everyone Loves to Read Classified Ads 3. How to Find a Money-Making Product 4. Write Classified Ads That Make Money 5. What I've Learned from Running Thousands of Classified Ads Month After Month, Year After Year 6. Classified Ads Can Help You Make Big Money in Multi-Level Programs 7. Two-Step Classified Ads Made Me a Multi-Millionaire and They Can Do the Same for You 8. One-Inch Display Ads Can Work Wonders for You 9. Full-Page Display Ads Can Make You a Fortune Overnight 10. Although I Live in California I Buy My Grapefruit from Florida! 11. Nuts and Bolts of Mail Order Success 12. What if You Can't Get Your Mail Order Business Running Successfully? What's Wrong? How to Correct It 13. The Melvin Powers Strategy for Mail Order Success

----

30-DAY MONEY-BACK GUARANTEE

Date_____

YES, I want to become successful making money with classified ads.

( ) Please send me *Making Money with Classified Ads* for $22.00 postpaid (CA res. $23.65).
( ) Please send me *Mail Order Millionaire* for $82.00 postpaid (CA res. $88.19).
( ) **Please send me both *Making Money with Classified Ads* and the *Mail Order Millionaire* audio tape course for $102.00 postpaid (CA res. $109.84).**

Enclosed is my ( ) cashier's check ( ) money order ( ) personal check, **payable to Melvin Powers** for $_____
Or charge to my ( ) Visa ( ) MasterCard. Call (818) 765-8579 to charge by phone.

Number_____ Expiration date_____

Name_____ Phone_____
                          (PLEASE PRINT)

Address_____
                          (PLEASE PRINT STREET ADDRESS FOR PRODUCT DELIVERY)

City_____ State_____ Zip_____

Mail to: Melvin Powers, 12015 Sherman Road, North Hollywood, California 91605

Discover how the Internet can put you on the fast track to making money . . .

101 BUSINESSES YOU CAN START ON THE INTERNET

Daniel S. Janal, Internet Consultant

<u>Contains the Fastest, Easiest, Most Effective Ways To Make Money on the Internet</u>

The Internet is *the* new frontier. It's gaining momentum at a phenomenal rate, creating a gateway to riches for those who capitalize on it. You can get in on the ground floor of this dynamic, new industry by using it to establish a new business or to advertise products and services for an existing one. The cost is nominal, or free when you place classified ads on free Web sites.

You'll receive e-mail inquiries and orders from all over the country and all over the world. With the incredible, day-after-day exposure the Internet provides, your potential business growth is unlimited.

Internet users are growing at an explosive rate every month. Many will take advantage of its entrepreneurial potential. You can have a decisive competitive edge in getting your message out there if you know how to do it right the first time. Where can you learn what to do? In *101 Businesses You Can Start on the Internet*.

UNLEASH THE PROFIT-MAKING POWER OF THE INTERNET

101 Businesses You Can Start on the Internet shows you how to take advantage of the Internet's incredible profit-making power. Whether you are considering supplementing your current income or creating an entirely new, full-time business, this practical, easy to-understand book contains all the information you will need to start generating revenue online. It tells you how to combine your interests, knowledge, and skills with online technology.

You'll get sound, practical, down-to-earth advice from more than 50 online entrepreneurs who are doing business—and making money—every day on the Internet. All have either started new businesses or moved their current location from a main street to the Internet. You'll learn why they decided to set up shop, what their start-up costs were, and what their typical business day is like.

YOUR BLUEPRINT FOR SUCCESS

Reading *101 Businesses You Can Start on the Internet* is like taking a seminar from 50 successful Internet entrepreneurs. They share their firsthand experience and know-how just as if you were sitting in front of them in a classroom. You find out exactly what works and what doesn't. Their experience becomes your experience. Their insights become your insights. Their enthusiasm will excite you, their success inspire you. They will stimulate your creative thinking. You'll become excited by your newfound knowledge and potential for success.

What better guide to your becoming successful could you possibly have than a blueprint that is working for others? Take the attitude that if they are doing it, you can too. Get started today and open up a whole new world of possibilities. Send for *101 Businesses You Can Start on the Internet*.

504 pages . . . $28.00 Postpaid (CA res. $30.06)

Send orders to: Melvin Powers, 12015 Sherman Road, No. Hollywood, CA 91605
For credit card orders: Telephone (818) 765-8579. Fax (818) 765-2922. E-mail: mpowers@mpowers.com

Discover how the Internet can put you on the fast track to making money . . .

ONLINE MARKETING HANDBOOK
Daniel S. Janal, Internet Consultant

How to Sell, Advertise, Publicize, and Promote
Your Products and Services
On the Internet and Commercial Online Systems

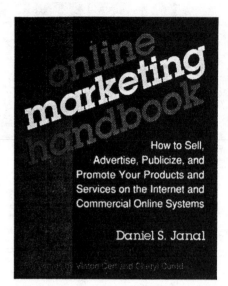

With a market of 30-million highly educated and affluent potential consumers, the Information Superhighway is an exciting promotional vehicle for anyone interested in mail order. Individuals running home-base businesses as well as marketers around the world are using the Internet and commercial online services to access a largely untapped audience while finding it less expensive and more effective, in many cases, than conventional media.

Online Marketing Handbook guides you through the essentials of online marketing from vital statistics on various online services to promotional devices that guarantee the best response rates. By learning how to take advantage of online technology, you can reduce costs, respond quickly to market conditions, and provide the convenience that your customers want.

Daniel S. Janal is a highly regarded marketer, entrepreneur, and professor. He instructs readers on how to use the Internet and commercial online services to create a successful marketing program. Reading his book is like taking his college course. You'll find out everything you need to know without having to be a computer wizard.

WHAT *ONLINE MARKETING HANDBOOK* DOES FOR YOU

•Brings you up to speed on the Information Superhighway, with complete information on how to successfully create and launch your online marketing program

•Investigates opportunities to enhance your marketing program and build customers' loyalty with services available only online, such as electronic stores, support centers, and electronic mail

•Provides case studies on how companies of all sizes promote their products and services online, giving real-world examples of what works best

•Explores the future of online advertising, how it will change and grow, and what it means to you as a viable way to promote your mail order or service business.

CLASSIFIED ADS CAN START THOSE ORDERS ROLLING IN

One of the most fascinating and informative chapters is "Selling Products and Services with Online Classified Ads." It tells you how to write effective classified ads and how to place them free or at minimal advertising rates. Online classified advertisements can help you announce new products, services, and sales to local, national, or international audiences. They are also great for testing headlines, body copy, call to action, and price. Classified ads are an easy, inexpensive way to start your Internet program. Order *Online Marketing Handbook* today and get started right away. You won't believe how excited you'll get when you open your electronic mailbox and it's filled with orders!

370 pages . . . $28.00 postpaid (CA res. $30.06)

Send orders to: Melvin Powers, 12015 Sherman Road, No. Hollywood, CA 91605
For credit card orders: Telephone (818) 765-8579. Fax (818) 765-2922. E-mail: mpowers@mpowers.com

THE TRAVEL BUSINESS IS BOOMING ... $400 BILLION A YEAR! HERE'S HOW TO GET YOUR SHARE OF IT

It's the Hottest New Money-Making Business Opportunity in Years!

Dear Friend:

Now, for the first time ever, you can become a travel agent and work from your own home or office. Because of deregulation and other exciting changes that have taken place in the travel industry in the last few years, you can enjoy all the advantages of being a fully accredited travel agent ... no matter what the size of your business or amount of your bookings ... even if you only operate in your spare time ... all with virtually no overhead or expenses. You can

- Earn Big Commissions
- Travel Free or at Huge Discounts
- Be Given VIP Treatment
- Get Tax Write-offs and Deductions

YOU CAN GET INTO THE TRAVEL BUSINESS OVERNIGHT

You'll need to work with a travel agency that is ARC (Airlines Reporting Corporation) appointed to provide you with airline tickets and other services,. And you'll need to learn what to do. That's where Keith Monen and Leisuretyme Travel—a division of San Diego Travel—can help.

You can become accredited immediately by becoming an independent outside travel agent for San Diego Travel through their Leisuretyme Travel division and you can start making commissions at once. Keith Monen, president of San Diego Travel, and founder of Hotel Express and Leisuretyme Travel—both highly successful discount travel clubs—has created a new, exciting, business opportunity program teaching people how to become travel agents on a part- or full-time basis.

NO EXPERIENCE NECESSARY

You don't need any prior experience in the travel business. Keith and his staff at San Diego Travel will teach you everything you need to know and help you every step of the way. Their experienced travel industry personnel will help you with any questions you may have on your bookings.

San Diego Travel has been in business since 1963 and is a fully bonded and accredited member in good standing of ARC (The Airlines Reporting Corporation) and IATA (International Air Transport Association). San Diego Travel is entrusted with the official ticketing plates from every major airline in the world. It is a member of ASTA (The American Society of Travel Agents), CLIA (The Cruise Line International Association), and IATAN (The International Airlines Travel Agent Network).

THE BEST BUSINESS OPPORTUNITY I'VE EVER OFFERED

As Keith's marketing consultant, I have participated in the phenomenal growth of his travel clubs and have seen firsthand the success of people who have become involved. Several years ago, I recognized the outstanding value of Keith's travel club business opportunity programs, and I made them available to entrepreneurs who were serious about becoming their own boss and building a secure future. Almost immediately, these programs became among the most successful I had ever offered.

Now Keith has really outdone himself! Never have I been as excited about any business opportunity as I am about his newest program that teaches people how to become independent outside travel agents. The program offers more profits, more fun, and more benefits—faster and easier than any other I've seen in my many years of helping people get into their own businesses. I'm putting my reputation behind this program because I know it works. If you have the motivation for success and want to have a great time achieving it, here's your golden opportunity.

KEITH'S FIRST 90 DAYS IN THE TRAVEL BUSINESS BROUGHT IN OVER $1,000,000!

In 1986 at age 28, with no prior experience in the travel business, Keith placed an ad that cost $126 in the Sunday travel section of the Houston Chronicle newspaper selling a $138 travel package. He received 200 orders in only 7 days—over $26,000 in sales. He took his profits from these sales and invested them in ads in the Sunday travel sections of the 19 largest newspapers in the country and brought in over $125,000 a week. His total sales in three months came to $1,046,000!

HE'S BEEN TAKING IN OVER $1,000,000 EVERY YEAR EVER SINCE AND WANTS TO SHARE HIS SECRETS OF SUCCESS

The special techniques Keith has perfected to sell travel are responsible for making him a lot of money. Keith's travel agent start-up kit will teach you the special techniques that have made him a big winner in the travel business. It contains everything you need to start earning commissions and taking full advantage of the VIP treatment, worldwide discounted trips, and the many other money-saving perks available to travel agents and their families.

LET THE MIDAS TOUCH RUB OFF ON YOU

Keith has dreamed the same dreams you have and wants to help you realize yours, as he has realized his. His years of successful business expertise is yours for the asking. And so is mine. Keith and I have both made millions of dollars in business, and we're ready to share our entrepreneurial know-how with you. You'll have two millionaire teachers at your side, showing you exactly what to do to be successful.

You'll be given a tested, proven blueprint to help you build your business from the first day. We want everyone who becomes affiliated with Leisuretyme Travel's new travel agent program to make more money, save more money, and have more fun than they ever have before.

THE EASIEST WAY EVER TO BOOK TRAVEL SERVICES

As an independent outside travel agent for Leisuretyme Travel, you'll be able to market all travel services, including airline tickets, cruises, car rentals, vacation packages and more. You simply call Leisuretyme for searches and reservations or fill out their travel request form and fax it to their office. They'll send your travel documents direct to you or to your customers by overnight courier or certified mail anywhere in the United States. You'll be paid 50% on all commissions Leisuretyme receives on your sales after your customers travel. It's that easy. San Diego Travel does all the work for you.

When you become a Leisuretyme travel agent you will be provided with a travel agent photo ID card containing their agency's in-house ARC/IATAN number, which will provide you with immediate access to all the services you will need to book travel and entitle you to all the fantastic perks available to travel agents. You will be entitled to attend hundreds of helpful travel training seminars put on by travel suppliers throughout the country. You'll also be able to receive trade magazines that will expand your knowledge and introduce you to exciting new horizons in travel.

MAKE EXTRA MONEY
THE EASY WAY

As an independent outside travel agent, you will be providing free service and advice which can save your friends, neighbors, relatives, club members, co-workers, and others a lot of time and the frustration of making their own travel arrangements ... and you'll often save them money at the same time. On the average, each of these people will spend between $1,000 and $1,500 per year on holidays, honeymoons, family visits, business meetings, and various other travel. In addition, many small businesses and corporations in your area will have travel needs requiring them to spend thousands of dollars.

As a Leisuretyme independent outside travel agent, you will learn about many exciting, new vacation packages, special fares and rates, and much more that will be of great interest to these people. You don't have to sell travel. It sells itself.

EARN $1,000 OR MORE
ON ONE GROUP BOOKING!

Groups are easy to sell and are very profitable. Leisuretyme training materials teach you everything you need to know to start booking group travel. You'll learn how to enlist sales people for free who will make contacts for you and promote and sell your group bookings. They receive a free vacation for two and you make the commissions. Often more business comes in as a result of group bookings, as travelers ask you to book their future personal travel and refer others to you. This is one of the ways you can build a substantial business.

MAKE THOUSANDS OF DOLLARS IN REPEAT BUSINESS

Corporate travel can make you thousands of dollars a year in commissions and provide dependable repeat business year after year. Most corporations have employees who travel frequently. Their average airline tickets cost between $500 and $1,200 because their travel arrangements are usually made at the last minute. The Leisuretyme independent outside travel agent program teaches you the easiest and most effective ways to get corporate business.

TAKE "FAM" TRIPS AT INCREDIBLY LOW PRICES
AND
BE TREATED LIKE A KING OR QUEEN

Many travel agents first become involved in the travel industry because of their desire to travel at greatly reduced prices. One of the perks that excites them most is what is known in the industry as fam (familiarization) trips. These are trips offered by cruise lines, airlines, tour companies, hotels, and resorts to acquaint you with them so that you will recommend them to your travel customers. Determined to make your experience with them an exceptional one, they'll shower you with VIP treatment.

Fam trips often include big discounts on transportation, meals, tours, and accommodations. As a Leisuretyme independent outside travel agent, you'll have hundreds of fabulous fams available to you, once you qualify. Fam trips are part of your ongoing professional education. What could be better!

ENJOY TREMENDOUS TRAVEL DISCOUNTS

Here are some of the big savings that you as a Leisuretyme independent outside travel agent will be entitled to on transportation, lodging, and entertainment.

Hotels & Motels—Up to 50% off, often with free upgrades to suites.
Cruises—Up to 50% to 75% off. Free cruise with most group bookings.
Airlines—Up to 75% off domestic and international flights—once you qualify.
Car Rentals—Usually 10% with unlimited mileage. Often upgraded free.
Condominiums—50% off and more at locations worldwide.
Theme Parks—Often free or discounted admission for you and your guests.

GET YOUR PASSPORT TO PROSPERITY

**Order your Leisuretyme Independent Outside Travel Agent Start-Up Kit today.
Here's what you'll get:**
• Instant certification as an independent outside travel agent
• A personal, laminated travel agent photo ID card with Leisuretyme Travel's ARC/IATAN number
• A certificate suitable for framing, identifying you as a certified travel agent
• 500 full-color travel agent business cards ready for your imprint
• 200 full-color letterheads ready for your imprint
• Camera-ready ads, full-color brochures and travel request forms
• An official travel agent manual
• A VHS training tape on booking and selling travel
• A Leisuretyme newsletter
• 100 Las Vegas, Hawaii, and Orlando $1,000 gift checks
• Three fun books valid in Las Vegas, Hawaii, or Orlando for $1,000 in free cash, chips, tokens, show passes,
  meals, recreation, entertainment, and discounts (cash and gambling benefits in Las Vegas only)
• A certificate valid for 3 days and 2 nights free accommodations in Las Vegas
• A certificate valid for 3 days and 2 nights free accommodations in Orlando

----

30-DAY MONEY-BACK GUARANTEE

Date_____

YES, I want to become a Leisuretyme independent outside travel agent.

( ) Please sign me up for $195 (CA res. $211.09) and send my Leisuretyme Travel Agent Start-Up Kit right away.
( ) Please also sign up my spouse or other person living at my address for the special discounted price of $100 (CA res. $108.25).
    (Includes a personal, laminated travel agent photo ID card and 500 full-color business cards ready for imprinting.)

Enclosed is my ( ) cashier's check ( ) money order ( ) personal check, **payable to Melvin Powers** for $_____
Charge to my ( ) Visa ( ) MasterCard. Call (818) 765-8529 to charge by phone.

Number_____Expiration date_____

Name_____Phone_____
                    (PLEASE PRINT)   (AREA CODE)   (NUMBER)

Address_____
                    (PLEASE PRINT STREET ADDRESS FOR PRODUCT DELIVERY)

City_____State_____Zip_____

Mail to: Melvin Powers, 12015 Sherman Road, North Hollywood, California 91605

Great Minds Prove
THERE IS MAGIC IN THINKING BIG!

*Success Is Determined Not So Much
By the Size of One's Brain
As it Is by the Size of One's Thinking*

It has been proven that anyone can increase the size of their bank accounts, happiness account, and general satisfaction account by increasing the size of their thinking. Think big and you will live big . . . in happiness. . . in accomplishment . . . in income . . . in friends . . . in respect.

Stay Off
Second Class Street

**IF YOU
THINK BIG,
YOU WILL
SUCCEED BIG**

If thinking big accomplishes so much, why doesn't everyone think that way? Because all of us, more than we recognize, are products of the thinking around us. And much of this thinking is little . . . so little in fact that it tugs at us relentlessly, pulling us down Second Class Street. Listen to successful people who have made it to First Class Avenue, rather than to the little thinkers who are stuck on Second Class Street.

Get Onto
First Class Avenue

You can fulfill all your desires and get from life all the good things you deserve by taking the simple steps presented in *The Magic of Thinking Big* audio tape. These steps are not untested theories. They are not one man's guesses and opinions. They are proven approaches to life's situations, and they are universally applicable steps that work, and work like magic. You'll get rid of paralyzing doubts, increase self-confidence, and present a winning image that will help you build the successful life you want. You'll learn how to sell yourself on yourself, how to look important, act important, think of your work as important, and visualize yourself accomplishing the undone and important tasks of the future.

The Average Man Has More Than
Enough Ability to Make it Big

Dr. Schwartz believes that brain power, the intelligence quotient, can create more problems than it can solve. He also believes—absolutely and provably—that man can vaccinate himself against failure by invalidating excuses based on health, age, opportunity, and natural ability.

With all his excuses for failure removed, man has no alternative but to succeed. If you think that reaching this pinnacle of potential successes sounds as if it is more the result of magic than of thinking big, you are in for a life-changing surprise.

YOU CAN FIND ANYONE, ANYWHERE
AND MAKE $1,000 PER DAY

In a surprisingly short time, you can step into one of the most fascinating, rewarding, and money-producing service businesses in the world—locating missing persons. Up until a short time ago, this powerful training material could only be purchased through a national association of private investigators. Now, for the very first time, you can obtain this knowledge that reveals hidden secret sources and techniques you can use to track down anyone, anywhere. Although many in the business have objected to this confidential collection of top investigative secrets being offered to the public, this material is now available in its newly released fifth edition, which includes free searches on the Internet you can use to find people.

THOUSANDS OF DOLLARS IN FINDER'S FEES—JUST WAITING FOR YOU!

Some types of missing persons cases bring the tracer so much money in finder's fees that a select group of professionals in the business have tried to keep the information secret. This book breaks that code of silence! You can choose to specialize in any one of a number of types of missing persons cases and reap the rewards, just as these people are doing:

• One unclaimed property case in California brought a tracer a finder's fee of $10,000 for a few days work.
• Another tracer, in Florida, makes $100,000 per year working part time locating missing heirs for estates and probate courts.
• A New England tracer locates lost loved ones and has the thrill of bringing people together again.
• Another tracer, in Texas, locates people who have skipped out on their car loans, and he gets tons of new assignments every week.
• Still another in Texas locates missing witnesses for attorneys in litigation cases. He has become so busy that he can't accept all the cases offered to him.
• Another tracer, in Virginia, tracks down people on the Internet.
• Recently, a husband-and-wife team placed national TV ads offering to locate missing persons for $95. These traces consist of a few computer searches that cost almost nothing and take only a few minutes!

HUGE WINDFALL PROFITS IN AN EXCITING, REWARDING BUSINESS

Imagine yourself working for an attorney and locating an important witness for a major legal case. Or what if you could locate someone to tell them that $100,000 or more is waiting for them in a missing heir's case? If you like excitement, there is lots of opportunity for that, too. Imagine the thrill of helping to bring in a fugitive from justice or locating a vehicle for a bank or loan company for repossession. These types of cases pay really big money.

Pat Rutherford of World Wide Tracers, based in California and Texas, read *How to Find Anyone, Anywhere* and chose to specialize in locating lost loved ones. Listen to his heartfelt words: "This is the most fun business in the world. I thank God for giving me the opportunity to play Santa Claus every day bringing loved ones together."

HOW TO FIND ANYONE, ANYWHERE
HAS BROUGHT FINANCIAL FREEDOM TO PEOPLE JUST LIKE YOU

We live in an extremely mobile society. The average person moves every three years. It's a sad fact that we have become a nation of strangers, but this trend has driven up the demand and need for all types of missing persons to be found. Businesses lose track of their clients and loved ones lose track of family members. Finding missing persons has become a gold mine business.

USED BY PROFESSIONALS . . . AND ACCLAIMED AS THE WORLD'S BEST BOOK ON HOW TO LOCATE MISSING PERSONS

How To Find Anyone, Anywhere features innovative information drawn by the author from his over 20 years of successfully locating missing persons. It also draws on the combined wisdom of thousands of private investigators from around the world and gives their best techniques and short cuts. You'll find all kinds of methods of access, address updates, and hundreds of professional techniques you can use. This book is really three books in one. It's a directory of sources you can use to track down missing persons. It's a technique manual on how to use little-known techniques to find people quickly, easily, and inexpensively. And it's a business manual that gives you extremely hard-to-find information on various areas of specialization and marketing techniques to obtain assignments.

THIS CONFIDENTIAL COLLECTION OF TOP INVESTIGATIVE SECRETS INCLUDES . . .

1. Hundreds of Little-known Professional Techniques That Usually Take Years to Develop.
2. Thousands of Sources of Information You Can Tap into.
3. Techniques to Find People Quicker, Easier, and with less Expense than Ever Before.
4. Great Tricks of the Trade from Top Investigators from Around the World.
5. Free Computer Searches You Can Tap into to Find People Fast.
6. Fee-based Computer Searches You Can Use and How to Gain Access to Them.
7. How to Find and Use People-Sources in Your Trace.
8. Types of Missing Persons Cases You Can Specialize in and How to Get Business.
9. Valuable Information on How to Be Successful in the Tracing Business.
10. New Types of Tracing Including How to Find People on the Internet.
11. Tons of Internet Sites and Resource Aids.
12. Places on the Net to Go to Get the Latest Updates to the Information in this Book.
13. Free People Searches on the Internet
14. Free Web Updates for *How to Find Anyone, Anywhere.*
15. A Free National List of Licensing Requirements to Become a Private Investigator: This valuable list gives you the name and address of the licensing authority for each of the 50 states and tells you which states require no licensing. Some states require you to obtain a private investigative license in order to locate certain types of missing persons. In that case, you can work, part or full time, for a licensed investigator, learn more about the business, and share the fees until you become licensed.

YES, I WANT TO LEARN THE SECRETS OF FINDING MISSING PEOPLE!

( ) Please send me *How to Find Anyone, Anywhere,* specially priced for Melvin Powers's entrepreneurs at $20.00 (CA res. 21.65) plus $2.00 S/H on a 30-day money-back guarantee. (Regularly sells for $35.00.)

Enclosed is my ( ) cashier's check ( ) money order ( ) personal check for $_____.
Or charge my ( ) Visa ( ) MasterCard. Call (818) 765-8579 to charge by phone.

Number_____ Exp. Date_____

Name_____ Phone_____
                         (PLEASE PRINT)

Address_____
               (PRINT STREET ADDRESS FOR PRODUCT DELIVERY)

City_____ State_____ Zip_____

Send to: Melvin Powers, 12015 Sherman Road, No. Hollywood, California 91605

How to Make a Fortune on the Information Superhighway

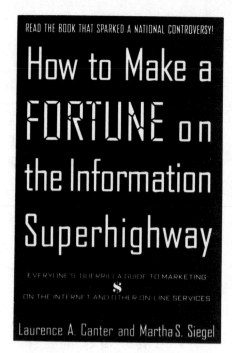

EVERYONE'S GUIDE
TO MARKETING ON THE INTERNET
AND OTHER ON-LINE SERVICES

In April 1994, two immigration attorneys in Scottsdale, Arizona did something no one had ever done before. They advertised their legal services to approximately 6,000 of the 9,000 discussion groups called "Newsgroups" on the Global Internet, reaching tens of millions of people. Their innovative, money-making venture netted over 25,000 customer inquiries for one night's work. The two Internet pioneers, by spending only $20.00—the price of this book—brought in $100,000 worth of business.

In *How to Make a Fortune on the Information Highway*, the authors tell you how to do what they did so successfully—making a fortune advertising on the Internet. You'll get the whole story, explained in clear, non-technical language. You'll discover that with some fairly simple ideas, a PC, a modem, and a telephone line, you can "Cybersell" your way to wealth. You can also advertise on the Internet without owning any equipment. There are companies that will provide this service for you.

The Internet puts small businesses on an equal footing with the largest corporations by making it possible to reach 30 million people with the touch of a button. Here is everything you need to know about using the Internet as the ultimate marketing tool for almost any product or service.

How to Make a Fortune on the Information Superhighway shows you how you can be a pioneer in an exciting future filled with marketing and sales opportunities.

CONTENTS
1. Getting Your Bearings on the Information Superhighway
2. A Busy Night in Cyberspace: The Green Card Incident
3. Selling to 30-Million People Who Call the Net Home
4. Products That Sell on the Net
5. Highway Red Light Districts
6. Free Advertising to Millions of People on the Usenet
7. E-mail and Electronic Mailing Lists: Paperless & Postage Free
8. Chat: Talk Your Way to Riches
9. The World Wide Web: Multimedia Advertising at Virtually No Cost
10. Gopher the Gold
11. FTP: Selling to the Whole Information Highway
12. Your PC—The Biggest Money-Maker You'll Ever Know
13. How to Get Yourself on the Net
14. Do It Yourself or Find a Geek
15. Crimes in Cyberspace. Why the Net Needs You
16. What It Means to Be a Pioneer

240 Pages . . . $15.00 postpaid (CA residents $16.07)
Send your order to: Melvin Powers, 12015 Sherman Road, No, Hollywood, CA 91605

Mail Order Bicycle Firm With $1,000 Start-Up Grossed $6.5-Million In Last Fiscal Year

By Jerrold Ballinger

NEW MIDDLETOWN, OH—An advertising man who enjoyed bicycling decided, in 1974, to invest $1,000 in an attempt to convert his hobby into a profitable mail order business. The resulting company, now Nashbar Associates, Inc., grossed $6.3-million in sales in the fiscal year ended Oct. 31, 1983, and the firm anticipates sales to jump to $7.5-million for 1983-84.

The company has grown completely through mail order stimulated by direct response advertising and the catalog that was developed and expanded in the evolution of the venture.

Catalog costs for 1983-84 have been projected at $300,000. The figure will cover five mailings during the year, according to Patricia DiVito, administrative assistant at Nashbar. An additional $120,000 has been budgeted for the company's space advertising. An inventory of $800,000 is planned, she stated.

The firm's first advertisement was 2½" x 5" in the August 1974 issue of *Bicycling*. It was hand-drawn, with drawings of the 12 accessories the new company—Bike Warehouse—was offering, said DiVito. The company operated at a loss that first year, she said.

Bike Warehouse operated out of the basement of Arni Nashbar's advertising agency in Boardman, OH, a suburb of Youngstown. Offered were such bike accessories as lights, water bottles, locks and cables, tools and T-shirts with the names of major brands of bicycles. The selling point was low prices, DiVito said.

The ad brought in 166 orders and the money was immediately reinvested in the company. Bike Warehouse had a loss of $2,200 at the end of its first year, "but it was on its way," DiVito said.

A six-page catalog using brown ink on white paper was included with the merchandise sold starting in November 1974. It had on its cover a picture of Arni, his wife Cheryl, who took care of the books, their five-year-old son Eric and the artist, Tim Anderson.

"The idea was to show that this was a family company," DiVito explained. While the pictures no longer are on the cover, all catalogs have pictures of the staff inside to continue the tradition, she said.

THE BUDGET JUMPED

In 1975, the budget jumped to $34,000 and revenue at the end of the year was $269,000 from 17,179 sales. "This time, there was a profit of $20,000," she said.

"It was all uphill from there," DiVito declared.

With an advertising budget of $22,000 in advertising and an inventory of $98,000, an estimated 22,982 sales brought in $421,000 in revenue in 1976.

Inserts were added to the catalog, expanding it to 36 pages by the fall of 1976, when three were still put out—all still inserted in response to sales or inquiries from advertisements.

By August 1977, the company had moved to its current location, eight miles away, in New Middletown, with 4,300 square feet available for warehouse and offices. The staff had risen from three to 15.

The following year, the business being "so successful that it called for his full-time efforts," Nashbar let the agency go. That year, sales rose to $1-million.

The first catalog had cost $541.52. In 1978, 45,000 were printed at a cost of $3,000, using different color inks.

In the same year, a toll-free telephone line was installed. Sales rose to $1.6-million, DiVito noted.

The catalog had been put in the hands of a manager, Hugo Dunhill Mailing Lists, Inc., New York, NY, and 138,000 were sent out by 1981. They now were being distributed four times a year, running 38 to 46 pages. The catalog was brought back in-house.

"There were many duplicates, as we kept adding names, and after cleaning the house list, 95,000 were sent out in 1982," DiVito said.

ADVERTISING EXPANDED

Advertising has expanded to other bicycling publications, but the main emphasis always has been on *Bicycling,* according to DiVito. "However, the size of these ads has increased, with most full-page," she said.

The inventory of merchandise expanded as the business grew, DiVito pointed out. Camping equipment was added and near the end of 1976, cross-country ski equipment was included.

To cover the expansion, the business name was changed from Bike Warehouse to Bike Nashbar in December 1981, "so that there was a name capable of being used for trademarking."

The skiing line is being phased out and is not included in new catalogs, DiVito said.

UNDER ITS OWN NAME

Late in 1981, Nashbar added raquetball and exercise equipment and a "Human Powered Vehicle."

In the spring of 1982, Nashbar began offering a bicycle under its own name. The firm always had handled bicycle frames. The bicycles, manufactured in Japan by Misuki, were sold at $345 each. The new bicycles, which are being featured with full-color, two-page spreads in February and March, sell for $349.

In the past year, Nashbar has returned to the use of a list manager—Direct Media, Inc., Edmond, OK. The house list totals 105,000 and approximately 25,000 other names from *Bicycling,* Vermont Bicycling Touring and Recreational Equipment, Inc., have been added, DiVito said.

As a result of the success of the computerization initiated in the spring of 1982, Nashbar is packaging software programs designed for mail order businesses. It can be used with all "pick" systems, DiVito explained.

The new programs will be sold by direct marketing, she said.

Cakes By Mail

Texas bakery builds $2 million overseas mail order business.

NINETY-ONE years ago, an itinerant baker carried a recipe from his home in Wiesbaden, Germany, to a small Dallas, TX, bakery. Today, the product of that recipe has not only found its way back to Germany, but is exported to 194 countries worldwide.

Perhaps even more impressive is the fact that the Collin Street Bakery has built a solid international mail order business on just that one product—fruitcake. Last year, more than 120,000 Original DeLuxe Fruitcakes were shipped to countries as remote as the Soviet Union, Czechoslovakia, Ecuador and Cameroon. "We've sent the fruitcakes to places where you couldn't pronounce the name, even if you were looking at it," says John Crawfort, director of marketing.

Collin Street has been cultivating its international mail order business for about 10 years. In the beginning, the company embarked on its overseas marketing campaign cautiously. Once it identified market potential, Collin Street went after overseas sales. Currently, overseas sales account for 10 percent of the bakery's $20 million sales volume. "We just kind of pecked around for awhile," says Crawfort, referring to the early years of the direct mail program. "In the last five years, though, we've been making considerable mailings."

In fact, the company's overseas mailing list has expanded from 50,000 names in 1976 to approximately one million names today. Americans living abroad are the target of most of Collin Street's mailings, though the bakery has developed a strong following among native foreigners. "Our primary goal is to market to the displaced Americans overseas. They are looking for us, and we want them to find us, so we go after them," Crawfort explains.

The bulk of Collin Street's mailing list is provided by a European list broker. And like many direct marketers, Crawfort is particular about the lists he rents. "We only want those people who want to hear from us. We look for people who buy through the mail. Of course, the ultimate list would be one of people who buy food through the mail. But such a list is not readily available at this time."

One list that's been particularly successful is of U.S. military personnel stationed overseas. Also effective is a list of people working in American embassies. After all, what's Christmas abroad without the ever-popular fruitcake?

Sales to Great Britain, Canada and Japan account for the bulk of the bakery's overseas business. Although the Japanese rank third in gross sales, when it comes to response rates, they really take the cake. "It's amazing. One mailer may be passed through five or 10 offices and each person will order on the same form and use the same credit card," says Crawfort. "We have lots of fun with them."

Collin Street has successfully penetrated the overseas market because customers have come to trust the integrity of the company. "Our lists will never be bandied around," says Crawfort, referring to the fact that Collin Street's lists are never rented. He believes this is why Collin Street has attracted many exclusive customers such as U.S. ambassadors, who can count on their gift lists being kept confidential.

Service is also an important ingredient of the bakery's direct mail effort. "We guarantee delivery, and if someone says the cake didn't get there, we don't hedge. We just ship another one. We do everything we can to maintain our good reputation," Crawfort notes.

From a creative point of view, producing the direct mailers is a piece of cake. Aside from minor modifications—changing the salutation, referring to a country's native currency and removing the U.S. toll-free number—the mailer is similar to the one used in the U.S.

Direct mail isn't Collin Street Bakery's only means of promoting its fruitcake. Space ads generate 15 to 18 percent of the bakery's international business. The ads are placed in English language newspapers and include a coupon. The bakery also counts on word-of-mouth advertising. The fact that the cakes aren't shipped with a brochure or price list isn't much of a deterent for the ardent fruitcake lover; recipients simply contact the bakery through the return address printed on the package.

The bakery has never had a problem clearing the cakes through customers. It simply prints the words, "Unsolicited gift, no commercial value" on the customs papers. "We have marvelous luck with this."

No doubt, the hundreds of Americans who awake on Christmas morning to find a fruitcake under the tree are evidence of the success of the bakery's overseas mail operation. But Collin Street has also received recognition by President Reagan, who presented the bakery with the "Presidential E Award" for seeking overseas trade.

Arnold Reuben, Retired Restaurateur Sells 10,000 Cheesecakes A Year

GREAT NECK, NY—Arnold Reuben, who once ran a popular restaurant called Rueben's in New York, has achieved a re-order rate of approximately 50 per cent with mail order sales of cheesecake favored by his patrons.

The retired restaurateur mailed 9,000 letters to his regular list in 1983, 1,000 more than in 1982, and expects that half of the individual customers and businesses will submit orders.

The cakes come in the seven-inch $13.50 variety or 11-inch at $26.60. Last year Reuben, a one-man mail order operation, sold close to 10,000 of the fluffy pastries by mail. He expects to sell the same amount this year, although he lost some corporate business accounts last Christmas because of recession cutbacks.

"Some of my business customers would order 300 to 400 cakes at Christmas time, last year they didn't. However, Thanksgiving more than made up for the falloff of orders of last year," he said.

Brochures with pictures and the story of the cake, order forms, cards and postage-free return envelopes go out to Reuben's in-house lists four times a year. On top of that he's gotten a lot of free publicity from such publications as *Money* and *The New York Times* with spinoffs to other publications and gourmet food television programs giving free plugs to his cheesecakes.

The operation is far from computerized. A typist types up labels and people are put on the mailing list. The cakes are wrapped in styrofoam containers and a corrugated overall cover and delivered via United Parcel Service or first class mail. All orders are delivered within two to two-and-a-half days.

Reuben's has its own bakery in Mt. Vernon, NY.

Reuben said that cheesecake lovers know no age, color or creed barriers but they tend to be in the upper scale brackets.

Mailing his cheesecakes is actually not a new endeavor for Reuben. He has been mailing them since 1929 when he had his restaurant at 58th and Fifth Avenue in Manhattan. The cheesecakes were made by a chef who came from Germany and baked them using an old German recipe.

Although he has no 800 number, Reuben accepts MasterCard, American Express and Visa.

Bakery Sold 1.5-Million Cakes By Mail In 45 Days

By Dan Abramson

CORSICANA, TX—Approximately 1.5-million Christmas fruitcakes were sold by mail during the 45 days prior to Dec. 25, 1984 by the Collin Street Bakery, according to John Crawford, vice president and co-owner. Crawford added that the bakery sells an additional 200 to 300 cakes per day for the remaining 320 days of the year, almost entirely due to direct marketing.

According to Crawford, the key direct marketing techniques that have made this operation successful have included classified ads in major upscale magazines, some radio advertising and mailings to a database of names that exceeds 500,000.

While most of this business is done in America, said Crawford, overseas mail, plus newspaper and magazine ads have extended the Collin Street Bakery operation to 194 foreign countries, "Which is not bad for a small town bakery which only bakes once a week during the off season," he said.

GOLDEN RUMCAKE SEASON

A small amount of "walk-in business" does contribute to the aforementioned totals, according to Crawford. However, he said that this is a minor factor in the organization's marketing strategy, which is both upscale and geographically diverse.

"We advertise in many of the more affluent magazines," said Crawford, who listed *New York Magazine, Better Homes & Gardens* and *Sunset* magazine as being among the better known. The ads for the bakery appear in the classified sections of those periodicals, he added. During the Christmas season, Crawford said that the company also takes ads in the Saturday and Sunday editions of more than 100 major newspapers around the United States.

"Our advertising doesn't really start until October," he said, in regard to the ads placed in the daily papers. "We really only exist for one day—Christmas."

The 800 telephone number used in these ads—800-245-9000—is soon to be changed, said Crawford. However, he added that the 800 number idea is going to remain the most common means of getting direct responses to the ads.

As far as lists are concerned, Crawford said he relies most heavily on the American Express credit card list, although others are used. The firm has also built up a considerable in-house list of recent customers over the years, although he decined to give a total.

As for overseas advertising, Crawford stated that the orientation is mostly toward English-language publications throughout the world. But the sales of Collin Street products are not limited by any media language barrier, he added. "We may not be able to advertise in Czechoslovakia," said Crawford, "but we certainly sell there."

He added that during January through March, the company also sells toasted pecan pies, while golden rumcakes are sold during the first six months of each year. "But fruitcakes are our primary business," he said.

FRUITCAKE HISTORY

The 1.5-million cakes mailed during the Christmas season weighed an aggregate of more than four-million pounds, according to a company source. The town itself, said this sources, has a population of 21,000.

How to Self-Publish Your Book & Have the Fun & Excitement of Being a Best-Selling Author

An expert's step-by-step guide to marketing your book successfully

Table of Contents

240 Pages...$22.00 postpaid

12015 Sherman Road
No. Hollywood, CA 91605

(818) 765-8579
FAX (818) 765-2922

HOW TO TRANSFORM AN ORDINARY SALESMAN INTO A VERITABLE GIANT!

Wouldn't you give almost anything to discover a way to stimulate your salesmen so they would pass up even a golf or fishing date to make a sale? The secret is revealed in this bestselling self-improvement book on the market today.

PSYCHO-CYBERNETICS
A New Technique for Using Your Subconscious Power
228 pages

On the back of this letter you will find a full description of this remarkable book. Read the table of contents and see for yourself what this book promises to do, which it also fulfills. Here is what two prominent business leaders say about this power-packed book.

"Dr. Maltz's discovery of Psycho-Cybernetics is an important and valuable contribution to man's knowledge of himself and to his ability to improve himself."
Louis Gruber, Chairman of the Board, P. Lorrilard & Co.

"Dr. Maltz shows us how to size ourselves up and outlines a plan of action that can help anyone to become a more effective person."
Thaddeous Hoinko, Managing Editor, Salesman's Opportunity Magazine

Place a copy of this dynamic book into the hands of every one of your representatives. Not only will this book lift up the struggling fledgling, but we promise it will put more muscle into your "star" salesmen.

Send $12.00 for your copy (CA residents $12.83) and you will be inspired to say, "I want my entire sales staff and office personnel to have a copy."

Sincerely,

Melvin Powers

Melvin Powers, President

P.S. The enclosed brochure contains a list of other powerful incentive books that are ideal for goodwill builders, premium and sales potential use, and for prospects, customers, and employees.

PSYCHO-CYBERNETICS
a new way to GET MORE LIVING OUT OF LIFE

LET THIS FAMOUS PLASTIC SURGEON'S remarkable discovery—*which vitally concerns your future*—guide you to the achievement of all your goals in life. Dr. Maxwell Maltz's experiments in the regrowth of injured tissues disclosed a little-known side-effect of plastic surgery: its revitalizing power on human personality. Removing outward scars and deformations produces a similar inward change on your temperament, abilities and Personality-Potentials, because it alters your "self image".

Built on this remarkable phenomenon, Dr. Maltz's new Self-Image Psychology works vast improvements on your personality thru *"emotional surgery."* This new psychology, the secret of PSYCHO-CYBERNETICS, performs this same crucial change by erasing *inner,* psychological scars. Through the amazing new techniques of emotional surgery, which are mapped out in detail in this book, you create a totally new image of yourself as a dynamic, happy, successful person—the sort of "born leader" who overflows with vigor and energy, plunges into every task with zest and unquenchable enthusiasm. You become a dynamic, vivid, colorful person who attracts fat paychecks, big promotions, admiring friends—swift success!

PSYCHO-CYBERNETICS awakes your sleeping abilities—galvanizes into life talents and powers you never dreamed were yours—fills you with such strength and new-found energy that you feel years younger, healthier, happier! Suddenly, you become overnight a Man of Power—your *latent potentials* have come to life—you zoom through tasks that would have stumped you before—you crash through obstacles and barriers that would have halted you before—you soar to new heights of achievement and wealth that seemed unscalable before PSYCHO-CYBERNETICS rebuilt your personality along "The Lines of Power"!

But better than this—PSYCHO-CYBER-NETICS touches into roaring life a hidden reservoir of latent energy that functions within you like an automatic machine. All you do is set up goals and this secret dynamo steers you to them—automatically, constantly, permanently—*even while you are asleep!* Fantastic? Yes! But THIS is the incredible power of PSYCHO-CYBERNETICS. Once you erase your "emotional scars" and trigger into action your "Success Mechanism"—overnight you will sleep better, work easier, feel happier and healthier and look younger than you have in years!

THANKS TO AN AMAZING NEW SCIENTIFIC INNOVATION THIS "NEW WAY OF LIFE" CAN NOW BE YOURS!

DR. MAXWELL MALTZ, M.D., F.I.C.S.,
DISCOVERER OF PSYCHO-CYBERNETICS

ABOUT THE AUTHOR: Dr. Maxwell Maltz, M.D., F.I.C.S., received his baccalaureate in science from Columbia University and his doctorate in medicine at the College of Physicians and Surgeons there. One of the world's most widely-known and highly-regarded plastic surgeons, he has practised in England, France, Germany, Italy and throughout Latin America. He has lectured before the University of Amsterdam, the University of Paris, and the University of Rome. He has been Professor of Plastic Surgery at the University of Nicaragua and at the University of El Salvador. He is the author of eight books previous to PSYCHO-CYBERNETICS, including ADVENTURES IN STAYING YOUNG and the famous bestseller, DR. PYGMALION.

YOU GET ALL THESE GIFTS—

• VIGOROUS, SPARKLING WELL-BEING!

• FREEDOM FROM FEAR AND GUILT!

• SUPERB, EBULLIENT GOOD SPIRITS!

• FINANCIAL SUCCESS AND SECURITY!

• RENEWED YOUTHFUL VIGOR!

• SERENE SELF-CONFIDENCE!

• NEW LOVE AND ROMANCE!

• DYNAMIC ENTHUSIASM AND WORK-ENERGY!

• A VITAL, COMMANDING NEW PERSONALITY!

• ADMIRATION FROM ALL YOU MEET!

• MONEY AND JOB SUCCESS!

83

Mail order boosts sales by 35 percent at Electronics Center

By Irene Clepper, contributing editor

LINCOLN, NE—Offering a mail order service has enabled Electronics Center to stretch its boundaries far beyond its Nebraskan roots and add 30 to 35 percent to its total annual volume.

To attract additional sales, the store also offers a layaway plan that has helped promote purchases among local college students. A liberal return policy keeps the customers satisfied. And a consistent, informative, occasionally humorous ad campaign keeps sales humming.

Finally, Electronics Center's sales approach is helpful, but not high pressured. It's not uncommon to have potential customers shop at the store two or three times before they buy.

Offers mail order

Mail orders account for 30 to 35 percent of Electronics Center's volume, according to Richard Musil, retail sales manager. The operation now runs its original store in Lincoln and a newly opened unit in Omaha. But mail orders have allowed its reach to extend coast to coast.

"We advertise in video, computer and ham radio publications," Musil explained. "We list WATS line numbers and have two people on duty all the time to handle the calls."

Customers pay either c.o.d., by credit or with a certified check to eliminate collection problems. The store uses United Parcel Service for most deliveries and ships orders within 24 hours.

"We've shipped everything from videotape to wide-screen TV sets all over the country," Musil said. "We pack and weigh the merchandise ourselves. If it's a factory package, we re-tape it for extra security. We prefer to handle the preparation for shipping ourselves—double checking the labels and the integrity of the package."

Musil reported all the store's customers have benefited from the mail order business, "because it enables us to buy in very large volume, which means low prices for everyone. With a national market like this, we're able to offer very good prices, even counting the delivery costs."

CHECKING OUT NEW GEAR at Electronics Center are Bob Eastwood (left), president, and Richard Musil, retail sales manager.

Being national keeps the company on its toes, as well. "Since we're in competition with retailers all over the country, we have to stay on top of the situation and be aware of trends, new models, prices," Musil said.

And for some customers, mail order is the only way a store can get their business. "For some people, it's the answer to 'shopping trauma,'" Musil explained. "If that person can phone or mail in an order and have it delivered, without having to spend time in a store, he is happy."

Another way of assuring customer contentment is through a layaway policy. By paying 20 percent down and making monthly payments, customers can have their purchases held for 90 days.

"Many of our customers are students at the University of Nebraska," Musil explained. "They may be waiting for money from home or from loans. A layaway plan allows them to take advantage of special sale prices."

Five percent of Electronics Center's business is now done on a layaway basis.

Finally, if a customer doesn't like his purchase once he gets it home, the store offers a liberal return policy.

Customers have seven days to bring back equipment if they are not satisfied. There is, however, a 15 percent restocking charge if they merely return it without exchanging it for something else, he remarked.

Before this policy was instituted, "We had people taking equipment out over the weekend, then returning it on Monday for a total refund," Musil said. "We had to protect ourselves against that type of thing."

Ads offer humor

Last year, Electronics Center doubled its advertising over the previous year, and sales grew accordingly. In-store promotions are also scheduled regularly to build excitement.

"We've done everything from hiring a couple of people to wear Mickey Mouse costumes and roller skate in front of the building to preparing very serious technical ads," said Musil. "We have a promotion ever week, and run a full-page ad in the Friday newspaper. We also use TV support during the weekend."

Sometimes, the store will zero in on a particular customer group. "For instance, we'll offer a free cassette deck as a prize to the fraternity and the sorority that do the most business with us during a 60-day period," Musil reported. "We present the prizes at a party we host for all members of each organization."

The store also injects humor into some of its advertising. "One of our radio spots stresses how many different lines we carry," noted Musil. "Supposedly, it's a robot reading the message. As he tries to crowd all the names into the spot his voice breaks, with all the sound effects you'd expect to hear when a piece of machinery fails."

One print ad asks the reader to put the ad up to his ear. "If he can hear music, he is then advised to see a doctor," Musil explained. "If not, we advise him he should see us."

In the store, customers find that they are being helped, not pressured into making a sale.

First, they are fully qualified by a salesman, who can then direct them to the equipment best suited to their needs.

"It's not uncommon to have people come back two or three times before making a decision," said Musil. "We don't put any pressure on them."

Clerks are willing to let a shopper listen to 25 receivers and 40 speaker systems in any combination they want to hear. "We're willing to spend as much time as they are. However, we aren't bashful about asking for the sale," Musil noted.

"In the end, we ask the customer if he has any questions," he said. "If not, we ask if he would like to take it with him, or have us install it."

Chapter Six

How to Copycat Successful Mail Order Operations

Becoming successful in mail order requires an inquisitive mind and a determination to become successful. You'll notice I have made the statement there are no secrets in the mail order field. Mail order successes are easy to spot because their ads are constantly repeated and their *modus operandi* is easy to discover. It's as simple as sending away for the product. Your job is to zero in on a product that interests you, send for it, evaluate it, and get on the mailing list. You know it's a winner because no one is going to continually spend thousands of dollars in advertising a loser.

Have you seen Joe Karbo's ad for *The Lazy Man's Way to Riches?* See page 93. How many times have you seen it? Undoubtedly, many. You know it's successful, because if you are at all cognizant of display ads, you've seen it a hundred times. That means many hundreds of thousands of dollars in advertising have been spent. On page 92 you'll find a United Press International story that appeared in newspapers throughout the country. Read it before continuing with your reading here.

Focus on the figures in the article: 175,000 copies of his book were sold at $10 each. That's $1,750,000. Note this is not Joe Karbo's first success. He also sold 100,000 copies of a $10 book on horse-race handicapping, and he has many other successful mail order books and products to his credit.

Newspaper and magazine articles like the one on him should immediately ring a bell in your mind. Don't just read the article and say, "That's nice." Consider its valuable information. If someone else can do it, so can you—and possibly do it better. Why not?

Your challenge is to create a book within your expertise, write a prize-winning ad, and have the pleasure of raking in the money. If you don't have a particular skill, don't worry about it. There's nothing wrong in collaborating with someone who has the skill or knowledge, and working on a royalty basis. What if you, or your collaborator, are not skilled in writing a book? No problem. Just drop me a line, and I'll refer you to some freelance writers. What if you are not skilled in writing advertising copy? Again, no problem. Contact a local advertising agency. If you don't get what you want, write to me again and I'll refer you to some freelance copywriters. Compare your job to that of a movie director bringing together a variety of talents to produce a money-making picture.

I often get good ideas for books, but don't have the time to write them. That doesn't keep me from producing the book. I'll contact a freelance writer and offer him the assignment. If he's interested, I'll pay him a royalty on each book sold. This is beneficial to him for several reasons. He has an opportunity to make money, he'll have an additional writing credit, and the quality of his work on this book can lead to other assignments from many publishers. As for me, I'm pleased because I have another book to promote. I suggest reading some books on book publishing. One I recommend is *The Self-Publishing Manual* by Dan Poynter. Dan Poynter is following his book's advice and making a fortune publishing such books as *The Self-Publishing Manual* and *Frisbee.* See page 80 for information on my book *How to Self-Publish Your Book and Have the Fun & Excitement of Being a Best-Selling Author.*

VIDEO CASSETTE TAPES

There are 60-million video cassette players in the United States. I'm in a drop-shipment program selling thousands of special interest videos. You could be doing the same thing.

I am very excited about the potential for building a substantial mail order business selling all kinds of videos. It's an opportunity to get started in a relatively new field that is not crowded and one in which you can use your creative ability to make big money.

Mail order is a great way to sell videos as it's difficult to find "how-to" videos in regular video rental stores.

CASSETTE TAPES

I buy cassette tapes every month, usually inspirational ones. I look for them in bookstores and buy them via mail order. I especially like those produced by Nightingale Conant, 7300 North Lehigh Avenue, Niles, Illinois 60648. The company produces a beautiful, full-color, 64-page catalog. If you are interested in selling cassette tapes, you can inquire about their dealer program. For customer service, call: 1-800-323-3938.

There are reference books at your main library or college library that contain a listing of 50,000 videos and their sources as well as reference books for cassette tapes, listing another 40,000 cassettes and their sources. The producers of these cassettes will be pleased to deal directly with you.

The names of the reference books are *Bowker's Complete Video Directory, Variety's Video Directory Plus,* and *Words on Cassette.* They are available from RR Bowker, P.O. Box 31, New Providence, NJ 07974-9904. Another reference book is *Video Source Books* available from Gale Research, Book Tower, Detroit, MI 48277-0748.

Look at pages 96 through 98. Have you ever seen this ad? Again, it's extremely successful. The *How To Wake Up The Financial Genius Inside You* ad has made a financial genius out of Mark O. Haroldsen. Read a writeup about him on page 99. It reads like Joe Karbo's article. Look at the important figures: 350,000 mail order copies at $10 each. That comes to $3,500,000. Not bad! In the third column of the article, Mr. Haroldsen tells you he was stimulated by William Nickerson's book, *How I Turned $1,000 into $3,000,000 in Real Estate—in My Spare Time.*

Let's examine the ads on *How To Wake Up The Financial Genius Inside You.* Notice the experimentation of three different photos. Which one do you think carries the most persuasive image? I'd vote for the one on page 97, showing a row of books in the background. This enhances the image by lending an air of authority.

Notice the coupon on page 98. Here Mr. Haroldsen is experimenting with a $12 price. But there must have been considerable resistance because all the ads now price the book at $10. Also note Haroldsen's ad offers a 30-day, free trial guarantee and promises the purchaser's check will not be deposited during the 30-day period. Observe the use of the notary public to authenticate the representations in the ad. Do you recall seeing those components in the ad for *The Lazy Man's Way to Riches?* The trick in copycatting the experts is to borrow those elements you believe are contributing to the success of the ads. The practice is permissible and makes good sense.

Notice in the ad on page 96 in which Lois and Mark Haroldsen appear together, all personal references have been changed from "I" to "we." The plural form has also been carried over into the order form. In the coupon you can order a deluxe, gold-embossed edition for $2 more. I'd be curious to know how many orders requested the gold-embossed edition. Not too great a percentage, I suspect, because it's been dropped from the ads. However, let's assume the response was good. Another dollar is made on the book simply by adding a line of copy. That is innovative.

On page 97, the ad is broken up with subheadings, contains a testimonial, and eliminates the mail order coupon. The very bottom line of the entire ad reads, **Inquire at your local bookstore for Mark Haroldsen's *How to Wake Up the Financial Genius Inside You.*** You will recall I did the same thing with my sales campaign for *Psycho-Cybernetics.* He is saying, in effect, "It's O.K. if you don't send me your $10. You can examine the book at your local bookstore and decide for yourself." I favor that approach. Obviously, he's cashing in on both retail and mail order business, plus his national distributor is selling his book to retailers all over the country. This additional exposure in the stores naturally adds up to more sales. It's a beautiful merchandising program.

I give Mark Haroldsen credit for continually trying to improve the response to his advertisements. He's not content to rest on his past successes. Save these ads and study them in detail to determine what makes them pull so successfully. When you learn why, applying the theory to your own product should be accomplished with ease.

Keep in mind these mail order entrepreneurs are spending hundreds of thousands of dollars on their advertisements. They wouldn't be spending it if the ads weren't paying off handsomely. They are experts in knowing and writing good advertising copy, and utilizing it in print to best advantage. Nothing is left to chance. Every headline, every subheading, every sentence, every phrase, and every word has been gone over carefully. It's there for you to study and digest. I urge you to start your advertising file today. I continue to accumulate ads, and the practice has served me well.

Note the theme of money in the ads that we have been discussing. Do you remember the title of the book you are reading at this very moment? Notice the money theme. Here's a good tip for you—let the theme of making or saving money direct your thinking to a book you can advertise. This theme is universal.

Joe Karbo, Mark Haroldsen, and Ben Swarez have all attended a private mail order seminar held annually in Los Angeles. They know round-table discussions stimulate the kind of creative thinking that can be translated into thousands of dollars. These mail order giants, entrepreneurs of the highest caliber, continue to share and seek information to increase their sales. It's all done in a very casual atmosphere, and we all delight in each other's success.

Success in mail order comes in getting an idea you think is valid and running with it. You can start from your kitchen table and become as successful as you want. I've given million-dollar ideas to some of the participants at the mail order seminars. The suggestions aren't always followed, as some of the individuals are as successful as they want to be. The idea of making more money isn't a strong enough inducement for them to work harder. I've also received excellent ideas from them in return. It becomes a question of time to implement them. Because of previous priorities, I may not be motivated to pursue ideas, even if they are winners.

At this point in my life, my creative challenge is to make successes of those interested in mail order. I'm doing that through my book and my mail order seminars. See page 236.

I've always been intrigued how various businesses can prosper through the application of mail order techniques. I used to rewrite ads I saw in magazines and send them to the advertisers with my compliments. I knew my thinking was right, but the suggestions were rarely followed and I seldom received a thank you. That seemed strange to me because I would be delighted if someone took the time and spent the energy to improve one of my ads. I changed my tactics. I wrote to the advertiser and told him I would guarantee to improve the pulling power of his ad for a fee. That brought the responses and the fees for a critique I had been willing to give away *gratis*.

An excellent exercise would be to lay out and write a full-page ad for an imaginary book dealing with instructions on how to make money in some activity of your own choosing. Here's one idea—a book called *How To Make Money Cooking and Baking At Home.* It tells how to cook and sell homemade meals for working mothers, who pick up the meals at your home upon returning from work.

Look at page 106. Here's another successful ad about losing weight. The name of the book is *Diet Secret.* The author, Nancy Pryor, even lists her phone number for the reader who has questions. The heading is powerful—*The Amazing Diet Secret of A Desperate Housewife.* Can you figure out why? Stop your reading and go back to the ad Think about it.

The Amazing Diet is greatly improved by the addition of the word *Secret.* This word has proved to be a winner in headlines. Would the headline be just as effective if the second line, *Of A Desperate Housewife,* were left out? I don't think so. The prize-winning element here is this second line. Some readers can identify with the two words *Desperate Housewife.* It compels them to read the ad. The entire headline captures the reader's attention, and as long as the rest of the copy is logical, the product will sell.

Try your hand at this writing assignment. Write a full-page ad on a book dealing with women finding sexual satisfaction. The headline reads: *The Secret Diary of a Sexually Frustrated, Desperate Housewife.* I have a book in mind that would be perfect for it. It's called *New Approaches to Sex in Marriage* by John E. Eichenlaub, M.D. If you think you've written a good ad, send it to me or use it yourself for an ad. If I use it, I'll pay you for it.

If the word *secret* isn't suitable for the headline, use it in the body of the copy. I published the following books with the word *secret* in the title. Read the titles aloud two ways—with, and without, the use of the word. Doesn't the inclusion of *Secret* improve the title?

Chess Secrets Revealed

Secrets of Winning Poker

Blackstone's Secrets of Magic

Secrets of Hypnotism

Numerology—Its Facts and Secrets

Palmistry Secrets Revealed

Secret of the Pyramids

Secret of Secrets

Secret of Bowling Strikes

Secret of Perfect Putting

Have you read the book *My Secret Garden* by Nancy Friday? It's about women's sexual fantasies and has sold over one million copies. The headline, *The Secret Diary of a Sexually Frustrated, Desperate Housewife,* would also serve as a perfect title for an article in the true confession magazines. Doesn't it convey a sensitive, emotionally-charged story? Could you write a novel based on that title? There's always a mass paperback sale in this genre. Who knows, you might wind up with a best seller.

Look at page 104. Here is a perfect example of Jim Everroad's creativity in writing and first publishing a 24-page booklet, *How to Flatten Your Stomach.* It was number one on the best seller list for many months. You can have no greater literary attainment than reaching #1 on the *New York Times Book Review* list and *Publishers Weekly.* Doing so is truly the epitome of success. As of this writing, the book has sold over 1,000,000 copies. While you are looking at the best seller list on page 104, note that *The Dieter's Guide to Weight Loss During Sex* is the #2 book. It combines two perennially good subjects to make a best seller. The book is in its 14th printing and has sold 415,000 copies.

The idea for the book came to Jim Everroad because he had a pot belly even though he was an athletic coach. Jim flattened his stomach by performing a series of exercises that he developed himself. The results of his exercise plan were enormously gratifying and did much to help others who had his problem.

Here's the fascinating part of the story, as told to me by Everroad. Using the psycho-cybernetics technique, he programmed himself one night to awaken the next morning with the winning title of a book he was going to write. He also programmed himself to take all the correct steps to make the book a best seller. When he awoke the next morning, the title popped into his mind, and he was on his way with a course of action to follow.

He published 2,000 copies of his booklet, and it was reviewed by one of the Columbus, Indiana local sportswriters. As a tag to his review, the sportswriter informed the reader copies of the booklet could be procured by writing directly to Jim Everroad at his home address. Jim received 500 orders in one week—a positive indication he had a tremendous winner.

I asked him what was to be the spinoff to the book. He told me he had none in mind, but subsequently he came out with a follow-up book, *How to Trim Your Hips and Shape Your Thighs.* I made the suggestion that he conduct classes teaching men and women how to flatten their stomachs. It could be fun to shed pounds and firm body muscles to the tune of disco or some other kind of music.

Read the ads on page 107 through 109. They have run for a considerable time and are undiminishing in their pulling power. Run the same ads five years from today and they'll pull just as well. When you appeal to men's and women's fantasies of love, you can be assured that you have a winner.

I published the book, *Cosmopolitan's Guide to Marvelous Men,* with a foreword by Helen Gurley Brown. Here's another writing assignment for you. Try to write a prize-winning ad that will instruct millions of women how to find true and lasting love. Your ad must be better than the three under discussion. Can you top the headlines of these ads? Think of the spinoffs. What about a mail order photo dating club? How about vacation trips for singles, cruises for singles, sports for singles, and seminars? The self-awareness courses you could sponsor by experts are endless. The catalyst to make it all happen is in the ad copy. The rest will follow once you build your list.

Go back to page 32 and look at the ad composed by Frederick's of Hollywood. Note he is asking two dollars for a one-year subscription to the catalog, a free gift to accompany this first issue. This company isn't sending out free catalogs. Someone paying two or three dollars is evidencing a genuine interest in a catalog. It would be great to be able to rent those names for similar or related products, such as the satin sheets advertised on the same page, to the left of Frederick's ad. If I were selling satin sheets, I'd make arrangements to rent all of Frederick's names.

Selling women's undergarments, bikinis, shoes, and accessories would be an easy operation to copycat. Once you've developed enough sales, you could manufacture some of your own garments. You are really selling the illusion, based on clever artwork and flattering photography, that every woman wearing the garment will be alluring and devastating. "How can he help but succumb to my charms?" Perfume ads imply this same message with their reference to tantalizing aromas. Frederick's ads state the message clearly. Look at some of the words in the copy: ALLURE! SEX APPEAL! SEXY BIKINIS and *SIN*-SUOUS SLINKS!

Assume you are interested in this merchandise as a possible mail order venture. Go to the reference publication, *Business Publications Rates & Data.* Under **Lingerie, section 34A,** you'll find a list of publications devoted to this subject. Send away for a free sample copy of every one, learn about the merchandise, produce your catalog and your ad, and you are in business.

I have the feeling Frederick's customers would be interested in astrology as a means to try and learn about the "true nature" of the men in their lives. I'd be interested to know what percentage of Frederick's customers are single, and what the average age is. I'd also like a profile on the average customer, disclosing her education, occupation, salary, and where she lives. Wouldn't you also like to know the amount of the average sale and the percentage of men buying garments as gifts?

TV ANTENNA

See page 110. Let's talk about some successful mail order products. I've seen this ad and variations of it for years. Probably you have, too. The fact you see full-page ads continually running is a sure sign they are winners. Note the copy in the coupon designed to sell you two or three antennas.

FOTO ROLL

See page 111. This item must be hot. I've seen the ad many times and in various sizes. The ad mentions a free mystery gift worth $5 to be sent if you buy the *Foto Roll.* Enticing the customer with such a gift is a good way to unload merchandise you are no longer selling.

30-YEAR KNIFE

See page 112. Stainless steel knives of every variety seem to sell extremely well. This one carries a 30-year warranty. Last week I watched a TV pitch selling a set of knives that were "Positively guaranteed for 50 years." I'd make the guarantee 100 years. My announcer would say, "Yes, we absolutely guarantee the knives for 100 years – for you, your children, and grandchildren. What a beautiful family treasure." (Can you imagine three generations accidentally cutting themselves with the same knife!)

The coupon offers a discount to the customer who buys two knives. I would like to see a statement about giving the knife as a gift. It could read, "A cherished gift that will last a lifetime." " A beautiful gift for the new bride." "Going to someone's house for dinner? Take this knife as a very special gift!" The ad could contain a statement about using the knife as a fund raiser. If you sell a product like this outside the scope of your ad, such as through retail outlets, enclose a card that must be returned by the purchaser to insure his guarantee with each item. This is another excellent way to build your mailing list. Send your catalog to these new names.

SLICK 50

On page 113 is a prize-winning advertisement that you should study and use as a model for one of your own products. SAVE GAS! CUT ENGINE WEAR IN HALF! are powerful attention-grabbing statements. The reader is immediately drawn into the ad. The first two paragraphs amplify the headline and keep the reader interested. Notice the word *secret* in the subtitle. It is one of my favorite advertising words. I've used it with great success in numerous ads and in titles of books I have published. Everyone is interested in secrets. Natural curiosity motivates the reader to find out what the secret is.

Next I offer seven benefits of using SLICK 50. If the prospective customer has read this far, chances are I have a sale.

Note that I use questions and answers rather than straight copy to tell the reader how to use the product. There's a subtle difference. I've used a question and answer format many times in writing advertising copy. It is very effective.

Now I am getting ready for the close. How do you like the subtitle **Internationally-Recognized Labs Unanimously Agree on Slick 50 Benefits?** Doesn't the statement lend an air of authenticity to the product? Starting with *Consumer's Digest Magazine,* I list the results of studies that prove my product claims. If the reader is still with me at this point, I have just about closed the sale.

Next come three terrific testimonials; one is from Andy Belmont, NASCAR "Rookie of the Year." Again, we are building product credibility.

The money-back guarantee is always important, no matter what you are selling. If the product is good, you'll rarely get a return. If you do, however, find out the reason. I like the statement **100% Money-Back Guarantee.** I'm using it now in all my ads, including those on television. It has a nice ring to it. I've noticed recently that some of the other television marketers have begun to use my phrase.

Note in the coupon that I do not confine my offer to only one bottle of SLICK 50. Now I am going to let you in on a secret that can greatly increase your future profits. Half of all SLICK 50 orders are for two bottles or more. Why? Because many of the readers have at least two cars in their family – a fact they are reminded of when they see the two bottle offer. Be sure to include a multiple sale offer in your ads and perhaps even suggest uses for extra product.

Offering Visa and MasterCard purchases helps increase sales. Many of our customers use their credit cards even when they order by mail.

I have been using 800 numbers in many of my prints ads and in all of my television ads. Because each phone order I receive costs me two dollars, I'm experimenting in some print ads with using my office number instead. Doing so may or may not prove to be cost effective, but testing new ways to increase profits is important to mail order success. On television, of course, an 800 number is a must. Although you'll find an address given in all direct response television commercials, I find that only about ten orders of every one thousand come through the mail.

This SLICK 50 advertisement has all the elements necessary to make it a winner, including a picture of the product and the powerful phrase AS SEEN ON TV. These elements can make your ad a winner, too. Remember that learning to write successful ad copy is one of the keys to mail order success.

Once your ad is bringing in orders for your product, should you stop there? Of course not! Try to find a related product or products to sell to your new customers. Doing so can convert many single sales into multiple sales. I do exactly that with SLICK 50. With every order, I enclose the two-sided circular seen on pages 114 and 115. The result, as you might guess, is a very high percentage of orders for the **Automatic Transmission Treatment** and **Gear Treatment For Manual Transmissions.** The entire advertising campaign works like a charm because of winning ad copy and perfectly suited follow-up products.

Using the SLICK 50 example, you, too, can be successful in the mail order business.

In thinking through all the possible markets for SLICK 50, I came up with the idea that it would be great for cars and trucks that pull horse trailers. On page 277 is a free publicity release that was run in *Western Horseman.* It generated thousands of dollars worth of orders. You could do the same with your products following the instructions in Chapter 13. Once you get your creative juices flowing, the potential for making money is unlimited.

I'm successfully using the ad copy on this one-page ad as a direct mail piece. I have also created a 30-minute infomercial for television based on the copy. I'm very excited about the results and am spending a great deal of time looking for more products to sell on television. Television marketing offers the potential to make big money in a short period of time. See Chapter 18 for details.

MONEY BELT

See page 116. Here's a beautiful mail order item that's been around for 100 years. You even get the belt personalized free of charge. If the product were mine, I would sell the belt as it is, and add a charge of $1 or $2 to monogram the belt. I think they are missing a chance for extra dollars. I would have preferred a line drawing of the belt to show it off effectively. The copy is excellent.

RADIO AND TELEVISION

It's difficult to create profitable mail order sales via radio. My suggestion is to consider this medium only when you have a smashing success on television. Use radio for leads, rather than selling the product.

An executive of a record company came to me with a problem. He was stuck with thousands of sets of the Bible recorded on records and couldn't sell them. I suggested that he try radio stations featuring religious programs, and sell only the first record, *Book of Genesis,* for $5. I also worked out some P. I. deals. The complete set sold for $30, and we gave credit on the $5 purchase. The conversion rate for the sale of the entire package was very high, because once the purchaser was pleased with the first record, it was only natural that he would follow up with the purchase of the set.

Have you seen *The Kiplinger Letter* advertised on TV? It sells for $10 for 21 introductory issues, and even if you cancel your subscription, you still get to keep the free books which come to you as a bonus for ordering the subscription. *The Kiplinger Letter* has been advertised for many years on TV; therefore, you know it must be paying off.

The most successful products advertised on TV are records and tapes. The ads are basically the same. Parts of the album are played, putting you into a receptive mood while the titles in the album are rolled on the screen. The announcer tells you of this outstanding collection that is offered only on TV. How can you pass it up when all you have to do is pick up your phone and dial a toll-free number? When you receive the album, you get a catalog of 100 other albums and tapes to purchase.

I spoke about seeing an ad for knives on TV with a 50-year guarantee. It must be paying off. How many times have you seen the commercial showing how to decoratively slice vegetables?

For study purposes, you can easily record TV commercials with a cassette tape recorder. You can sell the same or similar products that you see advertised. Once you can produce sales, record companies are willing to make deals with you. In the next chapter, you'll be told where you can buy remaindered records at a fraction of the original price. This will allow you to experiment on TV and be able to produce a record catalog as a follow-up to the initial sale.

Radio and TV obviously have proven successful for many advertisers, and they should be kept in mind as two of your options. If you go on TV or radio, you'll know within a week whether or not you have a winner. Run ten spots in the evening for a five-day period. If the mail count looks good at the end of a week, you'll know whether or not to continue. You might want to consider an additional schedule.

On page 117 you'll find a radio script that was helpful in promoting the book *Psycho-Cybernetics.*

I believe many space advertisers could be successful on TV if they pursued it diligently. We tend to stay with that which is familiar to us and has proven to be successful. If you try TV, don't go for prime time. The rates change after prime time in the evening and again after midnight. Try to work out a deal with your local TV station. Who knows, you might even get lucky and get a P.I. deal.

There are four publications you can research at your main library for advertising rates: *Spot Television Rates & Data, Spot Radio Rates & Data, Spot Radio Small Markets Edition* and *Network Rates & Data Serving the National Black Consumer.*

I'll share a personal mail order secret with you. I have an insatiable curiosity about the effectiveness of various types of advertising. I have posed some questions that came to my mind as we reviewed various advertisements. The purpose of this is to stimulate your thinking along similar lines. When you begin to ask the same type of questions, you are thinking like a pro and are on your way to riches.

Here's how I find out how an advertisement is pulling on TV or radio. I'll call the local TV or radio station and ask for the mail room. When someone answers the phone, I'll ask who it is. Here's the way my end of the conversation goes: "To whom am I speaking? Karen, this is Bill Smith calling from the advertising agency handling the XYZ account. That's the company selling the vegetable slicer. Would you tell me what the mail count is today? Did you say 102 orders? Thank you, Karen, I'll call back tomorrow." In most cases, the person in the mail room will give you the information. In case of toll-free numbers, follow the same procedure, asking how many orders were phoned in from all the stations around the country.

That is privileged information and shouldn't be given to anyone. Should you decide to run a radio or TV deal, or if you list a toll-free number, be sure to instruct the station and telephone service not to give out any figures unless the party knows the code word. You want to avoid Melvin Powers or anyone else calling to find out the count.

Finding out those figures is being a good mail order detective. If you were interested in pursuing a similar product, it could mean thousands of dollars in your pocket. You would have all the information you need to know if it were profitable.

Copycatting is O.K. for your initial attempts at mail order. But for your own enjoyment and full measure of gratification that is attached to creative endeavor, develop your own products, advertising copy, and unique way of doing business. You'll experience real satisfaction and feel good about yourself.

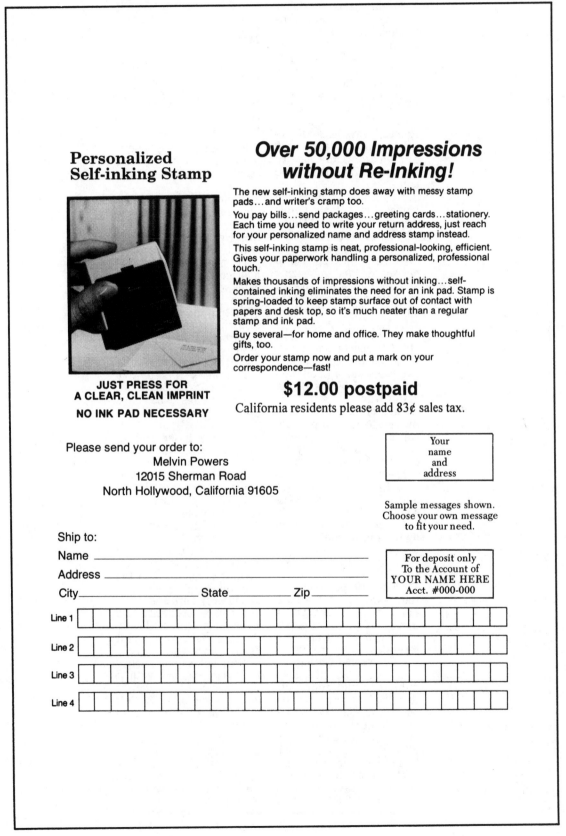

173,000 Sold

Author Cashes In On 'Lazy Way' Book

By United Press International

On the basis of dollar volume, Joe Karbo claims to have been the best-selling author in the United States in 1973, but you won't find the name of his book on the literary lists.

Karbo, author of a paperback called "The Lazy Man's Way to Riches," says he sold 173,-000 copies last year at $10 per. That adds up to almost $1.75 million, he notes.

"It's easy to figure," he laughs, presumably on his way to the bank. "That's why I made the price $10."

All his sales are by direct mail in response to newspaper and magazine ads. He took a fullpage ad in Time magazine to lure buyers with his soft sell.

Direct Response

He tells how he has a $100,000 beachfront home, a $30,000 mountain cabin, two boats and a Cadillac—all acquired by his "Lazy Man's Way."

Part of his pitch is a money-back guarantee. Karbo says he doesn't even cash checks or money orders for at least 31 days.

The book combines positive thinking principles and auto-suggestion plus sound and painstakingly detailed suggestions on operating a mail order business. He calls it "direct response business."

About 10 per cent of those who order the book request and get their money back, Karbo says, and this does not create a large dent in his profits.

Contracts Printing

He acts as his own publisher and contracts the printing. Actual production of the book costs him 50 cents a copy, he says, but that does not include the thousands of dollars spent on advertising.

This is not his first big seller, he says. He sold more than 100,000 copies of a book on horse race handicapping and about the same number on a book called "The Power of Money Management" at $3.95 a copy.

He is making plans to distribute the "Lazy Man's Way" in England and says, "We should sell three or four hundred thousand over there."

Basically, he says, he is an advertising man and his results indicate he knows the field.

In the book, he gives advice on writing ads and says the chatty approach—like writing a letter to a friend—is best.

The book tells how to get a discount on advertising rates with newspapers and magazines and also ways of getting radio and television time at reduced rates.

Karbo suggests picking a product for which there is a need or a service.

The book has drawn "hundreds of letters" from persons who have profited by it, he says.

Easy Way

"I had a letter from a man in Tulsa, Okla., who started a retail training institute by mail and has made a success of it," he says. "People think they have to work hard and deprive themselves to make money.

They don't set their goals high enough. My method is contrary to the Horatio Alger legend—you know, work hard and you'll get to be a supervisor or a managing editor. That's the long, hard way, and it doesn't work out too often.

"I'm not saying money is everything, but with it you have some freedom. I can take the afternoon off if I want to. I'm a very happy guy."

He also has a sense of humor. In light of the energy crisis, he says, "You know what—I just picked the wrong time to buy a Rolls Royce."

The Lazy Man's Way to Riches

'Most People Are Too Busy Earning a Living to Make Any Money'

I used to work hard. The 18-hour days. The 7-day weeks.

But I didn't start making big money until I did less—a lot less.

For example, this ad took about 2 hours to write. With a little luck, it should earn me 50, maybe a hundred thousand dollars.

What's more, I'm going to ask you to send me 10 dollars for something that'll cost me no more than 50 cents. And I'll try to make it so irresistible that you'd be a darned fool not to do it.

After all, why should you care if I make $9.50 profit if I can show you how to make a *lot* more?

What if I'm so sure that you *will* make money my Lazy Man's Way that I'll make you a most unusual guarantee?

And here it is: I won't even cash your check or money order for 31 days *after* I've sent you my material.

That'll give you plenty of time to get it, look it over, try it out.

If you don't agree that it's worth *at least a hundred times* what you invested, send it back. Your *uncashed* check or money order will be put in the return mail.

The only reason I won't send it to you and bill you or send it C.O.D. is because both these methods involve more time and money.

And I'm already going to give you the biggest bargain of your life.

Because I'm going to tell you what it took me 11 years to perfect: How to make money the Lazy Man's Way.

O.K.—now I have to brag a little. I don't mind it. And it's necessary—to prove that sending me the 10 dollars . . . which I'll keep "in escrow" until you're satisfied . . . is the smartest thing you ever did.

I live in a home that's worth $250,000. I know it is, because I turned down an offer for that much. My mortgage is less than half that, and the only reason I haven't paid it off is because my Tax Accountant says I'd be an idiot.

My "office," about a mile and a half from my home, is right on the beach. My view is so breathtaking that most people comment that they don't see how I get any work done. But I do enough. About 6 hours a day, 8 or 9 months a year.

The rest of the time we spend at our mountain "cabin." I paid $30,000 for it—cash.

I have 2 boats and a Cadillac. All paid for.

We have stocks, bonds, investments, cash in the bank. But the most important thing I have is priceless: time with my family.

And I'll show you just how I did it—the Lazy Man's Way—a secret that I've shared with just a few friends 'til now.

It doesn't require "education." I'm a high school graduate.

It doesn't require "capital." When I started out, I was so deep in debt that a lawyer friend advised bankruptcy as the only way out. He was wrong. We paid off our debts and, outside of the mortgage, don't owe a cent to any man.

It doesn't require "luck." I've had more than my share, but I'm not promising you that you'll make as much money as I have. And you may do better; I personally know one man who used these principles, worked hard, and made 11 million dollars in 8 years. But money isn't everything.

It doesn't require "talent." Just enough brains to know what to look for. And I'll tell you that.

It doesn't require "youth." One woman I worked with is over 70. She's travelled the world over, making all the money she needs, doing only what I taught her.

It doesn't require "experience." A widow in Chicago has been averaging $25,000 a year for the past 5 years, using my methods.

What *does* it require? Belief. Enough to take a chance. Enough to absorb what I'll send you. Enough to put the principles into *action*. If you do just that—nothing more, nothing less—the results *will* be hard to believe. Remember—I guarantee it.

You don't have to give up your job. But you may soon be making so much money that you'll be able to. Once again—I guarantee it.

The wisest man I ever knew told me something I never forgot: "Most people are too busy earning a living to make any money."

Don't take as long as I did to find out he was right.

Here are some comments from other people. I'm sure that, like you, they didn't believe me either. Guess they figured that, since I wasn't going to deposit their check for 31 days, they had nothing to lose.

They were right. *And here's what they gained:*

$260,000 in eleven months

"Two years ago, I mailed you ten dollars in sheer desperation for a better life . . . One year ago, just out of the blue sky, a man called and offered me a partnership . . . I grossed over $260,000 cash business in eleven months. You are a God sent miracle to me."

B. F., Pascagoula, Miss.

Made $16,901.92 first time out

"The third day I applied myself totally to what you had shown me. I made $16,901.92. That's great results for my first time out."

J. J. M., Watertown, N.Y.

'I'm a half-millionaire'

"Thanks to your method, I'm a half-millionaire . . . would you believe last year at this time I was a slave working for peanuts?"

G. C., Toronto, Canada

$7,000 in five days

"Last Monday I used what I learned on page 83 to make $7,000. It took me all week to do it, but that's not bad for five day's work."

M. D., Topeka, Kansas

Can't believe success

"I can't believe how successful I have become . . . Three months ago, I was a telephone order taker for a fastener company in Chicago, Illinois. I was driving a beat-up 1959 Rambler and had about $600 in my savings account. Today, I am the outside salesman for the same fastener company. I'm driving a company car . . . I am sitting in my own office and have about $3,000 in my savings account."

G. M., Des Plaines, Ill.

I know you're skeptical. After all, what I'm saying is probably contrary to what you've heard from your friends, your family, your teachers and maybe everyone else you know. I can only ask you one question.

How many of them are millionaires?

So it's up to you:

A month from today, you can be nothing more than 30 days older — or you can be on your way to getting rich. You decide.

". . . I didn't have a job and I was worse than broke. I owed more than $50,000 and my only assets were my wife and 8 children. We were renting an old house in a decaying neighborhood, driving a 5-year old car that was falling apart, and had maybe a couple of hundred dollars in the bank.

Within one month, after using the principles of the Lazy Man's Way to Riches, things started to change — to put it mildly.

- *We worked out a plan we could afford to pay off our debts — and stopped our creditors from hounding us.*
- *We were driving a brand-new Thunderbird that a car dealer had given to us!*
- *Our bank account had multiplied tenfold!*
- *All within the first 30 days!*

And today . . .
- *I live in a home that's worth over $250,000.*
- *I own my "office". It's about a mile and a half from my home and is right on the beach.*
- *I own a lakefront "cabin" in Washington. (That's where we spend the whole summer — loafing, fishing, swimming and sailing.)*
- *I own two oceanfront condominiums. One is on a sunny beach in Mexico and one is snuggled right on the best beach of the best island in Hawaii.*
- *I have two boats and a Cadillac. All paid for.*
- *I have a net worth of over a Million Dollars. But I still don't have a job . . ."*

Sworn Statement:
"On the basis of my professional relationship as his accountant, I certify that Mr. Karbo's net worth is more than one million dollars."

Stuart A. Cogan

Bank Reference:
Home Bank
17010 Magnolia Avenue
Fountain Valley, California 92708

Joe Karbo
17105 South Pacific, Dept. 88-R
Sunset Beach, California 90742

Joe, you may be full of beans, but what have I got to lose? Send me the Lazy Man's Way to Riches. *But don't deposit my check or money order for 31 days after it's in the mail.*

If I return your material — for *any* reason — within that time, return my *uncashed* check or money order to me. On that basis, here's my ten dollars.

Name _____

Address _____

City _____

State _____ Zip _____

© 1978 Joe Karbo

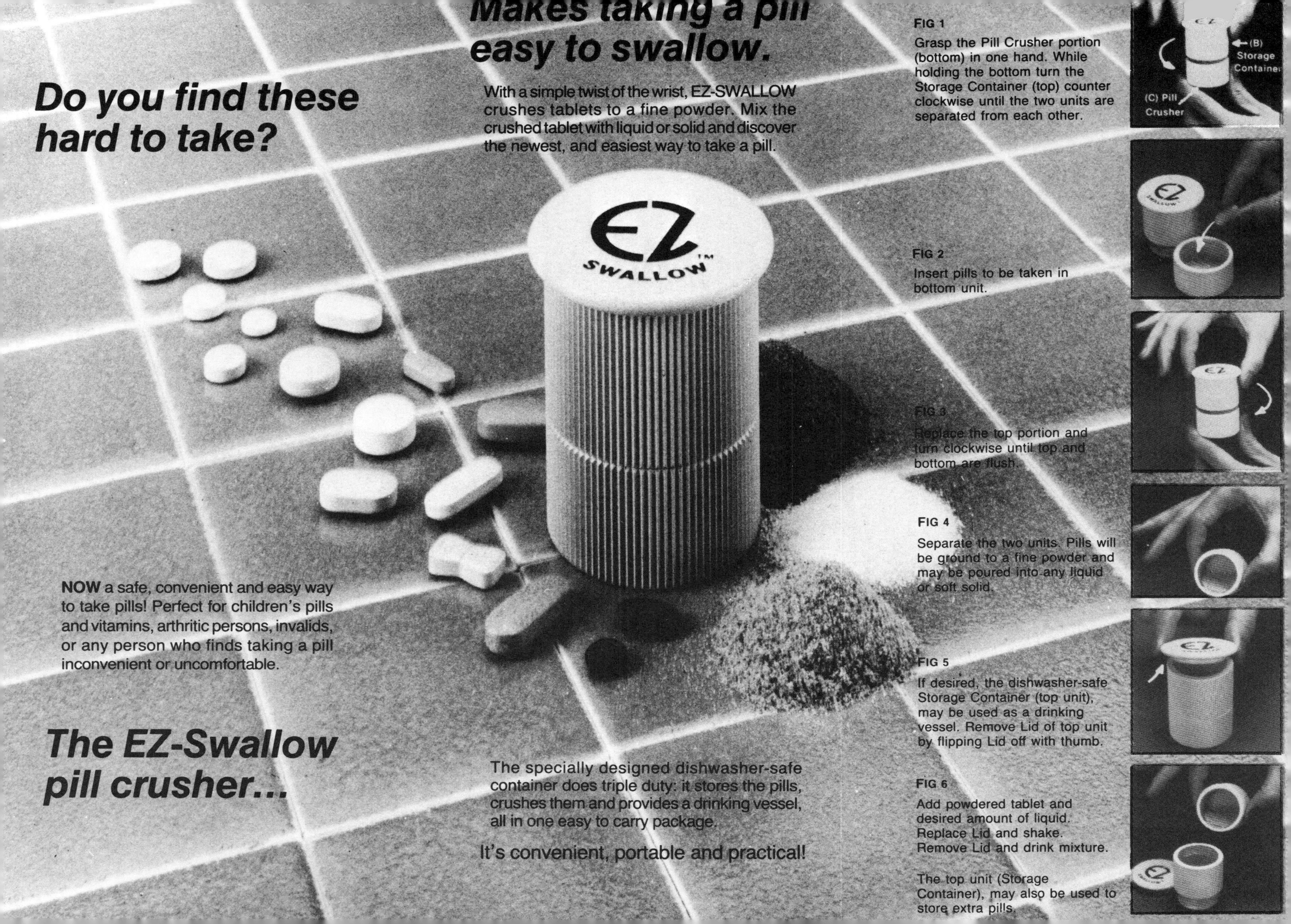

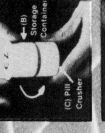

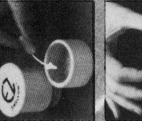

Makes taking a pill
easy to swallow.
Do you find these hard to take?
With a simple twist of the wrist, EZ-SWALLOW crushes tablets to a fine powder. Mix the crushed tablet with liquid or solid and discover the newest, and easiest way to take a pill.
EZ SWALLOW™
NOW a safe, convenient and easy way to take pills! Perfect for children's pills and vitamins, arthritic persons, invalids, or any person who finds taking a pill inconvenient or uncomfortable.
The EZ-Swallow pill crusher...
The specially designed dishwasher-safe container does triple duty: it stores the pills, crushes them and provides a drinking vessel, all in one easy to carry package.
It's convenient, portable and practical!
FIG 1
Grasp the Pill Crusher portion (bottom) in one hand. While holding the bottom turn the Storage Container (top) counter clockwise until the two units are separated from each other.
(B) Storage Container
(C) Pill Crusher
FIG 2
Insert pills to be taken in bottom unit.
FIG 3
Replace the top portion and turn clockwise until top and bottom are flush.
FIG 4
Separate the two units. Pills will be ground to a fine powder and may be poured into any liquid or soft solid.
FIG 5
If desired, the dishwasher-safe Storage Container (top unit), may be used as a drinking vessel. Remove Lid of top unit by flipping Lid off with thumb.
FIG 6
Add powdered tablet and desired amount of liquid. Replace Lid and shake. Remove Lid and drink mixture.
The top unit (Storage Container), may also be used to store extra pills.

How to Wake Up the Financial Genius Inside You

"Millionaires Are Not 100 Times Smarter Than You, They Just Know The Wealth Formula"

33 Year Old Millionaire and his 30 Year Old Wife (Mother of Five)

Millionaires are not 100 or even 10 times smarter than you, but it is a fact that millionaires are making 10 to 50 and even 100 times more than you.

Are these wealthy people working that much harder than you? No way!

If you are working only 20 hours a week, it would be physically impossible. (There are only 168 hours in a week, no one gets more.)

These questions used to really stump us. That was just a few years ago.

Lois and I then lived in Denver, Colorado, at 2545 South High Street. We paid $135 a month rent for a cramped, tumbled down house. We were expecting our second child and we were flat broke. We felt desparate and forced into a corner. We had to borrow $150 from my father and another $150 from my wife's father just to buy the groceries and pay the rent. If that wasn't enough, we were severeal thousand dollars in debt.

Things are much different now. Last year we could have retired and lived off the income of our one million dollars in real estate holdings. (Incidently, almost all of the income from the real estate is tax free).

Since I had worked 20 to 40 hours a week and my wife stayed home with the family, I know that we didn't work even 10 times longer or harder than you. And with my C-average from Ames High School (located in Ames, Iowa) and my wife's B-average from Twin Falls High in Idaho. I'm sure that we are not any smarter than you.

If hours, efforts, or brains are not what separates the rich from the average guy who is swamped with debts and very little income, then what is?

We learned the answer to that question from an old fellow in Denver that we met at our church. This fellow worked in a drug store stocking the shelves. Very few people knew that he had $200,000 in the bank, all of which he had earned starting from nothing.

Within a year after meeting him, we were told and shown the same thing by a young man who had recently earned over a million dollars. By this time, we began to realize that what we were being shown was truly a remarkable and workable way to grow rich.

We began to apply the principles and methods we had been shown. My wife, acting as a counselor, did her part by encouraging me when I was discouraged and pointing out where we could take some shortcuts. The results were amazing. We couldn't believe how easy it was, in fact, it seemed too easy.

But then we met an elderly lady (83 years old), who, had made $117,000 using the same formula.

We then figured our beginning wasn't luck. For three and one half years, we worked hard to refine and improve on the formula that we had been shown, so that it would be easy to get quicker results.

As we did this, our assets multiplied very rapidly (160% per year) to the point that neither of us had to work any longer.

I guess we're bragging now, but I did start spending alot of time in our backyard pool, traveling around the country, and doing a lot of loafing while my wife, with the aid of in-house help, was able to spend more time with our children besides being able to do all the things she had wanted to try for years.

Then one day a friend asked us how he could do what we had done.

So we began to outline the formula that we had improved to show him really how simple it was, and how he could do the same thing.

By the next time he approached us, we had written almost a complete volume on the easy way for him to copy our results.

We wrote this in simple, straight forward language so anyone could understand it.

This time our friend's questions were very specific. (He had already begun buying properties with the formulas we had been giving him). Now he had a property he wanted to buy, but was out of cash. How could he buy it?

We not only showed him how to buy without cash, but by the time the deal was complete, he had $5,000 cash in his pocket to boot.

We also showed him how to buy a $26,000 property for $75 down.

You, or anyone, can do exactly what we did, or our close friends have done; in fact, you may well do it better. (We began doing this in our spare time only.)

It doesn't matter where you live or the size of your town or city, our formula will show you exactly how to:

- Buy income properties for as little as $100 down.
- Begin without any cash.
- Put $10,000 cash in your pocket each time you buy (without selling property).
- Double your assets every year.
- Legally avoid paying federal or state income taxes.
- Buy bargains at 1/2 their market value.
- Allow you to travel one week out of every month.
- Borrow cash easily (my wife found out recently that with the new laws, borrowing can now be easily done by a woman alone).

When you send us a check or money order for $10, we will send you all our formulas and methods, and you are free to use them anywhere and as often as you would like.

Now if you were a personal friend of ours, we know you would believe us and not need any kind of guarantee, but since you don't know us personally, we will guarantee that you will be completely satisfied and that our formula will work for you if you apply it. We will back up that guarantee by not cashing your check for 30 days, and if you for any reason change your mind, let us know and we will send your uncashed check back.

You may well ask, why are we willing to share our formula for wealth? Well, because many of you will probably seek further consultation and direction from us as your wealth rapidly grows and the consultation fee adds to our fortune.

But you shouldn't care if we profit as long as you profit. And we guarantee that you will.

There is one small catch; you will have to apply some effort in order to get results from our formulas. But of course, nothing worthwhile comes without some effort, but let us assure you your efforts will be rewarded beyond what you believed possible. Besides the great monetary benefits, we find that by working on our financial future together, it greatly strengthens and improves our marriage and family life.

How To Wake Up The Financial Genius Inside You.

"I Have Helped More Than 250,000 People Discover Exactly How To Achieve Financial Freedom."

THE DIFFERENCE

If hours, efforts, or brains are not what separate the rich from the average guy who is swamped with debts and very little income then what is?

I learned the answer to that question from an old fellow in Denver. This fellow worked in a drug store stocking the shelves. Very few people knew that he had $200,000 in the bank, all of which he had earned starting from nothing.

Within a year after meeting him, I was told and shown the same thing by a young man who had recently earned over a million dollars. By this time, I began to realize that what I was being shown was truly a remarkable and workable way to grow rich.

THE BEGINNING

I began to apply the principles and methods I had been shown. The results were amazing. I couldn't believe how easy it was, in fact it seemed too easy.

But then I met an elderly lady (83 years old) who, although not very smart, has made $117,000 using the same formula.

I then figured my beginning wasn't luck.

For three and one half years, I worked hard to refine and improve on the formula that I had been shown, so that it would be easy to get quicker results.

As I did this, my assets multiplied very rapidly (160% per year) to the point that I didn't have to work any longer.

MORE LEISURE

I guess I am bragging now, but I did start spending a lot of time in our back yard pool, traveling around the country, and doing a lot of loafing.

Then one day a friend asked me how he could do what I had done.

So I began to outline the formula that I had improved to show him really how simple it was, and how he could do the same thing.

By the next time he approached me, I had written almost a complete volume on the

Mark O. Haroldsen became a millionaire in four years because he found a way to harness inflation to his benefit. Now it's your turn! *"I've found"* says Haroldsen, *"that most people just need a specific road map to follow...they can do what I've done."*

he had $5,000 cash in his pocket to boot.

I also showed him how to buy a $26,000 property for $75 down.

ANYONE CAN

You can do exactly what I did, or my close friends have done; in fact, you may well do it better. (I began doing this in my spare time only.)

It doesn't matter where you live or the size of your town or city, my formula will show you exactly how to:

■ Buy income properties for as little as $100 down.
■ Begin without any cash.

where and as often as you would like.

IT'S GUARANTEED

Now if you were a personal friend of mine, I know you would believe me and not need any kind of guarantee, but since you don't know me personally, I will guarantee that you will be completely satisfied and that my formula will work for you if you apply it. I will back up that guarantee by not cashing your check for 30 days, and if you for any reason change your mind, let me know and I will send your uncashed check back.

You may ask, why am I willing to share my formula for wealth? Well, simply because those of you who order my material will be helping to increase my net worth.

You shouldn't care if I profit as long as you profit. I guarantee that you'll be satisfied that my methods will help you or I'll send your money back!

"FINANCIAL FREEDOM"

To order, simply take any size paper, write the words "Financial Freedom", and send your name and address, along with a check for $10.00 to Mark O. Haroldsen, Inc., Dept. G-397, 2612 So. 1030 West, Salt Lake City, Utah 84119.

If you send for my materials now, I will also send you documents that will show you precisely how you can borrow from $20,000 to $200,000 at 2% above the prime rate using just your signature as collateral.

By the way, if you feel a little uneasy about sending me a check or money order for $10.00, simply postdate it by 30 days which will completely eliminate your risk.

*M3 © Mark O. Haroldsen, Inc. 1978

One of many unsolicited comments on my material:

" ... when it came I read it. Then I read it again, and have read it about once a week since it came. No magic. No secrets. A plain, easy-to-understand, 1-2-3 way for anybody with a little patience and common sense to become totally independent within a reasonable length of time. The one book I've been looking for for at least fifteen years ..."

—Jerry Donaho, Valdez, Alaska

---

easy way for him to copy my results.

EASY TO READ

I wrote this in simple, straight-forward language so anyone could understand it.

This time my friend's questions were very specific. (He had already begun buying properties with the formulas I had been giving him.) Now he had a property he wanted to buy, but was out of cash. How could he buy it?

I not only showed him how to buy without cash, but by the time the deal was complete,

■ Put $10,000 cash in your pocket each time you buy (without selling property.)
■ Double your assets every year.
■ Legally avoid paying federal or state income taxes.
■ Buy bargains at ½ their market value.
■ Allow you to travel one week out of every month.

When you send me a check or money order for $10, I will send you all my formulas and methods, and you are free to use them any-

Inquire at your local bookstore for Mark Haroldsen's "How to Wake Up the Financial Genius Inside You."

How To Wake Up The Financial Genius Inside You

"Millionaires Are Not 100 Times Smarter Than You, They Just Know The Wealth Formula."

Mark O. Haroldsen
Millionaire
in 48 Months

Millionaires are not 100 or even 10 times smarter than you, but it is a fact that millionaires are making 10 to 50 and even 100 times more than you.

Are these wealthy people working that much harder than you? No way!

If you are working only 20 hours a week, it would be physically impossible. (There are only 168 hours in a week, no one gets more.

These questions used to really stump me. That was a few years ago.

My wife and I then lived in Denver, Colorado, at 2545 South High Street. We paid $135 a month rent for a cramped, tumbled down house. My wife was expecting our second child and we were flat broke. I felt desperate and forced into a corner. I had to borrow $150 from my father and another $150 from my father-in-law just to buy the groceries and pay the rent. If that wasn't enough, I was several thousands dollars in debt.

Things are much different now. Last year I could have retired and lived off the income of my one million dollars in real estate holdings. (Incidently, almost all of the income from the real estate is tax free).

Since I had worked 20 to 40 hours a week, I know that I didn't work even 10 times longer or harder than you. And with my C-average from Ames High School (located in Ames, Iowa). I'm quite certain that I'm not any smarter than you.

If hours, efforts, or brains are not what separates the rich from the average guy who is swamped with debts and very little income, then what is?

I learned the answer to that question from an old fellow in Denver. This fellow worked in a drug store stocking the shelves. Very few people knew that he had $200,000 in the bank, all of which he had earned starting from nothing.

Within a year after meeting him, I was told and shown the same thing by a young man who had recently earned over a million dollars. By this time, I began to realize that what I was being shown was truly a remarkable and workable way to grow rich.

I began to apply the principles and methods I had been shown. The results were amazing. I couldn't believe how easy it was, in fact it seemed too easy.

But then I met an elderly lady (83 years old) who, although not very smart, has made $117,000 using the same formula.

I then figured my beginning wasn't luck.

For three and one half years, I worked hard to refine and improve on the formula that I had been shown, so that it would be easy to get quicker results.

As I did this, my assets multiplied very rapidly (160 per cent per year) to the point that I didn't have to work any longer.

I guess I am bragging now, but I did start spending alot of time in our back yard pool, traveling around the country, and doing a lot of loafing.

Then one day a friend asked me how he could do what I had done.

So I began to outline the formula that I had improved to show him really how simple it was, and how he could do the same thing.

By the next time he approached me, I had written almost a complete volume on the easy way for him to copy my results.

I wrote this in simple, straight forward language so anyone could understand it.

This time my friend's questions were very specific. (He had already begun buying properties with the formulas I had been giving him). Now he had a property he wanted to buy, but was out of cash. How could he buy it?

I not only showed him how to buy without cash, but by the time the deal was complete, he had $5,000 cash in his pocket to boot.

I also showed him how to buy a $26,000 property for $75 down.

You, or anyone, can do exactly what I did, or my close friends have done; in fact, you may well do it better.

I began doing this in my spare time only.

It doesn't matter where you live or the size of your town or city, my formula will show you exactly how to:

- Buy income properties for as little as $100 down.
- Begin without any cash.
- Put $10,000 cash in your pocket each time you buy (without selling property).
- Double your assets every year.
- Legally avoid paying federal or state income taxes.
- Buy bargains at ½ their market value.
- Allow you to travel one week out of every month.

When you send me a check or money order for $12, I will send you all my formulas and methods, and you are free to use them anywhere and as often as you would like.

Now if you were a personal friend of mine, I know you would believe me and not need any kind of guarantee, but since you don't know me personally, I will guarantee that you will be completely satisfied and that my formula will work for you if you apply it. I will back up that guarantee by not cashing your check for 30 days, and if you for any reason change your mind, let me know and I will send your uncashed check back.

You may well ask, why am I willing to share my formula for wealth? Well, because many of you will probably seek further consultation and direction from me as your wealth rapidly grows and my consultation fee adds to my fortune.

But you shouldn't care if I profit as long as you profit. And I guarantee that you will.

By the way, if you feel a little uneasy about sending me a check or money order for $12.00, simply postdate it by 30 days which will completely eliminate your risk.

---

9 L   ©Mark O. Haroldsen 1977

This column appeared in hundreds of newspapers across the nation during June 1978:

Real Estate: the key to wealth for average man

By JOHN CUNNIFF
AP Business Analyst

NEW YORK (AP).— Would you prefer to work for someone else at the rate of $1,000 a day for 35 days, or for yourself at an income beginning with 1 cent the first day and doubling on each succeeding day?

Wherever he goes Mark Oliver Haroldsen asks that question. Most people choose the $35,000 that comes with the first option, never realizing that the second would endow them with nearly $340 million.

He uses the illustration to prove the power of compounding, and how it works in real estate. While it's unlikely that anyone will double his money daily, he says, many people can do it by the year.

An example: An income property is bought for $50,000 with $5,000 down. Its value appreciates $5,000 to $55,000 in the first year, $ 100 percent gain. True, there are expenses, but there is income also.

Like himself, he says, many ordinary people can become millionaires by following his simple formula of buying income property, fixing it up, refinancing, and managing it wisely or selling at an opportune time.

The tremendous compounding comes from the leverage of using borrowed money, since some properties can be acquired for very little down, and in some instances for nothing at all.

Says Haroldsen, there aren't enough days in a year or years in a lifetime for most people to become millionaires while working for others. On thier own they can do it in remarkable short order.

Seven years ago the 34-year-old Salt Lake City resident owed $7,000. Recently he estimated his worth at $5.5 million, but that was before he bought an apartment house, he says, for $600,000 less than its value.

Haroldsen, a clean-cut, disarmingly direct and enthusiastic motivator, a Mormon, now seeks to arouse the dormant financial instincts in millions of Americans. And he hopes to make more millions doing so.

He has flooded the nation and intrigued hundreds of thousands in the past year or so with his magazine advertisements promising to demonstrate "How to Wake Up the Financial Genius Inside You."

That, in fact, is the name of a book Haroldsen wrote while working on his second million. He published it himself, and already, he says, has sold 350,000 mail order copies at $10 each.

The book is now making its way into bookstores, and Haroldsen says confidently: I'm sure it will be on the bestseller list." It already would be, of course, if sales by mail were included.

The book's reception, and the availability to him of mail order customers, convinced him to establish a monthly magazine, the "Financial Freedom Report." It too is a success, he states.

Haroldsen isn't the only one with the same insights about income property. He concedes a debt to William Nickerson, author of "How I Turned $1,000 into Three Million in Real Estate — in my Spare Time."

Haroldsen, however, might have the biggest goals of all. He has only begun, he states, and has every intention of continuing to compound his successes until he is one of the richest men in America.

What he and some other authors may fail to emphasize, however, is that most people lack the motivation. They can't accept the self-denial, financial sacrifices, disappointments, hard work, failures, fears.

Good intentions don't move you ahead unless you have a vehicle. Haroldsen found his when he discovered a stock market customer, Larry Rosenberg of Denver, had accumulated a fortune in properties.

He then borrowed as much as he could and bought small properties. For six months, he says, he didn't dare assess his progress. When he did, he found he was ahead. He quit his job.

The decision in 1975 to go fulltime into real estate, he says, was "the toughest decision I ever made, to leave a salaried job and depend totally on my own skill, ability and hustle."

HOW I MADE $1,000,000 IN MAIL ORDER

by E. JOSEPH COSSMAN

- HOW YOU CAN GO INTO THE MAIL ORDER BUSINESS
- HOW TO FIND NEW PRODUCTS
- HOW TO TEST YOUR PRODUCTS
- HOW TO DEVELOP AND PRODUCE YOUR PRODUCTS
- SELLING YOUR PRODUCTS
- ADVERTISING AND PROMOTING YOUR PRODUCTS
- TEN SECRET RULES TO WIN SUCCESS IN MAIL ORDER
- HOW TO GET THE MOST FROM TRADE SHOWS

- CASE HISTORY OF A MAIL ORDER SUCCESS
- MY BEST 35 MAIL ORDER LETTERS
- 23 TRADE SECRETS AND IDEAS
- HOW TO SELL YOUR PRODUCT OVERSEAS
- A SIMPLIFIED SYSTEM FOR KEEPING MAIL ORDER RECORDS
- HOW TO USE A BILLBOARD TO SELL YOURSELF AND YOUR BUSINESS

Preface, Introduction, Index

"The ideas in this book—and the practical, step-by-step system explained in detail—will give anyone who has an atom of persistence and creative imagination the key to financial independence in his own mail order business."

Elliott A. Meyer
President
NATIONAL DYNAMICS CORP.

"Joe Cossman is one of the two authentic geniuses I have met in 14 years in the business. Not only does he have an almost prophetic sense for picking winning items, even when they have been discarded as "worthless" by so-called experts, but he has an uncanny knack of squeezing the absolute maximum dollar profit out of each of them. If this book can convey even a fraction of 1% of his money-making ability, it will be worth 100 times its cost."

Eugene M. Schwartz
President
EXECUTIVE RESEARCH INSTITUTE, INC.

ABOUT THE AUTHOR Mention E. Joseph Cossman in mail order circles, and you get a reaction similar to mentioning Thomas Alva Edison to an electrical engineer. Joe Cossman is rightfully regarded as one of the "miracle men" of the field because of his amazing record of resounding successes.

Starting in his spare time, with a kitchen table for an "office", Joe Cossman built an international mail order empire that has made him a millionaire. He learned the ins and outs of mail order the hard way ... and you can benefit from his experience in these pages. Here Cossman tells you how he thought up—tested—marketed—produced—and sold his products. His mail order methods pulled an astounding total of *ten million sales* on six products alone—and that was just the beginning!

Today, Joe Cossman knows that anybody can find, advertise and sell a product in mail order. Capital—experience—even the product—all these are of secondary importance. The important thing is to know how to go about it—and that you will discover, spelled out in fascinating detail, in this book. Let this book be *your* first step towards starting your own company—in your spare time. In just a few years you may be wealthier than you ever dreamed!

30-DAY TRIAL PERIOD

As Joe Cossman says: "I know of no business in the world that requires such a small investment to start, and yet holds promise of such tremendous financial gains as mail order!"

The greatest business opportunities in the world today are in the booming field of mail order. That's the only field in which you can start small—with a minimum capital outlay—and build a fast-growing, money-making business right at home.

Joe Cossman, one of the biggest men in mail order, can tell you exactly how to do it. He shows you how to think up a product (with an infallible system responsible for his own list of successful products)—how to test the product—how to get lists—how to produce and sell the product ... and all of this can be done right in your own home!

Here are the professional "trade secrets" of a mail order giant who started small and wound up with one of the biggest mail order companies in America. He shows you how to do it, every step of the way. From getting the original idea, and writing the advertising, to how and which lists to rent, and where to get them. He details for you other successful mail order campaigns—shows you how other men started small and founded a booming business.

Cossman gives you valuable tips and pointers on how to produce your product inexpensively—and how you can branch out and develop new products.

If you've ever wanted to start your own business—here's the chance for you. Opportunities are actually unlimited in mail order. Nobodies have become millionaires overnight—and if anybody can show you how, Joe Cossman can.

If you follow his tested, fool-proof rules, you can start with little cash—working even in your spare time—and build a good income out of mail order. In a short time you can achieve the financial independence you have dreamed of ... and be your own boss, with your own business. This is your chance to break out of the old rut and hit the big time years earlier than you ever dreamed you would!

Contents

HOW I MADE $1,000,000 IN MAIL ORDER

tells how

YOU CAN MAKE $1,000,000 IN MAIL ORDER

WHAT THIS BOOK CAN DO FOR YOU

If you want to break out of the old rut—start your own business with little or no capital necessary—and be your own boss at last—mail order is the greatest business opportunity that can do this for you.

In this book I will show you how to think up a mail order product and test it inexpensively (following the advertising system given in these pages), produce it and market it. Starting with just one product, and working in your spare time or just on weekends, it is actually possible to bring in several thousand dollars a day in cash-in-advance orders!

That is what makes mail order the fastest-growing and most profit-making business in the world today. This book will show you how to go about it, from getting the first idea right on through to establishing an entire line of successful merchandise for your own mail order business.

I started out using the kitchen table as a desk and working on weekends while keeping my regular nine-to-five job. Today I own the office building in which I work and sit behind a $1,000 desk.

In these pages you'll discover how with common sense, imagination, and perseverance you can do the same, building a business with unlimited potential and adventure.

E. Joseph Cossman

MAIL NO-RISK TRIAL COUPON TODAY!

Please send your order to:
Melvin Powers
12015 Sherman Road
North Hollywood, California 91605

Gentlemen: Send me a copy of *How I Made $1,000,000 in Mail Order* by E. Joseph Cossman. $15.00 postpaid.

I will use this book for 30 days entirely at your risk. If I am not thoroughly pleased, I will simply return it for a full refund.

Enclosed is my check ( ) money order ( ) for $15.00.
California residents please send $16.07.

Name _____
(Please print)

Address _____

City _____ Zone _____ State _____

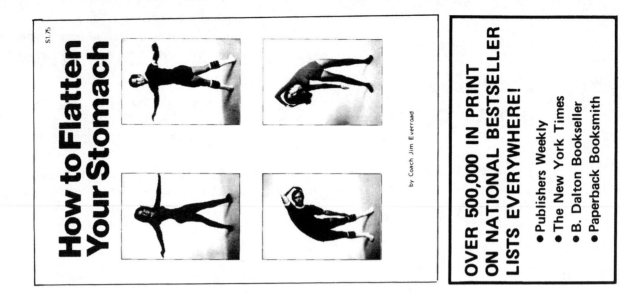

$1.75

How to Flatten Your Stomach

by Coach Jim Everroad

Paperback Best Sellers

MASS MARKET

Mass-market paperbacks are softcover books sold at newsstands, variety stores and supermarkets, as well as in bookstores. This listing is based on computer-processed reports from bookstores and representative wholesalers with more than 40,000 outlets across the United States.

1 **BLOODLINE**, by Sidney Sheldon. (Warner, $2.75.) Love and high financial intrigue on three continents: fiction.

2 **THE INSIDERS**, by Rosemary Rogers. (Avon, $2.50.) TV anchorwoman in the jungles of Los Angeles and New York: fiction.

3 **THE WOMEN'S ROOM**, by Marilyn French. (Jove/HBJ, $2.50.) A woman's rough road to liberation: fiction.

4 **MY MOTHER/MY SELF**, by Nancy Friday. (Dell, $2.50.) A discussion of the mother-daughter relationship.

5 **THE BLACK MARBLE**, by Joseph Wambaugh. (Dell, $2.50.) Cops and dognappers in Southern California: fiction.

6 **FINAL PAYMENTS**, by Mary Gordon. (Ballantine, $2.50.) After her father's death, a Queens girl comes to terms with herself: fiction.

7 **THE HOLCROFT COVENANT**, by Robert Ludlum. (Bantam, $2.75.) Nazi scheme to found a Fourth Reich: fiction.

8 **COMPROMISING POSITIONS**, by Susan Isaacs. (Jove/HBJ, $2.25.) Mystery and scandal in suburban Long Island: fiction.

9 **GOODBYE CALIFORNIA**, by Alistair MacLean. (Fawcett/Crest, $2.50.) Muslim plot to heave the state into the sea: fiction.

10 **THE HUMAN FACTOR**, by Graham Greene. (Avon, $2.50.) Spy novel with the Greene touch.

11 **THE AMITYVILLE HORROR**, by Jay Anson. (Bantam, $2.50.) Suburban haunted house.

12 **THE THORN BIRDS**, by Colleen McCullough. (Avon, $2.50.) Australian family saga: fiction.

13 **MIDNIGHT EXPRESS**, by Billy Hayes with William Hoffer. (Fawcett/Popular, $2.25.) Tie-in with the current film about an American jailed in Turkey for smuggling hashish.

14 **CENTENNIAL**, by James A. Michener. (Fawcett/Crest, $2.95.) Colorado from prehistory to the present day: fiction.

15 **THE IMMIGRANTS**, by Howard Fast. (Dell, $2.75.) Ambition and love in turn-of-the-century San Francisco: fiction.

TRADE

Trade paperbacks are softcover books usually sold in bookstores and at an average price higher than mass-market paperbacks. This listing is based on computer-processed reports from bookstores and wholesalers with more than 2,500 outlets across the United States.

1 **HOW TO FLATTEN YOUR STOMACH**, by Jim Everroad. (Price/Stern/Sloan, $1.75.) Exercises.

2 **THE DIETER'S GUIDE TO WEIGHT LOSS DURING SEX**, by Richard Smith. (Workman, $2.95.) Spoof on diet and sex manuals.

3 **JULIA CHILD & COMPANY**, by Julia Child. (Knopf, $8.95.) Recipes for dishes featured on her current television series.

4 **THE PEOPLE'S ALMANAC 2**, by David Wallechinsky and Irving Wallace. (Bantam, $9.95.) More odd facts from all over.

5 **THE JOY OF SEX**, by Alex Comfort. (Simon & Schuster/Fireside, $6.95.) With illustrations.

6 **THE CROWD PLEASERS**, by Rosemary Rogers. (Avon, $3.95.) High life in the worlds of politics, fashion and film-making: fiction.

7 **THE NON-RUNNER'S BOOK**, by Vic Ziegel and Lewis Grossberger. (Macmillan, $2.95.) Celebrating the joys of sitting.

8 **MURPHY'S LAW**, by Arthur Bloch. (Price/Stern/Sloan, $2.50.) Humorous explanations of why things go wrong.

9 **WHAT COLOR IS YOUR PARACHUTE?** by Richard Nelson Bolles. (Ten Speed Press, $5.95.) Guide for job-hunters and career-changers.

10 **THE COMPLETE GUIDE TO DISCO DANCING**, by Karen Lustgarten. (Warner, $4.95.) Illustrated exercise and dance guide.

11 **OUR BODIES, OURSELVES**, by the Boston Women's Health Book Collective. (Simon & Schuster/Touchstone, $4.95.) Illustrated guide.

12 **THE WOMAN'S DRESS FOR SUCCESS BOOK**, by John T. Molloy. (Warner, $3.95.) How-to.

13 **DOONESBURY'S GREATEST HITS**, by G. B. Trudeau. (Holt, $7.95.) Selections from the cartoon strip.

14 **OURSELVES AND OUR CHILDREN**, by the Boston Women's Health Book Collective. (Random House, $6.95.) The pleasures and problems of being a parent.

15 **A YEAR OF BEAUTY AND HEALTH**, by Beverly and Vidal Sassoon with Camille Duhé. (Simon & Schuster/Fireside, $4.95.) How to eat, exercise, reduce, etc.

How to Flatten Your Tush

$2

by Coach Marge Reardon

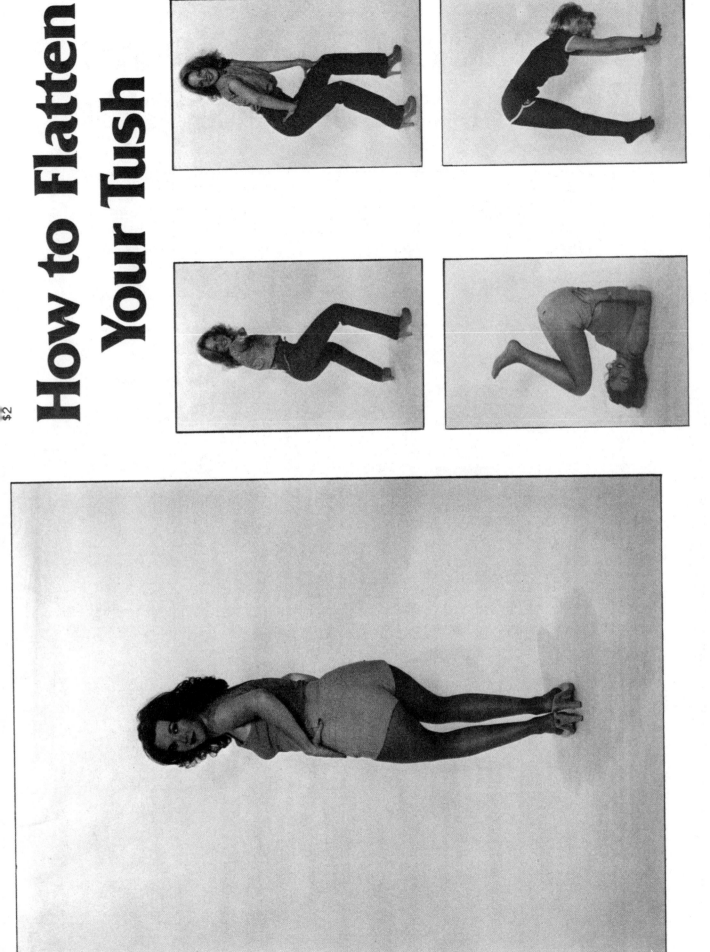

ISBN 0-87980-369-X

79

The Amazing Diet Secret Of A Desperate Housewife

My name is Nancy Pryor. I am 35 years old. I am a housewife and mother of three children. I would like to tell you something personal about myself.

One day last September I just broke down and started to cry.

I couldn't help it. I had reached my breaking point. I felt like I was going to have a nervous breakdown.

It happened one Monday morning right after I got on the bathroom scales to weigh myself. I had been on a strict diet for nearly 2 months. I had gone off the diet over the weekend to give myself a break and just to live like a normal human being for a couple of days. Now the scales said I weighed 188 pounds. I just couldn't believe it! That meant that in one lousy weekend I had more than gained back every single pound I had lost in the last 3 weeks.

Maybe this doesn't sound like a big deal to you, but to me it felt like a tragedy.

I had been trying to lose weight for the last 5½ years. I had tried liquid protein. I had tried fasting. I had tried hypnosis. I had tried exercise. I had tried sauna belts. For a while I even used dangerous diet drugs. As far as diets go I tried almost every one I heard about. The Adkins diet. The Stillman diet. The grapefruit diet. The Women's Ski Team diet. Etc. Etc. You name it — I tried it.

The results were always the same. I would struggle and struggle to lose a few pounds and then the very first time I would give myself a small break the weight would come right back on.

It had happened many times before, but somehow this time it seemed like the last straw. I didn't know where to turn or what else to try. I was about to give up.

Don't get me wrong. I don't want this to sound like a sob story. I'm not telling you all this because I want you to feel sorry for me. There is no need for that anyway. My story has a **very** happy ending.

My story has a happy ending because the very next day I made a discovery that has changed my entire life. I found an amazing way to lose weight that I never dreamed existed.

I **am** not going to tell you where I found this secret. However, I will tell you this much: I **did not** get this information from a doctor. I **did not** get this information from a diet book. I **did not** find this information in a magazine. I **did not** find this information in a newspaper. I **did not** get this information from any of the so-called "diet experts."

To tell the truth, I stumbled across this information totally by accident when I was looking for something else.

But all that doesn't matter. What does matter is that at last I have found an answer.

Let me tell you why I think my diet secret is so fantastic.

MELTS FAT FAST

First of all, this diet works fast. It literally burns off fat by the hour. If you go on this diet in the morning you will be losing weight before lunch. You will lose weight faster on this diet than if you ran 7 miles every day. You will be able to measure the difference in your waistline in 24 to 36 hours. I think this is the fastest safe diet in the world. If you can find a diet that works faster I will buy it from you and gladly pay you good money for it.

NO HUNGER

I'll tell you a secret. You will never lose weight and keep it off on **any** diet that leaves you hungry. Hunger is an irresistible force. Sooner or later, willpower always gives in to hunger. This diet brings hunger to a dead full stop. You will never be hungry. As a matter of fact, one of the unique features of this diet, makes it metabolically **impossible** for you to experience hunger. To me, it's like heaven.

76% MORE ENERGY

This diet converts body fat to body fuel. Starting on the 5th day of this diet your energy will begin to increase dramatically. It will increase every day until the 9th day when it begins to level off. After that your energy level will stay about the same. This new energy level will probably be about 76% higher than your level is now.

> *"... You will lose weight faster on this diet than if you ran 7 miles every day. You will be able to measure the difference in your waist line in 24 to 36 hours. I think this is the fastest **safe** diet in the world. If you can find a diet that works faster I will buy it from you and gladly pay you good money for it ..."*

SIMPLE AND EASY

This diet is very simple. It is easy to follow even if you eat in restaurants all the time. You do not count calories. You do not measure portions. The only thing you keep track of is how much you lose.

HEALTHY AND SAFE

This is not just a weight loss diet. It is a health diet also. It is safe. It is probably much safer than the way you eat right now.

Don't **ever** take a chance with your health. It's not worth it. Besides it is not necessary. You can lose weight fast with my diet **plus** get healthier every day you stay on it.

NO EXERCISE

You do not have to exercise to lose weight with this diet. However, since after the first few days you will have a lot more energy you will probably become more active. But you will lose weight very rapidly whether you become more active or not.

AUTOMATIC WEIGHT LOSS

Right after you go on this diet you start to lose weight automatically. You don't have to think about it all the time. Since you are never hungry you would probably forget you were on a diet if you weren't losing weight so fast.

As you can tell by now, I have come up with something pretty good. I think my diet is the best way to lose weight I have every heard about. You will lose weight very fast and you will never be hungry. You will not have to count calories or measure portions. You can eat out as often as you like. Your health will improve and your energy will increase. Except for when you weigh yourself you will probably forget you are on a diet.

In short, this diet is fast, safe and simple.

There are four reasons this diet works so well. These four reasons make this diet different from any other. Here are those reasons.

Reason #1 This diet makes liberal use of a natural food substance that eliminates hunger. This food substance is widely used in Europe but almost unheard of in the United States. It looks and tastes exactly like table sugar. You use it the same way. You can mix it in your coffee or sprinkle it on cereals or use it in recipes as a substitute for table sugar. This substance is perfectly safe. Remember — it is a food **not** a drug. It is much better for you than ordinary table sugar (sucrose) because it does not provoke an insulin response. When eaten regularly throughout the day this substance very dramatically reduces hunger. It also has a soothing effect on jangled nerves.

Reason #2 This diet has a different plan of attack. This diet forces you to form a very new habit. This new habit is pleasurable and fun. This habit makes it possible to stay on any diet for life without ever feeling deprived. This new habit makes everything easy. It is so simple you will wonder why you never thought of it yourself.

Reason #3 This diet contains 5 delicious foods that may very well be new to you. I am going to ask you to eat at least one of these 5 foods every day.

> *"... I have lost 75 pounds. My friends say I look 15 years younger. I enjoy a peace of mind I have never before experienced. I feel good all the time. Best of all, my husband has fallen in love with me all over again."*

All of them are what I call "natural food tranquilizers." At exactly the same time these foods are releasing new energy into your system they also work to release all tension from your nerves and muscles and give you an emotional lift. Believe me it is very hard to diet if you are upset and in a bad mood all the time!

Reason #4 This diet contains yet another unique food substance that releases the natural fat burning power of your system. This substance increases the amount of calories your body burns each day thereby allowing you to eat more without weight gain.

A SPARKLING NEW BODY

This diet has been a Godsend to me. I have a sparkling new body. I have lost 75 pounds. I now weigh 113 and I wear a size 6 dress. (I used to wear an 18). I have more energy now than I had when I was a teenager. I am in better health than I can ever remember. My friends say I look 15 years younger. I enjoy a peace of mind I have never before experienced. I feel good all the time. Best of all, my husband has fallen in love with me all over again.

Will this amazing little diet work for you? I am sure it will. All I ask is that you be open-minded enough to give me a chance to prove it even though I am an everyday housewife and not a diet doctor or anything like that.

I have written a book that tells you about my secret diet. It is easy-to-read. It tells you exactly what to do step-by-step. You can read my book in one evening. Then the very next day you can start losing weight so fast you just won't believe it.

NO RISK

Here's how you can read my book and try my diet without any financial risk at all. Go ahead and order my book by mail. Keep it 30 days and read it and check it out. Then if you are unhappy with it, send it back and I will return your payment to you quietly and without question.

If you are extra skeptical I suggest you postdate your check or money order by 30 days. I promise and guarantee I will not deposit it for a least that amount of time. Then if you decide to return my book I will send back your **uncashed** check or money order with no questions asked.

To order, write your name and address and the words "DIET SECRET" on a piece of paper and send it with $10.00 to me - Nancy Pryor. Dept. 168, 161 Maplewood Ave., P.O. Box 177, Maplewood, New Jersey 07040. I will send your book promptly by return mail. If you have any questions you can call me. My number is (201) 744-3777. Checks and money orders should be made payable to me - Nancy Pryor. (It is not a good idea to mail cash).

CHOOSE YOUR LOVER

HOW TO MEET AND DATE BEAUTIFUL WOMEN

You've seen ordinary guys who always seem to have sensational chicks to date. Have you ever wondered how the "other guy" manages to compile an up-to-date address book with an endless variety of live numbers to choose from? Well, it's no secret anymore. Starting now you can have all the action you could want.

JUST A PART OF THE AMAZING KNOWLEDGE YOU CAN GAIN FROM THIS BOOK

• How to turn the female's relentless trait of curiosity into a weapon that drives her to you like a super-charged leopard. • **What women look for most in a man.** • How to be so great on dates women will want to be with you again and again. • **Seduction techniques that warm up even the coldest girl and make her beg for more.** • Foolproof conversation techniques that make talking to any girl easy and remove forever the problem of not knowing what to say. • **How even a shy insecure man can handle women with dynamite confidence.** • The single most important secret for scoring with any type of girl. • **How to be so sexy, gorgeous chicks will be dying to get into bed with you.** • How to read those "special female signals" that tell you when to take her.

If you are a male with a strong desire to make out with the kind of beautiful women you see pictured on this page then this is the book for you. It's not just a storehouse of important facts and information but a complete and totally involved lesson-plan that outlines each step independently from the moment you first see her until she is eagerly satisfying your every desire.

A SMALL SAMPLE OF WHAT YOU'LL LEARN

• A simple rule that will triple the dates you get. • **Techniques that make picking up girls so easy anyone can do it.** • How to send subtle messages to a girl you've just met that let her know you are a dynamite lover. • **How to arrange to be introduced to exactly the right type of girl.** • How to radiate the kind of male magnetism women find irresistable. • **How an average guy can get dates with exceptionally desirable women.** • How to make a girl believe you are exactly the type of man she wants in her life. • **How to pick up sensational ladies without even trying.** • How to instantly draw romantic interest from girls you've never met before. • **How to convince "hard to get" girls to date you.** • How men who aren't good looking can become more sexually attractive than most handsome men will ever be. • **How to get pretty girls to take the initiative to try to meet you.**

Whatever your type, I have the technique to help you score. You know who you want, and my step-by-step instructions show you how to get her. The key to meeting and picking up beautiful women is a close as your mailbox.

Yes — send me. . . . . copies in a plain unmarked wrapper @ $8.95 plus $1.00 postage and handling. No COD's please. Money back guarantee. I am over 21 and am enclosing a ☐ check; ☐ money order.

Name. . . . .

Street. . . . .

City. . . . .

State . . . . .Zip . . . .

265

109

Electronic Invention Turn House Wires into Giant TV Antenna

MAKE THIS ONE MINUTE TEST
of an amazing new kind of TV antenna!

BEFORE

AFTER

Check these Super Features!

- Latest Model
- Safe! Improved!
- No Tools Needed!
- No Shock Hazard
- No Rabbit Ears!
- Installs in 1 Minute
- Works on New TV'S
- Works on Old TV'S

If worn, damaged, roof-top antennas or malfunctioning rabbit ears give you muddy, jittery TV reception, don't junk your old, worthy TV set! Restore its **RECEPTION POWER** with the latest, improved, **SUPER 77 ANTENNA** by Convertamatic. This invention, tested and proven in homes all over America, pulls in your favorite local programs, so sharp and clear, you won't believe your eyes and ears. **YES!** Crisp black and white, or vibrant color reception — without those frustrating rooftop or rabbit ear antennas!

HIGH RECEPTION POWER!

SUPER 77 ANTENNA is quite different from regular antennas — even the rotating type selling for $50.00 or more! Plug the **SUPER 77** into any outlet and it instantly changes your house wires into a **GIANT ANTENNA hundreds of feet long!** Yet it doesn't interfere with your electric current and never presents any shock hazard. It doesn't use up a penny's worth of electricity.

LASTS A LIFETIME

POWER 77 costs nothing to install ... nothing to operate. Has no moving parts to wear out. **Lasts a lifetime.** Yet costs less than a carton of cigarettes!

INSTALLS IN SECONDS!

No tools needed. Connect and plug into the nearest outlet and it's ready to operate instantly! This **IMPROVED MODEL** is perfectly **SAFE**. Plug has a **NEUTRALIZER** that effectively **BLOCKS OUT** electric current. It gets attached **OUTSIDE** the set. A shock is **impossible.** Yet it works fine!

SHARPER PICTURES!
RICHER COLOR!

Even older, functioning sets work better with a **SUPER 77 CONVERTAMATIC!** This invention harnesses hundreds and hundreds of feet of house wiring — converting it instantly into a **GIANT TV ANTENNA!** Naturally this gives you better reception on all local channels. Better pictures! Better sound! Richer, more brilliant color! So don't throw out your old reliable TV, just replace the old antenna with a genuine **SUPER 77 CONVERTAMATIC!** The moment you plug it in, you'll see the amazing difference!

TRY IT 30 FULL DAYS
WITHOUT RISKING 1¢

Why let an old, defective antenna spoil your TV fun? Send only 3.97 plus 82 cents postage and handling. When it arrives, get ready for a thrilling surprise! Suddenly fade-outs, streaks and ghosts are gone. All replaced by gloriously beautiful pictures! Even color and sound improve. Say goodbye to dangerous outdoor antennas and the high cost of needless antenna repairs! Enjoy **SUPER 77** for 30 days at our risk. Complete satisfaction guaranteed or your money back. **CAUTION:** Avoid cheap imitations! Get guaranteed, high quality **Super 77** today! Send handy coupon below for fast service!

Consumer Product Information

For best results use one **Power 77 Antenna** for **each** TV set or FM radio in your home. **Notice** extra savings on multiple orders. NOTE: You do not have to remove old rooftop antenna when using the Power 77.

CONVERTAMATIC DIVISION—1231-C
2425 Coles Sta., Fort Lauderdale, Florida 33303

FREE HOME TRIAL

BEWARE OF CHEAP IMITATIONS

CAUTION: Certain low cost, badly assembled models have been declared unsafe by the U.S. Consumer Protection Bureau. Trust Convertamatic quality product with a **NEUTRALIZER PLUG**

Now Display a "Lifetime" of Favorite Photos in the desk space of one!

only $4⁹⁸ *(we've seen a similar design in a 1977 gift catalog priced at an incredible $34.95!)*

No mounting or gluing – just slip photos in

Accepts sizes up to 3½" x 5"

Windows to hold 100 photos included

Capacity 500 photos – Extra windows available

Why leave these great photos buried in an album, or lost in a drawer? Now you can locate and admire [an]y of 500 photos simply by turning a knob! **Yet this ex[cit]ing FOTO-ROLL actually takes fewer square inches [of] table or desk space than a single unframed snapshot!** [Fo]r home or office — great gift idea too! Now relive all [tho]se vacation trips and fun times at the touch of a [fin]ger. A treasured gift for relatives, special friends, [esp]ecially grandparents, when filled with snapshots of [the] new baby or family activities.

[An] incredible bargain — you be the judge! What's the [dif]ference between our $4.98 model and that $34.95 [mo]del in the gift catalog? Well, theirs is made of plexi-[gl]ass — ours is crystal clear lucite. Theirs holds 600 [ph]otos, ours holds 500. For $34.95 they include windows [for] 240 photos and for $4.98 we only include 100. But [we]'ll sell you as many extras as you want at $1.50 per [se]t. Each set holds 60 photos, so figure it out for your-[se]lf! What's more, if you're not delighted with your order [in] every way, simply return it within 14 days and we'll [ref]und your money (except postage & handling). Mail [no]-risk coupon today!

ACT NOW! Get a FREE MYSTERY GIFT! worth up to $5⁰⁰ with each order while supply lasts! MAIL COUPON TODAY

111

AMAZING "30 YEAR KNIFE"

No Other Kitchen Knife You Can Own Is Backed By This Incredible Refund Policy:

"Butcher saw" edge cuts through the heaviest bone

Stainless steel blade for years of superb cutlery service

Clean-cutting chopping edge trims and minces delicate food neat and fast

Razor edge serrations slice fish, meat, and vegetables paper thin

Blunt safety edges won't cut your hand

Stainless steel rivets won't burst or tarnish

Molded grain, dishwasher-safe impact-resistant handle gives you the surest grip ever

Start using the "30 Year Knife" in your own kitchen now and if anytime in the next 30 years you're willing to part with it, we'll buy it back — no questions asked!

- No sharpening needed
- Overall length 10 inches

PLOWS THROUGH BIG TURKEY BONES

SLICES OVER-RIPE TOMATOES WAFER THIN

MINCES DELICATE HERBS IN SECONDS

Sound incredible? Not if you've seen this dishwasher-safe knife plow through big turkey bones . . . slice over-ripe tomatoes paper thin . . . mince delicate herbs in seconds — all without any sharpening!

The secret is the knife's super-durable blade of razor-sharp stainless steel. Forged and edged by masters, each must pass the most demanding inspectors before being exported for our exclusive distribution.

We've seen expensive look-alikes selling on New York's Madison Avenue at outlandish prices. How then, you ask, can we offer you the genuine stainless "30 Year Knife" for the unheard of price of just $4.95?

The answer lies in the massive economic power that we have as one of the nation's largest shop-by-mail retailers. Thousands will buy from this ad and make it possible for us to sell to you at this incredible price.

ORDER NOW, WHILE THIS AD IS RUNNING! GET YOURS AT OUR UNBELIEVABLE $4.95 PRICE!

DON'T BE FOOLED INTO PAYING RIDICULOUSLY OUTRAGEOUS PRICES FOR AN EXPENSIVE LOOK-ALIKE!

NOW!
GENUINE STAINLESS STEEL

FOR ONLY **$4.95**

113

GEAR TREATMENT FOR MANUAL TRANSMISSIONS

- Formulated with PTFE resins for long anti-wear protection
- Reduces friction and drag
- Lowers operating temperatures
- Extends gear life...cuts maintenance downtime
- Makes shifting easier, smoother
- Extra protection in high-stress conditions

Formulated with PTFE resins.

Slick 50 Gear Treatment from Petrolon is a remarkably superior formulation unlike any manual transmission lubricant. It is specially formulated with super-slippery PTFE resins that bond an incredible micro-thin layer of lubrication to working metal parts, significantly reducing friction, drag and heat build-up—the prime causes of transmission breakdowns.

Smoother, quieter, easier shifting.

This amazing lubricant blends thoroughly with gear oils, to provide a high new level of gear lubrication impossible to achieve with conventional products. Performance resulting from the noticeably-reduced friction and drag include smoother, quieter, cooler running gears. Users repeatedly report that the treatment has shown to quiet noisy, hot-running transmissions. Almost immediately noted is a new, effortless ease in shifting gears.

Extended transmission life.

Because Slick 50 Gear Treatment bonds to moving metal parts, it protects against dangerous metal-to-metal grinding and wear. Obvious benefits are extended gear and bearing life, fewer costly repairs and transmission replacements, less downtime.

Extra protection during hot/cold extremes & stresses.

This bonding protection is especially important during scorching and frigid conditions. These are periods when the best transmission oils lose lubricating properties, exposing gears and bearings to excessive wear.

Similarly, the Slick 50 treatment is especially effective where equipment is subjected to heavy load stresses or around-the-clock operational demands.

Used worldwide with satisfaction.

Millions of satisfied car/truck owners, countless fleet maintenance supervisors, both in the U.S. and abroad, report important benefits from using a Slick 50 treatment. They recommend and use this gear treatment in transmissions, transfer cases and differentials of various vehicles and equipment, including:

Automobiles	Construction equipment
Trucks	Farm machinery
Tractors	Industrial gear applications

Recommendations.

Change gear oil whenever possible. Refill with quality lubricant allowing for addition of the recommended amount of Slick 50. See container label for recommendations. DO NOT OVERFILL. Re-treat as needed.

CAUTION: DO NOT USE IN AUTOMATIC TRANSMISSIONS OR GEAR BOXES WITH ALL METAL CLUTCH PLATES.

SLICK 50®

AUTOMATIC TRANSMISSION TREATMENT

- Makes shifting easier and quieter
- Reduces transmission wear
- Lowers transmission operating temperatures
- Keeps seals soft and pliable to help prevent leaks
- Extends transmission life

Specially Formulated.
Slick 50 Automatic Transmission Treatment from Petrolon is specially formulated for use in all automatic transmissions to produce smoother operation and extended life. The results are significantly reduced wear and lower operating temperatures—the prime causes of transmission breakdowns and costly repair.

Smoother, quieter transmissions.
Slick 50 all but eliminates rough shift change patterns. Shifting is noticeably smoother and quieter, especially with older, noisier running systems.

Less need to drain fluid.
This amazing lubricant blends thoroughly with any transmission fluid, improving its thermal stability and increases its service life. Because of the lasting lubricating properties of Slick 50, there's less need to drain or replace transmission fluid.

Replenishes fluids & anti-wear additives.
Slick 50, in fact, replenishes all critical transmission fluid components. These include: anti-wear agents, anti-oxidants, dispersants/detergents, corrosion inhibitors, anti-foam agents, viscosity index improvers, seal swelling agents and low-temperature fluidity modifiers. And keeps seals soft and pliable to help eliminate leaks.

Extra protection in hot/cold stresses.
The ever-present protection of Slick 50 is especially important with vehicles driven in sustained hot conditions, when conventional fluid can overheat and lose its lubricating properties. Similarly, Slick 50 gives extra protection in cold extremes when sluggish fluid can expose gears and bearings to the dangers of wear.

Extended transmission life.
No other transmission product delivers the unique lubricant properties of Slick 50, which pay-off in extended service-life of the system. In addition, Slick 50 works to curb oxidation, corrosion, rust and sludge formations. Obvious long-term dividends include fewer costly repairs or transmission replacements and less downtime.

Many applications.
Slick 50 Automatic Transmission Treatment can be used in hydraulic systems—including power steering—of various vehicles and equipment, including the following:

Automobiles   Construction equipment   Light trucks   Farm machinery   Tractors

100% Money-Back Guarantee Order Form

SLICK 50 - Dept. 2
12015 Sherman Road
North Hollywood, CA 91605

Please send me:

___ One bottle (8 FL OZ) of SLICK 50 AUTOMATIC TRANSMISSION TREATMENT at $14.95 plus $2.95 shipping & handling.

___ Two bottles of SLICK 50 AUTOMATIC TRANSMISSION TREATMENT at $29.90. Free shipping.

California residents please add $1.01 per bottle sales tax.
Please make your check or money order payable to SLICK 50.

Name (PLEASE PRINT) _____

Address (FOR UPS DELIVERY) _____

City _____ State _____ Zip _____

SLICK 50 ®

115

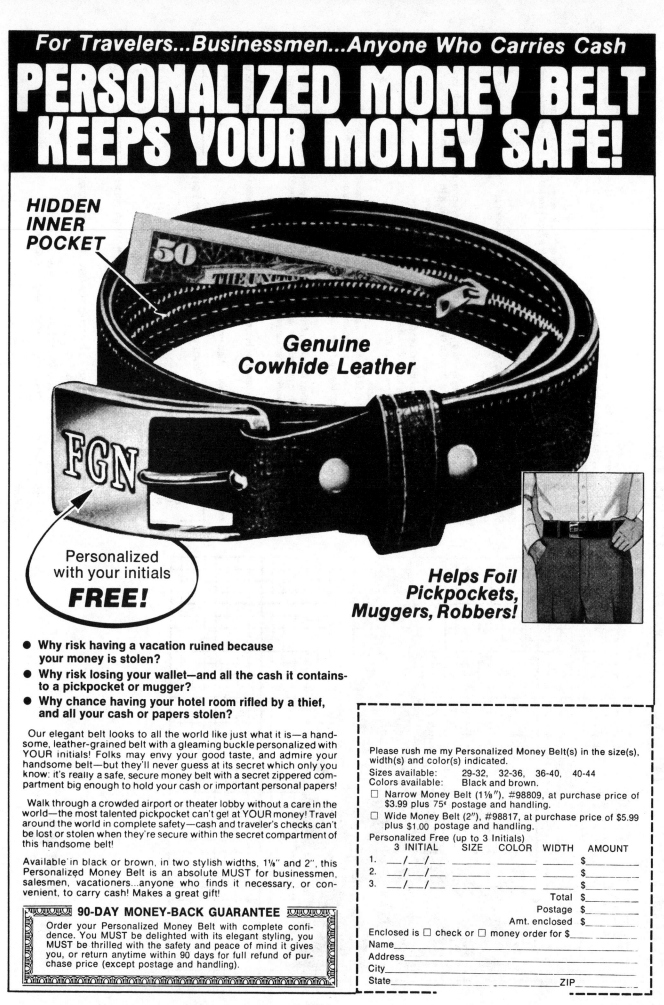

12015 Sherman Road
No. Hollywood, CA 91605

(818) 765-8579
FAX (818) 765-2922

ONE-MINUTE RADIO COMMERCIAL FOR *PSYCHO-CYBERNETICS*

Have you read *Psycho-Cybernetics*? If you haven't, you should! As reported by the *New York Times*, *Psycho-Cybernetics* has attained the distinction of ranking high among the all-time bestsellers. And not without reason. This brilliant, uplifting treatment of the new science of self-image psychology is without peer in the self-improvement field. Dr. Maxwell Maltz, the book's distinguished author, gives you his twentieth century technique for using the subconscious mind to help you develop your full potential. *Psycho-Cybernetics* is designed to help you discover your total capacities—those reserves of strength, talent, and ability that you are not using to the utmost, or that you may not even know you possess. The emphasis is on finding your hidden capabilities and developing them to a degree that will lead to a more vital, creative, and satisfying life. This amazing scientific innovation impels you, the reader, to program constructive suggestions into your subconscious that will work wonders for you.

Does is sound exciting? Well it is! And the theory, technique, and applications are yours in this practical guide for successful living.

Psycho-Cybernetics by Dr. Maxwell Maltz is in stock and available at your local bookstore for only $10.00. Or send $12.00 to Success Book, Radio Station_____ _City_____. Remember, *Psycho-Cybernetics* by Maxwell Maltz, M.D. is in stock and available at bookstores and newsstands everywhere. Or send $12.00 to Success Book, Radio Station_____ City_____. You'll be glad you did.

BEHIND THE BEST SELLERS
By Herbert Mitgang

Richard Smith ✓

Smith.

At last count, there were 3,000 diet books, 2,000 self-improvement treatises and 1,000 sex manuals, give or take a few hundred. Inevitably, someone had to come along to combine the three categories in one all-purpose book called "The Dieter's Guide to Weight Loss During Sex," — as Richard Smith has, in his new trade paperback best seller from Workman Publishing Company.

Included in the book are a "Height Report" for men and women (if you weigh 271 to 285 pounds, your partner ought to be 7 feet 7 inches tall), data about weight loss resulting from various sexual plays and ploys. For readers in a hurry, there's a pocket calorie counter with the book that gives information about sex and fat. Examples: Seducing partner if you are shy (15 calories); if you are rich (5 calories); if you are poor (164 calories).

Richard Smith, the 37-year-old author, who stands "6 feet 1 and change," says he was a 256-pound weakling until he discovered that shedding pounds in the most interesting way devised by mankind could bring him fame and a best seller. He now weighs 198.

Mr. Smith grew up on a farm in Parksville, N. Y., in the northern Catskills. In his youth, he worked as a busboy and waiter at resort hotels. He became "a good eater" while serving four meals a day (the fourth was a "midnight snack"), sampling between the kitchen and dining hall. The germ of the idea for the book was nurtured on the Borscht Circuit.

He discovered that waiting on tables for the big eaters and small tippers ("doctors and dentists — the worst") was not his glass of tea. But the Catskills, as one or two *tummlers* before him learned, were the mother lode for a would-be humorist; where no one was a straight man and anyone worth a half-sour pickle had to make out where it really counted — in the dining room and casino.

Mr. Smith went on to Orange County Community College, in Middletown, N. Y., where his main activity was playing the trombone in his own dance band. He became a dropout, drove a tractor-trailer for Pepsi-Cola, enrolled as an executive trainee at Alexander's department store in Manhattan and worked his way up to women's underwear buyer, became publicity director for an association whose aim was to persuade men to dress better. Somewhere along the line he was married once, a state of grace that no longer binds him. He is now a full-time humorist for several magazines.

Four years ago he devised a poster, "The Sensuous Dieter's Guide to Weight Loss During Sex." Privately printed, it sold tens of thousands of copies. The book, his first, followed inevitably.

Mr. Smith keeps in trim, for the most part, not as one might imagine from the author of "The Dieter's Guide to Weight Loss During Sex," but by running 60 miles a week in Central Park. He has to, because his favorite foods are pizza and halvah — "God, do I love halvah." He's been running for 11 years and is now preparing for a New York marathon. "There are two kinds of runners," he says, "the real ones and the civilians."

Mr. Smith is now working on a sequel to his book for Workman, in addition to other books. Two may turn out to be fiction: "About a man who is terribly afraid of women, and what will be the first Jewish Gothic. I've already got the title — 'The Isle of Murray.'"

His main activities now are writing, running and "keeping company with nice women." He was mortified when a woman reader proposed that they try out some of the weight-reduction activities in his book. "I said, 'Of course not,' but I took her telephone number, anyway." You can take the boy out of the Catskills, but not the busboy. ■

Paperback Best Sellers

MASS MARKET

Mass-market paperbacks are softcover books sold at newsstands, variety stores and supermarkets, as well as in bookstores. This listing is based on computer-processed reports from bookstores and representative wholesalers with more than 40,000 outlets across the United States.

1 **THE THORN BIRDS,** by Colleen McCullough. (Avon, $2.50.) Australian family saga: fiction.

2 **JAWS 2,** by Hank Searls. (Bantam, $2.25.) Female great white shark returns to familiar waters.

3 **THE LAWLESS,** by John Jakes. (Jove/HBJ, $2.25.) The Kent family saga reaches the glittering, corrupt 1890's.

4 **LOOKING OUT FOR #1,** by Robert J. Ringer. (Fawcett/Crest, $2.50.) Getting yours.

5 **TWINS,** by Bari Wood and Jack Geasland. (NAL/Signet, $2.50.) Twin doctors and their relationship in life and death: fiction.

6 **DAMIEN Omen II,** by Joseph Howard. (NAL/Signet, $1.95.) Evil child returns; sequel to "The Omen."

7 **THE INVESTIGATION,** by Dorothy Uhnak. (Pocket, $2.50.) Woman accused of murdering her children: fiction.

8 **THE BASTARD,** by John Jakes. (Jove, $2.25.) First book in the Kent family chronicles: basis of the recent TV series.

9 **THE DRAGONS OF EDEN,** by Carl Sagan. (Ballantine, $2.25.) How intelligence evolved.

10 **THE PROMISE,** by Danielle Steel. (Dell, $1.95.) Lovers separated by a tragic set of circumstances: fiction.

11 **CONDOMINIUM,** by John D. MacDonald. (Fawcett/Crest, $2.25.) Disaster hits a Florida key: fiction.

12 **DELTA OF VENUS,** by Anaïs Nin. (Bantam, $2.50.) Elegant erotica written for a wealthy patron: fiction.

13 **YOUR ERRONEOUS ZONES,** by Wayne W. Dyer. (Avon, $2.25.) Self-help pep talk.

14 **LOVE'S DARING DREAM,** by Patricia Matthews. (Pinnacle, $2.25.) From the Irish potato famine to romance in the Pacific Northwest: romantic fiction.

15 **SPLINTER OF THE MIND'S EYE,** by Alan Dean Foster. (Ballantine/Del Rey, $1.95.) The further adventures of Luke ("Star Wars") Skywalker.

TRADE

Trade paperbacks are softcover books usually sold in bookstores and at an average price higher than mass-market paperbacks. This listing is based on computer-processed reports from bookstores and wholesalers with more than 2,500 outlets across the United States.

1 **THE COMPLETE RUNNER,** by the Editors of Runner's World Magazine. (Avon, $4.95.) Advice by professionals.

✓ 2 **THE DIETER'S GUIDE TO WEIGHT LOSS DURING SEX,** by Richard Smith. (Workman, $2.95.) Spoof on diet and sex manuals.

3 **CROCKETT'S VICTORY GARDEN,** by James Underwood Crockett. (Little, Brown, $9.95.) Month-by-month guide.

4 **THE RUNNER'S HANDBOOK,** by Bob Glover and Jack Shepherd. (Penguin, $3.95.) Fitness guide for men and women.

5 **THE AUDUBON SOCIETY FIELD GUIDE TO NORTH AMERICAN BIRDS (Eastern Region)** by John Bull and John Farrand Jr. (Knopf, $7.95.) Illustrated.

6 **THE PEOPLE'S PHARMACY,** by Joe Graedon. (Avon, $3.95.) Guide to prescriptions, over-the-counter drugs and home remedies.

7 **THE JOY OF SEX,** by Alex Comfort. (Simon & Schuster/Fireside, $6.95.) With illustrations.

8 **STALKING THE PERFECT TAN,** by G. B. Trudeau. (Holt, Rinehart & Winston, $1.95.) Shifting political winds caught in cartoon form.

9 **ON DEATH AND DYING,** by Dr. Elisabeth Kübler-Ross. (Macmillan, $2.25.) Lessons to be learned from the terminally ill.

10 **OUR BODIES, OURSELVES,** by the Boston Women's Health Book Collective. (Simon & Schuster/Touchstone, $4.95.) Illustrated guide.

11 **THE TAMING OF THE C.A.N.D.Y. MONSTER** by Vicki Lansky. (Meadowbrook Press, Wayzata, Minn., $3.95.) Warning about "Continuously Advertised Nutritionally Deficient Yummies."

12 **IRELAND: A Terrible Beauty,** by Jill and Leon Uris. (Bantam, $7.95.) A "love song" in words and photographs.

13 **SHANNA,** by Kathleen Woodiwiss. (Avon, $3.95.) A stormy marriage: historical romance.

14 **BORN TO WIN,** by Muriel James and Dorothy Jongeward. (Addison-Wesley, $5.95.) How to apply Transactional Analysis.

15 **LIVE LONGER NOW,** by Jon N. Leonard, J. L. Hofer and Nathan Pritikin. (Grosset & Dunlap/Today Press, $2.95.) Diet-and-exercise regime.

PAPERBACK TALK

Continued from Page 19
women's historical romances.

Stomach flattener. Every year a thousand brave souls publish books of their own composition and attempt to sell them by mail or on consignment through bookstores. Every year several of them have a stroke of luck and achieve bestsellerdom. A recent example is Vicki Lansky's "The Taming of the C.A.N.D.Y. Monster," now on our trade paperback list.

The latest lucky self-publisher is Jim Everroad of Columbus, Ind. In 1974, after losing his job as a high-school athletic coach, Mr. Everroad thought he'd like to become a sportswriter. He spent the summer writing an article about something that had concerned him since he was a boy — his potbelly and the exercises he'd devised to flatten it. After selling it to a newspaper, he arranged to print an expansion of it in paperback — 6,000 words illustrated with two

dozen photographs — and sold out his 3,000 copies quickly. Euphorically, he then ordered 50,000 more copies, advertised the work more widely and persuaded a number of bookstores to stock it. After he'd disposed of 35,000 copies he was compelled to take a number of odd jobs, such as driving a Pepsi-Cola truck.

Then came his moment of luck. Late last year a new employee of Price/Stern/Sloan, the Los Angeles publisher, told its sales manager Chuck Gates, about the many copies of Mr. Everroad's book she had sold while working in a bookstore back in Indiana. Mr. Gates investigated, found it to be just the sort of checkout-counter item that is P/S/S's specialty.

P/S/S published "How to Flatten Your Stomach" last January and promptly discovered that America is full of people worried about their pot bellies. The book hopped onto our Best Seller List last week. Sales to date: 225,000. ■

Chapter Seven

How I Created a Best Seller
Using the Copycat Technique

I've hit the jackpot numerous times by publishing books that have made the best seller lists. I'm sure I'm on to a winner just as soon as I get a sixth-sense feeling that the proper elements have come together. It's like solving a jig-saw puzzle or knowing you are on the right track in working out a mathematical equation. .

While writing this book, I challenged myself to come up with another best-selling book to illustrate what I call the "copycat technique." The point was to demonstrate how I conceive a book idea and, with a minimal expenditure of money, make it evolve into a best seller by using direct mail techniques.

During the entire period I was writing this book, *How to Flatten Your Stomach* by Coach Jim Everroad was #1 on the best seller list. It seemed obvious that this was the book to copycat. Could I develop a similarly styled book featuring a different part of the anatomy—one that wasn't already the subject of another book? I chose the *derrière*.

Next, I needed the right title. *How to Flatten Your Derrière* occurred to me, as did *How to Flatten Your Rear End, How to Flatten Your Fanny;* and *How to Flatten Your Behind.* But none of them seemed right. It was during a brainstorming session that the specific word I wanted for my title came to me, and that perfect word was ... "tush." A widely known slang word for one's backside, "tush" is often preceded by an adjective such as "cute" or "beautiful" and the resulting expression is used in a frivolous manner. The word itself conveys humor, so the nature of my book would be lighthearted, as opposed to the serious tone of the original it proposed to imitate. "Tush" would allow for many a play on words and for *double entendres* that would get laughs.

But how could I be sure a humorous approach to the subject would sell the thousands of copies necessary for the book to be a winner? Another glance at the best seller list gave me all the reassurance I needed. In the #2 spot on the list was *The Dieter's Guide to Weight Loss During Sex* by Richard Smith. See page 104. *The New York Times* description of it, *Spoof on diet and sex manuals,* confirmed my feeling that with *How to Flatten Your Tush* I had the proper concept for a best seller—a "how to" exercise idea combined with a humorous parody approach. No other market research was required; the national best seller list contained all I needed to know. It was now clear to me that I had another winner. And remember—at this stage of the game, all I had was the concept and the title!

A concept is not hard to discover. It's a matter of asking the right questions, in whatever creative field you choose. In songwriting, for example, this technique enabled me to turn out hit songs. My partner and I would purchase all the top songs and listen to them over and over. We continually tried to answer these questions: What makes this song a hit? Is it mainly the lyrics or the music? What elements can we use as stimuli to write our songs? What hit song elements can we add to some existing songs we haven't had recorded to make them winners? Answering these questions during our brainstorming sessions helped us write award-winning songs.

Since I prefer to have a point of reference as I focus in on a book or song idea, I decide on the title right away. Before I wrote one word of the book you are now reading, I had to feel I had selected the right title for it. My choice was between *How to Make Money in the Fascinating World of Mail Order* and *How to Get Rich in Mail Order.*

Copycatting a book involves more than just choosing a concept and a title, however. In the case of *How to Flatten Your Tush,* I invented an imaginary author for the book, Coach Marge Reardon (note the "backside theme" in her name!) and dreamed up a personality for her. I also copycatted the cover design from *How to Flatten Your Stomach,* including its typeface. Compare pages 104 and 105 for similarity in cover design. These decisions, too, preceded the actual writing of the book.

Even advertisements should be written beforehand. Not a single word of this book, for example, existed at the time I made up the ads for it. Again, this Melvin Powers technique requires no more than a certain sense you get about your ads—when they feel right to you, your assignment becomes very clear. I knew I had to write a book to match the superlatives and promises of my "prize-winning" ads—nothing less would do. Do you have a book or other product in mind? Write the mail order ad. See how it feels to you.

If you're still not certain you have a potential winner, try another of my techniques. If possible, test your ad copy selling a similar product. That's what I did, using another book on mail order. When it pulled extremely well, I knew for sure at that point that I had a best seller. My market research was complete. Once I had finished the task of writing the book, it would just be a matter of time before I had another best seller.

When I had only page proofs from the printer for *How to Flatten Your Tush,* I sent a copy to the head buyer of the B. Dalton Bookstores chain, with a letter saying that I had designed a 24-copy counter display for the book. In reply, I received an initial order for 7,200 copies of the book—24 books in a counter display for 300 bookstores. See page 122 for the original order. That was it; I had a winner!

I immediately sent page proofs to other bookstores and jobbers. Walden's, another major bookstore chain, ordered a similar amount of books for 400 bookstores. Ingram, the major wholesale book distributor, ordered a like quantity. See pages 123 through 126 for some of the orders I received. My initial printing of 25,000 copies was sold out before I had printed one book. This was all accomplished by the use of direct mail.

My next job was to design an effective direct mail piece to be sent to the book trade. See pages 127 and 128. On page 127 you see the front and back covers of the book and on page 128, a brief description of it and some copy

about the imaginary author, Coach Marge Reardon. I was overwhelmed by the response to the circular. Now more than ever, I knew the book would hit the best seller list. On August 24, 1979, *How to Flatten Your Tush* came onto the B. Dalton best seller list at #23. See page 129.

In the meantime, I had made up a story about how the book evolved and I sent a publicity release, along with a copy of the book, to the major television and radio shows in Hollywood, as well as to the most important newspapers throughout the country. Jack Scagnetti, a well-known Hollywood literary agent, was pleased to lend "authenticity" to the story. See page 130.

The coordinator of the CBS-TV program, *Sunnyside,* contacted me about the book. On September 6, Dale Weintraub, an actress and vocalist posing as Coach Reardon, taped that show, and it was broadcast a week later. Nancy Gould, the hostess, went along with the gag, and this television exposure of the book to a national audience was terrific in terms of sales. See page 131 for photos of Dale Weintraub on the *Sunnyside* set. I have made a videotape of that show and sent it to the producers of the top TV talk shows, featuring Johnny Carson, Merv Griffin, and Dinah Shore.

More publicity for my book came in the form of contests and interviews. On September 5, for example, Dick Whittington, a popular radio personality, held a Tush Contest for Men, sponsored by radio station KGIL in the San Fernando Valley of California. Broadcast for one and a half hours, the contest was heard by thousands of listeners. The event also made the evening television news. See pages 132 through 134. Then, on October 3, Coach Reardon (alias Dale Weintraub) was interviewed by Paul Wallach on radio station KIEV. That evening the coach was the main judge at the 1980 Miss Tush Contest held at the Blue Moon Saloon in the Redondo Beach Marina. This was sponsored by the Tushery, a lingerie shop in Hermosa Beach. The evening was filled with fun, and Pauline Barilla, better known as Madame Tush, coordinated a perfect contest. See page 135. Two days later, Coach Reardon was interviewed by Jeff Hillary for *Earth News,* a program syndicated to over 500 radio stations. That same day, I received a beautiful order for 5,100 copies of *How to Flatten Your Tush* from Macmillan Company of Canada. See page 126. Keep in mind the fact that this sale was achieved solely by sending a copy of the book along with the publicity release. On October 7, our book was favorably reviewed in *The New York Times Book Review.* See page 136. This and other book reviews led to over 4,800 mail orders in a few weeks' time and a substantial number of orders from bookstores, as well as from a few wholesalers who had not, until then, ordered the book.

The following write-up appeared in the October 15, 1979 issue of *Publishers Weekly,* the leading trade book publication, which is circulated throughout the world. As a direct result of this publicity, I anticipate additional sales. The write-up was obtained by simply sending a copy of the book plus a brief publicity release to the editor of the magazine.

On How to Be Flat from Top to Bottom

Everyone knows we've had "How to Flatten Your Stomach" by Coach Jim Everroad ($1.75), Price/Stern/Sloan's long-lived best seller.

Perhaps fewer people know we also have **"How to Flatten Your Nose"** by "Coach" Vito Canoli as confessed to Don Lessem ($1.75). This paperback, similarly made up, similarly cover-designed to the title mentioned above, is published by Yuk, Inc., of Harvard, Mass. 01451. In the section entitled "How to Use This Regimen," the author advises, "The proper time to exercise the nose is in the morning, before it has been tired by a long day at the grindstone." Among the exercises advocated is the push-up, wherein the person with proboscis anxiety lifts body and head up until only nose and toes touch the ground. "How to Flatten Your Nose" is, says self-publisher Lessem, distributed by Baker & Taylor, Ingram and Golden Lee.

We also have **"How to Flatten Your Tush"** by Coach Marge Reardon ($2). This similarly made up, similarly cover-designed paperback is published by Wilshire Book Company. With a third printing, this title has 50,000 copies in print. In "How to Use This Program," Coach Reardon says bluntly, "Your goal is simply to maintain a flat tush. It won't be easy and it may take some time and patience. You won't be able to sit on your tush all day since you'll be using it in your exercise program." Among the exercises favored by the coach are Bottoms Up, Cheek to Cheek, Disco Tush and Tushdown.

By putting together the proper elements—by thinking creatively—I was able to produce a best seller. Systematic, logical thinking, in this case, paid handsome dividends. To be perfectly honest, I should tell you that I've had my share of unproductive books as a result of using the same, apparently cogent, reasoning. My advice, however, is this: when some of your projects are losers, take it as part of the creative process. Don't dwell on it too long; go on to the next project.

If you are interested in publishing a book, study the best seller list in your local newspaper. See if you can combine two elements to make up a new book. Try doing it as a creative exercise. You'll know when the idea is valid. It will feel right.

Be sure to visit your local bookstores, too. Introduce yourself and ask what kind of books are most popular. Listen to the feedback. On the front of the counter display for the book, *How to Flatten Your Tush,* I printed an obviously facetious line—*Soon To Be A Major Motion Picture.* Incredible as it may seem, I started getting inquiries; "Is it really going to be made into a movie?" and "How can you make a movie out of the book?" As a direct result of this, and to create further comment, on the third printing of the book I added the line in red on the cover, *Soon To Be A Major Motion Picture.* See page 137. I've also had an idea for a *Ms. World Tush Contest* and incorporated this idea in the third edition of the book in the form of an entry blank. I am getting many responses to the application form and I am considering sponsoring an actual contest. The publicity would be tremendous. See page 138. Remember, the best-selling status of *How to Flatten Your Tush* was accomplished by using direct mail techniques you can easily duplicate. I helped augment sales with my mail order solicitations, using the letter on page 139. Note that the last line refers the reader to his local bookstore. Newspaper reviews such as those shown on page 137 also pushed the sale of the book. There is nothing unusual about the entire campaign to sell the book. It follows a success pattern I've used many times and have written about in other examples in this book. The key element is the concept of the book. If that is viable, success will follow.

I highly recommend that you read *How to Flatten Your Tush* and copycat the format for a book idea of your own. Who says you can't create a book that will sell 100,000 copies or more and reap the profits from it? To do so is your exciting challenge.

Would you please let me know of your successes with any book or product of your own so I can share your experience with the readers of this book?

B. Dalton
BOOKSELLER
SAN 121-1579

INVOICE TO
****
* VENDOR ORDER RECAP *
****

TERMS	SHIPPING DATE	CANCEL DATE	BACK ORDER CODE
NET	AT ONCE	10-01-79	Y

SPECIAL INFORMATION

PURCHASE ORDER

NUMBER 006611   DATE 07-09-79   PAGE 1

SHIP TO
****
* VENDOR ORDER RECAP *
****

TO   WILSHIRE BOOK COMPANY
     ATTN MISS FREEDMAN
     12015 SHERMAN ROAD
     NORTH HOLLYWOOD CA 91605

TITLE OR ITEM DESCRIPTION	AUTHOR	ISBN OR ITEM CODE	QUANTITY	UNIT IDENT.	ITEM RETAIL	DISCOUNT %
				STORES		
HOW TO FLATTEN YOUR TUSH	REALDON	369X	7200	300	2:00	50.0
***DEPT. 1 TOTALS			7200		14400:00	
***DISC. SCH. P1 TOTALS			7200		14400:00	

| TOTAL LINES | TOTAL QTY | TOTAL EXT RETAIL |

ingram

INVOICE TO:

NASHVILLE ACCOUNTS PAYABLE DEPT.
INGRAM BOOK COMPANY
347 REEDWOOD DRIVE - P.O. BOX 17266
NASHVILLE, TENNESSEE 37217

PURCHASE ORDER

P.O. NUMBER	ORDER DATE	PAGE NO.	FORM NO.
NQ22925N	08/16/79	1	145956

FROM

INGRAM BOOK COMPANY
347 REEDWOOD DR
NASHVILLE, TN 37217

SHIP TO

INGRAM BOOK COMPANY
347 REEDWOOD DR
NASHVILLE, TN 37217

VENDOR

WILSHIRE BOOK COMPANY
12015 SHERMAN ROAD
NO HOLLYWOOD CALIF   91605

SHIPPING INSTRUCTIONS

SHIPPING DATE	CANCEL DATE	TERMS
SEE NOTE	SEE NOTE	

QUANTITY ORDERED	I.S.B.N.	TITLE	BIND	DISC. %	UNIT PRICE	EXTENDED PRICE
2000	0-87980-369-X	HOW TO FLATTEN YOUR TUSH	PA	50.0	2.00	2,000.00

SHIP WHEN BOOKS ARE AVAILABLE

TOTAL QUANTITY	# OF LINE ITEMS	VENDOR	BUYER	TOTAL EXTENDED PRICE	
2000	1		*S Walker*		2,000.00

123

Ingram

INVOICE TO:

NASHVILLE ACCOUNTS PAYABLE DEPT.
INGRAM BOOK COMPANY
347 REEDWOOD DRIVE - P.O. BOX 17266
NASHVILLE, TENNESSEE 37217

PURCHASE ORDER

P.O. NUMBER	ORDER DATE	PAGE NO.	FORM NO.
CQ20922N	07/27/79	1	142694

FROM

INGRAM BOOK COMPANY
16175 STEPHENS STREET
CITY OF INDUSTRY, CA
91744

SHIP TO

INGRAM BOOK COMPANY
16175 STEPHENS STREET
CITY OF INDUSTRY, CA
91744

VENDOR

WILSHIRE BOOK COMPANY
12015 SHERMAN ROAD
NO HOLLYWOOD CALIF   91605

SHIPPING INSTRUCTIONS

SHIPPING DATE	CANCEL DATE	TERMS
SEE NOTE	SEE NOTE	

QUANTITY ORDERED	I.S.B.N.	TITLE	BIND	DISC. %	UNIT PRICE	EXTENDED PRICE
2000	0-87980-369-X	HOW TO FLATTEN YOUR TUSH	PA	50.0	2.00	2,000.00
100	0-87980-368-1	JOKES FOR ALL OCCASIONS	PA	50.0	3.00	150.00

If this order cannot be billed at
the discount indicated, return to:

Francis Howell
Ingram Book Company
16175 Stephens St.
City of Industry, CA 91745

SHIP WHEN BOOKS ARE AVAILABLE

TOTAL QUANTITY	# OF LINE ITEMS	VENDOR		TOTAL EXTENDED PRICE
2100	2		BUYER	2,150.00

124

Ingram

INVOICE TO:

NASHVILLE ACCOUNTS PAYABLE DEPT.
INGRAM BOOK COMPANY
347 REEDWOOD DRIVE - P.O. BOX 17266
NASHVILLE, TENNESSEE 37217

P.O. NUMBER	ORDER DATE	PAGE NO.	FORM NO.
EQ22924N	08/16/79	1	145955

FROM

INGRAM BOOK COMPANY
BALTIMORE-WASHINGTON
INDUSTRIAL PARK
8301 SHERWICK COURT
JESSUP, MD 20794

SHIP TO

INGRAM BOOK COMPANY
BALTIMORE-WASHINGTON
INDUSTRIAL PARK
8301 SHERWICK COURT
JESSUP, MD 20794

VENDOR

WILSHIRE BOOK COMPANY
12015 SHERMAN ROAD
NO HOLLYWOOD CALIF   91605

SHIPPING INSTRUCTIONS

SHIPPING DATE	CANCEL DATE	TERMS
SEE NOTE	SEE NOTE	

QUANTITY ORDERED	I.S.B.N.	TITLE	BIND	DISC. %	UNIT PRICE	EXTENDED PRICE
1000	0-87980-369-X	HOW TO FLATTEN YOUR TUSH	PA	50.0	2.00	1,000.00

SHIP WHEN BOOKS ARE AVAILABLE

	TOTAL QUANTITY	# OF LINE ITEMS	VENDOR			TOTAL EXTENDED PRICE ▶	
1000 ◀		1		S Walker BUYER			1,000.00

N 142

125

western union **Mailgram**

1-129678G277 10/04/79 ICS IPMCNTA IISS LSAA
 CNF018 TORONTO ONT OCT 4/79 12.50HRS

▶ WILSHIRE BOOK CO
12015 SHERMAN RD
N HOLLYWOOD, CA
USA 91605

THIS IS AN ORDER-PLS SHIP USUAL ROUTING-OUR PO T3724
```
   3    879801042    BOND: NATURAL FOOD COOKBOOK   P
  60    879802987    CURTIS: HUMAN PROBLEMS HOW SOLVE THEM   P
   4    879801018    EDELMAN: MODERN ISRAEL   P
   8    87980159X    EDWARDS: TEN DAYS TO GREAT NEW LIFE   P
   5    879801166    FROTH: PALMISTRY SECRETS REVEALED   P
 100    879800720    GIBLIN: HOW YOU CAN HAVE CONFIDENCE   P
   3    879800372    GOULD: GOULDS GOLD SILVER GUIDE COINS   P
  50    879803673    HOU: GINSENG--MYTH " THE TRUTH   P
 100    879803568    JEFFARES: CALLILRAPHY ART BEAUT WRITING   P
 100    879803045    KNIGHT: YOUR ALLERGY WHAT DO ABOUT IT   P
  20    879800658    LECRON: HOW STOP SMOKING THRU SELFHYPN   P
  10    879802669    MCKNIGHT: HOW TO PICK WINNING HORSES   P
  10    879803207    MEADOW: SUCCESS AT HARNESS RACES   P
  10    879801964    MELLIN: ILLUSTRATED HORSEBACK RIDING   P
  10    879802634    MURRAY: TENNIS FOR BEGINNERS   P
   5    879801034    OMARR: MY WORLD OF ASTROLOGY   P
  10    879800798    ORTON: HYPNOTISM MADE PRACTICAL   P
   3    879802251    PITTENGER: RESCHOOLING THOROBRED   P
  20    879800801    POWERS: HYPNOTISM REVEALED   P
✓100    87980369X    REARDON: HOW TO FLATTEN YOUR TUSH   P
 200    879803681    SCHOCK: JOKES FOR ALL OCCASIONS   P
 200    879800925    SCHWARTZ: MAGIC THINKING BIG   P
  50    879800585    HOW TO DEVELOP EXCEPTIONAY MEMORY   P
✓5000   87980369X     REARDON: HOW TO FLATTEN YR TUSH   P
```
THANKS
STEPHANIE FARLETT
MACMILLAN CO OF CANADA LTD
70 BOND ST
NNN
12:12 EST

MGMCOMP MGM

5241 (R1/78)

$2

How to Flatten Your Tush

by Coach Marge Reardon

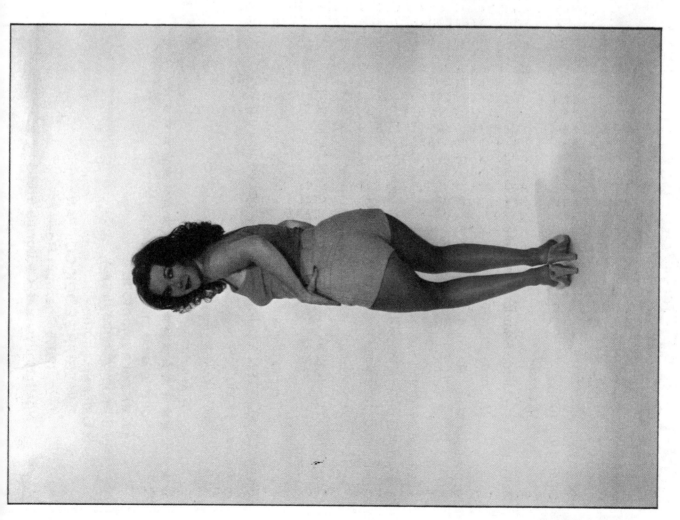

ISBN 0-87980-369-X

79

ABOUT THE AUTHOR

Coach Marge Reardon is a former army sergeant, and physical education instructor in the Des Moines, Iowa alternate schools. In 1977 she quit her job at Al's Nosherye to embark on a personal exercise program to flatten her own tush. Determined to help others with these successful tush exercises she wrote this book in less than three weeks.

The overwhelming response to Ms. Reardon's program led to an appearance on the Johnny Carson Show and national celebrity status. Tush Training Centers are now opening in Los Angeles and Kerhonksen, New York. HOW TO FLATTEN YOUR TUSH has been translated into five languages to date and will soon be a major motion picture.

★★

Comments on
HOW TO FLATTEN YOUR TUSH

"Yours is the Greatest."
M. Ali

"Since your appearance Ed and I are a little flatter in the tush and larger in the ratings."
J. Carson

"Tell it like it is—Marge Reardon is a veritable morsal of dorsal."
H. Cosell

"In praise of Marge Reardon, I could kiss my own tush."
B. Carter

"Greetings everyone! From Rodeo Drive to Malibu everyone in Hollywood is doing it these days. Flatten your tush is the biggest *in* Hollywood craze since forging your own check."
R. Barrett

"Marge Reardon in 1980. America needs someone to bring up the rear."
The Republican Party

"HOW TO FLATTEN YOUR TUSH has replaced running as America's #1 sport."
M. Wallace
57 Minutes

★★★★★★★★★★★★★★★★★★★★★★★★★★★★★★

- **Soon to be a major motion picture**
- **National author tour**
- 24-copy counter display
- Order now from:

WILSHIRE BOOK COMPANY
12015 Sherman Road
North Hollywood, California 91605

128

B. Dalton BESTSELLERS

Trade Paperback

August 24, 1979

NO.	TITLE	AUTHOR	PUBLISHER	LAST WEEK	RETAIL
1.	MARY ELLEN'S BEST OF HELPFUL	Pinkham	Warner	1	3.95
2.	HOW TO FLATTEN YOUR STOMACH	Everroad	Price Stern	2	1.75
3.	RAND MCNALLY ROAD ATLAS		Rand McNally	3	3.95
4.	JOY OF SEX	Comfort	Simon/Schuster	5	7.95
5.	IN SEARCH OF HISTORY	White	Warner	4	5.95
6.	MURPHYS LAW	Bloch	Price Stern	6	2.50
7.	HOW TO TRIM/HIPS/SHAPE/THIGHS	Everroad	Price Stern	7	1.75
8.	FREE STUFF FOR KIDS	Blakely	Meadowbrook	8	2.95
9.	SACAJAWEA	Waldo	Avon	9	8.95
10.	WHAT COLOR IS YOUR PARACHUTE		Ten Speed	10	5.95
11.	I, CLAUDIUS	Graves	Random	11	2.95
12.	WOMAN'S DRESS FOR SUCCESS	Molloy	Warner	14	3.95
13.	DIETERS GDE/WEIGHT LOSS/SEX	Smith	Workman	13	2.95
14.	HOW TO SURVIVE THE MONEY CRASH	Clark	Harvest House	20	1.95
15.	DO YOU KNOW YOUR HUSBAND?	Carlinsky	Price Stern	12	1.50
16.	MORE JOY OF SEX	Comfort	Simon/Schuster	26	7.95
17.	MAGIC OF THINKING BIG	Schwartz	Wilshire	17	3.00
18.	ELEMENTS OF STYLE	Strunk	Macmillan	19	1.95
19.	PREGNANCY AND CHILDBIRTH	Hotchner	Avon	21	6.95
20.	FOXFIRE 5	Wiggington	Doubleday	22	6.95
21.	DO YOU KNOW YOUR WIFE?	Carlinsky	Price Stern	15	1.50
22.	RAND MCNALLY INTERSTATE		Rand McNally	18	1.95
23.	HOW TO FLATTEN YOUR TUSH	Reardon	Wilshire	-	2.00
24.	OUR BODIES OURSELVES		Simon/Schuster	23	5.95
25.	MAGIC OF THINKING BIG	Schwartz	Simon/Schuster	17	2.95
26.	UP AND DOWN WITH/ROLLING STONES	Sanchez	Morrow	-	8.95
27.	ADRIEN ARPEL'S 3 WK CRASH	Arpel	Simon/Schuster	25	6.95
28.	NOTES TO MYSELF	Prather	Real People	-	2.50
29.	CLAUDIUS, THE GOD	Graves	Random	30	3.95
30.	ON DEATH & DYING	Kubler-Ross	Macmillan	28	2.45

B. DALTON BOOKSELLER Bestseller Lists are compiled from the weekly sales reports generated from 372 stores through computer report.

Melvin Powers
Wilshire Book Company

12015 Sherman Road
No. Hollywood, CA 91605

(818) 765-8579
FAX (818) 765-2922

How to Flatten Your Tush
Coach Marge Reardon

Price $2.00

How to Flatten Your Tush, a spoof on exercise and diet books, is off to a fast sales start, according to its publisher, Melvin Powers. President of Wilshire Book Company, Powers has a knack for picking best sellers. He thinks this original paperback has all the earmarks of a winner.

Initial sales of 25,000 copies to major book store chains sold out the first printing and sent the book back to press for an additional 25,000 copies. "We sold over 50,000 copies in one month," said Powers, who has 400 titles in print at his North Hollywood, California publishing headquarters.

Literary agent Jack Scagnetti of North Hollywood brought the book idea to Wilshire following an introduction at a Beverly Hills celebrity cocktail party and a chance remark to exercise coach Marge Reardon about her streamlined figure and tush. The book proposal quickly followed, with Coach Reardon authoring the text and Scagnetti shooting the photographs. He used three beautiful, professional models, including a former Miss California World.

The book features 20 exercises, with such titles as Bottoms Up, Cheek to Cheek, Tushdown, Tush Tone, and Disco Tush. The bibliography gives a clue to the tone of the book with its witty references to Backsides at the White House, The Best Rears of Our Lives and The Power of Posterior Thinking. Author Reardon includes herself, together with Marilyn Monroe, on a list of Famous Tushes.

A counter display for the book announces: "Soon to be a motion picture."

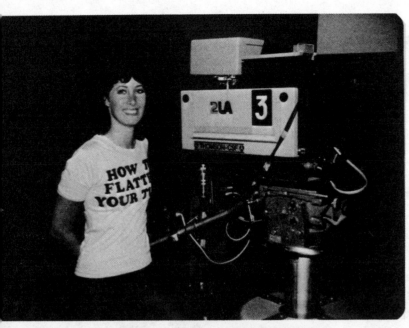

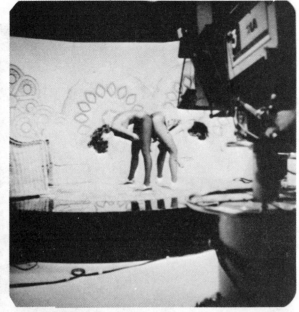

Paperback Best Sellers

MASS MARKET

Mass-market paperbacks are softcover books sold at newsstands, variety stores and supermarkets, as well as in bookstores. This listing is based on computer-processed reports from bookstores and representative wholesalers with more than 40,000 outlets across the United States.

1 **CHESAPEAKE,** by James Michener. (Fawcett, $3.95.) Four centuries of Maryland's Eastern Shore: fiction.

2 **SECOND GENERATION,** by Howard Fast. (Dell, $2.75.) The children of "The Immigrants" on the eve of World War II: fiction.

3 **THE FAR PAVILIONS,** by M. M. Kaye. (Bantam, $2.95.) Love and war in the high Himalayas: fiction.

4 **EVERGREEN,** by Belva Plain. (Dell, $2.75.) Jewish immigrant woman's rise from Lower East Side poverty: fiction.

5 **PULLING YOUR OWN STRINGS,** by Wayne W. Dyer. (Avon, $2.75.) Taking charge of your life.

6 **THE AMITYVILLE HORROR,** by Jay Anson. (Bantam, $2.75.) Suburban haunted house: basis of the current film.

7 **WIFEY,** by Judy Blume. (Pocket, $2.50.) A woman's search for emotional identity: fiction.

8 **EYE OF THE NEEDLE,** by Ken Follett. (NAL/Signet, $2.95.) Nazi spy vs. British professor in a World War II thriller: fiction.

9 **SCRUPLES,** by Judith Krantz. (Warner, $2.75.) A woman's rise in the fashion world: fiction.

10 **SISTERS AND STRANGERS,** by Helen Van Slyke. (Popular, $2.50.) Three siblings reunited at a golden wedding anniversary: fiction.

11 **THE WORLD ACCORDING TO GARP,** by John Irving. (Pocket, $2.75.) Comic, extravagant novel about the son of a famous feminist mother.

12 **THE ENTITY,** by Frank De Felitta. (Warner, $2.75.) A woman falls prey to a spectral rapist: fiction.

13 **METROPOLITAN LIFE,** by Fran Lebowitz. (Fawcett/Crest, $2.25.) Astringent observations on the New York scene.

14 **BLOODLINE,** by Sidney Sheldon. (Warner, $2.75.) Love and high financial intrigue on three continents: basis of the current film.

15 **A WOMAN OF INDEPENDENT MEANS,** by Elizabeth Forsythe Hailey. (Avon, $2.50.) Eighty years of an enthusiastic, stubborn woman who managed her own life: fiction.

TRADE

Trade paperbacks are softcover books usually sold in bookstores and at an average price higher than mass-market paperbacks. This listing is based on computer-processed reports from bookstores and wholesalers with more than 2,500 outlets across the United States.

1 **MARY ELLEN'S BEST OF HELPFUL HINTS,** by Mary Ellen Pinkham and Pearl Higginbotham. (Warner/B. Lansky Books, $3.95.) Ways to solve household problems.

2 **IN SEARCH OF HISTORY,** by Theodore H. White. (Warner, $5.95.) A journalist's memoirs.

✓ 3 **HOW TO FLATTEN YOUR STOMACH,** by Jim Everroad. (Price/Stern/Sloan, $1.75.) Exercises.

4 **WHAT COLOR IS YOUR PARACHUTE?** by Richard Nelson Bolles. (Ten Speed Press, $5.95.) Guide for job-hunters and career-changers.

5 **THE JOY OF SEX,** by Alex Comfort. (Simon & Schuster/Fireside, $6.95.) With illustrations.

6 **HOW TO TRIM YOUR HIPS AND SHAPE YOUR THIGHS,** by Jim Everroad and Lonna Moscow. (Price/Stern/Sloan, $1.75.) Exercises.

7 **SACAJAWEA,** by Anna Lee Waldo. (Avon, $8.95.) Indian woman shows the way West: fiction.

8 **OUR BODIES, OURSELVES,** by the Boston Women's Health Book Collective. (Simon & Schuster/Touchstone, $4.95.) Illustrated guide.

9 **MURPHY'S LAW,** by Arthur Bloch. (Price/Stern/Sloan, $2.50.) Why things go wrong.

10 **FOXFIRE 5,** edited by Eliot Wigginton. (Doubleday/Anchor, $6.95.) More folklore and how-to from Appalachia.

✓ 11 **THE DIETER'S GUIDE TO WEIGHT LOSS DURING SEX,** by Richard Smith. (Workman, $2.95.) Spoof on diet and sex manuals.

12 **FREE STUFF FOR KIDS,** by Pat Blakeley, Barbara Haislet and Judith Hentges. (Meadowbrook Press, $2.95.) A listing of samples and souvenirs to be had for the asking.

13 **ON DEATH AND DYING,** by Dr. Elisabeth Kübler Ross. (Macmillan, $2.25.) Lessons to be learned from the terminally ill.

14 **UP AND DOWN WITH THE ROLLING STONES,** by Tony Sanchez. (Morrow/Quill, $8.95.) Their stormy lives, recounted by a man who contrived much of it.

15 **THE WOMAN'S DRESS FOR SUCCESS BOOK,** by John T. Molloy. (Warner, $3.95.) How-to.

PAPERBACK TALK

Continued from Page 41
realistic sketches by Ron Toelke.

The Kent tradition. There are signs that the Kents may have fathered a new paperback genre. Consider:

¶Last February, Bantam inaugurated a new series, "Wagons West," four volumes about a family's westward trek. The author: Dana Fuller Ross, a pseudonym. The producer behind the scenes: Mr. Engel.

¶Next month, Bantam starts the "Colonization of America" series, about Indians and the early settlements. The author: Donald Clayton Porter, a pseudonym. The producer: Mr. Engel.

¶Next January, Playboy Press begins the "American Freedom Series," which the publisher says is "in the tradition of the Kent Family Chronicles." The author: George Smith (his real name), a Torrance, Calif., freelancer with eight science-fiction novels to his credit. No producer in this case.

Lampoons. Most books that succeed at the cash register invite a bit of kidding. Very few get what they deserve. Two worthy exceptions have been published lately.

✓ ¶"How to Flatten Your Tush," by Coach Marge Reardon. (Wilshire Book Co., North Hollywood, Calif., $2.) Exercises in punning and posturing by a former army sergeant, illustrated with posed photos of some of Hollywood's finest. You may not gain the great peace of tush this manual promises, but you'll surely get a good laugh.

¶"A Very Young Housewife" by Del Tremens. A Bogus Book. (Harvard Common Press, Harvard, Mass., $5.95.) An album of well-taken photographs that show the ways in which 9-year-old Chelsea Pendleton, an ordinary suburban kid, is training to join the ranks of the top U.S. housewives. These include scrubbing her mother's kitchen floor, meeting with "the girls" for a weekly chapter meeting of the BLAHs (Big League Amateur Housewives), doing her thing at the supermarket. What little girl would want to be a horseback rider, a gymnast or a dancer when she can have such fun as a housewife? ■

Reading Room

$2

SOON TO BE A MAJOR MOTION PICTURE

How to Flatten Your Tush

by Coach Marge Reardon

N.Y. Times
"One of the year's funniest books."

HOW TO FLATTEN YOUR TUSH by Marge Reardon. Wilshire Book Co., North Hollywood, Calif. 48 pages. $2. Call it a tush. Call it a derriere, a fanny, a rear end. Whatever you call it Ms. Reardon wants to get behind you and make yours a joy to behold.

Her power of posterior thinking depends mainly on a series of exercise illustrations. But, it's the witty asides that make this paperback worthwhile. Take her Tush Trivia Quiz, for example, and questions like "What tush would you like to see on the cover of *Reader's Digest*" and "Which president had

the largest tush?" There are no answers provided because with questions like that you don't need answers.

And, take some of her 20 Ways to Flatten Your Tush: "Shake it, bump it, twist it, lift it, use it, love it."

This is one book that really gets to the seat of a problem and, if you can stop laughing long enough, Ms. Reardon's exercises might accomplish what the book title promises. And to anyone prudish enough to pass up this gem, Ms. Reardon would probably just shake her fanny and say "Tush, tush."

George Beecroft
Asbury Park Press

* * *

Announcing
The First Annual
MS. WORLD TUSH PHOTO CONTEST

Rules:

1. Send a recent photograph of yourself.
2. Open to anyone from 9 to 90 regardless of race, religion, ethnic background or political affiliation.
3. This is an equal opportunity contest.
4. Finalists must be free to travel to Hollywood for screen test.

————————————————————————————————

Official Entry Form

Do you like to sing? _____ Do you like to act? _____

Do you like to dance? _____ Do you disco? _____

Are you free to travel? _____ Do you enjoy meeting people? _____

Are you presently under contract to a major motion picture studio? _____

Briefly write why you feel you should be selected as Ms. World Tush.

Name _____
             (Please print)

Address _____

City _____ State _____ Zip Code _____

Telephone number: Please give area code first. _____

Send all photos to:
MS. WORLD TUSH CONTEST
12015 Sherman Road
No. Hollywood, California 91605

In case of a tie, the photo baring the earliest tush will be awarded the prize. No photos can be returned and the decision of the judges is final.

This contest is void in Tibet.

Melvin Powers
Wilshire Book Company

12015 Sherman Road
No. Hollywood, CA 91605

(818) 765-8579
FAX (818) 765-2922

HOW TO FLATTEN YOUR TUSH
Coach Marge Reardon

This book shows you how to be the first one on your block to have a terrific tush! It's the living end! Haven't you always yearned to be the possessor of a beautiful, curvaceous bottom? You have? Well here's your opportunity to transform your secret fantasy into reality.

Enjoy the admiration of the opposite sex with your new, plush tush. Strangers will stare, then dare to seal a second glace at your lovely, firm fanny. Here's your chance to show off your assets and find true romance to boot. Back up your body with an elegant tush. You deserve it!

How to Flatten Your Tush also makes a great gift for someone you love or for someone you would like to love and for everyone you know—your lover, friends, mate, and business associates. It makes an uproariously funny gag gift. You'll have people falling flat on their tush laughing when you give this inspiring, practical, how-to-do-it book!

Here is our guarantee. Use our book for only 21 days. At the end of this time, if you're not as proud as a peacock with your transformed tush and have not increased your number of friends and admirers, we will refund your money.

What do you have to lose? Only flabby flesh! Don't just sit on your tush. Act today for tomorrow's delights. Today's action means tomorrow's reaction.

Send at once for your copy of *How to Flatten Your Tush* by Coach Marge Reardon. It will be sent to you discreetly wrapped in a plain manila envelope.

NO-RISK COUPON

Please send my copy of *How to Flatten Your Tush*.
Enclosed is my check ( ) cash ( ) money order ( ) for $4.00.

Name_____

Address_____

City_____ State_____ Zip_____

Mail to: Melvin Powers, 12015 Sherman Road, No. Hollywood, CA 91605

Waldenbooks

January 7, 1980

Ms. Frieda Freedman
Director of Marketing
Wilshire Book Company
12015 Sherman Road
No. Hollywood, CA 91605

Dear Ms. Freedman:

Your letter of December 19 to Margaret Peters was passed on to me, as Margaret is no longer with Waldenbooks.

Enclosed please find a copy of the theme ad on humor.

We measured sales velocity on titles in the theme tests the week prior to the promotion and the week following. Of the five theme tests, humor did best with a 375% increase. Your title, How to Flatten Your Tush, did even better, showing a 450% increase in sales.

Sincerely yours,

Alan Kellock

Alan Kellock
Vice President for Marketing

AK/ea

enclosure

201 High Ridge Road • Stamford, Connecticut 06904 • (203) 356-7500

THE KNIGHT IN RUSTY ARMOR

$5

Join a good, kind, and loving knight who faces a life-changing dilemma when he discovers that his shining armor can't be removed. As he searches for a way to free himself, he receives guidance from the wise sage, Merlin, the Magician, who encourages the knight to embark on the most difficult crusade of his life.

Chapter Eight

How to Start and Run a Profitable Special Interest Book, CD, Audio and Video Cassette Business

There are approximately 50,000 books published annuall. in the United States and another 50,000 published in England, Canada, and Australia. Let's assume a publisher printed 10,000 or more copies of a book and managed to sell only 5,000 copies. His problem then is to sell the rest of the books at any price. They are taking up space in the warehouse, and he has to recoup as much of his investment as he can. Some companies publish hundreds of books every year. You know they can't all be winners. These companies cannot afford to stock books that do not move, so they "remainder" the books or sell off the "overstock" at extremely low prices to companies who specialize in remainder books.

Once you start to sell books in sufficiently large quantities, you can also bid for the same books. Publishers periodically put out lists of the books they want to remainder, and you can request to be on their mailing list. Although the remainder list may contain several hundred book titles, you bid for only those books which are of interest to you and in the quantity you want. Sample books are also available for inspection at the publishers' offices.

Let's assume a remainder book was originally priced at $10.00. The publisher might be willing to sell off his stock at $1.00 per book. The remainder house might, in turn, sell the book to the book trade at $2.50 less 40% discount, making the cost to the bookstore $1.50 plus postage. The bookstore owner or mail order book dealer has the option of selling the book at whatever price he wants. As a matter of general business practice, the book dealer usually sells the book at the price suggested by the remainder house. In mail ordering these books, I would mark them up at least four or five times the cost. If the book costs $1.50, I'd list it in my catalog for $6.00, minimum.

Initially, your reason for dealing with remainder companies is you can get tremendous discounts, which you can then pass on to your customers. You can supplement your list with the books you can buy from various publishers. The standard discount is 40% plus postage. Once you start to use books in quantities, call or write the sales manager of the company telling him you are in the mail order book business and request an extra 10% discount for advertising. He'll generally give it to you with the result you will now be buying books at a 50% discount.

At one time I had a mail order catalog of hundreds of books in the field of psychology. I included numerous remainder books in this catalog and easily sold them at the full price. The reason? I had a captive audience interested in psychology books. If the customer wanted the book, the price was immaterial. Many of my customers were members of the healing arts, and they wrote the books off as a tax-deductible business expense. Remarkably, there were very few companies providing this service, and to this day there still are very few companies in this area providing it. I was servicing the customer with a special interest in psychological books. Not only was I selling the books to the general public, psychologists, psychiatrists, nurses, chiropractors, and osteopaths, but to universities and public libraries.

Here's how I proved to myself many times that price was secondary. Let's assume I purchased for $1.50 a hard-cover remainder book that had a retail price of $10.00. I'd run 15,000 copies of my catalog, broken down into three split runs, testing the retail price of $5.00, $7.50, $10.00. I would indicate in my catalogs that the book which was originally published at $10.00 is now available at the discount price of either $5.00 in one split run, or $7.50 in the other. Generally speaking, I found in testing the book on three price levels there was little, if any, appreciable difference in the sale of the book. I concluded there might even be a negative factor at work in selling books at discount.

Some people react adversely to a product which has been reduced in price. Do you believe selling books at a discount suggests a negative value of the books? I would be interested to learn of your results in price testing. Obviously, this same technique applies whether you're selling a product or a service. Incidentally, having a special sale once or twice a year is good business, and it helps to unload merchandise that isn't selling.

At the end of this chapter, you'll find a list of the names and addresses of companies specializing in the sale of remainder books. Some of them also carry music CDs. Write to them requesting their catalog and ask to be put on their mailing list. To get an education on how numerous companies are selling music via mail order, see the Web site: http://www.bizweb.com/keylists/music.html.

You will receive catalogs listing thousands of remainder books in numerous categories. You'll find books from virtually every publisher. Some catalogs list music CDs and cassette tapes that have been drastically reduced in price.

I suggest you decide on several categories of books and music to sell, preferably those in which you have an interest. Before you know it, you'll become extremely knowledgeable in these fields, enabling you to better serve your customers.

An excellent example of a mail order book company running a perfect operation is: Edward R. Hamilton, Falls Village, Connecticut 06031-5000. They put out a catalog of thousands of books in numerous categories. I, personally, have purchased hundreds of books from them. I urge you to send away for their catalog for two reasons: One, I want you to study their operation; and two, I know you'll be delighted buying books at great prices. If you are on the Internet, check out: http://www.amazon.com.

Here is how you would proceed if you wanted to get into the special interest mail order book business. Let's assume you are a sports fan and choose sports as your category.

To produce your catalog, you can offset the companies' catalog pages exactly as they are changing prices. Or you can make up your own catalog in whatever style you want. I've done extremely well with horse books.

I am particularly impressed with a catalog, *Ships & Sea,* put out by S.T. Preston & Son, Inc., Main Street Wharf, Greenport, Long Island, New York 11944. I am reproducing their colored cover in black and white on page 154 and also page 1 of the catalog. Doesn't it exude a certain warmth? That's the type of thing you want to inject into your catalog. Their 112-page catalog is a perfect example of an entrepreneur having found a specialized area and building a successful mail order business on that concept. The catalog is replete with beautiful gift items. Put it in the hands of someone interested in boats, and you have my guarantee that he'll find something he just can't do without.

You might want to incorporate a special section to include sports books for children. If so, research a book at your library entitled *Sports Books for Children* by Barbara K. Harrah. It contains an annotated bibliography of fiction and nonfiction books with grade-level descriptions.

Remember, I stated I found the price was immaterial when selling books by mail order in the psychological field. That was only after I had become established in this type of book business. Initially, I stressed the fact I was offering great values at big savings. The book service evolved over a period of years, and I discovered by trial and error I was actually offering an important personal service by providing a source for the purchase of books which could not easily be found in bookstores. I often heard the complaint from my customers that bookstores were not cooperative when it came to ordering a single copy of a book. Besides selling the hundreds of books in my catalog, I would get them any book in print and, on occasion, even try to find books that were out of print. In my opinion, that was providing a unique service. How could anyone not be successful doing the same thing? Follow it for your success.

Reproduced on page 155 is the front page of one of my catalogs. You might want to incorporate parts of it in your catalog. You'll note I invite the recipient to visit me and to examine the books I have for sale. Over the years, thousands of my mail order customers have accepted my invitation, with the result I have established a personal and very pleasant relationship with them. For my part, it gave me an ideal opportunity to get some valuable market research from them. This usually takes the form of questions and discussions about interesting and useful books they have discovered. If I like what they have to say about the books, I'll read them. Then if it seems advisable, I'll recommend them to my customers.

You'll note I invite correspondence. I can sell hundreds of books simply by recommending them in my personal correspondence. I don't need a circular about the book. You should keep that in mind as a sales technique. As a word of caution, however, recommend only books you feel are particularly worthwhile. Many of my customers write back to me, discussing the books, recommending others, and at the same time asking for my further recommendations. It's a two-way street paved with money.

All my books are sold on the basis of satisfaction guaranteed or money refunded. This might sound incredible, but I can't recall the last time anyone ever returned a book.

If there are no valid reasons not to do so, run your business under your own name, personalizing your business as much as possible. In some of your literature you might even want to display a picture of yourself, or of you and your spouse, or the entire family. Why not? It's fun to do, and it creates the friendly environment you want for your business. Doing business with the XYZ company is too impersonal.

My philosophy for the beginner is to keep things as simple and easy as possible, while spending a minimum of money to test the probability of success. When you run your catalog, print only 1,000 copies. In it, feature consideration for your customer through the savings of money and good buys. Once your business gets rolling, you can order books from any book company in the world and add them to your catalog. Once you have established credit, you can order on open account. When you are given this privilege, pay your bills promptly by the tenth of the month. You'll establish a good reputation, and the sales managers will be anxious to work with you. You'll get just as much attention and consideration as a large account.

Once your catalog has been put into circulation, buy only those books from the remainder houses for which you have actually received orders. You can do this once a week. Don't take the chance of getting stuck with inventory unless you see a selling pattern established. Some companies allow you to buy a few books at a time; others request a minimum order. Get started with the companies that have the most lenient terms. Be sure you read the terms of purchase for each company. They're stated in

their catalogs. With regard to those companies from whom you are going to buy books, either establish credit or, pending the establishment of credit, make arrangements to pay for the books as you order them. Don't be reluctant to call the credit manager or the sales manager. Tell them exactly what you are doing. They'll cooperate with you.

Now you have picked a category, printed your catalog and have made arrangements to purchase the books. You are ready for your customers' orders. How do you get them? There are several common approaches but if you can think of a unique way, try it.

You have your choice of running either a classified ad or display ad, using direct mail, or trying a combination of all. Assuming you want to run a classified ad pertaining to a sports category, your logical approach would be to run in sports magazines containing classified sections. If they don't have a classified section, run a one-inch display ad requesting readers to send for a free catalog of sports books at bargain prices.

To find the sports-related magazines, go to your library and you'll find the names, addresses, and advertising rates for 930 consumer and 200 farm publications in the reference publication, *Consumer Magazine and Farm Publication Rates & Data.* Under the category of sports, you'll find magazines you never knew existed and such publications as: *Baseball Digest, Baseball News, Boating, Field & Stream, Fishing & Hunting, Fishing World, Football Digest, Golf, Golf Digest, Hockey Illustrated, Motorcycle World, Outdoor Life, Pro Football Digest, Ring, Road & Track, Rudder, Sail Magazine, Salt Water Sportsman, Shooting Times, Ski, Skier, Skiing, Skin Diver, Snow Sports, Surfer, World Tennis, Yacht Racing,* and *Yachting.* This is just a sample of the type of magazines in which to run your ads. Besides magazines devoted to sports, there are numerous other publications in which you might want to run, such as *American Armed Forces Newspapers, Army Times,* and all kinds of men's magazines. You might also consider the *National Enquirer, Star,* and *Midnight Globe.*

Your aim is to create an interesting and provocative ad to invite inquiries about your catalog and to run the ad in the best-drawing publications. You could run a classified ad or a one-inch ad serving the two-fold purpose of selling one book and also mentioning your free catalog. Advertise that your catalog is free. You want the largest possible response. Run a few test ads to find out the number of inquiries received, the cost of the ads, the average cost of each inquiry, the number of orders received, the dollar value of the orders, the amount of the average order, the number of books requested in the average order, the percentage of orders received, the best magazines for bringing in inquiries and orders, and the profit or loss from the undertaking. Be sure to key each magazine.

Your classified ad should read something like this: FREE, interesting sports catalog. Fantastic savings. Great books for gifts. Write: Your name, address, and key. Since you're paying for each word, keep them to a minimum. Unnecessary words can cost you hundreds and thousands of dollars by the end of the year.

For a one-inch display ad, I'd run the following:

INTERESTED IN SPORTS?
Free, interesting sports catalog. Fantastic savings. Great books for your library or a perfect gift for the sportsman. Write today to:
Your name, address, and key.

You could rent a list containing names of individuals interested in sports and send your catalog to each of them with an introductory letter. Having a local mailing house handle the mechanics of the mailing will save you money.

Look for other categories of names. See page 198. These lists contain millions of names. Once your catalog is in the hands of the proper recipient, you are truly on the road to riches. That's the excitement of mail order. You're the guiding hand controlling your own destiny!

When you decide to use direct mail, be sure to consult people at your local mailing house before you print your catalog. There are some technical aspects to consider in regard to layout, folding, and printing your catalog. Because of their experience with numerous mailings, they can give you valuable information as to how to increase your response. They can also obtain mailing lists for you, or recommend a local or national list broker with whom you can work.

If you want to sell music, use the same techniques as with books, advertising in the appropriate media. There are two popular trade directories: *Phonolog* and *Recordaid.* Lots of money is being made selling music on the Internet. For a perfect operation see: http://www.cdnow.com. Does it give you any creative ideas to implement? Also be sure to check out: http://www.bizweb.com/keylists/music/html.

Examine the record titles available. You might want to consider running an ad on TV. Contact an advertising agency for assistance, and try your ad on a TV station where the rates aren't too high. You've often seen ads for all kinds of records. Be sure to include a toll-free number for impulse purchases. If you get a good concept for an album of music, you can deal directly with record companies. They are always anxious to deal with someone who can sell their music.

Recently, on one of the Los Angeles TV stations, there were nightly commercial spots plugging an album of Nelson Eddy and Jeanette MacDonald. This commercial appeared in print in the *Los Angeles Times Home Magazine* the same week and in the *Family Weekly.* I also saw the ad in *National Enquirer.*

You would be able to find out a great deal of information about the success of this TV ad, and others like it, by contacting the sales representative of the station handling the account. You would want to know how much did the TV spots cost, how many spots did they run, and how many records did they sell? What was the cost of the record in the mail? How many records were sold by the space ads? Was there a correlation between the pulling power of the TV ads and the space ads when both were run in the same city? If so, what was it? How much was the average order on the back end, and what percentage of customers ordered once, twice, and so forth?

If the above campaign was successful, has it been augmented with direct mail utilizing a variation on the same commercial that appeared on TV? Plastic records are very inexpensive, lightweight and unbreakable, and can produce further sales. Try some test mailings to the appropriate mailing lists.

Should you be interested in the use of plastic phonograph records to sell your product, write to: Eva-Tone, 4801 Ulmerton Road, Clearwater, Florida 33520. Telephone (813) 577-7000. They have plenty of success stories for you.

There are approximately 4,000,000 members in the various record clubs. The sales amount to $300,000,000. The most active record clubs are *Columbia Record Club,* the *Longines Symphonette* and the *Readers' Digest Record Club.* The music business is bigger than ever. Sales of all types of records have increased tremendously over the last few years. The end is nowhere in sight. You can compete with the giant record clubs if you specialize in a particular category of music and offer personalized service.

Hopefully, after a while, your book business will start to make money, and you will want to add more books to your catalog. Go to your library and ask for the reference book, *Subject Guide to Books in Print*. It contains 425,000 entries, 62,000 subject categories, and 53,000 cross references. Every library, without exception, has the set. It's a basic reference book they need. Look up the sports category. Under each sport, in alphabetical order, you will find thousands of books. It lists the title of the book, the author, publisher, and price. Volume II contains the names and addresses of the publishers. Write to the publishers for their catalogs and discount schedules, and ask for applications for credit.

One of my all-time, best-pulling, two-page circulars is reproduced on pages 152 and 153. Can you tell me why? What are the winning elements? Your challenge is to improve it. That's how you learn to write good advertising copy. It takes practice.

See pages 165 through 168. Here are examples of two-page, direct marketing sales letters that I have used with outstanding results. I mail these in response to individuals who write to me, saying how much they enjoyed *The Knight in Rusty Armor* and telling me about the many benefits they have derived. *Knights Without Armor* is the perfect follow-up book.

Offer your clientele the important service of being able to get any book in print or out of print. Any title in print can be found in the reference book, *Books In Print*. Every library has it. You can also call the librarian and ask for the publisher's name and address and the current price of the book. For out-of-print books, you can work with companies that specialize in this service, or you yourself can advertise in a weekly publication devoted to this service, *Antiquarian Bookman*, P.O. Box AB, Clifton, New Jersey 07015. Send for a sample copy and rate card. I run a one-inch ad, and invariably find the book I want. When the second-hand book dealers see your ad, they send you a card stating they have the book, describing its condition, and giving you the price they are asking for it. As you have probably surmised, there is no set price for the book, and the original retail price has no relationship to what may be asked. I always double the price to my customer plus the cost of the ad. The average bookstore proprietor isn't geared to finding out-of-print books, so the field is open for you to establish a highly valued service for your customers.

For future mailings to your customers, ask them in what category of sports they are particularly interested. Send special mailings to them. If your list isn't too long, write a personal note with the advertising literature.

Are you really ambitious? Here's an extension of your personalized sporting book business. What about getting into some phase of sporting goods merchandise, gifts, novelties, and clothing? Since you have a mailing list of potential customers, you might as well try it.

Assume you decide to specialize in books dealing with boating. A sample of a perfect follow-up catalog would be one put out by S.T. Preston & Son, Inc., Main Street Wharf, Greenport, New York 11944. It contains 112 pages and hundreds of beautiful nautical gifts. They carry a few books in their catalog, but their emphasis is on gifts. They also maintain a store.

You can find sources of merchandise by attending sporting goods trade shows. This information is available in various trade magazines devoted to sports. Write for the upcoming dates. Attend the shows located most conveniently to you and look for merchandise you feel could be successfully sold by mail order.

The possibilities for mail order success in sports are unlimited. If you can't attend the shows, you can subscribe to the various trade publications pertaining to your specialty. You can find the names of the trade magazines in the *Business Publications Rates & Data* at your library. Write the specific publication for a free sample and rate card. In the general sporting goods field, an outstanding publication is *Sporting Goods Business*, 1515 Broadway, New York, New York 10036.

One step leads to the next, and who would ever suspect that a small classified or display advertisement could lead to such a lucrative, money-making potential? It's all there waiting for you in whatever field you choose.

Here is the best part of all. When your catalog of specialized books and merchandise is successful, start working with a list broker to mail your catalogs to potentially millions of customers. If you can mail to outside lists successfully, you'll increase your business beyond expectations. My advice is to test no more than 5,000 names at a time. If the test is successful, go to 10,000, 20,000, 30,000 and various augmented increments. It may be tempting to complete the mailing all at once, but I strongly advise you to do it in stages and keep very accurate records of the returns. The initial names you purchase might be the company's very best and most recent names. Watch for the possibility of a diminishing return. For an example, you might want to do a mailing to the subscribers of *Sports Illustrated*.

When your mail order operation is running successfully, you could consider having a retail outlet. Many people like to actually see the products before purchasing them. Many successful mail order operations maintain retail stores. It means added business, the opportunity of getting personally acquainted with your customers, and the chance to do valuable market research with them. Mail order customers from all over the world visit me at my showroom and office. It's always a pleasant experience.

For many years, I have had excellent results using the four-page circular shown on pages 100 through 103 to sell the book *How I Made a Million Dollars in Mail Order* by E. Joseph Cossman.

I am now successfully selling the book *The Knight in Rusty Armor* by Robert Fisher by reprinting the first chapter. This technique is selling thousands of copies. People write that they got hooked on the story and are curious to know what happens. A high percentage of them are so delighted with the book that they reorder multiple copies to share with others. See pages 158 through 163.

The two-page circular on pages 156 and 157 is pulling in many orders. I had planned to write a four-pager but decided against it because of the outstanding success I am currently having selling the book *Brainstorming* with a two-page circular. See pages 152 and 153.

It's axiomatic with mail order professionals that four-page circulars always out-pull two-pagers, but I'm rethinking this philosophy because of my excellent results with the shorter format. You might try both to determine what works best for your particular product.

Help Yourself to Millions

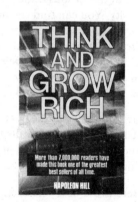

Setting and meeting goals are the key lessons in Think and Grow Rich *by Napoleon Hill.*

Many people are skeptical about the value of self-help business books. They may not work for everyone, but they certainly work for some people. A self-made real estate developer who worried about paying a $200 debt 10 years ago is worth about $6 million today because of a self-help book.

Greg B. Randle, owner and president of home-based Monex Land Development in Los Angeles, California, lives in a million-dollar house he paid for in one year and drives a Mercedes Benz 560 that he owns free and clear.

But it wasn't always this way. Twelve years ago his wife, Debbie, worked full-time as a nurse while Greg sold life insurance. When they had their first child, their bills quickly mounted, and buying a washer and dryer became their biggest goal.

Then Greg's boss and mentor, life insurance salesman Bob Larsen, introduced him to the book *Think and Grow Rich* by Napoleon Hill. "The book teaches you to set goals," says Randle.

Following the book's advice, Randle focused on a few goals at a time, writing them down and telling people about them. He pulls out a poignant memento: the index card on which he listed his first goals—paying off the $200 debt and buying that washer and dryer. Randle had the card laminated long ago, and he keeps it as a reminder of how far he's come.

After reading *Think and Grow Rich*, he continued selling life insurance and began buying fixer-uppers in downtown Long Beach, which was then in the early stages of redevelopment. An ex-marine exhilarated by physical labor, he razed or refurbished and rented those early junkers, all the time focusing on the big goal he had set. Randle was going to become a real estate developer and a millionaire.

Today he is both. "I owe it all to the book," he says, "and Bob Larsen." And to his own determination, one might add.

Randle is building a $10 million condominium complex this year and is working diligently toward attaining his next goal, "50 at 50." The 40-year-old intends to be worth $50 million by the time he's 50.

Think and Grow Rich sells for $12.00 postpaid and is published by Wilshire Book Company, 12015 Sherman Road, North Hollywood, CA 91605.

Here I am on television promoting the third edition of *How to Get Rich in Mail Order*. These pictures were taken on August 28, 1981 on Inez Pedroza's "Daybreak L.A." show on KABC-TV, Hollywood.

The picture on the bottom left shows Tomi Ryan and me holding one of her beautiful vegetable-floral arrangements. I showed this on television as the perfect example of a unique skill that could be taught with a booklet and easily sold through mail order.

Tomi is a well-known author, lecturer, caterer, and cooking instructor who teaches in the Los Angeles area. She is the resident teacher at the famous Everywoman's Village in Van Nuys, California.

See pages 333 through 336 for another example of selling specialized information by mail order. Why not try a similar approach in your area of expertise?

WHOLESALE MAIL ORDER PRINTING

- Low **Discount** Mailorder Prices
- **Professional** Lithographic Printing
- **Immediate** Service
- **FREE** Delivery
- **Charge** Your Order
- Satisfaction **Guaranteed**

SUPER LOW PRICES, Black Ink on 20# Bond Paper, 8½ x 11 only from your camera-ready copy.

	1 side	2 sides
250	13.00	19.00
500	16.00	24.00
1,000	22.00	33.00
2,000	36.00	53.00
3,000	51.00	75.00
4,000	64.00	96.00
5,000	76.00	112.00
add'l 1,000	15.00	22.00

POSTCARDS

Postcards measure 4¼" by 5½" and are printed in black ink on white 67 lb. vellum bristol from your camera-ready original.

	1 side	2 sides
1,000	38.00	48.00
2,000	56.00	76.00
3,000	69.00	99.00
4,000	82.00	122.00
5,000	94.00	144.00
10,000	154.00	254.00
add'l 1,000	12.00	22.00

COLORED CARD STOCK: Add $6.00 per 1,000 postcards.
TYPESETTING: We will typeset your postcard for $15 per side.

OTHER SERVICES

COLORED PAPER – Add $5.00 per thousand sheets. ($5 minimum per order).
☐ Canary ☐ Light Blue ☐ Light Green ☐ Salmon
☐ Buff ☐ Goldenrod ☐ Pink ☐ Ivory

FOLDING – Exact machine folding so your order arrives ready to mail. Add $5.00 per 1,000 sheets. ($5 minimum). Send a sample of how to fold.

CUTTING – Precise cutting. Add $2.00 per cut per thousand sheets.

FREE DELIVERY – We pay UPS shipping charges anywhere in the 48 States. WE MUST HAVE YOUR STREET ADDRESS. We will not ship to a P.O. Box or outside the 48 States.

CAMERA-READY COPY – Ship your original to us flat if possible. We will print exactly what you send us; no changes will be made. Photographs do not reproduce well, and will be printed only at customer's risk.

HOW TO ORDER – It's easy. Just tell the quantity and if you desire any optional services such as colored paper, folding, etc. Your order will be processed immediately, and your original will be returned to you. Please give us your phone number in case we have any questions.

PAYMENT – Full payment must accompany order. Money orders and credit card orders assure immediate processing. All checks are held for clearance (normally two weeks) until payment record has been established. Georgia residents must add sales tax.

CREDIT CARD ORDERS – You may charge your order on your Visa, Mastercard, American Express, or Discover if you wish. There is no extra charge. Print cardholder's name, credit card number, and expiration date. Cardholder's signature is required.

ENVELOPES

We use only the highest quality white wove 24# envelopes. These are not the cheap envelopes found in discount stores, drug stores, etc.

	500	1,000	2,000	2,500	5,000
#10 Regular	29.00	39.00	66.00	79.00	145.00
#10 Window	32.00	42.00	72.00	87.00	160.00
#9 Regular	32.00	42.00	72.00	87.00	160.00
#6¾ Regular	32.00	42.00	72.00	87.00	160.00

FREE TYPESETTING: We will print your camera-ready copy or we will typeset up to four lines absolutely free. Black ink on white envelopes only.

Send Your Order To: PRIME PUBLISHERS, INC.
P.O. Box 680-M • Swainsboro, GA 30401

QUESTIONS? Please feel free to write or call anytime – (912) 237-2422 • Fax (912) 237-3433

Call or write us for LOW WHOLESALE mailorder prices on booklets, business cards, professional typesetting, and our complete U.S.P.S. approved CASS/PAVE certified mailing service.

Wholesale Remainder Dealers

These firms are buyers of bulk remainder stock from publishers and other sources. Also included are selected outlets that handle limited quantities for retail sale.

Mark A Adams Inc
425 Riverside Dr, New York, NY 10025
Tel: 212-864-0416 Fax: 212-316-6496
Pres: Mark Adams
Technical & medical text remainders.

American Media Corp
219 N Milwaukee St, Milwaukee, WI 53202
Tel: 414-287-4600 Fax: 414-287-4602
Pres & Remainder Buyer: Laurence B Compton
Specialize in juveniles.
Warehouse: 2000 titles
Founded 1982

Assorted Book Co
230 Fifth Ave, Suite 1112, New York, NY 10001
Tel: 212-684-9000 Fax: 212-684-0590
Pres: Donn T Westervelt
Opers Mgr: Madge E Patterson
Wholesaler of remainder book & books-on-tape.
Founded 1992

Baker & Taylor
PO Box 734, Somerville, NJ 08876
Tel: 908-218-0400 Fax: 908-722-7420
E-Mail: BTINFO@baker-taylor.e-mail.com
Pres: James S Ulsamer
Sr VP, Opers & Mdsg: Marshall A Wight
Sr VP, Sales & Mktg: Michael E Strauss
VP, Mdsg: Jean M Srnecz
VP, Mktg Communs: Mary Shapiro
VP, Info Technol Group: Wendell Lotz
Contact: Linda Wilson
Buys bulk remainder stock from publishers & only handles limited quantities for resale to retailers & libraries.
Warehouse: 220,000 titles
Founded 1828

Barbour & Co Inc
1810 Barbour Dr, Uhrichsville, OH 44683
Tel: 614-922-6045 Fax: 614-922-5948
Pres: Tim Martins
VP: Mark Zobrosky
VP, Edit: Stephen Reginald
Christian books, bibles, reference.
Warehouse: 800 titles
Founded 1981

Beekman Publishers Inc
PO Box 888, Woodstock, NY 12498
Tel: 914-679-2300
Pres: Stuart A Ober
Warehouse: 5000 titles
Founded 1972

Black Dog & Leventhal Publishers Inc
151 W 19 St, New York, NY 10011
Tel: 212-647-9336 Fax: 212-647-9332
Contact: Helene Liss
Hard-cover & soft-cover nonfiction reference books.
Warehouse: 18 titles
Founded 1993

Book Sales Inc
Subs of Quarto Inc
114 Northfield Dr, Edison, NJ 08837
Tel: 908-225-0530; 800-526-7257 (orders)
 Fax: 908-225-2257
Pres: Melvin Shapiro
CEO: Joseph A Acosta
Treas: Jack Edelman
Discount, Chain & Mass Mktg Mgr: Frank Oppel
Sales Mgr: Joseph Fortin
Warehouse Supv: Deborah Kearney
Office Credit Mgr: Elizabeth Burke
Remainders, reprints & new publications.
Warehouse: 5000 titles
Founded 1952

Booksmith Promotional Co
100 Paterson Plank Rd, Jersey City, NJ 07307
Tel: 718-782-0405; 201-659-2768, 2317 Fax: 201-659-3631
Pres: Phil Hochberg
Exec VP: Barry Hochberg
Dir, Sales & Cust Serv Mgr: Annette Kaye
Remainders & promotional assortments to trade & institutional markets. Specialize in art, juveniles, quality paperbacks, textbooks, psychology & general nonfiction titles.
Warehouse: 5000 titles
Founded 1973
See ad in this section

Camex Books Inc
535 Fifth Ave, New York, NY 10017
Tel: 212-682-8400
Contact: Victor Benedetto

Daedalus Books Inc
4601 Decatur St, Hyattsville, MD 20781
SAN: 158-9202
Tel: 301-779-4102; 800-333-5489 Fax: 301-779-8112
Pres: Robin Moody
VP & Dir, Oper: Helaine Harris
Sales Mgr: Tamara Stock
Trade & scholarly remainders.
Warehouse: 1200 titles
Founded 1980

R Derstine Book Co
14 Birch Rd, Kinnelon, NJ 07405
Tel: 201-838-1109
Specialize in Americana, art, biography, history, science, sports, remainders, videos, university press.
Warehouse: 750 titles
Founded 1965

Diffusion Dimedia Inc
539 boul Lebeau, St Laurent, PQ H4N 1S2, Canada
Tel: 514-336-3941 Telex: 05-8275 43 Fax: 514-331-3916
Pres & Dir Gen: P Assathiany
French novels, literary criticism, human sciences. Wholesaler for French publishers: Le Seuil, Minuit & Boreal.
Warehouse: 8000 titles
Founded 1974

Fairmount Books Ltd
120 Duffield Dr, Markham, ON L6G 1B5, Canada
Tel: 905-475-0988 Fax: 905-475-1072
Pres: Marty Cutler
Dir, Sales: Paul Snow
Mktg Mgr: Marla May
Remainders & promotional books to trade & institutional markets. General trade (hardcover & quality paperbacks) & juvenile books; history, art, biography, reference & fiction.
Warehouse: 4000 titles
Founded 1983

Faro House
778 Genegantslet, Green, NY 13778
Tel: 607-656-8778; 800-729-3988 Fax: 607-656-8080
Owner: Sandra J Pulaski
Remainder Buyer: Lori Edwards
Specialize in women's studies, black culture, ethnic, gay/lesbian, family, Judaica, juvenile, related fiction & nonfiction, trade & university books.
Warehouse: 300 titles
Founded 1985

Granite Impex Ltd corp
Lower Mill Rd, Rte 3, North Stratford, NH 03590
Tel: 603-922-5105; 800-282-5413 Fax: 603-922-3348
Pres: Penelope Dewart
Mgr Mktg Progs: David Sturm
Sales Off(s): New York showroom, Publishers' Resources Inc, 95 Madison Ave, Suite 1303, New York, NY 10016. Tel: 212-686-8000 FAX: 212-686-7110
Home Office Showroom, 195 McGregor St, Manchester, NH 03102. Contact David Sturm, (603) 669-7032
Remainders in hardcover & paperback. Direct sales to retailers from home office or New York showroom. Granite's list contains 2000 titles covering a broad range of subject areas.
Warehouse: 2000 titles
Founded 1990

Hotho & Co
Box 9738, Fort Worth, TX 76147-2738
Tel: 817-335-1833 Fax: 817-335-2300
Pres: Donna Hotho
Founded 1961

Ingram Book Co
Subs of Ingram Distribution Group Inc
Box 3006, One Ingram Blvd, La Vergne, TN 37086-1986
Tel: 615-793-5000; 800-937-8100 TWX: 810-371-1092 Fax: 615-793-3825 (mktg), 361-0236 (ordering); 800-677-5116 (toll free Fax-lib serv)
CEO: Lee Synnott
VChmn: Steven J Mason
Pres, Ingram Intl & Ingram Lib Servs: John Ingram
Sr VP & CFO: Mike Lovett
Exec VP, Opers & Admin: Ray Taylor

Sr VP, Info Resource Mgmt: Wyatt H Pickler
Sr VP, Sales & Mktg: Sue Flaster
VP, Tele Sales & Mktg: Carol McElwain
VP, Book Prod: Steve W Little
VP, East Coast Opers: Jim Pierce
VP, West Coast Opers: Mike Focht
Dir, Mktg: W Neal Webb
Dir, Sales, Ingram Lib Servs Inc: Tom Harris
VP, Mktg, Ingram Library Servs Inc: Larry
  Price
Intl Specialist & Sales Mgr: Angela Schaadt
Sales Off(s): 8201-B Stayton Dr, Jessup, MD
  20794. Tel: 301-725-7110
20445 E Business Pkwy, Walnut, CA 91789.
  Tel: 714-595-2280
Library services & international wholesale
  trade books, elementary & secondary
  textbooks; library binds, prerecorded
  videocassettes & audiocassettes, compact
  disks, microcomputer software, hardware,
  peripherals & institutional educational
  software. Also associated inventory control
  & product identification systems, electronic
  ordering & retail services
BISG member.
Warehouse: 80,000 titles

Roy P Jensen Inc
986 Woodland Ave, Plainfield, NJ 07060
Tel: 908-757-4700 Fax: 908-756-4133
Contact: Roy P Jensen
Remainders, specializing in art &
  architecture, performing arts, natural
  history, general interest & coffee table
  books.

JLM Remainders
2370 E Little Creek Rd, Norfolk, VA 23518
Tel: 804-588-0699 Fax: 804-587-7421
Owner: John Lynch
Contact: Marie Roukas
Buying & selling remainders.
Warehouse: 1700 titles
Founded 1990

Landmark Books International
131 Hicks St, Brooklyn Heights, NY 11201
Tel: 718-624-6419 (voice & fax)
Pres: Diana Shelley-Prizeman
Primarily hardcovers. Specialize in art,
  photography, architecture & the decorative
  arts, cartography.
Warehouse: 50 titles
Founded 1993

Little Dania's Juvenile Promotions
Booksmith Promotional Co
100 Paterson Plank Rd, Jersey City, NJ
  07307
Tel: 201-659-2317; 718-782-0405 Fax: 201-
  659-3631
Pres: Phil Hochberg
VP: Barry Hochberg
Adv & Prom Mgr, Cust Serv & Dir, Sales:
  Annette Kaye
Juvenile promotions, reprints & remainders.
Warehouse: 2500 titles
Founded 1978

Magna Books Inc
95 Madison Ave, Suite 1303, New York, NY
  10016
Tel: 212-686-8000 Fax: 212-686-7110
Pres: Vance R Harvey
Sales for remainder & promotional books.
Warehouse: 4000 titles
Founded 1992
Formerly Publishers' Resources Inc

Milligan News Co Inc
150 N Autumn St, San Jose, CA 95110
SAN: 169-0272
Tel: 408-286-7604; 800-873-2387 Fax: 408-

286-3077
Opers Mgr: Sam Wallace
Books.
Warehouse: 15,000 titles
Founded 1935

National Learning Corp
212 Michael Dr, Syosset, NY 11791
Tel: 516-921-8888; 800-645-6337 Fax: 516-
  921-8743
Pres: Michael P Rudman
VP & Sec: Frances Rudman
Warehouse: 5400 titles
Founded 1967

Ollis Book Corp
Box 258, 28 E 35 St, Steger, IL 60475
Tel: 708-755-5151; 800-323-0343 Fax: 708-
  755-5153
Contact: Kenneth E Ollis
Founded 1965

Powell's Books Wholesale
1501 E 57 St, Chicago, IL 60637
Tel: 312-554-0431 Fax: 312-554-0360
Contact: Bradley Jonas
Scholarly & academic remainders.
Warehouse: 1500 titles
Founded 1990

Promotional Book Co
Div of Strathearn Books Ltd
36 Northline Rd, Toronto, ON M4B 3E2,
  Canada
Tel: 416-759-2226 Fax: 416-759-2150
Pres: R A C Dingman
VP: Toby Tenenbaum
Remainders & overstock.
Founded 1981

Publishers Overstock Unlimited Inc
149 Madison Ave, New York, NY 10016
Tel: 212-481-0055; 800-736-7336 Fax: 212-
  213-6074
Pres: Arthur A Bartley
VP: Elaine Kong
Wholesaler of remainder, reprints &
  promotional books.
Warehouse: 4000 titles
Founded 1985

Publishers' Resources Inc, *see* Magna Books
Inc

R & W Distribution Inc
87 Bright St, Jersey City, NJ 07302
Tel: 201-333-1540 Fax: 201-333-1541
Pres: Bert Wartelsky
Worldwide remainder magazines & comics.
Warehouse: 600 titles
Founded 1974

Random House Value Publishing Inc
Affil of Random House Inc
40 Engelhard Ave, Avenel, NJ 07001
Tel: 908-827-2700; 800-733-3000 Fax: 908-
  827-2691 (sales), 499-2279 (opers &
  admin); 410-848-1900 (sales)
Chmn of the Bd, Pres & CEO, Random
  House: Alberto Vitale
Chmn, Random House Juv & Mdse Div,
  Exec VP, Random House Inc: Gerald
  Harrison
Pres & Publisher: Harold Clarke
Exec Div VP & COO: Marshall Genger
Div VP & Dir, Field Sales: Jeanne Mosure
Div VP & Dir, Publg: Mo Stewart
Div VP & Dir, Sales & Mktg: Lynn Bond
Exec Dir, Prom Sales: Robert McGee
Div VP & Creative Dir: Donald Bender
Div VP & Edit Dir, Random House Value
  Publishing Inc: Kate Hartson
Div VP & Edit Dir, Gramercy Books:

Suzanne Jaffe
Div VP & Edit Dir, Glorya Hale Books:
  Glorya Hale
Publisher of books of all kinds; buyer & seller
  of remainders.
Warehouse: 2000 titles
Founded 1933

Riverside Book Co Inc
250 W 57 St, Suite 1117, New York, NY
  10107
Tel: 212-765-2680 Fax: 212-765-2682
Pres: Victor Eskenazi
Art, architecture/design, photography,
  gardening, cookbooks & reprints.
Warehouse: 30 titles
Founded 1987

S.A.V.E.: Half Price Books for Libraries
Subs of SAVE Suzie & Vic Enterprises
303 N Main, Schulenburg, TX 78956-0030
Tel: 409-743-4147 (voice & fax)
Pres: Suzie Barbee; Victor Hotho
Regional wholesale distributor to libraries.
Warehouse: 4000 titles
Founded 1989

Selective Books Inc
Box 1140, Clearwater, FL 34617
SAN: 204-577X
Tel: 813-447-0100
Pres: Lee Cusack
Business & moneymaking type books.
Warehouse: 25 titles
Founded 1969

John K Sharpe Inc
Box 522, Lake Forest, IL 60045-0522
Tel: 708-360-1577 Fax: 708-272-2051
Pres: Jack Sharpe
Founded 1970

Smithmark Publishers
Fieldcrest Ave, Edison, NJ 08837
SAN: 216-3241
Tel: 908-225-4900; 800-645-9990 Telex: 23-8449
Cable: FLOWERBOOK Fax: 908-225-6499
Pres: Phil Martinho
Chmn: Harvey Markowitz
VP, Publishing & Acq: Deborah Hastings
VP, Sales: Wendy Friedman
Cust Serv Mgr: Elizabeth Vandeveer
Remainders, reprints & promotional books.
Warehouse: 4000 titles
Founded 1979
Formerly Sunflower Books

Sunflower Books, *see* Smithmark Publishers

Texas Bookman
Div of Half Price Books, Records, Magazine Inc
8650 Denton Dr, Dallas, TX 75235
Tel: 214-350-6648 Fax: 214-352-0726
Mgr: Charles Dee Mitchell
Sales Mgr: Robert Wilkie
Scholarly & general remainders.
Warehouse: 1400 titles
Founded 1983

Trident Promotional Corp
801 12 Ave S, Suite 302, Naples, FL 33940
Tel: 941-649-7077 Fax: 941-649-5832
VP, Sales & Mktg: Richard Repass
Contact: Simon S Bailey
Sales Off(s): 95 Madison Ave, Suite 1303, New York, NY 10016
Remainders & promotional books.
Warehouse: 2000 titles
Founded 1989

True Remainders Ltd
Box 500, Jordan Station, ON L0R 1S0, Canada
Tel: 905-562-7767 Fax: 905-562-7828
Contacts: Jenny Hultink; John Hultink
Sales Off(s): Box 770, 240 Portage Rd, Lewiston, NY 14092. Tel: 716-284-7784
Wholesale children's books, coffee table books, cookbooks, computer books & novels.
Warehouse: 3100 titles
Founded 1988

Universal Sales & Marketing Inc
230 Fifth Ave, 12th fl, New York, NY 10001
Tel: 212-481-3500; 800-364-5403 Fax: 212-481-3534
Pres: Daniel Weiner
VP, Sales: Laura Sess
VP, Purch: Sara Matthews
Remainders & promotional books, assortments.
Warehouse: 5000 titles
Founded 1987

University Book Service
Div of UBS Inc
2219 Westbrooke Dr, Columbus, OH 43228
Tel: 614-777-2336; 800-634-4272 Fax: 614-777-2341
Pres: Suzanne Pusecker
Exec VP: Michael Pusecker
Books supplied to schools (K-12) & libraries with catalog cards.
Warehouse: 5000 titles
Founded 1957

WGP Distribution Co Inc
551 W Lancaster Ave, Suite 205, Haverford, PA 19041-1419
Tel: 610-525-9957 Fax: 610-525-3014
Pres: Ira J Pressman
VP: William Goldstein

Remainders & promotional books of all types - fiction, non- fiction, coffee table, children's, cookbooks, gardening books, self-help & mass market.
Warehouse: 166 titles
Founded 1992

Wilshire Book Co
12015 Sherman Rd, North Hollywood, CA 91605
Tel: 818-765-8579 Fax: 818-765-2922
Pres: Melvin Powers
Specialize in psychology, adult fables, inspirational & self-help; mail order, business, motivational & computer books.
Warehouse: 400 titles
Founded 1947

World Publications Inc
455 Somerset Ave, Bldg 2, North Dighton, MA 02764-0167
Tel: 508-880-5555 Fax: 508-880-0469
Pres: Jeffrey Press
Full range distribution of adult & children's remainders including fiction & nonfiction in hardcover & paper, art reference cookbook & mass-market titles.
Warehouse: 3000 titles
Founded 1984

X-S Books Inc
81 Brookside Ave, Amsterdam, NY 12010
SAN: 169-4634
Tel: 518-843-8144 (warehouse) Fax: 518-843-6220
Pres: Thomas Eliopoulos
Oper Mgr: Mimi Wheaton
Remainders & promotional books to trade & institutional markets; specialize in art & general trade titles, juveniles, songbooks, texts, clothbound & paperback; title-by-title & promotional assortments. Graphic design, comics, large print & graphic novels.
Warehouse: 1800 titles
Founded 1972

12015 Sherman Road
No. Hollywood, CA 91605

(818) 765-8579
FAX (818) 765-2922

THE SECRET
OF
BECOMING A MILLIONAIRE

Dear Mail Order Entrepreneur:

For years I have been fascinated by how some people become millionaires while others in the same business or profession never really reach the pinnacle of success. I wanted to know what millionaires think or do that set them apart from individuals who never quite seem to make it no matter how hard they try. I wondered if, perhaps, millionaires share a secret of success.

Over the years, I studied every success book I could find, and I interviewed over a hundred millionaires who had made it big in various fields of endeavor. What did I learn? That there are, indeed, specific attitudes and behaviors that helped make these people winners. Most were highly-motivated, positive thinkers who avidly read motivational and positive thinking books. And they had learned how to originate creative ideas that they diligently put into action. How did they come up with the ideas that made them millionaires? Their answers were always the same—by using a technique called brainstorming.

Brainstorming is a dependable, effective method of stimulating one's creative thinking. And creative ideas are a major component of success. Without them, achieving millionaire status is only an unlikely dream.

Let me share a few personal experiences with you. I spent a year as a songwriter. Although I had never before written lyrics or music, I came up with original song ideas and developed them into hits that made the charts. For one of those hits, I won a prestigious ASCAP award. I even sold an album to MGM Records for which I received a $15,000 advance. How did I do it?—by brainstorming.

I was in the Arabian horse business for many years. One of the horses I owned was a famous Arabian, double champion stallion named Asdar. I paid $20,000 for him and three years later was offered $175,000. Again, I have brainstorming to thank for my success. This time I used it to help me be creative in training, grooming, and developing Asdar, and in marketing his services.

My nephew, Fred Powers, bought a restaurant in downtown Los Angeles, now called Gorky's Cafe and Russian Brewery. He had never before been in the restaurant business, yet, in less than three years, he tripled both his profits and the physical size of his restaurant which now has additional seating, a bakery, and a micro-brewery. To what does Fred owe his astounding success? He attributes it to brainstorming.

A good friend of mine has a 23-year-old son, Robert Grad, who is bass-guitarist for "Kik Tracee," one of the thousands of rock bands trying to make it in Los Angeles. After five years of practicing nights and weekends, the band members began brainstorming sessions that in a few months produced an exciting, unique new sound for their music, a dynamic new image, and over a dozen original songs that incorporate the winning elements of current rock hits. Their efforts culminated in a major record contract with RCA. They are on their way to stardom thanks to brainstorming.

My success as a mail order entrepreneur and book publisher (I have sold millions of copies of such books as *Psycho-Cybernetics*, *The Magic of Thinking Big*, and *Think and Grow Rich*) is directly related to my use of brainstorming techniques. Where did I learn how to brainstorm?—from a book entitled *Brainstorming* by Charles Clark. I have used it as my business bible for the past 30 years. Fred Powers, "Kik Tracee," and an impressive list of well-known businesses and major corporations, such as General Motors, have done the same.

If you are serious about becoming a successful mail order entrepreneur or about achieving success in any business endeavor, you owe it to yourself to read *Brainstorming*. It can make the difference between success and failure.

Order your copy of *Brainstorming* now for only $12.00 postpaid. California residents send $12.85. It could be the best investment you've ever made in your future success. The book is also available on cassette tape for $55.00. California residents send $59.54. Or if you prefer to order by telephone, call (818) 765-8579 and use your Visa or MasterCard.

Feel free to call me when you finish reading the book and/or listening to the cassette tapes. I would be pleased to discuss specifically how you can use the brainstorming techniques you learned to join the ranks of millionaire entrepreneurs.

Good luck on your exciting new road to riches.

Sincerely,

Melvin Powers

Melvin Powers

P.S. Don't let this opportunity slip away. Brainstorming can make you a winner. It's helped others. Why not you?

View of Greenport from the harbor, 1857; Preston's location to right of wharf.

at Preston's - The Nautical charm of Yesterday - for the homes of Today....

At about the turn of the century, when many ocean going yachts put in to Preston's for final outfitting before setting sail to far-off places, six curious looking staffs, topped with a sharp brass fitting were left with us. They had been used to repel unwelcome boarders, and the ship's Captain asked us to hold them.

After almost 80 years, the staffs are still here, joining company with old ships figureheads, cannon and treasure chests from earlier centuries.

(This may seem to be a roundabout way of saying Preston's has been here in the same location for almost a century, and that anything you buy from us is protected by our absolute guarantee of satisfaction, or your money will be refunded.)

As our friends from every state in the Union and from many countries around the world continued to grow in numbers, so did Preston's grow in the diversity of its nautical merchandise.

This catalog is a representative selection of the Nautical items in our Store and Gallery — things that can bring a touch of the charm of the Sea to your home.

Individuals, companies and museums, both here and overseas are served by Preston's — from the South Pacific to Europe, from Alaska to South America — and most places in between.

We'd welcome the opportunity to serve you, too. Our Store hours are 9:00 a.m. to 5:30 p.m., Monday thru Saturday and we are open on Sundays, June thru Labor Day, 10:00 a.m. to 5:00 p.m.

PRESTON'S ABSOLUTE GUARANTEE: Regardless of the reason, if you are dissatisfied in any way with your purchase from Preston's simply return it to us by insured Parcel Post or prepaid Motor Freight within 30 days. You may either make another selection or have your purchase price refunded

# of SHIPS & SEA

Preston's Catalog of Ship Models, Nautical Brassware, Ship's Lights and Clocks, Figureheads, Marine Pictures and a Host of Decorative Nautical Ideas for the Home

PRESTON'S, Main Street Wharf, Greenport, Long Island, N.Y.

154

Melvin Powers
Wilshire Book Company

12015 Sherman Road
No. Hollywood, CA 91605

(818) 765-8579
FAX (818) 765-2922

900 KNOW-HOW

Dear Friend:

How would you like the telephone company to send you a check every month, month in and month out, year after year?

<u>You can start that money rolling in by becoming your own boss</u> in a part-time business you've probably read about in magazines and seen on television. <u>It's the amazing new 900 and 976 "pay-per-call" telephone business.</u>

Here's the Secret

Working with major telephone companies, 900-lines bring in literally thousands of calls per month and make their owners lots of money with every call. That means <u>large second incomes for many 900-line owners and whopping primary incomes for others</u>. And its all done with <u>no direct selling</u>—just by offering information that's in demand by the public!

Anyone Can Do It

Nine-hundred phone lines have become one of the most promising ways for entrepreneurs to cash in on the exploding field of telecommunications. <u>Anyone with information to offer the public</u>, such as horoscopes, financial information, employment news, entertainment and nightlife events, or sports updates, <u>can sell it over the phone and make substantial profits</u>.

<u>People from all backgrounds and income levels are jumping into this lucrative field to launch their own 900 and 976 lines</u>. The industry is just beginning to pick up momentum, and experts predict it will at least double in size over the next two years.

How can you <u>make big money with your own 900 or 976 line</u>? By learning the secrets of starting and running a successful telephone business from those who are already doing it.

Your Key to 900 & 976 Wealth

<u>A new in-depth book, *900 Know-How*, reveals all the insiders tips to starting your own money-making line</u>. This comprehensive book takes hard-to-get information from successful line owners and puts it all together, showing you how to:

* Evaluate your program ideas.

* Find existing programs that make money.

* Test your ideas.

* Determine what price to charge the caller.

* Deal with the phone company.

* Set up joint ventures with service bureaus.

* Get people to keep calling.

* Locate industry associations, trade publications, service bureaus.

Opportunity Is Knocking

900 Know-How comes with an <u>unconditional guarantee</u>. If you're not satisfied that this book reveals a wealth of insiders tips and knowledge, simply return it within 30 days for a complete refund.

<u>The 900 and 976 telephone business is already making some people very rich. More are destined to follow</u>. Will you be one of those who got in on the ground floor? <u>Take control of your financial future now</u>. Send $20.00 (CA residents $21.65) plus $2.00 S/H to:

Melvin Powers, 12015 Sherman Road, No. Hollywood, CA 91605

Chapter 1

The Knight's Dilemma

Once a long time ago, in a land far away, there lived a knight who thought of himself as good, kind, and loving. He did all the things that good, kind, and loving knights do. He fought foes who were bad, mean, and hateful. He slew dragons and rescued fair damsels in distress. When the knight business was slow, he had the annoying habit of rescuing damsels even if they did not want to be rescued, so, although many ladies were grateful to him, just as many were furious with him. This he accepted philosophically. After all, one can't please everybody.

This knight was famous for his armor. It reflected such bright rays of light that villagers would swear they had seen the sun rise in the north or set in the east when the knight rode off to battle. And he rode off to battle frequently. At the mere mention of a crusade, the knight would eagerly don his shining armor, mount his horse, and ride off in any direction. So eager was he, in fact, that sometimes he would ride off in several directions at once, which was no easy feat.

For years this knight strove to be the number one knight in all the kingdom. There was always another battle to be won, dragon to be slain, or damsel to be rescued.

The knight had a faithful and somewhat tolerant wife, Juliet, who wrote beautiful poetry, said clever things, and had a

1

penchant for wine. He also had a young, golden-haired son, Christopher, who he hoped would grow up to be a courageous knight.

Juliet and Christopher saw little of the knight, because when not fighting battles, slaying dragons, and rescuing damsels, he was occupied with trying on his armor and admiring its brilliance. As time went on, the knight became so enamored of his armor that he began wearing it to dinner and often to bed. After a time, he didn't bother to take it off at all. Gradually his family forgot how he looked without it.

Occasionally, Christopher would ask his mother what his father looked like. When this happened, Juliet would lead the boy to the fireplace and point above it to a portrait of the knight. "There's your father," she would sigh.

One afternoon, while contemplating the portrait, Christopher said to his mother, "I wish I could see Father in person."

"You can't have everything!" snapped Juliet. She was growing impatient with having only a painting to remind her of her husband's face, and she was tired from having her sleep disturbed by the clanking of armor.

When he was at home and not completely preoccupied with his armor, the knight usually delivered monologues on his exploits. Juliet and Christopher were seldom able to get a word in edgewise. When they did, the knight shut it out either by closing his visor or by abruptly going to sleep.

One day, Juliet confronted her husband. "I think you love your armor more than you love me."

"That's not true," answered the knight. "Didn't I love you enough to rescue you from that dragon and set you up in this

2

classy castle with wall-to-wall stones?"

"What you loved," said Juliet, peering through his visor so that she could see his eyes, "was the *idea* of rescuing me. You didn't really love me then, and you don't really love me now."

"I *do* love you," insisted the knight, hugging her clumsily in his cold, stiff armor and nearly breaking her ribs.

"Then take off that armor so that I can see who you really are!" she demanded.

"I *can't* take it off. I have to be ready to mount my horse and ride off in any direction," explained the knight.

"If you don't take off that armor, I'm taking Christopher, getting on *my* horse, and riding out of your life."

Well, this was a real blow to the knight. He didn't want Juliet to leave. He loved his wife and his son and his classy castle, but he also loved his armor because it showed everyone who he was—a good, kind, and loving knight. Why didn't Juliet realize that he was any of these things?

The knight was in turmoil. Finally he came to a decision. Continuing to wear the armor wasn't worth losing Juliet and Christopher.

Reluctantly, the knight reached up to remove his helmet, but it didn't budge! He pulled harder. It held fast. Dismayed, he tried lifting his visor but, alas, that was stuck, too. Though he tugged on the visor again and again, nothing happened.

The knight paced back and forth in great agitation. How could this have happened? Perhaps it was not so surprising to find the helmet stuck since he had not removed it for years, but the visor was another matter. He had opened it regularly to eat and drink. Why, he had lifted it just that morning over a breakfast of scrambled eggs and suckling pig.

3

Suddenly the knight had an idea. Without saying where he was going, he hurried to the blacksmith's shop in the castle courtyard. When he arrived, the smith was shaping a horseshoe with his bare hands.

"Smith," said the knight, "I have a problem."

"You *are* a problem, sire," quipped the smith with his usual tact.

The knight, who normally enjoyed bantering, glowered. "I'm in no mood for your wisecracks right now. I'm stuck in this armor," he bellowed as he stamped his steel-clad foot, accidentally bringing it down on the smith's big toe.

The smith let out a howl and, momentarily forgetting the knight was his master, dealt him a smashing blow to the helmet. The knight felt only a twinge of discomfort. The helmet didn't budge.

"Try again," ordered the knight, unaware that the smith obliged him out of anger.

"With pleasure," the smith agreed, swinging a nearby hammer with vengeance and bringing it down squarely on the knight's helmet. The blow didn't even make a dent.

The knight was distraught. The smith was by far the strongest man in the kingdom. If he couldn't shuck the knight out of his armor, who could?

Being a kind man, except when his big toe was crushed, the smith sensed the knight's panic and grew sympathetic. "You have a tough plight, Knight, but don't give up. Come back tomorrow after I'm rested. You caught me at the end of a hard day."

Dinner time that evening was difficult. Juliet became increasingly annoyed as she pushed bits of food she had mashed

4

through the holes in the knight's visor. Partway through the meal, the knight told Juliet that the blacksmith had tried to split open the armor but had failed.

"I don't believe you, you clanking clod!" she shouted, as she smashed her half-full plate of pigeon stew on his helmet.

The knight felt nothing. Only when gravy began dripping down past the eyeholes in his visor did he realize that he'd been hit on the head. He had barely felt the smith's hammer that afternoon either. In fact, when he thought about it, his armor kept him from feeling much of anything, and he had worn it for so long now that he'd forgotten how things felt without it.

The knight was upset that Juliet didn't believe he was trying to get his armor off. He and the smith *had* tried, and they kept at it for many more days without success. Each day the knight grew more despondent and Juliet grew colder.

Finally, the knight had to admit that the smith's efforts were useless. "Strongest man in the kingdom, indeed! You can't even break open this steel junkyard!" the knight yelled in frustration.

When the knight returned home, Juliet shrieked at him, "Your son has nothing but a portrait for a father, and I'm tired of talking to a closed visor. I'm never pushing food through the holes of that wretched thing again. I've mashed my very last mutton chop!"

"It's not *my* fault that I got stuck in this armor. I *had* to wear it so that I would always be ready for battle. How else could I get nice castles and horses for you and Christopher?"

"You didn't do it for *us*," argued Juliet. "You did it for *yourself!*"

The knight was sick at heart that his wife didn't seem to love him anymore. He also feared that if he didn't get his armor off

soon, Juliet and Christopher would really leave. He *had* to get the armor off, but he didn't know how to do it.

The knight dismissed one idea after another as being unlikely to work. Some of the plans were downright dangerous. He knew that any knight who would even think of melting his armor off with a castle torch, freezing it off by jumping into an icy moat, or blasting it off with a cannon was badly in need of help. Unable to find aid in his own kingdom, the knight decided to search in other lands. *Somewhere* there must be *someone* who can help me get this armor off, he thought.

Of course, he would miss Juliet, Christopher, and his classy castle. He also feared that in his absence Juliet might find love with another knight, one willing to remove his armor at bedtime and to be more of a father to Christopher. Nevertheless, the knight had to go, so, early one morning, he got onto his horse, and he rode away. He didn't dare look back for fear he might change his mind.

On his way out of the province, the knight stopped to say goodbye to the king, who had been very good to him. The king lived in a grand castle atop a hill in the high-rent district. As the knight rode across the drawbridge and into the courtyard, he saw the court jester sitting cross-legged, playing a reed flute.

The jester was called Gladbag because, over his shoulder, he carried a beautiful rainbow-colored bag filled with all sorts of things that made people laugh or smile. There were strange cards that he used to tell people's fortunes, brightly colored beads that he made appear and disappear, and funny little puppets that he used to amusingly insult his audiences.

"Hi, Gladbag," said the knight. "I came to say farewell to the king."

The jester looked up.

"The king has up and gone away.
To you there's nothing he can say."

"Where has he gone?" asked the knight.

"He's taken off on a new crusade.
If you wait for him, you'll be delayed."

The knight was disappointed that he had missed the king and perturbed that he couldn't join him on the crusade. "Oh," he sighed, "I could starve to death in this armor by the time the king returns. I might never see him again." The knight felt very much like slumping in his saddle, but, of course, his armor wouldn't let him.

"Well, aren't you a silly sight?
All your might can't solve your plight."

"I'm in no mood for your insulting rhymes," barked the knight, stiffening in his armor. "Can't you take someone's problem seriously for once?"

In a clear, lyrical voice, Gladbag sang:

"Problems never set me a-rockin'.
They're opportunities a-knockin'."

"You'd sing a different tune if *you* were the one stuck in here," growled the knight.

Gladbag retorted:

"We're all stuck in armor of a kind.
Yours is merely easier to find."

"I don't have time to stay and listen to your nonsense. I have to find a way to get out of this armor." With that, the knight kneed his mount forward to leave, but Gladbag called after him:

"There is one who can help you, Knight,

to bring the real you into sight."

The knight pulled his horse to a stop and, excitedly, he turned back to Gladbag. "You know someone who can get me out of this armor? Who is it?"

"Merlin the Magician you must see.
Then you'll discover how to be free."

"Merlin? The only Merlin I've ever heard of is the great and wise teacher of King Arthur."

"Yes, yes, that's his claim to fame.
This Merlin I know is one and the same."

"But it can't be!" exclaimed the knight. "Merlin and Arthur lived long ago."

Gladbag replied:

"It's true, yet he's alive and well.
In yonder woods the sage doth dwell."

"But those woods are so big," said the knight. "How will I find him in there?"

Gladbag smiled.

"One never knows be it days, weeks, or years,
when the pupil is ready, the teacher appears."

"I can't wait for Merlin to show up. I'm going to look for *him*," said the knight. He reached out and shook Gladbag's hand in gratitude, nearly crushing the jester's fingers with his gauntlet.

Gladbag yelped. The knight quickly released the jester's hand. "Sorry." Gladbag rubbed his bruised fingers.

"When the armor's gone from you,
you'll feel the pain of others, too."

"I'm off!" said the knight. He wheeled his horse around, and with new hope in his heart, galloped away to find Merlin.

Melvin Powers
Wilshire Book Company

12015 Sherman Road   (818) 765-8579
No. Hollywood, CA 91605   FAX (818) 765-2922

A PERSONAL WORD FROM MELVIN POWERS

Not since *Jonathan Livingston Seagull* first enthralled the reading public has there been a story that captivates the imagination so thoroughly as *The Knight in Rusty Armor*.

Since I first published *The Knight,* I've received an unprecedented number of calls and letters from readers, praising its powerful concepts and engaging style. I feel so strongly about this unusual book that I'm personally extending an invitation for you to read it.

Join the knight as he faces a life-changing dilemma upon discovering that his shining armor cannot be removed. As he searches for a way to free himself, he receives guidance from the wise sage Merlin the Magician who encourages the knight to embark on the most difficult crusade of his life.

With the help of an intuitive little creature named Squirrel and a loyal, clever pigeon, Rebecca, the knight travels the Path of Truth where he meets his real self for the first time. As he passes through the castles of Silence, Knowledge, and Will and Daring, the knight confronts the Universal Truths that govern his life—and ours.

The knight's journey reflects our own—filled with hope and despair, belief and disillusionment, laughter and tears. His insights become our insights as we follow along on this intriguing adventure of self-discovery. Anyone who has ever struggled with the meaning of life and love will discover profound wisdom and truth as this delightful fantasy unfolds.

In *The Knight,* the author, Robert Fisher, skillfully uses the wit and humor he mastered during his long and distinguished career writing for such comedy greats as Groucho Marx, Bob Hope, George Burns, Jack Benny, Red Skelton, Alan King, and Lucille Ball. Mr. Fisher has 400 radio and 1,000 TV shows to his credit, including episodes of "Alice," "Good Times," "All in the Family," "The Jeffersons," and "Maude."

The Knight is more than a book. It's an experience that will expand your mind, touch your heart, and nourish your soul. Treat yourself to the enchantment of *The Knight in Rusty Armor.*

$7.00 postpaid (CA residents $7.41)
Hardcover edition $12.00 postpaid (CA residents $12.83)

Slaying Dragons

Hiding beneath the protective armor there's a brave knight in each of us.

A FRIEND OF MINE RECENTLY recommended a book to me, called *The Knight in Rusty Armor* by Robert Fisher. The knight in the story considers it his sole and noble mission to be the best knight there is. When not saving damsels or slaying dragons, he is trying on his armor and admiring its brilliance.

As the story progresses, the knight grows to love his armor not only because it shows everyone who he is, but also—most importantly—because it keeps him from feeling anything. Furthermore, he wears the armor for so long he forgets how things feel without it. Then, when he tries to remove it, he can't—it won't come off. He asks the advice of Merlin, the magician, who helps him realize that the only way to rid himself of the armor is to *rust* it away. To do so he must feel something so deeply that he cries, thereby rusting the armor and causing it to fall away, part by part.

No matter how brave or strong we are, we all wear a type of invisible armor to protect us from some aspect of life. Fear is a significant, powerful force that we feel on many levels—physically, mentally and emotionally.

I admit, with apprehension, that fear is a significant part of my life. As a child with athletic tendencies, I learned to be strong physically, mentally and emo-

tionally. Being strong is comfortable for me. It is also my armor—it protects me from conflict, anger, pain and disappointment.

Learning to face and express these feelings is what I'm afraid of and what I deal with every day. However, I'm learning to move through this fear. I still have to remind myself every day that all feelings are OK, that I can feel safe if I recognize, acknowledge and deal with unpleasant feelings. I believe that fear is one of our greatest teachers. Whatever our fears, they are neither good nor bad—they just are. All we risk by uncovering them is becoming healthier, more fully human, and tasting another part of life.

I may climb mountains, strive to run a seven-and-a-half-minute mile and take care of the rest of my physical needs, but my daily training isn't complete until I've hiked a trail through my fears and tasted the waters at the summit, where my feelings continue to flow whether I recognize them or not.

It's scary to try something different, whether it's a walking program, in-line skating or expressing your feelings. Uncover your fears and what's behind them. Read "Overcoming Fear" on page 100, and learn to remove each small piece of your armor at a time, moving through your fears one by one, to a richer, fuller life.

Yours (and getting rustier),

Barbara Harris
Editor in Chief

RONI RAMOS

For every man and woman who loved *The Knight in Rusty Armor ...*

KNIGHTS WITHOUT ARMOR
A Practical Guide for Men
In Quest of the Masculine Soul

Aaron R. Kipnis, Ph.D.
Foreword by Robert A. Johnson

The Knight in Rusty Armor struggled to free himself with only Merlin, squirrel and Rebecca to help him. But you can get help and guidance from Dr. Aaron R. Kipnis, psychotherapist, leader of men's groups, and recognized expert in modern man's quest to define and live a new masculine role.

Readers of *The Knight in Rusty Armor*, both men and women, are enthusiastically acclaiming Dr. Kipnis's book that offers men guidance in living powerfully, yet fully and joyously, without their armor. Women readers gain new insights into the inner lives of men, deepen their understanding of the forces that shape the men in their lives, and learn how to support men's changes in a changing world.

SOMETHING IS STIRRING
IN THE HEARTS OF MEN

Many men feel angry and trapped by restrictive roles and jobs. They long for more authenticity and meaningful, impassioned relationships. Others are beginning to speak about their grief, their confusion, and their unrealized dreams. All are seeking new ways to express what it means to be a man in our time.

THE OLD ARMOR NO LONGER WORKS

The knights of ancient times were heavily armored from head to toe. These men were invincible in battle—until the crossbow was invented. Today, men in the marketplace have donned a new sort of armor. Many powerful men have constructed a heroic personality that is hard, inflexible and, like the armor of old, heavy to drag around. It is difficult to feel much pleasure or joy in life when one is burdened with a self-image that says: in order to be a man you must be tough and cold as steel. In today's society, however, men are discovering, like their medieval counterparts, that they are no longer impervious to the armor-piercing arrows slung by people who have lost connection to their souls.

Men are beginning to realize that in order to face the challenges ahead, they must find a way to remove the armor that immobilizes them. This armor makes it difficult to feel much and also renders men unable to tend their own wounds, which are festering beneath their hardened exteriors. In order to remain powerful without their armor, men must find a new way of being in the world. They must cultivate a new self-image that accurately reflects what it truly means to be a man, which is the quest undertaken by those whose lives are examined in this book.

SHEDDING THE MYTH OF THE LONE HERO

The myth of the lone hero, who conquers all through the force of his will, is no longer the image that inspires the modern man in search of his soul. And the idealized female—whether wife, mother, lover, goddess, or inner woman—is no longer seen as the sole source of nurturing, healing, and wholeness for man. A new myth for a new time emerges in this book, bringing a new dimension to the spiritual quest undertaken by the knights of other ages. The image that becomes apparent is of a soulful, life-generating, sensitive and joyful man who is also potent, fierce, and powerful in the world. Through cultivating male friends who risk revealing who they really are behind their iron masks, these men break out of the isolation that plagues so many contemporary men.

A NEW PSYCHOLOGY
FOR A NEW MILLENNIUM

Building upon all the work that has come before, the author represents a new generation of male psychologists who have gone beyond the patriarchal formulation of the nineteenth century and the feminist revisions of the twentieth century. Dr. Kipnis lays the foundations for a new male psychology that is more applicable to the challenges of a new millennium. His revisioning of male myths and intriguing perspectives on old stereotypes have opened a new door into the male psyche.

Knights Without Armor weds ancient myths of masculinity to the subjective experience of modern men and the objective perspectives of hundreds of studies from various scientific fields. What emerges is a fresh vision and new understanding of men that points the way for a new male psychology and spirituality. Dr. Kipnis's "Twelve Tasks of Men" guides men past the major problems they have in opening up their lives, and his "Male Manifesto" clarifies the positive image of masculine values.

This comprehensive and insightful work presents a rich adventure of self-discovery for the male reader who will undoubtedly hear many of his own issues expressed by the male voices in this book. And it will prove invaluable to any woman who wants to better understand her own quest for soul and that of the men in her life.

LIFETIME MONEY-BACK GUARANTEE

Order *Knights Without Armor* now and learn about the new, authentic masculinity and the effect it has on the lives of both men and women. If the book isn't all I've said it is—and more—you can return it at any time for a full refund. For a beautiful, 294-page hardcover edition, send $10.00 (CA res. $10.83) plus $2.00 shipping and handling to:

Melvin Powers, 12015 Sherman Road, North Hollywood, CA 91605

Three Magic Words Will Bring You Everything You Ever Wanted

Three Magic Words is a ground-breaking book about the greatest idea in the world—a secret revealed in just three words—an idea so simple, so startling, so wonderful that it can start you on an adventure that will forever change the way you see yourself, others, and life. Knowing the secret opens up a whole new world of contentment, fulfillment, joy and abundance.

What Are You?.... Why Are You Here?

This is the age of uncertainty. This is the time of emotional upset and nervous instability. This is the era when man, surveying the universe from atop the heap of his material accomplishments, sees his insignificance in comparison to the stars, understands how puny is his strength in comparison to nuclear power. This is the time when man, in his headlong rush to master the elements and harness nature's energies, has come far enough to know that he treads the wrong path to his own security. For there is no security in machines or electricity or electronics or nuclear power.

What am I? What caused me? Why am I here? Where am I going? These are the questions of the human soul that demand an answer.

For man is not an animal that exists upon the earth for a day, a freak of existence in a maelstrom of chaos. The human soul does not exist who at some cloistered moment has not reached out with timid fingers and touched God.

No circumstance or fact or event or thing exists that does not have a reason, and so it is with man. All harnessing of nature's elements and powers, all creation of material wealth and possessions are but passing fancies, things of the moment, for man enters into life naked, and naked he departs. The only thing, the single most important thing that concerns his existence on earth, is the discovery of his soul.

For man is not body alone. No human being can bear to live who regards himself as only a freak occurrence in a freak circumstance. Man is spirit, clearly and without dispute. Man is the essence of the mighty intelligence that guides and controls the universe. Man lives in this

167

intelligence; he is a part of it and the whole of it. He is as small as his temporal life and as great as his spiritual life, for the intelligence from which he comes is greater than all, greater than the far reaches of space, greater than the power that holds the planets in their courses. This intelligence is man's to use as he sees fit. It is God-given, a divine birthright, and is denied to no man except by himself.

Your Unlimited Power Over All Things

In the pages of *Three Magic Words*, you will learn of the unlimited power that is yours. You will learn how you can turn this power to work for you, here on earth, to make your life majestic and overflowing with good. *Three Magic Words* is not a religion or a sect or a society. In its entirety it is a series of essays aimed at revealing to you your power over all things. You will learn that there is only one mover in all creation and that mover is thought. You will learn that there is only one creator and that creator is the Universal Subconscious Mind, or God. You will learn that this creator creates for you exactly what you think, and you will be shown how you can control your thoughts, not only to obtain answers to your problems but to create in your experience exactly what you desire.

It requires only a few minutes of your time each day, a few minutes that will reward you with greater vistas in life, greater hope and promise than has ever been dreamed.

There is a cause! There is a reason! There is a power greater than you are, of which you are a part, that you can use to make your life good and great and vigorous and full of abundance!

A Promise of Success

If you read this remarkable book through, and do what it tells you to do, you cannot fail to accomplish what it promises. *Three Magic Words* is a book that many people carry with them for years, referring to it again and again to remind themselves of its powerful, life-changing message. Your life, too, will be affected, for once you learn the three magic words, you will feel compelled to live by them, every day of your life.

LIFETIME MONEY-BACK GUARANTEE

Please send me *Three Magic Words* by U.S. Anderson on a money-back guarantee basis. Enclosed is my check or money order payable to Melvin Powers for $12.00 postpaid (CA residents $12.83 postpaid).

Name_____ Date_____
                       Please Print

Address_____

City_____ State_____ Zip_____

Mail to: Melvin Powers, 12015 Sherman Road, North Hollywood, CA 91605

MAKE YOUR DREAMS YOUR GOALS

Chapter Nine

I Enjoy Selling Books by Mail—
Some of My Successful and Not-So-Successful
Ads and Direct Mail Circulars

I enjoy writing advertising copy to promote the sale of a book. The mere chance my ad might turn out to be a hit has the same excitement for me as the prospect of being a winner in the Irish Sweepstakes would have for someone else. I hope you, too, will be swept up in this kind of creative excitement once you've started promoting your products. Eventually, it will produce winners for you.

I am going to present several of my ads; some did extremely well, others did moderately well, and still others fizzled. It's important to note most ads don't continue to pull extremely well over a long period of time. Ads seem to run their cycle. You usually get the cream of the buyers, and then response begins to wane. I make this statement with the knowledge there are notable exceptions. Among these are Joe Karbo's ad, *"The Lazy Man's Way to Riches"* and Mark O. Haroldsen's ad, *"Wake Up the Financial Genius Inside You."* The responses to these ads increase rather than diminish with time.

Successful ads can be rejuvenated and again make a fortune. I've seen this happen many times. Recently, one of my mail order students asked my advice about purchasing, from a mail order entrepreneur, the rights to a product that seemingly had run its course. The item had been out of circulation for several years. Based on the successful sales record it had enjoyed earlier, I told him to go ahead. I felt the time was propitious to recycle the

product. He used the ads that made this product successful several years before and made a great deal of money.

If you are serious about being in the mail order business, start saving ads that have proven successful. You never know when you might want to redesign one or use part of it to improve your own copy. I should be reactivating some of my best-pulling ads, but I do not have time to devote my attention to all the projects I have in mind. That's the way it goes for many creative entrepreneurs, and I prefer to direct my creative talents to new products. A new challenge holds my interest.

I have previously suggested you read as many books as you can on current and out-of-print mail order books and search for ads in old magazines. It's an excellent way to find a product to bring back to life.

Besides having the product, you need good advertising copy to convey your message to the public. As you study my ads and comments, start thinking about how you could improve the ads. You may or may not agree with my comments. If you have suggestions that might improve any of my ads, I'll welcome your ideas. It's good practice for you. I want you to concentrate your creative endeavors on advertising copy and layouts. Bear in mind, your success lies not only in finding a product, but in developing or recognizing saleable advertising copy. Advertising copy is the catalyst that makes your operation successful. Spending a small amount of money with good ads will lead to success. Spending a fortune with ads that don't have a chance will spell disaster. Don't fall in love with your advertising copy. Be amenable to improvement through change.

Several months ago, I saved a mail order client $25,000. He had embarked on a direct mail campaign to sell a book that I believed was headed for failure. An advertising agency, not familiar with mail order, had designed a program for the sale of his book. They had missed many basic elements and were not even testing the advertising copy and various prices for the book.

He was about ready to start with the campaign when instead he decided to accept the ideas I had presented to him. I approached the campaign from a diametrically opposite position. I spent as little money as possible and tested many elements before going ahead. Although my client had the money to spend, my advice to him was to be slow in spending it, evaluating results as we went along. Even if you are sure you have a winner, use some test ads before you run a full schedule. The customers will always be there waiting. If it's a quick indication you want, run a newspaper ad. If it pays off in the newspaper, it will pay off handsomely in magazines. My client started on a reading program similar to the one I suggested to you. He worked on the assignments I gave him and made progress in a short period of time. We have redesigned the advertising copy and follow-up literature; the testing is proceeding in a logical manner; and we are obtaining much valuable information. He now has a winner, but I'm striving for the best returns possible.

My philosophy is to work *with* a client rather than *for* a client. I want to be of help, but I don't want him to be totally dependent on me for all future mail order campaigns. I enjoy the role of teacher, sharing my expertise.

THE SECRET OF BOWLING STRIKES

On pages 176 and 177, you'll find two of my most successful ads. I ran these ads for many years in *Bowling Magazine, Women's Bowler,* and numerous independent bowling newspapers.

Which of the ads pulled better? Before reading further, go back to the two pages and make your judgment. Why did you pick the one you did? If you picked the ad on page 177, you are on the way to becoming a mail order pro. The other bowling ad did well enough, but I wasn't pleased with the results. I felt the ad lacked an element of excitement, it was too stilted, and there wasn't enough action in it for a bowling ad. The answer came to me one day and I added the art work as shown on page 177. I also altered the layout slightly. These changes added considerably to the success of the ad. The results went from good to terrific.

When you have a good paying ad, try to get even better results. Didn't we observe Mark Haroldsen doing that

with his ad for *How to Wake Up the Financial Genius Inside You?* And he's sold $3,500,000 worth of books. You would assume he'd stop testing. Who wouldn't be happy selling that amount? But once you have become successful, it's the challenge rather than the money that becomes the prime attraction.

I'd like you to read the advertising copy of the bowling and other ads I'll present to you. What do you think about the advertising copy? Could you improve it? Here's your assignment for all the ads. Imagine you are now a mail order consultant being paid $100 per hour. Find a setting with no distractions, mentally set the mood for yourself, and completely immerse yourself in the task. As you do it from time to time, you'll become more proficient. You'll be delighted with yourself when you read an ad in a magazine and unconsciously come up with a better headline, subheading, layout and art work. This indicates you are making progress and are well on your way toward coming up with a winner for yourself.

Let's analyze the bowling ad. First is the promise to reveal *The Secret of Bowling Strikes.* What could be more valuable to you as a bowler? It's your dream come true. Above the title we have the lead-in copy: *Now available to you . . .* and *Available to you at last . . .* Those phrases help set up the headline. I could have written such phrases as: "An amazing discovery . . . Give me one hour and I'll give you . . . You can bowl like the pros with . . ."

I like putting the word *STRIKES* in the middle of the bowling pins being knocked over. It's graphic and effectively fits the illustration. Note I have the same type of illustration on the cover of the book.

I immediately followed up the title of the book with a reinforcing statement and guarantee. My second paragraph restates my claim and tells the reader: *"This remarkable new technique is thoroughly explained and can be easily understood and used by all bowlers."* That's an important statement. We are saying everyone can learn the secret of bowling strikes.

I like the subheading: HERE'S THE SECRET. The reader is hooked. It's impossible for a serious bowler to read the headline and not read the secret.

100 PHOTOGRAPHS is also a good subheading for this book. People who are into sports like action photographs for illustrative purposes. Read the second paragraph under this heading. It tells you the book is *for the beginning and advanced player alike.* That statement doesn't leave anyone out. Notice how the paragraph ends, restating the promise—*an exciting new approach that will help every bowler to achieve the kind of explosive action that results in pins toppling into strikes and in increasingly higher scores. Strikes* and *higher scores* are magic words to the bowler.

Go to TRY IT ENTIRELY AT OUR RISK! We tell the reader we know he may be hesitant about buying the book, so we make him an offer he can't refuse.

In the coupon we call for action. MAIL THIS COU-PON TODAY! That's a positive suggestion. I refer to the book as an amazing book although the word *amazing* has been used excessively in advertising copy. It still serves its purpose well. Again, there is the promise of a higher score. The price of the book is reasonable and would certainly not be a deterrent to someone who really wanted the book.

Everything about this ad has been thought out care-fully, and you could use it as a guide in writing one of your own. Couldn't you easily write an ad selling a tennis or racquetball book, using the same general layout and ideas?

I have sold tens of thousands of copies of this book and never had a single request for a refund. I also received lots of testimonial letters, but never used them in the ads. Are you convinced the average reader does not pay much attention to testimonials praising a book or product? Would you have added a few testimonials to the ad?

HOW YOU CAN BOWL BETTER USING SELF-HYPNOSIS

Read the ad on page 178 for *How You Can Bowl Better Using Self-Hypnosis.* How do you think it pulled, and why? Why didn't I use a photograph of the book? What is the purpose of using such a long ad instead of a brief one such as I used for *The Secret of Bowling Strikes?* If you are a bowler, would you be interested in purchasing the book? Why?

Let's analyze the pulling power of the ad. The subject of hypnosis has always been of keen interest to the general public. The promise of successfully combining the powers of hypnosis with bowling to help the bowler achieve higher scores is fascinating.

Every bowler can immediately identify with the head-line in a very positive way. He's had the experience of bowling a strike and feeling confident he has the know-how to follow it with successive strikes. I make a strong statement in the first few lines of the copy. I'm promising the bowler a very high score. It sounds incredible. I know it and the reader knows it, so I ask him to keep an open mind.

In the first paragraph, I give a familiar example with which he can easily identify. Under the subheading, *Here Is a Promise for Better Bowling,* I introduce the subject of hypnosis. I meet the possible objections under the sub-title, *What Will They Think of Next?* If the reader has read this far, he'll go onto the next subheading, *Here's the Secret.* I used this same subtitle in the ad for *The Secret of Bowling Strikes.* The subtitle of *Use Your Practice Game in League Play* is a powerful statement, and bowlers can easily identify with that. When they are more relaxed, they bowl better. I play tennis with the same group every week. During the warm-up period, everyone hits the ball like a professional. As soon as the game begins, the

beautiful strokes and shots seem to vanish. So far, this ad is all very positive, and the reader is ready for the proof. The next two subheadings do that with quotes from the experts. The copy under the last subheading again meets the possible objection to hypnosis.

I like the first sentence under *Try It Entirely At Our Risk*—"We know you may be hesitant about trying this new approach and because of this we make the following offer:" It's as if we are reading the reader's mind. I again state that the reader's bowling score will be higher. I do the same thing in the actual coupon. Calling for action, I tell the reader: *Act Today!* MAIL NO-RISK COUPON TODAY. It's a perfect ad containing all the ingredients for success. I didn't use a photograph of the book because I wanted the reader to get involved with the advertising copy. This style ad, one which is without a photograph or illustration, is known as a reading-copy ad. It has become very popular and has been used with great success. Joe Karbo used this style in his ad for *The Lazy Man's Way to Riches.* You might want to consider this type of ad for some of your own.

To complete the final phase of a perfect mail order program, I ran a series of classes for bowlers in the Los Angeles area teaching them self-hypnosis. The bowlers not only improved their averages, but received ancillary benefits.

THE SECRET OF PERFECT PUTTING

We have agreed you can determine if an ad is successful if you see it repeated. You can find out what's on the back end of the product by sending away for whatever is adver-tised. You can even find out how many orders the ads pulled by writing to the company or to a list broker saying you want to rent the names.

Why not copycat a successful ad with something sim-ilar? I suggested this in Chapter 6. It's exactly what I did with some of my ads, except I copycatted my own ads! I was selling tens of thousands of copies of my bowling books and the campaign was in high gear. The idea came to me—why not use a slight variation on the bowling ads to sell golf books?

Take a look at page 179 for the book, *The Secret of Perfect Putting.* Does it look familiar? Compare it with the ad for the book, *The Secret of Bowling Strikes,* on page 176. To paraphrase a popular statement, "Only the name has been changed to protect the innocent." The ad was extremely successful and ran for many years. I knew I had a winner even before I ran the ad because of the tremendous success of the bowling books. Look how closely I copied the bowling ad. That ad was successful, why not this one?

In Chapter 1, I suggested you read the book, *Brain-storming,* by Charles Clark. I used the technique to come up with two new book titles to merchandise. Your brain-storming sessions will help you develop new products. I'd be interested to hear what comes of your creative efforts using this technique.

HOW YOU CAN PLAY BETTER GOLF USING SELF-HYPNOSIS

Read the ad on page 180. This ad sold thousands of books. I knew it was excellent because I copied my ad on *How You Can Bowl Better Using Self-Hypnosis.* Look at the similarity. See page 178. It's virtually the same ad—the word "golf" is used instead of "bowling." I ran both golf ads in various golf magazines.

My headline, *Have You Ever Taken a Practice Golf Swing At A Dandelion?,* strikes a responsive chord with every golfer. He can immediately identify with this because all golfers do it, and when he does, his form is perfect. But replace the dandelion with a golf ball, and something happens to him.

See how I used the statements of experts to support my premise a person's golf game can be improved with hypnosis. See subheadings: *The Experts Agree* and *Here's More Proof from the Experts.* These statements were made by sophisticated golfers and lend credibility to my advertising copy. They blend in perfectly.

As a result of the ads on the book, I received a great deal of free publicity from sportswriters around the world. Their curiosity was aroused. They sent for copies and reviewed the book in their columns. I was surprised by all the publicity. I got major articles in golf magazines and in Sunday supplements. It was an unexpected bonus, resulting in more sales of the book. All of this was the direct result of the techniques of brainstorming and copy-catting.

Only one other book using the subconscious mind as a focal point for improving a sports game has had that much publicity—*The Inner Game of Tennis* by Timothy Gallwey, published in 1974 by Random House. It made the best-seller list and was the basis for many courses taught on the subject. Public TV in Los Angeles had weekly programs in which Mr. Gallwey explained and demonstrated his technique.

A PRACTICAL GUIDE TO BETTER CONCENTRATION

I trust you are beginning to understand the concept of copycatting as an initial way of putting your mail order skills to work. The real satisfaction comes in using successful ads as a springboard for your creative talent. Study the ads on pages 181 and 182. Only the headline and three subheadings have been changed on page 182. Which ad did better, and how do you think these ads pulled?

With the book, *Psycho-Cybernetics,* I not only had a best seller, but my ads were on a winning streak. I was headed towards selling a million copies of the book. I knew it and felt it. It was like having the touch of Midas.

Since the ads were going so well with the bowling and golf books, I started to think of another book with the idea of using the same technique. One day, I was reading my ad on *How You Can Play Better Golf Using Self-Hypnosis.* As I was reading the third line of the third column, "Your second mental problem is concentration," the answer came to me. I was to sell a book on concentration. The only problem was that I didn't have a book on the subject, and no one else had ever published one.

One would normally assume that the way to proceed is to get a book on concentration, and write an ad based on the book. It can be done that way, but it's not the way I usually go about it. Many book publishers send out very expensive mailing pieces based on a book they are thinking of producing. If the direct mail proves successful, they go ahead with the book. If the tests do not bring the desired results, they naturally refund the money with a letter of apology. The literature relating to this unborn literary child might read, "Pre-publication price $10.00, regular price $15.00."

My writing assignment was launched. Write a good ad and, if it appears I have a winner, write the book afterwards. That's exactly what I did. I wrote a book, *A Practical Guide to Better Concentration.* I decided to use the reading-copy format and follow the success pattern of the other two books. Although this is a completely different subject, look how I followed the layout exactly. Are you aware that the rhythm and style of the new ad is the same as that of the other ads? It's like putting new words to an old song.

So far the theory is excellent. The only problem is the pulling power of the ad was, at best, moderate. I changed the headline and a few subheadings, as shown on page 182, and although this improved the results somewhat, it wasn't enough to warrant my spending further time on it. For me, it was a signal to change directions.

Following the procedure of writing the ad copy before acquiring the product, I wrote a powerful ad based on a product for the home. I strongly felt the ad was a good one. All I needed was a product to live up to the claims of the ad. You might want to try the same thing.

MIND OVER PLATTER

See page 183. Does the layout look familiar? Of course. It's the same as in *The Secret of Bowling Strikes* and *The Secret of Perfect Putting.* I had very good results and ran it for a long time. I use the word "secret" in the headline (it's as though I can't escape the word). The copy under the headline is excellent. The book is based on help given to more than 2,000 patients and is written by a medical doctor. I use the subheading *Here's the Secret.* I'm using it because it's a winning component of my ads.

The little copy there is in the ad is all soft sell. I didn't use the reading copy type of ad because losing weight is itself a formidable problem, and I didn't want to create an ad that looked like a dissertation.

HOW TO ATTRACT GOOD LUCK

See page 184. This is my favorite layout with a different theme. However, I didn't have too much luck with the ad. Even so, let me point out some affirmative elements. I like the lead-in statement before the headline: *Even if you're a hard-nosed skeptic, I can prove how you can.* Hard-nosed skeptic is more descriptive than just the word skeptic. We have two excellent endorsements for the book with the names of Dr. Norman Vincent Peale and Edwin A. Locke, Jr. I changed the guarantee to 27 days instead of the usual 30, hoping to catch the reader's eye. Note the top line of the coupon: MAIL GOOD LUCK COUPON TODAY!

This is one of my favorite books, and I made it required reading for my Psycho-Cybernetics classes. The subject of good luck is also one of my favorite topics. Do you think you are lucky? Are you lucky in love? Are you lucky in work? Are you lucky to have the opportunity to change? Do you feel lucky reading this book, learning how to become a mail order success, or are you bemoaning the fact that there is so much work involved? How do you become lucky? It's all a matter of attitude. Be the optimist who sees the glass half full of water, rather than the pessimist who sees it half empty. Be the optimist who sees himself becoming successful in life.

Getting back to the ad, it obviously needs rewriting. I still think it's a good book to sell via mail order.

HORSE LOVERS' LIBRARY

See page 185. Here's an ad I'm running successfully in various equestrian magazines. I like the layout. If you use this type, keep track of the book titles that are being sold. Drop one or two of those that don't pull and substitute others.

SELL BOOKS BY MAIL

See page 175. Here's a perfect example of getting a lot of mileage out of a one-inch ad. It tells the story perfectly. My message—sell books by mail—tells what my ad is about in only four words. The right side amplifies my message. Note the key of Wilshire Mail Order Books instead of Wilshire Book Company.

I could easily spend the money for a two-inch or a four-inch ad. The results would not be any better. At the end of the year, I would have spent several thousand dollars

needlessly. Multiply that amount over several years, and it adds up to a sizeable amount of money. You develop a feeling for receiving the greatest returns from the smallest amount of space. This kind of economizing spills over into other areas of your operation. If you can discount a bill by paying within the discount period, do it. It's money in your pocket. Instead of keeping your working capital in an account that doesn't pay interest, put most of it into a transfer account that pays you interest. When you need the money, you simply telephone the bank to transfer your funds. It's a simple operation.

I ran the bowling ads for about 10 years. These were full-page ads. After the fifth year, I decided to run what is known as a junior page. That's two-thirds of a page. The rate is less, but, more important, I found the results to be the same as with the full-page ad. Therefore, using a junior page instead of a full page resulted in a savings of thousands of dollars every year without diminishing the pulling power of the ads. Although we may be getting ahead of ourselves with these comments concerning the outlay of money, bear it in mind because saving money spells GOOD BUSINESS.

I'm going to briefly present some ads that did not live up to my expectations, but I'm not going to speculate why. That's after the fact. As an analytical exercise, take the time to study these ads and try to determine why they failed.

One of my hobbies is to read best-selling books and try to decide if I would have published them had I the opportunity to do so. I find I would have picked only about 50%. There are unknown factors operating with every book that make it impossible to predict a winner every time. Some that you are sure will sell, bomb; and some that don't seem to have appeal become winners.

The same thing happens in the movie and music business. Millions of dollars are sometimes spent on a movie appearing to contain the necessary elements the public wants—but the public stays away in droves! The term "sleeper" is given to those movies that are successful without the fanfare that usually accompanies major studio productions.

At times, several hundred thousand dollars are spent on a music album that's certain to make it because of the big name of the recording artist. But something happens, and it fails. Only a small percentage of the music that is produced really makes money. Those records carry the nonproductive records.

Because you or I create ads that do not make money, or fail miserably, should not discourage us from going on to the next ad. Writing winning advertising copy is not an exact science. We can have a feel for it, but it's an impossibility to come up with a money-making ad all the time. I know some of the highest paid advertising copywriters in the country and they all have files full of ads that, for some unexplained reason, never made it.

AUTO BOOK

See page 186. This ad is very effective. Can you tell me why? Here's a creative challenge. Write a new ad. If I use it, I'll pay you a royalty based on sales derived from your advertising copy. Try it for fun and profit!

MARKETER'S FORUM

See page 187. I have had great success with this ad. Can you tell me why? Can you improve upon the ad? If so, how would you do it? Take it on as an assignment. Let me hear from you. It will help start yor creative juices flowing.

STAYING IN LOVE

See page 188. This advertisement did not do well. Do you know why? How would you improve it? Is the ad believable? Is the story believable? The challenge, of course, is to turn losing ads into winning ads.

Let's examine some direct mail literature that had various degrees of success.

SELF-THERAPY FOR THE STUTTERER

On pages 189 and 190, you'll find an excellent format for the 8½" x 11" front and back side of a direct mail circular for the book *Self-Therapy for the Stutterer*. The front side contains a brief summation of the book and contents; the back side gives you a complete description of the material in the book. Thus, the circular contains considerable information compacted into a good format. The two-fold fits conveniently into a regular size, #10 business envelope. This circular was included in the monthly newsletter *Letting Go*, which is sent to 7,000 members of the National Stuttering Project, 5100 East LaPalma Ave, Suite 208, Anaheim Hills, California 92807. Telephones: (800) 364-1677 (714) 693-7480. The results were excellent.

EXTRATERRESTRIAL INTELLIGENCE

See pages 191 and 192. I'm including a direct mail piece that did extremely well at certain times and poorly at others. Several years ago, there was considerable interest in the subject of extraterrestrial intelligence. This circular resulted in the sale of thousands of copies of the book over a period of one year. Then, without any apparent reason, the circular stopped pulling.

In 1979, the circular pulled extremely well again when we honored the century's pre-eminent scientist, Albert Einstein, on the occasion of the 100th anniversary of his birth.

This brings us to an observation. Depending upon public interest, the identical advertising copy can pull extremely well at one time and poorly at another. It's important to be aware of what is topical.

Can we therefore assume when you have a topical subject the advertising copy might not be that critical? Can we also assume when the public interest is low, the best advertising copy in the world isn't going to make it?

CHARISMA—THE ART OF ATTRACTING PEOPLE

See page 193. This ad has been extremely successful. Why?

HOW TO MEET THE PEOPLE YOU WANT

See page 195. This book has always sold well from this one-page circular. The title says it all in a very succinct way. Note the top of the book cover that reads, Friends & Lovers. That's powerful. The book *How to Win Friends and Influence People* by Dr. Vincent Peale is one of the all-time, bestselling books, having been translated into numerous languages. This book falls into the same category. It taps into a common desire of all people everywhere. When the title is powerful, you may not need reams of advertising copy.

THINK LIKE A WINNER!

See pages 196 and 197. I published this book in 1993, and it is currently my bestselling title. The two-page circular is selling thousands of copies of the book. Can you tell me why? Could you improve the circular? If so, try it as a creative exercise. The reorders on this book are extremely high. The multi-level companies are buying thousands of copies, and I predict I'll sell a million copies in a short period of time.

These experiences logically pose a question as to how long to stay with advertising copy that isn't pulling in orders. It depends upon the importance of the ad to you. If you've rewritten the ad several times, and the tests don't seem encouraging, perhaps the offer itself didn't make it at that particular time. Remember my reference to the advertising copy for my book, *Extraterrestrial Intelligence,* which pulled extremely well but only at those times when public interest was favorable. When the Fisher/Spasky chess tournament was at its height several years ago, all I had to do was to list my chess books in ads. The sales were unbelievable with little advertising copy.

Ask yourself if you are really excited about the advertising copy or by the offer. If you are not, it will probably be reflected in the copy. That's why I refuse to take on any assignments when the offer does not excite me. I've had prospective clients say to me, "Take on the mail order campaign, even if you are not sold on it." I refuse, because I know from my experience that my lack of enthusiasm will be reflected in the advertising copy. In the past, for some strange reason, this negative element manifested itself in copy even if I farmed out the assignment to some copywriters.

If you are not getting results from your ads, do some market research among your family and friends. When you ask for information, ask for a straight answer. My questions would be something like this: Would you buy this book (product or service) if you saw this ad in a magazine or received it in the mail? If not, why not? If the answer is yes, why? Did the ad hold your interest? Was it believable? Do you think you could benefit from the book (product or service)? How could the ad be improved? What are the weak points? What are the strong points?

It is not my purpose to prove I can always come up with a winner. That's just not possible. You should feel the same way.

I trust the discussion of the ads has been of help to you. You can learn from the ads that didn't make it as well as from those that did. Feel free to use the layouts and any part of the advertising copy for your ads.

IT COULDN'T BE DONE
by Edgar A. Guest

Somebody said that it couldn't be done,
  But he with a chuckle replied
That "maybe it couldn't," but he would be one
  Who wouldn't say so till he tried.
So he buckled right in with the trace of a grin
  On his face. If he worried he hid it.
He started to sing as he tackled the thing
  That couldn't be done, and he did it.

Somebody scoffed: "Oh, you'll never do that,
  At least no one ever has done it;"
But he took off his coat and he took off his hat,
  And the first thing we knew he'd begun it,
With a lift of his chin and a bit of a grin,
  Without any doubting or quiddit,
He started to sing as he tackled the thing
  That couldn't be done, and he did it.

There are thousands to tell you it cannot be done,
  There are thousands to prophesy failure;
There are thousands to point out to you, one by one,
  The dangers that wait to assail you.
But just buckle in with a bit of a grin,
  Just take off your coat and go to it;
Just start to sing as you tackle the thing
  That "cannot be done," and you'll do it.

177

Have You Ever Bowled A Strike And Said, "I've Got It!"?

What would your score be if you could bowl, all the time, with that same feeling? Pretty good? What would you say if we promised you that high score? Unbelievable? Incredible as it may seem, that is exactly what we promise.

If you are willing to keep an open mind for a new concept while you read this advertisement, we can point a way to help you improve your bowling score immeasurably as well as your enjoyment of the game.

The Mental Side of Bowling Crystallized into a Workable Formula

Have you ever rolled a gutter ball while concentrating on the theories of the proper stance, delivery, slide, release and follow-through? You know all there is to know about the mechanics of the bowling delivery and can recite the theories forwards and backwards. The only thing you don't seem to understand is your score. It seems the more you know and the harder you try, the worse you get.

If it is true that you know the fundamental movements of the bowling delivery and yet fail to bowl well, your failure must be in your mental play.

Here Is a Promise for Better Bowling

The pages of a new bowling book are dedicated to the mental side of bowling or, more specifically, to the use of self-hypnosis for control of the mechanical action of the bowling delivery. The use of self-hypnosis is a new concept and one that will help the bowler with all phases of his game. The reader will learn about the simplest, most effective technique ever devised to help him bowl consistently high scores.

What Will They Think of Next?

Your first reaction to the use of hypnosis for improving your bowling game will probably be a big smile followed by the comment, "What will they think of next?" Let us examine some interesting facts.

Book stores and libraries have racks filled with volumes on the physical side of bowling. Autobiographies by professional bowlers reveal, with the frankness of confession story writers, how they "feel" during every movement. Endless "tips" appear in newspapers and magazines aimed at improving the game of the average player.

Yet, why are there so many players seriously seeking improvement when the bowling delivery has been completely revealed, charted and plotted with the thoroughness of a geographical map?

The average player knows the fundamental movements of the bowling delivery, yet fails to play well. It must follow that his failure is in his mental play. Through hypnosis, the way to obtain a mental effect may be explained, understood and put to use. It reveals the mental side of bowling with the clarity that high speed cameras disclose the physical movements of the delivery.

Here's the Secret

Self-hypnosis helps the bowler to attain "the subconscious feel" which is imperative to good bowling. The subconscious feel has been described as the rhythm you have during a practice delivery, or that "sweet feeling" when a ball is thrown correctly. Any conscious effort usually produces muscle tension. This is what is meant when you are told "you are trying too hard." Your conscious mind is so concerned with the mechanical movements and your desire to spill the pins that it repeatedly produces muscle tension.

Use Your Practice Game in League Play

Keeping that important feeling is what you are going to learn from using self-hypnosis. It is the secret of the champions and high average bowlers who have discovered the means of taking their practice games into tournament and league play.

It is known as "the subconscious feel." Once you have learned how to activate this subconscious feeling and to bowl with the timing, relaxation and coordination possible in practice while under the tension of competition, most of your problems will be solved and you'll be well on the way to the high average you are capable of carrying.

The Experts Agree

Take it from Enrico (Hank) Marino, undefeated world champion, named Bowler of the Half-Century and a member of the Bowling Hall of Fame. Hank says, "It isn't until a bowler enters a tournament of competition, no matter how small it may be, that the mental side of the game asserts itself.

"The one thing that is impressive is the incredible change of temperament. This change of mental attitude almost makes a bowler a stranger to himself."

The great bowling master, Joe Falcaro, explains it as, "The kegler who feels he has a 300 game in the offing after two or three successive strikes will discover that every delivery gets tougher. His relaxation turns to tension and his muscles tighten. The ball seems to get heavier and more difficult to release. That's the mental side of bowling."

Every star writing on bowling or lecturing at clinics stresses that form is a highly individual matter. The only thing that really counts is being able to relax tension for a smooth delivery.

Carmen Salvino, who started bowling at 12, was in a Classic league at 17 and at 19 was the youngest American Bowling Congress (ABC) titlist, states: "I practice until the game becomes automatic. I don't have to think about what I intend to do with the ball, so I can be completely relaxed and natural when I am in competition."

Here's More Proof From the Experts

You could go right through the Bowling Hall of Fame and get identical advice from each of the greats. Ed Lubanski, Bowler of the Year in 1959, says, "Think what you are going to do as you take your stance. Then, don't think about anything in particular and just learn to spill the pins."

Only the phrasing changes as each of the champions gives advice. Buzz Fazio states it as, "Timing can make or break a bowler. The path to the foul line is short but is strewn with pitfalls if your timing is off."

Avoid stiffening. Be calm, relaxed and don't hurry your delivery."

The application of hypnosis to your bowling game was explained by Joseph Whitney in his popular King Features syndicated newspaper column, "Mirror of Your Mind." He wrote: "Properly performed, hypnosis is capable of changing mental attitudes at the conscious level. If faulty mental attitudes are responsible for an athlete's inadequate performance, a change wrought by hypnosis could improve his skill."

You Can Use Your Subconscious Mind for Better Bowling

Should the term hypnosis connotate mystery, black magic, stage trickery or fear, disregard it. Upon closer examination, you will find you are not only familiar with it, but you have been using it while thinking of it in other terms such as self-discipline, positive thinking, automatic response, muscle memory, suggestion or unconscious desire.

Hypnosis is not a new phenomenon. Its recorded history goes much further back in time than that of the ancient and honorable game of bowling.

The only thing new about hypnosis is when you, yourself, become aware of it. Then, its great power to influence the mind becomes known to you. You will learn to use it effectively, because you will understand how to channel its forces to tap the hidden resources of your subconscious mind. With the proper application of self-hypnosis, you will be able to bowl the best game you are physically capable of playing. The method of accomplishing this will be as normal as the automatic response while walking.

Try It Entirely At Our Risk!

We know you may be hesitant about trying this new approach and because of this we make the following offer:

TRY THE INSTRUCTIONS FOR 30 DAYS. See for yourself the unbelievable results. If you don't score higher, bowl consistently better and derive greater satisfaction from your bowling game — simply return the book for every cent of your money back. Fair enough?

The sound, authoritative instructions for using self-hypnosis to improve your bowling are presented in a clear, logical sequence and packed with new bowling aids in the book, HOW YOU CAN BOWL BETTER USING SELF-HYPNOSIS, by Jack Heise.

You have absolutely nothing to lose! Act today!

Have You Ever Taken A Practice Golf Swing At A Dandelion?

What would your golf score be if you could hit golf balls like you hit dandelions? Pretty good? What would you say if we promised you that score? Unbelievable? Incredible as it may seem, this is exactly what we promise.

If you are willing to keep an open mind for a new concept while you read this advertisement, we can point a way to help you improve your golf score immeasurably as well as your enjoyment of the game.

The Mental Side of Golf Crystallized into a Workable Formula

How many times have you heard the remark or, possibly, made it, "I can take a practice swing I know is just right, but put a golf ball down and I freeze."

What is there about the dimpled, white surface of a golf ball that should strike terror into a player about to smash it with a club? It can't move or strike back. It just sits there waiting patiently, inviting you to hit it.

The pages of a new golf book are dedicated to the mental side of golf or, more specifically, to the use of self-hypnosis for control of the mechanical action of the golf swing. The use of self-hypnosis for golf is a new concept and one that will help the golfer with all phases of his game. The reader will learn about the simplest, most effective technique ever devised to help him reduce his score.

What Will They Think of Next?

Your first reaction to the use of hypnosis for improving your golf game will probably be a big smile followed by the comment, "What will they think of next?" Let us examine some interesting facts.

Book stores and libraries have racks filled with volumes on the physical side of golf. Autobiographies by professional golfers reveal, with the frankness of confession story writers, how they "feel" during every movement. Doctors have written golf books dissecting the swing, with detailed descriptions of each part of the anatomy involved. Theorists treat the aesthetic qualities of both golf and golfers with nuances usually reserved for poetry. Endless "tips" appear in newspapers and magazines aimed at improving the game of the average player.

Yet, why are there so many players seriously seeking improvement when the golf swing has been completely revealed, charted and plotted with the thoroughness of a geographical map? Why do they find it so difficult to play their way around the course in less than 100 strokes? What keeps them from breaking 90 or coming close to par?

The average player knows the fundamental movements of the golf stroke, yet fails to play well. It must follow that his failure is in his mental play. Through hypnosis, the way to obtain a mental effect may be explained, understood and put to use. It reveals the mental side of golf with the clarity that high speed cameras disclose the physical movements of the golf swing. Self-hypnosis helps the golfer to attain "the subconscious feel" which is imperative to good golf.

The subconscious feel has been described as the rhythm you have during a practice swing, or that "sweet feeling" when a stroke is played right. Any conscious effort usually produces muscle tension. This is what is meant when you are told "you are trying too hard." Your conscious mind is so concerned with the mechanical movements and your desire to hit the ball that it repeatedly produces muscle tension. It is what golfers call "freezing" on a shot.

Here is a Promise for Better Golf

Why is it that the good golfer appears to hit the ball with such ease, while the duffer, "giving it everything he's got," appears to be using a rubber-shafted club and a steel ball?

Have you ever strewn divots all the way around a course while concentrating on the theories of the straight arm, steady head, hip turn and right elbow down? You know all there is to know about the mechanics of the golf swing and can recite the theories forwards and backwards. The only thing you don't understand is your score. It seems the more you know and the harder you try, the worse you get.

If it is true that you know the fundamental movements of the golf stroke yet fail to play well, your failure must be in your mental play.

The Experts Agree

"And just what," you ask, "is mental play?" Let's go to the experts to see what they have to say.

"The average individual," says sports writer Grantland Rice, "has given almost no attention to mental control, which in golf should be an absence of conscious thinking as the stroke is played." Psychologists call this automatic mastery a conditioned reflex.

"The subconscious mind is probably the most important factor in being a good golfer. It keeps distractions on the course from ruining a good round. You should practice, develop your swing, and do most of your thinking on the practice tee so that when you play in competition, you can hit the ball automatically." That's what Wiffy Cox, the nationally known pro at the Congressional Golf and Country Club in Bethesda, Maryland, has to say about it.

"Trouble shots are surprisingly easy if you activate your imagination. You simply must be able to imagine exactly what flight the ball will take before you can play any shot well," advises the great Walter Hagen.

The great "Slammin' Sam" Snead writes: "First and foremost, you must have confidence. Your second mental problem is concentration. Think the shot through in advance before you address the ball. Draw a mental image of where you want it to go and then eliminate everything else from your mind, except how you are going to get the ball into that preferred spot."

Here's More Proof From The Experts

In the popular King Features syndicated newspaper column, "Mirror of Your Mind," the question was asked of Joseph Whitney: "Can hypnosis improve your golf game?"

He answered: "Properly performed, hypnosis is capable of changing mental attitudes at the conscious level. If faulty mental attitudes are responsible for a golfer's inadequate performance, a change wrought by hypnosis could help him improve his skill."

"Much of anyone's game is played (or should be played) in the short six-inch course between the ears," said Louise Suggs, winner of both the American and British Open Crowns.

Even after you have been over a course many times, it isn't an easy layout to play, because most of the hazards are created by yourself.

Willie Ogg, instructor at the Professional Golfers Association school in Dunedin, Florida, lecturing on "Tensions and the Psychological Freeze," put it this way:

"One touch of jitters makes all golfers kin.

"The ideal is reached when one has only to think of mechanical control for the mechanical action. This is a matter of inducing self-hypnosis or complete concentration."

This is the essence of self-hypnosis. Hypnosis distracts the conscious mind and allows the subconscious to function. Through self-hypnosis comes the "subconscious feel." It is attained in the practice area as a measure for every shot. When you have this subconscious feel, then your swing becomes automatic.

Many professionals do refer to hypnosis. Bobby Jones described his iron-play as "so exceptional I felt I must have been hypnotized."

You Can Use Your Subconscious Mind For Better Golf

Should the term hypnosis connotate mystery, black magic, stage trickery or fear, disregard it. Upon closer examination, you will find you are not only familiar with it, but have been using it while thinking of it in other terms such as self-discipline, positive thinking, automatic response, muscle memory, suggestion or unconscious desire.

Hypnosis is not a new phenomenon. Its recorded history goes much further back in time than that of the ancient and honorable game of golf. Whereas some authorities claim golf originated with the early Romans in a sport they called "Paganica," references to hypnosis have been found on stone tablets, unearthed in Greece, dating back to 3000 B.C.

The only thing new about hypnosis is when you, yourself, become aware of it. Then, its great power to influence the mind becomes known to you. You will learn to use it effectively, because you will understand how to channel its forces to tap the hidden resources of your subconscious mind.

Would you like to curb that "killer instinct" off the tee? Would you like to thaw that psychological freeze when faced with hazards, cure the "jitters" on the putting green, and put both power and direction in your shot-making? This is what you may expect by applying self-hypnosis to your play.

Try It Entirely At Our Risk!

We know you may be hesitant about trying this new approach and because of this we make the following offer:
TRY THE INSTRUCTIONS FOR 30 DAYS. See for yourself the unbelievable results. If you don't cut strokes, play consistently better golf and derive greater satisfaction from your golf game—simply return the book for every cent of your money back. Fair enough?

The sound, authoritative instructions for using self-hypnosis to improve your golf game are presented in a clear, logical sequence and packed with new golf aids in the book, HOW YOU CAN PLAY BETTER GOLF USING SELF-HYPNOSIS, by Jack Heise.

You have absolutely nothing to lose! Act today!

Have You Ever Said, "I Just Can't Seem to Concentrate"?

If your answer is "yes," reading this advertisement may change the course of your life. What would you say if we promised to improve your powers of concentration so that you could master any subject? Impossible? Incredible as it may seem, that is exactly what we promise—and do.

If you are willing to keep an open mind for a new concept while you read this advertisement, you will learn about a dynamic method to improve your ability to concentrate, learn and memorize.

Is This You?

Have you ever made an honest and energetic effort to concentrate only to find your mind wandering? The more you tried to concentrate the more difficult it became. You seemed to know what to do in order to concentrate, but the ability to do it somehow eluded you.

It is no secret that knowledge cannot be obtained without concentration, yet millions of people blandly acknowledge they lack this prerequisite to learning. The expressions, "I just can't seem to concentrate" or "I never could concentrate" are so common they occasion very little comment. Indeed, many of those using these rationalizations sound as though they took a measure of pride in their deficiency. The implication by those who say they cannot concentrate is that they are suffering from a congenital condition beyond their control.

Do You Know Anyone Like This?

A good example of relativity in concentration can be made by comparing recreational and intellectual subjects. Consider the student who remarks that he cannot concentrate on his studies no matter how hard he tries, yet becomes so absorbed in watching a television program that he is oblivious to all around him. If it is a baseball game he is watching, he spontaneously, without effort, develops total recall for every play made during the game. Questioning would probably reveal that he knows the batting average of every player on his favorite team, and it is not unlikely that he knows similar statistics about every player in the league.

This same student may demonstrate equal facility in remembering football and basketball statistics, be up to the minute on the progress of twenty or more comic strips and be able to tell you all the details of a murder mystery he is reading. He keeps up with all these things with a zeal that would make him a top notch student in any field, yet he will tell you ruefully that he can scarcely remember the date of the War of 1812. Obviously, there is nothing wrong with his ability to concentrate. He has only to transfer his ability into more intellectual channels.

What You Should Know About Concentration

Most people profess to believe that the ability to concentrate is an inborn characteristic, as impossible to change as the general nature of their body structure or the color of their eyes. There is a great deal of evidence to indicate, however, that this is an unconscious rationalization or face-saving device which will not bear a searching and honest self-analysis. In a highly competitive world where one's resources are being constantly tried, it is comforting to be able to blame fate, heredity or circumstances for our shortcomings rather than place the stigma where it belongs — on ourselves. Psychiatrists are familiar with this sort of rationalization which occurs spontaneously to save the ego. Unfortunately, this unwitting form of subterfuge, while it may offer a measure of comfort, does nothing to eradicate the problem.

We believe that no one is born with the power to concentrate any more than one is born with a taste for exotic foods. It is an acquired characteristic and must be tended and nurtured every day. Anyone with normal intelligence can acquire it.

Psychological Factors in Concentration

Improving your ability to concentrate requires the formation of new thinking and behavior patterns. It may be that the individual with faulty concentration has inefficient study habits and a negative attitude in regard to his ability. Many times he will give up attempting anything that requires concentration because he feels it is futile to try to improve.

Developing the ability to concentrate and learn is a matter of harnessing the latent characteristics that everyone possesses. After all, poor students do become good students, and those who are successful in certain areas of achievement become proficient in areas where it was thought they had no aptitude. These changes are possible because the individual changes his feelings about himself and translates them into purposeful action. Our theme is that the initial impetus for improving your concentration must come from a changed attitude and increased self-esteem.

Here's the Secret

The pages of a new book on concentration are dedicated to an original technique for better concentration, or, more specifically, to the use of your subconscious mind for this pursuit. The reader will learn the most efficient method ever devised to help him concentrate more effectively.

When you achieve the ultimate results from using your subconscious for better concentration, studying or anything else, your powers for concentration will actually be effortless. Your built-in guidance system will be working perfectly.

The triggering stimulus for proper concentration need not be the actual undertaking of the problem itself, but the intense desire to reach your goal. As soon as this happens, it puts into motion favorable psychological factors which automatically help you. It is similar to thinking about a pleasant experience that you know will happen. We enjoy the anticipation of spending a pleasant vacation, weeks and months before the actual time.

Use Your Subconscious for Better Concentration

This statement, at first glance, may arouse a bit of confusion as to how the subconscious mind can be used for such a conscious pursuit as concentration. However, although it sounds contradictory, closer examination will prove otherwise.

It is likely that everything we do is regulated by an automatic mechanism. All we have to do, for example, to pick up a cup of coffee is to have the desire. The goal has been chosen and your subconscious, because of years of conditioning, automatically corrects the course of your hand to your mouth. A baby, with very little conditioning, makes many ludicrous errors as it tries to lift a cup to its mouth. Once it has performed the maneuver successfully, however, it will be "remembered" in the subconscious for future use.

We know that the mathematical genius uses his subconscious mind to solve complex mathematical problems in an incredibly short period of time. The information is fed to the subconscious, is worked on automatically and the answer reported back to the conscious mind. Everyone does this to some extent in solving mathematical problems or problem solving in general.

A Promise for Better Concentration

The fact that you are reading this advertisement indicates that you desire to improve your mental ability. With this motivation, you have the basic ingredient for better concentration. The rest can be learned.

Increasing your powers of concentration will do far more than help you in the accumulation of abstract ideas and the attainment of a higher cultural level. For the first time you will have the leisure and confidence to explore all the avenues of interest which add so much to the lives of those you have envied for the richness of their talents. Talent, unlike genius, can be uncovered in anyone who takes the trouble to try.

Our book offers you a practical formula that has already helped innumerable students and adults at all levels of achievement. The technique involved is a relatively new and unorthodox one, but it operates on proved psychological processes. If you faithfully follow the instruction, you can confidently expect to achieve goals you have always thought were impossible for you. Best of all rewards will be the exciting new feeling of self-esteem which will follow your mental accomplishments.

Would You Like To Have A Photographic Memory?

If your answer is "yes," reading this advertisement may change the course of your life. What would you say if we promised to improve your powers of concentration so that you could master any subject? Impossible? Incredible as it may seem, that is exactly what we promise—and do.

If you are willing to keep an open mind for a new concept while you read this advertisement, you will learn about a dynamic method to improve your ability to concentrate, learn and memorize.

Is This You?

Have you ever made an honest and energetic effort to concentrate only to find your mind wandering? The more you tried to concentrate the more difficult it became. You seemed to know what to do in order to concentrate, but the ability to do it somehow eluded you.

It is no secret that knowledge cannot be obtained without concentration, yet millions of people blandly acknowledge they lack this prerequisite to learning. The expressions, "I just can't seem to concentrate" or "I never could concentrate" are so common they occasion very little comment. Indeed, many of those using these rationalizations sound as though they took a measure of pride in their deficiency. The implication by those who say they cannot concentrate is that they are suffering from a congenital condition beyond their control.

Do You Know Anyone Like This?

A good example of relativity in concentration can be made by comparing recreational and intellectual subjects. Consider the student who remarks that he cannot concentrate on his studies no matter how hard he tries, yet becomes so absorbed in watching a television program that he is oblivious to all around him. If it is a baseball game he is watching, he spontaneously, without effort, develops total recall for every play made during the game. Questioning would probably reveal that he knows the batting average of every player on his favorite team, and it is not unlikely that he knows similar statistics about every player in the league.

This same student may demonstrate equal facility in remembering football and basketball statistics, be up to the minute on the progress of twenty or more comic strips and be able to tell you all the details of a murder mystery he is reading. He keeps up with all these things with a zeal that would make him a top notch student in any field, yet he will tell you ruefully that he can scarcely remember the date of the War of 1812. Obviously, there is nothing wrong with his ability to concentrate. He has only to transfer his ability into more intellectual channels.

What You Should Know About Concentration

Most people profess to believe that the ability to concentrate is an inborn characteristic, as impossible to change as the general nature of their body structure or the color of their eyes. There is a great deal of evidence to indicate, however, that this is an unconscious rationalization or face-saving device which will not bear a searching and honest self-analysis. In a highly competitive world where one's resources are being constantly tried, it is comforting to be able to blame fate, heredity or circumstances for our shortcomings rather than place the stigma where it belongs — on ourselves. Psychiatrists are familiar with this sort of rationalization which occurs spontaneously to save the ego. Unfortunately, this unwitting form of subterfuge, while it may offer a measure of comfort, does nothing to eradicate the problem.

We believe that no one is born with the power to concentrate any more than one is born with a taste for exotic foods. It is an acquired characteristic and must be tended and nurtured every day. Anyone with normal intelligence can acquire it.

Learn to Concentrate for a Better Memory

Improving your ability to concentrate requires the formation of new thinking and behavior patterns. It may be that the individual with faulty concentration has inefficient study habits and a negative attitude in regard to his ability. Many times he will give up attempting anything that requires concentration because he feels it is futile to try to improve.

Developing the ability to concentrate and learn is a matter of harnessing the latent characteristics that everyone possesses. After all, poor students do become good students, and those who are successful in certain areas of achievement become proficient in areas where it was thought they had no aptitude. These changes are possible because the individual changes his feelings about himself and translates them into purposeful action. Our theme is that the initial impetus for improving your concentration must come from a changed attitude and increased self-esteem.

Here's the Secret

The pages of a new book on concentration are dedicated to an original technique for better concentration, or, more specifically, to the use of your subconscious mind for this pursuit. The reader will learn the most efficient method ever devised to help him concentrate more effectively.

When you achieve the ultimate results from using your subconscious for better concentration, studying or anything else, your powers for concentration will actually be effortless. Your built-in guidance system will be working perfectly.

The triggering stimulus for proper concentration need not be the actual undertaking of the problem itself, but the intense desire to reach your goal. As soon as this happens, it puts into motion favorable psychological factors which automatically help you. It is similar to thinking about a pleasant experience that you know will happen. We enjoy the anticipation of spending a pleasant vacation, weeks and months before the actual time.

Use Your Subconscious for a Better Memory

This statement, at first glance, may arouse a bit of confusion as to how the subconscious mind can be used for such a conscious pursuit as concentration. However, although it sounds contradictory, closer examination will prove otherwise.

It is likely that everything we do is regulated by an automatic mechanism. All we have to do, for example, to pick up a cup of coffee is to have the desire. The goal has been chosen and your subconscious, because of years of conditioning, automatically corrects the course of your hand to your mouth. A baby, with very little conditioning, makes many ludicrous errors as it tries to lift a cup to its mouth. Once it has performed the maneuver successfully, however, it will be "remembered" in the subconscious for future use.

We know that the mathematical genius uses his subconscious mind to solve complex mathematical problems in an incredibly short period of time. The information is fed to the subconscious, is worked on automatically and the answer reported back to the conscious mind. Everyone does this to some extent in solving mathematical problems or problem solving in general.

A Promise for a Better Memory

The fact that you are reading this advertisement indicates that you desire to improve your mental ability. With this motivation, you have the basic ingredient for better concentration. The rest can be learned.

Increasing your powers of concentration will do far more than help you in the accumulation of abstract ideas and the attainment of a higher cultural level. For the first time you will have the leisure and confidence to explore all the avenues of interest which add so much to the lives of those you have envied for the richness of their talents. Talent, unlike genius, can be uncovered in anyone who takes the trouble to try.

Our book offers you a practical formula that has already helped innumerable students and adults at all levels of achievement. The technique involved is a relatively new and unorthodox one, but it operates on proved psychological processes. If you faithfully follow the instruction, you can confidently expect to achieve goals you have always thought were impossible for you. Best of all rewards will be the exciting new feeling of self-esteem which will follow your mental accomplishments.

Even if you're a hard-nose skeptic, I can prove how you can

ATTRACT GOOD LUCK & LIFE'S RICHES

One of the most startling scientific breakthroughs of our time in which it is proven that Good Luck can actually be made to order...attracted to you like a magnet...exploited and pyramided to become one of the most powerful success-tools ever invented!

"Based upon a very sound and substantial philosophy of life"—**Dr. Norman Vincent Peale.**

"One of the most helpful and worthwhile books I know"—**Edwin A. Locke, Jr.**, noted industrialist and former U.S. Ambassador.

HERE'S THE SECRET

Yes, it's true! Good luck is NOT a gift . . . NOT just a matter of chance . . . NOT anything at all to do with superstition. *The Art of Attracting Good Luck is a skill, and can be learned just as you'd learn any other skill!*

This is now a proven scientific fact, and this great new authoritative book brings you—for the first time—*the simple but incredibly powerful techniques of attracting—recognizing—and exploiting good luck to the fullest!*

YOU CAN BE A WINNER

Here, for instance, you learn the one unconscious mistake that MAKES most people unlucky—and how it can be eliminated overnight. Dozens of actual cases are presented in which chronic bad luck has been changed to good luck *in a matter of hours!* Nothing was demanded but a simple change in point of view—*a magnetic short cut to good luck that turned these men and women into WALKING RESERVOIRS OF GOOD FORTUNE!*

Here are the exact step-by-step methods (so simple that they will astound you) that enable you to set up *luck-channels,* where good luck can come to you automatically. How to turn *strangers* into sources of good luck, from the very first moment you meet them! The *Seven Golden Actions* that attract good luck—and the *Three Fatal Mistakes* that drive it away! How to recognize *hidden luck* in situations where ordinary people see nothing but disaster!

GOOD FORTUNE CAN BE YOURS

How to make every stroke of good luck do *double duty*—actually pyramid your good luck—make each stroke of good fortune actually produce another! *How to turn "bad luck" into good luck by TWISTING its results to your benefit!* How to develop *luck antennas* that can give you the reputation of being the luckiest man in your town!

Let me repeat: This is NOT a matter of superstition. This is a new psychological breakthrough—discovered only recently—and released to you only through this great new book! *The very first stroke of good luck it brings to you is worth years of hard work!* If you choose to put good luck to work on your side—success, happiness and riches can be yours!

Try It Entirely At My Risk!

So you won't hesitate about trying this new approach to luckier living and **who knows how lucky you can get**, I make the following offer.

TRY THE INSTRUCTIONS FOR 27 DAYS. If you aren't in a lucky cycle and on your way to riches in just 27 days, simply return the book for every cent of your money back. Fair enough?

This can be your lucky day if you act today!

184

GREAT HORSE BOOKS

**SAVE MONEY ON
THESE GREAT PAPERBACKS!**

HORSES—Selection, Care & Handling
By Margaret Cabell Self. Includes vices, riding, driving, first aid, selcting and much more $5

HOW TO BUY A BETTER HORSE And Sell Yours
By Jeanne K. Posey. Tells you where and how to look for another and how to dump yours. $4

HOW TO ENJOY YOUR QUARTER HORSE
By Willard H. Porter. We all know how this is done so why read it? Maybe we missed something $4

HUNTER IN PICTURES
By Margaret Cabell Self. If you like English riding, you'll enjoy this nice book. $3

ILLUSTRATED BOOK OF THE HORSE
By S. Sidney (8½ x 11) — You've got to really like these animals to pay this much! Great buy $11

ILLUSTRATED HORSE MANAGEMENT
By Dr. E. Mayhew. Some 400 illustrations on the horse are covered here. You'll enjoy it! $7

ILLUSTRATED HORSE TRAINING
By Capt. M.H. Hayes. The Captain thinks you can learn more with the use of pictures. He's right! $6

ILLUSTRATED HORSEBACK RIDING For Beginners
By Jeanne Mellin. An excellent Morgan horse artist and trainer as well. You'll really love this one. $4

JUMPING—Learning & Teaching
By Jean Froissard—The more you know about this subject, the better you can teach it. $6

KNOW ALL ABOUT HORSES
By Harry Disston—A ready reference about horses, horsepeople and horse sports. $4

LAME HORSE—Cause, Symptoms & Treatment
By Dr. James R. Rooney—236 pages in this fine book. A must for your library! $6

LAW & YOUR HORSE
By Edward H. Greene—You never know when you will need the law on your side! Don't wait! $6

MANUAL OF HORSEMANSHIP
By Harold Black—A reference guide to the many aspects of owning and raising a horse. $6

MOVIE HORSES—Fascinating Techniques of Training
By Anthony Amaral—An easy approach to train your horse to do things you'll enjoy $3

POLICE HORSES
By Judith Campbell—The training methods used by the police department get results. In case you ever run into a mob! $3

PRACTICAL GUIDE TO HORSESHOEING
A tech manual for the Army, but since horses have not changed that much, there's a lot to learn $6

PRACTICAL GUIDE TO OWNING YOUR OWN
By Steven D. Price. Everything is covered in this one, from buying to care and feeding. $4

PROBLEM HORSES
By Reginald S. Summerhays—A guide to cure the serious behavior habits of horses $5

REINSMAN OF THE WEST—Bridles & Bits
By Ed Connell—One of the most outstanding horsemen in our time. A must! $6

RIDE WESTERN
By Louis Taylor—Just in case you thought there wasn't any difference. Covers many subjects $6

SCHOOLING YOUR YOUNG HORSE
By George Wheatley—This is where it all begins. Many excellent training methods for those who are trying to train their own. $6

STABLE MANAGEMENT For the Owner-Groom
By George Wheatley—To make a business of it, or just to make sure things are going smoothly $5

STALLION MANAGEMENT
By A.C. Hardman—A guide for stud owners who are serious about breeding. $6

TEACHING YOUR HORSE TO JUMP
By W.J. Froud—Don't get off on the wrong foot. Also, in case you are having problems $3

TRAINING YOUR HORSE TO SHOW
By Neale Haley—There are many things to learn before going to the show. Here's how! $6

TREATING COMMON DISEASES of your Horse
By Dr. George H. Conn—The horse doctor doesn't leave anything out in this one. A must! $6

TREATING HORSE AILMENTS
By G. W. Serth—There are many things a horse-owner must know. You won't get it all from just one book! $3

**Mail your order to:
Melvin Powers
12015 Sherman Road
No. Hollywood,
California 91605-3781**

Name _____

Street _____

City _____

State _____ *Zip* _____

Quantity	Book Title	Price
	California residents add 6%	

Canadians please remit in U.S. funds.

Total Enclosed

A TREASURE CHEST OF HIGH PROFIT MAIL ORDER PRODUCTS

How would you like to have a treasure chest brimming with exciting mail order products that you could get at rock bottom prices? Over 40,000 people a month have their treasure chest appear on their doorstep — and so can you.

Marketers Forum is the most comprehensive, well-recognized national trade publication of its kind. It contains over 200 illustrated pages of innovative products from all over the world, including apparel, automotive, beauty aids, cosmetics, electronics, jewelry, leather goods, novelties, pet products, pictures, posters, records and tapes, sporting goods, knives, sunglasses, surgical instruments, tools, toys, videos and watches.

With each item **Marketers Forum** lists the manufacturer's or importer's name, address and toll free telephone number. Many of the importers are high-volume companies that make their products available to you below what you would pay to import them youself. They often have beautiful brochures and catalogs you can arrange to use. Some will drop ship your orders.

If you already have a product, you can use **Marketers Forum** to find new items to add to your line. Its large number of new readers each month makes it a great place to advertise. It has a list of trade shows, updated in every issue.

As a mail order entrepreneur, you need all the help you can get to find new products that will capture your imagination and catapult you to the pinnacle of success.

Take advantage of this opportunity to see for yourself how valuable **Marketers Forum** can be to your business. Send for your sample copy now, or subscribe for one year.

— — — — — **ORDER FORM** — — — — —

Mail to: Melvin Powers
12015 Sherman Road
No. Hollywood, CA 91605-3781

☐ Please send me a sample copy of
Marketers Forum $5.00
☐ Please send me a yearly subscription to
Marketers Forum $30.00

Enclosed is my check or money order for $_____.

Name _____
PLEASE PRINT
Address _____
City _____ State _____ Zip _____

187

What Is
the Secret
of
Staying in Love?

My name is Carol, and I'm a housewife with two children. I'd like to share a personal secret with you.

On Christmas Eve, when my family and relatives were downstairs getting ready to open presents, I was upstairs in my room, crying. At the time I wasn't sure why. Suddenly, I had become extremely depressed and my crying was uncontrollable.

With effort, I pulled myself together, joined the others, and was quiet until everyone had gone home and the children were in bed. Then I told my husband Michael I felt upset, as if something were terribly wrong. He said I would get over it and that I should try not to dwell on bad feelings.

But later in the quiet dark of night, unable to sleep, I tried to figure out why I felt so miserable. I could deny it no longer. I knew the cause of my depression: I was losing the man I loved.

THE ROMANCE WAS GONE

Oh, it didn't happen like it does in the movies. There were no clear-cut signs such as another woman calling on the phone or a big argument. For a long time Michael had slowly been slipping away. He never looked at me "that way" anymore. In fact, he seldom looked at me at all. Nor did he tell me about his day the way he used to. Every time I tried to get Michael to talk about our relationship, he retreated farther into his cocoon. When I really pressed him, he said, "You've been reading too many women's magazines," or something similar. The more evasive and withdrawn he became, the more alone I felt.

NO ONE TO TALK TO

I'm not one to talk over my marital problems with women friends nor to tell anyone in my family, so I was stuck with my dilemma. I wished that someone could understand what I was experiencing and, maybe, could help me decide what to do.

I HEARD MYSELF ON THE RADIO

And then one day as I was driving home from my children's school, I heard something on the radio that caught my attention. It was a woman's voice, and she sounded as if she'd been crying. I had tuned in to a call-in show hosted by a well-known psychologist. The woman caller was talking about her husband.

"He never talks to me anymore," she said. "He comes home, eats dinner, watches TV until he becomes sleepy, and then crawls into bed without kissing me good night."

The host was patient with her while she excused her tears. "Have you tried counseling?" he asked.

"A shrink? Are you kidding? My husband would never agree to that."

"Mine either," I found myself saying aloud.

Then the man on the radio said something interesting. He told the distraught woman that her problem was not unusual. "As a matter of fact," he said, "most people find that staying in love is not easy, but there is a wonderful book that tells how to go about it. Go to any bookstore and get a copy of *Staying in Love* by Dr. Norton Kristy. I have recommended it to many individuals who have found it to be exactly what they needed to reopen the lines of communication with their spouses and to revitalize their relationships."

I FOUND HELP AT MY LOCAL BOOKSTORE

I quickly made a detour to the shopping center and parked in front of a bookstore. They had the book. I took it home, skimmed through it, and became excited. I knew it could help Michael and me to straighten out our marriage.

That night, I used some of the techniques described in the book to get Michael to open up. Then, when the time seemed right, I turned to one of the book's helpful questionnaires. Michael and I each answered the questions about our relationship aloud, sometimes painfully, and we found out what had been bothering each of us.

WE FELL IN LOVE — AGAIN

Gradually, as we continued our searching conversations, Michael became able to talk freely about his feelings and really listened and tried to understand when I shared mine. As a result, we've grown closer to one another day by day and our marriage has become richer and fuller than ever before — even better than when we first fell in love. Finally, I am the happy wife I'd longed to be.

WE REMEMBERED HOW TO HAVE
FUN TOGETHER

Dr. Kristy's book not only helped to reopen the lines of communication between us, but it described ways to deal with a variety of problems that can arise in anyone's marriage. *Staying in Love* exposed us to a whole new world of adventures, and it reminded us how to have fun again — as friends and as lovers.

REINVENT YOUR RELATIONSHIP

Staying in Love presents unique, valuable ideas about how to deal with anger, jealousy, and infidelity. It offers suggestions about what to do with a partner who has closed the conversational door by saying, "I don't want to talk about it." And the book recommends ways to recognize and to stop "no-win" marital games. It tells you how to get your relationship on the right track and how to keep it there.

Some people believe that once the sizzle has gone out of a relationship, you can't ever get it back. Michael and I know this isn't true. Dr. Kristy showed us step by step how to get the most out of our relationship by putting the right things into it.

DO YOUR MARRIAGE A FAVOR —
LEARN THE SECRET OF STAYING IN LOVE

Staying in Love may well be the most important book you'll ever read. It can change your life forever.

I guarantee that this book will get you talking again — real talk that will make your marriage flourish.

256 pages ... $8.00 postpaid

$4.00

Self-Therapy for the Stutterer

Fifth Edition

MALCOLM FRASER
Director

SPEECH FOUNDATION OF AMERICA

To the Reader

There are always some stutterers who are unable to get professional help and others who do not seem to be able to profit from it. There are some who prefer to be their own therapists. In this book, Malcolm Fraser, Director of the Speech Foundation of America, has attempted to provide some guidance for those who must help themselves. Knowing well from his own experience as a stutterer the difficulties of self-therapy, he outlines a series of objectives and challenges that should serve as a map for the person who is lost in the dismal swamp of stuttering and wants to find a way out.

CHARLES VANRIPER

Distinguished Professor Emeritus and formerly Head, Department of Speech Pathology and Audiology, Western Michigan University

---

Contents

On Self-Therapy

If you are like most of the million and a half stutterers in this country, adequate clinical treatment will not be available to you. Whatever you do you'll have to be pretty much on your own with what ideas and sources you can use.
(Sheehan)

The first thing you must do is to admit to yourself that you need to change, that you really want to do something about the way you presently talk. This is tough but your commitment must be total; not even a small part of you must hold back. Don't dwell longingly on your fluency in the magical belief that some day your speech blocks will disappear. There is no magic potion, no pink pill that will cure stuttering.

Don't sit around waiting for the right time for an inspiration to come to you—*you must go to it*. You must see that the old solutions, the things you have done to help yourself over the years simply do not work. Ruts wear deep though, and you will find it difficult to change. Even though the way you presently talk is not particularly pleasant, it is familiar. It is the unknown from which we shrink.
(Emerick)

You must be willing to endure temporary discomfort, perhaps even agony, for the long range improvement you desire. No one is promising you a rose garden. Why not take the time and effort now for a lifetime of freedom from your tangled tongue? How can you do this? You break down the global problem of stuttering into its parts and then solve them one at a time. No one said it was easy. Shall we begin?

A valuable precondition for a successful therapy is the deep inner conviction of the stutterer in the manageability of his disorder, combined with a fighting spirit and a readiness to undergo hardships and deprivations if needed—hopelessness, pessimism and passivity being the deadliest foes to self-improvement.
(Freund)

---

192 Pages...$4.00 postpaid
Money-Back Guarantee

Please send your order to:

Melvin Powers
12015 Sherman Road
North Hollywood, California 91605

On This Approach to Self-Therapy

This book is written to and for the many adult stutterers in this country — and is addressed in the second person to describe what the stutterer can and should do to control his stuttering. We state confidently that as a stutterer you do not need to surrender helplessly to your speech difficulty because you can change the way you talk. You can learn to communicate with ease rather than with effort. There is no quick and easy way to tackle the problem but with the right approach self-therapy can be effective.

Experience has probably taught you to be skeptical about any plan which claims to offer a solution to your stuttering problem. You may have tried different treatment ideas and been disappointed and disillusioned in the past. This book promises no quick magical cure and makes no false claims. It describes what you can and should do to overcome your difficulty.

It offers a logical practical program of therapy for the stutterer based on methods and procedures that have been used successfully in many universities and other speech clinics. This approach to therapy has been shown to get results. If there were an easier or better way of learning how to control stuttering we would recommend it.

We start with two assumptions. One is that you have no physical defect or impairment of your speech mechanism. If you can talk without stuttering when you are alone or when not being heard or observed by others, it would be a fair assumption that you have no physical or organic defect causing your trouble.[1,2,3] Actually all stutterers have periods of fluency.

The other assumption is that you may not be in a position to avail yourself of the services of a speech pathologist, trained to help you work on your problem in the manner described in this book and that, as a result you need to be your own therapist. Even with competent guidance, authorities would agree that stuttering therapy is largely a do-it-yourself project anyway.[4,5,6,7]

[1]There is no physical reason why you can't learn to speak more easily and fluently than you do now. (Johnson)

[2]There is nothing wrong inside your body that will stop you from talking. You have the same speaking equipment as anybody else. You have the ability to talk normally. (D. Williams)

[3]Because you stutter doesn't mean you are biologically inferior or more neurotic than the next person. (Sheehan)

[4]No one but myself improved my speech. Others have helped me by providing information, giving emotional support, identifying bias, etc. but the dirty work of therapy is, and always has been, my responsibility. (Boehmler)

[5]Don't ever forget that even if you went to the most knowledgeable expert in the country, the correction of stuttering is a do-it-yourself project. Stuttering is your problem. The expert can tell you what to do and how to do it, but you are the one who has to do it. You are the only person on earth who can correct your stuttering. (Starbuck)

[6]The stutterer must conquer his own problems—no one else can do the job for him. (VanRiper)

[7]Needless to say, each stutterer must from the beginning of therapy accept the responsibility for his own difficulty. This implies self-therapy which is essential. (Stromsta)

If you are sincerely interested in working on your speech you will need to have a strong motivation to overcome your difficulty and a sincere determination to follow through on the suggested procedures and assignments. It will not be easy, but it can be done.

Obviously there is no way to promise success in this or any other program since no sure 'cure' for stuttering has yet been discovered, in spite of what you may have read. However, we believe that if you follow the suggestions and carry out the fluency procedures outlined in this book, you should be able to control your stuttering and speak easily without abnormality. Others have conquered their stuttering and you can too. But the best way for you to judge the effectiveness of any therapy program is to try it out and let the results speak for themselves.[1,2]

It should be mentioned that there are many differences among stutterers. Some cases are mild and others severe and in most cases the frequency and severity of stuttering tends to vary from time to time and from one situation to another. Sometimes a stutterer may be able to speak comparatively fluently with little or no difficulty and at other times he may have considerable trouble. That tends to make it a most frustrating disorder since it can and usually does become worse in certain environments and under certain circumstances.

[1]A major problem in the treatment of stuttering is how to encourage the stutterer to stay in and continue with the course of treatment. (Barbara)

[2]Based on your understanding choose the most appropriate therapy program you can, and work at the program with more consistency, devotion and energy than any other task you've ever tackled. As success is obtained, maintain it with equal vigor. (Boehmler)

Usually a stutterer is more apt to have difficulty when embarrassed or when anticipating trouble. This may be more noticeable when asked to state his name or when talking to people in authority like prospective employers or teachers; in making introductions; when speaking to groups or talking on the telephone, etc. On the other hand the stutterer may have little or no trouble when talking to himself or talking to a child or pet animal.[1]

It should also be recognized that stutterers may vary widely in their reactions and characteristics and in the conditions under which their stuttering may occur. No two persons stutter in the same manner since every stutterer has developed his own particular pattern of stuttering.[2,3,4] Your reactions may be different from others and accordingly we ask you to bear with us when you read about troubles which you may not encounter yourself but which may represent a problem to others.

Most all stutterers have certain abilities which are somewhat surprising. Practically all stutterers generally have little or no difficulty when they sing or shout or whisper or read and speak in unison with others.

---

[1]Some stutterers have difficulty reading aloud; others do not. Some can speak well when in a position of authority; others do not show their greatest difficulty here. Some can use the telephone without interference; others are completely frustrated by this situation. Speaking with members of the opposite sex causes great difficulty to one stutterer but results in fluency with another. Some speak well at home but not in other environments; with others the situation is completely reversed. (Ansberry)

[2]The old saying that no two stutterers are alike is undoubtedly true. (Luper)

[3]The speech behavior patterns that have usually been associated with or identified as stuttering vary from person to person, and from time to time with any given person. (D. Williams)

[4]We all have different personalities and our pattern of stuttering is distinct and interwoven in the unique personalities. (Garland)

In your case if you have no difficulty when you read or speak in unison with others, that would indicate that you have the physiological ability to speak normally. It would also make it evident that psychological factors are the cause of a lot of your stuttering.

In this connection we would add that this in no way infers that any mental deficiency is involved since it has been shown that the IQ (intelligence quotient) of the average stutterer is normal or above normal.

Equipment Desirable. For use in your work and study in this program it would help to have three items available. One is a reasonably large mirror (at least 15" x 18") which can be moved around unless it is now situated where you can observe yourself closely when talking on the telephone. And it would be most helpful if you could obtain the use of a small portable dictating machine or tape recorder of a size not much bigger than your hand which you can carry around with you to record your speech. It can be purchased at a fairly reasonable price. And you should also have on hand a small memorandum workbook.

Original Cause of Your Stuttering

One general comment is worth mentioning and should be of interest. There is no reason to be concerned about the original cause of your stuttering. Many theories have been advanced to explain its cause and nature, but none of them have been proven or seem provable. It may have been the result of environmental or hereditary factors or their interaction.

Whatever the cause, it is unlikely that it is still operating upon you or that it can be corrected at this late date. Therefore we do not believe that the original cause of your stuttering has or should have any bearing on or affect the therapy process.[1] You need to be concerned about what you are doing now that perpetuates and maintains your difficulty.

There is no reason for you to spend the rest of your life stuttering helplessly and making yourself miserable. Others have prevailed and so can you.

[1]Many stutterers have mistakenly believed that if only the "cause" could be found, a fast cure would result. (Murray)

Scientists Find Statistical Cues
For the Possibility of
Extraterrestrial Intelligence

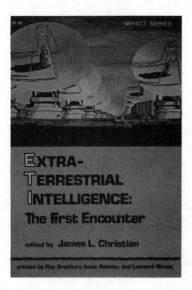

Dear Friend:

I'm excited by a new book that I think will excite you too. For centuries, from the earliest legends of the man on the moon, mankind has fantasized and speculated about other life in the universe. With the discovery of biochemical evolution which showed how life could evolve out of simple compounds, those speculations took on a new dimension. Most scientist now believe that it is possible there is other intelligent life in the universe.

What are the possibilities of our making contact with ETI's in the profound vastness of space? What will be the consequences to our images of ourselves and our world of the first proven contact with beings from another planet, since they are likely to be of superior intelligence? Could we still believe in the value of life as we live it? How would it affect mankind's religions, both Western and Eastern? Would it in fact mean, as Arthur C. Clarke has said, an end to mankind's childhood?

These and other questions are explored in *Extraterrestrial Intelligence: The First Encounter*—from the most practical issues, such as how the news of contact should be handled, to the most exciting and troubling questions of philosophy, religion, and science. *Extraterrestrial Intelligence* begins the search for a cosmic context for mankind. It leads the way in reflecting on the next stage in our gradual self-discovery.

Summer 1976 coincided with summertime on Mars. That's when Viking space probes 1 and 2 ventured out and became man's first attempts to locate extraterrestrial life. As we continue to explore the universe, the idea of life in space moves increasingly from the realm of science fiction into the domain of scientific possibility.

Scientific breakthroughs are often based on interdisciplinary research unfamiliar to the layman. Scientists, writers, and publishers need to supply the public with this important background information, so that new frontiers in science are made understandable. *Extraterrestrial Intelligence* is a book that does just that. It presents the views of fourteen men qualified to speculate on the vast implications of the subject. Contributors include well-known writers Bradbury, Frazier, Azimov, and Tennessen; distinguished scientists and academics Abell, R. Smith, and Desan; philosophers Royce, Christian, Tooley, and Angeles; and theologians Huntington, Hamilton, and Doss; and Leonard Lemoy, who was America's most popular extraterrestrial on the highly successful television series Star Trek. James Christian, editor, has selected his articles to cove a broad and provocative range of possible ETI phenomena, which (according to astronomer Carl Sagan) could confront mankind within the next fifty years.

That intelligent life is natural and inherent on a cosmic scale can be understood through a combined study of astronomical and biological discoveries of the last five decades. Authors Christian and Abell clearly summarize these findings: that advanced radio-telescope research estimates our galaxy to contain some 400 thousand million suns; that our universe contains some 200 billion galaxies; that it is common and natural for non-binary suns to produce planets; and that these planets are built of the same basic elements as our own. The experiments of Stanley Miller in 1953 gave the first indications that living organisms evolved form inorganic constituents. His theory (chemical biogenesis) would indicate that life can evolve anywhere that the basic chemicals and radiation exist. Since we have encountered no evidence of chemicals other than those found on earth in our telescopic exploration of deep space, we may assume that "the elemental constituents of living organisms are cosmic."

Extraterrestrial life exists: but does extra terrestrial intelligence? Can such intelligence cross the light years between even the closest neighboring stars? What are the implications of such an advanced technology? What is the lifespan of technological civilizations? And, should we encounter ETIs, would we be able to recognize them as intelligences? Smith and Tooley focus their articles on these scientific and philosophical questions.

Presuming that technology can advance far enough without destroying itself in the process, allowing ETIs to contact us, theologian Hamilton questions whether mankind could withstand the psychological impact. The implications may be devastating: mankind will have to re-philosophize and re-theologize. Contact with alien intelligence may totally alter our own concept of cognition, as psychologist Joseph Royce suggests in his article on the new dimensions of cosmic man.

Questions and possibilities raised by mere statistical inevitability of ETIs are endless and fascinating. As Azimov says:
> If we ever establish contact with extraterrestrial life, it will reveal to us our true place in the universe, and with that comes the beginnings of wisdom.

Send today for your copy of the exciting *Extraterrestrial Intelligence.*

NO-RISK COUPON

Please send me a copy of *Extraterrestrial Intelligence.* Enclosed is my ( ) check ( ) cash ( ) money order for $8.00 postpaid (CA res. $8.66).

Name_____

Address_____

City_____ State_____ Zip_____

Mail to:
      Melvin Powers, 12015 Sherman Road, No. Hollywood, CA 91605

How to Develop Charisma
The Art of Attracting and Influencing People

Have you ever wondered why some people seem to have incredibly attractive personalities? Why they draw others to themselves like a magnet? You know the kind of persons I mean—the natural spellbinders, the men or women whom everyone likes and who always make a lasting impression. In their personal lives everything seems to come their way; friends, lovers, followers, and mates all seem to gravitate towards them. Are these people born with the gift of charisma, the power to influence others, and the overwhelming good fortune to achieve their most cherished goals by the very force of their personalities? Or are these desirable qualities available to all of us if we are truly motivated to attain them?

I am firmly convinced that you can learn to be liked, to command attention, and to persuade others; in short, to have a magnetic personality. Some lucky individuals seem to have inherited their charismatic qualities but the truth of the matter is that most people, either consciously or otherwise, develop those captivating selves we so admire and wish to be like.

HOW DOES CHARISMA WORK?

Consider the following examples of how charisma operates in everyday life. There seems to be a certain undefinable, almost mystical, sense of power emanating from people who have developed magnetic personalities. Haven't you seen a guest on a TV talk show or a TV personality you'd never previously heard of, who kept your attention intensely focused on him or her the whole time he or she appeared on the show? You intuitively felt that that person possessed star qualities. To recognize this is the same job as that of the Hollywood talent scout whose aim is to discover future stars and superstars—the people with latent charismatic qualities. A superstar, in simple terms, is someone using charismatic power to its ultimate degree. We respond forcefully to that power, and a star is born.

Let's take a situation a little closer to home—the person you're introduced to for the first time. It could be a salesperson, a potential business associate, a potential friend or lover—a person in just about any capacity. The point is, you've only just met the person and yet—isn't it amazing?—you often have a good sense of whether you like or dislike him or her. I would like you to reflect for a moment on how utterly remarkable this phenomenon is, and how important it can be to understand its value. What made you form your instant opinion of this person you've just met? Can you really explain it? In most cases it probably had little or nothing to do with what he said or how he dressed. In the case of disliking the person, you were no doubt getting "negative vibrations." That's charisma working in reverse. If you liked the person, chances are you were responding to the subtle mystique of power that the likeable, attractive personality effortlessly exudes.

Do you see why this phenomenon of first impressions is a matter of such importance? How you are perceived, both consciously and subliminally, by the people with whom you come in contact is one of the keys to success in your personal and business life.

LEARN THE SECRETS OF CHARISMA

The secrets of developing a charismatic personality that will generate others' interest in you are yours now to learn and implement. Encompassing all areas of human development, various psychological techniques, intuition and powers of observation, the study of personal magnetism can result in great benefits to those of you who seek to change your life in dramatic ways by becoming "captivating." You'll learn from history's charismatic individuals as well as from living examples. Those seemingly magical qualities of power, the tremendous influence exerted upon others, will become clear to you as you begin to apply this wonderful knowledge to your own life.

MOTIVATION PLUS ACTION EQUALS SUCCESS

Does all this sound too good to be true? When I say you can actually learn to develop a charismatic personality do your shake your head in disbelief? Perhaps you've already tried to be popular, charismatic or to develop certain desirable character traits and failed to see any results. With the instruction available to you you'll have a far greater opportunity to succeed.

ACHIEVE PERSONAL HAPPINESS

Once you've felt the magnificence of your own charisma, your entire life will be changed. The warm glow of the sunshine of life will permeate everything you do. Its subtle influence will be felt in all your interpersonal relationships. When you develop yourself to the fullest, much becomes possible; your secret dreams can come true. This exciting prospect derives from the fact that no one can predict what your potential really is. It's in constant flux as you develop your vibrant charismatic powers. Once you set your mind to it, every goal becomes attainable. The thrust of a positive mental attitude, combined with the powerful propellant of charisma, makes for sheer explosive dynamism. To be lyrical, it can take you to the moon; you can touch the furthest stars.

MAKE THE MOST OF YOURSELF

This is the era of self-development. So why not live life to the fullest? Why not be a leader and decide right now to give yourself the chance to discover your potential. Successful people set goals for personal happiness and then go after them in a logical way. They are dreamers first, then they are doers. You can discard the limitations that you may have consciously or unconsciously imposed on yourself. You can succeed beyond your wildest expectations. You'll have an expert to guide you, and, with the proper motivation, your success is guaranteed.

EXPERT SHOWS YOU THE WAY

To help you achieve your charismatic powers to the utmost, we offer a book on developing a winning personality and three hours of cassette tapes on which you will hear Ms. Marcia Grad, an acknowledged expert in personality development, instruct you in the fundamentals, techniques and procedures of developing your charismatic powers and potential. These tapes were recorded live at one of Ms. Grad's stimulating college seminars. I urge you to take advantage of this remarkable opportunity to expand your horizons. It's exhilarating just to imagine what this material could mean to you. Provided you're motivated for success, we can positively help you. So get set for a thrilling adventure!

100% MONEY-BACK GUARANTEE

The book and tapes must dramatically and substantially help you to achieve your most secret and treasured aspirations or we'll refund your money. With your new charismatic vitality and awakened zest for life, you'll find that even goals that have always been elusive will become a reality. Yes, dare to dream because your dreams are about to come true!

Send today for the book, *Charisma—How to Get "That Special Magic,"* $8.00 postpaid and for *Marcia Grad's Three-Hour Charisma Seminar on Cassette Tapes,* $25.00 postpaid.

Mail to: Melvin Powers
12015 Sherman Road
No. Hollywood, California 91605

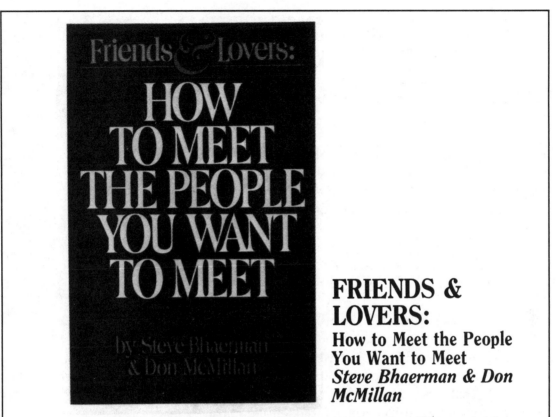

FRIENDS & LOVERS:
How to Meet the People You Want to Meet
Steve Bhaerman & Don McMillan

The pressure is on to meet people, right? WRONG!, say Steve Bhaerman and Don McMillan, who put their heads and experiences together and figured out that there's too much emphasis today on meeting people and not enough on simply *having fun*—and that's why most of the singles bar/singles get-togethers and "can't miss" methods fail miserably. In this new book, the emphasis is on how to do what's fun for you and *how that will naturally help you meet more of the people you want to meet*. Singles will learn how to:

- zero in on their favorite things to do, then translate those interests into a personal action plan of activities that will help them meet the people they want to meet
- clearly define who it is they want to meet
- keep from getting discouraged while finding that perfect match of interests and ambitions
- "grow their own fun" instead of waiting for it to come to them—with five ideas that are just crazy enough to work!

Above all, the authors help singles stop letting everyone else set standards for what to do and how to meet people, and set themselves free to remember what's truly fun for them!

Steve Bhaerman and Don McMillan are Ann Arbor, Michigan, singles who got tired of the disappointments of the dating game and decided to write their own rules. Bhaerman is a writer and humorist who met his fiancée as a direct result of writing this book (and practicing what it preaches!). McMillan holds a master's degree in social work and has served as a family therapist and now as a management consultant.

204 Pages ... $10.00 postpaid.

Send orders to:
Melvin Powers
12015 Sherman Road
No. Hollywood, California 91605-3781

Nothing is more exciting than the realization that you can accomplish whatever you want....
And nothing is more life changing than the tools to accomplish it.

THIS BOOK IS GUARANTEED TO CHANGE YOUR LIFE!

I am excited to announce I've just published a new book that has the rare elements necessary to propel it into the elite category of all-time, bestselling motivational classics. It's called *Think Like a Winner!* by Dr. Walter Doyle Staples, a highly acclaimed authority on human potential.

For years I have been fascinated by how some people become successful, while others in the same business or profession never quite seem to make it, no matter how hard they try. I wanted to know what sets them apart.

LEARN THE SECRET OF SUCCESS

I found that many successful people credit the shaping or changing of their thinking for putting them on the road to personal and financial success. Most remember a specific book that had great influence on their manner of thinking.... That's exactly what had happened to me. I read *Think & Grow Rich* by Napoleon Hill when I was only 16 years old, and I've never forgotten the impact it made.

I have been a book publisher for more than 40 years, specializing in motivational books. I've published such multi-million bestsellers as *Psycho-Cybernetics*, *The Magic of Thinking Big*, and *Think & Grow Rich* (which I published in trade paperback years after first reading it in hardcover). And I've read almost every motivational book that's been on the market. Though many have been interesting and helpful, only a handful have attained true greatness. *Think Like a Winner!* is destined for such greatness. Those who read it are profoundly affected. It's only a matter of time until *Think Like a Winner!* is cited by successful people as the book that changed their lives.

Of the many motivational books available, *Think Like a Winner!* has been chosen as the Bible of the Melvin Powers Wealth-Building Team—a group of motivated entrepreneurs participating in my money-making opportunities. Why are we using this particular book?... Because it teaches people how to think like winners and get the concrete results that winners get.

TECHNIQUES OF THINKING LIKE A WINNER

How do you think like a winner if you haven't been as successful as you'd like? In *Think Like a Winner!* Dr. Staples explains how the mind functions and specifically how you can achieve your personal and financial goals—even if you've repeatedly been unable to do so in the past. You'll learn how to reach your full potential, resulting in psychological and physiological changes that create a win-win life.

Dr. Staples compares the mind to a giant computer. Both are neutral. Both put out what has been put into them. Garbage in, garbage out—an expression well known to computer users—also applies to the human mind. Negative suggestions and experiences are the garbage that get programmed. Dr. Staples tells how to change one's programming so that what comes out is life enhancing ... the stuff of winners.

THE MOST IMPORTANT CHOICE YOU'LL EVER MAKE

What is the most important choice you'll ever make?... Your manner of thinking. And it is a *choice*. By choosing to think like a winner, you'll be choosing personal and financial success. You'll be open to opportunities that come your way—motivated and diligent in your pursuit of them. Eventually you'll catch the brass ring. I've seen it happen again and again with readers of my books and people who participate in my business opportunities. You are not only what you are today, but also what you choose to become tomorrow.

YOU'RE IN THE RIGHT PLACE AT THE RIGHT TIME FOR SUCCESS ... RIGHT NOW!

How many times have you heard that success is being at the right place at the right time? Well ... you're in luck. At this very moment you are at the right place at the right time. Begin to think like a winner and seize this opportunity to get on the road to success.

LEADING AUTHORITIES IN THE MOTIVATIONAL FIELD PRAISE *THINK LIKE A WINNER!*

Anthony Robbins — Author, *Unlimited Power*
"Helping people discover their richest possibilities and reach their greatest heights is an extraordinary gift, and the one that Dr. Staples shares."

Dr. Robert Schuller — Founding Pastor, The Crystal Cathedral
"If you want to maximize your life's potential and at the same time enhance the lives of others, *Think Like a Winner!* is vital reading."

Denis Waitley — Author, *The Psychology of Winning*
"A complete 'how to' success system for reaching new heights of personal excellence."

Dr. Norman Vincent Peale — Author, *The Power of Positive Thinking*
"*Think Like a Winner!* is a scholarly motivational book. It convincingly presents workable formulae for releasing your potential."

Dr. Kenneth Blanchard — Co-Author, *The One Minute Manager*
"Leaders are those who have a vision of excellence and have acquired the necessary skills to help themselves and others reach their full potential. By applying the principles of this book, you are taking a major step in this direction."

James Newman — Author, *Release Your Brakes!*
"The years of study and exploration which have gone into your book, *Think Like a Winner!* have produced a terrific course for personal growth. It will make a positive contribution to the life of every person who reads it."

Brian Tracy — Author, *The Psychology of Success*
"This book is a veritable encyclopedia of success ideas and concepts, and anyone could benefit by applying these ideas to his or her life."

A LIFETIME MONEY-BACK GUARANTEE

You'll be given a tested, proven blueprint for success. Follow it and your life will change forever. Order *Think Like a Winner!* If it isn't all I've said it is—and more—you can return it for a full refund at any time. Send $10 (CA res. $10.83) plus $2.00 shipping and handling to:

Melvin Powers
12015 Sherman Road
No. Hollywood, CA 91605

Chapter Ten

Five of My Most Successful Direct Mail Pieces that Sold and Are Selling Millions of Dollars Worth of Books

There is a saying, "We all learn by experience." It can refer to any aspect of living, from romance to career. I have reproduced numerous ads so you might learn from others' experiences and be that much further ahead in learning. The ads were carefully selected to illustrate certain points so that by concentrating on money-making ads and studying the elements that made them work, you would consciously or subconsciously absorb the formula for winning combinations.

PSYCHO-CYBERNETICS

The four-page circular and variations of it, illustrated on pages 203 through 206, enabled me to sell over two million copies of *Psycho-Cybernetics*. That's a clue that should prompt you to say to yourself, "What can I sell following the same patterns?" As a future mail order entrepreneur, you should continually ask yourself this question. You should be asking it every day as you peruse magazines and publications, spotting ads which, through their repetitive use, you know to be successful. Also scrutinize the ads on TV and the direct mail that you receive. Can you use the advertising concept as a springboard for your own product?

Everyone can be a Monday morning quarterback, knowing the precise reasons why things went right or wrong. Your job is to try to become an expert beforehand, before spending your time, energy, and money on a product. Now that you are becoming more sophisticated in your advertising expertise, can you judge why the four-page mailing piece did so well for *Psycho-Cybernetics?* Was it the subject matter, the advertising copy, or a com-bination of both? Which element do you think was most important? Would the circular have pulled just as successfully without page four (our page number 206)? Do you think the circular would have pulled just as well with the advertising copy on pages one, two, and three set in regular type and combined into one page, backed up with page four? That's an important question. If it had done the same job, I could have saved myself thousands of dollars in printing costs. I didn't do it because I was delighted with the result, and sensed that the personal feeling typewriter type gives to copy would have been lost.

Although I may sound redundant at times, there's a reason for it. I do it to emphasize and illustrate how you can make money in mail order by following professional mail order techniques. Most mail order success is predicated on follow-up sales. It's intended to get a customer interested in your product and sell him additional products by the use of a mail order catalog or direct mail literature. The additional sale is known as the spin-off, follow-up, bounce-back or back end.

Once you have a successful product, you should have or develop other products to sell. That's what I did following my incredible success with *Psycho-Cybernetics*. I published the following books: *Success-Cybernetics* by U.S. Andersen, *Dr. Psycho-Cybernetics* by Maxwell Maltz, M.D., and *Cybernetics Within Us* by Y. Saparina. Look at the covers on pages 207 and 208. The spin-offs of the three books amounted to over several million dollars in sales. It wasn't accomplished by accident; it was by design. That's what I want you to do once you have your winning product.

I'd like to digress for a moment to further illustrate the point of spin-offs in an entirely different field. In 1974, I took a year off from my publishing and mail order activities to devote my time and energy to being a songwriter. Although I had reached a very successful point in my business, I needed a new challenge. I'm always involved in several unrelated businesses because attempting to reach my goal in each is what piques my interest.

I wrote a very lively, danceable song called *Willie Burgundy,* based on my fantasy of being a good honky-tonk piano player. Since I'm from Boston, I chose to make the principal character in the song a Bostonian. The bounce and verve of the song make it almost impossible for the listener to sit still. One feels compelled to get up and dance. Teresa Brewer recorded the song and sang it on a George Segal TV special for NBC.

Because my creative training has programmed me to think in terms of spin-offs, my songwriting partner, Tommy Boyce, and I came up with the idea of an album of danceable music based on the unique sound we had created for the song, *Willie Burgundy,* a ragtime, rock-and-roll band featuring two pianos, a trombone, and tuba. On pages 210 and 211 you'll find the delightful results of that type of creative thinking.

Note the caption on the album cover, ON THE MID-NIGHT TRAIN FROM BOSTON. At the time we produced this album, Gladys Knight had a big hit with the song, *Midnight Train to Georgia.* I copycatted the idea from that song title. It seemed to fit perfectly. To keep in the entertainment mood, I'm including on page 209 a photo of Teresa Brewer, Tommy Boyce, and myself as a songwriter. I'm also including the sheet music of the song on pages 212 through 216.

Refer to pages 207 and 208. What do you notice about the design of all four covers? Do you think that was a good idea? Why? I purposely designed the covers of the follow-up books to resemble the look of *Psycho-Cybernetics.* I did this so there would be both a conscious and subconscious recognition of the design. My theory is that if the reader is pleased with the first book, he'll consider buying the follow-up books. It worked in both theory and practice.

I wrote a foreword for each of the four, identifying each as a Melvin Powers book. That's an important link. I have written forewords to many books, endorsing them. This has helped to sell many that otherwise might not have sold as well.

This is an original technique which, to my knowledge, has never been used by another publisher in merchandising his books. Either he didn't think of it, or he didn't think it was valid. If you are going to become successful, it's necessary to start being creative and test some innovations. I'll show you what I did in promoting the book, *Cybernetics Within Us.*

CYBERNETICS WITHIN US

First, I'd like to share a clever merchandising technique with you. Note the **1967 First Prize Award** for the book, *Cybernetics Within Us,* on page 207. On the rim of the award it reads **Wilshire Self-Improvement Library Series.** Doesn't the award look official? I gave the award myself to enhance the book's saleability. It worked effectively in helping to sell the book.

You might want to consider this same technique with a product of your own. You can call it *The Best Product of the Year Award.* It will help you get more mileage from the product. Don't movie companies take advantage of awards they get? Even a nomination will start the hard sell.

My job, even before I published *Cybernetics Within Us,* was to design an ad or direct mail piece that would stir a feeling of excitement about the book, one that was believable and would, in turn, motivate the reader to order the book. Publishing the book is easy. The problem is, what do you do with the books after you get them from the printer? I spent a great deal of time writing display ads, but somehow never felt I came up with a winner. I was writing and rewriting because I was indecisive as to which direction to take. Finally, I dropped the idea of running display ads and decided to sell the book using direct mail.

Once this was settled in my mind, I wrote the two-page personal letter. It had a good feel to it, so I continued and wrote the 12-page foreword to fill up the space in the circular. It is probably the world's longest foreword, but I believed if I wrote an interesting piece, the reader would order the book. And that's exactly what happened. When you see a product you want to mail order, visualize the content of your advertising copy.

Using a self-mailer has advantages you might want to consider. It eliminates the cost of an envelope to contain the circular, the need for a return envelope, and the need for a separate personal letter. These extra costs run into a lot of money when you are mailing out hundreds of thousands of circulars. Bear in mind your goal is to produce a profitable circular that can be mailed to outside lists totaling millions of names, and that's where the big profits are.

Practically every mail order book will instruct you to include a self-addressed envelope with your offer to make it easy for the recipient to order. I agree with that in principle, but it isn't imperative if your offer is strong and you are selling a low-ticket item. I've tested my mailings with and without return envelopes and haven't noticed an appreciable difference. From a practical point of view, if you can avoid the extra cost, it's more money in your pocket. This, of course is something to determine for yourself.

SALES CYBERNETICS

Examine the cover of one of my latest books, *Sales Cybernetics* by Brian Adams, illustrated on page 217. Compare this cover to that of *Psycho-Cybernetics* shown on the same page. The covers appear almost identical. This was purposely done so the cover of *Sales Cybernetics* would produce immediate recognition and conscious and subconscious recall of the cover on *Psycho-Cybernetics*.

I expect to sell millions of copies of *Sales Cybernetics* in a short period of time. I am using a self-mailer with great success and expect multiple sales. This mailer is being sent to sales training executives, sales and marketing executives, and sales people in numerous businesses ranging from clothing to real estate.

My foreword on pages 218 and 219 also serves as selling copy. See page 220 for the address panel carrying the line, "THIS BOOK CAN DOUBLE YOUR SALES". "Double your sales"—these three words embody the dream of everyone in sales. I have hit the bull's-eye with this copy and it has contributed to the excellent return on this circular.

Sales Cybernetics Cassette Tapes are being sold simultaneously and successfully with the book. See page 221.

Look at the order from B. Dalton for 2,000 copies of the book on page 222. I have sent complimentary copies to various businesses and anticipate volume sales. Page 223 contains a publicity release I sent to business magazines with a review copy of the book.

SELF-IMPROVEMENT CIRCULAR

One of my most successful mailing pieces is called *The Self-Improvement Circular*. It measures 11" x 34". That's like stringing together four 8½" x 11" pieces of paper. The basic plan is to divide each page into 15 boxes advertising various books. See pages 225 through 229 for the layout. Two panels are devoted to an order form containing the books I publish listed in various categories. See pages 329 through 334 in the back of the book.

This layout, and variations of it, are similar to the ones used in most gift-and-gadget mail order catalogs. It works very effectively. The idea behind this circular is that there is a book for everyone. Ordering of the book becomes an impulse purchase similar to buying impulse items at the supermarket. Our average order is for three books.

The sale of each book is tabulated daily, weekly, monthly, and yearly. Therefore, I know at all times how many copies of each book are being sold. If a book isn't selling well enough to devote a block of copy to it, I drop it and substitute another book. You would do the same thing if you were selling gifts and gadgets. Each block of copy must pay for itself, even though this catalog is your creation. You wouldn't continue to run a display ad if it didn't pull sufficient orders. The same goes for the pages and blocks of copy in your catalog.

JOIN THE WINNER$' CIRCLE

See pages 230 and 231. This circular uses the self-improvement circular format for the specific purpose of selling books pertaining to making money. The companies advertising various gambling systems use this circular very successfully as a package insert. It's a natural for them. Note how many times the word *win* is used in the titles of the books. I am advertising 23 books in this small amount of space and have had excellent sales for all the books. I have also had many orders for the complete set of books. That's truly an impulse purchase. You could adapt this layout for selling any category of books or products. I like it. It's clean-cut and effective. It's interesting to observe this circular does extremely well as a package insert for companies selling sex-oriented literature. I still haven't figured out the precise correlation. Such a company stamps its name and address on the blank order form or purchases a set of negatives from me, and then runs the circular with its imprint.

CHARISMA

See pages 232, 233, and 234. These three circulars and variations of them have helped put *Charisma* on the best seller list.

See page 235. This page represents a computer read-out of the best selling, quality, trade paperback books in 355 Dalton Bookstores throughout the country for the week of March 30, 1979. It is as accurate a sales picture as you can possibly get.

It's prestigious to get a book on this list. Any publisher would be very happy with that accomplishment. I'm proud to have three books on it: #5, *The Magic of Thinking Big*, #22, *Think & Grow Rich*, and #29, *Psycho-Cybernetics*. I feel it's a validation of my publishing acumen and makes me feel good.

Here I am on television promoting the first edition of *How to Get Rich in Mail Order.* The pictures were taken on June 27, 1980, on Alicia Sandoval's "Let's Rap" show on KTTV, Hollywood. My niece, Natasha Ryan, came along to give me a few tips on stage presentation.

Dear Friend:

Please listen to what I have to say about an amazing new discovery that can change your entire life. <u>Starting right now, you can begin to rebuild yourself—your personality, your outlook, even your appearance</u>—and fill your future with wealth, satisfying achievement, radiant well-being and long, rich years of happiness and contented fulfillment!

<u>I know this sounds fantastic but it's true</u>. An astonishing scientific discovery by Dr. Maxwell Maltz can be the magic key, opening vast new worlds to you. A zest for living, the superb feeling of good health, regained optimism and a new serenity, hosts of admiring friends, the happiness and success you were meant to enjoy—all these treasures can be yours at last—through the amazing power of psycho-cybernetics.

What is psycho-cybernetics? A fantastic new science based on the newly discovered law of self-image psychology. <u>A dynamic and miraculous program of personality rebuilding that can transform you into a magnetic personality</u>!

Psycho-cybernetics is built upon two astonishing new concepts that have already changed the lives, futures, and inner personalities of thousands of men and women no smarter, better educated, or harder working than you.

EMOTIONAL SURGERY
THE SECRET OF PSYCHO-CYBERNETICS

While doing research on the regrowth of damaged tissue, Dr. Maxwell Maltz, a famous plastic surgeon, noticed a strange psychological fact. That <u>when outward scars or deformations are removed, there is a corresponding inner change</u>.

Beginning with this phenomenon, he studied and worked for years exploring the borderlands of a new science. At last he found that the same amazing change in human personality and capability can be caused through emotional surgery—a repair process you can perform on yourself!

Thus the law of self-image psychology was discovered. It states that <u>every person has a mental picture of himself, his abilities, and limitations—and that to change himself he must change this mental image</u>. <u>That once you believe you can do something, suddenly you can do it</u>!

Dr. Maltz proves that the only limitations upon our abilities are those we impose upon ourselves. He cites the case history of Richard S., who thought he could never master a foreign language. Failing his college courses in French and Spanish, he was handicapped for many years by the self-image restriction.

But Dr. Maltz showed him this limitation was of his own making. Once he was convinced he could learn French, he took classes in the language. A year later, vacationing in

France, he could converse fluently with the natives—thanks to the magic of psycho-cybernetics!

What limitations are you imposing on yourself? Do you feel that you aren't capable of holding down a high-paying job? That you can't make new friends or find happiness in love and marriage? Are you convinced that you just can't get along with people? That you will never get rich? That you are too old for romance?

Whatever your self-image is, the chances are 100 to 1 that <u>emotional surgery, the secret of psycho-cybernetics, can change your potential abilities from minus to plus</u>! Prove to yourself that the power of psycho-cybernetics can give you the extra added impetus you need to:

Get a new job at higher pay

Find love, romance, friendship

Improve your health

Transform yourself into a dynamic, charismatic personality

Win the success, prestige, and happiness you have been denying yourself

PSYCHO-CYBERNETICS AND YOUR INNER SUCCESS-FINDING MECHANISM

Self-image psychology proves that within you and me and everyone is a success mechanism. The failure mechanism produces negative thinking, depression, narrow mental horizons, and the ingrained failure habit.

But <u>the success-finding mechanism is a dynamic reservoir of secret strength—an untapped fountainhead of hidden power</u>. This mysterious powerhouse is generally tapped only in extreme emergencies. You have read of bedridden people who got up and walked when their room caught fire—of paralyzed people who experienced miraculous cures under extreme emotional pressure—of ordinary people suddenly capable of feats of super-human strength in an emergency.

<u>*Psycho-Cybernetics* can show you exactly how to turn off the failure mechanism that has been guiding you all your life...exactly how to switch on the success mechanism...and the process is permanent</u>.

Best of all, the success mechanism actually operates just like an automatic radar tracker. Dr. Maltz shows you how to fix your sights on whatever goal or goals in life you most desire, then feed instructions to the success-finding mechanism (in much the same way an electronic data processor or computer is programmed) and then all you have to do is sit back and relax, confident that every moment your automatic success mechanism is guiding you unerringly towards those goals—even while you sleep.

The facts about psycho-cybernetics are so incredible that they sound fantastic at first hearing. No words of mine can possibly convince you of the amazing changes self-image psychology will work on you, your health and appearance, yours personality and abilities, your capacity for greater work energy, longer years, and increased happiness.

For this reason, I am eager to have you prove to yourself that everything I say is complete, undiluted truth! When your copy of this fascinating new book arrives, read and enjoy its amazing revelations of self-image psychology.

But don't just read it—put it into practice! <u>Set the giant force of psycho-cybernetics to work for you in your own life.</u> <u>Prove to yourself—in your regained optimism, your re-won spark, zest, and vigor—that this book can transform you into a new person.</u>

If for any reason you find that you are dissatisfied—that *Psycho-Cybernetics* does not contain the stimulating force we claim—then you are welcome to return the book to us at any time for a full refund.

Fair enough? <u>You are free to read and use this remarkable book for as long as you want, and then, if dissatisfied for any reason, just return it to us.</u> You can't possible lose a cent—and you stand to gain everything you want in life!

Wealth...success...vigor...love and romance...new friendships...the admiration of people you meet...financial independence and a glorious feeling of prosperity, achievement, and fulfillment!

Read *Psycho-Cybernetics* and prove to yourself that you can change your entire life!

Psycho-Cybernetics
A New Technique for Using Your Subconscious Power
Maxwell Maltz, M.D.
Foreword by Melvin Powers
288 pages...$12.00 postpaid

MAIL NO-RISK COUPON TODAY!

Please send me a copy of *Psycho-Cybernetics* by Maxwell Maltz, M.D. I will use this book entirely at your risk. If I am not completely satisfied, I will simply return it for a full refund.

I am enclosing my ( ) money order ( ) check for $12.00 (CA residents $12.83)

Name_____

Address_____

City_____ State_____ Zip_____

Mail to:

Melvin Powers
12015 Sherman Road
No. Hollywood, CA 91605

PSYCHO-CYBERNETICS
a new way to GET MORE LIVING OUT OF LIFE

LET THIS FAMOUS PLASTIC SURGEON'S remarkable discovery—*which vitally concerns your future*—guide you to the achievement of all your goals in life. Dr. Maxwell Maltz's experiments in the regrowth of injured tissues disclosed a little-known side-effect of plastic surgery: its revitalizing power on human personality. Removing outward scars and deformations produces a similar inward change on your temperament, abilities and Personality-Potentials, because it alters your "self image".

Built on this remarkable phenomenon, Dr. Maltz's new Self-Image Psychology works vast improvements on your personality thru *"emotional surgery."* This new psychology, the secret of PSYCHO-CYBERNETICS, performs this same crucial change by erasing *inner*, psychological scars. Through the amazing new techniques of emotional surgery, which are mapped out in detail in this book, you create a totally new image of yourself as a dynamic, happy, successful person—the sort of "born leader" who overflows with vigor and energy, plunges into every task with zest and unquenchable enthusiasm. You become a dynamic, vivid, colorful person who attracts fat paychecks, big promotions, admiring friends—swift success!

PSYCHO-CYBERNETICS awakes your sleeping abilities—galvanizes into life talents and powers you never dreamed were yours—fills you with such strength and new-found energy that you feel years younger, healthier, happier! Suddenly, you become overnight a Man of Power—your *latent potentials* have come to life—you zoom through tasks that would have stumped you before—you crash through obstacles and barriers that would have halted you before—you soar to new heights of achievement and wealth that seemed unscalable before PSYCHO-CYBERNETICS rebuilt your personality along "The Lines of Power"!

But better than this—PSYCHO-CYBERNETICS touches into roaring life a hidden reservoir of latent energy that functions within you like an automatic machine. All you do is set up goals and this secret dynamo steers you to them—automatically, constantly, permanently—*even while you are asleep!* Fantastic? Yes! But THIS is the incredible power of PSYCHO-CYBERNETICS. Once you erase your "emotional scars" and trigger into action your "Success Mechanism"—overnight you will sleep better, work easier, feel happier and healthier and look younger than you have in years!

YOU GET ALL THESE GIFTS—

- VIGOROUS, SPARKLING WELL-BEING!

- FREEDOM FROM FEAR AND GUILT!

- SUPERB, EBULLIENT GOOD SPIRITS!

- FINANCIAL SUCCESS AND SECURITY!

- RENEWED YOUTHFUL VIGOR!

- SERENE SELF-CONFIDENCE!

- NEW LOVE AND ROMANCE!

- DYNAMIC ENTHUSIASM AND WORK-ENERGY!

- A VITAL, COMMANDING NEW PERSONALITY!

- ADMIRATION FROM ALL YOU MEET!

- MONEY AND JOB SUCCESS!

THANKS TO AN AMAZING NEW SCIENTIFIC INNOVATION THIS "NEW WAY OF LIFE" CAN NOW BE YOURS!

DR. MAXWELL MALTZ, M.D., F.I.C.S., DISCOVERER OF PSYCHO-CYBERNETICS

ABOUT THE AUTHOR: Dr. Maxwell Maltz, M.D., F.I.C.S., received his baccalaureate in science from Columbia University and his doctorate in medicine at the College of Physicians and Surgeons there. One of the world's most widely-known and highly-regarded plastic surgeons, he has practised in England, France, Germany, Italy and throughout Latin America. He has lectured before the University of Amsterdam, the University of Paris, and the University of Rome. He has been Professor of Plastic Surgery at the University of Nicaragua and at the University of El Salvador. He is the author of eight books previous to PSYCHO-CYBERNETICS, including ADVENTURES IN STAYING YOUNG and the famous bestseller, DR. PYGMALION.

$5

CYBERNETICS WITHIN US

A Fascinating Scientific Exploration of Your AUTOMATIC SUBCONSCIOUS POWER

Y. SAPARINA

foreword by

WILSHIRE SELF-IMPROVEMENT LIBRARY SERIES
1967 FIRST PRIZE AWARD

$7

PSYCHO-CYBERNETICS

A New Technique for Using Your SUBCONSCIOUS POWER

By

MAXWELL MALTZ, M.D., F.I.C.S.

Foreword by

MELVIN POWERS

Based on an amazing new scientific innovation, this simple yet practical "New Way of Life" can be the most important influence in your life!

"An invaluable aid to the layman, offering a sound, scientific method of practical self-improvement."

Mark Freeman, Ph.D.
Clinical Psychologist

$5

DOCTOR PSYCHO-CYBERNETICS

Formerly titled Dr. Pygmalion

by **MAXWELL MALTZ, M.D.**

foreword by **MELVIN POWERS**

$7

SUCCESS-CYBERNETICS

Practical Applications of
HUMAN-CYBERNETICS

by **U.S. ANDERSEN**

Foreword by **MELVIN POWERS**

June 1974, at NBC taping of THE GEORGE SEGAL SPECIAL, featuring Miss Teresa Brewer singing an original song, "Willie Burgundy," written by the new and soon-to-be-famous team of Boyce & Powers. From left to right . . . Melvin Powers, Teresa Brewer, Tommy Boyce.

This is the front cover of the album, THE WILLIE BURGUNDY FIVE — ON THE MIDNIGHT TRAIN FROM BOSTON. From left to right . . . Michel running to catch The Midnight Train, and beautiful Linda Carter, better known as Wonder Woman, the female conductor, giving him a helping hand.

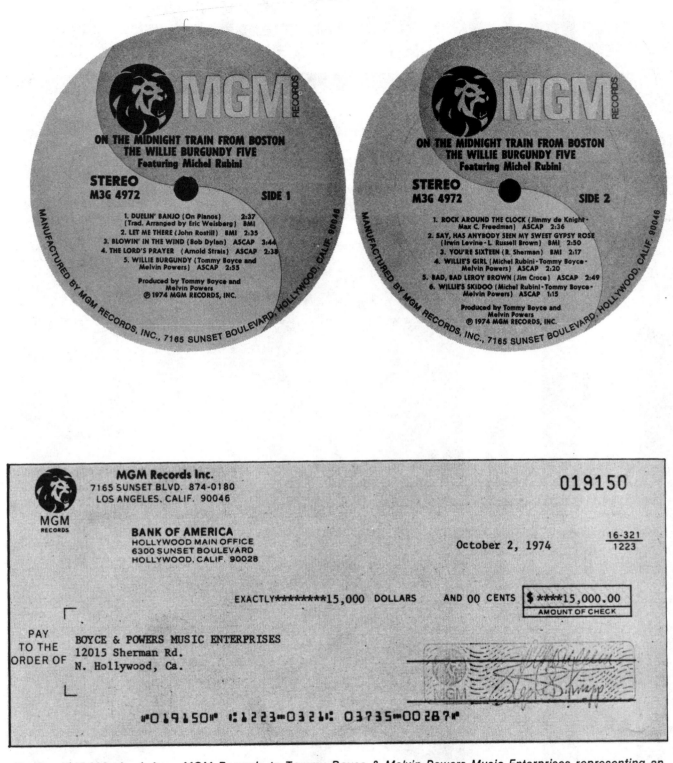

Here's a $15,000 check from MGM Records to Tommy Boyce & Melvin Powers Music Enterprises representing an advance against royalties for the album WILLIE BURGUNDY FIVE—ON THE MIDNIGHT TRAIN FROM BOSTON.

WILLIE BURGUNDY

Words and Music by TOMMY BOYCE • MELVIN POWERS

Recorded by TERESA BREWER on SIGNATURE Records

UNITED ARTISTS MUSIC CO., INC.
and BOYCE & POWERS MUSIC ENTERPRISES
Hollywood, Calif.

212

$1.50

Distributed by

WILLIE BURGUNDY

Words and Music by
TOMMY BOYCE
MELVIN POWERS

1988 - 4

if we asked you pret-ty please,__ would ya play our pi-an-o to-night.__

All eight-y-eight keys are in-tact__ fif-ty-two white and thir-ty-six

black and it's a gen-u-ine nine-teen eight-een brown up-right. Oh! It would
Oh!

thrill our hearts so much__ if our key-board you would touch__ with your el-e-gant__ Bos-
Wil-lie you play so nice__ if they gave a tro-phy you'd win first prize__ 'Cause you're the ver-y best__ hon-ky-

$7

SALES CYBERNETICS

New Scientific Techniques in MOTIVATIONAL SELLING

BRIAN ADAMS

Foreword by
MELVIN POWERS

$7

PSYCHO-CYBERNETICS

A New Technique for Using Your SUBCONSCIOUS POWER

By
MAXWELL MALTZ, M.D., F.I.C.S.

Foreword by
MELVIN POWERS

Based on an amazing new scientific innovation, this simple yet practical "New Way of Life" can be the most important influence in your life!

"An invaluable aid to the layman, offering a sound, scientific method of practical self-improvement."
Mark Freeman, Ph.D.
Clinical Psychologist

SALES CYBERNETICS

320 pages - $8.00 postpaid
by Brian Adams
Foreword by Melvin Powers

It isn't often that a publisher can honestly say that the book he is introducing is the best one on a particular topic that he has ever read. This is one of those rare occasions. *Sales Cybernetics* is the best book that I've read on the psychology of selling. And I've read a lot of them.

Sales Cybernetics draws its foundation from the "bible" of self-improvement — the classic *Psycho-Cybernetics* by Dr. Maxwell Maltz. Now the powerful principles of self-image psychology are focused by Brian Adams into the scientific techniques of motivational selling. It is my hope that the millions of persons who gained new ways of improving their personalities and erasing negative habit patterns from *Psycho-Cybernetics* will reap the same benefits from this new offering. In short, I hope it will open the way to new riches in your life, personally and financially.

Few things contribute more to an individual's well-being and sense of self-worth than his ability to stand on his own two feet, to achieve independence for himself and the ones he loves. Personal independence is difficult to attain without financial independence. Such independence can only come from your ability to make money. The more you make, the more your self-image will rise. I don't mean this to sound crass or mercenary, but it is undeniably true that one of the greatest joys in life is knowing that you are financially secure. I want you to be worth more by the time you finish reading this book. I want you to be able to make a lot more money; not just a fraction of what you earn at present, but *many times* more.

1

If you are content drawing an average salary for the rest of your life, accepting the fact that you will only have just enough to "get by," this book is not for you. But if you want your self-image *and* your bank balance to soar, study the time-proven, thoroughly researched methods of *Sales Cybernetics.*

There is only one area in the work force where you stand an excellent chance of making big money. That area is *business.* The great success stories of men like Carnegie, Rockefeller, Ford, and now Iacocca all spring from the field of business.

When I was starting in business, the giant corporations of America seemed overwhelming. There was no way I thought I could achieve the same greatness. But today, I have achieved some of that status for myself. I own a publishing company valued at millions of dollars.

How did I do this? By realizing two all-important things. First, I saw that success in business is primarily related to sales. All the rest is window dressing. The buildings, the staff, the logo, the letterhead, the image, and the advertising are there for only one reason — to sell a product.

Second, I saw that the art of sales is the art of interpersonal relationships. If people believe in you, they will believe in your product. I found that *Sales Cybernetics* explains how to sell both yourself and your product better than anything I've read. It so validated what I personally had learned, and so inspired me, that I was eager to share its secrets with the millions of persons who have bought my other books.

Written by an internationally acclaimed trainer in salesmanship at all levels of business, *Sales Cybernetics* exhaustively covers sound professional advice while putting sales techniques into a new, dynamic framework that works to produce electrifying results. It is action-oriented from the very beginning, a masterful synthesis of 15 proven formulas for getting people to say "yes" to you and your product. This "yes" can translate into untold dollars to anyone who puts the principles to work.

2

The first two formulas lay the groundwork by using computer programming principles to increase your sales productivity. Effective sales communication comes about through programming persuasive attitudes into your mental computer. An extremely important point is brought out in the discussion of the third formula; namely, that a poor concept of yourself is the biggest contributor to your failure. The chapter devoted to this formula shows you how to raise your self-image and match it with a better reality.

What you believe manifests itself in what you do. This is also true of your customer. If you wish to make a sale, it's important to know the belief system of your client — what motivates him to buy. Mr. Adams presents one of the best analyses of buying motives I have ever seen, and a powerful listing of the traits necessary to being a dynamic seller.

Further formulas tell you how to "get through" to people by making them like you; analyze the changing public tastes and preferences to make certain your product is always in demand; and prospect the market to find new avenues of business.

A truly extraordinary section is the one on how to handle objections through the psychology of harmonious human relationships. Blocks to your making a sale can be eliminated by using such techniques as *capitalizing*, making objections work in your favor, and *indirect denial*, a "yes-but" formula that lets you outflank your prospect's reasons for not buying by diverting his attention to why he *should* buy.

A book such as this is the result not only of many years of the author's experience, but lifetimes of experience of the most successful people in the business world. It is full of practical tips and secrets from leading authorities on how to increase sales. Following this advice can save you years in costly mistakes and help you start making big money. I believe that there is no substitute for experience in the field. This book is not meant to be such a substitute but, rather, a guide to potentiating your experience—making it maximally

3

effective and giving you time to make more sales and more money than you ever dreamed possible.

Sales Cybernetics contains aids to sales of every description, including many illuminating case histories. Read it carefully. Follow precisely the principles laid down and deliberately program yourself to sell until your subconscious mind takes over and makes you an "automatic" supersalesperson.

Brian Adams has written a book to show you how to *help yourself* to make more sales. You will have to exert the effort required to implement the principles. If you do, I can promise that the results will come back manyfold in proportion to the effort needed to produce them. These principles have helped thousands, and I have every confidence that they will now help you. Get ready. You are about to embark on the road to riches.

Melvin Powers
Publisher, Wilshire Book Company

12015 Sherman Road
North Hollywood,
California 91605-3781

4

The Author

Brian Adams' career reads like a page from his own book. He is an accomplished actor-writer-director. At the age of twenty-three he owned a chain of newspapers and a radio and television production company in Canada. He is an international lecturer on success and has hosted his own TV programs in Canada, America and Australia.

Born in Australia, he began his career as a copy writer for a Sydney advertising agency. Later he left on a soldier-of-fortune life that took him to many countries in the East, in Europe and to America.

After an absence of 15 years, Brian Adams was brought back to Australia by Sydney's Channel 10 to host their "Tonight" show for a year. Recently he set up BRIAD PRODUCTIONS AUSTRALIA to produce TV and film programs.

As a lecturer, he has conducted numerous seminars on 'salesmanship', the 'self image' and related success topics both in Sydney and abroad. In fact, he is considered one of the top ten motivational speakers in the United States. He has an impressive list of speaking credits which includes companies, men's and women's clubs, chambers of commerce and colleges.

Much of the lecture material is included in this book along with proven success techniques of other successful individuals.

Brian Adams knows the ingredients for health, happiness and prosperity and this book gives YOU the key for the expansion of YOUR life. At present he is working on another title—''Grow Rich with Your Million Dollar Mind''.

Sales Cybernetics Cassette Tapes

As a publisher of self-improvement books, I have listened to countless cassette tapes on the psychology and art of selling. So it is with utmost confidence that I recommend the *Sales Cybernetics* cassette tapes to you.

Author Brian Adams' dynamic techniques for motivational selling, coupled with the powerful principles of *Psycho-Cybernetics*, make these cassette tapes outstanding. Developing a good self-image, maintaining a positive relationship with others, and gaining insight so far as eliminating negative sales patterns is concerned will prove to be of tremendous benefit to you.

Although your enrichment will be immediate, it will progressively increase as you continue to adapt and implement the guiding principles and theories to your life. An indirect bonus quite apart from your business life is the potential for success in all your areas of interest. By the time you finish listening to them, you will know exactly how to enhance your self-image. This, in turn, will help you to achieve one of the great joys in life—financial security.

The *Sales Cybernetics* cassette tapes will prove to be the guiding light which will unlock and unleash your untapped talents and enable you to focus on successfully pyramiding your income. Basically, these tapes address two important ingredients for business success: The sale of the product and the buyer's perception of the person selling the product.

Produced by an internationally acclaimed trainer in salesmanship, the *Sales Cybernetics* cassette tapes offer sound professional advice and establish sales techniques within a new, dynamic framework that will help you bring about astonishing results. The tapes are action-oriented and describe in detail proven formulas to obtain positive responses. These formulas include ways to develop a persuasive attitude which, when programmed into your mental process, will result in easier and more lucrative sales productivity.

The tapes analyze buying motives and aptly describe the art of communicating effectively. A particularly helpful section outlines ways to handle objections by adeptly using sales psychology. The tapes describe in detail the sales techniques used by the author and other contemporary leaders in the business and financial communities.

In my judgment, the *Sales Cybernetics* cassette tapes are an indispensable aid to those who want to increase their sales potential. Listening to them will help you acquire confidence, self-esteem, and a dynamic selling style necessary to fulfill your ambitions and attain your dreams for financial reward.

Melvin Powers

Sales Cybernetics Cassette Tapes

$25.00 postpaid

SALES CYBERNETICS

New Scientific Techniques in
MOTIVATIONAL SELLING

BRIAN ADAMS

Foreword by
MELVIN POWERS

THIS
BOOK
CAN
DOUBLE
YOUR
SALES!

ORDER FORM

Please send immediately:

( ) Sales Cybernetics *Brian Adams* $ 8.00 _____
( ) Sales Cybernetics Cassette Tape   25.00 _____

Additional Motivational Books

( ) Magic of Thinking Success *David Schwartz, Ph.D.*   10.00 _____
( ) Psycho-Cybernetics *Maxwell Maltz, M.D.*   10.00 _____
( ) Success-Cybernetics *U.S. Anderson*   10.00 _____
( ) Think & Grow Rich *Napoleon Hill*   10.00 _____
( ) Think Like a Winner *Walter Doyle Staples, Ph.D.*   10.00 _____

Subtotal _____
CA residents add 8¼% sales tax _____
S/H: 2.00 per book _____
Total _____

Name _____ Title _____
           (Please print)
Company _____
Address _____
City _____ State _____ Zip _____

Please send orders to:
    Wilshire Book Company Dept. 543
    12015 Sherman Road
    North Hollywood, California 91605-3781

Satisfaction Guaranteed

P.S. The above listed books can also be obtained directly from all B. Dalton, Walden, Crown, and independent bookstores.

B. Dalton BOOKSELLER
SAN 147-000-00

PURCHASE ORDER

NUMBER C006221	DATE 08-05-85 PAGE 1

INVOICE
```
* * * * * * * * * * * * * * * * * * * *
    * VENDER ORDER RECAP *
* * * * * * * * * * * * * * * * * * *
```

SHIP TO
```
* * * * * * * * * * * * * * * * * * * *
    * VENDER ORDER RECAP *
* * * * * * * * * * * * * * * * * * *
```

TERMS	DO NOT SHIP BEFORE	CANCEL IF NOT SHIPPED BY	BACK ORDER CODE
NET	AT ONCE	10-30-85	Y

SPECIAL INFORMATION

TO
```
WILSHIRE BOOK COMPANY
ATTN MISS FREEDMAN
P O BOX 3952
NORTH HOLLYWOOD  CA  91605
```

TITLE OR ITEM DESCRIPTION	AUTHOR	ISBN OR ITEM CODE	QUANTITY	UNIT IDENT.	ITEM RETAIL	DISCOUN
				STORES		
SALES CYBERNETICS	ADAMS B	80412-2	2000	357	7 00	50.
***DEPT. 1 TOTALS			2000		14000 00	
****DISC. SCH. P1 TOTALS			2000		14000 00	

053688

DATE
09/24/85

Waldenbooks
WALDEN BOOK COMPANY, INC.
201 HIGH RIDGE ROAD
STAMFORD, CONN. 06904

PURCHASE ORDER

* SAN—

PURCHASE ORDER NUMBER

17630070

THIS ENTIRE (12 DIGIT) NUMBER & SAN MUST APPEAR ON INVOICE AND PACKAGES.

PLEASE REFER TO ROUTING GUIDE FOR SHIPPING INSTRUCTIONS

TO:
WILSHIRE BOOK COMPANY

SHIP TO:

MAIL YOUR ORIGINAL INVOICE TO:

WALDENBOOKS
ATTENTION: ACCOUNTS PAYABLE DEPT.
201 HIGH RIDGE ROAD
P.O. BOX 10218
STAMFORD, CT. 06904

FOR LOCATIONS 17, 18
OR 19 MAIL TO:
WALDENBOOKS
P.O. BOX 1170
STAMFORD, CT. 06904

ENCLOSE DUPLICATE INVOICE WITH PACKAGE.

DO NOT INSURE PARCEL POST SHIPMENTS.

DO NOT ENCLOSE ORIGINAL INVOICE WITH THE MERCHANDISE.

TERMS		SHIPPING DATE	09/24/85	CANCEL DATE	

THIS ORDER IS SUBJECT TO THE TERMS AND CONDITIONS SHOWN BOTH ON FACE AND BACK OF THIS ORDER.

S/C	TITLE/DESCRIPTION	I.S.B.N.	QUANTITY	PRICE	EXTENDED PRICE	DISC. %
	PURCHASE ORDER SUMMARY				NO. OF STORES	
	***********************	********	*****	*****	*****	*****
	SALES CYBERNETICS	0-87980-412-2	958	7 00	137	50 0
	COMP DEFENSIVE BRIDGE PLAYER	0-87980-287-1	1	10 00	1	50 0
	MODERN HYPNOSIS	0-87980-100-X	1	4 00	1	50 0
	BLACKSTONE'S SECRETS OF MAGIC	0-87980-260-X	4	3 00	1	50 0
	***********************	********	*****	*****	*****	*****

Melvin Powers
Wilshire Book Company

12015 Sherman Road
No. Hollywood, CA 91605

(818) 765-8579
FAX (818) 765-2922

To: Business Book Review Editors

SALES CYBERNETICS
Brian Adams

I am Melvin Powers, publisher of such multi-million bestsellers as *Psycho-Cybernetics* by Dr. Maxwell Maltz, *The Magic of Thinking Big* by Dr. David Schwartz, and *Think and Grow Rich* by Napoleon Hill. Now these great classics are joined by a new, equally powerful book, *Sales Cybernetics* by Brian Adams. Based on the proven principles of *Psycho-Cybernetics*, *Sales Cybernetics* teaches sales personnel how to dramatically increase their sales performance and motivates them to do so.

Sales Cybernetics brings new meaning to the psychology of selling. Written by an internationally-acclaimed salesmanship trainer, *Sales Cybernetics* is a masterful synthesis of 15 proven formulas that work in concert with customers' psyches to boost sales. And tried-and-true sales techniques are presented in a dynamic, new framework that multiplies their results many times over.

Sales Cybernetics adeptly employs sales psychology to overcome customer resistance. It presents invaluable techniques such as "capitalizing" which makes objections work in the sales person's favor; and "indirect denial," which outflanks a customer's reasons for not buying and diverts his attention to why he should buy.

It isn't often that a publisher can honestly say the book he is introducing is the best one on a particular topic that he has read. This is one of those rare occasions when a particular book deserves such praise. *Sales Cybernetics* is, without question, the most outstanding book I have ever read on the psychology of selling.

I am pleased to enclose a review copy of *Sales Cybernetics* and would appreciate your help in introducing it to the business community.

Melvin Powers
Wilshire Book Company

12015 Sherman Road
No. Hollywood, CA 91605

(818) 765-8579
FAX (818) 765-2922

GROW RICH
WITH YOUR MILLION DOLLAR MIND

Wealth Strategies For Those Who Want to Achieve Financial Success
Brian Adams

Today's successful entrepreneurs are amassing larger-than-life fortunes and achieving success where so many are failing because, whether they know it or not, they are tapping the extraordinary creative power of the human mind—the same power that you can use to achieve and attain everything you've ever wanted.

YOU CAN CHANGE YOUR LIFE

The power that controls your destiny is part of the creative you and can be used to turn failure into success. *Grow Rich With Your Million Dollar Mind* reveals how to release your subconscious power to quickly change the direction of your life. You will discover how to tap your creative power to attract opportunity, resulting in prosperity.

PUT PROVEN WEALTH-BUILDING TECHNIQUES TO WORK FOR YOU

Thousands of men and women from all parts of the world have amassed wealth by using Brian Adam's techniques. He has taught these techniques to great numbers of people in the United States, Canada and Australia and has witnessed the amazing changes in lifestyle of those who have diligently applied them. These same techniques are now available to you in a remarkable step-by-step guide, *Grow Rich With Your Million Dollar Mind*. This is your opportunity to learn these proven wealth-building secrets and how to use them for immediate results.

STIR THE GENIUS WITHIN YOU

You will discover how to release the creative genius within you. It doesn't matter who you are, what you are or where you are. You can be rich through the scientific use of your mental powers. This book shows you the way.

YOUR BLUEPRINT FOR FINANCIAL INDEPENDENCE

You'll learn how to become a success thinker, a shaper of your own destiny, a winner. You'll raise your self-esteem and expand your desire and capacity to achieve financial independence. With your creative mind operating at peak efficiency, your dreams and aspirations can become a reality. If you want to achieve more, accumulate wealth, and enhance your lifestyle—this book is for you. It's for every man and woman determined to start living a meaningful, rewarding, and outstandingly successful life.

Learn how to tap the power of your million dollar mind. Send today for your copy of *Grow Rich With Your Million Dollar Mind*. $9.00 postpaid (CA residents $9.58)

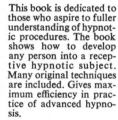

MELVIN POWERS SELF-IMPROVEMENT LIBRARY

ASTROLOGY

____ASTROLOGY—HOW TO CHART YOUR HOROSCOPE Max Heindel 7.00
____ASTROLOGY AND SEXUAL ANALYSIS Morris C. Goodman 7.00
____ASTROLOGY AND YOU Carroll Righter 5.00
____ASTROLOGY MADE EASY Astarte 7.00
____ASTROLOGY, ROMANCE, YOU AND THE STARS Anthony Norvell 10.00
____MY WORLD OF ASTROLOGY Sydney Omarr 10.00
____THOUGHT DIAL Sydney Omarr 7.00
____WHAT THE STARS REVEAL ABOUT THE MEN IN YOUR LIFE Thelma White 3.00

BRIDGE

____BRIDGE BIDDING MADE EASY Edwin B. Kantar 15.00
____BRIDGE CONVENTIONS Edwin B. Kantar 10.00
____COMPETITIVE BIDDING IN MODERN BRIDGE Edgar Kaplan 7.00
____DEFENSIVE BRIDGE PLAY COMPLETE Edwin B Kantar 20.00
____GAMESMAN BRIDGE—PLAY BETTER WITH KANTAR Edwin B. Kantar 7.00
____HOW TO IMPROVE YOUR BRIDGE Alfred Sheinwold 7.00
____IMPROVING YOUR BIDDING SKILLS Edwin B. Kantar 10.00
____INTRODUCTION TO DECLARER'S PLAY Edwin B. Kantar 7.00
____INTRODUCTION TO DEFENDER'S PLAY Edwin B. Kantar 10.00
____KANTAR FOR THE DEFENSE Edwin B. Kantar 7.00
____KANTAR FOR THE DEFENSE VOLUME 2 Edwin B. Kantar 10.00
____TEST YOUR BRIDGE PLAY Edwin B. Kantar 10.00
____VOLUME 2—TEST YOUR BRIDGE PLAY Edwin B. Kantar 10.00
____WINNING DECLARER PLAY Dorothy Hayden Truscott 10.00

BUSINESS, STUDY & REFERENCE

____BRAINSTORMING Charles Clark 10.00
____CONVERSATION MADE EASY Elliot Russell 5.00
____EXAM SECRET Dennis B. Jackson 7.00
____FIX-IT BOOK Arthur Symons 2.00
____HOW TO DEVELOP A BETTER SPEAKING VOICE M. Hellier 5.00
____HOW TO SAVE 50% ON GAS & CAR EXPENSES Ken Stansbie 5.00
____HOW TO SELF-PUBLISH YOUR BOOK & MAKE IT A BEST SELLER Melvin Powers 20.00
____INCREASE YOUR LEARNING POWER Geoffrey A. Dudley 5.00
____PRACTICAL GUIDE TO BETTER CONCENTRATION Melvin Powers 5.00
____PUBLIC SPEAKING MADE EASY Thomas Montalbo 10.00
____7 DAYS TO FASTER READING William S. Schaill 7.00
____SONGWRITER'S RHYMING DICTIONARY Jane Shaw Whitfield 10.00
____SPELLING MADE EASY Lester D. Basch & Dr. Milton Finkelstein 3.00
____STUDENT'S GUIDE TO BETTER GRADES J.A. Rickard 3.00
____TEST YOURSELF—FIND YOUR HIDDEN TALENT Jack Shafer 3.00
____YOUR WILL & WHAT TO DO ABOUT IT Attorney Samuel G. King 7.00

CALLIGRAPHY

____ADVANCED CALLIGRAPHY Katherine Jeffares 7.00
____CALLIGRAPHY—THE ART OF BEAUTIFUL WRITING Katherine Jeffares 7.00
____CALLIGRAPHY FOR FUN & PROFIT Anne Leptich & Jacque Evans 10.00
____CALLIGRAPHY MADE EASY Tina Serafini 7.00

CHESS & CHECKERS

____BEGINNER'S GUIDE TO WINNING CHESS Fred Reinfeld 10.00
____CHESS IN TEN EASY LESSONS Larry Evans 10.00
____CHESS MADE EASY Milton L. Hanauer 5.00
____CHESS PROBLEMS FOR BEGINNERS Edited by Fred Reinfeld 7.00
____CHESS TACTICS FOR BEGINNERS Edited by Fred Reinfeld 7.00
____HOW TO WIN AT CHECKERS Fred Reinfeld 7.00
____1001 BRILLIANT WAYS TO CHECKMATE Fred Reinfeld 10.00
____1001 WINNING CHESS SACRIFICES & COMBINATIONS Fred Reinfeld 10.00

COOKERY & HERBS

____CULPEPER'S HERBAL REMEDIES Dr. Nicholas Culpeper 5.00
____FAST GOURMET COOKBOOK Poppy Cannon 2.50
____HEALING POWER OF HERBS May Bethel 5.00
____HEALING POWER OF NATURAL FOODS May Bethel 7.00
____HERBS FOR HEALTH—HOW TO GROW & USE THEM Louise Evans Doole 7.00
____HOME GARDEN COOKBOOK—DELICIOUS NATURAL FOOD RECIPES Ken Kraft 3.00
____MEATLESS MEAL GUIDE Tomi Ryan & James H. Ryan, M.D. 4.00
____VEGETABLE GARDENING FOR BEGINNERS Hugh Wilberg 2.00
____VEGETABLES FOR TODAY'S GARDENS R. Milton Carleton 2.00
____VEGETARIAN COOKERY Janet Walker 10.00
____VEGETARIAN COOKING MADE EASY & DELECTABLE Veronica Vezza 3.00

____

GAMBLING & POKER

____HOW TO WIN AT POKER Terence Reese & Anthony T. Watkins 10.00
____SCARNE ON DICE John Scarne 15.00
____WINNING AT CRAPS Dr. Lloyd T. Commins 5.00
____WINNING AT GIN Chester Wander & Cy Rice 3.00
____WINNING AT POKER—AN EXPERT'S GUIDE John Archer 10.00
____WINNING AT 21—AN EXPERT'S GUIDE John Archer 10.00

HEALTH

____BEE POLLEN Lynda Lyngheim & Jack Scagnetti 5.00

____COPING WITH ALZHEIMER'S Rose Oliver, Ph.D. & Francis Bock, Ph.D. 10.00
____DR. LINDNER'S POINT SYSTEM FOOD PROGRAM Peter G Lindner, M.D. 2.00
____HELP YOURSELF TO BETTER SIGHT Margaret Darst Corbett 7.00
____HOW YOU CAN STOP SMOKING PERMANENTLY Ernest Caldwell 5.00
____MIND OVER PLATTER Peter G Lindner, M.D. 5.00
____NATURE'S WAY TO NUTRITION & VIBRANT HEALTH Robert J. Scrutton 3.00
____NEW CARBOHYDRATE DIET COUNTER Patti Lopez-Pereira 2.00
____REFLEXOLOGY Dr. Maybelle Segal 7.00
____REFLEXOLOGY FOR GOOD HEALTH Anna Kaye & Don C. Matchan 10.00
____30 DAYS TO BEAUTIFUL LEGS Dr. Marc Selner 3.00
____WONDER WITHIN Thomas S. Coyle, M.D. 10.00
____YOU CAN LEARN TO RELAX Dr. Samuel Gutwirth 5.00

HOBBIES

____BEACHCOMBING FOR BEGINNERS Norman Hickin 2.00
____BLACKSTONE'S MODERN CARD TRICKS Harry Blackstone 7.00
____BLACKSTONE'S SECRETS OF MAGIC Harry Blackstone 7.00
____COIN COLLECTING FOR BEGINNERS Burton Hobson & Fred Reinfeld 7.00
____ENTERTAINING WITH ESP Tony 'Doc' Shiels 2.00
____400 FASCINATING MAGIC TRICKS YOU CAN DO Howard Thurston 7.00
____HOW I TURN JUNK INTO FUN AND PROFIT Sari 3.00
____HOW TO WRITE A HIT SONG AND SELL IT Tommy Boyce 10.00
____MAGIC FOR ALL AGES Walter Gibson 7.00
____PLANTING A TREE TreePeople with Andy & Katie Lipkis 13.00
____STAMP COLLECTING FOR BEGINNERS Burton Hobson 3.00

HORSE PLAYERS' WINNING GUIDES

____BETTING HORSES TO WIN Les Conklin 10.00
____ELIMINATE THE LOSERS Bob McKnight 5.00
____HOW TO PICK WINNING HORSES Bob McKnight 5.00
____HOW TO WIN AT THE RACES Sam (The Genius) Lewin 5.00
____HOW YOU CAN BEAT THE RACES Jack Kavanagh 5.00
____MAKING MONEY AT THE RACES David Barr 7.00
____PAYDAY AT THE RACES Les Conklin 7.00
____SMART HANDICAPPING MADE EASY William Bauman 5.00
____SUCCESS AT THE HARNESS RACES Barry Meadow 7.00

HUMOR

____HOW TO FLATTEN YOUR TUSH Coach Marge Reardon 2.00
____JOKE TELLER'S HANDBOOK Bob Orben 7.00
____JOKES FOR ALL OCCASIONS Al Schock 7.00
____2,000 NEW LAUGHS FOR SPEAKERS Bob Orben 7.00
____2,400 JOKES TO BRIGHTEN YOUR SPEECHES Robert Orben 10.00
____2,500 JOKES TO START'EM LAUGHING Bob Orben 10.00

HYPNOTISM

____CHILDBIRTH WITH HYPNOSIS William S. Kroger, M.D. 5.00
____HOW TO SOLVE YOUR SEX PROBLEMS WITH SELF-HYPNOSIS Frank Caprio, M.D. 5.00
____HOW YOU CAN BOWL BETTER USING SELF-HYPNOSIS Jack Heise 7.00
____HOW YOU CAN PLAY BETTER GOLF USING SELF-HYPNOSIS Jack Heise 3.00
____HYPNOSIS AND SELF-HYPNOSIS Bernard Hollander, M.D. 7.00
____HYPNOTISM (Originally published 1893) Carl Sextus 5.00
____HYPNOTISM MADE EASY Dr. Ralph Winn 7.00
____HYPNOTISM MADE PRACTICAL Louis Orton 5.00
____HYPNOTISM REVEALED Melvin Powers 3.00
____MODERN HYPNOSIS Lesley Kuhn & Salvatore Russo, Ph.D. 5.00
____NEW CONCEPTS OF HYPNOSIS Bernard C. Gindes, M.D. 10.00
____NEW SELF-HYPNOSIS Paul Adams 10.00
____POST-HYPNOTIC INSTRUCTIONS—SUGGESTIONS FOR THERAPY Arnold Furst 10.00
____PRACTICAL GUIDE TO SELF-HYPNOSIS Melvin Powers 10.00
____PRACTICAL HYPNOTISM Philip Magonet, M.D. 3.00
____SECRETS OF HYPNOTISM S.J. Van Pelt, M.D. 5.00
____SELF-HYPNOSIS—A CONDITIONED-RESPONSE TECHNIQUE Laurence Sparks 7.00
____SELF-HYPNOSIS—ITS THEORY, TECHNIQUE & APPLICATION Melvin Powers 7.00
____THERAPY THROUGH HYPNOSIS Edited by Raphael H. Rhodes 5.00

JUDAICA

____SERVICE OF THE HEART Evelyn Garfiel, Ph.D. 10.00
____STORY OF ISRAEL IN COINS Jean & Maurice Gould 2.00
____STORY OF ISRAEL IN STAMPS Maxim & Gabriel Shamir 1.00
____TONGUE OF THE PROPHETS Robert St. John 10.00

JUST FOR WOMEN

____COSMOPOLITAN'S GUIDE TO MARVELOUS MEN Foreword by Helen Gurley Brown 3.00
____COSMOPOLITAN'S HANG-UP HANDBOOK Foreword by Helen Gurley Brown 4.00
____COSMOPOLITAN'S LOVE BOOK—A GUIDE TO ECSTASY IN BED 7.00
____COSMOPOLITAN'S NEW ETIQUETTE GUIDE Foreword by Helen Gurley Brown 4.00
____I AM A COMPLEAT WOMAN Doris Hagopian & Karen O'Connor Sweeney 3.00
____JUST FOR WOMEN—A GUIDE TO THE FEMALE BODY Richard E. Sand M.D. 5.00
____NEW APPROACHES TO SEX IN MARRIAGE John E. Eichenlaub, M.D. 3.00
____SEXUALLY ADEQUATE FEMALE Frank S. Caprio, M.D. 3.00
____SEXUALLY FULFILLED WOMAN Dr. Rachel Copelan 5.00

MARRIAGE, SEX & PARENTHOOD

___ABILITY TO LOVE Dr. Allan Fromme 7.00
___GUIDE TO SUCCESSFUL MARRIAGE Drs. Albert Ellis & Robert Harper 10.00
___HOW TO RAISE AN EMOTIONALLY HEALTHY, HAPPY CHILD Albert Ellis, Ph.D. 10.00
___PARENT SURVIVAL TRAINING Marvin Silverman, Ed.D. & David Lustig 10.00
___POTENCY MIRACLE Uri P. Peles, M.D. 10.00
___SEX WITHOUT GUILT Albert Ellis, Ph.D. 7.00
___SEXUALLY ADEQUATE MALE Frank S. Caprio, M.D. 3.00
___STAYING IN LOVE Dr. Norton F. Kristy 7.00

MELVIN POWERS'S MAIL ORDER LIBRARY

___HOW TO GET RICH IN MAIL ORDER Melvin Powers 20.00
___HOW TO SELF-PUBLISH YOUR BOOK Melvin Powers 20.00
___HOW TO WRITE A GOOD ADVERTISEMENT Victor O. Schwab 20.00
___MAIL ORDER MADE EASY J. Frank Brumbaugh 20.00
___MAKING MONEY WITH CLASSIFIED ADS Melvin Powers 20.00

METAPHYSICS & OCCULT

___CONCENTRATION—A GUIDE TO MENTAL MASTERY Mouni Sadhu 7.00
___EXTRA-TERRESTRIAL INTELLIGENCE—THE FIRST ENCOUNTER 6.00
___FORTUNE TELLING WITH CARDS P. Foli 10.00
___HOW TO INTERPRET DREAMS, OMENS & FORTUNE TELLING SIGNS Gettings 5.00
___HOW TO UNDERSTAND YOUR DREAMS Geoffrey A. Dudley 7.00
___MAGICIAN—HIS TRAINING AND WORK W.E. Butler 7.00
___MEDITATION Mouni Sadhu 10.00
___MODERN NUMEROLOGY Morris C. Goodman 5.00
___NUMEROLOGY—ITS FACTS AND SECRETS Ariel Yvon Taylor 5.00
___NUMEROLOGY MADE EASY W. Mykian 5.00
___PALMISTRY MADE EASY Fred Gettings 7.00
___PALMISTRY MADE PRACTICAL Elizabeth Daniels Squire 7.00
___PROPHECY IN OUR TIME Martin Ebon 2.50
___SUPERSTITION—ARE YOU SUPERSTITIOUS? Eric Maple 2.00
___TAROT OF THE BOHEMIANS Papus 10.00
___WAYS TO SELF-REALIZATION Mouni Sadhu 7.00
___WITCHCRAFT, MAGIC & OCCULTISM—A FASCINATING HISTORY W.B. Crow 10.00
___WITCHCRAFT—THE SIXTH SENSE Justine Glass 7.00

RECOVERY

___KNIGHT IN RUSTY ARMOR Robert Fisher 5.00
___KNIGHT IN RUSTY ARMOR (Hard cover edition) Robert Fisher 10.00
___KNIGHTS WITHOUT ARMOR (Hard cover edition) Aaron R. Kipnis, Ph.D. 10.00
___PRINCESS WHO BELIEVED IN FAIRY TALES Marcia Grad 10.00

SELF-HELP & INSPIRATIONAL

___CHANGE YOUR VOICE, CHANGE YOUR LIFE Morton Cooper, Ph.D. 10.00
___CHARISMA—HOW TO GET "THAT SPECIAL MAGIC" Marcia Grad 10.00
___DAILY POWER FOR JOYFUL LIVING Dr. Donald Curtis 7.00
___DYNAMIC THINKING Melvin Powers 5.00
___GREATEST POWER IN THE UNIVERSE U.S. Andersen 7.00
___GROW RICH WHILE YOU SLEEP Ben Sweetland 10.00
___GROW RICH WITH YOUR MILLION DOLLAR MIND Brian Adams 7.00
___GROWTH THROUGH REASON Albert Ellis, Ph.D. 10.00
___GUIDE TO PERSONAL HAPPINESS Albert Ellis, Ph.D. & Irving Becker, Ed.D. 10.00
___HANDWRITING ANALYSIS MADE EASY John Marley 10.00
___HANDWRITING TELLS Nadya Olyanova 7.00
___HOW TO ATTRACT GOOD LUCK A.H.Z. Carr 10.00
___HOW TO DEVELOP A WINNING PERSONALITY Martin Panzer 10.00
___HOW TO DEVELOP AN EXCEPTIONAL MEMORY Young & Gibson 10.00
___HOW TO LIVE WITH A NEUROTIC Albert Ellis, Ph.D. 10.00
___HOW TO MAKE $100,000 A YEAR IN SALES Albert Winnikoff 15.00
___HOW TO OVERCOME YOUR FEARS M.P. Leahy, M.D. 3.00
___HOW TO SUCCEED Brian Adams 10.00
___HUMAN PROBLEMS & HOW TO SOLVE THEM Dr. Donald Curtis 5.00
___I CAN Ben Sweetland 10.00
___I WILL Ben Sweetland 10.00
___KNIGHT IN RUSTY ARMOR Robert Fisher 5.00
___KNIGHT IN RUSTY ARMOR (Hard Cover) Robert Fisher 10.00
___LEFT-HANDED PEOPLE Michael Barsley 5.00
___MAGIC IN YOUR MIND U.S. Andersen 10.00
___MAGIC OF THINKING SUCCESS Dr. David J. Schwartz 10.00
___MAGIC POWER OF YOUR MIND Walter M. Germain 10.00
___NEVER UNDERESTIMATE THE SELLING POWER OF A WOMAN Dottie Walters 7.00
___NEW GUIDE TO RATIONAL LIVING Albert Ellis, Ph.D. & R. Harper, Ph.D. 10.00
___PRINCESS WHO BELIEVED IN FAIRY TALES Marcia Grad 10.00
___PSYCHO-CYBERNETICS Maxwell Maltz, M.D. 10.00
___PSYCHOLOGY OF HANDWRITING Nadya Olyanova 7.00
___SALES CYBERNETICS Brian Adams 10.00
___SECRET OF SECRETS U.S. Andersen 10.00
___SECRET POWER OF THE PYRAMIDS U.S. Andersen 7.00
___SELF-THERAPY FOR THE STUTTERER Malcolm Frazer 3.00
___STOP COMMITTING VOICE SUICIDE Morton Cooper, Ph.D. 10.00
___SUCCESS CYBERNETICS U.S. Andersen 7.00
___10 DAYS TO A GREAT NEW LIFE William E. Edwards 3.00
___THINK AND GROW RICH Napoleon Hill 10.00
___THINK LIKE A WINNER Walter Doyle Staples, Ph.D. 10.00
___THREE MAGIC WORDS U.S. Andersen 10.00

___TREASURY OF COMFORT Edited by Rabbi Sidney Greenberg 10.00
___TREASURY OF THE ART OF LIVING Sidney S. Greenberg 10.00
___WHAT YOUR HANDWRITING REVEALS Albert E. Hughes 4.00
___WONDER WITHIN Thomas F. Coyle, M.D. 10.00
___YOUR SUBCONSCIOUS POWER Charles M. Simmons 7.00

SPORTS

___BILLIARDS—POCKET • CAROM • THREE CUSHION Clive Cottingham, Jr. 10.00
___COMPLETE GUIDE TO FISHING Vlad Evanoff 2.00
___HOW TO IMPROVE YOUR RACQUETBALL Lubarsky, Kaufman & Scagnetti 5.00
___HOW TO WIN AT POCKET BILLIARDS Edward D. Knuchell 10.00
___JOY OF WALKING Jack Scagnetti 3.00
___LEARNING & TEACHING SOCCER SKILLS Eric Worthington 3.00
___RACQUETBALL FOR WOMEN Toni Hudson, Jack Scagnetti & Vince Rondone 3.00
___SECRET OF BOWLING STRIKES Dawson Taylor 5.00
___SOCCER—THE GAME & HOW TO PLAY IT Gary Rosenthal 7.00
___STARTING SOCCER Edward F Dolan, Jr. 5.00

TENNIS LOVERS' LIBRARY

___HOW TO BEAT BETTER TENNIS PLAYERS Loring Fiske 4.00
___PSYCH YOURSELF TO BETTER TENNIS Dr. Walter A. Luszki 2.00
___TENNIS FOR BEGINNERS Dr. H.A. Murray 2.00
___WEEKEND TENNIS—HOW TO HAVE FUN & WIN AT THE SAME TIME Bill Talbert 3.00

WILSHIRE PET LIBRARY

___DOG TRAINING MADE EASY & FUN John W. Kellogg 5.00
___HOW TO BRING UP YOUR PET DOG Kurt Unkelbach 2.00
___HOW TO RAISE & TRAIN YOUR PUPPY Jeff Griffen 5.00

WILSHIRE HORSE LOVERS' LIBRARY

___AMATEUR HORSE BREEDER A.C. Leighton Hardman 5.00
___AMERICAN QUARTER HORSE IN PICTURES Margaret Cabel Self 5.00
___APPALOOSA HORSE Donna & Bill Richardson 7.00
___ARABIAN HORSE Reginald S. Summerhays 7.00
___ART OF WESTERN RIDING Suzanne Norton Jones 10.00
___BASIC DRESSAGE Jean Froissard 5.00
___BEGINNER'S GUIDE TO HORSEBACK RIDING Sheila Wall 5.00
___BITS—THEIR HISTORY, USE AND MISUSE Louis Taylor 10.00
___BREAKING & TRAINING THE DRIVING HORSE Doris Ganton 10.00
___BREAKING YOUR HORSE'S BAD HABITS W. Dayton Sumner 10.00
___COMPLETE TRAINING OF HORSE AND RIDER Colonel Alois Podhajsky 10.00
___DISORDERS OF THE HORSE & WHAT TO DO ABOUT THEM E. Hanauer 5.00
___DOG TRAINING MADE EASY AND FUN John W. Kellogg 5.00
___DRESSAGE—A STUDY OF THE FINER POINTS IN RIDING Henry Wynmalen 7.00
___DRIVE ON Doris Ganton 7.00
___DRIVING HORSES Sallie Walrond 7.00
___EQUITATION Jean Froissard 7.00
___FIRST AID FOR HORSES Dr. Charles H. Denning, Jr. 5.00
___FUN ON HORSEBACK Margaret Cabell Self 4.00
___HORSE DISEASES—CAUSES, SYMPTOMS & TREATMENT Dr. H.G. Belschner 7.00
___HORSE OWNER'S CONCISE GUIDE Elsie V. Hanauer 5.00
___HORSE SELECTION & CARE FOR BEGINNERS George H. Conn 10.00
___HORSEBACK RIDING FOR BEGINNERS Louis Taylor 10.00
___HORSEBACK RIDING MADE EASY & FUN Sue Henderson Coen 7.00
___HORSES—THEIR SELECTION, CARE & HANDLING Margaret Cabell Self 5.00
___HOW TO CURE BEHAVIOR PROBLEMS IN HORSES Susan McBane 15.00
___HUNTER IN PICTURES Margaret Cabell Self 2.00
___ILLUSTRATED BOOK OF THE HORSE S. Sidney (8½" x 11") 10.00
___ILLUSTRATED HORSEBACK RIDING FOR BEGINNERS Jeanne Mellin 5.00
___KNOW ALL ABOUT HORSES Harry Disston 5.00
___LAME HORSE—CAUSES, SYMPTOMS & TREATMENT Dr. James R. Rooney 10.00
___POLICE HORSES Judith Campbell 2.00
___PRACTICAL GUIDE TO HORSESHOEING 5.00
___PRACTICAL HORSE PSYCHOLOGY Moyra Williams 10.00
___PROBLEM HORSES—CURING SERIOUS BEHAVIOR HABITS Summerhays 5.00
___REINSMAN OF THE WEST—BRIDLES & BITS Ed Connell 7.00
___RIDE WESTERN Louis Taylor 7.00
___SCHOOLING YOUR YOUNG HORSE George Wheatley 7.00
___STABLE MANAGEMENT FOR THE OWNER—GROOM George Wheatley 7.00
___STALLION MANAGEMENT—A GUIDE FOR STUD OWNERS A.C. Hardman 5.00
___YOU AND YOUR PONY Pepper Mainwaring Healey (8½" x 11") 6.00
___YOUR PONY BOOK Hermann Wiederhold 2.00

Please add $2.00 shipping and handling for each book ordered.

Enclosed is my check ( ) money order ( ) for $_____

Name_____
(Please print)

Street_____

City_____ State_____ Zip_____

For our complete catalog, visit our Web site at http://www.mpowers.com.

GROW RICH WITH YOUR MILLION DOLLAR MIND $7

You can change your life. The power that controls your destiny is part of the creative you and can be used to achieve riches. This book reveals how to release your subconscious power to change the direction of your life. This is your opportunity to learn wealth-building secrets and how to use them for achieving financial independence.

SECRET OF SECRETS $7

Make the impossible dream come true. You have a sleeping giant within you who can do anything. U. S. Andersen tells you how you can awaken this giant— the potential power of your subconscious mind. Step by step, you are taught the mental magic that is the dynamic source of all success.

SEVEN DAYS TO FASTER READING $7

A lack of reading s[kill] is the most serious [de]fect in American edu[ca]tion today. If you can[not] read fast and with co[m]prehension, you litera[lly] bar your own way [to] success. Here is a bo[ok] that makes reading [a] pleasure — and you [will] never read fast and [ef]fortlessly unless you [en]joy it.

VEGETARIAN COOKERY $7

Here are more than 777 new recipes. Soups, sweets, ices, cakes and biscuits. New uses for fruit and vegetable juices. And how to make for yourself in a few minutes the famous Janet Walker's Wholemeal Loaf. Her vegetarian recipes have brought her thousands of readers a wonderful new and delightful happiness.

SEX WITHOUT GUILT $5

Unquestionably, this is the most reassuring book on sex ever written, and it should be required reading for all those who are married or contemplate marriage. Dr. Albert Ellis, the world's foremost sexologist, has dedicated this book to the countless men and women who fight a losing battle against feelings of guilt.

SUCCESS-CYBERNETICS $7

Cybernetics is a magic word today. It has changed American life more than anything else, and you can use it to change yours. This book will teach you how to program your brain with techniques and ideas that will allow it to operate at its highest capacity — and you will solve problems and attain your ambitions with scientific precision

10 DAYS TO A GREAT NEW LIFE $3

Get a pencil and some paper and write down all the goals you would like to achieve. That's all you have to do to begin taking giant steps on the road to success. Utilizing sound and proven psychological principles, William E. Edwards explains how this simple act sets in motion a goal-directed chain of events. You literally write your own ticket to your chosen destination.

HELP YOURSELF TO BETTER SIGHT $7

Some vision can be improved without corrective eye glasses. If you are willing to make a conscientious effort, this new book by the foremost teacher of eye education may enable you to learn to see better. Relaxation is the secret of good vision. It is the secret of the Bates method, a highly successful system of eye training.

THINK AND GROW RICH $

The legendary Napole[on] Hill, advisor to two pr[es]idents and a friend [of] the richest and most [fa]mous man of the 20[th] century, spent 20 yea[rs] compiling the case h[is]tories and money-ma[k]ing methods contained [in] this book. No man ev[er] utilized more succe[ss] techniques, and the [re]sult was predictable. Th[is] book has become one [of] the best sellers of all ti[me]

THREE MAGIC WORDS $10

Just three words—and an idea so simple, so startling, so unique, it can change your life and make you happy as you have never been before. This unusual book by U. S. Andersen offers you the key to the inner peace and serenity that is locked within you.

THE SEXUALLY ADEQUATE FEMALE $3

A woman can be very passionate and still suffer from frigidity. Frank S. Caprio, M.D., an eminent psychiatrist, explains the physical and emotional causes of frigidity, how it can be cured, and how to achieve a satisfying sexual relationship. This book is a classic in the field of sexology.

THE SEXUALLY ADEQUATE MA[LE] $3

Impotence has become a disorder associated with modern civilization. The stress of everyday living can negatively permeate one's sexual activity. Frank S. Caprio, M.D., an eminent psychiatrist, explains the physical and emotional causes of impotence, how it can be cured, and how to achieve a satisfying sexual relationship. This book is a classic in the field of sexology.

HOW TO DEVELOP A WINNING PERSONALITY $7

Here is a complete, psychologically sound and eminently workable program of positive action for increasing your effectiveness in the whole area of human relations — in friendship, in romance and on the job. It outlines specific and practical techniques for breaking through the barrier of resistance. You are shown how to project the personal qualities that attract friends and lovers.

YOUR SUBCONSCIOUS POWER $7

The existence of the subconscious mind has been known for some time, but it is just beginning to be accorded the tremendous power it wields. Using its unlimited capacity to achieve anything the mind of man can imagine, there is literally nothing you cannot accomplish if you learn to utilize your subconscious.

HOW TO DEVELOP AN EXCEPTIONAL MEMORY $7

Memory is the most im[portant] portant function of the human mind. Without it we would be paralyzed by indecision and con[fusion] fusion because all future actions are based on pas[t] experience. This book outlines quickly mas[tered] tered memory systems including: How to easily remember names and faces. How to make rapid calculations. How to remember 100 objects

Practical stimulating books to help you achieve success, happiness and wealth.

JOIN THE WINNER$' CIRCLE

$$$$$$ *Pyramid Your Winnings with the Experts* $$$$$$

HOW TO PICK WINNING HORSES

$5

This author starts out on the "right track!" He maintains that the races CAN BE BEAT—and then he shows you how! And he knows! The author of many books on horse racing, he gives you the advantage of his years of experience and know-how. And he tells you how to pick the winners!—a unique method of handicapping which anyone can learn. This is our best selling horse racing book.

HOW TO WIN AT THE RACES

$5

The author of this book is nicknamed "The Genius" at the race tracks and he shares his secrets with you here. He tells you how he made many thousands of dollars at the horse races and all of the secrets which earned his rightful nickname of "The Genius." Complete with Appendix of Betting-Percentage Table.

SCARNE ON DICE

$15

The world's foremost gambling authority presents everything anyone would ever want to know about dice and dice games, including how to detect the latest cheating methods, with additional material on the dice.

MAKING MONEY AT THE RACES

$7

Here are all the rules and workouts for detecting "hot" horses, betting with the best odds, playing the longshots, how to win betting "place", and much more. Three select methods are described to help the reader become a winner at the races. One of these methods resulted in 100% winning for an entire month! Don't let this one pass you by. These are the "inside" secrets to winning.

HOW YOU CAN BEAT THE RACES

$5

Horse racing is an excellent hobby and this author tells you how to make it a profitable one as well as an enjoyable one! Develop a professional's standards of betting even while retaining your amateur standing. Use the methods the professionals use and become a steady winner!

SUCCESS AT THE HARNESS RACES

$7

No longer will you be a nine-bets-a-night amateur. This book clearly defines all the traps to avoid and outlines how to select winners. The author, a regular contributor to "Turf and Sport Digest", gives you professional hints on betting and on how to be a "controlled" winner. Accept his invitation to be a winner at the harness races! And good luck!

BETTING HORSES TO WIN

$7

The sequel to "Payday at the Races," this book is more than the author's fans could have expected. In response to all his readers' demands, he has come up with the most powerful means of selection that can be found anywhere and they are presented in a concise and easy to read method. Learn the new "power plays" and increase your percentage to the amazing degree experienced by hundreds of readers.

PAYDAY AT THE RACES

$7

This is the "easy way" to do it! The author has eliminated the work and given you every possible shortcut to winning! Beginners and even many once-a-week race-goers will find this book an invaluable companion to horse-race betting. Everything is explained in simple terms. Complete with glossary.

WINNING AT 21

$10

The greatest motivation for playing 21 is the enjoyment of the game. But it's even more fun if you are a winner! The author, in trying to master the strategies set forth by other masters, found innovations of his own. He found a shortcut, a key, for deriving useful ratios without having to keep a mental account of the cards. If you learn it, you will win. His is a *winning* method and it can be mastered by any serious player. His system promises a probability of always winning *something* every time you play!

ELIMINATE THE LOSERS— PICK THE WINNERS

$5

Subtitled "A Tested Method for Successful Handicapping," this book even tells you how to make a million! The author deals with betting the horse races, outlining a full system of controlled betting. He doesn't depend on luck but on skill and the knowledge of how to bet—for those who take their betting seriously!

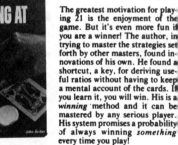

SMART HANDICAPPING MADE EASY

$5

This book goes farther than anything you have ever read on the secrets of the professionals! The crucial question of whether or not a horse is going to *try*—whether the stable is sending the horse today or prepping him for a race next week—is answered. You are told when to bet a horse and when to lay off. This book ties up "pure" handicapping with the inside betting activity of professionals. Here is the intelligent way to save money and win money at the races and it is written so simply that any beginner can learn all he needs to know!

THOUGHT DIAL

$7

"The value of the *Thought Dial* lies in the discovery—sooner or later—that all the answers to all questions must come from within. When one becomes truly aware of this ancient truth one will learn to ask the right questions. The first thing to find out is—*who* is asking what? *Second*, are you prepared to accept the response provoked?"
— HENRY MILLER

GROW RICH WITH YOUR MILLION DOLLAR MIND $7

You can change your life. The power that controls your destiny is part of the creative you and can be used to achieve riches. This book reveals how to release your subconscious power to change the direction of your life. This is your opportunity to learn wealth-building secrets and how to use them for achieving financial independence.

HOW TO WIN AT POCKET BILLIARDS $10

All the basic elements of the game you love to play, fully illustrated in 88 diagrams and over 40 photographs. From the most simple to the most complex points of pocket billiards, Mr. Knuchell, one of the prominent masters of the game, discusses every aspect in full and clear detail. Knuchell knows Pocket Billiards—and with this book, you will too!

THINK AND GROW RICH $10

7,000,000 readers have made this amazing book one of the all time best sellers! Behind the success of many of the wealthiest men in history is the secret revealed in this amazing book. The secret is real . . . and it works! The author spent 20 years researching and perfecting this secret, and it's all yours in the time it takes to read this book. Join the illustrious company of those who have already found the way to wealth and success!

WINNING AT POKER $10

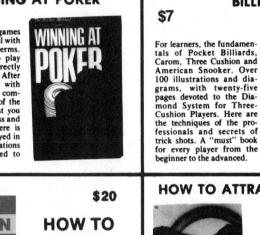

All of the popular poker games are described in full detail with a complete glossary of terms. You are taught how to play each of the games correctly and how to play to win! After only a short time spent with this book, you will be in command of the principles of the game. You will find that you are immediately losing less and winning more often. Here is modern poker as it is played in all of its forms and variations with the strategy needed to beat your opponents.

BILLIARDS $7

For learners, the fundamentals of Pocket Billiards, Carom, Three Cushion and American Snooker. Over 100 illustrations and diagrams, with twenty-five pages devoted to the Diamond System for Three-Cushion Players. Here are the techniques of the professionals and secrets of trick shots. A "must" book for every player from the beginner to the advanced.

HOW TO GET RICH IN MAIL ORDER $20

HOW TO ATTRACT GOOD LUCK $7

This book will change your ideas about the uncertainty of luck. If you "go by the book" (this one), you can't lose. Give yourself a weapon to aim at success; discover your "luck potential." A complete blueprint for success and the ability to achieve your goals is explained along with how to affect the power of chance and its influence on your luck. You can develop the lucky side of your personality to an extent that may seem miraculous!

MAKING MONEY WITH CLASSSIFIED ADS $20

THE SECRET OF SECRETS $7

Your key to subconscious power. Your secret self, that sleeping giant within you, can help you do anything and become anything. This book reveals the mental magic by which the power of your mind can be fully perfected.

MAIL ORDER MADE EASY $20

MAGIC OF THINKING SUCCESS $8

Dr. David Schwartz instructs us how to get ourselves onto the path that will bring happiness and satisfaction, and gives us a step-by-step guide to achieving personal happiness and wealth. You can make your dream life become a reality by applying the knowledge contained within this book.

How To Be Charismatic & Brighten Up Your Love Life

Dear Friend:

Have you been waiting for a special person to come into your life and fill it with love?

Why let love elude you when you can embrace it? Slip away when you can save it? Grow old when you can rejuvenate it?

Whether you are entering a new relationship or continuing in one you have had for years, you can now have one that is deeper, warmer, fuller, and richer than any you have ever experienced.

You can create love

Have you noticed the elusive way love can go from being overwhelmingly intense to being nearly non-existent — then returning as if it had a mind of its own?

You can sustain love

Do you wish your lukewarm love relationship were piping hot?

You can enhance love

You needn't succumb helplessly to love's whims. How we think and feel and what we say and do produces, maintains, augments or diminishes our other emotions. And so it is with love. The power to create, sustain, and enhance loving feelings is yours to use as you wish.

Have the love you've only dreamed of

There are people who enjoy the full, satisfying love relationship you'd like to have. Perhaps you've seen these happy couples — together for years, and still very much in love. They didn't find the perfect partner and live happily ever after just by luck. Rather, they learned how to get the most from their relationship and then did the things that made and kept it special. You can have their kind of love simply by learning what to do and putting that knowledge into practice.

You can have it all

Don't be one to compromise your dreams of love because you think a comfortable relationship must be dull. Don't expect or accept a disappointing facsimile of the relationship you really want. You need not give up excitement for security, freshness for reliability, or exhilaration for stability. You can have realistic, sensible, mature love that is enlivening and stimulating — even thrilling!

Why go through life enduring colorless love relationships? Why settle for black-and-white love when you can have Technicolor? Don't let another day pass without doing something to spice up your bland love life.

Your love fantasy can come true!

What else can you do after you've read all the books on love and on improving relationships you can find, used the information both directly and indirectly, but still do not experience the results you yearn to see? You know the right things to do and have tried them. You've learned communication skills and how to fight fairly. You've practiced your intimacy training and experimented with the newest sexual techniques. Still, your relationship doesn't sparkle.

Don't despair. You needn't resign yourself to an occasional weak spark of excitement. You can learn to enhance your partner's level of response and love as well as your own. You can boost his or her feelings of love. You can learn how to have your partner fall in love with you and feel the excitement and "cloud nine" feeling of being in love once again.

It sounds like an impossible dream. But that's exactly what we promise because our course of action is based on extensive, sound, and practical information and not just theory.

You can be charismatic, have the love relationship you really want, and be the person you have always secretly wanted to be.

You can put your charismatic power to work by employing special techniques based on widely accepted, sound psychological principles. Learn how from an exciting new, three-hour cassette tape, MARCIA GRAD'S CHARISMA-DEVELOPMENT SEMINAR. It is filled with suggestions on how to be charismatic. You'll learn to put the sizzle back into a relationship that's gone flat and how to turn the tide should love be ebbing. Listen to this exceedingly helpful cassette that can really change your life. Start immediately to feel your newly-found power and start to brighten up your love life.

You are what you choose to become tomorrow.

Send for the cassette tape, MARCIA GRAD'S CHARISMA-DEVELOPMENT SEMINAR, $25.00 postpaid. It's sold on a 100% money-back guarantee basis. It must accomplish what we promise or we'll refund your money.

------------------ **Order Form** ------------------

Please send me one MARCIA GRAD'S CHARISMA-DEVELOPMENT SEMINAR cassette tape $25.00 postpaid.

Enclosed is my check (   ) money order (   ) for $25.00.

Name _____
(Please print)

Address _____

City _____

State _____

Zip _____

Please send your order to:

Melvin Powers
12015 Sherman Road
North Hollywood, California 91605

CHARISMA
How to Develop the Power to Attract & Influence People

Charismatic people are not necessarily more interesting, talented, intelligent, or attractive than you, but it is true they are noticed, liked, and sought after. Material, professional, and personal success seem to gravitate toward them. What exactly do they possess that sets them apart from ordinary people? What is their secret of attracting and influencing people?

These questions really used to baffle me. For years I hung around the sidelines of life wondering what popular people had that I lacked. I thought certain people were born to be special, that they were innately endowed with a mysterious "something" that brought them more than their fair share of the good things in life —appreciation, love, and recognition. How I wished I could be like them. I longed to be the center of attention —poised, confident, and exciting to others. Instead, I became reconciled to my life style. I worked at a routine job, had little excitement in my personal life, and was puzzled as to why I was missing the sizzle.

Then something happened that changed my life dramatically. It was a rainy Saturday night and I was spending the evening curled up on the couch with nothing but my television set for company. My mind kept wandering as I aimlessly switched from one channel to another.

Suddenly I was captivated by a talk show devoted to personality development in which outgoing, stimulating men and women were being interviewed. Their personal stories had a common theme. They had once been shy, had had few friends, had not been getting what they were seeking out of life, and had seen no way to relieve their frustration until they became highly motivated to do something about it.

They told fascinating stories of how dramatic personality changes had gradually come about as a result of reading self-improvement books or by taking personality-development seminars. They developed one common characteristic. Each radiated what I would call—charisma.

To me that was dynamite—their stories were what I needed to hear. From that night on I was excited about the possibility that I, too, could develop charisma and a new life style.

I became determined to learn how I could become charismatic. I talked to people I considered to have charismatic traits. I asked how they had developed charisma, how it felt to have it, and how they used it. I spoke to psychologists and psychiatrists. I researched various psychological and image-enhancement techniques I thought might help me develop charisma.

Finally, my quest paid off. I discovered the secret of creating charisma—the magic I had yearned to possess all my life. From then on, every day became exciting, stimulating, and enjoyable because I became relaxed and self-confident.

Family and long-time friends were amazed by the new me. They said I had defied the axiom that people don't change. I no longer had to be concerned about how and where to meet new people. I met them everywhere and felt at ease. My relationships and life itself began to change for the better. Business and professional opportunities abounded as never before.

As a book publicist, I shared the secret with numerous authors as we worked together to build their charismatic qualities. Interestingly, their personal lives began to flourish. What had worked for me obviously worked for others.

Eager to share the secret with more people, I began teaching college classes throughout the Los Angeles area on how to develop charisma. I now conduct workshops and lecture to all types of groups. From this evolved a step-by-step charisma-development program that has been used successfully with people from all walks of life, including entertainers, politicians, and business and professional people.

You can do exactly as my authors, students, clients, and I have done. You can be as you've always wished to be — self-assured, in control in social and business situations, and energetic and stimulating to others. You can be popular, noticed, liked, and sought after.

It's exhilarating just to imagine what is waiting for you. Get set for a thrilling adventure—the development of the charismatic personality within you.

The cassette tapes I offer were recorded live at one of my three-hour college seminars on charisma. They outline the highly effective charisma-development program that has helped so many people change how they feel about themselves and how others feel about them. Also offered is a supplementary book on how to develop a winning personality.

Take that first step toward your secret dream by ordering now.

THE SECRET OF CHARISMA

CHARISMA
How to Develop the Power to Attract & Influence People

208 Pages . . $8.00 Postpaid

Can you really get "that special magic"? Emphatically, "Yes!" says Marcia Grad, author of *Charisma*. And she has impressive research, clinical evidence, years of experience, and common sense bolstering her claim. She is a well-known image consultant who conducts workshops and lectures at seminars on the subject of charisma and how to get it. Marcia has turned numerous shy, introverted, and unpopular adults into magnetic personalities. How this magic is accomplished is the main subject of this book.

Her message is dazzlingly clear: Charisma is neither an accident of genes, nor is it luck. The potential for charisma is our birthright — a natural gift given to each of us. But if this is the case, why do so few seem to possess it? Because most often it lies quietly dormant deep within the individual — held down, undeveloped, and hidden from view.

Until now, we have found it difficult to explain what charisma is and why some people seem to have it in abundance while the majority of others seem to have little or none at all. And we have been curious about how some people have charisma as children, then lose it, while others first get it later in life. And what about those who have it only at certain times — when at work, for example, but not in social situations, or, as is the case with many entertainers, when on stage but not when off?

This book first unravels these mysteries and then teaches us how to awaken the charismatic force within us, how to enhance its power, and how to sustain its magic. Development of our potential for charisma is a skill, we are told — a skill we can study, practice, master, and absorb as a part of ourselves. Anyone can do it and many individuals already have, simply by following Marcia Grad's highly effective, step-by-step Charisma Development Program.

What is this program that can help a shy person to become confident, an apathetic person to become enthusiastic, a dull person to become exciting, and everyone to have command of his or her own innate magnetism? The author uses a multidimensional approach. She explores the many pieces of the charisma puzzle, each essential to its solution — thoughts, attitudes, perceptions, social behavior, sexuality, physical presentation, and personal habits. We are urged to probe, to question, and to change longtime beliefs about ourselves, about others, and about the world that may be blocking the flow of our natural charisma. Then we are ready to start cultivating habits basic to building "that special magic." You will gain some surprising insights into how you behave in your daily life, and will be given specific techniques which will help to make charismatic feelings, behaviors, and qualities become second nature to you. Once mastered, these techniques work automatically, on a subconscious level. They become an integral part of your total being.

This book reflects the personal flair of its author whose enthusiasm and conviction that people can and do change have served as an inspiration to her many students and clients. The same expert guidance and continuous encouragement that have been invaluable to them are now available to you, the reader.

I'm especially pleased to endorse Marcia's book because I've seen the amazing results of her techniques. They work. Her students are now out in the world realizing their dreams. And what happened to them could happen to you.

You needn't become reconciled to remaining as you are. You can be as you've always wished to be — self-assured, in control in social and business situations, energetic, and stimulating to others. You can be noticed, be liked, and be sought after. You can meet the people you want to meet and bring them into your life. You can become involved in relationships you previously thought were beyond you, and you will be able to reach for business opportunities never before within your grasp.

If you've previously believed that only a select few individuals are capable of powerful personal magnetism and that, unluckily, you are not one of them, you are about to embark upon a unique and eye-opening journey. It's exhilarating just to imagine what is waiting for you — achievement of all those goals and aspirations you once thought impossible. This is your chance for a new beginning, for a new and better you, for a new and better life. I wish you success in achieving your goals.

Melvin Powers
Publisher, Wilshire Book Company

B. Dalton BESTSELLERS

Backlist Trade Paperback

March 30, 1979

NO.	TITLE	AUTHOR	PUBLISHER	LAST WEEK	RETAIL	SKU
1.	JOY OF SEX	Comfort	Simon & Schuster	1	$6.95	110-4268
2.	MAD LIBS ASSORTMENT		Price Stern	3	1.50	133-5235
3.	SIMPLIFIED CALORIE COUNTER		Webster	2	.98	104-1754
✓4.	WHAT COLOR IS YOUR PARACHUTE		Ten Speed	4	5.95	110-9928
5.	MAGIC OF THINKING BIG	Schwartz	Wilshire	5	3.00	163-6561
6.	LO-CARBO DIETER		Webster	6	.98	114-1791
7.	NEW WESTERN GARDEN BOOK	Sunset	Lane	7	8.95	160-6166
8.	ON DEATH & DYING	Kubler-Ross	Macmillan	8	2.45	147-4103
9.	OUR BODIES OURSELVES		Simon & Schuster	11	4.95	114-3565
10.	PARENT EFFECTIVENESS TRAINING	Gordon	NAL	–	5.95	114-3468
11.	ELEMENTS OF STYLE	Strunk	Macmillan	–	1.95	139-1410
12.	MORE JOY OF SEX	Comfort	Simon & Schuster	9	6.95	114-3115
13.	ROYAL CANADIAN EXERCISE BK		Simon & Schuster	10	2.95	163-1284
14.	HOW/PREPARE COLL ENT EXAM	9TH ED	Barrons	30	5.50	142-8845
15.	NOTES TO MYSELF	Prather	Real People	18	2.50	158-6203
16.	CROCKETTS VICTORY GARDEN	Crockett	Little Brown	14	9.95	121-6260
17.	WHY AM I AFRAID TO TELL YOU	Powell	Argus	12	2.75	159-1568
18.	HOW TO KEEP YOUR VW ALIVE	Muir	Book People	24	7.50	163-7177
19.	SECRET OF STAYING IN LOVE	Powell	Argus	16	2.95	106-5106
20.	THE PEOPLE'S PHARMACY	Graedon	Avon	20	4.95	119-7266
✓21.	BIRDS OF NORTH AMERICA	Robbins	Golden	23	4.95	153-1107
22.	THINK AND GROW RICH	Hill	Wilshire	–	3.00	161-5165
23.	LIVE LONGER NOW	Leonard	Grosset	19	3.95	118-4075
25.	HOPE FOR THE FLOWERS	Paulus	Paulist	–	4.95	100-4077
26.	PEARL		Grove	–	2.95	180-5037
27.	BEAT THE DEALER REVISED	Thorp	Random	–	2.45	123-1553
28.	ROBERTS RULES OF ORDER	Robert	Morrow	–	2.95	162-2617
✓29.	PSYCHO CYBERNETICS	Maltz	Wilshire	–	2.00	161-7826
30.	ANGRY BOOK	Rubin	Macmillan	–	1.95	161-8288

B. DALTON BOOKSELLER Bestseller Lists are compiled from the weekly sales reports generated from 355 stores through computer report.

THESE TOP EXPERTS WILL SHARE THEIR SECRETS WITH YOU

A Tradition at Orange Coast College That Attracts Overflow Audiences of "Hopefuls", Amateurs & Professionals Every Year!

Last fall, over 200 disappointed mail order enthusiasts were turned away from this popular lecture event, which has become a tradition, both for Orange Coast College and the Southern California mail order community.

This year, with paid admissions, it will be possible to reserve your place at this exciting event — but you should act early, and avoid disappointment.

The question and answer format which proved so popular at the last three seminars will be retained, but a change in the format will allow each panelist to give a 20-minute talk before the question and answer session begins.

Speakers will include the ever-popular Joe Karbo, a favorite of the last seminar, Mel Powers, and for the first time, one of Southern California's outstanding women in mail order, Diane Diamond — together, with Stuart Williams, instructor in mail order at Orange Coast College and coordinator of this widely acclaimed series.

THE BIG MAIL ORDER EVENT IN SOUTHERN CALIFORNIA! . . . DON'T MISS IT!

Saturday, Sept. 27
SCIENCE HALL
9 a.m. - 1 p.m.
Admission: $5.00

236

JOE KARBO

When you think of Joe Karbo, you naturally think of *"Lazy Man's Way to Riches"*, the bestselling book he authored and promoted with an ad that has become a classic example of mail order copy (and proved it by selling a million and a quarter books!)

But Joe is more than a one-ad phenomenon. A product of Pasadena Playhouse, he began his career in television, but switched to print media when the TV bubble burst. In addition to *"Lazy Man"*, his other mail order successes include a book he wrote, *"The Power of Money Management"*, a diet plan, a horse race handicapping system, a book on swap meets and garage sales and a newly launched newsletter for small business projects.

In addition to his money-making activities, Joe finds time for Little Theater work. He is also Honorary Chairman of United Way for West Orange County and recently was keynote speaker at the USC Graduate School of Business.

MELVIN POWERS

Melvin Powers is a professional mail order consultant, founder and president of Wilshire Book Company, which specializes in selling books by mail. A successful entrepreneur for 25 years, he is often referred to as the "dean" of mail order publishing.

Mr. Powers is the publisher of many well-known bestselling books, such as *"Psycho-Cybernetics," "Magic of Thinking Big", "Think and Grow Rich"* and many others. His most recent book, which he authored, *"How to Get Rich in Mail Order"* has been adopted as a text for the basic course in mail order at Orange Coast College, and is gaining widespread acceptance all over the country, and promises to be a runaway bestseller.

DIANE DIAMOND

In an industry long dominated by men, Diane Diamond has proved that a woman can more than hold her own. Widely known and respected by mail order people, Diane heads up the Advertising Department of Specialty Merchandise Corporation in Woodland Hills.

She not only uses direct marketing and mail order to recruit thousands of wholesale customers for her company, but also helps set up most of them in the mail order business on their own, selling many of the 2500 products provided by Specialty Merchandise Corporation to mail order companies.

An honor graduate of the Art Institute of Pittsburgh, and the Armed Forces Institute School of Journalism, Ms. Diamond worked in publishing, fulfillment and advertising,

all phases of this fascinating business. He has been involved with almost every kind of product and type of service.

During the past 25 years, he has served as an account executive, consultant or has worked for more than 60 different firms and been involved with many more products than this. During that time, advertising that he prepared has brought a response from *one out of every nine Americans!*

In addition to his activities as a consultant, Williams also has taught courses in basic mail order at Orange Coast College for the past four years, and served as coordinator for the popular annual seminars on mail order.

STUART WILLIAMS
Coordinator

Stuart Williams is a mail order man's *mail order man.* As a consultant to some of the biggest names in mail order, he is familiar with

Seminars are the "Frosting" Have A Piece Of The Cake, Too!

It's fun to go to seminars, but for deep-rooted learning, it takes classroom study. Orange Coast College is one of the few institutions of higher learning in the world that offers courses in mail order selling. Two courses are available: Course 142, *"Selling by Mail,"* a basic course for beginners which meets every Tuesday evening; and course 143, *"Advanced Mail Order"* for those who have completed the basic course or have some previous experience. *"Advanced Mail Order"* meets on Wednesday evening. Classes begin September 9, so you still have time to register.

Chapter Eleven

Melvin Powers' Mail Order Success Strategy— Follow It and You'll Become a Millionaire

I consider this to be one of the book's most important chapters, because it presents a unique facet to the game plan which forms the foundation of your mail order operation. It includes a detailed description of the additional money-making opportunities inherent in courses of instruction or seminars in specialized fields patronized by those who have ordered the book, newsletter, or service. In many cases, it's one of the natural follow-ups. It's the frosting on the cake.

We have concluded, for the most part, it is extremely difficult to sell just one item via mail order and make a profit on it. It's possible, of course, but why not utilize your buyer's name as a prospective customer for more products? Maximum profits are the result of multiple sales. Most companies make it a practice to advertise one product, then follow it up with a catalog of similar or related items. As a potentially successful mail order entrepreneur, it would be to your financial advantage to develop a product line to serve as a logical follow-up to your principal product.

Past experience has taught me the customer who buys a book in a particular category will invariably buy more books on the same subject. It is this inevitability which makes for added profits. I personally employ, and heartily endorse, any plan which makes for added profits through multiple sales. When I am interested in a subject, I'll buy every book I can find on the subject. I'll even go to used book stores looking for out-of-print books. I like doing this, and I have the added pleasure of building a library.

When you develop a sufficiently large number of customers, you can rent your names, an option that will net from 30 to 50 dollars per thousand. Income thus derived is added profit. Another part of your money-making plan is to try to make your catalog profitable to outside lists. Once you do that, your potential for making money is unlimited.

In Chapter 6 we discussed Mark Haroldsen's ad for *How to Wake Up The Financial Genius Inside You.* Last year he sold 250,000 copies of the book at $10 each. That's $2,500,000 gross income. I met Mark several years ago at a private mail order seminar in Los Angeles. He told a small group of us that he had sold $900,000 worth of books in one year. I made the suggestion he should try to improve the ad and experiment by running it in various publications. I predicted he'd have sales of $2,000,000. He followed my suggestion and the dollar results were even greater than the prediction.

Would you be content to sell millions of dollars worth of books and stop there? I hope not. Mark not only rents his names, but he follows up with more books, tapes, and a personal course of instruction. It's the personal course of instruction that is of particular interest to us. He could be making another fortune easily from this. He's running seminars in various cities throughout the country. If you can't attend the class, you can buy a tape of the course. It's a perfect operation, and I congratulate Mark on his success.

Let's have some fun speculating on the Mark Haroldsen operation. I do not know the volume of the back end of his business. Let's assume he takes in another $5 per name from the rental of the names, additional books, his newsletter, tapes, and courses. For every $1,000,000 in sales, he'll take in another $500,000. Assuming the book in the mail costs him $2 a copy, how much money can he afford to pay for every order? Can he pay $8 an order and not make one cent up front? Can he even lose money on the front end?

See page 241. Here Mark is extending his mail order operation to the retail trade in bookstores. He is doing everything just right, and represents the ideal example of the Melvin Powers mail order success strategy: a good pulling ad, rental of names, follow-up with additional books and tapes, a newsletter and course of instruction where applicable, jobber sales, and finally, retail sales in a store outlet.

WILLIAM NICKERSON & DR. ALBERT J. LOWRY

See pages 242 and 243. The book, *How I Turned $1,000 Into $3,000,000 in Real Estate—In My Spare Time,* was a best seller for many years. Originally, the title was *How I Turned $1,000 Into $1,000,000 in Real Estate—In My Spare Time.* I guess inflation escalated the value of the property. *How You Can Become Financially Independent by Investing in Real Estate* by Dr. Albert J. Lowry is also very well known. These two authors teamed up to teach several courses on how to make a fortune in real estate. The strategy of the ad is to invite you to a free lecture. You are then given the opportunity to sign up for the class. There is also an advanced course available after the first course has been completed.

These gentlemen are not in the mail order business *per se.* The publicity and sales of the books stimulate interest in their courses. On January 29, 1979, ABC television evening news program reported Al Lowry's income at $5,000,000 per year. Mark Haroldsen credits the book, *How I Turned $1,000 Into $3,000,000 in Real Estate—In My Spare Time,* with supplying the impetus that enabled him to acquire his millions.

E. JOSEPH COSSMAN

See page 244. Here is another example of good follow-through based on a book. E. Joseph Cossman, author of the book, *How I Made $1,000,000 in Mail Order,* invites you to a free lecture on making money in the mail order field. After the lecture, you are invited to take his course. The fee is several hundred dollars.

Basically, Joe Cossman's book tells you how to find and then sell your products to mail order companies. It's one of the very best books in the field and very worthwhile reading. I've known Joe for 25 years. During that time, I've seen him take products others discarded and make millions with them. That's his specialty. You can get his book at the local library, and if you ever get the opportunity to take his course, do so. It's worth one hundred times the investment. He's made millions of dollars from teaching classes, while making others wealthy.

MELVIN POWERS

The idea for this book stemmed from my experience as a speaker on the subject, "How to Make Money in Mail Order." The speech took place in connection with a business exhibit and symposium held last year at the Los Angeles Convention Center. 36,000 people attended the three-day exhibition. There were 125 exhibits and 12 speakers covering various subjects. Besides the admission fee, there was a $10 charge to attend each two-hour seminar. Over 500 people attended my lecture. I was inundated with requests for a course and a book of instruction. That was all the unexpected market research I needed.

Because of the overwhelming response to my lecture, I knew I could not fail. I was challenged to write a book on mail order based on my perspective, area of competence, and on my specialty, which is publishing and merchandising books. That's what this book is about. I'm sharing my trade secrets in the hope you'll gain insight into how professionals make money using mail order techniques.

JOSEPH SUGARMAN

Read the write-up about Joe Sugarman on page 245. Now read page 246. Joe Sugarman does a volume of $50,000,000 and still is interested in teaching classes on how to make money in mail order. You know he can't possibly be in it for the money. He simply enjoys sharing his knowledge.

Joe attended last year's mail order experts' seminar in Los Angeles. Despite his busy schedule, he took the time to attend the seminar and share his expertise, as well as to learn from others. This is the reason he is doing $50,000,000 annually. In truth, one good tip from the seminar can be translated into millions, not thousands, of dollars.

In Chapter 14, I'll show you how my ideas for some changes of copy in the ad, *How You Can Become Financially Independent by Investing in Real Estate,* can translate into tens of thousands of dollars. I guarantee it. This is the type of information that is shared freely with other mail order experts at the seminar.

HOWARD J. RUFF

Howard J. Ruff sells a financial newsletter and advisory service via mail order. The subscription fee is $95 annually. He has 70,000 subscribers. He also has a 58-station, nationally syndicated TV and cable show. I watch the program because he is provocative, has interesting guests, and I appreciate the packaging of his service.

Here's the twist—he reversed the usual process of publishing a book and following it with a newsletter. Mr. Ruff's book, *How to Prosper During the Coming Bad Years,* was published on January 23, 1979. On February 12, 1979, it was #12 on the best-seller list, having sold 100,000 copies. On April 16, 1979, the paperback reprint rights were sold to Warner Books on a $350,000 guarantee, with escalators to a possible $450,000. On May 21, 1979, the book was #3 on the best-seller list. You can be sure it will go to #1. No doubt his TV show, plus the popularity of his newsletter, contributed to the immediate success of his book.

This is the part in which we are interested for our discussion. See page 247. This appeared in the February 18, 1979 issue of the *Los Angeles Times.* The ad announced a course to be given by Howard Ruff and others. The cost was $95 for an individual, $170 for a couple. It is important to note that it is not a free lecture. One is charged $10 for the opening night session; this may be applied to the full course fee. Here's the good news: 4,000 people signed up for the course. I'll let you estimate how much money was taken in at the seminar. It staggers the imagination.

That's not all. See page 248. The course is available on tape for $95. How would you like to develop a program like that? Howard Ruff did it by himself. He's prospering by helping others to prosper.

MELVIN POWERS

When the sales of the book, *Psycho-Cybernetics,* were at their peak, I taught classes based on the precepts of the book. I had the mailing list of purchasers of the book, and it was a simple matter to send out a mailing to those individuals. See page 250 for the direct mail piece that was used. Also see newsletter, pages 251 through 254.

The readers of the book were happy to have the opportunity to get together with similar-thinking individuals. We all learned from the class and derived considerable benefit from the cross-fertilization of many ideas for self-improvement.

When I conducted classes in *Psycho-Cybernetics,* I told my students if the course wasn't worth ten times what they paid for it, I would immediately refund their money. When the class ended, I sent each student a letter requesting his appraisal of the class, asking for a statement pointing out the weak and strong points and suggesting how the class could be improved. I incorporated that information into my next class, always trying to improve the curriculum. I do the same thing with the books I publish. On page 328 of this book, I ask for feedback on this book. The purpose is aimed at constant improvement and constitutes taking pride in one's work. You might think in terms of a follow-up letter for whatever you are doing.

In the course of conducting market research, I used the letter on page 255 and questionnaire on page 256 to find out some very valuable information. The answers led to publishing specific books which, in turn, resulted in excellent sales. My sales were assured because I knew exactly what my readers wanted.

WALTER DRAKE & SONS, INC.

See page 257. Walter Drake & Sons, Inc., one of the country's leading mail order companies, is doing market research on the possibility of publishing a special catalog of items for left-handed people.

Mr. Drake says he'll publish the catalog if there is enough interest. Remember we talked about publishers offering a book at pre-publication prices to test the market? Naturally, those responding will comprise a valuable mailing list to start the operation. Note this is not a pre-paid post card, probably to discourage curiosity seekers. It would have been too easy to fill out the card and mail it in, and the mailing list would not have been valid. The results of the survey were favorable. See page 258.

One of my students recently took a class in calligraphy, the art of beautiful handwriting. She suggested to her teacher, Kathy Jeffares, that she write a book on this subject, and that she would publish it. My student published the book several months later and has had good success with it. The book has been adopted by several school systems and by a number of calligraphy teachers, assuring the sale of several thousand copies a year. Because of the book and attendant publicity, the author's classes are filled to capacity. She can't handle all the jobs she has for calligraphy work and is subcontracting work with her best students.

If you take a class of instruction, always be aware that the subject matter might make a good mail order book. To keep the cost down and test the validity of your sales potential, you could mimeograph the first edition instead of printing it in book form. You might want to look through the catalogs of extension courses being offered at your local schools. One of those courses could spark your interest for a mail order program. If it does, speak to the instructor and go from there.

Your success in mail order will come from adopting a strategy that is unique, rather than one used by everyone else. You need some element of individuality, such as I have illustrated in this chapter.

Taking the lead from some of the most successful mail order entrepreneurs, I suggest you give some thought to class instruction based upon your knowledge in a specialized field. People with common interests are anxious to get together with others to learn and exchange ideas. Your course of instruction can be the natural extension of your mail order program. The possibilities are unlimited, and you should give some thought to it. Think of yourself as an educator. If you don't have the expertise, or if you feel you might not be comfortable as a teacher, make arrangements with someone to work with you.

When you read in the paper about a class announcement or seminar, such as I have shown in this chapter, be sure to attend the first evening. See how the program is handled. Note how many attend, how many sign up for the course, the presentation of the speakers, and the demeanor of those in charge of the program. Get to talk to some of the people attending the meeting.

Do you want to find out the count of those signing up for the particular course? Attend the first meeting of the actual course and place yourself unobtrusively outside the classroom. Take the count. When I want to check on the pulling power of someone's ad or other factors, I'll send someone else to get the information, if I am unable to go myself. On one such occasion I sent someone who went with his wife and another couple. They were so impressed by the speaker and the program they all signed up for the course! (I'm still waiting for my commission.)

As a personal note, I like to take courses in all kinds of subjects and have been doing this all my life. I find it stimulating. I recently took a course in Chinese cooking. Preparing the dishes with other members of the class was a delight, exceeded only by the pleasure of eating the delectable food. I'm presently taking instruction in music composition and arranging.

Once you establish yourself in a mail order operation, take surveys of your customers' interests. It will give you a tremendous amount of information, and you'll be able to zero in on products or services tailor-made for them. In this way, you'll be doing market research that can result in your coming up with substantial winners.

Start taking courses of interest to you. Make notes as to how they can be improved. Use that information for your classes. When you start teaching a course, don't be bashful about asking for feedback. That information will improve your course and result in making more money for you. Let your students know when your next class will begin. If they are pleased, they will recommend it to their friends. For years, most of the students for my *Psycho-Cybernetics* classes came from recommendations of former students. They became my representatives. Although I had anticipated running only one class, I instituted several courses simply because the members of the class wanted to continue. It was an unexpected bonus, all starting from the sale of a $2 book.

If you need some help getting organized with your classes, feel free to write or call. If you start a class, send me your literature.

As a final note, use the success patterns of others in the instruction field to encourage you. It's easy to copycat, because their entire program is laid out for you. Are you sufficiently motivated to take action? If you are, there's a fortune waiting for you.

Subsequent to publishing *How to Get Rich in Mail Order,* I developed a one-day seminar directed to the theme, "How to Start and Operate a Successful Mail Order Business in Your Spare Time." My mailing list for prospective students was composed of the names of persons who had purchased my book directly or had written to me after purchasing it elsewhere. I ran ads in newspapers announcing details of the class and was fortunate to receive free publicity in local newspapers, resulting in television and radio interviews espousing the merits of mail order.

To reach even more people, I contacted private schools and local colleges in the Los Angeles area. I now have a busy schedule teaching one-day mail order seminars, but find time to also participate as guest lecturer to marketing classes at various colleges and at other seminars devoted to mail order, direct mail, advertising, and book publishing.

Announcements of my mail order seminar are listed in over a million catalogs sent out every semester by the colleges and schools where I teach. In the catalog class description, I recommend that it is preferable my book, *How to Get Rich in Mail Order,* be read prior to enrollment, noting it can be purchased at any bookstore in Los Angeles or obtained free at public libraries. The result? My book has excellent sales.

I find it rewarding that colleges and schools are delighted with my class enrollment and that bookstores and libraries are pleased with requests for the book. I thoroughly enjoy imparting information to help people supplement their incomes in an exciting endeavor with a minimum of risk capital and relish the feedback received from personal visits, letters, and phone calls not only from the United States but from all over the world.

My mail order seminar is recorded on cassette tape and is sold worldwide, retailing for $87 postpaid. Ths sales are excellent, and I'm reaching more students through this distribution than I do in my classes.

So you can see, it's a never-ending cycle that generates larger seminar enrollment and book sales as time goes on. I suggest you consider presenting your own seminars, following the success pattern just described. Or, follow the other patterns mentioned in this chapter. The opportunities are unlimited.

THE ANSWER IS IN THIS BOOK

Over 250,000 Sold Last Year

TWO ANSWERS:

1. **A big seller for the book store (if you're the buyer, they'll call *you* the "Financial Genius.")**

2. **America's Best step-by-step guide how to cash in on inflation.**

WHY THIS HAS HAS SOLD BIG AND WHY IT WILL SELL FOR BOOK STORES

In the heart of everyone is the burning desire, the crying need to be free from financial worry.

Millions want to buy this book this year. Do yourself and your customers a favor. Sell them this book.

How to Wake Up the Financial Genius Inside You

Mark O. Haroldsen became an author as an afterthought. His net worth had soared to over one million dollars in only forty-eight months. He realized that although his money-making approach was not unique, how quickly he was able to accumulate wealth was.

Here is a method the author calls his "Wealth Formula", that anyone can follow. *How to Wake Up the Financial Genius Inside You* is the very specific road map to guide you or anyone to that very sought-after goal of financial independence.

This book specifically reveals what every American is interested in — How to Achieve Total Financial Freedom in today's inflationary economy.

36488 Hard Cover
$10.00

ONE MILLION DOLLAR ADVERTISING BUDGET!

- Advertised by full page ads in all major national publications
- National television advertising campaign starting in June 1978
- One million dollar advertising budget for 1978
- Full color poster available for window and store display (Order through Ingram Book Company)
- Price: $10.00

Available exclusively through:

INGRAM BOOK COMPANY
Title Code: 36488
Call Toll Free:
1-800-251-1200

Display this book with your best sellers. It already is one!

E. JOSEPH COSSMAN, M.B.A., author of "How To Get $100,000 Free Services From U.S. Government" and best-seller "How I Made $1,000,000 In Mail Order" (now in 21st printing); conductor of world-trade marketing seminars to Japan, Europe, Africa, South America and Russia.

FREE LECTURE!
IN PERSON
E. JOSEPH COSSMAN
Self-Made Millionaire

HOW I MADE $1,000,000 IN MAIL ORDER

Selling Ideas, Products And Services!
Starting In My Spare Time!
Working On My Kitchen Table!

The public is invited to attend a FREE lecture entitled 'How You Can Make Money in Mail Order with Your Ideas, Products and Services." The lecture will be given by world famous author E. Joseph Cossman. He will explain in his easy-to-understand manner the most simple, safe and sure methods of making money in many phases of mail order.

The enlightening illustrated FREE lecture will be held at 8 pm this week only (see dates and location). There are no education or age requirements. Everyone is invited. Bring your spouse or bring a friend. Come as as you are. The lecture is strictly educational. NO investments will be offered or sold.

The purpose of the 90-minute FREE lecture is to expose the public to the many extremely profitable money-making opportunities that exist all around you in mail order. It also serves as an introduction to a dynamic Cossman seminar that will be discussed and offered at the conclusion of this FREE lecture.

Who Should Attend This Free Lecture?

If you are on salary, working for a living, and want to be your own boss ... if you want to make additional income in your spare time ... if you have a product, or an idea for a product, and want to know how to market it ... if you are in your own business and want to increase your sales ... then don't miss this opportunity to attend this lecture. If could be the most profitable, as well as the most exciting time you have ever spent in your entire life.

Little-Known Secrets Could Make You Rich!
Learn over 300 of them that will show you how to make money doing what you like to do.

How to turn your skills, experience and talents into a 2nd income.
- Run a "Disguised Ad" for your product in one hundred top magazines, for as little as 26c each!
- Receive a free list of hundreds of brand-new products every month that you can tie up for a song.
- Sell a product by mail order, with no risk of losing any money on the ad.
- Five ways to test a new product before you invest a cent in it.
- Protect a hot new idea, so you can show it to big companies and they haven't the slightest chance to steal it.

©1978 COSSMAN SUCCESS SYSTEMS

- The 3 best ways to get free front page publicity on your company, or your product, or yourself.
- Get national distribution for your product in just one evening.
- Get the U.S. Government to display your products in foreign lands, FREE!
- Appear with your product on up to 200 TV stations for $50!
- Exhibit at a trade show, even if you don't want to pay a penny for the space, the travel, or the personnel to get there!
- How to get your product displayed in front of the cash register—FREE!
- How to get FREE ART WORK for your ads, from now on.

8 pm—Each Night At Six Locations

Sunday Jan. 15
LOS ANGELES
Convention Center
1201 S. Figueroa St
At Pico Boulevard

Monday Jan. 16
LONG BEACH
Queen Mary
Grand Salon
Pier J at End of
Long Beach Freeway

Tuesday Jan. 17
ANAHEIM
Inn At The
Park Hotel
1855 S. Harbor Blvd.
Off Santa Ana Freeway,
next to the Anaheim
Convention Center

Wednesday Jan. 18
NORWALK
Saddleback Inn
Santa Ana Freeway
and Firestone Blvd.

Thursday Jan. 19
LOS ANGELES
Hotel Sheraton
L.A. Airport
9750 Airport Blvd.
One Block North of
Century Boulevard

Friday Jan. 20
NEWPORT BEACH
Airporter Inn
18700 McArthur Blvd.
Opposite Orange County
Airport

Joe Sugarman's Mousetrap Store

What Sears and Wards are to the catalog business, Joe Sugarman is to print media marketing.

LOOKING for an unusual gift for a loved one? How about a laser beam mousetrap, yours for a mere $1,500? Or a jogging computer that keeps tabs on your speed and mileage as you run your legs off in the basement, for only $149.95? For the kiddies, how about a home pinball machine, at $650?

Should any of these catch your fancy, call or write to Joe Sugarman, a young soft-spoken Chicagoan who hawks such items through "print media mail order"—catalog selling, but without the catalog. In the $75-billion direct-marketing industry, Sugarman has carved a unique niche by finding unusual products (he manufactures nothing himself) and promoting them in full-page ads in magazines and newspapers. Buyers call a toll-free number to order an item. If some of the above products seem far-fetched, consider this: Set up just seven years ago, Sugarman's JS&A Group, Inc., privately owned, now does an estimated $50-million-plus sales and nets perhaps $5 million on it.

Sugarman's canny eye for a hot item is one key to his success. He was among the first to mass-market pocket calculators. In 1976, he says, he probably sold more high-quality digital watches than any retailer in the U.S.

Moreover, Sugarman deals almost exclusively in high-priced electronic goods. That's quite a novelty in direct marketing, which is more accustomed to pitching automobile seat covers and grapefruit. Because his products are more expensive, Sugarman doesn't require the repeat business other direct sellers need to cover costs.

"We like to pioneer," Sugarman explains. "When a product reaches its peak, we get out." For example, JS&A began selling pocket calculators in 1971 at $29.95. Now they're down to $14.95, and Sugarman has long since moved on to home computers at $220.

"My competitors are Sears and Wards," says Sugarman, "not because we're selling the same customer, but because they're jumping into products we're already selling." Unlike retailers and catalog houses that must make longer-term commitments, Sugarman has maximum flexibility in the faddish consumer electronics field: "We can be in and out of a product in ten days."

Good as he is in choosing merchandise, Sugarman may be even better at advertising it. He writes his own ad copy—most of his 50 employees man the phones and process orders—and boldly fills nearly a full page with snappily written text to explain his product. Favorite

Marketing Guru: Is Joe Sugarman's ad copy good? It supports a $50-million-plus business in consumer electronics.

publications for pitching his goods to higher-income audiences are the *Wall Street Journal, Popular Science* and airline magazines. "I'm the world's highest-paid copywriter," he crows. "He uses the medium brilliantly," says John Canova of Time-Life Books. James Mabry of the Horchow Collection, the prestigious catalog house, concurs: "We tried space-selling but were never successful. We never had anybody who could write copy well enough."

Sugarman himself can't be accused of thinking small. "When I started out I thought that if people saw expensive items advertised by a company with a big ad, they'd think we were a big company. If they saw small ads they'd think we were a small company. I had the guts to say, 'Okay, let's look like we're big.'" Sugarman carries that notion further. His operation is based at "JS&A Plaza," which conjures thoughts of marbled walks, Henry Moore sculpture and glass skyscrapers. JS&A Plaza is actually two single-story buildings and a warehouse at the end of a badly paved side street in suburban Chicago.

Suppliers, however, love Sugarman's "big company" image. "He's put our name in front of the consumer like no one else has," bubbles Ross Scheer, marketing director for Bally Manufacturing, the slot and pinball machine maker that now produces those $650 pinball games.

Sugarman came to the mail order business with an odd set of credentials. A University of Miami dropout who studied electrical engineering, he served three and a half years with Army Intelligence and the Central Intelligence Agency and returned to civilian life as an adman for a small consumer electronics firm. Sugarman tried to get the outfit to sell a new product, pocket calculators. The company refused. So in 1971 Sugarman set up JS&A in the basement of his home with the help of $12,000 from investors from whom he has since parted. After failing badly with a direct-mail pitch for the calculator, he placed an ad which made a $20,000 profit on orders in ten days.

Sugarman merchandises these successes and failures (the laser beam mousetrap bombed) in a spinoff venture: one-week seminars, limited to 15 students who pay $2,000 a head, held twice a year at Sugarman's Wisconsin estate, a rustic English Tudor homestead on a 30-acre spread. One pupil is Richard Viguerie, the political fund raiser who has headed up direct-mail campaigns for candidates like George Wallace and recently turned Capitol Hill upside down with all the mail he helped generate in opposition to the Panama Canal treaties. "My $2,000 went for a very worthwhile experience," says Viguerie. "Joe has some unorthodox marketing approaches, but they work." ∎

FORBES, JUNE 26, 1978

Am I giving away my trade secrets?

by Joseph Sugarman, President   JS&A Group, Inc.

JS&A is America's leading print media mail order company—devoted strictly to advertising in national magazines and newspapers. We advertise in a greater variety of national magazines and newspapers than any other direct response organization.

A typical JS&A advertisement will move millions of dollars in merchandise, generate substantial profits, provide good corporate exposure and greatly influence a market place. The JS&A Group consists of four separate companies offering everything from collectables and expensive space-age products to low-priced mass market merchandise.

Our success in marketing is a matter of record. We introduced the first pocket calculator, literally creating a new industry. We have consistently led all retailers in the sale of digital watches, and we are at the forefront of every major new product or mail order development.

To achieve these results we have concentrated our efforts on doing only one thing and doing it well—sell products and services directly to consumers through full-page ads in national magazines and newspapers. The procedures, sales approach, organization and disciplines required to do this took us five years and plenty of mistakes to develop. I now wish to divulge this information to a group of people in a small seminar I plan to give at my estate in Minocqua, Wisconsin.

WHY AM I DOING THIS?

You might call it a philosophy. I have no trade secrets. I don't believe in them. For the past three years, for example, we have publicly announced our top ten most responsive national magazines. I openly discuss our techniques and philosophies at seminars. If you've ever heard one of my speeches, you know that I freely answer any question no matter what the topic, no matter how secret the information may seem.

One of the keys to our success is my copy which, of course, is public and available for all to see and study. JS&A is truly an open book which can contribute to our industry and assist others so that they may someday contribute.

My seminar is a profit-making extension of this philosophy and a method of gathering the most serious-minded people and guiding them. Hopefully, my efforts will bring more respectability and expertise to the mail order industry—the same industry to which I owe my success.

In my seminar I show you how to organize the basics and develop the disciplines to enhance your chances of success. I take you through our entire creative process in which we study a checklist of 40 elements all advertisements should have to be effective.

Testing, the single most important phase of any program, is covered with examples and techniques. Other topics I discuss include: product selection, analyzing reponse, use of the telephone and computer, how to maximize profits, how to reduce paperwork and keep your staff small and efficient, how to select, evaluate and buy media, and many of my marketing philosophies.

We will have projects, workshops and discussions. And my time will be available to each participant to discuss his or her own specific problems or programs.

IN THE NORTH WOODS

You will study at my thirty acre estate in Minocqua, Wisconsin, where, during your free time, you may play tennis, go boating, swim, water ski, fish, hike or relax.

We will select only 15 people for this five-day seminar to be held from July 31st through August 5th of this year. I will charge each participant $2,000 for attending, which includes motel and most meals. Participants may fly into our local airport from Chicago on Sunday evening where they will be met at the airport and driven one half hour to a very comfortable motel across the lake from my estate.

Announcing a five-day seminar for those interested in furthering their knowledge of print media mail order advertising.

If you are interested in my program and in a course outline, please write me. If you definitely wish to attend and participate in this seminar, simply send a deposit of $500 made payable to the JS&A Wisconsin Mail Order Seminars. I will personally acknowledge your deposit, and my staff will take care of your reservations and advise you of the details.

If your company is considering advertising in print as a new form of direct marketing, or if you want to discover the best techniques of print media direct response advertising, I believe the JS&A Seminar will be a very rewarding experience—rewarding even if all I do is prevent you from making just one mistake. I look forward to welcoming you as my guest, and I urge you to respond early.

One JS&A Plaza   Northbrook, Ill. 60062   (312) 564-9000

©JS&A Group, Inc.,1977

Over 4,000 people attended the most informative, penetrating convention yet held concerning your future.

Held the last week in February—the participants will be talking about this convention. . .the information. . .the predictions. . .and making successful decisions based on startling, but sound statements on

- Political events worldwide
- World monetary systems
- Your financial survival
- Investment shockwaves
- Real Estate and You
- Self-sufficiency and the Family

Your financial position, where you live, what you invest in, what you purchase, how you vote. . . what your entire future is could be dictated by the information from "A WORLD TURNED UPSIDE DOWN" . . .

YOUR HEALTH, WEALTH AND INDEPENDENCE COULD WELL BE EFFECTED BY COMING EVENTS. . .HAVING THIS INFORMATION MAY BE THE MOST IMPORTANT DECISION YOU HAVE MADE!

And Now it's YOURS! on Audio Cassette Tapes.

All the stimulating, spellbinding material on these tapes will be yours. . .to listen to straight through, to refer back to, and to use as research on specific problems and decisions which every one of us will face now, and in the very near future.

You'll know what the insiders know. . .and what the predictions are from behind the scenes by people in-the-know:

HOWARD J. RUFF, Author of the nation's fastest growing financial newsletter and advisory service, as well as, the best seller "*How to Prosper During the Coming Bad Years.*" His predictions have made millionaires and saved small investors from tragic errors and he predicts a "period of national and personal testing" for the near future.

CONGRESSMAN PHILIP M. CRANE, Presidential Candidate, Chairman of the American Conservative Union and 10 year member of the House of Representatives looks at politics and politicians, the current state of the union and its problems, plus solutions from a Free Market prospective.

HANS SENNHOLZ, expert in the fields of economics and political science explores taxation and inflation as a method of redistributing the wealth, as well as, real estate.

ROBERT BLEIBERG, Editor of Barron's National Business and Financial weekly reveals some of the thinking behind government regulation of the economy, and the stock market outlook for 1979.

SENATOR ORRIN HATCH, member of the Committee on Separation of Powers and one of the most successful freshman senators in history takes conservative view as it applies to "'A WORLD TURNED UPSIDE DOWN''.

PLUS—Terry Jeffers • Richard Russell • James Blanchard • Dr. Gary North • B. Ray Anderson • Norvel and Joann Martens • R.E. McMaster • Bernard Cirlin • Maury Kravitz • Jesse Cornish • Mark Skousen •

Fill this order form out today. This is a regular $125 value which will pay for itself time and again. . .and it's available to you, our members, at only $95 if you mail this order form now!

Learn to Hold an Audience Spellbound
and
Master the Art of Casual Conversation

Speaking expressively and effectively to other people is an enviable trait that guarantees you an attentive and respectful hearing when you express an opinion. It opens doors of business opportunity that might otherwise remain closed. And it assures you of a warm welcome in the best social circles. Like it or not, the way you speak largely defines who and what you are in the minds of others.

Today, regardless of your field, you must be able to speak in public. Whether you are making presentations to business organizations or sales forces, customers or colleagues—or conversing with friends and family, how well you speak greatly affects your professional and personal success.

Public Speaking Made Easy is a down-to-earth, practical guide for anyone, young or old, amateur or professional, who finds that he is required to or wishes to speak in public. It is also teaches how to become a polished casual conversationalist. The book was written by Thomas Montalbo, a seasoned public speaker with over 25 years of speaking and speech-writing experience. His proven formula for speech writing and delivery will take your speech capabilities to new heights. Whether you want standing ovations from large groups of executives or want to achieve a new level of casual conversation at small gatherings of friends or family, you can do it better, sooner, and easier than you ever thought possible—using the tools and techniques found in *Public Speaking Made Easy*.

You'll discover the secrets of history's most effective speakers. This indispensable guide is a Speaker's Hall of Fame, revealing invaluable research about the speech writing habits and platform styles of scores of illustrious figures, amplifying this with excerpts from their greatest speeches.

You needn't stumble from one platitude to the next, nor punctuate your speech with ahs...ums...and y'knows, groping for words to express what you want to say. It's easy to speak eloquently when you use the tools and materials found in *Public Speaking Made Easy*. Try them and see! You'll learn how to:

•Select a subject

•Locate suitable content

•Organize and write speeches

•Control Tension

•Sound professional

•Develop stage presence

•Add clarity, force, and conviction

•Use wit and humor to best advantage

To order your copy of *Public Speaking Made Easy*, send $12.00 (CA res.$12.83) to:

Melvin Powers
12015 Sherman Road
No. Hollywood, CA 91605

Announcing...

Courses in Applied Psycho-Cybernetics

Dear Friend:

Since the publication of *Psycho-Cybernetics* by Dr. Maxwell Maltz, there have been many requests for a course in the principles and practices of psycho-cybernetics. I am pleased to announce that such a course in now available.

There has been a deserved and enthusiastic response to the writings of Dr. Maltz, and it is the aim of this course to supplement his writings with a practical and proven program for better living. Elaboration of the psychological concepts and principles found in *Psycho-Cybernetics* will provide practical approaches to the problems and situations encountered in everyday living.

This course includes lectures and discussions about psychological techniques that can help students to lead a more rewarding, well-adjusted, and richer life, and to reach their highest potential. Among the many topics is why we resist change and, more important, what makes change possible—with a particular emphasis on the role of applied psycho-cybernetics. There are also fascinating demonstrations and a stimulating exchange of questions and answers which helps them to explore their own feelings and attitudes. This course examines a variety of interpersonal relationships from the point of view of various schools of psychology. It helps expand understanding and aids in developing necessary skills.

There are no prerequisites for joining the class. All that is needed is an inquiring mind and a sincere desire for self-improvement. If you would like to attend, please fill out the enrollment form and include your check for $50 payable to Melvin Powers.

Classes will be held on five consecutive Tuesday evenings from 8:00 pm to 10:00 pm., beginning _____. Classes are also available on five consecutive Saturday mornings from 10:00 am to 12:00 pm., beginning _____.

The location is in West Los Angeles, in the conference room, Suite 270, of the Kirkeby Center—an informal setting, conducive to stimulating discussion and study. It is located at 10889 Wilshire Blvd. at the northeast corner of Wilshire and Westwood Blvd. The Kirkeby building is located five minutes from the University of California at Los Angeles.

You need not live in Southern California to attend classes. Qualified instructors are available in all parts of the United States, who will form a class whenever twelve students express an interest in attending. If interested, let us know. In New York City, Dr. Maltz himself will teach weekend courses. If you live in or near this area, don't miss this opportunity to study with the famous "father of psycho-cybernetics."

For further information, please call (818) 765-8579 or write:

Melvin Powers
12015 Sherman Road
No. Hollywood, CA 91605

NEWSLETTER

VOL. 1 NO. 1

AMERICAN PSYCHO-CYBERNETICS ASSOCIATION

12015 Sherman Road,
No. Hollywood, California 91605

A Message of Welcome from Dr. Maxwell Maltz

From left to right, Maxwell Maltz, M. D. & Melvin Powers

I am happy to take this opportunity to welcome you to your Psycho-Cybernetics group. These groups are an unexpected but gratifying aftermath to the publication of my book, and, although I did not envision this result, I must confess that their formation is pleasing to my own self-image. This, of course, puts me in the position of a physician who receives the greatest benefit from his own advice, but I would not change this paradoxical situation because I truly believe psycho-cybernetics can be of value to everyone.

The fact that you have evidenced an interest in joining or forming one of these groups indicates that you have already taken the first step toward self-improvement. You were one of those who were quick to see the benefits of such a program and are anxious to join the thousands of others in America and other parts of the world who are already putting its principles into practice. Incidentally, these pioneer members are proving that the techniques of psycho-cybernetics really work, and they will work equally well for you.

Group psychotherapy came into being partly because of a shortage of psychologists and psychiatrists and is now part of the practice of most progressive psychotherapists. It was not, however, intended for serious mental illness, and I hope that no one with deep-seated mental disorders will attempt to cure himself by participating in group discussions with those who are seeking to improve their personalities and solve emotional problems which afflict us all from time to time. Psycho-cybernetics can help a vast majority of those whose lives are not as meaningful as they would like because their self-image is inadequate. It was not designed to aid those who have seriously defective behavior patterns.

Fortunately, psycho-cybernetics can be of great value to most individuals who feel they are unable to fully achieve worthwhile goals because they lack confidence and self-esteem. Examining themselves rigorously and honestly with the help of a group that is similarly motivated will help provide them with the answers they need. It was Alexander Pope who said, "Know then thyself...the proper study of mankind is man." These words are as timely today as they were nearly 250 years ago, and you may be sure Pope was not referring to the usual superficial examination to which most people subject themselves. Self-improvement depends on looking deeply into yourself, avoiding the usual excuses and rationalizations and freely admitting your mistakes. You will find this much easier to do when you are in a group dedicated to rooting out its faults so that high goals may be obtained.

One of the surprising things you will discover in group discussions is that in helping others you help yourself. Using the techniques of psycho-cybernetics, you will find you can logically provide answers for others that are equally applicable to you. And you will, to your astonishment, find you have strong assets beneath the many layers of failure that you have piled up because you lacked the proper method to reverse your negative habit patterns. Eventually, through regaining the dignity and self-respect that are inherent in all of us, you will reach self-fulfillment.

Self-fulfillment is the only way to achieve true happiness. Aspiring to realistic goals and then attaining them is the most rewarding emotion a human being can feel. These goals, if properly chosen, encompass everything in life that is right and good. Psycho-cybernetics can help you achieve them.

We live in an age which is now dedicated to discovering the secrets of outer space. What a blessing it would be if we could also discover the secrets of ourselves, learning through psycho-cybernetics the potential of our own minds.

Seeking the great treasures within yourself can be for you the greatest voyage of discovery of all time. Will you join me in seeking these treasures? I promise you it will be the greatest experience in your life. I wish each one of you the best of luck and success in your new self-improvement program.

In more than 20 years devoted to teaching classes in self-improvement, I have seen the astonishing results that can be achieved when individuals within a group relate their problems to others who have similar problems. Invariably, the discussion that ensues helps to solve the problems of all, particularly if the moderator is able to direct the group thinking into ever new channels of personality analysis and suggests solutions.

Because of the efficacy of this form of self-improvement which has been adopted by psychologists and psychiatrists everywhere, I have long sought a book that would serve as a guide for those who desired to start self-help groups. There were many excellent books dealing with specific factors involved in self-improvement (guides to better concentration, memory and positive thinking were especially plentiful) but it seemed to me that no single volume contained enough proven techniques to effect a complete reorganization of the personality. Such a change is indicated for many individuals whose lives are not meaningful or goal-directed.

The book, it seemed to me, would have to provide answers for those whose self-esteem was so low that they were perpetuating a failure pattern which had become so much a part of their personalities that it constituted a conditioned response. It was obvious that the solution to such problems would have to be derived from a method so penetrating that old habit patterns would be buried beneath new habits of thinking, feeling and acting that would allow the individual to function effectively and successfully in an environment that has become increasingly competitive.

Finding a book that I felt fulfilled all the specifications necessary for a self-improvement group to operate was no small task, but my search was rewarded when I read *Psycho-Cybernetics* by Dr. Maxwell Maltz. Dr. Maltz, a renowned plastic surgeon, had conducted a long search of his own, directed toward finding a method by which the personality strength of his post-surgical patients could be raised to the point where it matched his cosmetic results. Briefly, many of those whose ugliness had been transformed by Dr. Maltz' surgery still *felt* ugly, and the able surgeon could not rest content until their self-image was strengthened to coincide with their new image.

It was thus that "Psycho-Cybernetics" was born, but it did not happen overnight. There was a long period of gestation during which Dr. Maltz examined all the scientific disciplines—both physical and social—seeking the synthesis of techniques he felt was necessary to accomplish the results he envisioned. Many times, as he sought to go beyond the "closed systems" of many art-sciences, he thought the solution would elude him, but the plight of his patients spurred him on and late in 1960 he published his unique method of implementing and making more certain the benefits of "Self-Image" psychology.

The book was an instant success and the steady demand for it resulted in the printing of many editions. It was my hope, however, that this valuable book would eventually be made available for many more persons who needed it through the medium of an inexpensive edition which everybody could afford. This has been done by the Wilshire Book Company, and I am happy to report that it is available to all who wish to try a new and exciting method of self-improvement.

In closing these remarks in the *Newsletter,* I again compliment Dr. Maltz on the remarkable synthesis of techniques he has evolved to make self-improvement in every area of the personality more certain.

You who have already started or joined "Psycho-Cybernetics" groups know how effective this new approach can be in instigating and carrying through a program directed toward a more meaningful and successful life. Those who are not members of a group should hasten to join one or, if necessary, form a new group. The dividends will exceed your most optimistic expectations.

How To Organize A "Psycho-Cybernetics" Group

The easiest way to organize a Psycho-Cybernetics group is to enlist the help of the parent Psycho-Cybernetics group which can furnish you with the names, addresses and phone numbers of several people in your area who have already expressed a desire to start such a group.

There are many reasons for using the facilities of the parent organization to found local groups. It is, for one thing, more convenient, but beyond that it is of great help to those who might find the mechanics of starting a group present insurmountable obstacles. For instance, if one of your personality problems is shyness, procrastination, lack of ability to make up your mind or an inordinate fear of calling or meeting strangers, it will be of inestimable value for you to know that you will have a great deal in common with those you call to join you in becoming charter members of a group.

Such persons may not have exactly the same problems as you, but you can be sure they have problems they feel they can solve through sharing them with a group and applying the techniques of *Psycho-Cybernetics*. In brief, regardless of the area in which you wish to improve, you will be surrounded with individuals whose goals parallel your own.

Persons called under these circumstances will not, in fact, be strangers. They will have already written of their wish to start or join a group. They will have evidenced their desire to meet others similarly motivated. They will hope and expect to receive a phone call. This is a far different situation than that facing an individual who wants to start or join a group but has no idea of who may be interested. The people you call will have read *Psycho-Cybernetics* and will be anxious to start discussing and practicing its principles as soon as possible.

A phone call is sufficient for the first contact. At that time plans can be made for a place to meet and discuss the forming of the group. Meeting places can be arranged almost any place where at least semi-privacy can be maintained.  Many groups rotate meetings, gathering in the home of a different member each week. Other groups arrange permanent facilities in community recreation halls, the local "Y," church social rooms or even clubs and offices. The only thing really necessary is an atmosphere free of undue interruption.

There are no hard and fast rules for conducting meetings. The only requisites are a sincere desire to honestly conduct an inventory of your liabilities and assets with the help of others who are engaged in the same task, and then apply the knowledge of *Psycho-Cybernetics* to effect the changes necessary to achieve your goal.

Most groups appoint a different moderator each week who selects a portion or a particular therapeutic technique from Dr. Maltz' book, *Psycho-Cybernetics,* for discussion. Each of the members contributes his own comments. Each also discusses his results using psycho-cybernetic principles so that many aspects and uses of the technique are brought to light. It is astonishing how many different and yet valid ways there are of practicing a methodology, and that, of course, is the reason why groups often achieve results so much faster than individuals. Alcoholics Anonymous, for instance, with its 700 chapters and 300,000 members has proved the efficacy of the group approach through the 30 years of its existence. Such groups are an unlimited expansion of the adage that, "Two heads are better than one."

One of the amazing aspects of group discussion is the ease with which you will be able to relate the nature of your problem and seek the help of others. Even the most inhibited individuals find they can discuss their personality problems without embarrassment in a group which treats their revelations in a friendly, confidential and helpful way. This is because each member has his own particular problems and is deeply aware that he is not in a position to criticize others unless his criticism is constructive and free from malice.

All of this is not meant to imply that joining a group will automatically afford you instant relief from firmly entrenched personality problems. It does mean, however, that right from the beginning you will start to consciously change your negative and goal-inhibiting habit patterns and gradually impress correct habits of thinking and acting which will penetrate the subconscious mind and eventually become automatic. It will take time to completely reorganize certain aspects of your personality but it is hoped that you will attain tangible results from the beginning so that you will never lose confidence in your ultimate success.

Members of Psycho-Cybernetics groups should feel free to call on the parent organization for further literature, help or advice at any time. Questions of general interest will be printed and answered in this *Newsletter*. There is never any obligation on your part for these services. Your only duty and obligation is to yourself and your group. Our only desire is that the tremendous potential for self-improvement contained in *Psycho-Cybernetics* is made available to as many individuals as possible. We are positive the sincere application of its methods will result in a startling improvement in your total life situation and enable you to attain the goals that you thought have always been beyond your reach.

Remember, this is your organization. Please keep us informed of the progress of your group. It may well prove an inspiration to others. We welcome and shall print your information, questions, comments and suggestions in the *Newsletter*. Please feel free to write.

If you are interested in the growth of the Psycho-Cybernetics movement, you can help by participating in its program. A good way to start is to form or join a Psycho-Cybernetics discussion group or give this newsletter or a copy of Dr. Maltz's book, *Psycho-Cybernetics*, to someone you believe would be interested in it. The book can be obtained from your local bookstore or ordered directly from Wilshire Book Company, 12015 Sherman Road, No. Hollywood, California 91605. ($12.00 postpaid)

> "When you have decided what you believe, what you feel must be done, have the courage to stand alone and be counted."
>
> —*Eleanor Roosevelt*

Question: What is the meaning of the word "psycho-cybernetics"?

Answer: On page 17 of *Psycho-Cybernetics,* Dr. Maltz defines the word as follows: "When we conceive of the human brain and nervous system as a form of servo-mechanism, operating in accordance with cybernetic principles, we gain a new insight into the why and wherefore of human behavior.

"I choose to call this new concept 'Psycho-Cybernetics': the principles of cybernetics as applied to the human brain.

"I must repeat. Psycho-Cybernetics does not say that man *is* a machine. Rather, it says that man *has* a machine which he uses."

Question: What is cybernetics?

Answer: The word "cybernetics" stems from a Greek word meaning "steersman," and this is an extremely cogent definition. Through the application of cybernetic principles you literally steer yourself to success, avoiding the shoals of failure by utilizing the goal-directed feedback mechanisms of the brain which operate with the same mathematical exactitude as an electronic computer. It is simply a matter of programming the proper suggestions, ideas and mental pictures into your subconscious mind so powerfully that they afford a certain and permanent guide to your goal. Deviations from your predetermined path are corrected automatically, and your imagination, not your will power, is the key to success.

Question: What can I expect from the study of psycho-cybernetics?

Answer: It is my belief that the application of psycho-cybernetic principles will effect a remarkable change in your life. It is literally impossible to conscientiously employ the techniques in Dr. Maltz' book without developing a more dynamic and positive personality. Your self-image will change through the development of new habits in thinking, imagining, remembering and acting which, in turn, will activate your potential success mechanism.

No matter how convinced you are that you are destined to fail in attempting to reach a pinnacle of self-realization and success, you owe it to yourself to read *Psycho-Cybernetics.* The very first chapter will convince you that all things are possible to those with imagination enough to see themselves as invincible in their mind's eye. It's as simple as that.

Question: Mr. Powers, what is your personal experience in teaching psycho-cybernetics?

Answer: I was profoundly impressed with Dr. Maltz' techniques and immediately incorporated them into my classes devoted to developing positive personality patterns which lead the individual to function adequately and maturely in a society where the incidence of neurosis is increasing alarmingly. Negative failure patterns, I found, yielded to the application of psycho-cybernetics, and, like most effective therapies, its success depends on potentiating qualities which all people possess rather than stressing the increase of will power or the acceptance of metaphysical concepts.

Most important, I discovered that Dr. Maltz' synthesis of visual imagery with the principles of cybernetics effected a rapid change for the better in the individual's self-image. Through correctly visualizing themselves surmounting obstacles, acting in a confident manner and making mature and critical decisions, they soon were able to alter their self-perpetuating failure patterns to one of achievement and wishfulfillment. In short, they were enabled to evoke a *feeling of success* which soon became permanent and automatic, giving them the confidence to encompass the goals that had eluded them so long.

Question: Why should I join a Psycho-Cybernetic group?

Answer: By comparing your experiences in applying this new approach to self-improvement, you will supplement and add new dimensions to your understanding of the program. These groups are specially designed to activate productive discussion which will lead to a more rewarding, deeply meaningful and totally successful life.

You will be delighted with the pleasure and help you will receive from these discussions keyed to realizing the full potential of the most effective self-improvement method ever devised. And you will make lasting friendships which are necessary to acquiring the self-esteem you need to be successful at anything.

Question: Can you recommend another book in the cybernetics field?

Answer: I am pleased to recommend CYBERNETICS WITHIN US by Y. Saparina, a Russian science writer. It is a remarkable volume which both complements and augments Dr. Maltz's book which has already become a classic in the self-improvement field. The author enumerates physiological processes that produce psychological changes in man's opinion of himself and his destiny.

Melvin Powers
Wilshire Book Company

12015 Sherman Road
No. Hollywood, CA 91605

(818) 765-8579
FAX (818) 765-2922

Dear Friend:

We were highly gratified recently when *Psycho-Cybernetics* became a bestseller, climbing into fourth place on the *New York Times* list of general book sales. We were pleased that our high opinion of the book had been proved by so many people, and that we had played a part in helping those people to achieve their highest potential.

We still think *Psycho-Cybernetics* contains the most positive techniques yet devised to enable man to utilize his subconscious power. You, as a reader of the book, probably think so too, judging from the many readers' letters we have received praising the book. None of the letters, however, mentioned why the writer had decided to purchase the book. This has made us veteran book people very curious. We are also curious to find out what type of scientific information and techniques people would like to see in future books that we publish. The best way is to ask. And since readers like you are the only ones qualified to furnish us with the reasons for *Psycho-Cybernetics* having become such an unprecedented success, we have sent you a questionnaire in hopes that you won't mind answering the few questions for us.

Your answers will have an extremely important bearing on the titles and contents of future books we will publish in the field of self-improvement. We want our new books to reflect your needs. We want to provide the information you want and need to continue fulfilling your ambitions.

We sincerely hope you will help us in this project. We are enclosing a self-addressed envelope to make your task a little easier.

The questionnaire need not be signed. We appreciate your taking the time to answer. You have our most sincere thanks.

Sincerely yours,

Melvin Powers

Melvin Powers, President

Psycho-Cybernetics
Questionnaire

1. How did you come to possess *Psycho-Cybernetics*? Did you purchase it yourself or was it given to you as a gift? If someone recommended it or gave it to you, who was it? Did you read about it in an advertisement?

2. If you purchased the book yourself, why were you attracted to it? How did you react to the scientific, technical-sounding title?

3. Had you heard of or read *Cybernetics*, a book written by the late Dr. Norbert Weiner, a theoretical mathematician who taught at Massachusetts Institute of Technology? Did you realize that his studies were the inspiration of *Psycho-Cybernetics*?

4. Do you prefer scientific titles rather than the more usual self-explanatory type? An example of the latter would be *How to Win Friends and Influence People*.

5. Would you be interested in a book which would describe more techniques to supplement and amplify those explored in *Psycho-Cybernetics*?

6. Can you suggest specific problems that you would like to have discussed in a scientific but understandable book, which would help assure success if its techniques were followed?

257

Chapter Twelve

How to Sell Your Products to Mail Order Companies, Retail Outlets, Jobbers, and Fund Raisers for Maximum Distribution and Profits

A number of mail order companies maintain retail outlets as a source of additional revenue and collect names to be used and listed for rental. Many retail stores develop mail order operations for the same reasons. If a retail outlet is successful, the chances are the potential for mail order sales is extremely high.

Here's a Melvin Powers mail order technique: When you develop a product to sell, think of selling it through the mail, not only to the mail order consumer but to other outlets as well. You can sell to other mail order companies, retail outlets of all kinds, jobbers, and as a fund-raising device. In this way, your product will get maximum distribution.

For example, I have a line of tennis books which I sell to tennis shops and tennis clubs. I have a line of health books which I sell to health food stores and health-oriented mail order businesses. I have a line of bridge books which I sell to bridge clubs. I recently published a book on racquetball, and I'm successfully selling the book to racquetball clubs and to colleges where the sport is taught. Some schools are using it as a textbook and have made it required reading.

One step in your mail order operation will lead to another, and it's best not to restrict yourself to a single way of merchandising your product or service. Keep alert constantly to the fact that you can develop all kinds of outlets by taking advantage of your mail order know-how. Because of the success of my tennis and health books in specialized outlets, I started to show books at industry trade shows. Here I had contact with the proprietors and buyers of this type of merchandise. Not only did I sell books, but I used the opportunity to do some market research as to what specific subjects their customers were

interested in. That information is extremely valuable, since it enables you to catch a trend at its inception.

Here's how my effort in some market research resulted in the sale of thousands of books and continues to produce a large volume of sales. At a health trade show in San Diego, a health food store owner suggested I publish a low-priced vegetarian cookbook with hundreds of recipes. He said his customers were always looking for a good book on that subject, and it would make an excellent impulse, point-of-sale purchase. He himself was a vegetarian and was looking for such books all the time.

I had assumed the market was flooded with good books on vegetarian cooking, so it never occurred to me to publish such a book. Thanks to his suggestion, I published a book called *Vegetarian Cookery* by Janet Walker. The book contains 777 delicious recipes, and I priced the book at $3. It immediately became a good seller. It received excellent reviews in magazines relating to health, which further enhanced the sale of the book.

I not only sold the book via mail order at the retail level, but embarked on a direct mail campaign to promote the book to health food stores and health food jobbers. At the trade show, I contacted some jobbers and they agreed to take on the book along with other books from my list. That's merchandising in a good business way, and that potential is also available to you. I haven't had the time to explore the premium market, but I know sales in that field are tremendous. There are premium shows where you can exhibit. You can share a booth or contact a distributor. I prefer being present at the trade shows. If you are not there, your product might not get the proper attention, and a possible winner could easily get lost.

I've seen this very thing happen time and again at the international trade book shows in Jerusalem and Frankfurt. Though companies will agree to exhibit your books, it takes the personal touch of someone really interested to consummate the deals. I've been to many other types of trade shows, only to find that the representatives of some companies aren't nearly as diligent as they might be about showing and selling their products. Attend every show you decide to patronize. There is no substitute for that personal touch.

HORSE LOVERS' LIBRARY

Here is an example of how I developed a line of 70 horse books. The technique is similar to that used in developing a line in any other category. If I were developing and merchandising products, I would do the same thing. An additional merchandising element is to call on department store and specialty buyers. The feedback acquired from them is extremely valuable, and you never know when you might get an order.

It is important to research the market yourself to determine the sales potential of your products. Even if you can afford the services of an established marketing survey company, do it yourself. Remember how many times the pollsters are wrong? Major companies have lost millions relying on information they could not substantiate. I do not advocate executives should eliminate the use of market research companies, but it might be better were they to get out in the field themselves. Get other executives to do the same thing. You might get an entirely different set of answers. A chance remark by someone you are interviewing might be the key to your success.*

The advisability of developing a line of horse books came to me when I was trying to purchase some books on the Arabian horse. I had just bought an Arabian stallion and wanted to become knowledgeable in the field, but I discovered that there weren't any paperback horse books. Why hadn't any publisher thought of it? There were plenty of paperback books on dogs, cats, fishes, hamsters, and rabbits. Was there something I didn't know?

To get the answer, I was compelled to do some market research. I visited a number of riding and equipment stores and training stables in the Los Angeles area and spoke to numerous riders and trainers. I also called on the riding instructors at the local colleges where horseback riding is taught.

They all deplored the high cost of horse books and told me they would welcome low cost, quality paperback books. I constructed a profile of a potential buyer, and decided it would be a young girl, between the ages of 10 and 17, with the responsibility of caring for her horse. She would have limited funds and be unable to buy expensive books. She would want to improve her riding ability and look for practical information about the general care and

feeding of her horse. She would also be interested in acquiring a better horse.

In doing the survey, I found horsemen very cooperative. At times I was involved with a small group eager to answer my questions. They were brainstorming on my behalf. I'd ask such questions as: What subject matters would you like to see covered in quality paperback horse books? What would you be willing to pay for such a book? Where would be a convenient place for you to purchase such books? Would you purchase several books if you thought they were worthwhile? My best selling titles came from those discussions. Another benefit came in the form of volunteer models for my books. They were all pleased with the fun and pleasure of being on a book cover with their horses and offered these services without charge.

Before I had published even a single book on the subject, I knew that I had a new winning category of books. I was so confident I published 20 different titles all at the same time. I didn't have to wait for the results. Based upon my research, I knew exactly what book titles would sell, the proper price, and where to concentrate my selling efforts. It couldn't have been easier.

The books were enthusiastically received, something which encouraged many publishers to imitate me. The mistake made by most publishers was to assume anyone owning a horse could easily afford the hardcover books. That thinking was correct, except that it was the children, not the parents, who were involved with the horses.

To properly maintain a horse, one has many on-going expenses, such as stabling, feed, grain, food supplements, veterinary care, medicines, worming, shots, shoeing, equipment, saddles, bridles, blankets, grooming equipment, clothing, riding lessons, training lessons, entry fees for shows, trailers, and insurance. Hardcover books are at the bottom of the priority list.

Here's how I capitalized on what I had. The instructors with whom I spoke adopted some of the books as required reading. I subsequently acquired a list of all the schools, colleges and camps where courses in horsemanship were offered. I sent my list of books offering free review copies to the instructors. After they examined them, back came the orders. There are now numerous schools where my books have been adopted as required reading. Those sales add up. I received an enthusiastic response from the librarians in the Los Angeles area, and subsequently sold my books to local libraries, as well as to many throughout the country.

When the books first came out, I called on all the riding goods stores in and around Los Angeles. I made sales everywhere I went and the re-orders soon followed. It was obvious I had a winner. Now to move forward on a national basis.

See page 185. Mail order ads in horse magazines paid off handsomely. I received many unsolicited letters

---

*This paragraph was written in 1979. Do you suppose an executive at Ford Motor Co. read this in my book? See newspaper article on page 263 dated October 1, 1980.

thanking me for publishing such beautiful and reasonably priced horse books.

The next step was to broaden my scope in order to reach the riding goods dealers everywhere. Using *Business Publications Rates and Data,* I advertised in the trade publications patronized by riding goods dealers. I carried full-page ads in those publications every month for several years. It was impossible to miss them. On page 264, you'll find the type of ad I ran in color. The response to the advertising campaign was gratifying. The orders poured in, and so did the re-orders. I offered a 24-pocket, revolving stand at a very nominal price to display the books and sold hundreds of them. That produced additional sales since the books were prominently displayed face out. As I developed more books, I offered a 48-pocket stand.

I learned about various trade shows featuring riding goods. One of the big shows was in Denver, Colorado. I decided to take a booth and show my books. To spice up my exhibit, I equipped the booth with a very attractive, vivacious, blond model, named Candy, and a 2' x 4' framed picture of her, *au naturel,* leading a Palomino horse. See page 265. She was the show-stopper. My booth was crowded everyday. The atmosphere was like that of a lively cocktail party. Buyers brought other buyers to see the picture and meet Candy. She held their attention long enough for one of us to take orders for the books. The results were excellent, and we introduced our books to a large number of new riding goods stores.

While I was there, I lined up jobbers from Australia, England, Canada, and the United States to handle our books. I also hired some salesmen to act as our representatives for calling on the trade. The show produced marvelous results.

Here's where I used mail order techniques to produce even more sales. Refer to page 264. You'll note I introduced our Arabian stallion, Asdar. His sire, Naborr, was owned by Wayne Newton. Asdar attracted a good deal of interest and earned The Legion of Merit, an award given to horses that have earned sufficient points in horse shows to qualify for excellence.

See page 265 and 266. This represents one side of an 11" x 17" circular. The other side has a full-size order form and pictures of various books. This self-mailer and others like it were sent to 15,000 riding goods stores on a regular basis with good results. I was able to get complete saturation of the market with my trade ads, direct mailing pieces, jobber and salesmen representation, and our recognition at the trade shows. I had the only book display.

Let's talk about pages 265 and 266. Don't they convey a friendly feeling? I'm engaged in my favorite pastime of doing market research. I did receive some excellent suggestions for horse books, and based on those suggestions I published books that answered a public need. On page 266, I talk about Asdar's progress and show a picture of him under saddle with Gary Cohen and me. See the invitation to visit. Look how nicely I introduce the new book, *Stable Management.* The recipient gets to meet Florence Cohen as well.

This page of copy gives the personal touch. Introduce members of your family, and talk about your hobbies or interests. Let people get to know you. As a result of this personal approach, and the prompt shipment of books, I received numerous letters saying how nice it was to do business with my company. In return, I also received correspondence and pictures of families and horses. It was something I thoroughly enjoyed.

Using a direct mail circular to sell books to riding goods stores is an obvious approach. How can you utilize the circular to sell the same books to their customers? Just make a few changes in it. Leave out the discount, use a slightly different order form, and imprint the name of the store for their use in sending out statements, packages, and special mailings. It can also be used as an enclosure with all purchases in the store and as printed matter contained in a counter display which reads: FREE—TAKE ONE.

I suggest you do not imprint the circulars free of charge. This gesture will not be appreciated, and the circulars may not even be used. I've had the unfortunate experience of printing thousands of free circulars for all kinds of accounts, but for some reason, they were never used. Some store owners were not the least concerned about my expense in producing these circulars as a favor to them and the cost of postage involved. My policy now is to make a minimal charge. In this way, the store owner has a vested interest, and he'll make it a point to use the circulars and assess their value. He'll be pleased with himself when the sales come in, and, as a result, he'll wind up ordering more circulars.

This was not the end of my sales campaign. I instituted mailings to 8,000 public libraries and 15,000 bookstores, featuring the horse books. The books met with immediate acceptance. I also supplied book racks to the bookstores. I featured the books for several years at various book conventions. There are many companies selling horse equipment and clothing by mail. I contacted every one of them, and they, in turn, displayed and sold my books in their catalogs. If I didn't get an answer, I contacted them by phone and told them of the success of the books. I got the accounts.

Have you reached the point where you are beginning to ask the question, "Is there no end to this campaign?" There is but one answer. As long as your creative vitality persists, there are no limits, no boundaries. You're calling the shots. It's all up to you. I'm still at it, finding new outlets, such as 4-H Clubs and various kinds of horse shows. An interesting footnote to my being enterprising is that I published a series of tennis books several years ago when interest in tennis was at its peak, and successfully duplicated the same campaign. I'm saying, "Don't limit yourself to retail mail order sales. Take advantage of the other outlets."

WILSHIRE MAIL ORDER BOOKS

When you develop your own products, mark them up a minimum of four or five to one. If the product costs you $2.50, retail it for $10.00 minimum. This will allow you to wholesale and sell the product to other mail order companies at a discount of 50%. Selling your product at $5.00 will still give you a $2.50 profit.

Joe Cossman, author of *How I Made A Million Dollars in Mail Order*, made his millions mainly by selling his products to mail order houses. His products were priced to account for the discounts. It was as though he was getting free ads in several hundred million catalogs annually. Hundreds of magazines ran space ads on his products. What's wrong with that? Nothing. Everything was right—and it made Joe Cossman a millionaire several times over.

All my books are priced on a four-to-one ratio, allowing me to wholesale and sell my books to other mail order companies. I supply the mailing pieces, and the companies imprint their name and address. They can also buy a set of negatives so they can print their own circulars locally or make up their own layouts. This is all done at cost. When the companies get the orders, they are sent to me, and I drop-ship at a discount of 50% plus postage. See page 275 for a letter that I send out answering inquiries from my one-inch ad on page 175.

I also accompany the letter with a sample of the circulars that are available. See pages 267 and 268 for the *Sexually Fulfilled Woman* circular and pages 269 and 270 for the *Sexually Fulfilled Man* circular. Other drop-shipment circulars included are *Join the Winners' Circle* on pages 271 and 272, *How to Write a Hit Song and Sell It* on pages 273 and 274, and the *Self-Improvement Circular*, shown partially on pages 225 through 229.

Some companies preparing catalogs for mail order customers have this as their main source of business profits, not the products. Don't make that mistake. Supply your catalogs at cost, or give your customers the option of making their own. You are in the product business, not printing business. I sell 100 circulars for $5.00 postpaid. You can't beat those prices, and it gives the prospective drop-shipper the opportunity to test the circular on his clientele at a minimum cost. I'm looking for a long-range relationship that will mean repeat sales and profits for both of us. That philosophy and technique has enabled me to develop a relationship with customers that sells millions of my books. You can do the same thing.

My average drop-shipment order is for three books and averages $30.00 retail. I am sent $15.00 plus the postage, which has been included by the purchaser. The mail order company sending me the order makes a profit of $15.00 and I make a profit.

I also suggest to my mail order clients they make their products available to competitive companies. This usually produces a negative reaction until I explain it's impossible to advertise in every publication. Any time you can double your money on a product, you are making good business sense. Joe Cossman was in the drop-shipment business, which gave those who were new in mail order the opportunity to test the saleability of the products before investing in inventory. That technique helped him to become a millionaire. Let's hope it will do the same for you.

Let us assume you have a product and have designed a mailing piece, allowing room for a mail order dealer to imprint his name and address. Make sure the fold containing the space for the imprint is on the outside, making it easy for the dealer to rapidly rubber-stamp his name and address. You now need a mailing list. My suggestion is you go to those publications where you would normally advertise. Then send your literature to everyone who is running an ad, along with a sales letter such as the one I use.

If you have a product for a gift-and-gadget company, pick up a copy of *House Beautiful* or *Better Homes & Gardens* and send your literature to everyone advertising in the magazines. If you are getting a good reaction, send away to the magazines for the October or November issue of the previous year. These months contain the greatest amount of advertisers, and you have a beautiful, current mailing list.

I suggest you also adopt the following procedure, which is one I use. I mail my drop-shipment offer regularly to everyone advertising in *The National Enquirer, The Star,* and *Midnight Globe.* This includes display and classified ads. Periodically, I'll buy dozens of magazines at my local newsstand and send my mailing to all their advertisers. Using this type of random mailing has brought in some excellent accounts. Many of them are companies I might not have considered before because I would never have expected them to be interested in selling my books. It's always a pleasant surprise.

When you produce your drop-shipment circular, send one to me with your sales letter. I have a daily volume of mail going out of my office, and I'll be able to get a fast reading on the saleability of your product to my type of clientele. I hope it will result in sending you an abundance of orders and dollars.

YOUR PRODUCT AS A FUND RAISER

Fraternal and church groups are constantly selling merchandise to raise money. Haven't we all purchased Girl Scout Cookies to help send a girl to summer camp—or pot holders, key chains, pens, cakes, miniature license plates, and other products? Why not try to get some such organizations to use your product as a fund raiser for some worthy cause? It's easier than you think.

Look in the Yellow Pages of your phone book under the two headings, fraternal organizations and churches. Here is your ready-made mailing list. Address your letter to the chairman of the fund-raising committee. Tell him about your product and how ideally suited it is to raising money for charity. Give him a discount of 50%. Send out the literature you have for the mail order houses or for yourself. If you have no brochure, photograph the product and make up an inexpensive brochure.

Once you start to move your product as a fund raiser, the prospects are endless. You can easily acquire the names and addresses of fraternal organizations and churches through list brokers. Fund-raising is one of the major industries in America.

I remember receiving a large, free bar of delicious chocolate candy from a charitable organization. In return, they asked for $1. The candy bar was extremely tasty and, as a result, I ordered a dozen of the bars. Periodically, I'd receive literature from the organization, suggesting I re-order, and asking for a donation. My order for more candy would be in the return mail! This went on for years. I can't remember the purpose of the charity, but the taste of the candy lingers on. (Now that I think about it, I wish they would start sending the candy again!)

Los Angeles Times

Wednesday, October 1, 1980

Ford Executives Take to Field to Help Sell Escort

By PATRICK BOYLE, Times Staff Writer

DETROIT—Henry Ford II, retired chairman of Ford Motor Co., sold the first 1981 Escort in Belgium this past weekend, and on Friday the company's top executives will get their chance to hand a set of keys to a buyer of the new model.

Sending top officers into the field to sell cars is believed to be unprecedented in an industry where nearly every sales gimmick imaginable has been tried at least once.

Chairman Philip Caldwell has decreed that Ford's 55 vice presidents and other top officers will be in dealer showrooms the day the car goes on sale for a front row seat in the company's effort to steal sales from the imports. Caldwell will be visiting dealers in Los Angeles, the strongest small-car market in the country and the one where Ford officials would like the Escort to make its best showing.

Ford officials said Caldwell and his colleagues may not necessarily accompany a potential customer on a test drive, but the executives will visit a number of dealerships and manufacturing plants in their assigned metropolitan areas, talking to dealers, car buyers and company employees about the Escort.

Officials acknowledged that selling cars will be an unusual experience for those Ford executives who have worked their way to the top through the manufacturing and engineering ranks of the company.

"There's no question it will be a little bit of a new experience for some of them," said Gordon B. MacKenzie, vice president in charge of the Lincoln-Mercury division, who will spend Friday with dealers in Cleveland. "Some were surprised at it, but we've given them some pointers so they can talk up the good things we've got."

Dear Friends:

Thank you for your very nice reception to our line of horse books. Should you have suggestions on horse books to publish, please write.

If you know anyone interested in writing a book on some phase of horsemanship, tell him to drop me a line. I am particularly interested in a comprehensive book about Palominos.

We are interested in purchasing a Palomino riding horse. If you know one for sale we would appreciate hearing about it.

Hi Neighbor:

I'm Candy, the girl with the blue eyes leading the Palomino horse.

I'll be at the WAEMA show in Denver and at the Columbus show as well. I'm looking forward to meeting you personally as I recently did at the riding goods show in Las Vegas.

I hope it isn't too cold in Denver and Columbus. I just love the warm California weather. See you soon.

Candy

P. S. Can I help it if I'm an outdoor gal who loves the sun?

A PERSONAL NOTE TO FELLOW HORSE LOVERS
IN ANSWER TO INQUIRIES ABOUT ASDAR'S PROGRESS

I'm pleased to tell you that our Arabian Stallion Asdar (*Naborr x Miss Dior) is progressing just beautifully. At the Fall Arabian Horse Show at Santa Barbara, Asdar placed first at halter, winning over 27 of the finest Arabian stallions in the country. He also took first place blue ribbon in driving and under park saddle. It was a thrilling day.

If you are in the vicinity of Los Angeles, my partner, Dr. Harvey Cohen, and I welcome your visiting us and saying hello to Asdar at the Champion Arabian Farms, Jim Bridger Road, Hidden Hills. The coffee pot is always on the fire and the donuts are delicious.

Asdar is proving to be a popular sire getting a nice number of bookings for this year.

Melvin Powers

P. S. Gary Cohen is astride Asdar and I'm standing.

Hi Folks:

Since this is a family affair, I might as well get into the act as well.

I'm Florence Cohen, Dr. Harvey Cohen's wife, a friend of Asdar and the chief groom. Oh yes, that's yours truly on the book cover on the left, STABLE MANAGEMENT FOR THE OWNER-GROOM.

Don't tell the fellows, but I know my impeccable grooming of Asdar helped him win first place at the Fall Arabian Horse Show at Santa Barbara. Besides, I needed a blue ribbon to decorate the barn.

When you come to the ranch I'll be pleased to autograph a copy of the book for you. You never know when you might need some expert advice on grooming your horse.

Florence Cohen

P. S. Am I supposed to get a modeling fee?

Melvin Powers
Wilshire Book Company

12015 Sherman Road
No. Hollywood, CA 91605

(818) 765-8579
FAX (818) 765-2922

A Practical Guide to Becoming
THE SEXUALLY FULFILLED MAN
Dr. Rachel Copelan

What man hasn't dreamed of being a completely fulfilled and fulfilling lover--of scaling peaks of ecstasy, with his woman right up there beside him? In his wishful thinking, man is always superb, but in reality, he sometimes secretly wonders if he is even normal.

There's a wide expanse between being "normal" and reaching one's top potential as a lover, and few men manage to bridge that gap in their lifetime. Yet, the difference between being grossly inept and highly skilled as a sexual partner is simply a matter of know-how and practice.

Although today's women are assuming increasing amounts of responsibility for their own sexual pleasure, "satisfying a woman" is still considered by society to be the criterion for judging whether or not a man is an adequate lover. A woman's body is in his charge and he is "supposed" not only to satisfy himself, but to guarantee that she will also enjoy sex and reach an orgasm. No matter in what other areas of endeavor he may succeed, a man still strives for a woman's stamp of total approval, the assurance that he is "all man."

No one becomes an expert at anything instinctively. The art of lovemaking is not transmitted automatically by genetic inheritance. It is a behavior pattern that anyone with sufficient desire can master. A good lover is self-made by becoming consciously aware of his role in relation to his partner. He is thoughtful about her needs and confident that he has sufficient control to make the experience memorable. This kind of awareness goes beyond the body's instincts. It combines training the mind and body, involving the emotions, and freeing the spirit.

The Sexually Fulfilled Man tells you exactly how you can make each sexual encounter an improvement over the preceding one, until you become the best lover you are innately capable of being. You will do it not merely by altering techniques, but by altering your basic thinking and improving your physical ability to bring pleasure to yourself and your partner. In addition, you will learn what a woman expects from a man and what you, in turn, should expect from her.

Don't miss this opportunity to become the lover you have always wanted to be. Send for *The Sexually Fulfilled Man* today.

A Practical Guide to Becoming
THE SEXUALLY FULFILLED MAN
Dr. Rachel Copelan

CONTENTS

$7.00 postpaid (CA residents $7.41)

Melvin Powers
Wilshire Book Company

_____

12015 Sherman Road
No. Hollywood, CA 91605

(818) 765-8579
FAX (818) 765-2922

A Practical Guide to Becoming
THE SEXUALLY FULFILLED WOMAN
Dr. Rachel Copelan

This book has been written for:

1. The nine out of ten women who are not able to reach orgasm every time they have sexual intercourse.
2. The many women who fake orgasm sometimes, and the others who fake it all the time.
3. The vast majority who are limited to clitoral sensation and believe that sex offers nothing more.
4. Every woman who wants to reach her highest potential of sexual responsiveness and satisfaction.

This fascinating and informative book emphasizes woman's role in improving her sex life. Of course, a man can help by being unselfish and by providing effective preliminary stimulation, but the woman herself must eliminate the basic cause of her resistance and become proficient at maximizing her enjoyment.

Women who want to live fully must get to the deeper truth about themselves. They must be more aggressive about learning how their genitals work and how to release the dynamic power of the orgasm. Ultimately, a woman must free herself, because it is her own inside thinking which shuts off the instinctual peak of feeling necessary for orgasm to occur. She must be aware of how her mind and body affect each other. And she must then bring them back into harmonious concert—the natural state before negative conditioning sets in.

Unfortunately, this is not taught in schools. A woman must learn it for herself. This book has been written to help her do just that. No matter how severe a woman's negative conditioning, it can be corrected. And it's never too late. One is never too old to love or to be loved.

Dr. Copelan's sexual reconditioning program gives step-by-step guidance on how to attain greater heights of sexual happiness—no matter at what level one begins. It teaches how to develop good sexual habits and eliminate old, self-defeating ones. It helps restore woman's ability to function as nature intended—freely, sensuously, spontaneously, and capable of great satisfaction and fulfillment.

Treat yourself to the gift of full sexual satisfaction. Send for *The Sexually Fulfilled Woman* today.

$7.00 postpaid (CA residents $7.41)

A Practical Guide to Becoming
THE SEXUALLY FULFILLED WOMAN
Dr. Rachel Copelan

CONTENTS

$7.00 postpaid (CA residents $7.41)

Famous songwriter reveals secrets:

Would you like to write a hit song? If your answer is yes and if you are willing to devote some time to a pleasant and fun-filled hobby, you can be successful in the exciting world of music. Your dreams of songwriting success can come true! Listen to this.

Songwriter with 22 Gold Records Tells You How

Tommy Boyce, an internationally known hit songwriter, who has earned millions of dollars in royalties, has written a book called *How to Write a Hit Song and Sell It*. It's a complete course of instruction in which he reveals professional songwriting tips for the beginner and up-and-coming songwriter. You'll find out how he wrote six of his biggest hits, see step-by-step how the music and lyrics were developed, and learn how you can use the same techniques to write your own hit songs.

This one-of-a-kind book tells it all. It even includes some of Tommy's actual royalty statements from around the world—something that has never been published in any other book. And you'll see personnal photographs of Tommy and many of his celebrity friends.

Here are some of the songs that Tommy Boyce has written: *Last Train to Clarksville, Come a Little Bit Closer, I Wanna Be Free, Valleri, I Wonder What She's Doing Tonight, Lazy Elsie Molly, Be My Guest, Pretty Little Angel Eyes, Alice Long, I'm Not Your Stepping Stone, Peaches 'N' Cream, Words,*

She, the Monkees' theme song, and the theme song for the ever-popular TV show "DAYS OF OUR LIVES."

Here are the chapter titles:
1. Who Am I? 2. Can the Amateur Songwriter Reach Stardom? 3. How to Begin with or without a Musical Background. 4. Moods, Titles, and Melodies 5. Where Do Songs Come From? 6. Which Comes First, the Lyrics or the Melody? 7. Analyzing Hit Songs. 8. What Makes a Hit Song? 9. Professional Songwriting Tips for the Amateur and Up-and-Coming Songwriter. 10. How I Created Six of My Hit Songs. 11. Evaluating Your Music. 12. Rewriting Before Presenting Your Song. 13. Promoting Your Own Songs 14. Copyright, ASCAP, BMI. 15. The Business Side of Music. 16. How to Sell Your Songs in Person or by Mail.

The Easy Way to Rhyme Lyrics The Songwriter's Companion

Songwriters' Rhyming Dictionary, which contains thousands of rhymes, will be of tremendous help with your lyrics. Organized for quick reference, it contains rhymes for single and multiple syllable words.

Amateur Songwriter Hits it Big

Melvin Powers, publisher of Tommy Boyce's book, was fascinated by the manuscript when it was first presented to him. As a direct result of reading the book in its manuscript form, he

wrote two country-western songs that made the charts. His song *Mr. Songwriter* was recorded by Sunday Sharpe on United Artists Records and *Who Wants a Slightly Used Woman?* was recorded by Connie Cato on Capitol Records. He even won an award from ASCAP for *Who Wants a Slightly Used Woman?*. What this remarkable, instructive book did for new amateur songwriter, Melvin Powers, it can do for you.

Don't delay. Get started in the fascinating, fun world of songwriting and music. Send for both books: *How to Write a Hit Song and Sell It* - $12.00 postpaid and *Songwriters' Rhyming Dictionary* - $12.00 postpaid.

A PRACTICAL GUIDE TO SELF-HYPNOSIS

by

Melvin Powers

All of us like to think that our actions and reactions are a result of logical thought processes, but the fact is that suggestion influences our thinking a great deal more than logic. Consciously or unconsciously, our feelings about almost everything are largely molded by ready-made opinions and attitudes fostered by our mass methods of communication. We cannot buy a bar of soap or a filtered cigarette without paying tribute to the impact of suggestion. Right or wrong, most of us place more confidence in what "they," say than we do in our own powers of reason. This is the basic reason why psychiatrists are in short supply. We distrust our own mental processes and want an expert to tell us what to think and feel.

Despite this tendency to adopt our attitudes from others, man has always been dimly aware that he can influence his own destiny by directing his thoughts and actions into constructive channels. He has always, to some extent, known that his mind exerts a powerful influence on his body, and that thoughts can have harmful or helpful effects on his emotional and physical health. The ancient Egyptian sleep temples and the attempts by early physicians to drive evil spirits out of the body were both attempts to influence the body through the mind.

The unprecedented sale of *The Power of Positive Thinking* by Norman Vincent Peale and other inspirational literature proves that millions of modern people recognize the efficacy of constructive thoughts. What most of them do not recognize is that they are capable of implanting these beneficial thoughts in their own minds without reference to any outside agencies. This can be done through self-hypnosis.

In modern society we have many cults, religions and methodologies which have mental discipline as their goal. The best example of a methodology is psychosomatic medicine which deals with the interrelationship of the mind and body in the production of mental or physical illness. The rapid growth of hypnosis in the last few years is another example, and it is gratifying to see that the emphasis in this field is now shifting from hetero-hypnosis to self-hypnosis.

Self-hypnosis is a highly suggestible state wherein the individual can direct suggestions to himself. It is a powerful tool in any therapeutic process, and highly motivated subjects can parallel the success of hetero-hypnosis through their own efforts. Self-hypnosis can be used as a palliative agent and can even afford lasting results in many areas of the organism. Self-hypnosis can alleviate distressing symptoms, substitute strong responses for weak responses, help overcome bad habits, create good habits and help one's power of concentration. The total personality is eventually changed to the point where it can function adequately in an increasingly difficult environment.

In learning self-hypnosis, the subject does not relinquish control of himself as is commonly believed. Actually, more control is gained. Self-sufficiency and self-confidence are inevitable results. It is well to remember, however, that even good things may be overdone, and good judgment is necessary for favorable results. Neither hypnosis nor self-hypnosis should ever be used indiscriminately. The effectiveness of self-hypnosis depends upon many factors. Strong motivation, intelligent application of suggestions and diligence are prerequisites.

This book is written in terms that are comprehensible to the layman. The step-by-step instructions should afford the reader a means of acquiring self-hypnosis. The necessary material is here. The reader need only follow the instructions as they are given.

It is the author's hope that you will, through the selective use of self-hypnosis, arrive at a more rewarding, well-adjusted and fuller life.

Contents are as follows

128 Pages ... $7.00 postpaid

Melvin Powers
Wilshire Book Company

12015 Sherman Road
No. Hollywood, CA 91605

(818) 765-8579
FAX (818) 765-2922

YOU CAN MAKE MONEY
SELLING BOOKS BY MAIL

USE OUR PROVEN MAIL ORDER CIRCULARS

There are a variety of circulars to choose from for books on popular subjects. You get a whopping 50% off the book prices shown. Include the circulars in all your outgoing mail. Simply stamp your name and address in the blank space provided. When ordering circulars from us, be sure to print your name and street address for UPS delivery. We can drop-ship for you or send you the books and you can fulfill your own orders.

INSTRUCTIONS FOR DROP-SHIPPING

As you receive each order, send us a label addressed to your customer, showing your name and return address. On the back of the label, list the names of the books ordered. Add up the dollar amount and deduct 50%, which is your discount. Add $2.00 postage per book. We will process your order immediately.

CIRCULAR NAMES	PRICE PER 100	PRICE PER 1000
Auto Book	$5.00	$50.00
How to Get Rich in Mail Order	5.00	50.00
Join the Winners' Circle	5.00	50.00
Making Money with Classified Ads	5.00	50.00
900 Know-How	5.00	50.00
Self-Improvement Books (Includes all book titles.)	10.00	100.00
Think Like a Winner!	5.00	50.00

ACT TODAY FOR TOMORROW'S PROFITS

Order your circulars now. It could be one of the best investments you'll ever make. Should you have any questions, please feel free to call my office and ask for a service representative. Be sure to visit our Internet site: **http://www.mpowers.com**

HOW TO START AND OPERATE
YOUR OWN SUCCESSFUL MAIL ORDER BUSINESS

Here is your opportunity to learn the winning techniques of getting your own mail order business up and running successfully. You can save precious time and money by taking advantage of my many years of experience in the business. Order my book *How to Get Rich in Mail Order* ($22.00 postpaid—CA residents $23.65) or my complete *Mail Order Millionaire* cassette and book course. (See enclosed 4-page circular.)

Author Grad spreads happiness through her book, lectures, life

NORTHRIDGE — Marcia Grad is going to be a June divorcee, her marriage of 23 years fractured beyond repair.

She doesn't have a boyfriend.

So, is she depressed because, on Valentine's Day, she is not likely to be receiving cards, flowers and candy from a beau? Heck no.

"As a single person, I really see Valentine's Day as an opportunity to celebrate my love of life," Grad said enthusiastically. "And with the person I've become through much effort, (I can) appreciate and enjoy the lovely relationship I have with my family and friends. I think it's wonderful to celebrate whatever love you have in your life."

If she sounds unusually upbeat, don't be surprised. The 43-year-old Northridge resident is somewhat of an expert on being happy, something she taught herself to be.

Grad has been passing this trait on to others for more than four years via seminars at community colleges, and is aiming for a broader audience as the author of "Charisma, How To Get That Special Magic."

Grad did not always have an abundance of personality, so she knows how painful it can be to think you are not popular, loved or liked, especially at times like Valentine's Day when the emphasis is on being with someone special.

"I think very often (people) do get depressed," she said of these types of occasions. "I hear that very often in class, and certainly on a day when everyone focuses on that."

Whether people are upbeat or downbeat depends on the attitude they take toward life in general, she said. Grad makes it clear in conversation, her seminars and her book that the attitude should always be positive.

Charisma is something a person can be born with and lose or not be born with and acquire, she points out in her book. The Greeks originally thought it was favor or divine gift, like the ability to heal the sick or peer into the future. German economist and sociologist Max Weber defined charisma as the quality of people with innovative personalities to amass followings.

Grad says there are three types of charisma: pseudo charisma, exemplified by actors, politicians, professional speakers, auctioneers and sales people; situational charisma, which develops when a person gets turned on by an event; and genuine, sustained charisma.

To develop or expand charisma, she endorses a five-step program of thinking and speaking non-critically for 30 minutes, making a list of your good qualities and past successes and reading it at least three times daily, doing one thing you've been embarrassed to do in the past, participating in a childlike activity and greeting at least one new person a day.

Once a person has acquired charisma, Grad suggests hanging onto it by developing a "treasured self-friendship," making a habit of being happy, projecting positive energy and surrounding yourself with positive people.

Grad has not always followed her own advice. She had polio as a child and was not as outgoing as some of her classmates. Her first child died, then she and her husband separated once before eventually agreeing to a divorce.

But she does not believe that once a person develops a personality it is set in concrete. "It's not true that people cannot change," she said. "The (charisma development) program really evolved out of testing and trying and getting feedback from people over a period of nine years."

Grad received a degree from California State University, Los Angeles, and taught school off and on over the years. Then she went to work promoting the authors of self-help books for Wilshire Publishing Co. in North Hollywood, the house that published her book.

"I wanted to be around that (atmosphere) and work with those types of authors," she said. "Very often they were not quite what I expected. There are some who are the very embodiment of what they are preaching and teaching, and of course there are some that are not."

About four years, ago Grad started conducting three-hour seminars each Saturday on different community college campuses. Three years ago, she decided to put her ideas in a book.

MARCIA GRAD

She began practicing what she preached out of a sense of self protection.

"The whole thing started out as a self-development program for myself," she said. "I wasn't happy. I was kind of disappointed with the way my life was going."

Her marriage has evaporated since then, but she is not about to dwell on any negative aspects of the situation.

"This (the divorce) is something I've thought about for several years," Grad said. "I know it was right for me. I have a full, beautiful life and I like to make every day as full and rich and beautiful as I can."

She might not have a date on Valentine's Day, but she'll be smiling.

Chapter Thirteen

How to Get Free Display Ads and Publicity that Will Put You on the Road to Riches

Numerous consumer and trade magazines and newspapers have new product display sections. This usually consists of a photograph of the product, the price, a small write-up, and the name and address of the company.

The consumer magazines run this section under a variety of headings, such as: Mail Order Shopping, What's New, Mailbox Shopping, New Products, Shop-by-Mail, Gifts and Things, Shopping Guide, Buyer's Guide, Armchair Shopper's Guide, Family Shopper, and Shopping Scout.

Every write-up you get is like a free display ad. Here's how you get publicity for your product that could put thousands of dollars in your pocket. This technique also gives you the opportunity to test the saleability of your product with a minimal expenditure of money. Use this technique for every new product on the market.

Assume you have a new product that you want to publicize. Ask the manufacturer for a glossy print or line drawing of the item. He'll be pleased to send it to you. When you get it, contact a photographic service that can run duplicates of the picture. You need the photographs to send to the magazines for reproduction purposes. Most mail order books will instruct you to send 8″ x 10″ photographs. Don't do it. Instead, send 4″ x 5″ photographs. First of all, the smaller size is adequate, the prints will cost you less, and you'll save postage. Since this size and your publicity release can fit in a regular business envelope (#10 size), it can be sent first class mail with no extra postage. Mark your envelope New Products Editor.

I use the following two duplicate photographic service companies. Write to them for their latest price list: Duplicate Photo Lab., 1522 No. Highland Avenue, Hollywood, California 90028 and Quantity Photos, Inc., 5432 Hollywood Blvd., Los Angeles, California 90027.

Try your library, or purchase a copy of *Consumer Magazine and Farm Publications Rates & Data* which has a list of 300 magazines carrying mail order shopping sections. You'll find magazines that you never thought about for your publicity releases. It lists 1,000 consumer and 200 farm publications that might run a story on your product.

While at the library, look at the *Ayer Directory of Publications*. This directory contains the names of editors in various categories, such as automotive, business, finance, food, and sports. The directory is published by N.W. Ayer & Son, Inc., West Washington Square, Philadelphia, Pennsylvania 19106. Another excellent reference book available at all libraries is *The Working Press of the Nation*, published by the National Research Bureau Inc., 221 No. La Salle Street, Chicago, Illinois 60601. Check out some books on publicity and read them carefully. There are many good ones, and the effort will give you an insight into some of the techniques you can use to publicize your products.

Here are elements to include in the publicity release on your product:

1. Name of your product (such as Pet Rock)
2. A 100- or 200-word description of your product
3. A good sharp 4″ x 5″ glossy photograph of your product
4. Special features of your product
5. Price of your product postpaid
6. The statement, "Satisfaction guaranteed"
7. Your business name and address
8. Your personal name and phone number
9. A P.S. which says, "We'll be pleased to send you a sample for your inspection."
10. An accompanying letter stating any important information not covered in the publicity release

Mail order shopping editors are definitely interested in new and unusual products. They want you to get a good response so that it will encourage you to advertise. When you run a paid advertisement in a magazine having an editorial new-product section, always ask for a free editorial on the product being advertised, or some other product. If it's for the same product, request they run the editorial the following month. Be sure to key the address in the editorial, so you'll be able to draw a comparison between the amount of orders from the paid and the free ad.

Here's a good tip for you. Rarely does an editor receive a thank you note for including the product in the publication as a free publicity release. Be sure to do this, letting him know your results. When I have had good results from an editorial, I'll call the publication, get the name of the mail order products editor, introduce myself, remind him of the product, and tell him about the response. I'll do this about four weeks after I have received my first order.

When I call, it invariably means I'm placing a paid ad in the magazine. That's what he likes to hear, and I've made a friend. I've been told many times that I'm the only one who has ever called to say, "Thank you." Don't forget, the editor is also curious to know the results and is pleased when he has picked a winner to publicize.

Most of the publications are in the East. Because of the time difference, I call before 8:00 A.M. Los Angeles time, which is 11:00 A.M. Eastern time. There's a special rate for direct calls at this time, so for $1 I've made myself a friend. I've been told more than once, "If you have anything else, send it in to me." Then the next time I send a publicity release, I include a personal letter to the editor. You may be sure my publicity release gets preferential consideration. Follow this technique and you'll find yourself with a minimal expenditure for advertising. I have received thousands of dollars worth of free publicity ads because I have taken a few minutes to thank the editor.

Let us assume your publicity releases have paid off, and you are now getting orders for your product. You want to determine if advertising the product would be worthwhile. Say the publicity release consisted of a one-column, four-inch space. Go back to the *Consumer Magazine and Farm Publications* and look up that magazine's rates for that amount of space. You can also write directly to the magazine and ask for their latest advertising rate card.

To illustrate, assume the ad costs $300 and you received 100 orders for a $10 product. Your cost in the mail is $5 each. Your gross is $1000 less $300 for the ad and $500 for the products, leaving you a profit of $200. You also have a good list of 100 customers to whom you can sell other products. You have a winner, so run the paid ad. Also try a similar publication. Be sure you key each ad. You might also want to experiment with the price of the product.

Don't look only at the $200 you made from the advertisement. It's also important for you to know how much each customer's name is worth in additional profits. Even if it's worth only $5 per name in profits from sale of other items and rental of names, that would give you another $500. This, added to the $200 from the ad, makes a total of $700 profit. If each name were actually worth more, so much the better.

If you have an inexpensive item, you might want to consider sending out a sample of it along with your publicity release. I always do this with my books, and I've done it with most of the products I have sold. You increase the probability of getting editorial mention.

PUBLICITY RELEASES TO TRADE PUBLICATIONS

When you have an exclusive on a product, you want to get the publicity releases not only in consumer magazines but in trade magazines as well. This is what I did with the latest horse book I published, *You and Your Pony* by Pepper Mainwaring Healey. See page 293. It contains the publicity release that was published in the January 1979 issue of *Tack 'n Togs Merchandising,* a trade publication for stores carrying horseback riding equipment, clothing, and accessories. The retailer circles the number 234 on a postage-free, business reply card included with the magazine. The magazine firm, in turn, sends us a computer read-out of the names and addresses of all those who circled our number.

I then send the retailer a free copy of the book, along with a dozen covers of my other horse books and an order form. In my accompanying letter, I tell him the book is free, and to test the saleability of the book I suggest that he display it on his counter, next to the cash register. He's delighted when he sells the $6 book which he received free of charge. It usually results in an order to me, and then I'm delighted. Taking this a step further, I send the names and addresses of the riding goods stores to my sales representatives.

The simple act of sending out some publicity releases with a sample of the book has brought me substantial sales for my entire line of 70 horse books. It adds names to our list of customers and gives our representatives excellent leads. All the buyers remember the free book, and it provides a good conversational opening.

TRANSLATING CALCULATOR

Read the publicity release on the translating calculator on page 21. It's perfect. If you have a unique product, call your local newspaper and ask to speak to the business editor. Tell him about your product, your company, and yourself, and perhaps he'll assign a reporter to cover the story. For out-of-town newspapers, you can send a publicity release, photograph, and an interesting story about your product. Also tell them about yourself. That, combined with the product, could make a good human interest story. The headline of the story might read: *Housewife with unusual product dreams of mail order riches. Part time mail order novice ready to strike it rich with unusual new product. Mail order beginner positive she'll find pot of gold with unique product.*

THE PET ROCK

Remember the pet rock craze? Gary Dahl is the gentleman who created the Pet Rock. He sold 1,000,000 of them without spending one cent on advertising. It was all done with a perfectly conceived publicity campaign. The Pet Rock sold for $4 because Gary Dahl wanted to make $1 on each sale. The first test of the Pet Rock came when it was exhibited at a gift show in San Francisco and then New York. In San Francisco he sold 3,000 units and in New York 1,500 units. His first big order came from Neiman-Marcus in Texas for 500 units. When that happened, he knew he had a winner. During the peak of the craze, he was selling 10,000 Pet Rocks per day.

Here's how Gary Dahl hit the $1,000,000 jackpot. He sent out press releases writing about the Pet Rock craze as an interesting phenomenon. He wrote about the Pet Rock as if it were an animate object, telling how much easier it was to keep than a dog or cat. That was his hook and, fortunately, it worked.

His publicity release was picked up by *Newsweek,* and in the November 10, 1975 issue they gave him almost a full-page write-up, including his picture. That did it!

Newsweek has a circulation of 17,973,000 readers. Following the publicity release in *Newsweek,* he was inundated with requests for interviews. He did 300 interviews on radio and TV, and had 1,400 stories written about him and the Pet Rock in newspapers and magazines around the world.

Isn't that an interesting story? I mean it when I say, "You, too, can get lucky and sell 1,000,000 units of a product." But it isn't luck that does it; it's being aware of all the channels for publicity and distribution and promoting your product accordingly.

A black-and-white page advertisement in *Newsweek* costs $29,275. That was the minimum value that Gary Dahl received for being aware of the fact that *Newsweek* and other magazines would find his story of interest. His success can be duplicated. Let's hope it happens to you.

GUINNESS BOOK OF WORLD RECORDS

After I had sold *The Willie Burgundy Five* album to MGM, Inc., Jimmy Bowen, president of the company, asked Tommy Boyce and me to write a song for Dean Martin as he was going to record an album of country-western songs.

We wrote a song, *San Antonio, Texas,* especially tailored for Dean Martin, made a demo of it, and presented it to Jimmy Bowen. Dean Martin loved the song and we were told it was going to be the single release from the album. What a stroke of good luck! The only problem was that weeks and months went by and Dean Martin never did record the album or the song.

Several years later, hearing that Snuff Garrett, one of Hollywood's top music producers, was going to record an album of country-western music, I sent him a demo and lead sheet of *San Antonio, Texas.* The same week I received a phone call saying he would like to record the song.

My first royalty check for the song was for four cents, representing the sale of two albums during a brief period. This struck me as being humorous, and I had the check laminated, framed, and hung it on my office wall. What a far cry from the tremendous royalty checks I had envisioned when Dean Martin was scheduled to record the song!

As I was writing this chapter, the thought came to me that I had probably received the world's smallest royalty check. Wouldn't it be fun to get into the *Guinness Book of World Records?* That was my challenge. I sent a photograph of the check and a letter explaining the small amount to the publisher of the book.

To my delight, a photograph of the check and write-up was included in the 1980 edition of the *Guinness Book of World Records.*

Do you realize that if my aunt in Miami Beach and one of my brothers in Boston hadn't purchased the album at that time, I never would have made the *Guinness Book of World Records*? Give yourself a challenge and go after it. It's creative, fun, and productive.

119510

CBS RECORDS
A Division of CBS Inc.
51 WEST 52 STREET
NEW YORK, N. Y. 10019
ROYALTY ACCOUNT

P
1-12
210

CHEMICAL BANK
ROCKEFELLER CENTER OFFICE
NEW YORK, NEW YORK 10019

PAY EXACTLY ************ DOLLARS AND 04 CENTS DATE 11 15 78 $ **********.04**

TO THE •
ORDER
OF
BOYCE & POWERS MUS ENT
T BOYCE & M POWERS E
12015 SHERMAN RD
NORTH HOLLYWOOD
CA 91605

COUNTERSIGNATURE REQUIRED $5000.00 AND OVER
Peter Washura

SMALLEST ROYALTY PAYMENT

Melvin Powers of Northridge, California, received this four-cent check as royalty payment for his song, *San Antonio, Texas*, which was included in the CBS Records album, *The Boys in the Bunkhouse.*

Chapter Fourteen

How to Make Your Advertising Copy Sizzle to Make You Wealthy

Good advertising copy is what makes mail order work. It is the most important element in your entire mail order campaign, even more important than the product itself. To be successful in the mail order business, you must become well versed either in writing good advertising copy or in being able to recognize good advertising copy. You, as the copywriter, must cultivate a vigorous curiosity about ads and what makes them successful.

Start saving mail order ads from magazines and newspapers. Keep a file of different types of ads, and when you write your own, review them. Study them carefully, trying to pick out the winning elements. I still save ads, and find it is important to do so in order to keep up with new trends, choice of words, layouts, typeface, headlines, coupons, illustrations, and guarantees. When I see a new ad, I automatically assess its chances of becoming a winner. Often, I see such glaring mistakes in the advertising copy, I instinctively know it won't sell. The advertiser must take the responsibility for the advertising copy. He can save himself thousands of dollars if he does some market research. Instead, he may become soured on mail order and its successful elements remain elusive.

Your library contains a large number of books on all phases of advertising. The lifeline of your business is to read them. Your enthusiasm for becoming knowledgeable in advertising will be reflected quickly in mail order dollars.

I have discussed the easiest way of writing advertising copy, which is to copycat the successful elements of various ads, particularly those bearing some relationship to your product. The copycat method will do as a start, but it's not the beginning and the end. I hope you can become as creative as possible. This will insure your chances of becoming successful. Imitation ads look exactly like what they are—imitation ads, and soon they lose the punch inherent in originality. The public is quick to recognize and shun imitation.

The consummate reward from creative writing is to come up with a winner. I recently wrote an advertisement based on copy and layout which had worked successfully for someone else. I knew I was using a winning ad, but I also knew it lacked my personal touch. I berated myself for not being as creative as I might be, discarded the copy, and started anew. I needed the creative challenge, and fortunately the new ad subsequently proved to be a real winner.

If, after a diligent effort, you find you don't have the flair for writing advertising copy, don't be reluctant to get professional help from someone else. I employ freelance copywriters all the time. My procedure is to give three copywriters the same assignment. I, too, write copy and select the best of all four ads to make up the new ad. I then have the three copywriters rework that composite ad. When, again, I incorporate the best of what the three have come up with, I have my final ad. I'll send a copy of all the material that has been written by everyone to all of the copywriters, so they can evaluate what I have done. They appreciate this practice of sharing, and it's a good learning experience. If one of the writers is still not satisfied with parts of the ad, we'll talk about it, and I may once again rewrite the advertising copy. It is at this point I'll conduct my market research, testing the ad. If I'm not getting favorable responses, I'll meet with my writers in my office and conduct a brainstorming session. Each writer, including myself, is assigned the task of improving the ad based on my findings. I'll go through the same process again, including market research. While this process might sound laborious to you, it does produce good results when, finally, I run the ad.

Another thing I do is live with the ad for a few weeks to see if I can possibly improve on it by changing a word, possibly a phrase, possibly a sentence. I'll then have everyone in my office read the copy and give me an opinion or reaction. We'll then jointly discuss the strong and weak points of the ad. It becomes another brainstorming session. It's a stimulating, creative, and enjoyable exercise. The fact I've spent a great deal of time on an ad never deters me from changing it again if we do not agree that the ad is just right.

THE SUCCESS FORMULA FOR WRITING YOUR DISPLAY AND DIRECT MAIL ADS

There are four requisites in writing the ad. They are:
1) Capture the reader's attention with an eye-catching headline.
2) Generate interest by persuasively describing the benefits of your product or service.
3) Stimulate desire with proof, testimonials, or a further explanation of the benefits.
4) Solicit orders, spelling out your guarantee.

YOUR HEADLINE—75% OF YOUR SUCCESSFUL AD

Your ad is competing with many ads in the same publication. To entice the potential customer to read your ad, something in it must capture his attention immediately. This is usually accomplished with a strong provocative phrase or a promise to the reader of some benefit he will enjoy.

If your headline is weak, the prospective customer is never going to read the rest of the ad. It's the first impression that counts. It's like meeting someone new. The body of your ad might contain the work of a genius, but if there is no punch to the headline, you've lost the order.

When you run your ads, test different headlines against each other. Continue to rework it until you know by the returns you've come up with a winner. You can do this in your magazine ads as well as with your direct mail. This is known as a split run. Assume the publication has a 200,000 circulation. Run 100,000 with one heading and another 100,000 with a different one. Be sure to change the key so you'll know which of the two headlines pulled better.

DETERMINING THE BEST PRICE FOR YOUR PRODUCT

By using the technique of split runs, you can also determine the best selling price for your product. Keep all the elements the same, except the price. In addition to determining which of the two prices is going to produce more orders, you want to know how much each name is worth for the back-end purchases and rental of names. You may

be wise to settle for less on the front end if the back end is so lucrative. This is the way the professional thinks, and it's the way I'd like you to start thinking.

SOME TIPS FOR WRITING GOOD BODY COPY

When you have momentarily captured the attention of the reader with a clever headline, he'll begin to read what your offer is all about. The first few paragraphs must sustain his interest or you will lose him. It's like the first 30 seconds of a song, or the teaser for a TV show. If it doesn't grab you at once, you'll turn to another station. One technique is to write in the first person, which will make your ad as personal as possible. This is the technique employed in the prize-winning ads of Joe Karbo, Mark Haroldsen, Ben Swarez, and Nancy Pryor. Each of their ads tells a personal story.

Make sure your grammar and spelling are correct. Your credibility will be tarnished if you make mistakes. Don't hesitate to seek help from an English or journalism teacher. Ask that the ad be rewritten, improving it as much as possible. If you can get an advertising agency to work with you, so much the better.

Describe clearly what the product or service is all about and the benefits to be derived from it. Elmer Wheeler, an expert in the field of selling, said, "Sell the sizzle and not the steak." Tell the reader in glowing terms what benefits can accrue to him in a personal way. This sales message is amplified in the article, *Mail Order Success Story Sells The Promise, Not the Product.* Read pages 288 through 295. Let the success story of Ulla and Harvey Rothschild be an inspiration to you. Here's a list of common desires: better health, wealth, personal power, sexual power, better physical appearance, better emotional feelings, personal magnetism, how to be more beautiful, live longer, save money, be your own boss, have a business of your own, make money in your spare time, win at the horse races, dice tables, or blackjack.

HOW TO LEND CREDIBILITY TO YOUR ADS

Do you have proof that what you are saying is true? If so, state it clearly. Do you have letters from satisfied customers? If so, use important excerpts or even the entire letter. Do not use the letter without written permission. You might want to use a photograph of the individual. Again, get written permission. Be sure to keep these letters on file. You might be questioned some day by the FTC (Federal Trade Commission), a governmental agency that monitors ads for proof of credibility. Have some of your statements notarized. If you don't have laudatory letters, simply write to your customers asking how they feel about your product. When you receive favorable letters, request permission to use them.

ASK FOR THE ORDER ALONG WITH THE GUARANTEE

State the guarantee clearly. These are good examples: "If you are not convinced these are the best, your money will be refunded without question." "I won't cash your check until 30 days after I have sent you your order." "If not completely satisfied within 30 days, write to me and I'll return your check." "365-day, money-back guarantee."

USE A NOTARY FOR YOUR CLAIM

Use a notary's seal in an ad when it is appropriate for purposes of authenticity. It can effectively support your claim. Use a statement from your bank manager, accountant, lawyer, or president of your local chamber of commerce if it will enhance the credibility of your ad. You can also show part of your income tax return, proving a point. Assume you were selling a real estate book. One of your statements might be: "I made $251,396 in real estate last year and I'm willing to share my secrets with you. In fact, I'm willing to prove it by showing you part of last year's income tax return."

THE USE OF FREE 800 TELEPHONE NUMBERS

You must test the usefulness of an 800 number yourself. There is a fee connected with the service, and it's up to you to determine whether it's worth the extra expense. The easiest way to find out is to place some split-run ads giving the 800 number. I favor the lines which read, "Call this free telephone number day or night, and place your order. Telephone operators are waiting for your call."

CALL FOR ACTION

Try to get the customer to order your product as soon as he finishes reading your ad. You might want to offer him an incentive, such as a free product, a reduced price for prompt action, or a courtesy reminder that the price is going up after a certain date. Among the more persuasive phrases calling for prompt action on the part of the customer are: "Act today for one of the best investments of your life." "Send for your order right now while you are thinking about it." "Don't put it off another day. Tomorrow may be too late." "Get your check book, fill in this coupon, and send off for the offer that can change your life."

COPYRIGHT YOUR PRIZE-WINNING ADS

If you think you have an ad with great pulling power, copyright it at once.

Secure form TX by writing to the United States Copyright Office, Library of Congress, Washington, D.C., 20559. The form is free. Fill it out and send it back with your check for $10, payable to the Register of Copyrights. Use of the copyright notice is the responsibility of the copyright owner and does not require advance permission from the Copyright Office. The required form of the notice for copies generally consists of three elements: (1) the symbol "©", or the word "Copyright", or the abbreviation "Copr.", (2) the year of first publication, and (3) the name of the owner of the copyright. For example: "Copyright 1980 by Melvin Powers."

CONTACTING AN ADVERTISING AGENCY

The easiest way to contact an advertising agency is through the Yellow Pages of your phone book. Ask the agency people if they have had any experience in handling mail order accounts. For a complete list of agencies, go to your main library and look at a copy of *Standard Directory of Advertising Agencies,* published by the National Register Publishing Co., Inc., 5201 Old Orchard Road, Skokie, Illinois 60077.

SET A GOAL FOR YOUR ADVERTISING

I like to set a goal for my ads. You should think about doing the same thing. It's an exhilarating experience to discover you have reached your goal, and even if you don't reach it, it's fun trying. Do you want your ad to bring in 50, 100, 200, 500 or 1,000 inquiries or orders? Set realistic goals that will result in success.

If you are not getting the results you anticipated, do some analyzing. Are you communicating your exact message through the ad? Is it persuasive? Does it have good selling copy? What is the mood created by the ad? Should you use an illustration, a better illustration, or no illustration at all? Have you accented the unique features of your product? Have you involved the reader? Is there a rhythm to your ad, or is it choppy? Do you have a good name for your product? Is the name easy to remember?

No one can write good pulling copy with every try. There are too many variables. It may be something inherent in the product, or it might be a matter of timing—the wrong time to advertise the product. If you keep writing and trying to improve your advertising copy, you'll eventually come up with success. However, I want to stress that if your ad is not pulling in orders, don't keep running it hoping for better results. Rewrite it or get some professional help with it; you are in business to sell your product. Admit it when your advertising copy is wrong and try to find out the reason. This will save money for you.

A LESSON IN IMPROVING ADS

Let us now direct our attention to the practice of analyzing ads for the purpose of improving the responses.

Imagine yourself a mail order advertising expert. Two clients have come to you for suggestions to improve the ads they are running. Although they are spending a great deal of money on ads, the orders are not coming in as they had anticipated. See pages 243 and 296. After you have carefully studied them, write down your suggestions. Now compare them with mine.

Let's talk first about the ad for the book, *How You Can Become Financially Independent by Investing in Real Estate*. This is an excellent book, now in its 10th printing, having sold 184,000 copies. The sales have been generated mainly by the author, Albert J. Lowry, through the Lowry Investment Seminars. The mail order ad, in my opinion, could be greatly improved. It has a poor headline, and I do not care for the illustration. The combination gives me the feeling of an absentee owner getting rich on tenants in slum dwellings. Who wants such a situation? Where's the pride of ownership? While it may be an attractive investment, the illustration conjures up too much of a negative response. I'll give you the perfect headline which is now being used as a subheading. On top of the ad, where it normally should appear, place these two sentences—ONCE I WAS A BUTCHER IN A SUPERMARKET. 7 YEARS LATER, I WAS RICH ENOUGH TO BUY THE SUPERMARKET. That sounds interesting. I'd fill up the space where the picture of the building appears with testimonials of people who have used the technique to accumulate wealth. I would also run the ad without the picture of the book. I'd rather intrigue the reader with advertising copy. I might even consider eliminating the coupon. While the two-week, free examination period sounds fine, I get the feeling of being rushed. What about a 30- or 60-day free examination period? I might even consider a one-year guarantee. That sounds like I'd have the opportunity to put the theories into practice.

And if you never follow a single one of my suggestions except this one, you'll have learned a very good point— get rid of the $9.95 price. Make it $10.00. It looks and sounds better. Don't let anyone tell you differently. I've sold millions of books all quoted at round figure prices. Can anyone prove to me that the sales would have been better if the books had been priced at $1.95, $2.95 or $9.95? The prize-winning ads we have discussed in this book all carry round figures of either $10 or $20, and that makes sense. The copywriters are experts in theory and practice.

Finally, the ad is like too many others I've read. It makes a good start, but then loses my interest. I'd like to see some figures showing the street addresses and prices of some buildings he actually purchased, and the sale prices after he renovated them. I'd like to hear more about his pride in doing this. I'd like to hear that because of his background and because of all the money he makes, he

sends 100 orphans to summer camp every year—if that were the case. It's a throw-away line that has impact. I have no idea how the ad pulled. I know I haven't seen it repeated in national publications, and that's a pretty good indication it might have needed the services of a new copywriter with a different perspective. This full-page ad ran in the *New York Times Book Review*. The cost for a one-time insertion is $5,950. I wonder how much market research was spent on this ad.

Now let's examine the ad on *Bobby Baldwin's Winning Poker Secrets*. Making the $9.95 price quote part of the headline concerns me. Sell the product first, and then tell me it's going to cost only $9.95. I'd use this headline: WORLD POKER CHAMP REVEALS WINNING SECRETS. Or, I MADE $379,000 IN POKER TOURNAMENTS IN TWO YEARS. I'M REVEALING, FOR THE FIRST TIME, MY POKER STRATEGY. Here's a headline we might consider: WINNING MONEY PLAYING POKER IS EASY IF YOU USE MY INFALLIBLE SAVVY. HERE'S HOW I MADE $379,000 IN POKER TOURNAMENTS IN ONLY TWO YEARS.

I dislike the advertising copy because it capitalizes on the mistakes of players, their bad habits and negative subconscious feelings. I would eliminate all the copy that refers to it. Instead, put more emphasis on the winning secrets that Bobby Baldwin gives you in his book and what this will mean to you—more money than you can spend. The ending of my last sentence gives me another good headline: BOBBY BALDWIN, WHO MADE $379,000 IN POKER TOURNAMENTS IN TWO YEARS, REVEALS HIS SECRETS ABOUT HOW TO MAKE MORE MONEY THAN YOU CAN SPEND! I'd buy that one.

Eliminate the subheading, *Everything Bobby Baldwin Knows About Poker, You Can Learn for Less Than $10*. It again stresses the wrong selling point. What about *I Made $210,000 Playing Poker in a Few Days. I'm Willing to Show You How I Did It*? That, too, would make a good headline.

The headline states the price of the book to be $9.95. The subheading says it costs less than $10. But when I get to the order form I discover it's actually going to cost me $9.95, plus $1.00 for postage, or a total of $10.95. Why not sell the book for $11.00, stating the price one time only? State the price of the book, sell the dream of riches and all that it is going to mean to the buyer.

The toll-free number comes too soon in the ad. First sell the reader on the proposal you are making. Then follow up with the toll-free number. I would also change the 30-day guarantee. Let's consider this guarantee: *Play 12 games of poker on me within one year. If you are not making more money than you dreamed possible, return the book for a full refund and your winnings are still yours. I'm willing to take the gamble. Are you? You have nothing to lose.*

Look at all the variations of type in the ad. The result is jarring, the copy is not easily read, and there is no rhythm to the ad. For argument's sake, let's assume the ad is making money. I'd still like to test it with my new copy ideas. I know the suggestions I've enumerated would result in more orders.

For practice, I suggest you do the same thing with various ads you come across. Study them as I have and rewrite them to incorporate the best parts. As you do this, you'll improve your copywriting ability. Feel free to send me the original ad, your criticism, and rewrites. I'd like very much to see them.

EVENING IN PARIS PERFUME

One of my objections to the ad on poker is it stressed the wrong elements. It didn't conjure in my mind an exciting picture of what would happen when I won all that money. There was no sizzle to it.

I previously spoke about a good product name. How do you like the name of the perfume *Evening in Paris*? Doesn't it immediately send you romantic messages? The name has style and sparkle. Any ad copy after that is bound to seem anticlimactic. If I were running the advertising campaign, I'd show only a beautiful picture of a couple in Paris at night, with the perfume bottle and name clearly identified in one corner. That would be it.

Do you want another campaign? How about this copy? *Put just one drop behind each ear. When he's with you, it will be like an evening in Paris.* Does it sound corny? Just think of the perfume ads that you see on TV or in magazines. They are all selling sexual fantasies. And doesn't that daring woman on TV selling perfume put a drop at the top of her cleavage!

The point I'm making is to sell the sizzle, the fantasy, the dream, and ego gratification. Use emotional appeal in your advertising, and incorporate subtle and not-so-subtle hidden persuaders.

HOW TO WRITE A HIT SONG AND SELL IT

See page 273. Here's your opportunity to criticize one of my ads. Do it for the fun and practice of it. Point out to me the weak and strong points. Tell me how to improve the ad. In what magazines and publications would you like to advertise the songwriting book? Would you prefer running a classified ad such as: Learn to write a hit song and sell it. Write to: Name and address? As you receive the inquiries, you will send the circular. Can you think of any mailing lists that you might appropriately use when sending the circulars?

JOSEPH SUGARMAN

The mail order expert who best exemplifies what we have been talking about in this chapter is Joseph Sugarman. He's a master when it comes to putting sizzle into his advertising copy, aimed primarily at selling electronic equipment and gift items. I refer to him as the man with the golden pen, because his creative advertising copy is directly responsible for generating $50,000,000 worth of sales a year. You can't do much better than that, although you can be sure his sales will surpass even that impressive figure.

Study his catalog as the perfect example of how to produce a prize catalog and use it in writing advertising copy. Study every ad and every page. It represents an amalgamation of perfection. If the cost of the catalog were $100, I'd still urge you to buy it. You just can't put a price on the mail order expertise that went into producing the Sugarman catalog.

I first met Joe Sugarman and saw his catalog when he attended a seminar for mail order experts last year in Los Angeles. He spoke eloquently at the seminar, sharing his mail order know-how. My first reaction to his catalog was what I might have experienced if I were looking at a Rembrandt. I needed nothing more than a cursory examination to know Joe had produced a masterpiece. The proof is in the $50,000,000 in sales it has generated.

Now read a write-up about him on pages 299, 300, and 301. He writes his own advertising copy and even does his own art work. Please note his initial mail order effort was a total failure, but that didn't stop him. He tested ten different mailing lists; two lists were profitable. His success came in continuing the mailing with those two lists. The article states that although Joe has an excellent sense of choosing merchandise, he excels in advertising it. That's the real secret of his success, and it should become your aim. His ads have no coupons. I'd like to see the results of his tests using split runs.

Isn't it gratifying to know that a man like Joe Sugarman, who does $50,000,000 a year in business with a profit of $5,000,000, will still take time out of his busy schedule to teach a mail order seminar? That's what I call responding to a creative challenge.

PERSONAL SATISFACTION FROM A WINNER

I'm sure you are beginning to discover mail order success doesn't happen in a haphazard way. Learning the business aspects of mail order is no different than learning the fundamentals and intricacies of any other business. Your challenge is to become familiar with them and turn them into a success. It's really not as difficult as it might at first appear. To help you in your pursuit of success, there is an abundance of informative books, magazines, courses, and experts on the subject.

Your initial task is to find a viable product for which you have genuine enthusiasm, and create saleable advertising copy for it. Mail order to me represents an extremely exciting business. I can hardly wait to see the results of each new offer. Every mail order campaign holds the promise of a gold strike. Sometimes, having put together all the elements for success, the strike does occur, and with it comes the wonderful feeling of elation and personal satisfaction that money can't buy.

MELVIN POWERS' PERSONAL CHALLENGE

Since we are approaching the end of the book, I want you to relax while I share with you a personal goal that I achieved.

My vocation is that of a book publisher. My avocation is that of a mail order consultant, selling not only books, but just about everything and anything that can be sold by mail order and direct mail. For as long as I can remember, I've been giving people advice on how to become a successful mail order entrepreneur, or how to enhance their business with mail order techniques.

In 1974, I published a book by Tommy Boyce, *How to Write A Hit Song and Sell It.* I was so intrigued with the manuscript and opportunities it presented for becoming a songwriter, I half-jokingly asked the author if he thought I could write a hit song. He was very encouraging and assured me writing music was no different from any other pursuit. It required study, application, and dedication. All I needed to know, he went on to tell me, was in his manuscript. If I were to study it and follow his instructions, there was no reason why I couldn't become a songwriter.

I was so taken with the idea I decided to devote most of my time to it. There was the added incentive of a chance to be on the selling end of a new creative endeavor. I wanted to see where it would take me. Suddenly, the idea of writing a hit song became a creative challenge to me, and I asked Tommy Boyce for his guidance.

As I became involved with songwriting on a full time basis, I soon realized it was very much like writing a good display ad. Both needed a good headline or title, and both needed good body copy, or lyrics, to grab and hold the reader's or listener's attention immediately. Could the reader or listener identify with it? As I have previously said in connection with writing advertising copy, make it personal whenever you can. So it is with songwriting.

My very first song, *Willie Burgundy,* was recorded by Teresa Brewer, and I got world-wide play on it. I also got a cover record by Diane Solomon in England. It was a stroke of good luck. My next song, *Mr. Songwriter,* was recorded by Sunday Sharpe on United Artists Records, and was on the charts for several months. I was euphoric listening to my songs on the radio. Being "an overnight success," I was deluged with requests from songwriters whom I met in songwriting classes I was taking, asking me to examine their lyrics and music. I could hardly believe what was happening.

It was at this point I took on the challenge of writing an award-winning, country-western song. During one of my brainstorming, songwriting sessions, I came up with the song title, *Who Wants a Slightly Used Woman?* I was using the same technique as in writing an ad. A good headline encourages me to write the ad. I never write the body copy until I'm satisfied with the headline.

I knew I had a hit song before I had written a single word of it. It's like instinctively knowing when you have a superb headline for an ad. Once you have that great headline, it's almost impossible to miss with the rest of the copy. I did my share of market research on just the title. Because of the words "slightly used," the feedback was so negative it reinforced my positive feelings I had something hot. Everyone asked what the song was all about. Their curiosity was piqued. I had even planned a campaign to subject radio stations to an onslaught of phone calls demanding that they stop playing the song because of the demeaning two words. No other songwriter would ever dream of doing a thing like that, but I figured it would stir up a great deal of controversy and get it played even more. It's like getting a book or play banned in Boston.

When Tommy and I finished writing the song, we sang it wherever we went. We always carried our guitars with us. The response was very favorable. We knew we had written a chart song. It was time to get it recorded.

Unfortunately, we signed a six-month contract for exclusive agency representation with a song promoter who assured us he personally knew every top female singer in Nashville and guaranteed ours would be the #1 song on the charts within a matter of weeks. What could be sweeter? Looking back, I wondered why we signed for six months.

Six months later we were still waiting! I knew I could sell the song if I went to Nashville and contacted the record companies and top singers. The day the contract expired, I decided before leaving for Nashville I'd use my mail order techniques to sell the song since it had worked in getting the song *Willie Burgundy* recorded. I sent a demo, a lead sheet, and a glowing cover letter to all of the artists and repertoire departments of every record company in Nashville. A week later, we hit two jackpots. The A & R department heads of two major record companies called me for permission to record *Who Wants a Slightly Used Woman?*

The song was recorded by Connie Cato on Capitol Records, went to #36 on the charts, and won an award for being one of the outstanding songs of the year. See pages 302 and 303. I'm including sheet music of *Who Wants a Slightly Used Woman?* and *Mr. Songwriter.* See pages 304 through 312. I hope you like the songs.

I became a successful songwriter using the rules that apply to writing good mail order copy. I sold some of my songs using direct mail techniques. Before I started writing songs, I had never given songwriting a thought. I followed the suggestions of a professional songwriter, took classes in songwriting and music, read all the books I could find on all phases of the subject, did my homework and assignments with enthusiasm, rewrote my songs when necessary, and applied myself to attaining the goal of writing some hit songs for the sheer pleasure and the creative challenge of it.

Basically, I'm encouraging you to do the same thing in the mail order field. I realize most of you cannot devote full time to developing a mail order business, so, for those of you who can't, get into it on a part-time basis and set realistic goals for yourself. Take classes in advertising, read the many books available to you at the library, be curious about successful mail order operations, start in a small way, and learn by your mistakes as well as your successes. One success will make you "an overnight expert." There's nothing mystical in becoming successful in any field of endeavor. All it takes is work and diligence. One day, success will come to you.

RECOMMENDED READING

How to Write A Good Advertisement by Victor O. Schwab
One of the very best books on the subject. Highly recommended. The book contains a short course in copywriting that can be adapted for your mail order advertising program.

The Compleat Copywriter by Hanley Norins
A comprehensive guide to all phases of advertising communication.

Advertising by Hugh G. Wales, Dwight L. Gentry & Max Wales
This is a self-teaching book that concentrates on the fundamentals of good advertising. It shows how copy, layout, and typography are combined to achieve a single effect in the successful advertisement.

Breakthrough Advertising by Gene Schwartz
Available at your library. Be sure to read it.

Tested Advertising Methods by John Caples
John Caples is the famed writer of the classic mail order ad, "They Laughed When I Sat Down at the Piano." This book is extremely worthwhile reading.

Systematic Approach to Advertising Creativity by Stephen Baker
Most behavioral psychologists say creativity is a basic skill rather than a unique gift bestowed on only a few. The author shows you how to acquire and develop your powers of creativity.

SUCCESS

Success is in the way you walk the
   paths of life each day;
It's in the little things you do and in
   the things you say.
Success is not in getting rich or rising
   high to fame;
It's not alone in winning goals which
   all men hope to claim.
Success is being big of heart and clean
   and broad of mind.
It's being faithful to your friends and,
   to the stranger, kind.
It's in the children whom you love
   and all they learn from you;
Success depends on character and
   everything you do.

"Reprinted from May 1979 ZIP. The Magazine of Effective Lists/Mailing/Fulfillment."

From Sore Feet to Comfortable Profits

Mail-Order Success Story Sells the Promise, Not the Product

Harvey Rothschild's mailing list of over 700,000 inquirers expands at the rate of 7000 a week. Its demographics are precise: most persons are over 50 years of age, have an average or better income, have admitted a need for relief from foot pain, are not hesitant to buy products by mail costing nearly $60—and more than 17% already do business with Harvey's company, Featherspring International Corporation.

Accumulation of the computerized list is a side benefit of a "second career" Harvey launched after retirement, all because his feet hurt while visiting Hamburg, Germany. In just over two years, the business has expanded out of Harvey's home and into a $5 million operation employing over 60 persons in an industrial park in Seattle, Wash. Featherspring International's promotional strategies now yield a 50% return on advertising investment.

To this direct marketing effort, Harvey and his wife, Ulla, apply many of the "piecework" principles learned in their former garment business. They have also applied the principles of mechanized paper handling offered to them by a trained mail systems specialist, who helped them *lower inquiry handling costs* from $1.80 to less than $1 each.

"The Miracle of Hamburg"

Direct mail success stories aren't all that rare, but Harvey Rothschild's is both fascinating and instructive. Closing his garment manufacturing plant after a heart attack, he wanted something to do. A Stanford Law School graduate, he thought it would be good to put his mind to work. So he went to Germany, his wife's home country, to learn the language. As he tells it in Featherspring International's ads: "It was the European trip I had always dreamed about. I had the time and money to go where I wanted—see what I wanted. But I soon learned that money and time don't mean much when your feet hurt too much to walk. After a few days of sightseeing, my feet were killing me."

While he was sitting in a language classroom, his instructor responded to Harvey's sore-feet laments by removing one of her shoes. She lifted out a support made of metal and plastic, and launched into a discourse in German of how comfortable it made her feet feel.

Fascinated, he decided to try a pair himself. Later he went to meet the manufacturer in Hamburg, requesting U.S. distribution rights.

"They almost laughed me out of the office when I said I would find a way to sell these supports by mail so they could manufacture customized orders for my customers in America," says Harvey.

There was also skepticism when Rothschild stated that he would offer customers a *money-back guarantee* if they were dissatisfied, and that he would allow customers to *make purchases on credit*.

Harvey applied his garment-background pattern experience to the task. He developed a sell-by-mail kit that included a cardboard device that could be moistened, covered with supplied carbon paper, and stepped on to record clear foot imprints. These impressions, along with a questionnaire completed by customers, are sent on to West Germany, where orthopedic technicians make individually customized, flexible Featherspring foot supports from specially-formulated Swedish steel.

Start-up Pains

Setting up shop out of his home in Seattle, Harvey went to work on

Harvey Rothschild and his wife Ulla, with a Featherspring foot support in one hand and dozens of testimonial letters in the other.

the marketing end. He contacted a local advertising agency, and they worked out a "technically correct" ad that was placed in local newspapers and selected magazines, aimed mostly at the over-50 audience. "Altogether, we put almost $100,000 into that advertising effort, and it almost bankrupted me," sighs Harvey. "If I knew then what I know now, I could have launched my business successfully on less than a third of that!"

The ad stressed the product, and asked for the order. It tried to do the entire selling job, and simply wasn't delivering enough orders to even pay for itself.

Harvey was almost ready to throw in the towel when he got a call from a satisfied customer, a New Yorker named Irv Spurling who happened to be a publisher's representative. "Your supports are out of this world," he told the Rothschilds, "but your advertising program stinks. You need a whole new approach!"

At that point, Harvey couldn't have agreed more. But what to do? Irv made a suggestion: there was a fresh young agency in the Chicago area, Fisher & Zivi, and an emerging hotshot there named Bud Fisher, fresh from a dynamite campaign that was selling thermal underwear by the bushel through the mails. The agency was small, flexible, and creative—and 95% of its business experience had been related to direct mail.

Harvey called Bud, and got him excited about the product and its potential. He patiently explained, though, that there wasn't much money left for testing and research—that whatever path was chosen would be the only (and perhaps final) effort. Bud scribbled down all the details, asked for a kit and copies of the previous advertising, and hung up.

Several weeks later, an ad layout appeared in Featherspring's mailbox. "Nice looking ad," said wife Ulla, "but it's hard to judge how effective it will be without seeing the copy." The layout showed a foot, obviously in pain, and bulls-eye areas with aches. The Rothschilds waited.

Another two weeks, and there

was a call from Fisher & Zivi: "We're booked into the regional *Wall Street Journal* in the midwest, and also the *National Observer* with a 210-line ad. You must have loved the copy, since we never heard back from you at all."

"What copy?" shot back Harvey; "you didn't send us any copy!" Somewhere between the Xerox machine and the envelope, the ad copy had gotten lost, and an ad carrying all the hopes (and most of the remaining bankroll) of Featherspring was running in two major publications.

The ad didn't try for anything except the attention and readership of people with recurring foot pain. Its tone was personal, almost folksy. It described the Featherspring foot supports, but didn't try to sell them. The headline: "My Feet Were Killing Me . . . Until I Discovered the Miracle of Hamburg!"

The strategy was to aim for large quantities of inquiries, and then to follow up with a complete "package" of information in the mail. Harvey was to prepare brochures, patterns, a detailed guarantee promising money back if not satisfied, and a three-page personalized letter (designed for word processing equipment) that spelled out what he was trying to do and how Featherspring could bring the "corrective comfort" that inquirers sought. It was basically a two-stage sale, with conversion being made through the mail follow-up.

"It sounded great to us over the telephone, but all we could do at *(continued)*

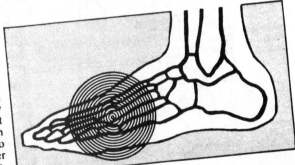

My Feet Were Killing Me ...Until I Discovered the Miracle of Hamburg!

It was the European trip I had always dreamed about. I had the time and money to go where I wanted—see what I wanted. But I soon learned that money and time don't mean much when your feet hurt too much to walk. After a few days of sightseeing my feet were killing me.

Oh, I tried to keep going. In Paris I limped through Notre Dame and along the Champs-Elysées. And I went up in the Eiffel Tower although I can't honestly say I remember the view. My feet were so tired and sore my whole body ached. While everybody else was having a great time, I was in my hotel room. I didn't even feel like sitting in a sidewalk cafe.

The whole trip was like that until I got to Hamburg, Germany. There, by accident, I happened to hear about an *exciting breakthrough for anyone who suffers from sore, aching feet and legs.*

This wonderful invention was a custom-made foot support called Flexible Featherspring. When I got a pair and slipped them into my shoes *my pain disappeared almost instantly.* The flexible shock absorbing support they gave my feet was like cradling them on a cushion of air. I could walk, stand, even run. The relief was truly a miracle. . . . . one pair was all I needed. I learned that . . . with sandals and open

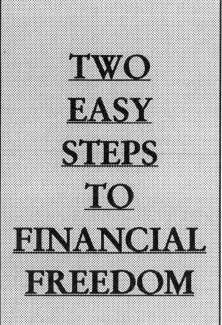
Direct Mail "Miracle" *(continued)*

A model 3166 six-station inserter with an on-line mailing machine is used to automatically insert and meter stamp the multi-part follow-up mailings that go out every three weeks to non-respondents.

that point was pray," recalls Ulla. They didn't have very much time for praying, though, because the mail started to roll in, and all those follow-up packages had to be prepared.

"I had read in a book on direct mail that it is common to overestimate the prospective customer's knowledge, and to underestimate his intelligence. I figured that the kind of people who had gone to the trouble to answer the ad would sit still for some in-depth information on feet and foot pain, so I researched the subject thoroughly, and put together a very complete package to help them understand the causes of their discomfort, and precisely what the Featherspring supports would do for them," he says.

With the help of this package, which originally cost a total of $1.80 each to process and mail, sales zoomed. Featherspring asked for only a small amount down with the order and the foot impression, with the balance of the $59.95 price to be paid upon receipt of the product. Installment payments were offered, too. In only a few months, sales blossomed from thirty supports a week to more than 1400!

Then a funny thing happened: people started sending in testimonial letters by the armload. Bartenders, beauticians, stewardesses, mailmen all wrote, telling the Rothschilds how much the supports had helped them. The letters were very personal and warm in tone.

"It occurred to me that we could improve the whole operation even more by utilizing some of this personal appeal," says Harvey. He and Bud Fisher wrote a new ad, using Harvey's picture and some of the testimonials. They placed test ads in *Parade, Family Weekly, Moneysworth, TV Guide, Travel*, and several other publications to assess the results against the proven "bullseye" approach.

The results were fast in coming: business picked up more than 15%.

"We were convinced from that point on that we could establish a unique and ongoing relationship with our customers," says Harvey. "We began to think in terms of making the customers into a secondary sales force." Ten thousand personalized letters were prepared for the list of satisfied buyers, asking them to share their new discovery with friends. For every set of foot supports that they helped sell, Featherspring would send them a check for $8. More than four thousand orders came back within just a few weeks!

Later testing found that a $5 offer worked just as well, and this type of pass-along has continued successfully up to the present. Also in the works is a whole line of foot-related products, to be sold by mail not only to satisfied customers, but to all of those who answered the ad. "These people all have one thing in common," notes Rothschild; "they all have problems with their feet, and they're by far my most likely prospects." Foot creams, scrubs, cleaning lotions, and related aids are formulated and packaged for Featherspring by a California lab, and are sold strictly by mail. The results to date have been very encouraging.

Ending Paperflow Pains

With inquiries growing, the Rothschilds knew that they had problems in the office. "Ulla and I found ourselves stuffing ad response materials by hand, trying to achieve a quick turnaround in responding to each inquiry we had received. That was certainly no way to retire from a heart attack!" exclaims Rothschild.

"As the number of inquiries grew, so did our problems with costs, speed of reply, and space to get all the work done in. We had developed a progressive bundling system (as I had set up when making dresses), with each job organized down into its basic component parts. Our staff was increased to meet the demand, and we could have kept on adding people and stockpiling more response materials endlessly. But that would simply have created even more storage and supervisory problems."

Harvey called on several mailing consultants, finally deciding to act on the suggestions of the Pitney Bowes expert, Gary Parsons, who reviewed the entire mailing and order-processing operation before making suggestions. Once Parsons could identify specific areas where mechanization could lower costs and expedite inquiry responses, he was able to make suggestions on new systems and equipment that exactly suited the operation. Since Parsons had been trained as a postal consultant as well as a systems analyst, he was able to foresee other problems that could be expected to emerge as the firm's operations grew, and he designed a "modular" system that allowed for orderly growth.

One example was the change to an electronic postage meter mailing machine that was faster and had a greater flow-through capacity than the previous equipment, which was only a desk-top model. (Later on, they added on a yet more powerful mailing machine, keeping the first one as a back-up.) In only a short *(continued)* while, workers had stopped hand-gathering and stuffing materials into envelopes: a high-speed, six-station Pitney-Bowes model 4166 inserting machine was put on-line to get the many different pieces required into the envelopes.

High-Volume Folding Machine

They decided to go with a high volume folding machine, too—PB's Model 1861. "The speed of the folder, plus the fact that its consistent accuracy meant fewer stoppages, were the deciding factors in our selecting it over other models," says Harvey. At the next stage, they also added a ten-bin collating machine and an on-line stapler, to help prepare the many versions of their multi-page, direct-mail letters.

From the beginning, the Roths-childs have found an electric mail opener indispensable to the handling of the flood of inquiries received every morning.

Harvey had learned in the garment business that if a machine is critical to an operation, it often pays to have two. That's because, with the bundle system, one person has to complete a job before another can handle it, and so on down the line. Now he has put in two folding machines and two postage meter machines for peace of mind and peak work-flow periods.

"The Pitney Bowes people showed us how to achieve the kind of paperwork system we wanted, and at the same time helped us cut our paper-handling costs almost in half by mechanization instead of handwork. Incidentally, even our postage meter works extra hard for us, with a meter ad carrying the sales message 'Treat your feet to comfort.'

"We could probably save more money if we did our *printing* in-house too, but that would require a large initial expenditure. I prefer to work with small printing firms, giving them large orders, so that they can buy paper in bulk, store it, and bill us only when a job is delivered," says Harvey.

Follow-up Yields More Orders

If there is no response from inquirers within 21 days after the information packet has been mailed, prospects receive another two-page letter to motivate them to place an order. The letter makes it very clear that Featherspring guarantees and stands behind its product. Along with this letter, the inserting machine stuffs a two-page summary of additional testimonials, along with a reply card in case a new set of foot-impression material is needed. The card also asks for referrals (others to whom material could be sent).

The second follow-up, surprisingly, pulls as well as the first, going out three weeks later. It is less than a page long, and reminds the reader that it has been two months since Harvey originally sent them material. The letter inquires if their foot problems still exist and, mentioning overseas inflation, advises them to order before prices increase. A testimonial sheet is included, but no reply card. The prospect has to *ask* for another order form by mail!

"We may use a third and fourth follow-up, and will soon have a fifth and sixth, each at 21-day intervals. We keep records on the efficiency of each follow-up letter, and will add them until they cease to be profitable," Harvey reports.

Ads Work for Seven Months

Advertising has been built up to about the $90,000-per-month level, yielding about 7000 inquiries a week. Data shows that an ad pulls best the first time it runs in a publication; the second and third time, inquiries drop somewhat, and they then level off by the fourth run. A good weekly magazine can pull con-

Promotional literature is in many forms: some of it is pre-printed at an outside shop; some is generated by the firm's own computer and word processing equipment; and other material comes from outside. The various "packages" are collated, stapled, and folded on this P-B machine.

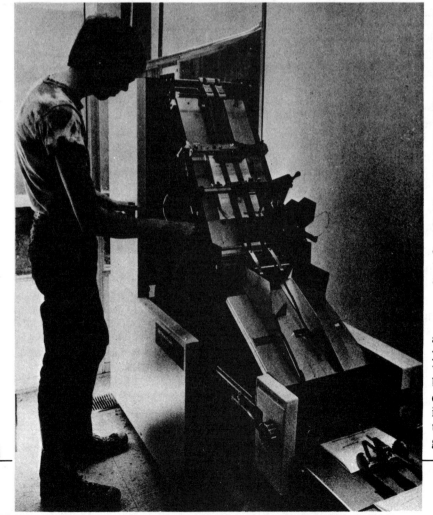

sistently for Featherspring if an ad runs only once a month.

Weekly newspaper supplements, over-the-counter publications like the *National Enquirer*, and several monthly consumer magazines are currently their main source of new leads. Other publications are considered and tested if they offer a demographic median age of 45 or more.

A Little Help From IBM

"Keeping track of this whole operation, and deciding when to send what to whom to optimize our sales and follow-up was just about driving us crazy," reflects Harvey. He started talking to computer professionals, and decided to install an IBM System 32 with a 13½ megabyte disk memory. "As soon as we got the bugs out, we realized that this was too small," he says, so a System 34 was immediately ordered, with more than twice the capacity. IBM trained Featherspring's own people to operate the computers, and directed them to a local software firm which wrote programs.

An experienced full-time computer operator was later added to the staff, and Featherspring continually finds new uses for its computer, including the printing of shipping labels and a tie-in to the above-mentioned word processing equipment. The machines now give weekly media analyses, administer the complete billing and follow-up programs, and generate accounts-receivable reports. Information on the sex, age, weight, and occupation of each customer and prospect is maintained in the files.

Featherspring has now begun mailing re-order offers to customers who want supports for other shoes. The mailing list also serves as a major resource for the possible marketing of other related products in the future.

But for now, thanks to a well-accepted product and a well-planned, smoothly running internal operation, Harvey and Ulla Rothschild are able to spend large chunks of time at their new vacation-retirement home in the Hawaiian Islands—with their shoes off, feet comfortably in the sand. ▭

Pony book

The Wilshire Book Co. publishes *You and Your Pony* for people interested in ponies. The publisher says the book covers the topic for beginners and experienced rider alike.

Circle No. 234 on ACTIONCARD

My Feet Were Killing Me...Until I Discovered the Miracle in Germany!

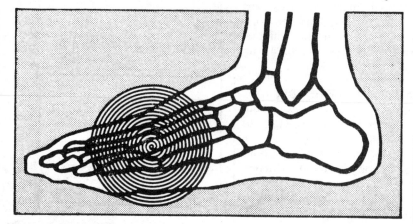

I was retired from business and traveling in Europe, but not enjoying it at all because my feet were killing me. I hurt all over. I guess God must have had his arms around me because almost by accident I found a device in Germany that gave me instant relief when I put them in my shoes. They were called Flexible Featherspring Foot Supports, and the flexible shock-absorbing support they gave my feet was like cradling them on a cushion of air. I could walk, stand, even run. The relief was truly a miracle. And just one pair was all I needed.

I was flabbergasted to find that they were only sold in Europe, so almost right then and there made arrangements to bring them to America.

Today thousands of Americans have found this blessed relief from foot problems just like V.W., of Cambridge, Maryland, who says: "*I am delighted with the supports. The second day I had them I wore them in three different pairs of shoes, from 7 A.M. to 10 P.M., which included two hours at a cocktail party. It's the first cocktail party I have left in years without wishing I could crawl out on my knees.*"

Here's why Feathersprings work for all of us and why they can work for you. These supports are different from any you may have seen before. They are custom fitted and made for your own feet. They actually imitate the youthful elastic support that nature originally intended your feet to have.

DOCTOR RECOMMENDED

Even doctors are amazed. As Dr. C.O.C., of Tucson, Arizona, wrote us: "*Received my wife's Feathersprings two days ago. They are super—neither of us can believe the results. She has had terrible feet for years; already no pain. Incidentally, her sore knee is better . . . as a retired physician, this result is amazing.*"

Maybe all this sounds too good to be true, but H.S.H., of Louisville, Kentucky, writes: "*I have checked your corporation with (A Consumer Protection Agency) and received an excellent report.*" And Mrs. E.G.C. wrote us and said: "*I didn't know such immediate relief could be obtained for the painful calluses on my foot. I've lived with that pain for years and was told by a podiatrist that foot surgery was the only proper course of treatment. I've been wearing your supports for* about two months, and I've not had even a twinge of pain from those calluses. Furthermore, they are shrinking in size and feel softer. I find I am able to stay on my feet for considerably longer periods of time, and I no longer have that 'tired' backache every evening. Thank you again for the vast improvement your product has made in my life.*"

NO RISK OFFER

If you're suffering pain with corns, calluses, old injuries, pain in the balls of your feet, burning nerve ends, painful ankles, backaches or just generally sore, aching feet, Flexible Feathersprings will bring you relief with every step you take or your money back without question if you are not completely satisfied.

Don't suffer pain and discomfort needlessly. If your feet hurt, we can help you.

Write for more detailed information; there is no obligation whatsoever. A Canadian, Mr. J.K., of Ontario, said: "*I'm glad I did try them for they proved to be everything you claimed them to be.*"

Just fill out the coupon below and mail it today—like Mr. J.K., you'll be glad you did!

It's mail-order music lessons

By SEAN M. GRADY
Daily Press Business Writer

APPLE VALLEY — The idea of getting music through the mail usually extends just to records, tapes and compact disks ordered from television ads or record clubs.

It normally is not connected with learning how to play an instrument, and much less with learning to do so in one day. But Eddie Star, an Apple Valley musician who has been teaching guitar, piano and other instruments by mail, has found it to be better in some ways than using the traditional approach.

Star offers a series of instruction books and recorded tapes, which he sells to beginners who want to play the piano, as well as to professional musicians who want to break out of a creative rut.

Though private music lessons generally are one-on-one affairs with students and teachers in the same room, Star said he has not run into any problems with students learning from his mailed instructions.

"I have found that these mail order tapes are amazing things. The students can keep playing them over as much as they need," Star said. Thus, they can repeat a lesson as many times as they want, something that would be more difficult in person.

And students do not have to worry about missing lessons or driving out of their way to get to a teacher's house, Star said.

Star's books and cassettes include such topics as "How to Write and Play Beautiful Music in One Evening," a beginning lesson, and "The Art of Guitar Improvisation," for more advanced musicians.

Star also will be offering a correspondence course called "Stars in Progress," where students will be able to send him taped "homework" for his critiques.

SUSAN D. PRICE / Daily Press

Eddie Star poses in his Apple Valley home after discussing his new mail-order music lesson system.

Unfortunately, the business is not all pleasure for Star.

Not all musicians who go into the mail order business stay in it, Star said.

"A lot of them go into it thinking they can make a quick buck, but it's usually not there. It's a business, and it takes a lot of hard work."

He not only has to keep track of what materials need to be mailed and who has paid their bills, but he also has to respond to the "Stars in Progress" homework tapes, listening to his students' lessons and answering any questions they have.

Though he has been a music teacher for more than two decades, he did not start working on his mail order business until roughly two years ago, after he had devised his own teaching system.

He based his work on that of Joseph Schillinger, a mid-20th century academician who studied music as a mathematical problem.

"Schillinger was a Da Vinci of our time, who applied mathematics and science to music," Star said.

Star incorporated Schillinger's system and others in his lessons, which he feels allows his students to grasp the fundamentals of music more easily than more traditional teaching methods.

"They learn that the chord tones are the most important parts of the melody," Star said. They then learn how to combine different chords — groups of notes that harmonize — in new patterns, and thus to come up with their own melodies.

Star said he is looking more for creativity in his students, rather than for the ability to follow rules or notes on a page. And most of his lessons involve learning to play by ear.

"Creativity moves me. It's like a flower opening up," he said.

Star and his wife, Lynn, moved to California two years ago from Minnesota, where he taught music at the college level.

He and his wife eventually settled down in Apple Valley for its slower pace and wide-open spaces. "I know some people like living in the big city, but that lifestyle is just not for us," Star said.

When he decided to start up his business, he had help from Lynn, who had owned a Christian gift and book store in Minnesota.

Star's students include judges and music professors, with ages ranging from 16 to 70 years old. "It's wonderful. You get to meet people from all over the United States," he said.

When he is not teaching, either in his Apple Valley home or through the mail, Star performs at the Spring Valley Lake Country Club or for smaller groups, like the Desert Knolls Convalescent Hospital.

But while he enjoys that part of his work, Star said he likes teaching the best. "I think that if I did not have the ability to teach, I would not enjoy music as much," he said.

For further information, write or call:

Eddie Star
P.O. Box 1957
Helendale, California 92342

Telephone: (619) 952-1071

A single pair of sunglasses makes a whole company shine

NORTHBROOK, ILL.—Thanks to a pair of sunglasses, things are looking a lot sunnier for the JS&A Group these days.

As travelers might know from reading its direct response ads in airline magazines and other media, cataloger and mail order specialist JS&A Group switched its emphasis four years ago to the fitness market.

But since discovering the appeal of BluBlocker sunglasses, they have become the star attraction in the company's health and vitality product lines, according to Joseph Sugarman, president and CEO.

"It all started," he says, "when I was driving in Los Angeles with a man who said, 'Joe, you should try these glasses—it makes things appear clearer and sharper.' I tried on the pair and was amazed."

He was so impressed he tracked down the manufacturer and did a direct response ad to run in some consumer magazines and his own catalog. "The results were so good that I decided to do two things—make the sunglasses myself in Taiwan and conduct one of the biggest ad campaigns in the history of sunglasses," Sugarman says.

The ad he created was called "Vision Breakthrough" and it dealt with BluBlocker sunglasses whose lenses block blue light." I wrote that when

you block blue light, your vision improves, you can see clearer and further and you protect yourself from the sun's dangerous ultraviolet light," Sugarman says.

The ad ran in his own catalog and he used it in direct mailings. Over six months, more than 100,000 pairs were sold—a nice piece of business since the glasses are priced at $60 a pair.

Once he decided to concentrate on BluBlockers, Sugarman looked for an advertising medium that could combine his penchant for showmanship and long-winded sales messages. "I had never considered TV because I use long copy to sell my products and television was not a good medium because I could never do a proper selling job in just a minute or two," he says.

That is until he discovered the half-hour infomercial.

It was appealing, he says, because he could get national television exposure on cable TV, as well as some local broadcast stations. And he'd have enough time to entertain the audience while delivering his commercial messages.

Sugarman's first effort was billed as a consumer information show. It ran for a year and a half. It didn't win any Emmys, but it did sell 100,000 pairs of glasses in a month—or six times faster than his magazine ad cam-

paign had.

No wonder the half-hour commercial became his favorite medium. After the initial show had run its course, Sugarman created a new one called "The making of a national commercial," with a new show host.

What he needed next, he reasoned, was a new product feature to exploit. "That's when we came up with a new idea for a pair of sunglasses that lets you see behind you," he says.

Hollywood got wind of the product and BluBlocker was asked to make futuristic sunglasses for "Back to the Future II," a movie set in the year 2015.

"When we learned that Pizza Hut was also going to be seen in the movie," Sugarman says, "we got permission to pitch them on doing a continuity program where BluBlocker glasses would be sold at a discount to customers who bought a pizza in their restaurants."

The point-of-sale promotion in the pizza stores advertised the glasses as, "Seen in the movie, Back to the Future."

Pizza Hut tested the idea, loved the results, and wound up ordering 10 million pairs for their stores worldwide. It was the single biggest sunglasses order in sunglasses business history, Sugarman claims.

The eloquent Joe Sugarman sold more than 100,000 sunglasses in a month via a 30-minute infommercial.

Currently, Sugarman says, the company is spending about 80 percent of its advertising budget on television, and most of that on local cable TV.

When asked if shrinking availability of time slots for half-hours, particularly on the cable networks, is causing any problems, he says, "It always has." But it hasn't deterred him, either. "We create a new half-hour commercial every year," he says, and they continue to star BluBlockers as seen through the eyes of on-camera personality, Joe Sugarman. ∎

Sunglass
ILLUSTRATED

BluBlockers go gold—page 15.
Lenses tougher than a speeding bullet—page 19.
Sunglasses follow the rainbow—page 5.

products that think.

Intelligent robots that understand English and toys that talk back. A revolution in electronics is about to hit the consumer market.

by Martin Sheridan

As chief guru of the consumer electronics industry, JS&A's Sugarman unveils his extensive line of new consumer products.

Are you lucky! What is about to invade the American marketplace will provide more conveniences and more excitement than in any other period in our history.

Remember the small integrated circuit (IC) that made pocket calculators and digital watches possible? That same IC will provide a new series of miracle products that sound almost too incredible to believe.

Imagine talking to your typewriter and having it recognize your voice and type out what you say. The teaching machine shown on page one of this supplement is the first step in this direction. Called "Speak and Spell," it contains two-hundred-thirty of the most frequently misspelled words in order of difficulty.

Speak and Spell asks you to spell a word which it clearly pronounces. As an example, let us use the word "language." You enter the letters of that word, and as you do so, the unit pronounces those letters. When you finish the spelling, you press a button, and if you are right, the unit says, "That is correct. Now spell 'treasure.'"

Had you spelled the word wrong, the unit would have said, "Wrong. Try again," and you would have had a second chance. If you spelled it wrong the second time, the unit would have said "Wrong again. The correct spelling is L-A-N-G-U-A-G-E."

The teaching machine uses two newly developed memory devices called 256K ROMs, which is the equivalent of five hundred thousand transistors — almost impossible to imagine.

Texas Instruments recorded a professional announcer's voice to pronounce and spell all the words and letters used in the unit. These sounds were converted to digital information and stored on the two 256K ROMs. The digital information is converted into audible speech patterns through the use of an integrated circuit synthesizer and then amplified through a speaker. There are no strings to pull, no tapes to wear out, no records to replace. The entire system is solid state and as dependable as today's pocket calculators.

Once you develop a system of producing sounds from IC's, the next step is to recognize sounds.

Within a few years products will be developed with powerful memories that will use this technology to recognize complete words, letters and even entire dictionaries and then type out these words as you talk. It will recognize accents, differentiate between words that sound the same and make hyphenation decisions.

The next logical step will be robots that recognize not only words but phrases as well, and then respond to commands. And the incredible part is that the technology is here — now. It's just a matter of time before the IC's become even more powerful and the applications expand.

OTHER EXCITING PRODUCTS

The future looks exciting, but consider what is in store for us this year.

A language computer that translates seven thousand words, enables you to carry on complete conversations without ever speaking a language and fits in your pocket.

A television so small it actually fits in your pocket.

An electronic system that controls all the electrical appliances and lights in your home — and can be carried in your pocket.

And the list goes on.

The prime mover in marketing these exciting consumer products is a Northbrook, Illinois, company called JS&A. Started just eight years ago, the firm has pioneered the introduction of the calculator, digital watch, plus a multitude of other space-age products.

JS&A doesn't manufacture anything. It is strictly a marketing organization that translates this new, complicated technology into understandable advertisements that appear regularly in the *Wall Street Journal*, *Popular Science*, *Scientific American* and hundreds of other U.S. publications including these inflight magazines.

"There is no company in the United States more responsible for the advancement of recent electronic technology than JS&A," says Bernard Gittelson, an electronics industry consultant. "The firm has started more trends and successfully introduced more new products than many of the large consumer electronic manufacturers."

Indeed, JS&A has been a major factor in modern consumer electronics. Even more incredible is the JS&A story.

HUMBLE BEGINNINGS

JS&A now occupies two modern buildings on a tract of land twenty miles north of Chicago. Their advertisements reach sixty million people each month, and their annual sales volume (which they keep confidential) is rumored to be approaching $50 million.

JS&A is the brainchild of a former advertising man, college drop-out and ex-CIA agent, Joseph Sugarman, forty, who started the business in the basement of his home.

"I was reading a copy of *Business Week* and noticed that a manufacturer was reducing the size and cost of electronic calculators so they would fit in your pocket and cost only $240," reminisces Sugarman.

"At that time I was in the advertising business, and one of my accounts was a consumer electronics mail-order company. I presented the idea of having them sell the electronic calculator, but they rejected it. They claimed it was too costly, too new and besides, they said it was impossible to sell a $240 electronic item through the mail."

Sugarman refused to abandon the idea. He felt that with his own advertising ability, personal confidence and faith in the product, he couldn't help but succeed. So he contacted the manufacturer, Craig Corporation, who dispatched their local sales representative to call on him.

Sugarman bought his first sample and created a direct mail piece for a national mailing. "I couldn't afford to send the mailing out," he says, "so I called a few of my friends to chip in $12,000 to help me.

"The financial arrangement offered them was simple. They would double their investment before I made a penny on the deal. As soon as they got their money back, I was free to continue on my own."

So Sugarman put together a beautiful full-color mailing piece, rented fifty thousand names from a mailing list broker, and sat back to wait for the big response, which was slow in coming and far below what he had hoped for. In fact, he experienced a nearly total failure.

"I was told to look for a 2 percent response from my mailing," Sugarman recalls. "That was a typical direct mail response rate, according to the experts. All I needed was two-tenths of 1 percent to break even, so I thought I was really on my way to making a fortune.

"Imagine my disappointment when I lost most of the money and had to face my investors with the bad news. But I did one thing right. I had tested ten different mailing lists and coded the response cards to let me know which lists did the best.

"Two of the lists did well enough to make a profit, but the others were such disasters, I lost my shirt."

But Sugarman didn't give up. He went back to his investors and urged them to stay in the program. "I told them about the results and the fact that the price of our calculator was dropping to $180. I was convinced that we would do well with a new mailing to a proven list of prospects at this lower price."

The investors stayed in, and when the results of the second mailing were in, Sugarman and his group had realized a nice profit.

"I now had my own business," Sugarman explains, "but I realized that with calculator prices dropping so fast, I couldn't continue to send out mailing pieces. By the time I would receive my first orders, the cost of the calculator would be much lower."

So Sugarman took out a large mail order advertisement in the *Wall Street Journal* and featured his Craig calculator. Within a week, he had sold as many calculators as he had in his entire direct mail campaign. "I couldn't believe the response," he recalls. "It was more than I thought I deserved."

That first mail-order ad convinced Sugarman to concentrate on what he calls "print mail-order advertising."

In the eight years since he started, Sugarman has gained the respect of the advertising community, the entire electronics industry and even the retailing giants like Sears, Wards and Radio Shack.

"When Joe starts on a campaign for one of his new products, it doesn't take long be-fore Sears, Wards and retailers across the country start clamoring for it," says Gary Braver, a Chicago area manufacturers' representative. "He has started major trends and has been credited with the creation of industries almost overnight."

Indeed, Sugarman has been responsible for many electronics fads. When Bally Manufacturing couldn't get any distributor or major retail chain to buy its consumer pinball game, the Northbrook, Illinois, direct marketer created a mail order ad for the product that shattered all mail-order traditions. Nobody had ever sold such an expensive and large item through the mail.

When Sears and Wards saw the JS&A ads, they hopped on the bandwagon, too. Soon there were no less than six manufacturers entering the pinball business. "He's put our name in front of the consumer like nobody else has," reports Ross Scheer, marketing director for Bally.

"My real competitors are Sears and Wards," says Sugarman, "not because they're selling the same customers, but because they're always competing with me for new products at the manufacturers' level."

One of Sugarman's secrets to success is his keen ability to spot a potentially hot product, jump on it and single-handedly make it a huge success.

"We are pioneers. We create trends," he boasts. "If there is one thing I'm proud of, it's that we have called the shots in mic-. roelectronics since we started. Sears, Wards and Radio Shack keep a close eye on everything we do."

The *Wall Street Journal*, in a front-page article on Sugarman, noted that the giant mass merchandisers often follow his lead. When Sugarman began selling the Brearley Company's scale, for example, both Sears and Wards were pleading for it within a few months.

The big retailers agree that he is a powerful force, but some don't like to admit it. "Sugarman's success or lack of success doesn't guarantee our success or lack of success," says Bernard Appel, vice-president of Radio Shack, a unit of Tandy Corporation. "His decision to sell a product is *a* factor, but not *the* factor in determining whether Radio Shack will stock a product."

Al Barsimanto, national sales manager at Midex Corporation, contends that Sugarman has more than the Midas touch when it comes to picking winners. "He's an institution. We couldn't sell our burglar alarm system in a mail order campaign until he took hold of it. Now JS&A protects more homes than any other security company in the country."

As good as he is in choosing merchandise, Sugarman may be even better at advertising it. He writes his own copy, sets his own type and does his own artwork.

His advertising breaks many of the normal mail-order traditions. His ads have no coupons. They have a great deal of text and very clearly explain complicated products to the consumer with no big hype or exaggerations.

According to Cecil C. Hoge, Sr., a mail-order consultant, "Joe Sugarman has married space-age science to mail-order. He has become a bit of a space-age Sears in pioneering mail-order methods, a Thomas Edison in introducing electronic products, a P. T. Barnum in his flair for public relations. In eight short years he has introduced one breakthrough product after another and scored several major breakthroughs in mail-order selling."

Robert Silverman, president of the Cleveland Direct Marketing Club, referred to Sugarman in a recent speech, "Joe represents everything good about mail-order. He's honest, he services his customers, he's a true entrepreneur, he has innovated and contributed to his industry and he represents the true American dream."

Robert Stone of Stone and Adler, a large direct marketing firm, calls Sugarman "the new breed of mail-order entrepreneur."

Sugarman claims that he wouldn't be where he is today if it weren't for his very capable staff. His executive vice-president, Mary Stanke, remarked, "Mr. Sugarman handles the creative aspects of the company, but he's left everything else for me to handle."

As his top executive, Stanke has four managers reporting to her and plays a major role in screening products. "We run a well-disciplined operation here. Everybody is referred to by his last name, and we are probably fifty of the most productive

Manufacturers look to JS&A to introduce their products first. Shown here are two ITT representatives presenting Sugarman their various telephone products.

people you'll find in any company," says Stanke.

"We know that a few mail-order companies don't answer correspondence unless it might mean a sale. Our policy is to answer everything and respect customers as if they were the single most important asset of our company. And they are," she emphasizes.

FAILURES TOO

Not all JS&A ads are successful. In 1975 Sugarman thought he could create a fad around a Mickey Mouse calculator. In the end, he was stuck with five thousand unsold units. During the same year he also lost $250,000 promoting a checkbook calculator that bombed.

More recently, he lost money on his $1,500 Laser Beam Mousetrap which was targeted towards top executives. "It will go nicely in any office, boardroom or rodent-infested area," the ad proclaimed. He didn't sell one.

$2,000 SEMINAR

Despite his early failures, Sugarman continues to roll up success after success. In 1977, he decided to capitalize on this success and conduct a seminar to disclose the secrets of his unorthodox style of advertising. He charges each participant $2,000 to attend a five-day course, which he holds at his large lakeside estate in Northern Wisconsin.

The demand to attend his first seminar was so great, he had to hold three additional ones shortly after the first. The participants have all expressed great enthusiasm for the sessions.

Harvey Cinamon, an advertising agency president, stated, "I have attended many seminars during my thirty years in the advertising, direct mail and promotion business, but never have I come away from any seminar with the degree of enthusiasm and the feeling of having gained as much as I did from Joe's."

Richard Viguerie, the famous political fund raiser, was quoted recently in *Forbes Magazine* as saying, "Joe has some unorthodox marketing approaches, but they work." Viguerie was a student at Sugarman's first seminar.

Sugarman claims that his seminar produces real winners. "I've had individuals attend from companies that could never make advertising work for them, let alone mail-order. After my course, they succeeded even beyond my expectations."

In his space advertisements for the seminar, Sugarman lists several success stories that resulted from attending the seminar. And the list of endorsements in the ad reads like a "who's who" of the top people already in the mail-order industry. "Joe's an incredible guy," says Joe Karbo, a successful mail-order entrepreneur even before he attended the seminar. "I learned a tremendous amount from just being around him for five days."

His students have come from as far away as New Zealand, Australia, Germany and Monaco. They've included individuals from large corporations like Atlantic Richfield to advertising agency executives interested in Sugarman's unique advertising philosophies.

SPACE-AGE IMAGE

Sugarman lives the image that his products represent — space-age technol-

Sugarman writes his own copy, sets his own type and does his own artwork in his well-equipped art studio.

ogy. He flies a twin-engine Aerostar with a $70,000 onboard navigational computer. He's a ham radio operator with a one-thousand-watt station and one-hundred-foot telescoping antenna. His company processes orders using the latest in state-of-the-art computer and microfilm technologies.

He is also an accomplished speaker and was recently selected as one of the top speakers at the International Platform Speakers Association Convention in Washington.

His number one philosophy is honesty. "If there is one very powerful force that has made our company successful, it is my insistence on honesty throughout our entire organization," he says.

COPY CATS

There are many companies trying to copy JS&A's style and techniques, but Sugarman remains quite calm about it. "Competition is good," he says, "as long as it's fair. I'm always concerned about an unknown mail-order company cheating one of my customers. That customer may not want to buy through the mail again from me, even though we treated him properly."

Sugarman has seen too many companies come and go. "There isn't one electronics mail-order company still in business that was around when we started, and I've counted twenty-three that have already disappeared. Selling microelectronic products through the mail is a difficult job requiring a great deal of customer service. We really work at it and are proud of our efforts."

FEW COMPLAINTS REPORTED

JS&A advertises constantly in the *Wall Street Journal,* where Robert Higgins is the executive in charge of product acceptance and investigation of any complaints about advertised products. When readers are dissatisfied they may complain about quality, failure to ship, late shipments, exaggerated claims or for other reasons. Competitors are usually the first to point out errors on claims.

Higgins does not recall a single complaint from a reader, whether user or competitor, regarding JS&A advertising claims — competitive or otherwise. Higgins also ranks JS&A high on its performance in handling customers.

JS&A'S FUTURE

What about the future? The world of microelectronics has grown so rapidly that Sugarman can hardly keep up with the new products he advertises. He has published a catalog called "Products That Think" and is selling the fifty-two-page, full-color, magazine-type publication for $1.00 through the mail.

The catalog contains all the latest developments in microelectronics and has become the bible of what's happening in the electronics industry.

"I don't consider my catalog a catalog," says Sugarman. "It's really a magazine. There are a lot of pages in the publication that don't sell products but are there to paint a picture of the microelectronic revolution. In our current issue we even reprinted our Laser Beam Mousetrap ad—the one that didn't produce a single sale — just to show that we do have failures."

Several of JS&A's advertisements, which appear quite often in this publication, follow on the succeeding pages. The company usually runs these advertisements throughout the issue; however, this month we have included some of them in this article. They are paid advertisements.

What's in store for JS&A's future? "Plenty," according to Sugarman. "Our customers will be part of a new elite group which will hear about new products before they are presented to the general public. To accomplish this, we are initiating a direct-mail campaign to keep our customers informed and we will also be expanding our catalog.

"The space-age product revolution is indeed a revolution. More exciting products are coming our way now than at any other time in our history, and the future will only dazzle the imagination."

If Sugarman is right, JS&A is indeed the company to watch.

ABOUT THE AUTHOR
MARTIN SHERIDAN

Martin Sheridan has been associated with the consumer electronics industry for over twenty years. He was formerly vice-president of Admiral Corporation, a consultant to the Consumer Electronics Shows, author of two books and contributor to over two hundred and fifty publications. He was also a Boston Globe war correspondent during World War II.

AMERICAN SOCIETY OF COMPOSERS, AUTHORS AND PUBLISHERS

TWO MUSIC SQUARE WEST

NASHVILLE, TENNESSEE 37203

OFFICE OF
REGIONAL EXECUTIVE DIRECTOR

September 20, 1976

Dear Melvin:

Congratulations

On behalf of President Stanley Adams and the American Society of Composers, Authors and Publishers, we are pleased to announce that you will be a recipient of a 1976 Country Award for:

WHO WANTS A SLIGHTLY USED WOMAN

As you may know, awards are made annually in Nashville by the Society to those songs which have sustained chart action in the trades. They will be presented to all who have had a part in the hit song, including the songwriter, publisher, producer, and artist.

On Wednesday, October 13, the Awards Dinner will be held at the Armory with cocktails at half after six and dinner at eight. We sincerely hope you will be able to attend; however, if you are unable to accept in person, your award will be forwarded to you. No substitutes, please.

Best wishes and appreciation.

Cordially,

Edward J. Shea

Mr. Melvin Powers
12015 Sherman Road
North Hollywood, Calif.

Who Wants A Slightly Used Woman?

Words and Music by TOMMY BOYCE and MELVIN POWERS

Recorded by CONNIE CATO on CAPITOL Records

BOYCE & POWERS MUSIC ENTERPRISES/ADVENTURE MUSIC

No. Hollywood, California

Distributed by

$1.50

WHO WANTS A SLIGHTLY USED WOMAN?

Words and Music by
TOMMY BOYCE
MELVIN POWERS

To - day my di - vorce ___ be - came fi - nal.

Sev - en years ___ of my life ___ have slipped a -

way. And would you be - lieve it

2342 - 4

wom - an? _____ With a dar - ling, blue-eyed daugh-ter { by her _____
{ named Su

side. _____ I can cook and I can sew _____ and I'm still full of
zanne. _____

lov - in', _____ So tell me _____ who wants a

slight - ly used { bride. _____
{ wom - an. _____

1.

In my

2.

MR. SONG WRITER

Words and Music by TOMMY BOYCE • MELVIN POWERS

Recorded by SUNDAY SHARPE on UNITED ARTISTS Records

'S MUSIC CO., INC. /
ERS MUSIC ENTERPRISES
W YORK. N.Y.

$1.50
Distributed
by
big3

MR. SONG WRITER

Words and Music by
TOMMY BOYCE
MELVIN POWERS

With words soft and sweet and a phrase hid-den deep say-ing I love you. I'll sing it to a man I know, a man that I've been lov - ing so, I want to tell him how much, how much he means to me. You can make my life

2. Mister Song Writer, oh, Mister Song Writer,
   Won't you teach me to write a pretty love song with sweet country rhyme.
   A verse with lots of pretty words, words only you and I have heard,
   So when I bring it to my love and sing it he'll want me all of the time.
   I'm hoping he'll understand, I want him to be my good lovin' man,
   I want to tell him how much, how much he means to me.
   Mister Song Writer, you can make my life brighter,
   If you teach me to write a love song the way that you do.

Chapter Fifteen

Questions and Answers to Help You Get Started Making Money in Your Own Mail Order Business

Before publishing this book, I gave copies of the manuscript to many of my mail order students for their criticism and questions. This was done to further ensure the book would encompass a comprehensive treatment of the subject. The following represents a cross-section of the most commonly asked questions:

Question: Do I need an office?
Answer: No. Conduct your business from your home until the volume dictates the practicality of moving into your first business quarters. You want to keep your overhead to a minimum.

Question: How do I know how much inventory to order?
Answer: Initially, whenever possible, make arrangements to drop-ship your merchandise to your customers until you can estimate how much inventory to carry. Assume you decide to sell a unique watch. Don't order 100 units in anticipation of orders. Should your mail order campaign not work out, you would be the unhappy owner of a surplus of watches.

When I was in the gift-and-gadget business, I always ordered minimum quantities; you can always reorder. When you are out of stock, write to your customers, advising them their orders will be shipped in two or three weeks. Everyone understands it's possible to run out of inventory. By keeping your customer informed, you maintain good relations.

Question: What is the best way to get started selling books?

Answer: Pick a category and contact publishers selling that particular type of book. You'll find this information at your library in the reference book, *Subject Guide to Books in Print*. Inquire whether the publisher will drop-ship the books for you. If he will not, order the books as you receive your orders. When you determine what books are selling, order small quantities, gradually building your inventory.

You might want to consider my drop-shipment plan for selling books. If so, write to me for complete information. Ask for the *Selling Books by Mail Kit*. I'll send you complete details and my latest mailing pieces.

Question: I can't seem to get moving in a mail order program. I keep procrastinating. What can I do?

Answer: I'd recommend a good physical fitness program. I jog, swim, or take a brisk walk every morning. I get high from exercising. It induces productivity and creativity. You might consider joining a health club, getting involved in swimming, handball, racquetball, an exercise class, or any other activity. Treat yourself to some massages. It's good for your body and mind and affords you some time for meditation. You might want to take a dance class to get your body moving.

If you are overweight, lose some of those extra pounds. Your weight is draining too much energy from your body and is making you sluggish. The obvious suggestion is clearly one of the best—eat less. Forget the crash diets.

If you smoke, give very serious consideration to stopping. I realize it's easier said than done. Smoking plays havoc with your body and mind; in fact, it may be reducing your powers of concentration.

Read some inspirational books such as *Magic of Thinking Big* by David Schwartz, Ph.D., *Exuberance* by Paul Kurtz, Ph.D., *Psycho-Cybernetics* by Maxwell Maltz, M.D.

Question: I have a vague feeling I will not be successful even though I understand the principles and procedure to follow. Do you have any comments?

Answer: Inability to succeed is a common apprehension among neophytes in any field of endeavor, because success seems so far down the road. Don't worry about it; instead, proceed one step at a time. Initially, set only minimal challenges for yourself. You'll get a feeling of exhilaration when the first order puts you into the mail order business. Your potential for success is as great as anyone's. There is no mystery to becoming successful. Follow the many suggestions I have given in this book. Your first attempts might not be successful, but you are learning. I would suggest reading the following books: *A Guide to Developing Your Potential* by Herbert A. Otto, Ph.D. and *A New Guide to Rational Living* by Albert Ellis, Ph.D. & Robert Harper, Ph.D.

Question: What are the most common reasons people are not successful in mail order?

Answer: I have found the common denominator to be a lack of information or a lack of conviction as to what would make a good mail order product. If they had a good product, they were often lacking in the essential, persuasive advertising copy. Poor returns left them bewildered. That's why I'm so much in favor of an ongoing reading program and studies in advertising, copywriting, and marketing courses. From these informative methods, you'll gradually develop insight as to what will make a winner and how to properly advertise it.

Question: You have suggested so many books to read. Which ones would you recommend that I read first?

Answer: They are all important. My suggestion is to take advantage of your public library and read whatever books they have in the various categories I have recommended. You can learn from every book. If you find a particularly good book I have not recommended, I would appreciate your telling me about it so I can read it, and, if suitable, include that information in the next edition of this book.

Question: I am interested in raising money for my favorite charity, using mail order techniques. What would you suggest?

Answer: Write a personal letter plus an in-depth story of what the organization is doing. Tell a story of how one person was helped. Use photographs whenever possible. Besides asking for money, invite the recipient to become active in the good work of the organization. See page 320 for sample letter. See page 321 for the type of literature I recommend. It measures 11″ × 17″. The letter and circular not only brought in cash donations, but donations of riding equipment, clothing, horses, ponies, and cowboy hats that delighted the children.

The local sheriff responded by attending the annual Christmas party, dressed as Santa Claus with bags full of gifts. He came in a sheriff's car with the sirens screaming and the spinning colored lights illuminated the faces of all the children. The excitement was contagious.

Question: How can I further develop a sense of what might be a good mail order product?

Answer: By studying the repeat advertisements in publications, by analyzing the direct mail that you receive, by reading success stories in publications, and by reading books dealing with all phases of mail order. Eventually you'll develop that indefinable sixth sense for knowing what is right.

Question: I've found a product and have written an ad. How do I know if I've written a good pulling ad?

Answer: I'm not being evasive when I say, "You'll develop a sixth sense about it." Do the market research I previously suggested. My favorite book on advertising is *How to Write a Good Advertisement* by Victor O. Schwab. If your library doesn't have a copy, you can obtain it through my office. The book sells for $22 postpaid. Also establish a working relationship with a freelance copywriter who can be of assistance to you. He'll make money for you with his expertise.

Question: Can you recommend a good freelance copywriter who will work with a beginner?

Answer: I'm pleased to recommend a prolific, freelance copywriter who does excellent work. He's creative, diligent, and completes his assignments on schedule. His clients include beginners as well as major mail order companies. Do yourself a favor and contact him for your ads and mail order program. He has his own syndicated weekly business opportunity radio show. Talk to him about advertizing your product on the air. Write or call: Sheldon J. Swartz, 508 Glenwood Drive, W. Palm Beach, Florida 33415-2084. Telephone: (561)) 686-2133.

Question: Can you recommend a printer to help me get started in the mail order business?

Answer: I am pleased to recommend my printer who does an outstanding job for me. He does beautiful work, his service is excellent, his prices are reasonable and he completes jobs when promised He is extremely efficient and conscientious. Call, write or fax Jim Dunn, the owner of Prime Printing, P.O. Box 680-M, Swainsboro, GA 30401. Phone: (912) 237-2422, Fax: (912) 237-3433. See page 148.

Question: I have a product/service that I would like to advertise on the Internet. Can you help me get started?

Answer: I'd be pleased to be of service to you. Call or send me all the particulars and I'll send you full details on how to get started including the cost of setting up a Web site, promoting it, and maintaining it. It's important to get the best marketing strategy for your Internet business. We can determine monthly how many people viewed your site. It's an exciting challenge and your chances of success are as good as anyone else's. You can view my Web site at: http://www.mpowers.com.

Question: You seem to be successful in whatever you do. You even made reference to having the Midas touch. How do you account for it and what advice would you give to enable another to develop the same ability?

Answer: As you become successful in small ways, you gradually develop a success-oriented aura. The dictionary defines the word aura, as "A distinctive quality that characterizes a person." Over the years, I have developed a winning attitude about everything I do. I know that once I put my creative energies into any venture, it will succeed. I have proved it many times.

Philosophically, I feel fortunate to have the opportunity to meet the challenges of life. It hasn't always been easy for me. I don't dwell on the unhappiness, sorrow, mistakes, and missed opportunities of the past. It drains too much energy and can make you depressed. I view it as part of the natural flow of life, putting it into its proper perspective, trying to learn from it, while concentrating on the present.

I have read, and continue to read, practically every book published in the field of positive thinking and am a great believer in programming oneself for success. The secret—it's all in an attitude. One of my favorite books is *How to Attract Good Luck* by A.H.Z. Carr. That book had a constructive effect on my life.

My suggestion is to make friends with the inexhaustible supply of self-improvement books at your library. Make it your business to get involved with a long range, continuous, reading program. Do it at your own pace. It's pleasant, constructive, and rewarding. It will pay handsome dividends. Before long, you'll develop a winning, zestful sense of well-being that will constructively permeate your entire personal and business life. Then the Midas touch will rub off on everything *you* do!

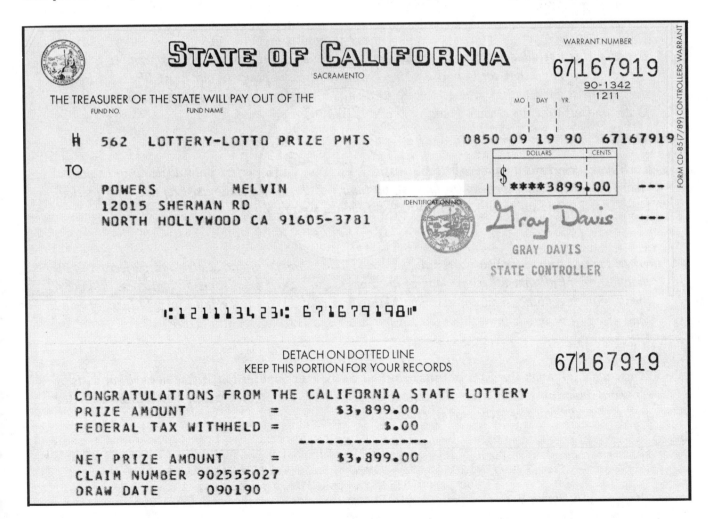

The First Sacred Scroll

These Truths We Hold to Be Self-Evident . . .
Yet Most Often They Are Not

I

We are, first and foremost, children of the universe—whole, beautiful, perfect in every detail—for we are as the Infinite meant us to be. As such, it is our birthright to be worthy of respect and love, and our obligation to accept nothing less.

II

As the whole of the ocean is in every droplet of water, so do we contain the whole of life. As the sea ebbs and flows, so shall we ebb and flow with the tide of life, accepting that the only constant is change, and being resolute that all is as it is meant to be, even when we know not why.

III

Within the arms of weakness is strength, eager to burst free. Within the grasp of pain is pleasure, waiting just to be. And within the path of obstacles lies opportunity. For all that these teachers bring to life, shall we be ever grateful.

IV

There is a grand design of which we are a part that does not rely upon us to be in charge of it. Everyone and everything has a rightful place in this grand design, and a reason for being.

V

Experience is not always truth, for it is colored by the eyes through which it is seen. It is in the silence of our mind that we hear truth. The gentle voice that speaks to our heart like a whisper is the Creator stirring within, trying to make us aware of all that we truly are, all that we are meant to do, and all that we already know.

VI

Each new moment is a banquet of fresh possibilities. Each day a perfect plum waiting to be picked. Again and again, shall we reap the harvest, partaking of the plenty while wasting not—for precious is all that is. And all that is, shall all too soon be all that was.

VII

When we walk upon the Path of Truth, we feel flowing through us the beauty and perfection of all that we are, of all that others are, and of all that is. Our chosen way is one of gentleness, kindness, compassion, acceptance, and appreciation. With these shall our mind be full. Such fullness of mind shall create love in our heart. And love in our heart shall create love in our life.

VIII

When we walk upon the Path of Truth so shall we be ever mindful that what lies within us is of far more importance than what lies behind us or before us. For that which lies within us is the greatest of all treasures—the magnificence of the universe itself.

From *THE PRINCESS WHO BELIEVED IN FAIRY TALES* by MARCIA GRAD
Trade paperback, 208 pages, $12.00 postpaid
Wilshire Book Company, 12015 Sherman Road, No. Hollywood, CA 91605

How to Succeed With Your Own 900 Number Business

900 KNOW-HOW

"Nothing will guarantee success in this business, but reading this book will go a long way toward maximizing the chance for success."

W. Brooks McCarty, President
Information 900 Services Corp., Palm Springs, CA

Contents

Four Facts You Should Know About 900 Numbers:

1 Dial-a-porn is on the way out, and even now accounts for only 3% of 900 programs. The future in this industry will be with legitimate information and entertainment services with good perceived value.

2 Many new 900 programs fail because they are launched by people who have not done their homework to learn the business or to find out what it takes to succeed. Because the 900 business has so many truly unique advantages, the lure of easy profits has been irresistible, and too many would-be entrepreneurs have jumped onto the bandwagon completely unprepared.

3 There is a lot of hype and blatant misinformation out there surrounding the 900 industry, perpetuated by snake oil hucksters who are fleecing naive opportunity seekers. For example, you cannot "own" a 900 number, and the government does not limit the quantity of 900 numbers that are available.

4 Established businesses are getting into the 900 industry in ever growing numbers. Virtually every business has access to unique, timely or specialized information that can be sold by means of a 900 number. A 900 number is a convenient, efficient information delivery medium, for both the caller and the information provider.

Here's a partial listing of only a fraction of the well-known companies and organizations that have joined the 900 industry:

Sports:	*USA Today, Sporting News, Sports Illustrated,* Coors
Financial:	H&R Block, AM Best, *Fortune,* Dow Jones & Company
Entertainment:	MTV, HBO, *Spin Magazine,* NBC, Paramount Pictures
Health:	Whitehall Laboratories, PMS National Network Support Assoc.
Consumer help:	*Consumer Reports, Car & Driver,* Better Business Bureau
Technical advice:	Novell Netware, Technical Software, Inc.
News & Politics:	ACLU, *Newsweek,* Freedom International, Inc.
Fundraising:	March of Dimes, Amnesty International, World Vision

About the Author
Robert Mastin

Robert Mastin is an entrepreneur in the truest sense of the word. For more than 15 years he has run several successful small-business enterprises based in Newport, Rhode Island. His achievements include the organization of a residential design and development firm whose projects have been featured in *Popular Science Magazine, Builder Magazine,* and *The New York Times.* Mr. Mastin has successfully developed his own 900 number information service and currently has several more under development.

A graduate of the U.S. Naval Academy and the recipient of a master's degree in accounting from the University of Rhode Island, Mr. Mastin began researching the 900 pay-per-call industry with a view toward launching a tax preparation service. Quickly he discovered that reliable, honest information about the 900 industry was scarce — and difficult to find, at best. After establishing his own 900 number business, he decided to write a book about his knowledge and experience: ***900 KNOW-HOW.***

With acknowledged expertise in the area of telecommunications and voice information, Mr. Mastin is currently working on yet another book; this one about launching an 800 number order-processing service.

A Personal Note From The Author

"When I first got into the 900 business, accurate information was scarce and very difficult to find. As I waded through all the hype and misinformation, I decided that serious entrepreneurs needed honest, useful information about the industry. That's why I wrote 900 KNOW-HOW — for people like me. I wish such a book had been available when I jumped into the business myself - it would have saved me a lot of time, effort and money."

He's Sailing off Maui, Making Money Around the Clock!

The Ideal Home Business

Launch your own 900 number business and sell pre-recorded information over the telephone to a national market—24 hours a day, 365 days a year.

Learn the secrets to one of the most exciting business opportunities of the century—this industry exploded from zero to $975,000,000 in only four years! And it has only just begun.

Easy to Start

You will be amazed how easy it is to start your own 900 number business. Very low start-up costs. Work part-time from home, from anywhere in the country. The only equipment needed is a touch-tone telephone.

Enormous Potential

Your potential market is huge - the entire country - only a telephone call away. And best of all, the telephone company collects all your money for you—collection costs are zero!

Learn How

To launch a profitable 900 program, you must learn the secrets to success. What 900 programs work, and why. What pitfalls to avoid. You need honest advice from experts—people who have seen the mega hits as well as the flops.

You need **900 KNOW-HOW: How to Succeed With Your Own 900 Number Business**. This new book is crammed with 174 pages of honest, straightforward, nuts-and-bolts information.

Endorsed by Experts

Here's what some of the leading industry experts say about **900 KNOW-HOW:**

"I have been involved in the audiotex industry for over 5 years and 900 KNOW-HOW is one of the best books on the pay-per-call industry that I have seen. The information provided is accurate and concise. This book is a must for anyone contemplating getting into the business."

Bill Gundling, Vice President
The Nine Call Corporation, Newton, MA

"Well written and informative for new or experienced IPs (Information Providers). We even use it as part of our training for new salespersons."

Robert Bentz, Director of Marketing
Advanced Telecom Services, Wayne, PA

Ironclad Guarantee

You can't lose. If not 100% satisfied with your copy of 900 KNOW-HOW, simply return it within 30 days for a full refund. No questions asked.

Act today! Join other successful entrepreneurs in this explosive industry. Earn money while dozing on the beach, while playing tennis, or while vacationing at Disney World. But you can't get started until you know how.

( ) YES! Please rush my copy of 900 KNOW-HOW. I'd like to learn more about the 900 business. If I'm not completely satisfied, I can return the book for a full refund.

Enclosed is my ( ) check ( ) money-order for $20.00 (CA res. $21.65) plus $2.00 postage.

Name_____

Address_____

City_____ State_____ Zip_____

Please make your checks payable to:

Melvin Powers
12015 Sherman Road
North Hollywood, CA 91605

Here's What They're Saying About *900 KNOW-HOW:*

"It was only a matter of time until somebody wrote a frank, no-hype book on launching a 900 pay-per-call business. The author is experienced 900 number entrepreneur Robert Mastin and the title is '900 KNOW-HOW'...."
--Joyce Lain Kennedy
Nationally Syndicated Careers Columnist

".... a superb job of gathering and conveying the information....crammed full of information which is concise and accurate....I highly recommend it for anyone contemplating going into the 900 number business...."
--Ed Durham, Editor
Home Income Reporter

".... Solid advice to anyone wanting to start-up the business....a good starting place for 'infopreneurs' who want to get in the game....presented in a factual, concise manner that can be easily understood and digested...."
--Bruce Jones, Book Reviewer
Mailer's Review

"The book is fantastic....the answers you need for going into this business....I am glad to recommend this book to you because it contains the information you need to become successful in your own 900 number business...."
--Bob Barnes, Book Reviewer
Jackpot magazine

".... This book provides HONEST information about what it takes to be successful in this business....Get the REAL facts...."
--Bob Riemke, Editor
The Real Entrepreneur

".... 900 KNOW-HOW explores this explosive industry in-depth, including how to start and operate a 900 business, what pitfalls to avoid, the costs involved, and what kinds of 900 programs have been successful...."
--Business Bookshelf
Business Opportunities Journal

"Medium-to-small businesses could profit from the acquisition of a 900 number, and this title is a good place to begin. It's a detailed examination of the 900 pay-per-call option which offers detailed advice on how to succeed with a 900 number -- and what to avoid...."   --The Bookwatch
The Midwest Book Review

".... Really offers the readers non-biased information....This has to be one of the best, well written and informative books on the subject.... 900 KNOW-HOW is a must...."
--John Moreland
The Dream Merchant

"Everything one needs to know to start a 900-number phone service is surveyed ....Starting a 900 number service is relatively easy, but its success depends on the additional factors of marketing research, customer service, and costs which are also dealt with in this introductory guide."
--The Small Press Book Review

"Here's an exploration of one of America's growth industries. The author covers how to start and operate such a business, pitfalls, costs and marketing....a good primer on starting a business based on the 900 telephone numbers...."
--Jeff Rowe, Business Book Editor
Orange County Register

"The book provides honest information about what it takes to be successful in this business, and clearly debunks some of the hype and blatant misinformation surrounding the 900 industry...."   --MAIL PROFITS Magazine

".... a good primer if you have ever dreamed of making your fortune with a 900 number.... This book will help focus your thoughts and give you the resources to study how to build a successful 900 number service...."   --Kathy Mathews
Stepping Stones

".... you'll get a nuts-and-bolts guide to starting and operating a 900 service....start-up and monthly operating costs....ways to effectively market a 900 service....details on types of services that are successful...."
--Barbara Kaplowitz, Editor
What's Working in DM and Fulfillment

"This is the bible of an industry that shot from $0 to nearly $1 billion in annual sales in only four years...."
--Duncan Anderson, Book Reviewer
SUCCESS Magazine

"....explores the pay-per-call industry in depth....and what makes a successful 900 program...."   --FOLIO Magazine

"... 900 KNOW-HOW is a comprehensive guide that helps the start-up information provider..."
--The Newsletter on Newsletters

".... the author shoots straight from the hip in his clearly understandable approach to the business, showing you what can and cannot be done, how and how not to do it... an extraordinary accomplishment... read it before you act..."
--Entrepreneur's Digest

"If you're interested in launching a 900 pay-per-call information or entertainment service, you will find this book helpful."   --Galen Stilson, Publisher
The DIRECT RESPONSE Specialist

"This is a valuable book to have on your bookshelf."
--Mail Order Entrepreneur

"... provides in-depth coverage of the 900-number industry..."
--Sales and Marketing Strategies & News

"... the first comprehensive how-to book about launching a 900 pay-per-call business... explores the ever growing pay-per-call industry, including pitfalls to avoid, effective marketing, the most successful programs to start, and much more."   --Income Opportunities magazine

Melvin Powers Television Marketing

12015 Sherman Road
No. Hollywood, CA 91605

(818) 765-8529
FAX (818) 765-2922

IN HELPING OTHERS, WE ARE FULFILLED

Dear Friend:

I've had the pleasure of becoming acquainted with an inspiring humanitarian who is devoting his time, energy, and money to bring happiness to numerous handicapped children.

For more than 30 years, "Cowboy John" Carpenter has almost single-handedly operated the Heaven on Earth Ranch for Handicapped Children in Lake View Terrace (San Fernando Valley), California.

Children with varied afflictions and handicaps are able to forget their disabilities for awhile when they are riding specially trained horses at the stable and enjoying the activity and the exhilaration of being one of Cowboy John's "sheriffs." Their eyes and laughter tell you they are experiencing a rare joy. After riding their favorite horses and going on wagon rides, the children are treated to lunch or refreshments at the ranch house.

Most importantly, the children receive Cowboy John's love and attention. The pleasure derived from this special, educational playground has a remarkably beneficial effect on the well-being of the children. They, of course, can hardly wait until their next visit to the ranch.

Over the years John Carpenter and a few friends have shouldered the financial responsibility of this unique program. Now, due to spiraling costs, the gates to the ranch may soon be closed. Since I have become aware of the remarkable results that accrue to the children, and since I believe the operation of this ranch to be a much-needed humanitarian project, I am inviting you to share in this work whether through donations or by becoming personally involved. Your reward will be the loving smile on a child's face.

We welcome your visit to the ranch and your active participation in any way. Please send your contributions directly to: Heaven on Earth Ranch for the Handicapped, 11469 Tiara Street, #8, North Hollywood, California 91601.

John and I look forward to hearing from you. We hope you will want to join us in giving a helping hand.

Sincerely yours,

Melvin Powers

Melvin Powers

All donations are tax deductible.
Internal Revenue Service #23-7092538

Heaven On Earth Ranch for the Handicapped

by Charles R. Moseley

Tucked away near the entrance to the Big Tujunga Canyon at the east end of the San Fernando Valley in Lake View Terrace, California, is a small parcel of land with an old weather-beaten sign proclaiming this spot to be "Heaven on Earth."

A stranger passing by might look at the run down, ramshackle place and say, "That place looks more like Hell." Both terms are right. There is no place on earth where one may see more happiness, joy and laughter and without turning one's head see pain, despair and hopelessness.

The happiness, joy and laughter are reflected in children's faces as they see, pet and ride horses, donkeys and mules for perhaps the first time in their lives. They may also play on old wagons or wander in and around a setting of a small old western

The Heaven on Earth Town Square.

town, or maybe ride on a hay wagon. All of these things are free. There is never any charge.

The pain, despair and hopelessness are there too. An observer needs only to watch to become filled with emotion. Picture, if you will, a small child in a pint sized wheel chair, with braces on both legs, arms at odd angles, head not sitting on the shoulders properly, and with an expression on his face as if he is angry at the world. Then up walks a rough looking old cowboy type who says, "Are you ready for your ride, Timmy?" With a worried look the small child grunts in agreement. The cowboy raises the child over a waiting cow pony and the child's father pulls the braced legs apart and Timmy slips down into the saddle. A few ties are made to hold the boy upright and then the horse with Timmy aboard is lead off for a few time around the riding ring. The light in Timmy's eyes and his bright smile are a reward beyond compare.

Timmy is typical of the children who frequent John Carpenter's Heaven on Earth Ranch. It is dedicated to handicapped children and all of them are crippled, mentally retarded, blind or afflicted in one way or another.

Let us go back to 1967 when I first met John Carpenter. He was pointed out to me as a horse trainer. I was having a problem with my horse and I wanted to talk to him. John was standing beside a three foot jump instructing a young man in the art of jumping. I had to wait. Watching the instruction, I felt there was something odd about the lesson. John would say "to the right a little, ok, turn 90 degrees left now, you are set, go." As the rider approached the jump, John yelled, "Now!" Then as the jump was cleared, he proceeded to direct the rider back for another try. It was not long before I realized the rider was totally blind.

A month or so later I realized the significance of what I had seen. A small article in a local newspaper published the fact that John Carpenter had been working with the handicapped for many years and was supporting his work with his small disability pension.

I went looking for John again, this time to see if I could be of some help to him. Being a working man I did not have much to offer,

Al Franklin, a blind Explorer Scout, with the help of John Carpenter and a willing Quarter Horse experience the free feeling of taking a jump.

but I felt I would do what I could. The expression on John's face was one of sheer amazement as I made him the offer of my assistance. It turned out that I was the first person who had offered him any kind of help at all in all the years he had been doing this work.

It was decided transportation was the most urgent need. John was working with a special troop of explorer scouts (all handicapped) and he wanted to take them camping. Because most of these boys were

This picture with the empty wheel chair in the shadows serves better than any words can to capture the spirit of John Carpenter's Heaven on Earth Ranch for handicapped children.

from very poor homes, he often had to drive to the boys' homes and pick them up for meetings and other outings.

With the help of a couple of my friends and a very sympathetic neighborhood Chevrolet dealer, we purchased an older pick-up truck with a shell camper on it and presented it to John. We added a couple of benches down the sides of the camper and we had what he needed. In it he could carry 10 to 12 boys.

This was the start of what was to become Heaven on Earth Ranch. John became more and more involved. He rented the property where the ranch now stands. The truck became a means of realizing his dream of a special place where the handicapped children could come and maybe forget for a little while their handicaps in the sheer enjoyment of the surroundings.

John Carpenter takes pride in having built the ranch with his own hands. The heaven on earth diner where visitors can have lunch or a snack is one of the most recent additions.

John started picking up used lumber and junk from any place that would let him have it. He hauled it to the ranch and built most of the mini western town with his own hands. John worked so hard that several times he ended up in the hospital to recuperate.

A little help started to come in. Mostly from working men like myself plus a very nice lawyer who donated the work required to form a corporation so donations would be tax deductible. The donations so far have been small and not much help. Television and the press have come to the ranch for stories and pictures, but all of them have failed in the most needed area of gaining financial help for the ranch. John keeps on trying and will continue to do so as long as possible.

During the past year there have been approximately 10,000 children visit Heaven on Earth Ranch. Many times they arrive by the bus load. One of those times, about two months ago, a bus load of forty children arrived at the ranch at 10:00 a.m. in the morning. By lunch time the children were enjoying themselves immensely. There

was laughter and broad smiles all around. Then disaster struck. Someone had forgotten to bring the children's lunches. John with his big heart exposed for everyone to see grabbed the phone and called a local hamburger stand. Forty hamburgers and miles later the fun and games resumed. The money to buy that food came from John's own pocket and shortened his own small disability fund.

The other day I received a call from John. It seems with the approach of winter, darkness was coming too soon and some of the children had to leave early. I am able to help in this sort of way, so I gathered the material I needed and went over to the ranch. As I was working to install some additional lighting, I noticed two healthy looking teenage boys with rakes and shovels cleaning up around the place. I said to John that it was sure great to see some young people taking an interest in the place and helping out a bit. John took me aside to tell me the story.

The two boys were caught in the act of vandalizing a local school and had caused some serious damage. The youth authority and the L.A.P.D. Foothill Division Captain felt that as part of the disciplinary action against the boys, they should be required to do some work in the public interest to partly repay the community for the damage they had caused. John's big heart was out front again, because it was either

John Carpenter with Randy Horton—a boy whose positive attitude to life is an inspiration.

let the boys work or have them go to a correctional facility.

It might be said now that John is expanding to helping healthy young men. Those two boys are not afflicted. Or are they?

I feel that I have seen a little of Heaven on Earth through my association with John Carpenter's Heaven on Earth Ranch. Of all those he has helped, it may be that I have been helped the most by possibly becoming a better man for the experience. ⟨⟩

The noblest question in the world is, What good may I do in it?

Melvin Powers Television Marketing

12015 Sherman Road
No. Hollywood, CA 91605

(818) 765-8529
FAX (818) 765-2922

$10,000 Reward

Dear Friend:

$10,000 will be paid to each person who sends in a video of a product we use on TV in a "successful" two-minute direct response commercial or half-hour infomercial.

Just video tape the hottest selling item or items from your fair and send us the tape. If we like the product, obtain rights to it, and go national as described below, you get your $10,000 reward. If you submit more than one "successful" product, you will receive $10,000 for each one.

Why are we offering this reward? Because we need your help. Although we spend a great deal of time every year searching fairs, trade shows, and publications, and reviewing submissions to find new products to present on television, it is impossible to find every potential winner that may be out there.

Each video tape submitted must be clearly marked with submitter's name, address, and telephone number and must list names of products and demonstrators. Each video tape must be submitted with an attached list that sets forth the following:

1. Submitter's name, address, and telephone number.
2. Product names, manufacturers' names, addresses, and telephone numbers.
3. Demonstrators' names, addresses, and telephone numbers.
4. Date sent or delivered.

Terms and Conditions

Melvin Powers Television Marketing (MPTM) is continuously searching the marketplace for new products in connection with its video marketing programs. This is not a contest or sweepstakes, but a nationwide search for products. We spend thousands of dollars in our search, and we are willing to pay a "reward" to individuals who provide us with a video demonstrating a "new" product. "New" means that the product has not appeared on national or regional cable television. There is no limit on the number of tapes that can be submitted, but the format must be VHS or 8mm. All tapes submitted become the property of MPTM. Submitter warrants and represents that he or she has the legal right to make such submission and will hold MPTM harmless against any third party claim. In the case of duplicate products being submitted, MPTM will be the sole judge of the recipient of the $10,000 reward. In the case of multiple "successful submissions" of distinctly different products, multiple rewards will be awarded. To qualify for the reward, the product submitted must be accepted by MPTM, and at the sole discretion and judgment of MPTM, after appropriate evaluation and testing, be aired on national cable as paid programming for at least 12 consecutive weeks as a two-minute direct response commercial or half-hour infomercial. The $10,000 reward is completely separate of any ongoing royalty or similar arrangement that may be negotiated with and paid to the actual owner of the rights to the "successful" product. MPTM has the right to require the name and photograph of reward recipients for use in its future promotional activities as a condition to the reward. Any dispute, controversy, or claim between submitter and MPTM will be arbitrated in Los Angeles in accordance with the rules of the American Arbitration Association, and judgment upon may be entered in any court having jurisdiction thereof. Submitter must be over 18 years of age and this offer is not valid in states or territories where it would be prohibited.

SHIRLEY WOODCOCK GOTTSCHALK

Carpenter and Randy Horton at the Heaven on Earth Ranch

Handicapped kids respond magically to this cowboy who cares

John Carpenter and His Miracle Ranch

BY EARL C. GOTTSCHALK, JR.

THE SIGN ON THE GATE read: "John Carpenter's Heaven on Earth Ranch for Handicapped Children." And, as Marie and Armando Perello stood at the end of the corral, a sturdy cowboy with a weather-beaten face and a white hat strode over, picked up their seven-year-old son Carl and set him on a big black horse. "Okay, cowboy, let's take a ride," he said and began to lead the horse around the corral. The boy grasped the saddle horn and meekly followed John Carpenter's instructions.

Carl was an autistic child, who from age two had spoken only gibberish and was given to fits of screaming. His wild behavior caused even close friends and relatives to shun the Perellos, who lived in a state of constant fear and isolation. Marie Perello had tried everything to control Carl and teach him to talk properly, but nothing worked. Neither doctors nor speech therapists had been able to help. Finally she heard about Carpenter, who let handicapped children ride horses at his ranch in Lake View Terrace, Calif., 20 miles northwest of Los Angeles.

One weekend, after months of regular visits, Marie left the family at the corral and went off to do errands. When she returned, her husband and their two other children were shouting with glee. It seemed that Carl had wanted to ride the horse outside the corral and, as Carpenter led the horse near the gate, the boy had said clearly and unmistakably his first meaningful words: "Open the door, Carpenter."

Not only did Carl continue to talk more and more, but he became calm. By age eight he had become so proficient a rider that he could stand on the saddle as the horse walked around the corral. Carpenter had provided Carl with something that doctors and specialists couldn't: the feeling that he was normal. *There was something in the mystique, the magic of the horse, rider and teacher,* Marie thought.

Carl is only one of dozens of autistic and spastic children who have spoken their first words at the ranch. An incredible total of 750,000 handicapped persons have visited since Carpenter opened the ranch in the early 1940s.

Among them was Randy Horton, whose motor functions were so impaired by cerebral palsy that he could not walk and could speak only a few words. His hip sockets had been damaged, and doctors said they might have to be replaced with plastic-lined metal sockets. The Los Angeles teen-ager had spent all his life indoors—at home, in special schools and hospitals. A sullen figure crouched in his wheelchair, Randy never smiled. His mother brought him to the ranch to see if that might cheer him up.

At first Randy just sat watching the activity: spastic children riding horses; handicapped children leading other handicapped children around on horses; children wearing braces and protective helmets riding in a stagecoach.

Then Carpenter appeared. With his usual greeting, "Hi, cowboy," he slapped a Stetson on Randy's head. During his first stagecoach ride, Randy's twisted body was tense; his features were contorted in fear. But as Carpenter snapped the reins and the mules pulled the coach, Randy began to relax.

At the end of half an hour a smile spread across the youngster's face. With every subsequent visit, he was involved in more phases of riding. He started on a mule sidesaddle. Later Carpenter got him astride a well-trained horse. Leather straps held Randy upright. He tilted strangely in the saddle, his head cocked. But slowly, through Carpenter's patient commands, the boy learned to direct the horse. Soon he was riding alone around the corral.

One December Randy performed at the ranch's Christmas party. Sitting stiffly but proudly in the saddle, Randy trotted his horse for the audience. He tugged on the reins, and his horse turned left. Another tug, and the horse moved smartly to the right.

"Okay, cowboy, show them what you can do!" Carpenter shouted. Randy tugged the reins again, and the horse pranced forward and backward, then pirouetted. The crowd cheered, as Randy's mother beamed. *A miracle,* she thought. *John Carpenter accomplishes miracles here.*

Carpenter also puts on shows for the handicapped. Vans and buses arrive at the ranch, and nurses roll wheelchair patients down the dusty streets of a ramshackle western town Carpenter built. In Gruesome Gulch, the clock is turned back 100 years. A rinky-tink piano plays in the Mangy Dog Saloon. A dance-hall gal in a frilly red-and-black dress strolls out through the swinging doors. Pack mules wait in front of Higgins General Store.

Suddenly hoofbeats echo through the town. Gunshots ring out. Astride a black horse, Carpenter thunders into view, his six-gun blazing. Hot in pursuit are two scroungy bad guys. Carpenter turns and fires. One mustachioed villain—a stunt man donating his time—falls from his horse into a pile of hay. His horse does a trick fall, too, onto its side. The kids cheer!

Carpenter would be performing a great service even if he charged for such outings. But the children pay nothing. Carpenter's Social Security plus donations from friends, relatives and organizations pay the $42,000 annual operating costs. But coming up with the money is a constant struggle.

The ranch is a one-man operation. Carpenter, who looks 15 years younger than his 68 years, labors seven days a week. He feeds the animals, mucks out the stalls and corrals, prepares cookout meals and handles reservations. The only time he gets a day off is when it rains. Some days Carpenter is so tired that friends have to help him onto his horse. It has been that way ever since he started the ranch.

John Carpenter grew up in Dardanelle, Ark., and learned to ride horses on his father's farm. An incident back then helped form the philosophy he has practiced all his life. Besides the farm, John's father ran a butcher shop. One day a neighbor with nine children stopped in, said he had no money and asked the elder Carpenter if he would buy his milk cow. John's father gave him $40 for the animal.

Later he asked John to return the cow. John was puzzled. "Someday you'll understand," his father said. "They need that cow a lot more than we need the forty dollars."

A close brush with death also helped develop John Carpenter's empathy for the handicapped. When he was 18, a car careened out of control and ran over him. His left leg was broken in seven places, his back in two places, and he had internal injuries. In a body cast for 119 days, Carpenter experienced the isolation of the handicapped. As he lay helpless, he made a pact: if God would let him walk again, he would spend his life helping the handicapped. When the cast came off, his father suggested that he strengthen his leg by riding. Even though he couldn't walk without crutches, he could still ride.

Carpenter then moved to California and found work at a stable. The riding slowly strengthened him, but eight years passed before he was able to throw away his crutches.

In time, he gained a reputation

around Los Angeles as a handsome cowboy who had skill with a horse. He began stunt riding in movies. Carpenter also started writing, directing and producing his own "B" westerns—and he opened a stable. One day four young blind men came to the stable and asked if they could ride. Despite misgivings, Carpenter saddled up four horses and, to his surprise, the men rode slowly around the corral.

Timing and balance turned out to be more important than sight in horseback riding. The horse, after all, *can* see. The blind men came back three or four times a week and kept getting better. Eventually, with Carpenter's training, they became quite a sensation at rodeos and parades.

By the 1960s B westerns were passé, and Carpenter's avocation became his full-time, nonpaying job. Visitors are impressed with his achievements. "It's hard to put your finger on just what it is," says Hal Hubbard, a sociologist at California State University at Long Beach. "John creates a mood, and the kids relax. Sometimes we forget that kids need to have a good time."

Carpenter believes that, deep down, handicapped kids want to participate in the same kind of action sports as normal children do. "Just like the rest of us, they'd like to jump on a horse, shoot the bad guys and ride off into the sunset," he says.

The horse is just a device Carpenter uses to help handicapped children grow. Says Marie Perello, "The kids respond to horses. If only we could get state institutions for the handicapped and retarded turned into ranches, we might see some real progress."

The handicapped youngsters know what Carpenter has done for them. Carl Perello has now grown into a strapping 18-year-old who speaks well. Rated "high functioning," he lives at a home for autistic young adults. His parents believe Carl eventually will be independent, a big achievement for a person afflicted with autism.

The ranch has been a miracle not only for thousands of youngsters but also for John Carpenter himself. "The Bible says, 'As you sow, so shall you reap.' Well, I've reaped two-hundredfold," he explains. "I've gotten more satisfaction out of this ranch than anything else I've ever done. Everything I own is on my back. Yet because of the ranch, I can get up every morning and walk down the street like a king. The ranch, for me, is a spiritual thing. If I get to heaven, it'll be on the coattails of these kids."

Chapter Sixteen

A Personal Word from Melvin Powers

Now that we have explored the fascinating world of mail order, I hope you will be inspired to use this book as a constant source of practical information and helpful suggestions.

The opportunities in the fertile and fascinating field of mail order are endless—limited only by your imagination, your drive, and your initiative. Admittedly, taking the *first* decisive step to strike out in new territory is the most difficult of all. But once you have made the initial plunge and have started to work as a mail order entrepreneur, you will be carving a new career for yourself that holds the promise of wealth, security, and personal esteem, which are the inevitable rewards of success in the world of business.

I am glad to know you are using this book as a reference guide to mail order success. If you conscientiously study it and the recommended supplementary reading, earnestly practice the principles set forth, and work with steadfast application, I guarantee success will be yours. But remember that success is the result of a combination of resourcefulness, dedication, and hard work. Once you have schooled yourself in the basics, the odds are in your favor.

This book is the fruition of my many years as a successful mail order entrepreneur—years of trial and error, setbacks, and triumphs. Use my experience to your advantage. The fundamentals of mail order, which have taken me years to assimilate, are set forth in explicit capsule form. Digest them, use them, apply them to your own business. They work—if you will work.

Keep this book at your fingertips. It could prove to be the first break for you in the fascinating field of mail order. If you're serious about making your fortune in mail order, begin with the facts, principles, guidelines, and examples that I have given you. Exert your best effort and reap the rewards. They are monumental, perhaps beyond your expectations; rewards above and beyond dollars and cents—the delight of knowing that you've met the challenges and mastered them!

MELVIN POWERS'
TEN-HOUR MAIL ORDER SEMINAR
ON CASSETTE TAPES

Here is an opportunity for those of you unable to attend my mail order seminar to hear me discuss many aspects of running a successful part-time or full-time business. In the privacy of your home, office, or car, you'll hear the same seminar that thousands of entrepreneurs all over the country have attended. The ten hours of audio tape instruction will answer many of the questions you have wanted to ask. It will teach you how to successfully become your own boss.

After listening to the tape program, you will better understand mail order fundamentals and procedures, and will have an overall plan that will help you start making money right away in your own mail order business. The tape program is sold on a one-year, money-back guarantee. It must be of tangible help in teaching you how to make money in mail order, or I'll refund your money—no questions asked.

Here's how to gain maximum benefit from the tapes: (1) Listen to the material several times to fully comprehend the practical suggestions and information; (2) Put into practice the specific elements to be incorporated in your mail order plan; (3) Run your first classified or display ad; (4) Do a test mailing to one thousand or as many as three thousand people who would logically be interested in your product; (5) Evaluate the results; (6) Call or write to me to discuss your mail order plan and receive my suggestions for increasing your chances to attain success.

Send for Melvin Powers' Mail Order Seminar on Cassette Tapes. Price $65.00 postpaid.

A PERSONAL WORD FROM MELVIN POWERS, PUBLISHER, WILSHIRE BOOK COMPANY

My goal is to publish interesting, informative, and inspirational books. You can help me to accomplish this by sending me your answers to the following questions:

Did you enjoy reading this book? Why?

What ideas in the book impressed you most? Have you applied them to your daily life? How?

Is there a chapter that could serve as a theme for an entire book? Explain.

Would you like to read similar books? What additional information would you like them to contain?

If you have an idea for a book, I would welcome discussing it with you. If you have a manuscript in progress, write or call me concerning possible publication.

Melvin Powers
12015 Sherman Road
North Hollywood, California 91605

(818) 765-8579

Chapter Seventeen

How to Get Started Making Money in Mail Order

My name is Sheldon Swartz. I am an associate of Melvin Powers, who helps individuals become successful in mail order. I have my own weekly, syndicated, business opportunity radio show that emphasizes mail order. I'm always looking for products to advertize on my show, so please feel free to contact me with yours.

Since my expertise is in mail order radio advertising, I am in direct communication with people who want to possibly add radio advertising to their campaign.

As a result of feedback from these individuals, I find that beginners, after reading books such as *How To Get Rich In Mail Order,* are sometimes overwhelmed by the wealth of material and need further clarification as to how to start making money with the least risk capital. So, the purpose of this guest chapter is to present an appropriate marketing plan and to recapitulate in capsule form the key money-making ideas of this book.

Step #1: Select a product or line of products you would like to sell. Numerous ideas are contained in this book, with many more to be discovered as you attend trade shows and read trade magazines. An excellent way to become aware of available products is to visit your library and ask for two publications — *Standard Periodical Directory* and *Standard Rate & Data Business Publications.* The first book is on the shelves of most libraries; the second is more likely to be found in the main library of your city. These two reference sources contain the names and addresses of thousands of business publications in various categories. Using your letterhead stationery, request a sample copy and an advertising rate card and you will receive any of the magazines free.

Write to the manufacturers who advertise in these magazines. They all look for sales outlets and will be eager to answer your request for their catalogs and information about discount schedules and minimum order amounts. They can tell you whether they will drop ship merchandise to your customers and supply you with product literature. If so, you, in turn, can then mail the literature to your prospective customers. This is desirable as there is a savings to you in this method

The magazines will include dates for forthcoming trade shows. Go to as many as your schedule permits. Your attendance will prove to be an excellent educational and business experience. Going from booth to booth, tell the representatives you are starting a mail order business and ask about discounts, advertising literature, and drop shipments.

Expenses incurred traveling to and from trade shows are fully tax deductible, even though you haven't made five cents. Keep accurate records of expenses such as stationery, telephone charges, automobile mileage and expense, attendance at seminars pertinent to your business, travel, hotel and food expenses, books, tapes, subscriptions, and magazine expense — anything connected with starting your business is a *bona fide* deduction. Uncle Sam encourages business entrepreneurs and will help you get started in every possible way. Why not? When you start making money, you will be creating jobs, helping the economy, and paying taxes.

Step #2: When you decide on a product, you might want to send out a publicity release to consumer magazines. Editors are pleased to inform their readers of new products, and there is no charge for this exposure. They will even key your publicity release so you'll know the origin of your orders. This is an excellent way to determine the sales potential of your product. If the response is good, go back in that publication with a paid advertisement. At the same time, send them another publicity release about another of your products. Since you are now paying for an ad, they'll be pleased to cooperate with you.

Step #3: Does your product lend itself to a two-step mail order technique? If so, pick out the most logical publications — those where others are selling products in the same general category via mail order. Choosing the minimum space offered, run a classified or small display ad requesting the reader to send for free details or for further literature about your product. This approach is extremely successful for both small and large mail order companies. It gives you the opportunity to promote the selling points of your product with as much or as little literature as you think necessary and, at the same time, do some market research. You can test your item with different prices, sales letters, brochures, headlines, or guarantees. When your return literature proves successful, pick out the winning combination and use it in full page display ads. These can lead to big money.

In my opinion, the two-step approach is the best and least expensive way for the mail order novice to start. Study the classified and small display ads in various publications which request the reader to send for further information. Answer some of the ads to see how long it takes for a response. Read and study both the initial and the follow-up material. Always key your inquiry with a suite or a department number or include a middle initial in your name. Record the key code and keep a record of the returns. With this important information, you will know when your name is being rented and to what company. Rental of names can be a profitable ancillary business — the rental falling into two categories: inquiry names and customer names. Customer names rent for more than inquiry names.

Step #4: Does your product lend itself to direct mail? If so, rent a small quantity of names and try a test mailing. See page 198. Joy, a knowledgeable service representative, will be pleased to be of assistance to you and give you recommendations. Send your mailing package to her. Once it is successful, you can "roll out" with thousands of names. Wait for the results of each mailing before proceeding to the next. Discussing your results with Joy can help improve subsequent mailings.

In your direct mail, you can test various prices, advertising copy changes, and different mailing lists. When Melvin Powers' mail order book first came out, we tested 20 different mailing lists of 5,000 each; then continued mailing to only those lists that had proved successful. We evaluated and tabulated the results for subsequent mailings. If there was a drop in response in one, we eliminated that list.

If your mailing is not successful, the reason lies in either the offer, the price, the advertising literature, the guarantee, or, perhaps, the mailing list itself. When results are not what you believe they should be, seek professional help. The services of a mail order advertising specialist can be of inestimable value.

Once you are making money with direct mail, use your advertising copy for display ads in appropriate publications. Now you can pyramid your success. Try a few publications at a time and expand only after you know you have a winning ad. But remember, a winning ad successful in one publication might not prove successful in another. Be creative and try this ad in publications you normally might not consider. Experimentation may lead to a bonanza. This type of thinking will reward you with a personal sense of satisfaction. And you'll derive still more satisfaction when you add an eye-catching feature to your ads such as an illustration which can help to increase response.

Step #5: Perhaps you have purchased Melvin Powers' mail order book from a full page ad in a newspaper. My monthly assignment from Mr. Powers is to increase his newspaper response. This might be accomplished by adding a word or words to the headline, by changing the body copy, the subheads, the price of the offer, or the layout. Success might come by running the ad in color or by changing the guarantee and the type face. There is no end to the creativity that goes into a full page newspaper or magazine ad.

To me, full page ads are one of the most exciting ways to advertise. As a beginner, you probably aren't ready to spend the necessary money, but you should keep them in mind once you begin to make money. The advantage of newspaper ads is that you can test your copy immediately. With magazines or national tabloids, there is a two- or three-month wait. As soon as you have a winner, you can cover the nation with your money-making ad. It's exciting to receive thousands of checks and money orders from all over the country.

Step #6: What about advertising on TV? I'm sure you have seen the Ginsu commercial which promotes a set of knives that are guaranteed for 50 years. Is it successful? You know it is! Think how many times and for how many years you have seen it. Recall records and tapes you've seen advertised on TV. Isn't it easy to order just by calling the free "800" number and being billed later? I realize that not every product lends itself to TV ads, but when one does, the response can be incredible! So consider the medium. Of course, I can almost hear you say, "I don't have that kind of money to spend." I just want you to be aware of the possibilities to expand your advertising campaign from your minimum classified or one-inch display ad beginning.

Step #7: One of the best ways to begin your mail order operation is by the drop-shipment method. This means you don't need to purchase and warehouse expensive inventory in anticipation of sales that may not even come.

I recommend that you send for free information from Mail

Order Associates. They'll drop-ship 500 products for you. See their ad on page 15.

I also recommend that you send for free information from Specialty Merchandise Corporation. They'll drop-ship 3,000 products for you. See their ad on page 19.

If you are looking for a special product, to manufacture a product inexpensively, contact the Hong Kong Trade Development Council. For the address of the office nearest you, see page 28.

You can also contact the Far East Trade Service, 3660 Wilshire Blvd., Los Angeles, California 90010. Telephone (213) 380-3644. They deal with products mainly from Taiwan. You'll receive prompt, efficient, and courteous service from foreign government trade representatives. See page 345 for the names, addresses, and phone numbers of additional foreign consulates.

The best general monthly product magazine is *Marketer's Forum*. It's truly an encyclopedic source of products from the Orient. It will allow you the greatest profits for your mail order sales. Send for a sample copy. You'll find it stimulating and fascinating reading. See page 187.

Think about selling lingerie through the mail. Other companies are doing it successfully. So can you. Send for free copies of trade magazines and wholesale catalogs listed on page 33.

Perhaps you would be interested in selling advertising specialties. There is big money in it because the products that are given away free create repeat sales for you. See page 53.

Audio cassette tapes have a good mail order track record. They are certainly worth your consideration.

The hottest new product in mail order sales are video tapes. Tens of thousands of homes now have video players. People are hungry for tapes of all kinds, yet, video stores mainly have movies. Millions of consumers find it difficult to locate the thousands of quality special interest and "how-to" tapes that have been produced.

You can sell virtually anything by mail, from peanuts to elephants. The challenge you now have is to find a product that is of special interest to you. The genuine enthusiasm you will generate by your efforts to market something you are excited about is the secret ingredient that can propel you to success in the mail order business and, subsequently, to financial independence.

Step #8: A catalog is the key to a profitable mail order operation. As the successful entrepreneurs have, you, too, will eventually have a catalog, but it will be earmarked with *your*

personality. It will be distinguishable from others — the ads will have a new twist.

Initially, your catalog can be a simple, one-page, black-and-white flyer. Since your repeat customers will provide you with easy profits, very little advertising expense is involved. As your business progresses, you can add pages to your flyer and, in time, it can, at your discretion, ultimately develop into a beautiful, four-color catalog. Your growth is determined strictly by your own needs.

And now we come to the moment of truth! What is your potential for success? Can you really succeed in making money in mail order? The answer is that it really depends upon what you put into it in terms of time, energy, enthusiasm, dedication, and common sense business practice. Throughout this book, Melvin Powers recommends a continuous reading program by checking out books on mail order and advertising from your public library. The more information you accumulate, the better able you will be to make valued judgments in your mail order business. I recommend the same. (I took his advice myself and have read virtually every book on mail order and advertising in print. I also have an extensive library on these subjects and continue to read every new book that is published in these fields.)

Success does not depend upon your investing large sums of money in your mail order operation. Rather, both Melvin Powers and I advise you to start in a small way with a minimum investment of money but with a substantial investment in research.

It's the advertisements, sales letters, brochures, and personal letters you use that will spell either failure or success. The greatest product in the world isn't going to sell if your advertising copy doesn't influence the reader to buy it. On the other hand, you can sell an ordinary product if you can pique the prospective customer's imagination. Effective advertising copy persuades the reader to send for your product. That's the job of a copywriter, and that's where I can help you.

I am intrigued every day with the wonderful opportunities available in mail order. I hope you will get excited about these ever-present possibilities. Keep in mind that if someone else can be successful selling a product or service, there is no reason why you can't be as well if you approach your business in a logical way.

I wish you much success as you embark on your exciting mail order adventure. Should you want to discuss your mail order plans, feel free to write or call. I can also be of help if you want to advertise on the Internet. I'm as close as your telephone. Call or write: Sheldon Swartz, 508 Glenwood Drive, W. Palm Beach, Florida 33415-2084. Telephone: (561) 686-2133.

Mail Order Made Easy

Due to space limitations in my book, *How to Get Rich in Mail Order,* I searched for a mail order book that would add important information on the mechanics of the everyday operation of a part-time or full-time mail order business.

I am pleased to say that I have found such a book, *Mail Order Made Easy* by J. Frank Brumbaugh. I enthusiastically recommend it as supplemental reading.

Mail Order Made Easy is extremely valuable containing numerous professional mail order tips. This practical knowledge can help spell successs for you, leading to subsequent financial independence.

Take time to read this interesting table of contents:

208 Pages· · ·$21.00 postpaid

Send your orders to:
Melvin Powers
12015 Sherman Road
North Hollywood, California 91605

12015 Sherman Road
No. Hollywood, CA 91605

(818) 765-8529
FAX (818) 765-2922

A 5-MINUTE PHONE CALL
CAN DRAMATICALLY CHANGE YOUR LIFE!

Dear Friend,

I'm going to give you some great news that will make it possible for you to make more money, sooner than you ever thought possible. But first, I want to tell you about the three elements that can guarantee your success.

Three Golden Keys to Getting Rich

Have you ever wondered how so many people who start with nothing, become financially successful?
1. They look for a good opportunity until they find one.
2. They get someone to teach them what to do.
3. They do it.

You can do what they have done, but just any opportunity won't do...and neither will just any teacher. Your chances of success are best if the opportunity is unique, powerful, easy, and proven to work...and if the teacher is experienced, successful, and dedicated to helping you make it.

Here's your chance to seize the right opportunity and the right teacher. It couldn't be any easier...I've already found them both for you! All you have to do is take advantage of the opportunity being offered to you.

Your Own Personal Teacher
Will Stand by Your Side
And Help Make You Successful

Have you ever had a successful person say to you, "I'm going to teach you how to become financially successful and guide you every step of the way"? Well now someone is saying exactly that. Laura Grad, a dynamic, full-time, Los Angeles multi-level supervisor and seminar instructor is dedicated to helping people who dream of riches and want to get their bank accounts to overflow with cash, checks, and money orders. Like so many other things in life, it seems so easy when you know how. So difficult—sometimes impossible—when you don't.

Most individuals who achieve success are "ordinary people." They start out with dreams, probably much like yours. Dreams of extra money to buy larger homes, new automobiles, travel, and pay for college educations. Dreams of becoming their own boss and working as much or as little as they wanted. Dreams of finding their work rewarding, challenging, and fun.

This Opportunity Has Every Element Necessary to Qualify it As a Virtual Gold Mine

There are thousands of millionaires in the United States. Interestingly, a great many of them made their fortunes in the last ten years in multi-level sales. In fact, more millionaires have been created in the last decade by network marketing than by any other form of business.

Fortunately, the company involved with the business opportunity is a multi-level marketing company. This means that in addition to making a profit from selling products yourself, you can make money on other people's sales.

Every one of your happy customers is a potential distributor as he or she enthusiastically tells amazing success stories to friends and relatives.

Infinite Level Bonus Plan Sets a New Industry Standard for Distributor Compensation

The money-making opportunity is great because of the company's unprecedented new marketing plan. It provides an infinite level bonus, rather than the three to five levels offered by other multi-level companies. Since its adoption, the plan has dramatically increased the amounts of money being earned.

Many Motivated Entrepreneurs Have Been Transformed into Millionaires

Individuals who learned of this innovative company's products in the early 1980s when they were first introduced, and who chose to put their energy into marketing them, have become rich beyond imagination. They knew the time was right for what they had to offer. And once again, the time is right.

The company is on the cutting edge of scientific technology for the 1990s. They have 14 years of invaluable experience with substances from the plant world that medical researchers are now looking to for solutions to our most puzzling health problems. The scientific community's interest in preventative health care and natural means of dealing with illness and disease is growing larger every year...and health care is now one of the largest industries in America. Market conditions couldn't be better.

They Have Changed Their Lives Forever... It Can Happen to You

In countries throughout the world, thousands of people have had the foresight to recognize this opportunity as the life-changing event it truly is.

Students, homemakers, accountants, engineers, teachers, police officers, construction workers, waitresses, market checkers, truck drivers, retired and disabled people have taken control of their lives. They found out what works from someone who knows, and they did what it takes to make it. As a result, they have achieved financial freedom while doing something they find satisfying and which makes a worthwhile contribution to mankind. You can do what they have done.

All You Need is...

A good attitude.
A willingness to take direction.
A desire to take control of your life.
A dedication to consistency and perseverance.

You Will Become Valuable

Do you know how much you are worth in the marketplace? <u>You are worth what you're being paid</u>. How valuable do you think you are? Why do you think corporation presidents are paid hundreds of thousands or millions of dollars a year? Because they are valuable!

<u>Laura will teach you skills that will make you valuable</u>. And you will bring value to the marketplace...with products that make people feel great...and with an opportunity that helps others to change their lives, follow their dreams, and take control of their futures.

Rich People Are No Smarter Than You

They just know the techniques of making money. <u>Laura will teach you how to be a money maker</u>—and how to have a Rolls Royce mentality, rather than that of a wage earner. You'll develop the Midas touch and have a winning attitude in everything you do. <u>You are no different from those who are making unbelievable sums of money</u>. What's their secret? They are motivated for success and are willing to follow a proven plan while keeping their sights on their long-term goals.

You'll Be Given a Tested, Proven Blueprint to Follow

<u>Laura will give you a plan that works—a plan that has already made many people very wealthy</u>. If you do what they did, you'll get what they got—and more—because she has committed her years of successful marketing experience to multiplying the earning potential of the plan.

<u>Your success will be her success</u>. <u>She will be available to you at all times to help you every step of the way</u>. She'll hold your hand and guide you as you build your business from the first day on—for as long as you want her help. This plan makes sense. It's working. It's growing every day.

What Is the Secret of a Winning Team?

It has been my experience that the most successful teams are comprised of members who believe in their ability to be successful, are enthusiastic about the project at hand, have pride in a job well done, and have a vested interest in the outcome of their efforts. In plain language, this means that <u>each person has a positive attitude, works hard to do his or her best, and has the opportunity to share in the profits</u>.

An Unusual Promise When You Join
The Laura Grad Wealth-Building Team

<u>Laura is inviting you to take a wealth-building journey with her that will change your life in ways you may never have imagined</u>. Becoming more valuable, making a lot of money, and feeling satisfied with

with what you have chosen to do in life are only part of what the Laura Grad Wealth-Building Team offers. As a member, you will get a sense of belonging to a new family that is supportive of your goals and self-development. A family you will find psychologically uplifting. A family with an ongoing personal growth program that will empower you to reach both your personal and financial goals. The continuing personal contact with her will help you become a winner in this endeavor…and in life.

Don't Neglect Your Future

If you want your life to change, you must change. If you want things to be different, you must do something different. Be good to yourself—allow yourself to be a winner. You have the chance to associate with winners and to be part of a winning team.

Where will you be one year from today if you don't join her? Two years from today? Think about it. Take 100% responsibility for where you are and where you want to go. Take charge of your future. Remember, you are not only what you are today, but also what you choose to become tomorrow.

Think Like a Winner
You Are at the Crossroads of Success

Don't lose one precious minute. Those who get in on the ground floor of this once-in-a-lifetime opportunity will flourish. Don't be left out.

Be ready to feel great. Be ready to spread the word to others. Be ready to be successful faster and easier than you ever imagined possible. Be ready to have others spread the word for you. Be ready to cash in on your mounting sales and on the sales of others. Be ready to take loads of cash, checks, and money orders to the bank. And be ready to lead the life you've dreamed of, but never really thought possible to attain.

This Is the Moment of Truth
A Pot of Gold is Yours for the Asking

If wishing could make money for you, you'd already be rich. Now is the time to do what it takes to get what you want. You have the opportunity to join a winning team. Create a miracle in your life by taking the steps that have made fortunes for others. Do yourself a favor and make a 5-minute phone call that can dramatically change your life! Call Laura at (818) 597-0097 to find out how you can get started making money immediately. You have a wonderful adventure in store for you.

Laura looks forward to welcoming you to her wealth-building team.

Melvin Powers
Publisher

P.S. The secret of success in life is to be ready for opportunity when it comes. I hope you're
    ready…because it doesn't get any better than this! Good luck.

Chapter Eighteen

Selling Products on Television
An Exciting Challenge

Your challenge is to turn a minimal investment into a fortune by advertising a product on television. The opportunity for riches is unlimited if you can find a suitable product and then produce a television commercial that will motivate the viewer to call your toll-free 800 number to be given at the end of the commercial.

Let's look at the sales figures of some successful television mail order products: Ginsu knives—$30 million, Armourcote pots and pans—$60 million. Even if we did not know the sales figures, we could assume these commercials were successful because of their longevity.

These and similar household products are sold successfully on television only because of interesting commercials extolling their unique features. The commercials hold our attention, reveal benefits to be derived, assure us that life will be better because of the purchase, and convince us we are getting a good deal for only a small sum of money. What could be better?

Many products advertised on television are very ordinary; however, the commercials entice the viewers to watch by attributing extraordinary qualities to the product, usually with clever action demonstrations.

As an example, in the early 1950s, Samuel J. Popeil and his brother Raymond began demonstrating gadgets on late-night television. In those days, station managers were offering that time for as little as $7.50 a minute. Their most famous item, the Veg-O-Matic, used to slice vegetables, sold over 11 million units.

Another idea, a collapsible "Pocket Fisherman," came to Popeil after he saw a boy almost poke out his eye while carrying a conventional fishing pole. The Popeils sold more than two million of the $19.95 fishing poles in 1973, the first year they were advertised on television.

In the 1950s, Charles Antell sold millions of dollars' worth of a hair preparation that captured the attention of the public.

Think of all the television commercials you've seen for the hit songs of the 50s, 60s, 70s, for the "100 greatest country-western hit tunes sung by your favorite artists," and for other types of music.

We have all seen television commercials for records and tapes. Since I am fond of Spanish music, whenever I see and hear a commercial for an album of favorite Latin tunes, I'm always tempted to call the 800 number.

The announcer's statement, "These records and tapes are not available in the music stores and can be purchased only by calling the special 800 number," is correct—they wouldn't sell well in the stores because the listener usually needs to hear bits of the music before making his purchase.

WHAT CAN YOU SELL ON TV?

You can sell anything for the home, garden, and automobile. You can sell anything to make you feel or look better. Knives and gadgets to sharpen knives are good items. Weight-control products always do well. Glass cutters and non-dripping paint applicators have sold into the millions. Food blenders and health-related items have been extremely popular. Beauty products of all kinds have sold successfully. Garden tools have excellent sales. Finally, songbooks and easy-playing piano and guitar books, among others, have had good sales.

Your research endeavor is to find products suitable for television. Perhaps you can revitalize a product that has been discontinued. Interest in products goes through cycles, and many items can be brought back to life. There are really very few new products; what you see is generally an old product with a new twist.

The television product should have broad appeal, possess clearly defined benefits and, if at all possible, lend itself to demonstration. If the product doesn't have this last requisite, you can show before-and-after pictures, talk about the benefits, and load your commercial with testimonials. This technique is used extensively in the sale of pills to make one feel better, to lose weight, to stop pain, and to relieve a host of ailments.

THE TELEVISION COMMERCIAL FORMULA

Pitchmen at carnivals, fairs, and boardwalks were the forerunners of the sophisticated advertising that we see on television today. The sequence is similar to a display ad: 1. Capture the listeners' attention with an attention-getting statement. 2. Talk about the problem and its solution. 3. Mention the benefits to the listener. 4. Make the commercial personal, as though you were talking directly to the viewer. 5. Demonstrate the product, if possible. 6. Give testimonials and/or implied testimonials from authoritarian figures ("approved by leading doctors"). 7. If appropriate, give the listener a reason for ordering immediately (limited quantity, offer ending on certain date, introductory offer, special price this week only, not to be offered again this season). 8. Ask for the order. 9. State the guarantee. 10. Offer money-back guarantee if not satisfied—no questions asked.

All direct-response advertising is geared to getting the prospective customer to take action—to purchase the product that is advertised immediately. Late-night television spots are perfect because the person watching is probably relaxed and in a receptive mood. It's his quiet time. You, personally, must be enthusiastic about your product. If not, your commercial will reflect it. It will lack the element of believability or "sizzle." An important subliminal element will be missing.

Do not go on major TV stations. It will generally not prove cost effective. There are published TV advertising rates, but you can negotiate. Rates are flexible because if the station's time is not sold, it is lost forever. You can make a deal to run your commercial at lower rates, such as when there is unsold time. There are also P.I. or P.O. (per inquiry or per order) deals where the station runs the commercial and you pay a fixed rate for every order. This is usually done after the commercial has a successful track record. You might prefer paying for the time to insure that the commercial runs. P. I. or P. O. deals run only when the station has open time. Don't be reticent about asking for it.

WILL YOUR PRODUCT MAKE IT?

It's alway problematical whether or not a product will make it on television, in consumer publications, in newspapers, or through direct mail. I've had my share of losses—it's all part of the creative process. One of the jobs in television advertising is to match the city to the product. Not all cities will pull the same. Similarly, match the product to the season. Not all products are suitable for all seasons.

My best success in television came during a bowling program when I ran an offer for a bowling book and record called *The Secret of Bowling Strikes*. It was the perfect combination of product and audience. Because of having some perfect P.I. deals, I've had excellent success selling name-and-address labels, records, and razor blades on the radio.

Television advertising gives you an immediate answer. You'll know the same evening or the next morning if you have a hit or a miss. When you are on target, it's the dream come true. Your bull's-eye can make a fortune for you in a very short time. I've hit the jackpot many times in my business career, and it's a marvelous feeling to know your creativity has produced a winner. And you, too, are in for a treat. Nothing can match the glorious feeling of shaking checks, cash, and money orders out of stacks of envelopes addressed to you! It's an exhilarating experience that I trust you will enjoy in the future.

HOW DO YOU START ON THE ROAD TO RICHES?

Your first step is to start paying attention to direct-response television commercials. If possible, record the commercials, type out the exact words, and do a storyboard of them. A storyboard usually has drawings arranged in sequence that show the visual continuity of a commercial. Under each illustration describe the video action and the words that are spoken, with appropriate comments or instructions. Or, you can draw a straight line down the center of a piece of paper. On the left side write VIDEO and on the right side write AUDIO. This will accomplish the same thing for your purpose. Instead of a drawing, you describe the video. Under audio, write the words to be spoken and whatever comments and instructions are necessary.

STUDY MONEY-MAKING COMMERCIALS

I want you to analyze and study the composition of proven, money-making commercials. You'll know they are making money when you see them continually repeated. Can you improve the commercial? Try it as an exercise in creativity. Can you figure out the winning elements? When you do, incorporate them into your own commercials.

Remember, nothing is left to chance in a winning commercial. There isn't an extra word or movement. Every second is important. The commercial must keep building interest. Keep in mind that millions of dollars may be riding on what you say and show in a two-minute commercial. The first minute and 40 seconds tells your story. The last 20 seconds, known as the tag, tells the viewer how to order. Be sure the announcer repeats the toll-free 800 number three times in the tag. Keep the number on the screen the entire time, as well as your company name and address, the price of your product, and the money-back guarantee statement.

You'll know the results of your commercial immediately. But even with success, your task is always to improve the commercial. Television commercials make shopping easy and convenient. What could be easier than calling a telephone number and having the product delivered to your door?

CREATIVITY SPELLS BIG DOLLARS

Good, effective television commercials take plenty of time to write and to make. Foremost is the thinking process concerning what you will say about your product. What are the necessary elements in your commercial that will motivate the television viewer to act? Don't forget you have a relatively short time to influence him. Don't let him run off to the refrigerator.

Mail order sales amount to billions of dollars. Wouldn't it be nice to get your slice of that money? You can! – because in many families husbands and wives both work, leaving less time for shopping. Families look for convenient ways to shop. That's part of the reason for the tremendous growth of mail order sales.

Part of the popularity of mail order shopping can be attributed to the lack of service and courtesy in most stores. Here's an exception. A new department store, Nordstrom, recently opened in the San Fernando Valley on Topanga Canyon Boulevard. Everyone is talking about it. Why? *Because they give service*. I went there myself just to check it out. Sure enough, I was greeted warmly in every department. The sales personnel is perfect. I bought some merchandise, although that was not my original intention, and I'm going to continue shopping there. From this example, it would seem that your attitude should be that you are rendering a service by offering your product on television.

COOPERATE WITH HOME TOWN STORES

An alternative to selling your product directly through the television commercial is to send the viewer to a local store. Call on the store or chain of stores in your home town that you think would appropriately tie in with your product. Tell the buyers about your television campaign. They are familiar with this type of merchandising and will welcome the opportunity to work with you. Work out an appropriate discount. Get them to give you a good display. Your ads will draw people into their stores, not only for your product but for other merchandise. The use of the store name in your commercial lends credibility to your offer. You'll also get some point-of-purchase impulse sales. Add signs to your store display reading AS SEEN ON TV or AS ADVERTISED ON TV.

Another way to go is to use 30- and 60-second commercials. This can be of great help as you can purchase many more spots, and the cost, of course, is less than for the longer spots. Start paying attention to those commercials that direct you to stores. Recording and studying them is an excellent method of learning.

Assume your television campaign is successful. You then go to the TV stations in another of the chain's cities, gradually expanding throughout the country. Don't think for one minute that you can't do it. You can. Let's see how you can get started logically with as little money as possible.

DEVELOP A WINNING ATTITUDE

The first requisite concerns your mental attitude rather than the product. Starting right now, I want you to adopt a winning attitude. A positive mental attitude can do wonders for you when you fortify it with well-thought-out steps that can help you to achieve your goals. Along with this positive mental outlook, I want you to consider yourself an entrepreneur. That, again, implies a certain mental attitude. An entrepreneur doesn't wait for someone to give him an opportunity for success. He goes after it in a determined way, learning from others, from books, from courses and seminars, and from wherever else necessary to reach his goals. No one is born an entrepreneur — one acquires the necessary ability through osmosis. It's a gradual conscious and subconscious process — assimilation of knowledge put to work to achieve the ultimate goal.

THE NUTS AND BOLTS OF TELEVISION PROFITABILITY
STEP #1: WHAT TO SELL?

What to sell is always the big question. You must decide that yourself. I can't tell everyone to promote macadamia nuts from Hawaii. At my weekly seminars, I'm asked by my students, "What's a good item to sell?" My answer is, "Everything can be sold profitably by mail. Right now someone is probably selling whatever product might come to your mind." If someone is selling or has sold one of your choices profitably, that's good news for you. It means your idea is valid. Your challenge is to come up with a new ad or commercial to sell the product. It should have your imprint.

You need a new angle to help sell the product. Perhaps there's nothing new under the sun, but you can make it appear to be new if it is approached from a different angle. Can you make it smaller, larger, wider, or narrower? Can you take away or add something to it? Can you give it some "sizzle" in a demonstration?

Your hard-earned money will be riding on your commercial, so it is important that you be genuinely enthusiastic about whatever it is you have decided to sell. Those with whom you work will catch your excitement and this, in turn, will help spark their creativity.

STEP #2: YOUR MINIMUM MARKUP

You need at least a minimum four-to-one markup to be successful on television. If the item sells for $20.00, it should cost you no more than $5.00. You can work on a two-to-one markup with catalog sales. If the item costs you $10.00, you sell it for $20.00. There's nothing wrong in doubling your money. The discount from manufacturers for mail order dealers is usually 50%.

Go to all kinds of trade shows where you might find some close-out or surplus merchandise. Don't worry about selling it out. Ask if you can make arrangements for buying more if your television campaign is successful. There are many costs involved in advertising on TV and you can't possibly make it at a 50% discount. You need the greater discount of at least 75%. If the item sells for $20.00, you need to buy it for $5.00. That's easy to say but difficult to find. The manufacturer must also make a profit.

THE WHAT, WHERE, AND HOW OF FINDING TELEVISION PRODUCTS

The answer lies in such products as cosmetics, facial creams, nail polishes, vitamins, diet pills, body lotions, items such as super-strength glues, roach powder, insecticides, flea collars, animal products, car polishes, car products, tarnish removers, vinyl cleaners, food slicers, fishing lures, fuel additives, records, tapes, and books.

You can manufacture your own product. Write to the nearest convention centers and get on the mailing lists for trade shows. In case you are going to Las Vegas, go when there is a trade show of interest to you. For a schedule of trade shows, write to the Las Vegas Convention Center, 3150 Paradise Road, Las Vegas, Nevada 89109. Refer to page 16. Visit the nearest trade center where you'll find representatives from numerous countries who are eager to help you find products. There is no charge for this service, and they will immediately make your wishes known to the appropriate manufacturers. In a matter of weeks, you'll receive stacks of catalogs, product magazines, and correspondence from sources willing to be of assistance to you. Refer to page 16 again. Call your nearest U.S. International Trade Administration district office. Employees there will be very helpful to you as well. You might want to contact your Small Business Adminstration and Chamber of Commerce.

Refer to pages 28 and 29. Send away for sample trade publications of interest to you. If you live in the Los Angeles area, write to Los Angeles Convention & Exhibition Center, 1201 S. Figueroa Street, Los Angeles, California 90015, enclosing a self-addressed, stamped, legal-sized envelope. Ask for a list of trade shows open to the public and also for major trade shows and conventions not open to the public. You can go to all the trade shows since you are now a mail order entrepreneur. All you need is a business card.

Look in the Yellow Pages of the phone book under importers. Contact those that deal with Taiwan, Hong Kong, Korea, and Singapore. You'll be able to get your biggest markups on products imported from those countries.

BOOKS ARE WINNERS

Remaindered books are excellent to sell. Write to Outlet Book Company, 225 Park Ave. So., New York, New York 10003, asking for their wholesale catalog and telling them you are in the mail order business. Let's assume you find a book, advertise it, and sell out. Don't worry about more supply. You have several choices. Contact the Outlet Book Company and tell them about your television promotion, inquiring if you can get more books. If they can't supply you, contact the original publisher and negotiate for the mail order rights. Pay no more than a five percent royalty. If the book sells for $10.00, you pay a royalty of 50¢ to the publisher when the book is sold. These royalties are usually paid twice a year, during January and July.

If, for some reason, you can't negotiate with the publisher, look in *Subject Guide to Books in Print* at your local library for a similar book. Write to its publisher and tell him you want to advertise the book on television, negotiating the best discount. If it isn't high enough, inquire about obtaining the mail order rights. If you get the rights, do not publish the book with a hard cover and a jacket as this would add unnecessary costs. Publish it in the same format as this book — with a soft cover. Call me if you would like an immediate quotation on printing.

YOU CAN PUBLISH THOUSANDS OF U.S. NON-COPYRIGHTED BOOKS

You can also sell books published by the United States government and receive a discount. Send for the free Catalog Number R-4; the number changes periodically however, so you may get a catalog with a different number, but it will be a current one. It will contain 1,000 of the most popular books sold by the government. That's very important information as it will help you in deciding which books to sell. Write to Superintendent of Documents, U.S. Government Printing Office, Washington, D.C. 20402. I'm including some pages from this catalog for your perusal and suggest you visit a government bookstore if convenient. See pages 350 and 351.

As a test only, you might want to sell a government book not at the proper television markup. The reason for this would be to test the pulling power of your TV commercial. You can reprint any book published by the government and pay no royalties because the books are not copyrighted. You may change the cover and put any price you want on it. This will also afford you the opportunity of becoming a book publisher and selling your book to bookstores and libraries throughout the United States and the world. When you reach this point, you might wish to call me and discuss some details.

STEP #3: GETTING YOUR COMMERCIAL OFF THE GROUND

Let us assume you have found your product and are ready to make your television commercial. Our game plan is to spend as little money as possible in making the commercial and in testing it for one week in one or two cities.

Call your local independent or cable television station. Explain that you are just getting started in television marketing and would appreciate some help in producing a two-minute commercial for your product. Naturally, you are going to run the commercial for one week or more as a test on their station. If your commercial is uncomplicated and can be shot in the TV studio, they might do it at a reasonable cost in order to get your advertising. Don't hesitate to inquire regarding the cost. Remember you are an entrepreneur. Act it. Make an appointment to see the sales representative. The television station will want to help you. When you are successful, it will mean additional revenues to them.

The station will also be able to give you help in writing the commercial. Assuming the cost of making the commercial is reasonable and that the station is ready to give you a "deal" in running your commercial for a week, the moment of truth has arrived. Will you go ahead with it? Don't make an emotional decision — make a business decision. Sleep on your choice for 48 hours. Then, if you still feel your decision is right and if you are getting good cooperation from the station, go for it.

UNCLE SAM WILL HELP YOU GET STARTED

Here's the good news. All expenses incurred in producing your television commercials, such as costs of television time, products, professional help, and selling your products, are fully deductible from your income. The cost of this book, other books, tapes, miscellaneous expenses, subscriptions to magazines, and expenses incurred during your attendance at seminars, trade shows, and business meetings are fully deductible.

For further information write to Internal Revenue Service, 5045 E. Butler Avenue, Fresno, California 93727. Ask for Publication 587 — Business Use of Your Home. It's free.

I am hoping that you will be very successful and that you will be looking for tax shelters. When that time comes, do not invest one cent until your accountant and attorney have given it their O.K. If it sounds too good, pass on it!

If you use one room of your apartment or home exclusively for your mail order business, you can deduct that portion of your rent or mortgage. Mail order and its many ramifications offer you an excellent legal method for sheltering pre-tax dollars. Confer with your accountant, who can save money for you by telling you about other items that you can legally deduct, such as a percentage of your automobile and telephone expenses.

Uncle Sam wants you to be successful in your mail order venture and to that end offers you these incentives. He loves entrepreneurs. He knows what he is doing, and he isn't entirely altruistic. Don't forget — when you start making money, he becomes your silent partner.

PRODUCING THE MONEY-MAKING COMMERCIAL

Making the right commercial is like setting out to write a hit song, a best-selling book, a hit box-office movie, an award-winning television series. It's done all the time, but it is truly difficult to predict success with certainty.

Let us suppose that money is no object in getting the commercial done and that you hire six of the top advertising agencies in the country to write and produce the commercial. There's still no guarantee that they will capture the essence of the product to produce a money-making commercial.

Start studying the commercials that you see on television. They might be technically correct in form, but are they effective in producing sales? Fortunes are spent on television commercials, but how many can you clearly remember? How many of the thousands that you have seen have persuaded you to buy the products? I'm sure you'll say, "Not too many." At the end of the evening, all the commercials tend to become one big blur. Sponsors keep changing advertising agencies to get better results. They keep getting pretty commercials, but what does this mean in terms of concrete sales? That's our bottom line.

In direct-response television advertising, you know the effectiveness of your commercial immediately. You know the precise cost of each order. Your judgment of a commercial can be as valid as the experts'. Listen to everyone, but make the final decisions yourself. Write some television commercials for the fun of it. If executed, would they be just as good as the ones you've seen? Are they better? Are you adding a different twist? Are you creatively different? It's not as easy as it sounds to come up with something different, but that's precisely how you have to start thinking to get some results. You don't want the viewer to fall asleep during your commercial.

TV COMMERCIAL CHECK LIST

1. Do you have the right product?
2. Is there a need for the product?
3. Do you have the right markup?
4. How many orders do you need to break even?
5. Is the cost of the commercial too expensive? (It's never too expensive if it makes money.)
6. Is the cost of the TV time too expensive? (It's never too expensive if it makes money.)
7. Do you have the right spokesperson or people in the commercial?
8. Do you start with an interesting or provocative statement or question?
9. Do you state the problem, if there is one, and how your product can solve it?
10. Does your commercial progress in a logical sequence?
11. Do you peak too early?
12. Do you show the product in action?
13. Do you have testimonials?
14. Is your commercial believable?
15. Are you "selling the sizzle?"
16. Is the commercial rushed?
17. Are the benefits clearly stated?
18. Would the product sell better at half the price?
19. Would the product sell better at a higher price?
20. Do you state that the viewer can use his VISA or MasterCard?
21. Do you have a local telephone number for your test commercial? (You don't need an 800 number for your test.)
22. Do you allow 20 seconds for the tag?
23. Do you repeat the phone number three times?
24. Do you show your local address and price of the product?
25. Do you give a reason to order immediately?
26. Do you give a money-back guarantee?
27. Did you pick the right city or cities for your test?
28. Would music enhance your commercial?

FULFILLING YOUR ORDERS

When volume makes it necessary, you can hire a mailing house or a fulfillment house to handle the mechanics of preparing credit card paper work, typing shipping labels, sending out merchandise, and reporting daily sales from all over the country. These organizations will even bank money in your account every day and give you a regular inventory report.

Successful mail order entrepreneurs rarely handle the mechanics of the operation themselves. They spend their time more profitably, in such activities as refining even a successful commercial. They will ponder the possibility of improvement and if they can't accomplish this, they'll make a new commercial and test the results against the first one.

Once you are successful, you'll be amazed how people will gravitate to you with all kinds of products. Only some of the ideas will be winners, but you'll start thinking in terms of a commercial immediately as you evaluate the products. The question always is how the product can be presented to motivate a person to get up from his chair or bed, make a telephone call, charge a purchase on his credit card, and feel good about it.

ADDITIONAL REVENUES FROM BUYERS

Don't forget there's a fortune to be made in selling a mailing list of the names of people who respond to your offers. Furthermore, you can develop a catalog of related merchandise that you can send to your customers. Once they are satisfied with an item, they'll purchase more products from you. That's the nature of the mail order buyer. So, a never-ending cycle produces more and more revenue for you.

YOU'VE RUN YOUR TEST COMMERCIAL FOR ONE WEEK AND THE RESULTS ARE TERRIFIC. WHAT DO YOU DO?

Congratulations, you've hit the jackpot! Keep studying your commercial and checking the sales results every week to catch trends—an increase or a slowing down in sales. Continue to run with the cities that are making it and add new television stations in those cities. If feasible, add new cities and their stations.

Make sure you are keeping current with your product inventory. It's also necessary to project your forthcoming needs. In other words, don't get caught short but, at the same time, don't overbuy.

Start thinking of other items you can sell to your customers. Contact a list broker to start selling your mailing-list names. The fun has just begun.

YOU'VE RUN YOUR TEST COMMERCIAL FOR ONE WEEK AND THE RESULTS ARE DISAPPOINTING. WHAT IS WRONG? WHAT DO YOU DO?

What do you do if your first attempt at television mail order advertising does not succeed? Do you give up? Do you say, "It's not for me. I can't do it."? I hope not. Look at it not from an emotional but from a business standpoint and try to determine how you can improve your response. My advice would be the same if you ran a small inexpensive classified ad and were disappointed with the results. There is a logical answer. Your job is to try to find it.

Meet with your TV sales representative and discuss the results with him. Get his feedback and ask for his suggestions. Try to get what is known as a "make-good." When advertising results are not good, publications and radio and television stations may, at their discretion, run your advertising again without charge if they feel it is to their advantage (not to lose an account). Perhaps a new commercial from a different perspective might turn the tide. Talk to your account executive about it.

If you break even on your first attempt, I would be pleased. Go for another week. You hope to build viewer identification and overcome initial resistance. If after two weeks your orders have improved, you can be cautiously optimistic. If your results should be discouraging, stop running because it's now time to reevaluate your television commercial and campaign. The answer can lie in the product itself (it just doesn't make it), in the price of the product, in the commercial itself (the wrong story line or execution), in the cost of the TV time (the cost per order is too much), in exposure during an inappropriate time of the year, in using the wrong television station (the demographic characteristics of the audience are not right for the product), or in a commercial run in the wrong time-slot (too much competition from other stations resulting in too few viewers).

Obviously, there are many variables, but we must start with the product and then the commercial. If you are still enthusiastic about the product, try getting the TV station's cooperation in producing a new commercial. If you receive an insufficient amount of enthusiasm for this idea, you might want to consider a different TV station. Show them the first commercial and tell them what time-slots were used and your sales figures. They might come up with just the right commercial. Good luck.

WHAT ARE YOUR CHANCES FOR SUCCESS?

Ultimately, you'll produce the winning commercial. In the meantime, look at your experience as a learning process. Success or fame represents the culmination of this ongoing process. You are beginning to think creatively, which starts your conscious and subconscious juices flowing. This energy will produce ideas and some of them will be winners.

Perhaps my experience will help you. Previously in this book, I referred to my songwriting career because it represents a perfect example of putting one's creative talent into a new area of endeavor. It's similar to your making your first TV commercial.

While I was producing my first album of music, some friends said to me, "What do you know about producing an album of music?" My answer was, "Absolutely nothing, but I believe I have an excellent concept for the album—one that I'll be able to sell to a major company for distribution." The concept, like the product, was the key for my enthusiasm.

I picked the songs to be recorded, including several of my own, engaged the best musical arranger I could find, conveyed to him the exact unique sound that I had in mind, and delegated all of the details to him. I went first class with my presentation and finally sold the album to MGM Records, Inc. for an advance of $15,000 against royalties. See page 211. That made me feel terrific—to me it was worth one million dollars.

Your creative challenge is to come up with a product that will sell because of the commercial that you'll make about it. There's plenty of good technical help available to produce a television commercial, but your input as to its contents is very important. Orchestrate the overall plan and seek whatever expertise you need.

TAKE RESPONSIBILITY FOR YOUR SUCCESS

Newspapers, magazines, books, and television programs are filled with true stories of successful people who started with very little money, who had practically no education, and who sometimes did not even speak the language. Yet they managed to accumulate fortunes in business. I personally know many such individuals.

The common characteristics that they all shared were the motivation for success and a positive attitude, not only for business but for life itself. They were "up" people. They were dreamers first—then they were doers. They all overcame obstacles. No one handed them success.

Every challenge became an opportunity for success. They logically and methodically went after their goals—one step at a time. They may have stumbled and faltered, but they straightened out, ultimately reaching their goal. Eleanor Roosevelt once said, "It is better to light one candle than to curse the darkness." No one said that the achievement of success in any field is easy. It requires determination, motivation, and logical steps.

TAKE THE LONG-RANGE VIEW

Successful people also take the long-range view of business. Every day becomes a learning experience.

When performers or actors finally become successful, they speak of "having paid their dues." This philosophy is generally necessary in becoming successful in mail order, although we both know you can become extremely successful almost overnight, once the proper ingredients come together.

NOW IS THE RIGHT TIME FOR TV

I know successful direct-response television entrepreneurs who are making a carload of money every month. I recently met with two of these highly successful persons in my office. Did you ever hear the expression "walking on air?" I swear that's exactly what they were doing. They had the "success aura." Why not? They were making millions of dollars.

They agreed that the chances of success for direct-response television advertising are greater now than ever before because the public has accepted the idea of ordering products they see advertised on television as a normal way of purchasing merchandise.

THE MIDAS TOUCH LIBRARY

Over a period of 25 years, I have been asked numerous times to recommend a reading program to develop a winning attitude to achieve success. You'll note throughout this book that I place great importance on one's attitude toward mail order success. It is as important as the product itself. Under the category of SELF-HELP & INSPIRATION on page 227, you'll find a list of books that can have a tremendous effect upon your psyche.

It is my suggestion that you pick out a dozen books and read one book per week. These outstanding books are psychologically motivational and comprise one of the most inspirational reading programs I know. Taking the material seriously could give you the success lift-off that you need as you will be programming both your conscious and subconscious mind for success.

Benjamin Franklin said, "An investment in knowledge pays the best dividends."

HELP FROM THE AUTHOR

The purpose of this chapter is to give you a brief introduction to the exciting world of television mail order advertising. To me, it's like a fascinating puzzle that needs its pieces in the correct positions in order to become whole. When it does, it's like winning the Irish sweepstakes. The possibilities for success are limited only by your imagination.

If you are contemplating selling books, I'm willing to sell you some of my books at a long discount, for your television offers only. I'll work out the details with you on an individual basis.

IT'S LIKE WINNING A LOTTERY!

Dear Entrepreneur:

Imagine what your life would be today if you had been paid $1.00, $.50, or even $.25 for each of the 40-million dollars worth of Ginsu knives sold on television or for every "top tunes" record album sold for years on those familiar commercials that roll hit song titles on the screen while playing a few bars of each.

If only you had known the secret . . . these product sales could have made you wealthy—without your having been responsible for producing the shows, getting them on the air, fulfilling orders, and without it having cost you one cent!

This secret can make you rich. Does making a fortune on television product sales seem like the impossible dream? A dream, maybe, but certainly possible. People are doing it every day—with no experience and no investment. And so can you. Here's how.

Get your slice of the TV money pie. The growing popularity of cable television has made TV marketing the hottest money-making opportunity in recent times.

Likely you have heard or read about or seen advertisements on cable stations that are raking in the money as fast as it can be counted. The airways are alive with powerful one- and two-minute spots and innovative half-hour and one-hour, long-format commercials that inform and entertain as they sell. What does all this have to do with you? Read on.

You can cash in on the Melvin Powers Midas Touch. I've made BIG MONEY in mail order and I plan to make even BIGGER MONEY in television marketing. I need people to help me find desirable products. Just think about all the items yet to be advertised—items that can mean FINANCIAL INDEPENDENCE for some individuals . . . why not for you? You are as likely as anyone to find a winning product. When you have found that winner, your part of the job ends and mine begins. I will put my time, effort, and expertise into making your product a hit. As a Melvin Powers product agent, you will be paid a royalty on each sale. What could be better? You'll be making money even while you sleep.

The treasure hunt that pays and pays. Products that sell best fill a common need or desire and are of benefit to a broad spectrum of the public. They can be demonstrated easily and interestingly and have impulse appeal. They offer a four times mark-up above the manufacture price and still represent good value to the customer. These items have unique features that set them apart from, and make them more desirable than, similar ones that are readily available. (What made an ordinary knife, mixer, and wok TV cash register bonanzas?—they were made to appear extraordinary by the magic of creative commercials.)

Kitchen gadgets like the V-slicer, small appliances such as the vacuum-pack food sealer, closet organizers, small exericse equipment like the Gut Buster, and automotive care items are all examples of excellent TV products. Items that have proven successful in print often do extremely well on TV.

It's easy to get started. Begin to consider every product you see or hear about as a possible TV money-maker, and measure each against the criteria above. Think about products made and/or sold by your business, the company you work for, your friends' businesses, or those that you frequent. Look for items being demonstrated at trade shows, county fairs, and swap meets. When you find a product you believe would be strong on TV, find out the name of it and the manufacturer's name, address, and telephone number. If the demonstrator would be effective on TV, get his or her name, address, and telephone number, as well.

Highly successful long-format commercials have sold written information and cassette tape courses on a variety of topics, ranging from real estate investing and developing self-confidence to improving one's study habits and losing weight. The best resources for finding courses that may make it on TV are business opportunity and self-improvement lectures and conventions. As with products, business opportunity and self-improvement programs should fill a common need, have wide appeal, and appear exciting, practical, and credible. In addition, the spokesperson or instructor must make a strong positive impression that would come across on TV. If you find such a program, get the name of the program and the name, address, and telephone number of the person presenting it.

How to build a network of people to find products for you. Tell everyone you know that you are a TV product agent. Explain what you are searching for and offer to pay a royalty on any item or program they find that is accepted for sale on TV. You bring the item to me and split the royalty with the person who brought the product to you. This technique will greatly increase your exposure to potentially hot products.

You've found the perfect product...now what? You can get an immediate answer as to its TV marketability by calling me. Or, if you prefer, write to me describing the product or program and include any brochures you may have.

If I accept your product or program, I will send you a contract, produce the show, air it, fulfill the orders, and send you monthly royalty payments.

Start today to think like a television marketing entrepreneur. Remember, success begins with the belief that you can do it, setting your wheels in gear, and getting moving! Decide right now to reach out for this rare opportunity to MAKE BIG MONEY, FAST.

Sincerely,

Melvin Powers

Melvin Powers
President

MELVIN POWERS:

The Man with the Midas Touch

Skeptics might scoff at a self-help book like
"How to Get Rich in Mail Order," but its
author is living proof that these theories work.

By Randall D. Schultz

Make no mistake about it, Melvin Powers has the Midas touch. Sure, he does things differently—some would even say he does things wrong. Yet in the process of doing everything "wrong," he's made himself a very rich man.

Melvin Powers publishes books. Not just any kind of books, special interest books. Books about bridge, chess, pets, sports and hobbies. But his Wilshire Book Company is best known for its line of self-help and inspirational books, the kind that most other publishers don't quite know how to handle. And the world headquarters for Wilshire Book Company is located not in a fancy New York City high-rise, but in a modest office/warehouse building in North Hollywood.

In an age of million-dollar advances and lavish book tours for superstar authors, Melvin Powers's Wilshire Book Company inauspiciously sells more than half of its books by mail. Mail-order selling is Powers's first love, and it's how his multi-million dollar publishing empire began.

As a teenager in Boston, Powers subscribed to *Popular Science* magazine, and occasionally read the classified ads in the back. An avid chess player, he noticed an ad for a chess book and mailed away for it. When it arrived, he decided he should sell books by mail, too.

"I started in the mail-order business when I was 16 years old," says Powers. "It was my hobby, running classified ads in the same magazines that I was reading—*Popular Science* and *Mechanix Illustrated*. I began selling books on chess, then one-by-one, added new titles and new subjects."

At first, he bought books from publishers at wholesale cost and sold them for retail. When he got one order, he sent it out with a flyer advertising the other books that he had. And he's still basically doing the same thing—running almost the same ad. "The formula is still working after all these years," he says, with a chuckle.

His first venture into publishing was a book called *"Hypnotism Revealed,"* which he wrote himself. "There's no money in having someone else publish your book," Powers explains. "I was an entrepreneur, so instead of getting a small percentage as a royalty from another publisher, I decided I might as well print the book and sell it myself."

It was a good decision. Now, 40 years after moving to Southern California to start Wilshire Book Company, Powers publishes all of the books he sells. Wilshire Book Company, which began on Wilshire Boulevard near downtown Los Angeles (hence the name), is privately held by Powers, and he is reluctant to release financial information. The company employs 21 people, and sells "a couple million books a year," says Powers.

Powers's first big publishing success came in the early 1960s with *"Think*

and Grow Rich" by Napoleon Hill. Even though it had been published in hardcover years before, it was Powers who first asked the question, "Why isn't this book available in paperback?" He bought the "trade paperback" rights and has since sold more than 7 million copies of the book. This trade paperback format—a larger size than the "mass market" paperbacks that fit into racks in supermarkets and drugstores—accounts for virtually all of Wilshire Book's sales.

His biggest coup, however, was snatching up the trade paperback rights to *"Psycho-Cybernetics"* by Dr. Maxwell Maltz.

"'Psycho-Cybernetics' wasn't doing anything in hardcover," says Powers. "Zero. But, I read a couple a pages of the book while standing in a bookstore and said to myself, 'This is a multi-million best-seller.'"

He was right. The Wilshire Book trade paperback edition of *"Psycho-Cybernetics"* jumped onto the best-seller lists, and to date has sold more than 3 million copies. It's still one of the company's steady sellers. And ever since the back-to-back mega-successes of *"Think and Grow Rich"* and *"Psycho-Cybernetics,"* self-help and inspirational books have been the company's primary editorial focus and biggest selling line of books.

Powers still goes to bookstores every week or two to read the hardcovers, looking for his next big find. He knows that the big New York publishers, with hundreds and sometimes thousands of books on their lists, sometimes let a good one slip through the cracks without being properly promoted. But bookstores aren't the only places he finds new books to publish.

Twenty years ago, when a friend asked him to buy an Arabian horse, Powers went to the Calabasas Saddlery and asked to see the horse books. He was shown a section of hardcover books.

"Where are your paperback books?" he asked.

"There aren't any," said the salesperson.

"There aren't any?" he asked, incredulously. "How come?"

"Everybody who has horses has money," said the salesperson. "They can afford to buy hardcover books."

When Powers heard that, he knew he had found another gold mine. He quickly wrote to the publishers of the hardcover books, negotiated the paperback rights and brought out a line of 70 horse-related books as fast as he could. He sold them by mail, in bookstores, in the 17,000 riding goods stores across America and Canada and got sales reps to sell them at the major riding goods trade shows. Mr. Midas had struck again.

Powers has also demonstrated his golden touch in the music business. When songwriter Tommy Boyce came into his office 15 years ago with a manuscript called *"How to Write a Hit Song and Sell It,"* Powers not only published the book but decided to try his hand at songwriting. With some personal coaching from Boyce, and some classes in composition and lyrics at U.C.L.A., Powers cowrote some songs with Boyce that made it onto the country and western charts. Teresa Brewer recorded his "Willie Burgundy," and he was invited to Nashville to accept an award for his song, "Who Wants a Slightly Used Woman."

He also used his songwriting experience to get into the *"Guinness Book of World Records"*—for getting the world's smallest royalty check.

"It was for a song called 'San Antonio, Texas,'" he says. "I got this check for four cents. Other people might have hidden it, but I got a big kick out of it. So I called the Guinness people and made it in the 1980 edition of the book." The four-cent check is still proudly displayed on his office wall.

As you might expect from someone who has made millions of dollars by selling books by mail, Powers is now a renowned expert in mail-order sales. The book he wrote and published, *"How to Get Rich in Mail Order"* is the all-time best-seller on the subject, and is considered the bible of the mail-order industry. He has taught seminars on mail-order techniques at virtually every community college in the Los Angeles area. Despite his understated approach and low-key personal style, he is truly a super salesman.

So, it isn't surprising that his newest endeavor is called "Melvin Powers Television Marketing," which sells products on TV. For many years he has been sought out as a consultant, working behind-the-scenes to help the companies that offer Ginsu steak knives, exercise equipment, vegetable slicers and other hard-to-resist goodies on TV. Now he's actively seeking products that his new company can sell on cable TV.

"That means traveling to housewares and food shows, trying to find a product with the potential for mass appeal," says Powers. "It might be a new kitchen gadget or small appliance, or even an automotive product or a course of instruction in a book or on tape. Believe it or not, sometimes television exposure generates so many orders that the manufacturers can't keep up."

In other words, Melvin Powers may be about to open up another gold mine.

Not that he's giving up the publishing business. Far from it. Last year Wilshire Book Company published 12 new books to add to its total list of about 450. This year, if he can find another dozen good books he'll publish them, too. But he's not on any quota system, so he'll only publish the books that he cares about.

Of all the books he's published, he's proudest of *"How to Get Rich in Mail Order."* "It's helped a lot of people leave their jobs and start a business for themselves and become financially independent," he says. He also mentions *"New Guide to Rational Living"* by Albert Ellis, and of course, *"Psycho-Cybernetics."*

"I'm happy with the books I've published because every week people tell me how their lives have been changed by them," says Powers. "It's a nice feeling." **VM**

Before you close this book, will you turn to page 175 and read aloud my favorite poem "It Couldn't Be Done" by Edgar A. Guest?

I wish you good luck and much success as you contemplate and implement your mail order television plans. "May the road rise to meet you and the wind be always at your back...."

I'll look forward to toasting you and welcoming you into the Mail Order Entrepreneurs Millionaires Club!

FOREIGN GOVERNMENT TRADE REPRESENTATIVES

ARGENTINA
Argentina Trade Office 623-3230
707 Wilshire Blvd., Ste. 4850, LA 90017
Ricardo A. Alurralde,
Senior Trade Commissioner

AUSTRALIA
Office of the Australian Trade Commissioner
Australian Consulate General 380-0980
3550 Wilshire Blvd., Ste. 1744, LA 90010
Richard Fletcher, Senior Trade Commissioner
Anton H. Meyer, Trade Commissioner

AUSTRIA
Austrian Trade Commission 380-7990
3440 Wilshire Blvd., Ste., 515, LA 90010
Alexander Lifka, Trade Commissioner
Walter Patzl, Assistant Trade Commissioner

BELGIUM
Consulate General of Belgium 385-8116
3921 Wilshire Blvd., Ste., 600, LA 90010
Ralph Esquivel, Commercial Officer
Louis Verhaeghe, Commercial Officer
Willy Robyn, Commercial Officer

BRAZIL
Brazilian Trade Center 628-7291
350 S. Figueroa St., Ste., 240, LA 90071
Luez Antonio Dubeux Fonseca, Director

CANADA
Canadian Consulate General
Commercial Division 627-9511
510 West 7th St., LA 90014-1377
David E. F. Taylor, Consul and Sr. Trade Com.
Leo R. Leduc, Consul and Trade Commissioner
Robert W. Craig, Consul and Trade Com.
Rodney B. Johnson, Consul and Trade Com.
Roger J. Mailhot, Vice-Consul and Asst. Tr. Com.

CHILE
Consulate General of Chile 624-6357
619 S. Olive, Ste. 203, LA 90014
Carmen Castro, Honorary Chancellor
Patrick Madariaga, Commercial Attache

DENMARK
Royal Danish Consulate General 387-4277
3440 Wilshire Blvd., Ste. 904, LA 90010
George D. Rasmussen, Commercial Attache
Peter Jensen, Senior Commercial Officer
Carsten Heering, Commercial Officer

FINLAND
Consulate of Finland 203-9903
1900 Ave. of the Stars, Ste. 1060, LA 90067
Asko Karttunen, Trade Commissioner

FRANCE
French Govern. Trade Commission 879-1847
1801 Ave. of the Stars, Ste. 921, LA 90067
Andre Lambert, Trade Commissioner
Gilles Della Guardia, Deputy Trade Commissioner
Bernard Charvet, Assistant Trade Commissioner
Bernard Lozevis, Assistant Trade Commissioner
Judy Szyf, Asst. Trade Commissioner

GERMANY
German Consulate General 852-0441
6435 Wilshire Blvd., 4th fl., LA 90048
Eberhard Hesse, Head Economic Affairs
Robert Grief, Consular Attache

German American Cham. of Comm. 381-2236
3250 Wilshire Blvd., Ste. 2212, LA 90010
Michael Lehmann, Director
Sigi Carlton, Operations Manager

GREAT BRITAIN
British Consulate General 385-7381
3701 Wilshire Blvd., Ste. 312, LA 90010
Jack C. Sloman, Deputy Consul General
and head of Commercial Section
Brendan Donnolly, Vice-Consul (Commercial)
Jim H. McIntyre, Vice-Consul (Commercial)
D. Henry Ford, Commercial Officer

GREECE
9555 Van Alden Avenue 993-3477
Northridge, CA 91324
Nicholas Conteas, Commercial Attache

HONG KONG
Hong Kong Trade Development Council
Los Angeles World Trade Center
350 S. Figueroa St., Ste. 520, LA 90071 622-3194
Anthony Wong, Los Angeles Trade Representative
Peter Leung, Marketing Officer

INDIA
Engineering Council of India 622-8548
727 W. 7th St., Ste. 658, LA 90071
Santosh Misra, Regional Manager

INDONESIA
Indonesian Trade Promotion Centre 617-9398
350 S. Figueroa, Ste. 272, LA 90071
Achbad Achmad, Director
Frank S. Dharmawan, Marketing Officer

ISRAEL
Israel Invest. and Export Auth. 658-7925
6380 Wilshire Blvd., Ste. 1700, LA 90048
Abraham (Avi) Rosental—until Sept. 1983, Consul

ITALY
Italian Trade Commissioner 879-0950
1801 Ave. of the Stars, Ste. 700, LA 90067
Mario Castagna, Trade Commissioner
Massimo Ludovisi, Deputy Trade Commissioner
Philip Baca, Senior Trade Analyst

JAPAN
Consulate General of Japan 624-8305
250 E. First St., Ste. 1507, LA 90012
T. Inoue, Consul
S. Morinobu, Consul

Japan Trade Center (Jetro) 626-5700
555 S. Flower St., LA 90071
Akira Tsutsumi, Director General

JORDAN
Jordanian Consulate 557-2243
2049 Century Park E., #3050, LA 90067
Frank Jameson, Consul
Karyl Dickinson, Vice Consul

KOREA
Korean Consulate General 931-1331
5455 Wilshire Blvd., Ste. 1101, LA 90036
Keunyi Suh, Consul for Economic Affairs

LUXEMBOURG
Consulate 394-2532
516 Avondale Ave., LA 90049
Marie-Anne Pitz, Consul

MEXICO
Trade Commission of Mexico 655-6421
8484 Wilshire Blvd., Ste. 808, Beverly Hills 90211
Cesar Lajod, Trade Commissioner
Damian Correu, Asst. to the Trade Commissioner
Guadalupe Barba, Asst. to the Trade Comm.

NETHERLANDS
Consulate Gen. of the Netherlands 380-3440
3460 Wilshire Blvd., Ste. 509, LA 90010
J.H.W. Fietelaars, Consul General
Ivan Charles De Johgh, Commercial Affairs
and Trade Commissioner

NEW ZEALAND
New Zealand Consulate General
Commercial Office 477-8241
10960 Wilshire Blvd., Ste. 1530, LA 90024
Jon Neas, Consul (Comm.) and Trade Com.
Jane Patterson, Assistant Trade Commissioner
and Vice-Consul (Commercial)
Kent M. Dolan, Marketing Officer
Sydney Cruce, Marketing Officer

NORWAY
Consulate General of Norway 626-0338
350 S. Figueroa St., Ste. 360, LA 90071

PHILIPPINES
Philippine Consulate General 383-9475
Office of the Foreign Trade Promotion Rep.
2975 Wilshire Blvd., Ste. 450, LA 90010
Cristina Ortega, Trade Representative
Manuel B. San Luis, Foreign Trade Analyst
Hermenegildo Borja, Trade Consultant
Ofelia Q. Nituda, Market Analyst

PORTUGAL
Portuguese Govt. Consulate 277-1491
1800 Ave. of the Stars, Ste. 307, LA 90067
Edmundo Macedo, Consulate

SINGAPORE
Singapore Trade Office 617-7358
350 S. Figueroa St., Ste. 170, LA 90071
Geoffrey Lim, Director

SOUTH AFRICA
Consulate General of South Africa 858-0380
9107 Wilshire Blvd., Ste. 400, Beverly Hills 90210
Nick Sounes, Consul (Commercial)
Pierre Von Geusau, Marketing Officer

SPAIN
Commercial Office of Spain 628-1406
350 S. Figueroa St., Ste. 946, LA 90071
Carmen Ferrer, Commercial Officer

SWEDEN
Swedish Trade Office 475-4501
10880 Wilshire Blvd., Ste. 914, LA 90024

SWITZERLAND
Consulate General of Switzerland 388-4127
3440 Wilshire Blvd., Ste 817, LA 90010
Rene J.C. Rode, Consul and Trade Commissioner

TAIWAN
Taiwan Commercial Division 380-3644
Co-ordination Council for N. American Affairs
3660 Wilshire Blvd., Ste. 918, LA 90010
C.Y. Liu, Trade Representative
S.S. Chang, Assistant Trade Representative
Luke Lu, Assistant Trade Representative
Angela Chu, Assistant Trade Representative

THAILAND
Thai Trade Center 380-5943
3440 Wilshire Blvd., Ste. 1101, LA 90010
Chamnan Malisuwan, Director
C. Popien, Assistant Director

TURKEY
Consulate Office 855-1278
8730 Wilshire Blvd., Ste. 210, Beverly Hills 90211
Suat Cakir, Consulate General

ABBREVIATIONS
A.C.C. – Acting Commercial Consul
C.G. – Consul General
D.C.G. – Deputy Consul General
A.C.G. – Acting Consul General
C. – Consul
V.C. – Vice-Consul
C.A. – Commercial Attache
C.C. – Commercial Consul
C.O. – Commercial Officer
T.C. – Trade Commissioner
T.D. – Trade Delegate
T.R. – Trade Representative

D.C.G. – Deputy Consul General

Who We Are

Each year the departments, offices, and agencies of the Federal Government prepare and release thousands of publications, which range from small pamphlets to multi-volume reports. Many of these documents are printed and sold through the Sales Program administered by the Government Printing Office. The Superintendent of Documents is responsible for the operation of the Sales Program, with a current staff of nearly 1,000 professionals, technicians, and clerks whose sole purpose is to serve the public.

The Superintendent of Documents currently has a sales inventory of more than 16,000 titles. It is a very dynamic inventory, with new items being added and backlist titles being dropped at the rate of 2,000–3,000 per year. Among the Government publications we sell are more than 500 subscriptions—a service adjudged the largest in the United States.

Reference Service

While we make every effort to identify any publication requested, we do not maintain a research staff and cannot provide extensive information or reference service on either phone or written inquiries. If you do not have an exact title, GPO stock number or GPO catalog number, we suggest that you request assistance from the nearest Depository Library or from your local public library.

Government Bookstores

GPO operates 24 bookstores all around the country where you can browse through the shelves and take your books home with you. Naturally, these stores can't stock all of the more than 16,000 titles in our inventory, but they do carry the ones you're most likely to be looking for. And they'll be happy to special order any Government book currently offered for sale. All of our bookstores accept VISA, MasterCard, and Superintendent of Documents deposit account orders.

ALABAMA
Roebuck Shopping City
9220–B Parkway East
Birmingham, Alabama 35206
(205) 254–1056
9:00 AM–5:00 PM

CALIFORNIA
ARCO Plaza, C-Level
505 South Flower Street
Los Angeles, California 90071
(213) 688–5841
8:30 AM–4:30 PM

Room 1023, Federal Building
450 Golden Gate Avenue
San Francisco, California 94102
(415) 556–0643
8:00 AM–4:00 PM

COLORADO
Room 117, Federal Building
1961 Stout Street
Denver, Colorado 80294
(303) 837–3964
8:00 AM–4:00 PM

World Savings Building
720 North Main Street
Pueblo, Colorado 81003
(303) 544–3142
9:00 AM–5:00 PM

DISTRICT OF COLUMBIA
U.S. Government Printing Office
710 North Capitol Street
Washington, D.C. 20402
(202) 275–2091
8:00 AM–4:00 PM

Commerce Department
Room 1604, 1st Floor
14th & E Streets, NW
Washington, DC 20230
(202) 377–3527
8:00 AM–4:00 PM

Dept. of Health and Human Services
Room 1528, North Building
330 Independence Avenue, SW
Washington, DC 20201
(202) 472–7478
8:00 AM–4:00 PM

Pentagon
Room 2E172
Main Concourse, South End
Washington, DC 20310
(703) 557–1821
8:00 AM–4:00 PM

FLORIDA
Room 158, Federal Building
400 W. Bay Street
P.O. Box 35089
Jacksonville, Florida 32202
(904) 791–3801
8:00 AM–4:00 PM

GEORGIA
Room 100, Federal Building
275 Peachtree Street, NE
Atlanta, Georgia 30303
(404) 221–6947
8:00 AM–4:00 PM

ILLINOIS
Room 1365, Federal Building
219 S. Dearborn Street
Chicago, Illinois 60604
(312) 353–5133
8:00 AM–4:00 PM

MASSACHUSETTS
Room G25, Federal Building
Sudbury Street
Boston, Massachusetts 02203
(617) 223–6071
8:00 AM–4:00 PM

MICHIGAN
Suite 160, Federal Building
477 Michigan Avenue
Detroit, Michigan 48226
(313) 226–7816
8:00 AM–4:00 PM

MISSOURI
Room 144, Federal Building
601 East 12th Street
Kansas City, Missouri 64106
(816) 374–2160
8:00 AM–4:00 PM

NEW YORK
Room 110
26 Federal Plaza
New York, New York 10278
(212) 264–3825
8:00 AM–4:00 PM

OHIO
1st Floor, Federal Building
1240 E. 9th Street
Cleveland, Ohio 44199
(216) 522–4922
9:00 AM–5:00 PM

Room 207, Federal Building
200 N. High Street
Columbus, Ohio 43215
(614) 469–6956
9:00 AM–5:00 PM

PENNSYLVANIA
Room 1214, Federal Building
600 Arch Street
Philadelphia, Pennsylvania 19106
(215) 597–0677
8:00 AM–4:00 PM

Room 118, Federal Building
1000 Liberty Avenue
Pittsburgh, Pennsylvania 15222
(412) 644–2721
9:00 AM–5:00 PM

TEXAS
Room 1C50, Federal Building
1100 Commerce Street
Dallas, Texas 75242
(214) 767–0076
7:45 AM–4:15 PM

45 College Center
9319 Gulf Freeway
Houston, Texas 77017
(713) 229–3515
10:00 AM–6:00 PM

WASHINGTON
Room 194, Federal Building
915 Second Avenue
Seattle, Washington 98174
(206) 442–4270
8:00 AM–4:00 PM

WISCONSIN
Room 190, Federal Building
517 E. Wisconsin Avenue
Milwaukee, Wisconsin 53202
(414) 291–1304
8:00 AM–4:00 PM

RETAIL SALES OUTLET
8660 Cherry Lane
Laurel, Maryland 20707
(301) 953–7974
8:00 AM–4:00 PM

All stores with the exception of Houston are open Mon-Fri (Houston, Mon-Sat)

To Order

1. To help speed your order, be sure to use the special order forms in this catalog. Please use separate order forms when ordering both subscriptions and regular publications. Photocopies of the form are acceptable.

2. Type or print your complete name and address, your order number (if any), your Superintendent of Documents deposit account number (if applicable), your VISA or MasterCard number (if applicable), and expiration date in proper places at the top of the form. If order is to be shipped to a third party, fill in address at bottom of form. Please include your office/home telephone number.

3. When ordering non-subscriptions, type or print the stock number (the number preceded by "S/N" at the bottom of each annotation), quantity, title, price, and total payment enclosed. Allow 4 weeks for delivery (longer for international orders).

4. When ordering subscriptions, type or print the quantity, list ID, title, unit price, and total payment enclosed. Allow 4–6 weeks plus mailing time for processing. All subscriptions are for one year unless otherwise noted. Subscribers will be notified in ample time to renew.

5. Include total payment with your order. Please make checks or money orders payable to the Superintendent of Documents. You may charge your order using your Superintendent of Documents deposit account or your VISA or MasterCard account. Do not send cash or stamps.

6. Shipping is by non-priority mail. United Parcel Service (UPS), first class, and airmail services are available for an additional charge. Please contact us in advance for rates if you desire this service (202-783-3238) and indicate on your order if you desire special postage.

7. Mail this form (or a photocopy) to: Superintendent of Documents, U.S. Government Printing Office, Dept. 33, Washington, DC 20402.

8. Please do not call to inquire about your order until at least 6 weeks have elapsed. After that, to inquire about subscriptions, write to the Subscription Service Section, Stop SSOM, U.S. Government Printing Office, Washington, DC 20402. To check on orders for non-subscriptions, write to the Publications Service Section, Stop SSOS, U.S. Government Printing Office, Washington, DC 20402. You may also call (202) 275-3050 for non-subscription inquiries and (202) 275-3054 for subscription inquiries.

9. If our shipment is incorrect, return the shipping cards for adjustment. PLEASE DO NOT RETURN BOOKS UNTIL NOTIFIED TO DO SO. All claims must be submitted within 6 months.

Bookdealers

Designated bookdealers and educational bookstores are authorized a 25-percent discount on the domestic price of any publication or subscription when delivered to the dealer's normal place of business. This rule applies to single as well as multiple copies of a publication, pamphlet, periodical, or subscription service, except on items sold at a special quantity price, on items specifically designated "no discount allowed," or on items shipped to a third party (except in single-title quantities of 100 or more). The maximum discount allowed is 25 percent, but note that GPO pays freight.

Orders for 100 or More Copies

Any customer ordering 100 or more copies of a single publication or subscription for delivery to a single destination will be allowed a 25-percent discount on the domestic price of the item, with the exception of those items specifically designated "no discount allowed." The maximum allowable discount is 25 percent, so discounts may not be "combined."

Deposit Accounts

Over 30,000 customers find that a prepaid Superintendent of Documents deposit account is a convenient way to do business. Upon receipt of an initial deposit ($50.00 minimum), an account will be established and a unique account number will be assigned. Future purchases may be charged against this deposit account number including telephone orders, as long as sufficient funds are available in the account. Order blanks are provided and monthly statements are mailed to customers with active deposit accounts. For more information and necessary authorization forms, write to: Special Accounts Branch, Stop SAOS, U.S. Government Printing Office, Washington, DC 20402 (202) 275-2481.

International Orders

In order to provide the special handling required by international mailing regulations, a surcharge of 25 percent of the domestic price will be added on all items shipped to a foreign address. Remittance in U.S. dollars must accompany every order and be in the form of a check drawn on a bank located in the U.S. or Canada, a UNESCO coupon, or an International Postal Money Order made payable to the Superintendent of Documents. NOTE: Due to a recent change in Treasury Department regulations, we can no longer accept checks drawn on Canadian banks for less than $4.00 (U.S. dollars). If your order totals less than $4.00 (U.S. dollars), we suggest that you use your MasterCard or VISA account. International customers may also charge their orders to a prepaid Superintendent of Documents deposit account. Please include the expiration date of your credit card with your order. Orders are sent via surface mail unless otherwise requested. Should you desire airmail service, please contact us in advance by letter, telephone (202-783-3238), or Telex (#710-822-9413; ANSWERBACK USGPO WSH) for the total cost of your order. Foreign currency, checks on foreign banks, and postage stamps will not be accepted. All orders must be in English.

Melvin Powers' Mail Order Library

HOW TO WRITE A GOOD ADVERTISEMENT

by Victor O. Schwab

Contents:

Chapter 1: GET ATTENTION—How Important Is the Headline? What Kinds of Rewards Do Good Headlines Promise? 100 Good Headlines and Why They Were So Profitable. The Attraction of the Specific. How Many Words Should a Headline Contain? The Primary Viewpoint—the "Point of You." Don't Worry about a "Negative" Approach. Neophobia?—Americans Don't Suffer from This Ailment! Stale News to the Advertiser May Be Fresh News to the Reader. MAKING YOUR LAYOUT GET ATTENTION Two Ways to Do It. The Use of Pictures. Show Product in Use. What the Illustrations Should (and Should Not) Do. QUIZ ON CHAPTER 1. **Chapter 2:** SHOW PEOPLE AN ADVANTAGE—You're on Both Sides of the Counter. What Do People Want? Psychological Background Behind These Desires. New Trends for Old. HOW SHALL WE SELECT OUR COPY APPEAL?—Judy O'Grady and the Colonel's Lady. Eliminating the "Testing of the Obvious." IMPORTANCE OF YOUR FIRST PARAGRAPH—Two Examples—One Bad. QUIZ ON CHAPTER 2. "TELL ME QUICK AND TELL ME TRUE." **Chapter 3:** PROVE IT—Why You Need Facts—and Where. Two Forces Are Needed to Pull a Sale. Never Forget This Psychological Truth. The Heart Dictates to the Head. The Kind of Facts to Get. The Missing Ingredient in Many an Otherwise Good Advertisement. How to Present Your Facts. QUIZ ON CHAPTER 3. **Chapter 4:** PERSUADE PEOPLE TO GRASP THIS ADVANTAGE—A $600,000,000 Example. A Simple Illustration of It in Action. How a Salesman Uses This Factor. It May Be Negative or Positive. The Sixth Prune. Aim at the Hardest Target. QUIZ ON CHAPTER 4. THIRTEEN AGAINST THE GODS. **Chapter 5:** ASK FOR ACTION—The Gap Between Reading and Acting. What Kind of Action Shall We Ask For? Guarantees Get Action. "Delay Is the Enemy of a Sale." The Fallacy of "Sometime." Not What People Say—but What They Do. The Battle for the Bucks. QUIZ ON CHAPTER 5. **Chapter 6:** HOW LONG SHOULD THE COPY BE?—Platitudes Won't Answer This Question. Eight Milestones to a Sale. The Qualities of Quantity. How Far Will You Carry the Majority? The Vital Key Word. The Quantity of Quality. 22 Ways to Hold Interest Longer. How To Make It *Look* More Inviting. The Form vs. Substance Mistake. A Condensed Recapitulation. HOW TO DECIDE THE BEST COPY LENGTH—It's Easier to Get Attention and Interest than to Hold It. The Everlasting Yea and Nay. If It Isn't There It Can't Do Any Work. When Shorter? When Longer? And Now You're Going to Cut—or to Expand. You Need This Additional Guidance. THE LOWLY SUBHEAD—How to Make Them Do More Work. Use Questions—Sequence. Let Them Speak Out Strongly. QUIZ ON CHAPTER 6. **Chapter 7:** HOW TO GET MORE INQUIRIES—Inquiries—the Cornerstone of Many Businesses. Ten Ways to Increase Them. HOW TO REDUCE THE NUMBER OF INQUIRIES—A Delicate Balance. What to Decide First. How to Decide Whether to Reduce Them. Ten Ways to Reduce Them. HOW TO MAKE THE INQUIRY COUPON ITSELF DO A BETTER JOB—Three Kinds of Prospects. Ten Ways to Improve Your Coupon. COUPON RIDERS—WORTH MUCH, COST LITTLE OR NOTHING—Allow People to Trade Up if They Want to. SEVEN OTHER FACTORS WHICH INFLUENCE THE EFFECTIVENESS OF AN ADVERTISEMENT—Size of Advertisement. The Use of Color. When It Appears. Position. The Effect of Big News Events. The Effect of Weather. And the Most Important Factor of All. QUIZ ON CHAPTER 7. **Chapter 8:** HOW TO SIZE AN ADVERTISEMENT—Your Vision May Be Too Narrow. Look Beyond the "Nuts and Bolts." If You Are Testing a New Product. QUIZ ON CHAPTER 8. **Chapter 9:** DO COPY APPEALS HAVE A SEX?—"Longer-Haul" Thinking. "Shorter-Haul" Thinking. Do Your Observations Check with This One? Why It Has Bearing on Your Copy. QUIZ ON CHAPTER 9. **Chapter 10:** FACTS OR FANCIES—WHICH SHALL YOU FEATURE? "The Most Wanted Product in the World." Some Ads Don't Need Much Factual Underpinning. QUIZ ON CHAPTER 10. **Chapter 11:** FOURTEEN INTERESTING AND INSTRUCTIVE SPLIT-RUN TESTS—Sufficiently Conclusive—if Properly Handled. Differences Should "Scream"—not "Whisper." The General Application of Split-Run Experience. QUIZ ON CHAPTER 11. **Chapter 12:** "CUMULATIVE EFFECT"—A COMMON ALIBI FOR POOR ADVERTISING—Why Multiply Zero? False Reliance upon the "Series" Idea. What's Profitable about Procrastination? What's the Cumulative Cost in Time and Money? You're Not in an Endurance Contest. QUIZ ON CHAPTER 12. **Chapter 13:** THE HARD-BOILED ATTITUDE—AND HOW TO ACQUIRE IT—What's Behind This Attitude? But There Are Two Compensations. When Is an Ad "Good"? Knowing and Avoiding That Which Is Most Likely to Fail. More Nays than Yeas. The Tougher the Job, the Better the Copy. Doubt Makes Demands. A Hair Shirt Worth Wearing. Not What They Think, but What They Do. QUIZ ON CHAPTER 13. **Chapter 14:** RANDOM OBSERVATIONS—INDEX

256 Pages . . . $22.00 postpaid

MELVIN POWERS' TEN-HOUR MAIL ORDER SEMINAR ON CASSETTE TAPES

Here is an opportunity for those of you unable to attend my mail order seminar to hear me discuss many aspects of running a successful part-time or full-time business. In the privacy of your home, office, or car, you'll hear the same seminar that thousands of entrepreneurs all over the country have attended. The ten hours of audio tape instruction will answer many of the questions you have wanted to ask. It will teach you how to successfully become your own boss.

After listening to the tape program, you will better understand mail order fundamentals and procedures, and will have an overall plan that will help you start making money right away in your own mail order business. The tape program is sold on a one-year, money-back guarantee. It must be of tangible help in teaching you how to make money in mail order, or I'll refund your money—no questions asked.

Here's how to gain maximum benefit from the tapes: (1) Listen to the material several times to fully comprehend the practical suggestions and information; (2) Put into practice the specific elements to be incorporated in your mail order plan; (3) Run your first classified or display ad; (4) Do a test mailng to one thousand or as many as three thousand people who would logically be interested in your product; (5) Evaluate the results; (6) Call or write to me to discuss your mail order plan and receive my suggestions for increasing your chances to attain success.

Send for Melvin Powers' Mail Order Seminar on Cassette Tapes. $65.00 postpaid.

Send your order to:

Melvin Powers
12015 Sherman Road
No. Hollywood, California 91605